Arms

and

Armour

The Dollar conversions have been made at the rate of exchange prevailing at the date of the sale.

ISBN: 0-8256-9672-0
ORDER NO.: 450017

Copyright ©Lyle Publications MCMLXXIX
Glenmayne, Galashiels, Scotland.

Printed by Apollo Press,
Dominion Way, Worthing, Sussex, England.

Bound by Newdigate Press, Vincent Lane,
Dorking, Surrey, England.

Distributed in the U.S.A. by
Quick Fox,
33 West 60th Street,
New York, N.Y. 10023.

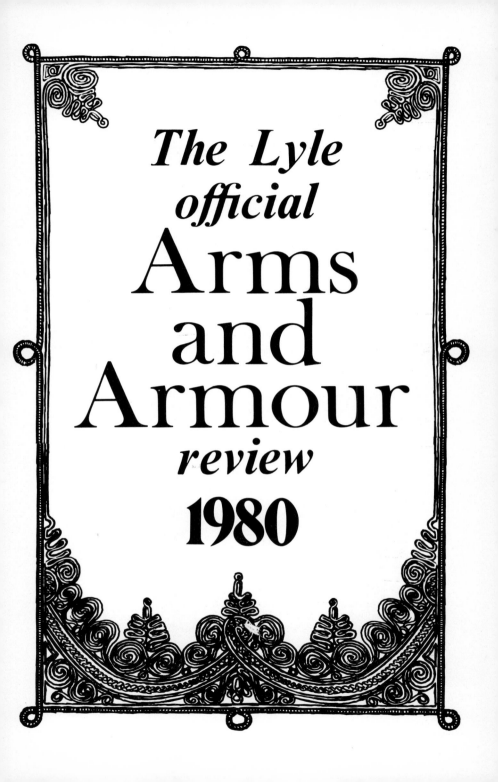

The Lyle
official
Arms
and
Armour
review
1980

Acknowledgements

EDITED BY TONY CURTIS
COMPILED BY MARGARET ANDERSON

Janice Moncrieff
Carmen Milivoyevich
May Mutch
Elaine Harland
Alison Morrison
Susan Lower

All photographs and text throughout this book relate
to recent sales at the Lewes Auction Room of
Messrs. WALLIS & WALLIS
to whom the publishers are deeply indebted.

INTRODUCTION

As the interest in all things antique widens steadily from year to year, the tendency towards specialisation becomes ever more marked. This is a tendency which has been fostered by a wealth of beautifully produced, highly informative books published at very reasonable prices.

No longer has the would-be-specialist to spend long periods tracking down obscure, out-of-print volumes in search of information fundamental to the pursuit of his interest; a few pounds wisely spent will equip him with works of considerable scholarship on any chosen subject.

But scholarship is rarely at ease in the market place, and there are relatively few publications available whose sole, or even primary, aim is to accurately indicate the current values of the objects they describe. This is a task not to be undertaken lightly, for it is one that requires encyclopedic knowledge coupled with a ready understanding of market trends. In achieving this rare blend, the publishers are deeply indebted to Messrs. Wallis and Wallis of Lewes, possibly the world's leading specialist auctioneers of all things military.

This, the Lyle Official Arms & Armour Review 1980, is the fifth edition of an annual review of current values in a field which is gaining a steadily widening circle of devotees.

TONY CURTIS

Contents

Arms
and
Armour
review

It is hard to guess how much Colonel James Bowie paid for his lethal knife which he wielded with great effect in bloody battles of the American West in the early 19th century — but one thing is certain — if Colonel Bowie knew that a knife like his could fetch today as much as £1,000, he would have given up Indian fighting in favour of knife buying.

Bowie knives are among the most rapidly growing areas of collecting interest in the Arms and Armour world and in America there are clubs and organisations with newspapers and magazines devoted to the subject of knife collecting.

The cognoscenti are also interested in hunting and trappers' knives but it is the Bowie knife that arouses the greatest enthusiasm. These knives were popularised by Jim Bowie, a friend of Davy Crockett, who died with him at the Battle of the Alamo. Bowie was a byword in the West for the savagery and accuracy of his use of the large, sinister blade and many a would-be knife fighter went to the local blacksmith to order "a knife like Bowie's." The Bowie knife was born but to be the real thing it

A Victorian Bowie knife, blade 8in. $614 £310

should, like the first one carried in the Colonel's bloody fist, have come from Sheffield in England. The knives were popular because a man armed with one had no danger of running out of ammunition and it was a lethal weapon. Veteran knife fighter C. M. Clay of Kentucky wrote this chilling description of fighting with a Bowie knife ....

"One should drive to the hilt on a line with the navel – a move which produces great shock and almost invariably puts an end to the encounter."

The great shock today is however in the ever rising price of those knives which 19th century Sheffield cutlers produced in thousands for the American market.

Collectors avidly seek out knives from well known firms like William Butcher, Marshes and Shephard, James Rodgers, Charles Gongreve, Unwin and Rodgers, Samuel Wragg and George Wostenholm. Prized examples have their blades etched with the messages of their original owners – "I'm a real ripper", "Arkansas Toothpick" or "A Sure Defence."

So, if it is a defence against inflation that is being sought instead of a defence against Red Indians or gambling enemies, a Bowie knife would make a very enviable asset.

Mr Butler, head of Wallis and Wallis in Lewes, Sussex, one of the world's biggest and most knowledgeable auction houses dealing with the sale of Arms, Armour and Militaria can foresee that the already high price of Bowie and hunting knives will go up even more. A definitive catalogue on the subject is now under production by American expert William R. Williamson of Santa Barbara, California, who himself owns over two hundred Bowie knives. When the book is issued it will be a standard work on the subject and should encourage even more interest in the knife collecting field.

All in all, the past year seems to have been the Year of the Knife. Apart from the ever rising interest in the Bowie knife and others of its type, there has been a significant increase in the price of World War I and World War II trench and fighting knives. Recently these changed hands at about £1 or £2 but now they fetch between £20 and £50. Several catalogues on these knives have been produced and people are searching them out from attics or off the shelves of garden potting sheds.

More exotic examples of this "cut and thrust" market are the Eastern weapons which too have risen spectacularly recently. There has been a great increase in the past year of the number of high quality Indian weapons appearing for sale. These lovely daggers and swords, many of them hilted with precious or semi-precious stones and with filigreed and inlaid blades, have been sent for sale to this country by influential Indian owners whose families have owned them for centuries. Because of the difficulty in exporting weapons it is usually only the finest which come up for sale here unlike Middle Eastern weapons which are often bought by people visiting the Middle East and many of which prove to be forged or poor examples of their type.

The Indian weapons have entrancing names – tulwars, a kind of sword; katar – a thrusting dagger; pia kaetta, a Sing-

An Indian dagger kard, blade 12¼in.   **$168 £85**

alese knife. The chilanum is a curved sword with a raised central rib and the choorz is a T-shaped Indian dagger. The kard is an Indian knife and a phurbu is a Tibetan dagger used by priests for exorcising purposes. At one time the only Indian weapon people knew much about was the kukri, carried by the Gurkhas, but now the rare weapons, often with silver covered blades embossed with floral and foliate patterns, are appearing for sale and demanding high prices. A pia kaetta with a seven inch long blade and silver mount sells for around £50 and is regarded by collectors as a good investment because it is very much a rising market. The Malayan kris is also a good buy — today they change hands for around £30 to £50. More expensive are the long Caucasian knives called kindjals which used to be carried by the Cossacks. They were often silver mounted and decorated in foliate patterns and can fetch between £100 and £200 at the moment, with even more for exceptional examples. If any of these Indian, Malayan or Cossacks' knives have been known to have belonged to an eminent person, their prices will be even higher than those quoted.

The fascination of collecting Militaria continues to draw in more and more people every year. Salerooms all over the country are starting to hold special sales of Arms and Armour and collectors are avidly bidding for everything from suits of armour to military books and pictures.

A Singalese pia kaetta, blade 7½in.   **$119 £60**

A Caucasian dagger kindjal, blade 16in. $832 £420

Mr Butler of Wallis and Wallis is confident that Britain is the centre of the world for this type of article. "We policed the world for so long and almost every British soldier who came home brought a souvenir of his career with him, so we are the best source for military artefacts," he said. His confidence is fully justified as buyers from all over the world come to this country seeking out treasures. The best customers seem to come from Germany, Switzerland and Belgium — rich countries with people who have the leisure and resources to take up collecting seriously. Every year Mr Butler travels to Europe and America where Militaria collectors are also active, persuading enthusiasts not only to come here to buy but to send their collections to Britain to be sold. Now, although fifty per cent of the goods bought in his own saleroom go abroad, he is happy to note that approximately twenty per cent of the lots are sent in for sale by sellers living outwith this country. An example of this was the magnificent helmet of an

officer of the 1st Regiment of the Suffolk Yeomanry dating from around 1812 which was sent in for sale by a German collector who knew that it would fetch the best price in Britain. The helmet was worth at least £2,000.

"There are fine examples of Arms and Armour still in this country," said Mr Butler, "and we are also happy to see that we are becoming a centre for the re-dispersal of collections."

He forecasts that in the next ten to twenty years, collections which were built up after the Second World War will start to appear for sale. Already he has noticed that collectors from that period are either dying or capitalising on their collections and he recently was instructed by an amateur collector in the Midlands to sell a collection which fetched over £36,000. He had originally paid only a fraction of that price for his mixed collection of headdresses, uniforms and weapons. With regret collectors now acknowledge that in the future there will be fewer of these "mixed collections" built up. When they were first amassed, prices were much lower and sellers were not so aware of the value of their goods so bargains could be found more easily. Today with the media informing people about the value of the contents of their dusty cupboards and attics, it is difficult to pick up treasures unless you are very rich. Collections will, of necessity, also be more specialised, because more people are buying in the field.

Only twenty years ago Glengarry badges were found in the oddment trays

A Georgian officer's tarleton helmet of the 23rd Dragoons. **$7,920 £4,000**

An other rank's Glengarry badge of the 78th Highland Regiment of Foot.
$83 £42

of junk shops for around ten shillings — today a Glengarry badge will sell for between £25 and £50. The metal helmet of an officer of a cavalry regiment used to fetch about £10 — now it would be impossible to buy one for less than £200 to £500. A cloth covered helmet with spike of a line officer could be bought in the 1950's for £5 — today you would not get a decent one for under £100.

In spite of the rise in prices however, collecting is booming. Prices continue to rise steadily and auction houses and dealers all admit with confidence that "trade is good." Some items that enjoyed spectacular rises in past years have quietly held their price over the past twelve months, particularly blunderbusses, duelling pistols and pepperbox revolvers. They have not fallen in price however and seem to be drawing breath for their next spurt forward. People interested in buying, as an investment or to sell again, would be best advised to stick to swords, especially Japanese swords, which are still showing a good return over a short period of time. The Japanese sword market is particularly strong with the best quality weapons going back to Japan.

Here a word of warning should be given to would-be collectors — study your subject before you start to buy because, as in so many areas of the collecting world, forgeries can appear for sale. The signature of the maker engraved on the tang of a Japanese sword does not alone authenticate it. Often these signatures were only put on when the sword was first made to show that it was a weapon of high quality, just as the name Ferrara was carved on the blades of swords which were not made in that city. However, in the field of Japanese swords it is obvious that a signed sword has to have a blade of first class quality and the knowledgeable will know at a glance whether that is the case or not — so study the subject first.

A Victorian officer's blue cloth spiked helmet of the King's Own Royal Lancashire Regiment. **$238 £120**

A post 1902 officer's helmet of the Household Cavalry.   **$792 £400**

ten is not worth the modern craftsman's time to reproduce the item unless it is sure of fetching a very high price indeed. Collectors all know that when American Colt revolvers began to rise in value, reproductions of them appeared for sale. Often they were only too easy to pick out but the question became more difficult when the forgers had taken the trouble to "distress" the weapons, bruising the butts and making them appear much older and more used than they actually were. Again the advice given to would-be buyers was "study the subject" — knowledge in the field of collecting is never a dangerous thing unless it is only scanty. People buying older weapons than Colt pistols can usually buy with greater confidence. It would be a dedicated forger who could turn out a fine hand-made copy of a Queen Anne pistol.

Forgeries also appear in other areas of the market but again, to pass the eye of the real collector, the forgery has to be of such high quality that it very of-

Making their appearance now in many salerooms and specialist shops all over the country are toy soldiers — no longer for the enjoyment of small boys at Christmas, but sought after by very knowledgeable collectors. The most desirable among the mass produced toys

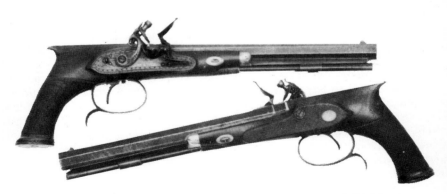

A pair of 34-bore saw-handled flintlock duelling pistols by H. W. Mortimer & Son.   **$1,980 £1,000**

15

Mounted Artillery Gun Detachment. $97 £50

are those made by Britain's at the beginning of the twentieth century. A mounted toy soldier by Britain's in good condition can sell for around £3 to £10; a model of a foot soldier will fetch between £1 and £5. Collectors are however warned against trying to repaint toys that they find. Because they were bought for children and because their original prices were only fractions of what they sell for today, toy soldiers too often bear the signs of wear and tear — chipped paint, missing legs and arms, snapped off gun barrels. To make the best prices, they have to be in good condition but collectors should not try their hand at home restoration because copying the original colours and markings is extremely difficult and can always be detected by the specialist. A repainted soldier will make less money than it would with its original paint chipped and worn.

Finally, military collectors do not confine themselves to buying only arms and armour, uniforms and toy soldiers. There is growing interest in books, letters, pictures and other oddments like cigarette cards providing they have a military theme. Recently sixty-four cigarette cards of military badges and military scenes sold for £16 — not bad considering they were originally put into packets of cigarettes for nothing. The

world of books with military themes ranges from bound copies of the Army List — recently the New Annual Army List for 1863 made £34 at auction — to copies of small boys' "Wonder Book of Aircraft" and "Wonder Book of Ships". Two copies of the latter, rathern worn and browned at the corners made £6 in a Militaria sale recently. More unusual books like pictorial souveniers of regiments in India and histories of specific corps like the Royal Marines can command prices of between £60 and £90 depending on their condition and rarity. In recent years because of the break-up of many households with connections in the Army and the East, these books have started appearing on the market and will certainly repay a bit of judicious buying now.

Of course the big favourite of military collectors — fine uniforms, helmets, medals, badges, guns, swords, suits of armour, pikes and halberds continue to demand steadily appreciating prices. Anyone who owns any of these things or who has some to sell can survey their future price with steady confidence. The advent of nuclear weapons has done nothing to diminish the appeal of a well burnished broadsword — at least as far as the price is concerned.

LIZ TAYLOR

EDGED

WEAPONS

BAYONETS

A scarce Martini Henry pattern 1875 Artillery sword bayonet, short fullered single edged, saw-backed blade 18in., steel crossguard, diced leather grips.$59 £30

A fine Nazi Wehrmacht carbine dress bayonet, plated, clipped back blade, 7¾in., by Albert Loscher Hamm, plated mounts, stag horn grips, 'eagle's head' pommel, red felt liner to bayonet slot, in its black painted metal scabbard. $79 £40

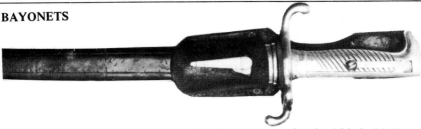

An 1871 pattern Prussian brass hilted bayonet, single edged blade 18½in., stamped on back-strap with crowned 'W' above '78', crossguard stamped '51.RR.9.165', in its brass mounted leather scabbard. $79 £40

A fine and rare Nazi fire department carbine dress bayonet, saw-backed plated blade, 7½in., with 'knight's head' maker's mark, plated crosspiece 'eagle's head' pommel, diced black grips, in its black painted metal scabbard. $119 £60

A French 1866 Chassepot bayonet, blade 22½in., etched on back-strap 'Mre Impale de Mutzig Janvier 1868', plated hilt, in its steel scabbard. $119 £60

A fine Nazi Army dress bayonet, plated blade 9½in., by Eickhorn, plated mounts and 'eagle's head' pommel, diced black grips, with red felt bayonet slot, in its black painted metal scabbard. $119 £60

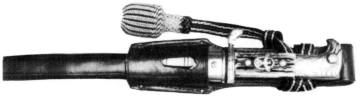

A fine Nazi Police dress bayonet, plated blade 13in., by Carl Eickhorn, plated mounts, stag horn grips, crossguard stamped 'S Kol 213', red felt in bayonet slot, in its brown leather scabbard with plated mounts. $119 £60

A scarce carbine length Police dress bayonet of the Weimar Republic, plated, clipped back blade 7½in., white metal shell guard with Eagle device, white metal cross piece 'eagle's head' pommel and mounts, stag horn grips, in its black painted metal scabbard. $129 £65

A Nazi Police dress bayonet, plated blade 13in., by E. & F. Horster, plated 'eagle's head' pommel and mounts, the crosspiece and top sheath mount stamped 'L.D. 96', stag horn grips, in its brown leather scabbard with plated mounts. $152 £77

A good Nazi Police dress bayonet, plated blade 13in., by F. W. Holler, white metal mounts, 'eagle's head' pommel, the crosspiece stamped 'S.D.V. 214 R.I.', stag horn grips, in its black leather scabbard with white metal mounts, the top mount with repeated issue stamps, with leather frog stamped 'Gebr Graf 1940 Kuchenheim', with dress knot. $158 £80

A Nazi Wehrmacht presentation dress bayonet, plated blade 9½in., by Eickhorn, etched with Army Eagles 'Zur Erinerung An Meine Dienstzeit' in scroll, oak leaf border, plated mounts, 'bird's head' pommel, diced black grips, in its black painted metal scabbard. $178 £90

A rare all steel dagger bayonet for the Le-Mat revolver, single edge straight blade 8¼in., with false edge. Steel cruciform hilt engraved with scrolling foliage, reverse side slotted with channel for bayonet fitting. $218 £110

A fine Nazi Police dress bayonet, plated blade 13in. by E. & F. Horster,
plated mounts, 'eagle's head' pommel, stag horn grips with Police Eagle,
bayonet slot, in its black leather scabbard with plated mounts.$218 £110

A very fine mid 18th century French fusil socket bayonet, spear point, double
edged blade 8in., the facetted socket of solid silver, also with frond engraved
bands, the blade mount in the form of a Turk's head wearing turban, in patent
leather scabbard with plain, white metal mounts. $300 £145

A rare Nazi Police parade bayonet, plated blade 16½in., by A.C.S., plated
mounts, the shell guard with badge of the Weimar Republic, stag horn grips
with Nazi Police Eagle, 'eagle's head' pommel, in its leather scabbard with
plated mounts. $297 £150

An early 18th century plug bayonet, plain, double edged spear pointed
blade 8½in., squared steel cross piece, plain horn hilt with swelling base, in
its steel scabbard with belt loop. $297 £150

A good English late 17th century plug bayonet, double edged, tapering blade
8¼in., struck with 'Turk's head' mark, reversed gilt bronze crossguard, ivory
hilt with swelling base and inlaid with silver pique stud patterns, gilt bronze
mounts. $620 £300

A mid 18th century Continental dragoon broadsword, plain, straight, single edged blade 33½in., stamped with small mark at forte 'O.M.'. Steel basket guard with thumb ring and flattened pommel, steel wire bound grip. $148 £75

An English Cavalry trooper's broadsword, circa 1750, double edged blade 32in., with short fuller, with traces of etched decoration of crown 'GR' and foliage, with maker in one fuller 'Woolley', iron basket openwork guard with oval trailing rein panel, flattened ovoid pommel, old leather covered grip. $188 £95

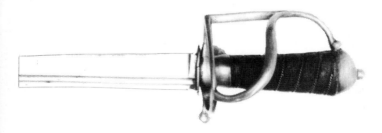

A good mid 18th century European Cavalry broadsword, long, tapering, plain single edged blade 33½in. with two narrow back fullers, plain brass half basket guard with thumb ring, flattened brass wire bound fish-skin covered grip, plain brass mounts. $198 £100

A Victorian Scottish officer's broadsword, double edged, part double fullered blade 32in. by Henry Wilkinson, Pall Mall, steel basket hilt of traditional pattern with pierced designs, wire bound fish-skin covered grip, in its steel mounted leather scabbard. $158 £80

A Victorian Highland officer's broadsword, double edged, double fullered blade 31½in., etched with royal cypher within foliate panels, steel full basket guard, the panels pierced with heart motifs, ovoid pommel, fish-skin grip, red cloth over buff leather liner and tassels, in its plated scabbard. $178 £90

A Scottish broadsword, circa 1770, straight, single edged, multi fullered blade 34½in., iron basket guard of traditional form, with large oval trailing rein panel, fluted conical pommel, cord bound grip. $188 £95

A Scottish broadsword, circa 1770, double edged blade 33in., iron basket guard of traditional form, pierced with traditional patterns, flattened domed pommel, wood grip.   **$238 £120**

A Victorian Scottish basket hilted broadsword, straight, double edged blade, 34¼in., with broad central fuller, full basket hilt the panels pierced with stylised hearts and circles, pommel, copper wire grip.   **$238 £120**

A Scottish broadsword, circa 1800, double edged blade 32½in., with central fuller, sheet steel basket guard of traditional form, pierced with traditional patterns, original red liner, the pommel replaced with a nut retaining blade.
                                                $257 £130

A late 18th century Highland officer's broadsword, double edged blade 33½in., short fullers with geometric star patterns, steel basket hilt, fluted conical pommel with screw knurl, wire bound fish-skin covered grips, old leather backed crimson cloth lining with blue edge-binding. $340 £170

A good late 18th century Scottish officer's broadsword, earlier double edged blade 34in., short fullers at forte signed 'Andrea Ferara', steel basket guard pierced with traditional patterns, large cigar shape back quillon, old red liner, conical pommel, wire bound spiral fish-skin covered grip, in a leather scabbard. $436 £220

A late 18th century Scottish broadsword, double edged, tapering blade 32in., of flattened diamond section, engraved 'Vive Le Roy', with traces of brass inlay, iron pierced basket guard of treditional pattern, flattened pommel, brass wire bound fish-skin covered grip. $436 £220

A late 18th century Scottish officer's regimental basket hilted broadsword, double edged blade 34in., struck in the fullers with armourer's marks and 'Andrea Ferara', with running wolf mark on each side. Basket guard formed as woven basketwork around central shield section which is engraved with Georgian Crown above Scottish thistle. Ribbed dome shaped pommel, wire bound shark-skin covered grip with steel ferules. $495 £250

A Scottish officer's broadsword of the Breadalbane Fencibles (1st. Bn.) circa 1880, broad double edged blade 32in. with traces of etching and large maker's name 'Marshall-Perth', central fuller, steel basket guard pierced with thistles and with central panel engraved with crown 'BF 1 Bn', and motto 'Nemo Me Impune Lacessit', old red liner, wire bound fish-skin covered grip, fluted pommel, $574 £290

A late 18th century Scottish officer's broadsword, double edged, fullered blade 32in., signed 'Andrea Ferara', gilt basket guard pierced with traditional patterns, flattened circular pommel, part of old red liner, wire bound fish-skin covered grip, in its leather covered scabbard, small copper gilt locket. $594 £300

A 19th century twig dagger, slim, clipped back blade 5½in., with blued etched decoration of foliate scrolls and 'Recuerdo de Toledo', traces of gilt, spring catch with disguised release button. **$40 £20**

A 19th century Scottish dress hunting dagger, single edged blade 6in. with scallop back edge, scroll reversed copper crosspiece, stag horn hilt with brass pommel cap decorated with Celtic pattern, in its leather covered sheath with brass top mount, brass belt loop, the chape with Celtic pattern. **$83 £42**

An early 19th century Spanish knife dagger, spear blade 11in., with short deep fuller, chiselled at forte with foliate scrolls and dated '1810', white metal single quillon in the form of a 'dog's head', old ivory, spiral fluted grip, white metal pommel cap. **$119 £60**

A composite dagger in the style of the late 17th century, double edged flattened tapered blade 11in., cast brass crossguard with short langets and recurved monster head quillons, the hilt of carved bone. **$148 £75**

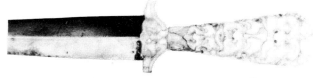

A Dieppe ivory hilted dagger, double edged, plain, tapering, spear point blade 8½in., the hilt and guard of carved ivory, crosspiece in the form of a buffalo mask, the hilt of grotesque masks balanced one upon the other. **$257 £130**

A rare Austrian Air Force officer's dagger, plated blade 8in., by Zeitler, Wien, plated, rectangular, stepped crosspiece with circular badge enamelled in Austrian State colours, set in stylised eagle, rounded white grip, spring catch, beaded, plated pommel and mounts. $287 £145

A good, scarce Spanish Main gauche fighting dagger, tapering double edged blade 19¼in., with single fullers, tri-fullered at forte. Swollen cross piece terminals, large single shellguard, swollen oviform pommel, wire bound grip with 'Turks' Heads'. $693 £350

DHA

A Burmese dha, curved blade 24½in., inlaid for entire length with silver foliate scrolls and animals within panels, copper inlaid outer border, white metal covered hilt decorated with human figures within oval panels, conical pommel, in its white metal sheet covered wooden scabbard. $158 £80

A Burmese sword dha, heavy curved single edged blade 22¼in., the cylindrical wooden hilt entirely overlaid with Eastern sheet silver, mushroom shaped pommel, in its wooden sheath. $158 £80

A good silver mounted Burmese dha, curved blade 19in., the wooden hilt covered in Eastern silver, pierced with foliate and floral patterns, beaded ring mounts, conical pommel, in its wooden scabbard also covered in Eastern silver. $475 £240

A Celebes kleewang, single edged blade 21½in. of watered steel, horn hilt with ornate foliate carved pommel, in its wooden sheath. $75 £38

An old bronzed Tibetan exorcising dagger Phurbu, triangular blade 3in., issuing from elephant head, surmounted by thunderbolt symbol, the top of three masks surmounted by hound's head, over 8in. $129 £65

A good Tibetan dagger, single edge, multi-fullered blade 13in., with spear point, small beaded oval crossguard, Eastern silver wire bound grip, the pommel of silver gilt pierced with scrolls of traditional pattern, in its sharkskin covered wooden sheath with two Eastern silver mounts. $166 £84.

A scarce Japanese dagger Wedung, curved laminated blade 8½in., heavily sheet gold damascened ferrule integral with blade, facetted elephant's tooth grip, in its wooden sheath with gilt wire binding, applied floral embossed silver badge and horn belt hook. $168 £85

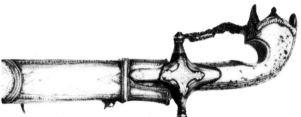

An old Arab silver mounted Saif, curved, single edged blade 29in., with half moon mark and double back fulllers, the hilt of Eastern silver, white metal chain guard, in its leather covered wooden scabbard with two large mounts of Eastern silver. $218 £110

An Indian foot dagger Bichwa, recurving blade 5in., with reinforced point, the grip with gold damascened foliate decoration.   **$238 £120**

An attractive Japanese dirk Aikuchi, blade 19¼cm., mumei, two mekugi ana, hiri zukuri. Wooden tsuka and saya inlaid with eighteen various insects and reptiles.   **$317 £160**

A fine Indian Pesh Kabz, watered steel blade 9½in., the hilt decorated overall with silver floral and foliate patterns, with green enamel background, gold damascene decoration at base, in its red cloth covered wooden sheath with two small silver gilt mounts decorated with floral patterns.**$356 £180**

FASCIST

An Italian Fascist 1st model MVSN leader's dagger, bright steel blade 6½in., aluminium hilt with 'eagle's head' pommel, black grips inset with Fasces and mounted with Eagle, in its metal sheath and braid hanging loop.
      $257 £130

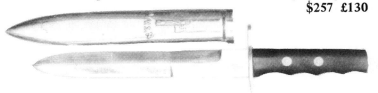

A rare Italian Fascist MVSN dagger of the 'Musketeers of the Duce', plated blade 8in., with facsimile inscription in the autograph of Mussolini and with his signature, plated crosspiece and mounts, shaped black wood grips, in its plated metal sheath.   **$713 £360**

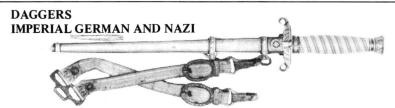

A Nazi Army officer's dagger, plated mounts, yellow ivorine grip, in its plated sheath with original hanging straps and belt lug, clips and lug with 'D.R.G.M.' mark. $83 £42

A Nazi Army officer's dagger, tapered diamond section blade by 'W.K.C. Solingen', down curved crosspiece with Eagle holding Swastika, yellow spirally ribbed grip with diecast pommel, embossed with oak leaves. $99 £50

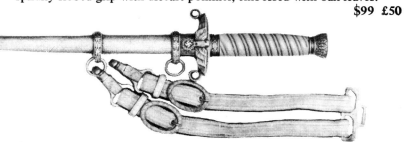

A Nazi Army officer's dagger by R. W. Holler, blade retaining much original polish, plated mounts, yellow ivorine grip, in its plated sheath with original hanging straps and belt clip, the clips marked 'D.R.G.M.' $99 £50

A good Nazi S.A. dagger by Bontgen & Sabin, German silver mounts, in its metal sheath with white metal mounts, and scarce double hanging loops and belt clip. $109 £55

A Nazi Army officer's dagger by Eickhorn, plated mounts, orange grip, in its plated sheath, with hanging straps and belt clip, and with bullion dress knot. $119 £60

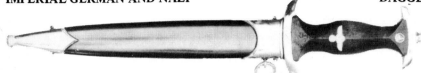

A good Nazi S.A. dagger, the blade with R.Z.M. mark, and 'M. 7/72/39', plated mounts, in its metal sheath with plated mounts. $119 £60

A Nazi Luftwaffe 2nd pattern officer's dagger, by W.K.C., grey metal mounts, silver wire bound orange ivorine grip, in its metal sheath with original hanging straps and belt clip. $129 £65

A Nazi 2nd pattern Luftwaffe officer's dagger, by Rudolf Buchel, grey metal mounts, white grip, in its grey metal sheath with original hanging straps and belt clip and with bullion dress knot, the clip marked 'D.R.G.M.' $129 £65

A good Nazi N.S.K.K. dagger by Carl Wusthof, plated mounts, in its metal sheath with plated mounts, with single hanging strap and belt clip. $139 £70

A good Nazi N.S.K.K. dagger, blade with R.Z.M. mark and also marked 'M. 7/37', plated mounts, in its metal sheath with leather frog suspension and with belt clip. $139 £70

A Nazi Army officer's dagger, by E. & F. Horster, plated mounts, orange ivorine grip, in its plated sheath. $148 £75

A Nazi S.A. dagger, fitted with imitation damascus etched blade by Eickhorn, German silver mounts, the hilt with original Eickhorn seal on tag, in its metal sheath with German silver mounts and with single loop and belt clip and with the additional belt loop and clip attached to hilt. $148 £75

A fine Nazi S.A. dagger, by S.M.F., German silver mounts, area stamp on reverse of crosspiece, in its metal sheath with German silver mounts and with single hanging strap and belt clip, stamped 'D.R.G.M.' $158 £80

A good Nazi S.A. dagger, blade etched with R.Z.M. mark and 'M. 7/83', German silver mounts, the crosspiece stamped '16/3744', in its German silver mounted metal sheath with single suspension loop and belt clip and with odd Nazi bullion dress knot. $158 £80

A Nazi 1st pattern Luftwaffe Officer's dagger, by Gebr. Heller, stamped '195' at forte, plated mounts, wire bound blue leather covered grip, in its blue leather covered metal sheath with plated mounts and hanging chains and belt clip, the top chape throat stamped: 'III F L 157' $178 £90

A scarce Nazi N.S.F.K. dagger by S.M.F., white metal mounts, blue leather covered grip, in its blue leather covered metal sheath with white metal mounts, single hanging strap and belt clip. $188 £95

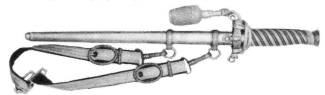

A Nazi Army officer's dagger by A.C.S., plated mounts, orange ivorine grip, in its plated sheath, with original staff officer's hanging straps and belt lug, buckles, swivels and mounts with some gilt and bullion dress knot.
$208 £105

A good Nazi 1st pattern Luftwaffe officer's dagger, plated blade by Gebr. Heller Marienthal B: Schweina Thr., with inspection stamp, German silver mounts, wire bound blue leather covered grip, in its German silver mounted, blue leather covered metal sheath with original hanging chains and belt clip.
$228 £115

A fine Nazi Red Cross man's dagger, the blade marked at forte 'Ges Geschutz', plated mounts, in its black painted metal sheath with plated mounts, with original leather frog, stamped 'Carl Busse Mainz 1941'.
$228 £115

A Nazi Red Cross man's dagger, blade marked at forte 'Ges Geschutz' and retains all original polish finish, plated mounts, in its black painted sheath with plated mounts. $238 £120

A Nazi N.S.F.K. dagger by S.M.F., plated mounts, leather covered grip, in its leather covered metal sheath with plated mounts, the locket with mark of the Luftsport-Verband. $257 £130

A Nazi 1st pattern Luftwaffe officer's dagger, by F. W. Holler, the blade retaining virtually all original polish, plated mounts, wire bound leather covered grip, in its blue leather covered sheath with plated mounts and suspension chains and belt clip, with bullion dress knot. $277 £140

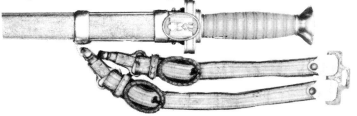

A Nazi Red Cross man's dagger, blade retaining much original polish and stamped 'Ges Geschutz' at forte, grey metal mounts, in its metal sheath with chrome plated mounts. $277 £140

A Nazi N.S.F.K. dagger by SMF., German silver mounts, blue leather covered grip, in its blue leather covered metal sheath with German silver mounts, the throat stamped with Nazi Eagle control mark. $287 £145

A Nazi National Hunting Association dress dagger, single edged blade 10in. by Eickhorn, etched with hunter shooting at deer within forest, plated shell guard with Turkey Cock, stag horn hilt mounted with 'D.J.' emblem.
                    $287 £145

A good Nazi N.S.F.K. dagger by E. A. Helbig Steinbach, blade retaining some original polish, plated German silver mounts, leather bound grip, in its leather covered sheath with plated mounts and hanging strap and belt clip. $317 £160

A scarce Nazi Railway Protection Force, 1935 model, officer's dagger by Robt Klaas, plated mounts, black grip, in its plated sheath. $337 £170

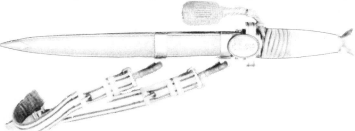

A Nazi Red Cross officer's dagger, plated blade and mounts, yellow ivorine grip, in its plated sheath with rare original hanging straps and belt clip, with bullion dress knot. $416 £210

A rare Nazi Land Custom's officer's dagger by E. & F. Horster, blade retaining some original polish, bright metal mounts, green leather covered wire bound grip, in its green leather covered metal sheath with metal mounts and bullion dress knot. $426 £215

A scarce, Nazi R.L.B. man's 2nd model dagger, German silver mounts, enamelled emblem to grip, in its black painted metal sheath with German silver mounts. $436 £220

A scarce, Nazi R.L.B. man's 2nd model dagger by E. & F. Horster, plated mounts, enamelled emblem to grip, in its black painted metal sheath with plated mounts and with bullion dress knot. $446 £225

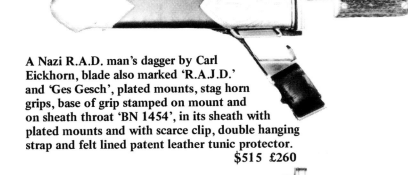

A Nazi R.A.D. man's dagger by Carl Eickhorn, blade also marked 'R.A.J.D.' and 'Ges Gesch', plated mounts, stag horn grips, base of grip stamped on mount and on sheath throat 'BN 1454', in its sheath with plated mounts and with scarce clip, double hanging strap and felt lined patent leather tunic protector. $515 £260

An extremely fine Nazi Red Cross officer's dagger, the blade retaining virtually all original polish, plated mounts, ivorine grip, in its plated sheath, with bullion dress knot, with original paper packet. $515 £260

A Nazi R.L.B. 2nd model officer's dagger by Paul Weyersberg, bright steel mounts, enamelled badge to leather covered grip, in its leather covered metal sheath with steel mounts and with original hanging straps and belt clip. $634 £320

A Nazi Teno man's dagger, by Eickhorn, also etched with Teno Eagle and
'Ges Gesch', grey metal mounts, white grips, in its black painted metal
sheath with white metal mounts.   **$634 £320**

A Nazi Railway Protection
Force officer's dagger, by
Eickhorn, blade retaining some original
polish, black grip, plated mounts, in its metal
sheath, with rare original hanging straps and belt lug
and bullion dress knot.   **$693 £350**

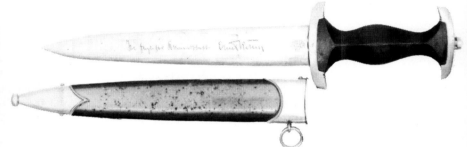

A Nazi S.A. dagger by Carl Eickhorn, the blade retaining nearly all original
polish, and with complete un-erased Roehm inscription, plated mounts, in
its metal sheath with plated mounts.   **$792 £400**

A Nazi S.S. 1936 model officer's dagger, blade retaining much original
polish, and etched with 'R.Z.M.' and '1196/38 S.S.', plated mounts, in
its metal sheath with original suspension chains of S.S. and death's head
links and with belt clip and leather tongue strap with belt clip.**$911 £460**

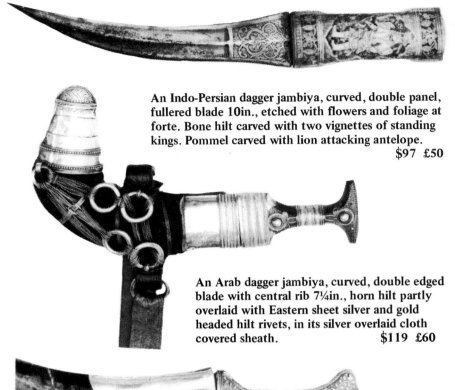

An Indo-Persian dagger jambiya, curved, double panel, fullered blade 10in., etched with flowers and foliage at forte. Bone hilt carved with two vignettes of standing kings. Pommel carved with lion attacking antelope.

$97 £50

An Arab dagger jambiya, curved, double edged blade with central rib 7¼in., horn hilt partly overlaid with Eastern sheet silver and gold headed hilt rivets, in its silver overlaid cloth covered sheath. $119 £60

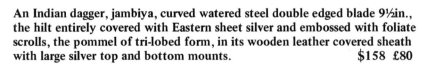

An Indian dagger, jambiya, curved watered steel double edged blade 9½in., the hilt entirely covered with Eastern sheet silver and embossed with foliate scrolls, the pommel of tri-lobed form, in its wooden leather covered sheath with large silver top and bottom mounts. $158 £80

A good 18th century Islamic dagger jambiya from Turkestan, slightly curved double edged watered blade 10½in., with sections of single and treble fullers, slightly waisted oval sectioned steel hilt. $356 £180

An Indo-Persian dagger kard, watered steel blade 8¾in. with swollen point. Grip strap and forte chiselled with foliage and scrolls, two-piece bone grips. In its leather covered sheath. $103 £52

An Indian dagger kard, straight finely watered fullered blade 12¼in., with gold damascened decoration at forte, steel mounted marine ivory grip, the mounts damascened similarly to blade, in its velvet covered copper mounted sheath. $168 £85

KHANJAR

An Indian ivory hilted dagger khanjar, recurved double edged watered blade 9½in., gold damascened at forte. Ivory hilt carved as a 'lion's head', open mouthed. In its velvet covered sheath. $238 £120

An Indian ivory hilted dagger khanjar, recurved double edged watered blade 10in., gold damascened at forte, ivory hilt carved as a bridled 'horse's head' with foliage at base, in its fabric covered sheath. $257 £130

An early 19th century Russian dagger kindjal, straight fullered double edged blade 12½in., iron hilt and sheath, iron suspension band around sheath top, two iron rivets to grip. $148 £75

A Caucasian white metal mounted dagger kindjal, multi-fullered double edged blade 13¼in., with traces of etched decoration at forte, horn hilt with white metal mounts engraved and decorated with geometric nielloed patterns, white metal mounts leather covered wooden sheath. $158 £80

A Caucasian kindjal, double edged, multi-fullered blade 13in., with spear point, horn grips mounted with niello decorated German silver, in its leather covered wooden sheath. $158 £80

A large Caucasian kindjal, long, double edged blade 24½in., with deep central fuller and with some silver inlaid foliate scroll decoration, plain horn grips with iron mounts and mounted with six Persian coins, in its leather covered sheath. $198 £100

A Cossack white metal and nielloed kindjal, double edged blade 15¼in., multi-fullered, and struck at forte with armourer's mark, white metal hilt with two tall stud mounts, oblong domed mount, in its wooden lined white metal sheath. $228 £115

A Caucasian dagger kindjal, double edged tapered blade 14in., with a mark at forte, silver mounted horn hilt with decorated rivet heads, in its silver mounted leather covered wooden sheath. $297 £150

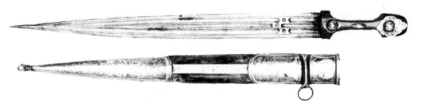

A Caucasian silver mounted dagger kindjal, tri-fullered blade, 18½in., etched with artificial damascus, struck with three cutler's marks. Hilt and sheath mounts of nielloed silver including large Turkish toughra. $356 £180

A large Caucasian kindjal, broad, single edged, multi-fullered blade 23in., with clipped back tip, struck with armourer's mark at forte, plain horn grips, Eastern silver beaded straps, in its leather covered wooden sheath.$416 £210

A fine Caucasian dagger kindjal, double edged fullered, tapered blade 16in., ivory part horn hilt with nielloed silver mount, in its leather covered nielloed silver mounted wooden sheath with companion knife. $832 £420

DAGGERS
KLEEWANG

A silver mounted celebes kleewang, straight, single edged, watered steel blade 26½in., elaborately carved foliate horn pommel, grip covered with Eastern sheet silver. $139 £70

A silver mounted Celebes kleewang, single edged, multi-fullered blade 30½in., stamped at forte 'W. Klanberg, Solingen'. Elaborately foliate carved horn pommel with grip sheathed in Eastern sheet silver. In its wooden sheath with Eastern silver ring mounts and horn throat mounts. $158 £80

A good kleewang, single edged blade, 22½in., with long clipped back edge, Eastern silver covered hilt with floral and foliate patterns, elaborately foliate pierced horn pommel, in its wooden sheath with seven silver band mounts and with horn throat and bottom chape. $198 £100

KNUCKLEDUSTER

A World War II brass hilted Middle East Commando knuckleduster dagger, single edged, straight blade 7in., with single fuller, flattened plain grip. $119 £60

A scarce World War II Middle East commando knuckleduster dagger, single edged blade 5½in., brass, flattened knuckleduster hilt, in its original leather sheath with belt loop and flap. $238 £120

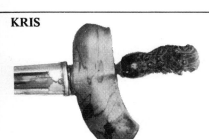

A Javanese kris, straight, double edged, watered steel blade 14½in., well floral carved wooden hilt with small brass base mount, in its part white metal clad wooden sheath. $83 £42

A good Moro kris, broad, double edged, slightly wavy blade 21¼in., with two silver decorative bands at forte, bone hilt of typical Moro form, in its part cane bound plain wooden sheath. $91 £46

A Javanese kris, double edged, wavy, watered steel blade 15½in., well carved ivory hilt and with flattened turned brass base mount, in its plain wooden sheath. $99 £50

A Sumatran kris, straight, double edged, watered steel blade 14in., well carved ivory garuda hilt, pierced in relief with foliate patterns and set in a white metal base mount, in its polished wooden sheath. $119 £60

A Sumatran kris, wavy, watered steel blade 12¼in., intricately carved, stylised garuda wooden hilt with Eastern silver cup mount, in its Eastern sheet silver covered sheath. $139 £70

A good Sumatran executioner's kris, double edged, straight blade 19½in., carved ivory grip with chiselled brass cup mount, in its sheath set with thirty-four Eastern silver bands, the lower section being of ebony.
$168 £85

A Sumatran kris, wavy, watered steel blade 11in., stylised garuda hilt, covered in copper gilt sheet, in its Eastern sheet silver covered sheath.
$178 £90

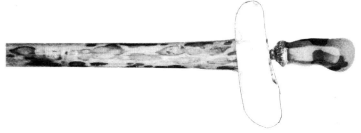

A good Malay kris, straight, double edged blade 13½in., carved with two tone wood grip with gold cup mount set with rubies, in its two tone wooden sheath with large single piece ivory boat shaped top mount. $495 £250

A Nazi Naval officer's dirk, plain fluted blade, brass mounts, brass wire bound white grip, in its brass sheath.　　　　　　　　　　$119　£60

A Nazi Naval officer's dirk by Eickhorn, blade etched with fouled anchor, foliage and entwined dolphins and gilt mounts, in its gilt metal sheath with original dress knot.　　　　　　　　　　$148　£75

A Nazi Naval officer's dirk by F. W. Holler, gilt mounts, wire bound white grip, in its gilt metal sheath.　　　　　　　　　　$148　£75

A Nazi Naval officer's dirk by W.K.C., brass mounts, wire bound grip, in its hammered brass sheath, with bullion dress knot.　　　　　　　$150　£76

DIRKS
IMPERIAL GERMAN AND NAZI

A Nazi Naval officer's dirk, plain fullered blade, by A.C.S., brass mounts, wire bound white grip, in its brass sheath with roped hanging ring mounts.

$154 £78

A Nazi Naval officer's dirk by E. & F. Horster, etched with fouled anchor, brass mounts with traces of gilt, in its brass sheath and with one original black velvet lined suspension strap. $168 £85

A Nazi Naval officer's dirk, by Clemen & Jung, blade etched with fouled anchor, gilt mounts, wire bound white grip, in its gilt metal sheath with bullion dress knot. $178 £90

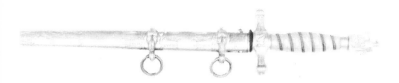

A Nazi Naval officer's dirk by W.K.C., blade etched with sailing ships, gilt mounts, orange grip bound with brass wire, in its brass sheath, the suspension rings with knotted rope mounts. $218 £105

A Nazi Naval officer's dirk by W.K.C., brass mounts, brass wire bound white
ivorine grip, in its brass sheath with original naval bullion dress knot.
$208 £105

A Nazi Naval officer's dirk, by Eickhorn, the blade retaining most original
polish and etched with foliage, fouled anchor and entwined dolphins, gilt
mounts, brass wire bound white grip, bullion dress knot, in its brass sheath
with original hanging straps. $208 £105

A Nazi Naval officer's dirk by Eickhorn, etched with fouled anchor, gilt
mounts, wire bound white grip, in its gilt sheath with original black velvet
lined hanging straps. $238 £120

A Nazi Naval officer's dirk by W.K.C., the blade etched with fouled anchor,
gilt brass mounts, wire bound orange ivorine grip, in its hammered gilt
sheath with black velvet lined hanging straps and original dress knot.
$356 £180

An attractive Georgian Midshipman's dirk, flattened, tapered blade 9in.,
turned ivory grip with gilt mounts including oak leaf and acorn, embossed
crosspiece and lion mask pommel. $63 £32

A Georgian Naval dirk, circa 1800, plain, single edged, long curved blade
18½in., with narrow back fuller, plain reversed crosspiece and shield langets, ribbed bone grip, brass 'lion's head' pommel. $75 £38

A Georgian Naval type dirk, plain blade 15¾in., with narrow back fuller,
brass wire bound ivory grip, brass crossguard with up and down swept
quillons, brass pommel. $75 £38

An early 19th century Continental (French?) Naval officer's dirk, tapering,
single edged blade 12½in. of flattened diamond section, small brass crosspiece with turned quillons, spiral black grip with brass oval escutcheons,
fluted pommel, in its brass mounted leather sheath. $129 £65

A Georgian Artillery officer's dirk, straight, single edged blade 15¾in.,
etched with military trophy, brass armee and scrolls. Copper gilt hilt, cannon
ball finialled pierced quillons, oval langets engraved with cannon centred
military trophies. Engraved ferrule and stepped pommel, diced ivory grip.
                                                                   $158 £80

A Georgian 'Nile Club' Naval officer's dirk, curved blade, copper gilt
guard with side loop incorporating openwork crocodile design, copper gilt
mounts and crocodile head pommel, diced ivory grip. $168 £85

A good post-1902 Naval officer's dirk, blade 17½in. by Gieves, etched with
crown fouled anchor. Gilt crosspiece, 'lion's head' pommel and mounts. Gilt
wire bound white fish-skin covered grip. In its brass mounted sheath.
                                                         $178 £90

An Imperial Russian Naval officer's dirk, blade 8¾in. of diamond section,
etched at forte with Imperial Russian Eagle and crowned cypher of Nicholas
II, plain, reversed crosspiece and squared brass mounts, flattened rectangular
ivory grip, in its patent leather covered wooden sheath with three plain brass
mounts. $178 £90

A Georgian Naval officer's dirk, double edged, tapering blade 7½in. etched
within scrolls: 'Alexander Glen, Royal Navy, Malabar 1832-1834, Wolf
1834-38, Obit Malta 1842, Aatat 25', with foliate sprays, copper gilt crosspiece chiselled with acorns and oak leaves, spiral turned ivory hilt, in its
leather sheath. $267 £125

A Georgian Naval dirk, tapered, double edged blade 7¼in., of flattened
diamond section, blued and gilt and engraved with foliage and trophies
of arms, chiselled copper gilt circular guard, copper gilt mounted turned ivory
grip, in its copper gilt sheath with two suspension rings. $327 £165

An early 19th century Scottish dirk, plain, single edged blade 13½in., stamped at forte with ordnance mark, back fuller, corded wood hilt with central swelling, carved at top with thistles, and mounted with iron studded decoration, steel pommel engraved with thistles, steel ring mount at hilt base, in its leather covered metal sheath with four steel mounts. $89 £45

A Victorian military Scottish piper's dirk, single edged blade 12in., with double fullers, corded wood hilt with German silver studded decoration, plain German silver pommel and mounts, the ring base mount engraved 'N52'. $119 £60

A Victorian silver mounted Scottish dirk set, plain blade 11in., corded wood hilt with plain silver mounts, the pommel engraved with a family crest, in its leather covered sheath with four plain silver mounts and with companion knife and fork.
$307 £155

A post-1902 officer's silver mounted Scottish dirk set of a Commonwealth Scottish Regiment, blade 11¼in., with short fuller and scallop back edge, corded wood black grip mounted with silver studded decoration, silver base mount decorated with Celtic pattern, the pommel with badge of facetted star surmounted by KC, motto: 'Per Ardua Stabilis Esto', in its leather covered sheath. $346 £175

A mid 18th century Scottish dirk set, single edged blade 10½in., by 'Jn. Bell Perth', scallop back edge, corded wood hilt, some brass studded decoration, pewter mounts, glass panel pommel containing silver paper, in its leather covered metal sheath with four pewter mounts engraved with thistles and with companion knife and fork. $356 £180

A good, late 18th century silver mounted Scottish dirk set, single edged blade 12¾in., stamped 'Cocker', scallop back edge, the back fuller pierced with holes, corded wood hilt with silver stud decoration, silver base mount with thistle engraved pattern, circular silver pommel inset with facetted glass stone pommel, in its leather sheath with four silver mounts decorated with thistles, together with companion knife and fork. $346 £200

A Victorian Scottish dirk set of the 21st Regiment (Royal Scots Fusiliers), single edged blade 10½in., with double fullers and scallop back edge, by 'Peter Henderson, maker, Glasgow', corded wood hilt with German silver mounts, the pommel engraved with thistle and 'XXI', in its leather covered wooden sheath with four German silver mounts, together with companion knife and fork. $396 £200

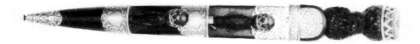

A late Victorian silver mounted Scottish dirk set, blade 11½in., with pierced fuller, scallop back edge, by 'Ferguson and McBean Inverness', corded black wood hilt carved with thistles, silver mounts engraved with Celtic patterns, silver claw mount inset with facetted yellow glass pommel, in its leather covered wooden sheath with four silver mounts and with companion knife and fork. $693 £350

A Victorian silver mounted Scottish officer's dirk set of the 93rd Regiment, single edged, tapering blade 12in., with pronounced clipped back point and part scallop back edge. Corded wood hilt set with silver studs. Silver mounts chiselled with thistles, facetted glass pommel. In its leather covered wooden sheath with four silver mounts, the top chape with embossed numerals '93' and engraved on back 'Prosser, London'. Together with companion knife and fork. $752 £380

A late Victorian Scottish officer's silver mounted dirk set of the Gordon Highlanders, single edged blade 12in., with single fuller and scallop back edge. Corded wood hilt set with silver studs. Silver base mount decorated with thistles. Elaborate openwork pommel mount with facetted coloured glass pommel supported on fronds, etc. In its leather covered wooden sheath with four hallmarked silver mounts. The top chape with badge of the Gordon Highlanders. The reverse with maker's stamp 'R. & H. B. Kirkwood, Thistle St., Edinburgh' and with hallmark 'Edinburgh 1899', together with companion knife. Contained in purple velvet lined fitted leather covered case with companion skean dhu. $772 £390

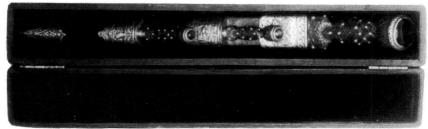

A Victorian Scottish officer's silver mounted dirk set of the Argyll & Sutherland Highlanders, single edged blade 10in., with scallop back edge. Corded wood hilt mounted with silver stud decoration. Silver mounts decorated with Celtic patterns, facetted coloured glass stone in pommel. In its leather covered wooden sheath with four chased and cast silver mounts, by 'Anderson & Sons, George St., Edinburgh'. Together with companion knife and fork. $990 £500

A 16th century German halberd, flattened crescent blade, 6½in., pierced with some holes, flattened beak struck with an armourer's mark, diamond section spike 23in., two brass rosettes at base, long straps, mounted on section of original haft, overall 6ft.2in.   **$198 £100**

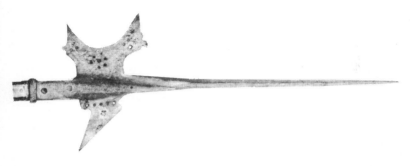

A late 16th century German halberd, head 20in., spike 15in., of diamond section, beak and blade pierced with holes, traces of quatrefoil armourer's stamp to beak, long straps, on a section of haft, overall 6ft.6in.**$287 £145**

A rare French or Swiss etched halberd, circa 1550, head 21in. overall with diamond sectioned spike 15½in. Pierced crescent cutting edge, pierced back-spike wrought with three integral claws of square section, on its brass studded octagonal haft and crimson silk tassels and fringes.   **$673 £340**

A hanger, circa 1775 (possibly American revolutionary period), plain single edged, slightly curved blade 25in., with broad and narrow back fullers and with hatched pattern to backstrap, plain iron, single flattened knucklebow and mounts, plain wood grip. $69 £35

A silver gilt hilted Georgian officer's hanger, circa 1770, curved, double fullered blade 24½in., with clipped back point, wavy slotted guard, fluted knucklebow, 'lion's head' pommel, the guard base with some stamps, spiral horn grip. $79 £40

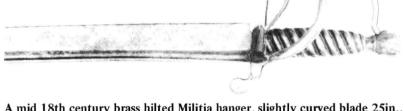

A mid 18th century brass hilted Militia hanger, slightly curved blade 25in., with traces of 'BO' and ordnance arrow at forte. Brass heart-shaped guard, plain knucklebow with double side loop. Ribbed spiral grip, ovoid pommel engraved 'CNLM4'. $89 £45

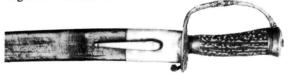

A 17th century English hunting hanger, slightly curved, single edged blade 19in., deeply struck with fleur-de-lys cutler's marks. Brass guard, integral foliate finialled quillon, crowns and fleur-de-lys on knucklebow. Natural stag horn grip, pommel with 'cherubs' heads' and fleur-de-lys. In later brass mounted leather scabbard. $99 £50

An early 18th century English brass hilted hunting hanger, slightly curved, single edged fullered blade 24in. Brass knucklebow, shellguard and quillon with swollen terminal. Natural stag horn grip with brass ferrule and pommel. In its brass mounted blind tooled leather scabbard. $99 £50

A hanger, circa 1770 (possibly American revolutionary period), curved blade 23in. with pronounced clipped back point, blade pierced with small hole pattern and double orb and cross, steel guard with slotted base, wire bound, ribbed bone grip. $99 £50

A late 18th century American/European hanger (probably U.S. revolutionary period), curved blade 18in., iron hilt with single knucklebow and side bar with sheet guard at base, octagonal bone grip, thumb ring. $117 £60

A mid 18th century brass hilted Danish military hanger, curved blade 26in., engraved on backstrap 'S. & T. in Solingen' and etched with crowned 'FR' cypher and foliate scroll heart-shaped guard, single knucklebow, spiral grip, ovoid pommel. $123 £63

A late 18th century Imperial Russian brass hilted hanger, single edged, slightly curved blade 26in., etched in Russian script at forte 'Tula' and with crowned cypher of Catherine II with traces of date '1778', heart-shaped guard, Imperial Eagle stamp to back quillon, single knucklebow, ovoid pommel, spiral grip. $139 £70

A mid 18th century brass hilted Militia hanger, slightly curved, single edged blade 24½in., with back fuller, ordnance crown stamp at forte, heart-shaped guard engraved '4/3M = Huntingdon', double loop guard, plain knucklebow, spiral grip, ovoid pommel. $139 £70

A late 18th century Dutch Naval hanger, slightly curved blade 24in., etched with date '1793', crossed anchors and 'AR' and foliate scroll, brass hilt with plain knucklebow and sideloop, engraved on backstrap 'N 2026'. Brass wire bound leather covered grip. In its leather scabbard with brass mounts. $139 £70

A Russian 1817 pattern brass hilted 'Briquet' Naval hanger, curved blade 27in., engraved on backstrap in Russian and dated '1831' with Russian stamps at forte and struck with anchor, plain single knucklebow brass ribbed grip, in its leather scabbard with brass top mount with belt lug. $158 £80

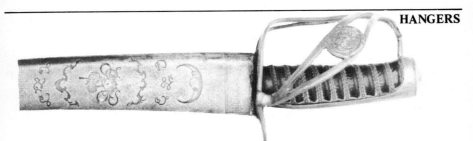

An interesting 18th century hanger, broad, curved, single edged blade 26in., with clipped back point etched with 'Turk's head', crescent moon, foliate sprays, Talisman symbols, standing Ecclesiastical figure, traces of gilt, single knucklebow, slotted guard, openwork sideloop with cartouche bearing arms of the Papal States, brass mounts, wire bound leather covered grip. $297 £150

An English silver hilted hunting hanger, curved blade 23½in., with clipped back point, the knucklebow and mounts of silver (knucklebow hallmarked London 1777), maker's stamp 'W.K.', flattened black wood grip, in a leather scabbard with silver top mount. $436 £220

A Georgian Naval officer's hanger, circa 1790, curved blade 26in., 'Warranted' copper gilt hilt with scrolled sideloop and plain knucklebow and mounts, fluted ivory grip, copper gilt oval escutcheon inset, engraved with crown and fouled anchor, in its blind tooled leather scabbard, with three copper gilt mounts. $554 £280

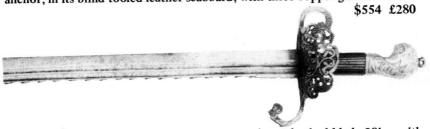

A fine English mid 17th century hanger, curved, saw-backed blade 28in., with 'King's head' mark, with double fullers and signed in the fullers 'Fide Sed Cui Vide', finely foliate scroll pierced and chiselled double shellguard, reversed scrolled quillons chiselled with human mask terminals, fluted bone grip, silvered chiselled brass pommel in form of 'lion's head'. $792 £400

HUNTING CUTLASSES

A late Naval boarding cutlass, slightly curved blade 31in., with clipped back tip, ordnance stamps at forte, and date '02' by Mole, Birmingham, sheet steel guard, ribbed iron grip, in its leather scabbard with brass bottom chape.

$99 £50

A Georgian figure-of-eight Naval cutlass, slightly curved blade 25in., with single back fuller, and struck with crown 'GR', sheet iron guard, ribbed iron grip.

$103 £52

A scarce, late 18th century American or British Naval boarding cutlass, 29in. straight, single edged blade with narrow fuller, iron figure-of-eight guard impressed with maker's name 'H....SER', plain tubular iron grip. $111 £56

A Georgian Naval cutlass, curved blade 32in., iron figure-of-eight guard, ribbed iron grip.

$119 £60

A Georgian Naval cutlass, circa 1790, single edged blade 28in., with back fuller, ordnance stamp at forte, figure-of-eight sheet iron guard, sheet iron bound grip. $119 £60

A Nazi era hunting cutlass, blade 16in. by Carl Eickhorn, lightly etched with military trophies and foliage, brass shellguard, reversed hoof crosspiece, stag horn grip mounted with three brass acorns, brass mounts, in its brass mounted leather sheath. $139 £70

A unusual early 19th century boarding cutlass, broad, slightly curved, single edged blade 21½in., with narrow back fuller, stamped '22 Harvey' at forte, integral cast iron hilt with 'D' knucklebow. $148 £75

A large late 19th century cutlass, broad, single edged, slightly curved blade 33in., black painted sheet steel guard, plain wood grips, in its leather scabbard with brass bottom chape. $158 £80

HUNTING CUTLASSES

A 19th century German hunting cutlass, straight, single edged blade 19½in., by A.C.S., lightly etched with military trophies and foliate scrolls, small brass shellguard decorated with hounds attacking boar, brass reversed hoof quillons with central device of boar's head, slightly curved stag horn hilt, in its brass mounted leather sheath. $158 £80

A 1900 pattern Naval cutlass, single edged blade 27½in. by Mole, model date '00' on backstrap, ordnance stamps at forte, solid steel guard with turn-over edges, diced leather grips, in its steel mounted leather scabbard with brass frog button. $158 £80

A Nazi era forestry official's dress hunting cutlass, single edged blade 13in., by Carl Eickhorn, etched with scenes of stag and boar hunt etc., fluted gilt shell-guard, gilt knucklebow and mounts, hoof back quillons, stag horn grips mounted with three acorns, in its leather sheath with gilt metal mounts. $198 £100

A late 18th century European hunting cutlass, plain, single edged blade 19in., with narrow back fuller, copper gilt plain shellguard with loop, reversed copper gilt hoof quillons, copper gilt mounts, flattened hilt with ivory grips, in a leather covered wooden sheath with plain copper and brass gilt mounts. $218 £110

A Japanese sword katana, blade 56cm., mumei, two mekugi ana, ito suguha hamon. Iron mounted tape bound same tsuka, menuki as dragon with ken, iron tsuba and whirled rim, in its black lacquered saya. $396 £200

A Japanese sword Katana, blade 69½cm. signed 'Kashunoju Tachibana Katsuiye Saku'. Chu gunome hamon with broad nie clusters, O kissaki, itame hada. Iron mokko tsuba, tape bound same tsuka, iron fuchi kashira. In its black lacquered saya. $673 £340

A Japanese sword katana, 72cm. signed 'Bishu Osafune Noju Kiyomitsu', two mekugi ana. Itame hada, chu suguha hamon. Iron tsuba with radial chiselling. Tape bound same tsuka, iron fuchi kashira with clouds in katakiri. In its black lacquered saya with red clouds. $841 £425

A heavy Japanese sword katana, blade 65cm., signed Hizen Nokuni Minamoto Munetsugu with two mekugi ana. Broad gunome hamon, straight itame hada, broad nie clouds. Gin hitoye habaki, iron mokko tsuba with gilt tendrils. Shakudo fuchi kashira with gilt and copper horses, good floral menuki to tape bound same tsuka. In its birch lacquered saya with iron kojiri, $2,277 £1,150

KNIVES
BADE BADE

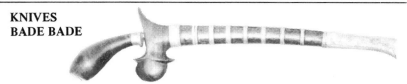

A Malayan knife bade bade, single edged, curved blade 10in., wooden globose pommel, in its pewter mounted wooden sheath, the bottom mount decorated with scrolling foliage design, the top section of a different colour wood.

$32 £16

A silver mounted bade bade, blade 7¼in., horn tulip carved hilt with Eastern silver cup mount, in its wooden sheath with Eastern sheet silver and silver band mounts embossed with geometric patterns, carved horn mount at top.

$99 £50

A silver mounted bade bade, slightly curved blade 7½in., tulip hilt overlaid with Eastern sheet silver decorated with foliate sprays, in its wooden sheath, with two Eastern silver mounts similarly decorated.

$148 £75

BICHAQ

An Armenian knife bichaq, down curved, single edged blade 6¼in., brass mounted gold damascened hilt, decorated with scrolls and down turned pommel, in its wooden red leather covered sheath with large embossed top and bottom, silver mounts.

$34 £17

A silver mounted Armenian dagger bichaq, blade 7in., etched with a snake, the hilt covered in Eastern silver, embossed with foliate and other patterns and with stud decoration, eared pommel. In its sheath of solid Eastern silver cast with floral patterns.

$67 £34

BOWIE

A bowie knife, clipped back blade 6in., marked at forte 'Wilson Hawksworth Ellison and Co', 'Patent Handle Kindner Bros', white metal oval crossguard, white metal hilt embossed with foliate patterns. $20 £10

A bowie knife, clipped back blade 6¾in., with traces of maker 'Jameson & Co. Patent', small oval German silver crosspiece, stag horn grips, in leather sheath, sheath stitching AF. $75 £38

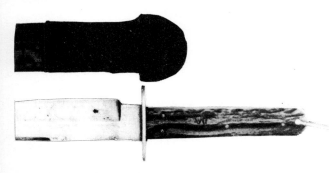

A good, old Victorian bowie knife, plain, single edged blade 8in., with pronounced clipped back tip, small plain oval German silver crosspiece, stag horn grips, in its leather sheath. $89 £45

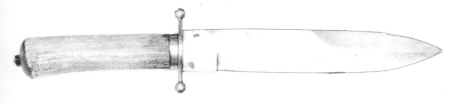

A heavy Victorian bowie knife, broad, straight blade 7½in., with clipped back tip. Steel crosspiece with ball finials, natural stag horn grip with steel ferrule and pommel. In its leather covered sheath with sprung retaining catch.
                    $129 £65

A good Victorian folding bowie type knife, single edged blade 4½in. by Edward Barnes & Sons, white metal crosspiece, embossed with foliate spray and 'Liberty and Union' with scroll, plain horn grips, inset with two mother-of-pearl plaques and German silver pommel, thumb spring release catch.

$178 £90

A good Victorian bowie knife, single edged, clipped back blade 10in., stamped at forte with maker's name and Sheffield address, small scalloped crossguard, brass hilt decorated with wheat ears against striated ground, in its white metal mounted leather sheath.

$178 £90

A good Victorian bowie knife, long, single edged blade 10¼in., with clipped back edge, scalloped and crossed along back of blade. Elliptical steel crosspiece with scalloped edges, finely foliate and scroll engraved en suite with oval pommel. Steel ferrule, natural stag horn grip.

$208 £105

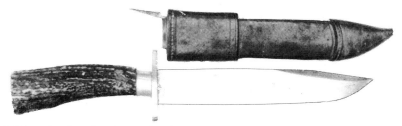

A Victorian London bowie knife, clipped back blade 7in., stamped 'V.R. Underwood, Haymarket, London'. White metal crosspiece, ferrule and pommel, natural stag horn grip. In its leather sheath with sprung steel catch reciprocating through crosspiece.

$228 £115

A good Victorian bowie knife, blade 8¾in., with pronounced clipped back
point, faintly etched with U.S. Eagle and: 'I Ask For Nothing But What Is
Right' by 'I. Read, Lambert Street, Sheffield', the hilt side panels of white
metal, small up-turned crosspiece, in its leather covered cardboard sheath
with plain white metal thoat mount. $396 £200

A good, old folding bowie knife, single edged blade 4½in, white metal small
crosspiece, stag horn grips, white metal pommel in form of a horse's head
with anchor above cannon. $515 £260

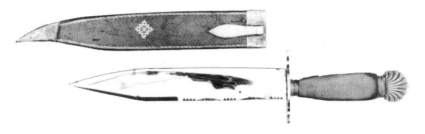

A good Victorian bowie knife, broad, clipped back blade 9¼in., with clipped
back point and part scalloped back edge, flattened German silver crosspiece,
flattened back horn grip, scalloped German silver pommel, in its leather
covered sheath with plain German silver mounts. $544 £275

A good Victorian bowie type knife, broad, shallow, diamond section, double
edged blade 8in., panel etched with 'A sure defence' against scrolled ground.
Hallmarked silver ferrule, ball finialled crosspiece, spiral carved ivory grip. In
its silver mounted sheath with gilt tooled green Morocco leather covering.
                                                           $614 £310

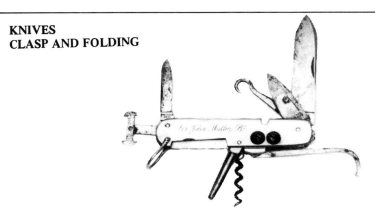

A good, old combination penknife, plain German silver sideplates, one engraved 'Sir John Miller B.T.' and with long and short blades, 2in. and 3½in. by 'Clements Liter St E.C.', corkscrew button hook, gouge, horse's hoof stone remover, screwdriver, two others, frame length 4¾in. $32 £16

A good Victorian bowie type folding knife, plain, single edged blade 4in. and small blade, white metal crosspiece embossed with foliate and floral pattern with similar design to pommel, mother-of-pearl grips. $218 £110

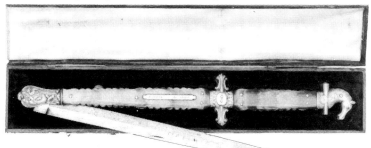

A fine presentation folding clasp knife, straight, single edged blade of flattened diamond section 10½in., with spring lock, the white metal mounted grips inset with escutcheon engraved 'R. Higgin from Mrs Cobden', the pommel in the form of a horse's head surmounting cannon barrel and anchor, the crenulated horn grip panels (four) separated in centre by an additional white metal embossed mount and contained in a close fitted blue velvet lined case. $1,534 £775

A South American gaucho knife, tapered, clipped back blade 7½in., stamped 'Gebr Ortmann Solingen' at forte, white metal hilt with ribbed decoration, in its white metal sheath.   **$40 £20**

A good South American (Argentina) gaucho knife, single edged, tapering blade 10½in., with sun mark and maker 'Broqua Scholberg & Cia Rosario', the hilt of German silver, the top decorated with foliate sprays, in its leather sheath with two large German silver mounts, with broad belt hook of foliate form. **$128 £65**

A silver mounted South American gaucho knife, spear blade 7in., etched with mythical bird amidst foliage, wolf and hound etc. South American silver hilt embossed with foliage etc., pommel with leopard masks in its solid silver sheath with belt hook.   **$139 £70**

A silver mounted South American gaucho knife, spear blade 4¾in., retaining nearly all original polish, by Franz Wenk, the hilt of South American silver with gold mounts: Arms of Uruguay, floral patterns, dog and gaucho, in its sheath of solid silver with '800' hallmark.   **$169 £85**

KNIVES
HUNTING

A rare 17th century Dutch or English hunting knife, slightly curved, single edged blade 11½in., with clipped back edge, struck with king's head, 'playing card' mark. Recurved brass crosspiece with dragon's head quillon terminals. Brass ferrule and pommel with classical busts and cherubs amidst scrolls. Natural stag horn grip. $356 £180

KUKRI

A Gurkha kukri, curved single edged blade 12in., white metal mounted horn hilt, in its Eastern silver mounted leather sheath, the top and bottom mounts embossed with sprigs of foliage flowers, the top chape mounted with a silver gilt coat of arms. $99 £50

PIA KAETTA

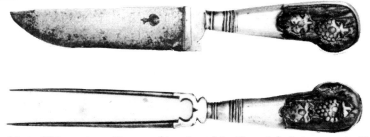

A fine Singalese knife pia kaetta, blade 7½in., inlaid with panels of intricately foliate chiselled silver. Brass forte mount intricately scroll chiselled and inlaid with silver scrolls. Scroll carved and pierced horn hilt with scroll silver pommel and rivet heads. $119 £60

TROUSSE

A good late 17th century German (Augsburg) knife and fork trousse, knife blade 4in., struck with cutler's mark of a fir cone within an orb. Two pronged fork, both mounted on stepped German silver hilt with integral grip straps, natural stag horn grips with rivet heads in the form of fir cones.
$267 £135

A rare 18th century Chinese parrying weapon, iron head 18½in., double edged leaf shaped blade 9in., scalloped at base. Crescent supported by two integral bars emanating from brass ball on stem, brass dragon's head above socket. On its wooden haft. $71 £36

A Japanese horseman's disarming polearm Sode Garami, iron bound head 18in., with three spiked iron lames, six barbed iron hooks at top. On its original wooden haft. $109 £55

A late 17th century French polearm Partizan, head 12½in., stamped with maker's name 'Praiaia' (?), with three crescent and flamboyant side projections, raised central rib. Now fitted on a 22in. section of musket barrel from which a haft projects. $129 £65

A good 16th century Italian polearm Coresque or Runkas, head 31in., auxiliary blades 7in., with an 18th century velvet covered haft and neck with bullion embroidered tassels. $240 £120

A good Victorian copy of a cup-hilted rapier
used by John George, 3rd Earl of Durham at
a Dress Ball at Devonshire House, 2nd July
1897, at which King Edward VII was present
as Knight Hospitaler of Malta, the 34in. blade
etched with later inscription to that effect,
brass multi bar hilt. In its brass mounted velvet covered scabbard. $119 £60

A Spanish 18th century cup-hilt rapier, slim blade
34½in., of diamond section, short fullers, plain
steel cup guard, long circular plain quillons, plain
'D' shaped knucklebow, plain, small pommel,
wood grip. $198 £100

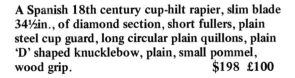

A Spanish 18th century rapier, tapering, double
edged blade 34½in., with running wolf mark and
signed in short fullers: 'Inti Domini', iron, pierced
double shellguard, long turned crosspiece, plain
'D' knucklebow, fluted ovoid pommel, wire bound
grip. $198 £100

A fine Spanish cup-hilt rapier, circa 1670, shallow diamond sectioned blade 37in., struck on the fluted ricasso with 'Vapfr'. Cup with turned over brim. Plate and guard secured by crossed bun headed screws. Long quillons with baluster terminals, integral cup supports with foliate and ribbed supports. Baluster knucklebow terminal and mid section. Bun pommel on stepped baluster foot. Wire bound grip with steel ferrules.
$693 £350

A good Italian (Milanese) swept-hilted rapier by Caino, circa 1615, straight, double edged blade of alternate diamond and flattened section 43½in. Swept-hilt of good form, comprising octagonal sectioned bars, small buckled shell-guard, octagonal lemon shaped pommel. Wooden grip with iron 'Turks' heads'. $713 £360

A fine Spanish 18th century silver mounted cup-hilt rapier, straight, slightly tapering, double edged blade 36in., of flattened diamond section, signed in the short fullers 'Rtung in C:uir htcl'. Steel bowl chiselled with foliate, floral and semi-circular patterns, the rim mounted with Spanish silver has central gold band decorated with studs, long, straight rounded quillons, plain rounded knucklebow and a flattened circular pommel of silver has a gold rosette mount. $832 £420

A late 19th century Prussian Mounted Artillery trooper's sabre, curved blade 29½in., retaining most original polish, stamped on backstrap 'W. 97'(1897), steel stirrup guard and mounts, the crosspiece stamped 'R.A.R. 13. I.L.M.K.87', plain steel mounts, ribbed leather covered grip, in its steel scabbard. $51 £26

A Nazi Police sabre, plain, plated curved blade 34in., by Puma, also stamped 'No. 9', plain, plated stirrup knucklebow and mounts, wire bound ribbed black grip, in its black painted metal scabbard.$59 £30

An Indian Army, late 19th century, Foot Artillery sabre, plain curved blade 30in., stamped on backstrap:'London Made'. Plain brass stirrup knucklebow and mounts, ribbed iron grip, the top of back quillon stamped: 'FA 1.05', in its brass mounted leather scabbard. $79 £40

A late 19th century Turkish Officer's sabre, slightly curved fullered blade 29½in., retaining most original polish, etched with complex trophy and foliage patterns, the etching also covers the back of the blade, ornate brass stirrup guard with eagle quillons, one langet with star and cresent, the other escutcheon, 'lion's head' pommel, wire bound fishskin covered grip, in its steel scabbard with single suspension ring. $91 £46

An Imperial German Artillery officer's sabre, slight curved plated blade 32in., etched with Prussian Eagle, military trophies, foliage, mounted artillery team and regiment 'I. Grossh Hess Feldartill Reg No 25' on blued panels, plain steel stirrup guard and mounts, ribbed fish-skin covered grip, in its metal scabbard.

$99 £50

An Imperial German Mounted Artillery officer's sabre, plain, curved, pipe-back, clipped back blade, 33in., etched on backstrap 'M. Schreiber, Hanover', brass hilt with traces of gilt, square langets with crossed cannon, the knuckle-bow decorated with foliage etc. 'Lion's head' pommel, wire bound fish-skin covered grip, in its steel scabbard.

$99 £50

A Nazi sabre, curved blade 33in., by Horster, plain brass stirrup guard and mounts with Nazi Eagle Waffen AMT stamps, 'E. & F. H. 38' and '2597', brass wire bound black ribbed grip, in its black painted metal scabbard.

$99 £50

A U.S. Society sabre, curved, plated blade 30½in., by Henderson Ames, Kalamazoo, etched with Masonic temple and scenes, foliage etc., gilt triple bar guard, 'lion's head' pommel, wire bound, fish-skin covered grip, in its plated scabbard with three elaborate gilt Gothic mounts of warriors etc.

$99 £50

SABRES

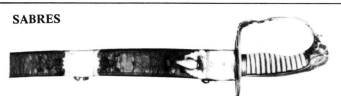

A Georgian 1803 pattern officer's sabre, plain, curved blade 30in., copper slotted guard and knucklebow incorporating crown 'GR' cypher, copper mounts, 'lion's head' pommel, ribbed ivory grip, in its leather scabbard with blind tooled decoration, including Prince of Wales' feathers device and with three plain copper mounts, the top mount marked 'Prosser, Charing Cross' with belt lug. $111 £56

A U.S. officer's sabre, circa 1820, possibly Naval. Curved blade 28½in., gilt hilt with openwork slotted guard and fluted knucklebow, 'eagle's head' pommel, fluted black grip. $119 £60

A pre-Nazi Artillery officer's sabre, slightly curved, plated blade 33in., by E. Pack & Sohne, etched with horse's head, mounted artillery team wearing steel helmets, foliage, military trophies and 'I. Reit Batterie Artl Regt 22', plain, plated stirrup guard and mounts, wire bound black ribbed grip, in its plated scabbard. $119 £60

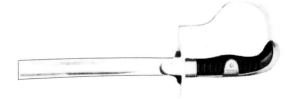

A good Imperial Bavarian officer's sabre, curved, plated blade 34in. by A.C.S., etched 'In Treue Fest' within scroll and foliage, plated, plain stirrup guard and mounts, wire bound, ribbed black grip, in its plated scabbard. $128 £65

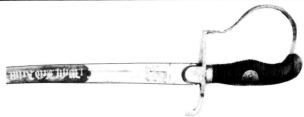

An Imperial German Artillery officer's sabre, plated, curved blade 35in., etched with military trophies, foliate scrolls and the regiment '1 Westf. Feld Artill. Regt No 7', and with mounted artillery team, both on blued panels, plated hilt with stirrup guard, wire bound fish-skin covered grip, in its metal scabbard. $129 £65

A scarce Imperial German, 19th century Baden Infantry officer's sabre, curved, pipe-back, clipped back blade 32in., etched with furled standards and military trophies, crowned 'M' (for Maximilian), foliage etc., plain brass mounts, stirrup knucklebow, back quillon with two slots for dress knot, wire bound fish-skin covered grip, in its metal scabbard. $129 £65

A French 1822 pattern Light Cavalry trooper's sabre, curved blade 36in., engraved on backstrap 'Mre Nle de Chatt – Mars 1871 – Cavrie Lre Mle 1822', triple bar brass guard, brass mounts, ordnance stamps, brass wire bound leather covered grip, in its steel scabbard. $129 £65

A French 1829 model Mounted Artillery sabre, curved blade 32½in., plain brass knucklebow struck with numerals and ordnance mark and obliterated date '1887', brass mounts, brass wire bound leather covered grip, in its metal scabbard. $158 £80

A late 18th century French (revolutionary era) Cavalry sabre, curved blade 32in., with stamp at forte, etched 'Jainse Rep.', brass hilt with single knuckle-bow with stamps, long, plain langets, ribbed leather covered grip. $158 £80

A French AN XI Light Cavalry sabre, curved blade 35in., engraved on back-strap 'Manufacture de Solingen K.S. & C.', brass triple bar guard, brass mounts and langets, knucklebow stamped 'Versailles', ribbed leather covered grip.
$158 £80

A Prussian 1811 Cavalry trooper's sabre, curved blade 32½in., heavy steel stirrup knucklebow and plain mounts, crosspiece stamped 'A.M. VI 2 15', leather bound ribbed grip. In its heavy steel scabbard. $178 £90

A 19th century Victorian Indian Army officer's mameluke sabre, slightly curved blade 30½in., with faint traces of etched decoration of foliate patterns, gilt crosspiece decoration with scrolls and foliage, ivory grips mounted with two gilt rosettes, grip strap decorated with oak leaves, in its velvet covered wooden scabbard with three large gilt mounts. $178 £90

A Georgian 1803 pattern Light Company officer's sabre, curved blade 30in., gilt hilt incorporating stringed bugle over 'GR' cypher, 'lion's head' pommel, wire bound fish-skin covered grip.　　　　　　　$194 £98

A French 1822 pattern Light Cavalry sabre, curved blade 35½in., engraved on backstrap 'Mre d'Armes de Chat Juin 1874 Caulre M. 1822', triple bar brass guard, brass mounts, brass wire bound leather covered grip, in its metal scabbard.　　　　　　　$198 £100

A 1796 Light Company Volunteer Cavalry officer's sabre by Gill, London, curved, single edged blade 30¼in., panel etched 'Gill's Warranted'. Steel stirrup hilt, wire bound leather covered grip, in its steel scabbard.
　　　　　　　$198 £100

An 1803 pattern Georgian general officer's sabre, curved blade 30in., etched with crown 'GR', military trophies, foliage, 1801-16 Royal Arms, traces of blueing, copper gilt hilt, 'lion's head' pommel, wire bound fish-skin covered grip, in its leather scabbard, with three copper gilt mounts.　　$198 £100

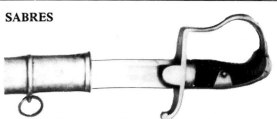

A good Prussian 1811 pattern Cavalry trooper's sabre, plain, curved blade 33in., stamped on backstrap '339', heavy, plain steel hilt with thick stirrup knucklebow, stamped on crosspiece with regimental markings 'R.P.C. 21. 18' and '339 R.', ribbed leather covered grip, in its steel scabbard.

$208 £105

A Nazi officer's sabre, plated, curved blade 31in., plain, plated stirrup knucklebow and mounts, brass wire bound black ribbed grip, in its metal scabbard.

$208 £105

A 1788 Light Dragoon officer's sabre, curved blade 35½in., engraved on backstrap 'R. Solingen'. Etched with mounted cavalryman, military trophies and 'Light Dragoons'. Plain steel guard, langets and mounts, ribbed fish-skin covered grip.

$228 £115

A late 18th century German Napoleonic era officer's sabre, curved blade 32in., etched at forte 'Sohmelbusch & Sohn'. Brass plain hilt with single knucklebow and long, oval langets, wire bound leather covered grip. In its brass scabbard.

$238 £120

An early 19th century Austrian Cavalry trooper's sabre, plain, curved blade 30in., marked at forte 'Fischer' and '821', plain steel guard, single plain knucklebow, plain mounts, ribbed leather covered grip, in its steel scabbard stamped at top 'Eisenbach'. $246 £124

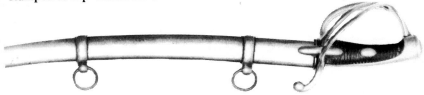

A Russian 1826 pattern Cavalry trooper's sabre, plain, curved blade 34½in., with Russian script on backstrap and date '1826', Russian stamps at forte, triple bar brass guard, plain brass mounts, ribbed leather covered grip, in its steel scabbard. $267 £135

A Georgian officer's sabre, circa 1790, plain, curved blade 30½in., with pronounced clip back tip. Steel hilt with squared knucklebow, broad flattened pommel and langets of fluted bowl pattern, leather covered grip mounted with three steel rosettes, in its leather covered scabbard with three plain steel mounts. $277 £140

A 1788 pattern Light Cavalry trooper's sabre, curved blade 33in., with traces of etched decoration of 'Woolley', crown, 'GR' and '7D.G.', plain steel knucklebow, langets and mounts, wood grip, in its steel scabbard.$287 £145

A late 18th century French sabre, plain, slightly curved blade 27in., with narrow back fuller, plain brass single knucklebow and mounts, small diamond shaped langets, the pommel in the form of a plumed cavalry helmet, copper wire bound grip, in its brass mounted leather scabbard. $297 £150

A rare Georgian officer's sabre of the 52nd Oxfordshire Light Infantry Regt., circa 1803, slightly curved blade 31in., with clipped back tip, etched within panel with Royal Arms and crown above strung bugle with figure '52' within foliate spray, plain steel hilt, with shield langets and stirrup guard, shagreen covered grip. $297 £150

A Georgian 1803 pattern Light Company officer's sabre, curved blade 29½in., blued and gilt etched decoration of crown, 'GR', Britannia, 1801-16 Royal Arms and maker's name 'Underhill and Cooper' in scrolls. Stamped 'G.G.' at forte, copper gilt guard, 'lion's head' pommel, wire bound leather covered grip, in its leather scabbard with three copper gilt mounts. $328 £165

A rare Georgian officer's sabre, circa 1795, of the Warwick Light Dragoons, curved blade 33in., etched on backstrap 'Gill's Warranted' and retaining some blued and gilt etched decoration of crown, 'GR', scrolled 'W.L.D.', mounted cavalry trooper, military trophies. The Arms of Warwick within a shield, steel hilt of Light Dragoon pattern, oval langets, flattened knucklebow, diced black wood grip. $346 £175

A Russian 1826 pattern Cavalry trooper's sabre, plain, curved blade, 34½in., stamped at forte 'A.P.' in cyrillic script, triple bar brass guard, plain brass mounts, leather covered grip, in its heavy steel scabbard. $346 £175

A Victorian 1831 pattern general officer's mameluke sabre, curved, clipped back blade 30½in., by Wilkinson, Pall Mall, gilt crossguard, straps and grip rosettes, ivory grips, in its brass scabbard. $346 £175

A Georgian officer's mameluke sabre, curved blade 31in., with clipped back point etched with floral and foliate sprays, copper gilt crosspiece engraved with squared pattern and central device of Star of David, gilt mounts, ivory grips, in its leather covered wooden scabbard. $356 £180

A good 1788 pattern Light Cavalry sabre, curved blade 36in., engraved on backstrap 'J. J. Runkel, Solingen' and etched with mounted hussar, Cabalistic and Talisman symbols, Turkish bonnet and military trophies, iron hilt with single flattened knucklebow, ribbed leather covered grip, in its iron mounted scabbard with openwork panels with wooden insert. $356 £180

SABRES

A good 1796 pattern Light Company Georgian officer's sabre, curved blade 30in., with pronounced clipped back point, with etched decoration of strung **bugle**, crown, 'GR' and military trophies, steel hilt with plain stirrup guard, sideloop and mounts, small langets, wire bound fish-skin covered grip, in its steel mounted leather scabbard. **$376 £190**

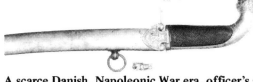

A scarce Danish, Napoleonic War era, officer's sabre, curved blade 32in., with clip back point, etched with military trophies and floral sprays. Brass hilt with shield langets, one with crowned 'FRVI' cypher, bordered with lions, back quillon with 'monster's head' finial. Stirrup knucklebow decorated with lion mask and foliate spray. 'Lion mask' pommel, diced black grip. In its brass scabbard. **$396 £200**

A mid 18th century English Dragoon sabre, slightly curved blade 30in., stamped 'S. Harvey', single back fuller, steel basket guard with diamond panel. Flattened circular pommel, brass wire bound fish-skin covered grip. **$396 £200**

A Georgian officer's mameluke levee sabre, circa 1810, mounted with Indian curved blade 30½in., inlaid at forte with maker's mark within panel, copper gilt crosspiece engraved with sunburst, ivory grips, inset with two copper gilt rosettes, copper gilt mounts, in its fine, shagreen covered wooden scabbard, with three ornate copper gilt shapes, the long bottom chape engraved with foliate and floral sprays. **$416 £210**

A Georgian Cavalry officer's sabre, curved, broad fullered blade 26in., blued and gilt for most of its length, etched with crowned 'GR' and post 1801 Royal Arms figure of Britannia, foliage, military trophy, 'Warranted' and 'Thos Bate Sword Manufacturer to the Honble Board of Ordnance', copper gilt stirrup hilt, 'horse's head' pommel, chequered ivory grip, in its copper mounted leather scabbard with two hanging rings. $416 £210

A rare 1803 pattern flank company officer's sabre, Grenadier Guards, curved blade 32in., etched in large lettering 'Grenadier Guards', crown, 'GR', 1801-16 Royal Arms, 'For My Country and King', roses and foliate sprays, copper gilt hilt, wire bound fish-skin covered grip, in its leather scabbard, with three copper mounts with traces of gilt. $416 £210

A good Georgian 1803 pattern officer's sabre, curved blade 32in., retaining approximately eighty per cent original blued and gilt etched decoration of crowned 'GR', military trophies and foliage, 1801-16 Royal Arms, copper gilt hilt, 'lion's head' pommel. Silver wire bound fish-skin covered grip. In its leather scabbard with three large copper mounts. $436 £220

A French Cavalry officer's sabre, circa 1770, slightly curved blade 30in., etched with crown, fleur-de-lys, foliate scroll, etc. and 'Veuve Gaze Et Fils Marchands E Courbusseurs A Onze 17', copper hilt with multi-looped semi-basket guard, wire bound ribbed wood grip, in its copper gilt mounted leather scabbard. $436 £220

SABRES

A Georgian officer's sabre, circa 1795, of the Leeds Light Dragoons, curved blade 34in., engraved on backstrap 'I. Woolley & Co.', and etched with scrolled 'L.L.D.', ram's head, military trophies, Prince of Wales' feathers and pre 1801 Royal Arms, steel hilt of Light Dragoon pattern, lozenge langets, flattened knucklebow and diced wood grip. $495 £250

A Georgian officer's sabre, circa 1800, curved blade 30in., engraved on backstrap 'J. Runkel, Solingen' and etched with pre 1801 Royal Arms, crown 'GR', military trophies and foliage. Copper gilt hilt with circular langets with lion mask. Knucklebow with beaded decoration. 'Lion's head' pommel, finely diced ivory grip. In its leather scabbard. $495 £250

A 1796 pattern officer's sabre of the Loyal Birmingham Light Horse Volunteers, curved blade 33in., etched 'H. Osborn' and dated '1797', also etched with Caduceus, initials 'L.B.L.H.V.' motto 'Ducit Amor Patria', crown 'GR', pre 1801 Royal Arms etc., plain steel stirrup guard and mounts, wire bound leather covered grip, in its steel scabbard. $495 £250

A rare Grenadier sabre, circa 1800, of Captain Close of the Royal Manchester and Salford Volunteers, curved blade 30in., retaining most original blued and gilt etched decoration initials 'R.M. & S.V.', pre 1801 Royal Arms, Turkish bonnet, crown 'GR', foliate scrolls and Cabalistic symbols, copper gilt guard with sideloop, plain knucklebow, 'lion's head' pommel, wire bound ribbed ivory grip, in its leather scabbard. $515 £260

A good Victorian 1831 pattern general officer's mameluke sabre, curved, clipped back blade 30½in., retaining nearly all original polish, by Pulford & Co., 65 St James' St, London, well etched with crown 'VR', general's insignia and foliage, gilt crosspiece with scrolls, rounded ivory grips, in its brass scabbard.

$535 £270

A Georgian 1796 pattern Light Cavalry officer's sabre, curved blade 33in., retaining nearly all blued and gilt etched decoration of 1801-16 Royal Arms, mounted cavalry trooper, crown, 'GR', military trophies and foliage, plain steel stirrup guard and mounts, silver wire bound, leather covered grip. In its steel scabbard. $574 £290

A rare 1796 (variation) Georgian Cavalry officer's sabre of the 19th Light Dragoons, circa 1810, curved blade 31in., with pronounced clip back point etched within panel 'XIX L.D.' within foliate sprays with crown above elephant and Assaye battle honour. Plain steel stirrup hilt and mounts. Silver wire bound fish-skin covered grip. In its steel scabbard. $614 £310

A rare Georgian Cavalry officer's sabre of the 10th Prince of Wales' Own Light Dragoons, circa 1810, curved blade 31in., with pronounced clipped back tip and retaining some original polish, etched with imitation Eastern type Cabalistic symbols and inscriptions. Copper gilt hilt with large silver Prince of Wales' feathers on langets, plain knucklebow, copper wire bound fish-skin covered grip, in its steel scabbard. $634 £330

A rare Georgian Naval officer's sabre, circa 1810, of Commander John Bernhard Smith, R.N., curved blade 28½in., retaining much original blued and gilt etched decoration of Britannia, crossed fouled anchor and flag, Naval trophies, Neptune mask, standing Victory, foliate sprays, maker 'Osborn & Gunby, Sword Cutlers to his Majesty; The Hon. Board of Ordnance'. $673 £340

A rare 1803 pattern officer's sabre of a flank company of the 1st Royal Regiment of Foot (The Royal Scots), plain, curved fighting blade 30½in., copper gilt hilt of 1803 pattern, wire bound fish-skin covered grip, the base of guard inset on either side with regimental badges, a crowned garter with the motto 'Nemo Me Impune Lacessit' above a scroll, 'The Royal' (pre 1812 badge and title), in its leather scabbard with three copper mounts. $673 £340

A rare Georgian flank company officer's sabre of the 42nd Royal Highland Regt. of Foot (The Black Watch), circa 1800, slightly curved blade 32½in., etched on backstrap 'J. J. Runkel, Solingen' and with crown, 'GR', pre 1801 Royal Arms, military trophies and foliage, copper gilt half basket, looped scroll guard and mounts, fluted ivory grip, with band and oval cartouche engraved with St. Andrew, '42' and 'Nemo Me Impune Lacessit', in its leather scabbard. $733 £370

An extremely fine 1796 Georgian Light Cavalry officer's sabre, curved blade 32½in., retaining nearly all original blued and gilt etched decoration of crown, 'GR', mounted trooper with drawn sword, 1801-16 Royal Arms, military trophies and foliate sprays and much original polish, plain steel hilt with stirrup knucklebow, silver wire bound fish-skin covered grip, in its plain steel scabbard. $772 £390

A rare Naval officer's dress sabre, probably for a Lieutenant, circa 1805, curved blade 25in., retaining much original blued and gilt etched decoration of crown, 'GR', classical urn, military trophies and foliage, copper gilt hilt with langets engraved with fouled anchors, the stirrup guard with laurel spray, 'lion's head' pommel, wire bound black ebony grip, in its leather scabbard with three copper gilt mounts. $772 £390

A rare Georgian officer's mameluke sabre, of Major General Robert Cheney (dated 1810) mounted with Indian curved, multi-fullered blade, 22in., with pronounced clipped back tip, plain copper crosspiece with traces of gilt, ivory grips mounted on each side with three gilt rosettes, in its leather covered scabbard bearing four copper mounts. $792 £400

A rare 1796 (variation) Georgian Cavalry officer's sabre of the 19th Light Dragoons, circa 1810, curved blade 31in., with pronounced clipped back point, retaining most original polish and etched within panel 'XIX L.D.', foliate sprays, crown and elephant with Assaye battle honour, plain steel stirrup hilt and mounts, ribbed fish-skin covered grip, in its steel scabbard. $812 £410

A rare 10th Light Dragoon officer's sabre, circa 1810, broad, curved blade 33in., with imitation damascus pattern for half length and etched with talisman symbols, copper guard with traces of gilt, the langets with applied silver Prince of Wales' feathers, stirrup knucklebow, wire bound fish-skin covered grip, in its copper scabbard with locket of 'Prosser, Charing Cross, London'. $832 £420

A rare and attractive Georgian Naval officer's sabre, circa 1795, curved blade 32in., engraved on backstrap 'J. J. Runkel, Solingen', and retaining approximately fifty per cent original blued and gilt etched decoration of crown, 'GR', pre 1801 Royal Arms, foliage and military trophies, copper gilt semi-basket guard, with two scrolled sideloops decorated with laurel sprays and supporting oval cartouche with openwork design of fouled anchor, copper gilt mounts, diced ivory grip, in its leather scabbard. $930 £470

A fine Georgian Naval officer's sabre, slightly curved, pipe back, clipped backed blade 27½in., with imitation damascus steel finish and retaining most original polished finish, with bright steel panel, the backstrap recessed at forte to accommodate push-button retaining catch on top mounts, fine copper gilt hilt with oval langets, stirrup knucklebow, 'lion's head' pommel, diced ivory grip, in its shagreen covered scabbard. $990 £500

A fine, early 19th century European mameluke sabre, curved blade 31in., of German or Russian make, with clipped back tip, retaining approximately seventy-five per cent blued and gilt etched decoration of military trophies, foliate sprays, stand-of-arms, two oval panels containing military trophies, the other a foliate spray, cornucopia, Fasces, etc., and engraved at forte, 'N. Hanquel inc.', gilt crosspiece, mother-of-pearl grips, in its shagreen covered wooden scabbard. $1,010 £510

A fine Regency period officer's sabre, multi-fullered, curved, clipped back blade 32½in., of false damascus pattern, etched with Cabalistic inscription on both sides, fine copper gilt hilt, shield langets with affixed devices of ox skulls, the knucklebow of twisted oak leaf pattern, twist pommel, in its leather scabbard with three fine copper gilt mounts, roped suspension rings.$1,188 £600

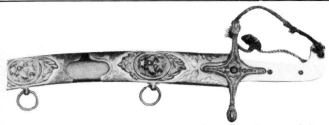

A rare and interesting Georgian Cavalry officer's mameluke sabre, circa 1810, believed of 19th Hussar Association, curved blade 30in., with gilt etched decoration of 1801-16 Royal Arms, crown, 'GR', military trophies, mounted trooper, foliate scrolls and Horse of Hanover, copper gilt crosspiece, ivory grips, in its full dress fish-skin covered wooden scabbard. $1,287 £650

A rare Georgian Lancer officer's full dress 1822 pattern mameluke sabre of the 17th Lancers, curved, pipe-backed, clipped back blade 31in., by Moore, Late Bicknell & Moore, Old Bond St., London, etched with crown, skull and crossbones, crossed lances and 'Or Glory' and 'XVII Lancers', gilt crossguard, gilt straps, ivory grips and two gilt rosettes in its blue velvet covered wooden scabbard with large gilt chape.. $1,307 £660

A Georgian Volunteer officer's presentation sabre, 1808, curved blade 28½in. by 'Woolley, Deakin, Dutton & Johnston' with much original blued and gilt etched decoration for entire length of standing figure of Britannia, military trophies, Prince of Wales' feathers, crown, 'GR', etc. Fine copper gilt hilt, the knucklebow of divided form of stylised wheatsheaf form, in its leather scabbard with three large copper gilt mounts. $1,336 £675

An extremely fine Victorian hallmarked silver mounted presentation officer's mameluke sabre, presented to Major General Sir N. R. Stewart, curved blade 32in., by Henry Wilkinson, Pall Mall, retaining all original polish and finely etched with foliate scrolls, blank panel, and panel containing presentation inscription 'Presented to Major General Sir N. R. Stewart from the officers who served under his command, Indian Army 1897', silver gilt crossguard (hallmarked London 1897), ivory grips, in its scabbard of solid hallmarked silver (Birmingham 1897, maker's initials J.F.ᴸ.).. $1,782 £900

A 19th century Military sidearm (possibly Artillery), plain, curved blade 30in., stamped on backstrap at forte 'Robt. Mole & Sons, Birmingham', plain brass stirrup knucklebow and mounts, ribbed iron grip. $59 £30

A Prussian 1864 model brass hilted Infantry sidearm, curved blade 17in., reversed crossguard stamped 'FW66' and '11.T.F.7.72', hatched grip, 'bird's head' pommel, in its brass mounted leather scabbard, top mount stamped '19.A.6.43', leather bayonet frog. $59 £30

A late 18th century French brass hilted Grenadier sidearm, plain, curved blade 23in., single knucklebow, ribbed grip, 'bird's head' pommel. $69 £35

An unusual Continental Military sidearm, probably Scandinavian, circa 1800, broad, double edged, fullered blade 20in., brass hilt with swollen crosspiece, angular pommel and ribbed grip. $70 £40

A French early 19th century brass hilted Naval briquet sidearm, curved blade 24in., engraved on backstrap 'Manufre Nle de Chatellerault . . .', plain brass knucklebow, ribbed grip, stamped at base with anchor in its brass mounted leather scabbard. $109 £55

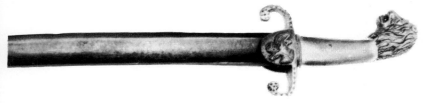

A late 18th century Swiss sidearm, broad, straight, single edged blade 27in., gilt brass hilt, with down drooping crosspiece, stamped with floral patterns, langet with device of plumed helmet and military trophies, 'lion's head' pommel. $109 £55

A late 18th century French brass hilted Grenadier sidearm, plain, curved blade 21½in., backstrap with traces of engraving, single knucklebow, ribbed grip with 'bird's head' pommel and reverse langets, stamps to knucklebow.$119 £60

A U.S. brass hilted 1833 pattern Foot Artillery sidearm, double edged, spatulate blade 19in., with short fullers, stamped at forte with U.S. Eagle and 'N. P. Ames Springfield', brass scaled grip, U.S. Eagle on pommel. $129 £65

SIDEARMS

A French pioneer sidearm, circa 1790, broad, straight, saw-backed blade 27in., brass hilt with broad straight crosspiece, the grip in form of eagle's neck and head. $139 £70

A late 18th century French revolutionary period brass hilted briquet sidearm, curved blade 24in., etched with cockerel standing on circular panel inscribed 'Liberte' and military trophies, plain knucklebow, ribbed grip. $148 £75

An unusual French sidearm, circa 1830, double edged, slightly spatulate blade 22½in., with fullered panels, copper crossguard with central device of eagle's claw, 'lion's head' pommel, spiral wire bound leather covered grip. $198 £100

A good Coast Guard sidearm, circa 1850, single edged blade 26½in., etched within panel 'E.S.C. 11', and retaining some original polish, brass stirrup knucklebow with sideloop, ribbed iron grip. In its brass mounted leather scabbard with belt lug and original leather frog also stamped 'E.S.C. 11'. $228 £115

A late 18th century Georgian officer's spadroon, plain, straight, double edged blade 30½in., of flattened diamond section, plain copper fighting hilt with single guard and solid sideloop, ribbed ivory grip. $99 £50

A Georgian officer's spadroon, circa 1780, straight, single edged blade 31in., etched with crown, 'GR', foliate sprays and military trophies, plain steel knucklebow and mounts, small feathered langets, wire bound ribbed grip.
$109 £55

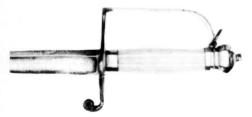

A Georgian officer's spadroon, circa 1780, straight, single edged blade 32in., engraved on backstrap 'J. J. Runkel, Solingen', etched with crown, 'GR', pre 1801 Royal Arms, military trophies and foliage, copper gilt guard with plain single knucklebow and sideloop, fluted ivory grip. $139 £70

A late 18th century Georgian officer's spadroon, straight, single edged blade 31½in., with traces of etched decoration of crown, military trophies, lion in shield and thistles, copper gilt, with plain knucklebow and sideloop, plain mounts, fluted ivory grip with band and oval cartouche inset, engraved 'R.P.V. I.D.' (Royal Perth Volunteers). $139 £70

SPADROONS

A Georgian officer's spadroon, circa 1795, of The Royal Dublin Volunteers, straight, double edged blade 32in. of flattened diamond section, etched with pre 1801 Royal Arms, military trophies and 'For My Country And King'. Plain steel hilt with single sideloop and plain knucklebow, urn pommel, fluted ivory grip, inset with silver band engraved with crowned garter belt. $158 £80

A Georgian officer's silver hilted spadroon, circa 1770, straight, single edged blade 29in., etched with crown, 'GR', military trophies and foliage, plain silver knucklebow, large langets and mounts, silver band bound horn grip, old white hide dress knot, in a steel mounted leather scabbard for a Scottish sword. $158 £80

A Georgian officer's silver hilted spadroon, 1787, straight, single edged blade 31½in., etched with crown, 'GR', military trophies and foliage, the guard of solid silver, with plain knucklebow, sideloop and urn pommel, with hallmark below guard for 'London, 1787' and initials 'W.K.', fluted ivory grip. $198 £100

An unusual Volunteer/Militia spadroon, 1798, straight, single edged blade 32½in., frost etched 'Osborn Warranted 1798' and with Turkish bonnet above crown, 'GR', a Piratical figure, Winged Victory, pre 1801 Royal Arms etc., steel masonic style flattened crossguard, fluted ebony grip, octagonal steel pommel. $218 £110

A Georgian officer's dress spadroon of The 16th or Queen's Light Dragoons, circa 1795, straight, single edged blade 32½in., etched on backstrap 'J. J. Runkel Solingen', retaining some blueing and gilt and with etched decoration of crown, 'GR', pre 1801 Royal Arms, military trophies and foliage, steel hilt with plain knucklebow, fluted ivory grip. $218 £110

A Georgian officer's 'five-ball' spadroon, circa 1780, straight, single edged blade 33in., etched with crown, 'GR', military trophies and foliage, copper gilt guard with sideloop and knucklebow, fluted bone grip, in copper mounted brown leather scabbard. $247 £125

A Georgian Naval officer's 'five-ball' spadroon, circa 1790, straight, single edged blade 32in., retaining much original polish, the backstrap etched 'J. J. Runkel Solingen', and etched with crown, 'GR III', pre 1801 Royal Arms, military trophies and foliage, fine copper gilt guard with sideloop and knucklebow incorporating 'five-ball' design. $752 £380

A Naval officer's spadroon, circa 1795, believed to have been awarded to Admiral Lord Nelson by HRH The Duke of Clarence (later William IV), straight, single edged blade 30in., retaining most original blued and gilt etched decoration, gilt hilt, lozenge shaped langets, flattened pommel and knucklebow, silver wire bound grip, in its leather scabbard. $1,723 £870

A Victorian copy of a 16th century sword, double edged plain blade 31in., iron twisted double ring guard and down drooping crossguard, spiral ovoid pommel, wire bound, leather covered grip. $32 £16

An early 19th century brass hilted bandsword, slightly curved double fullered blade 25in., solid brass hilt with 'lion's head' pommel, pineapple finial crossguard, langets with stylised thistle device, in its brass scabbard. $55 £28

A good dyak headhunter's sword, mandau, blade 22in., with pierced scrolls on back edge at point and with simple decoration and brass stud inlay, bone hilt elaborately carved in horse's head form part rattan bound, in its part rattan bound wooden sheath with part openwork carved design. $63 £32

A pioneer sword, circa 1830, broad, slightly curved, saw-backed blade 22in., stamped 'Gill' on backstrap, solid brass hilt, with plain stirrup guard, 'lion's head' pommel, ribbed grip. $109 £55

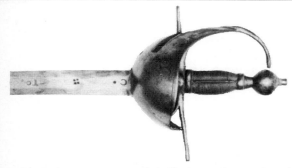

An 18th century Spanish 'Bilbo' sword, tapering, double edged blade 30½in., struck with crown above 'R' and 'Cs. IV to. 1801', steel cup guard, plain crosspiece and knucklebow, ovoid pommel, copper wire bound grip.

 $317 £160

A rare 13th century medieval sword, double edged blade 32½in., with traces of central fuller, straight iron crossguard of square form, 'Brazil nut' pommel, in excavated condition (blade tip missing). $535 £270

A scarce Prussian 1735 model Dragoon pallasch, straight, broad, tapering, single edged blade 32in., semi-basket brass guard, thumb ring, 'eagle's head' pommel, ribbed, leather covered grip. $594 £300

An English flintlock sword pistol, circa 1765, slightly curved, single edged, bi-fullered blade 26¾in., frizzen spring screwed to left side of blade. Pierced steel shellguard, integral knuckle. Turn-off barrel 2¼in., with cannon muzzle, proved at breech. Pan and foliate finialled bow with baluster. Natural stag horn grip, fluted steel pommel. $832 £420

A mid 18th century English horseman's backsword, single edged blade 34in., with narrow and broad fullers, and long, clipped back point, iron basket with circular loops, rectangular side panels, circular flattened pommel, brass wire bound fish-skin covered grip, in its leather scabbard. $178 £90

A Scottish Infantry backsword, circa 1770, tapering, single edged blade 29in., with narrow back fuller and stamped with crown, 'GR' and 'Drury', iron basket guard, conical pommel, wood grip, in its brass mounted leather scabbard, with slightly later leather shoulder belt with brass buckle. $198 £100

An early 18th century Scottish basket backsword, single edged blade 35in., without fullers. Basket-hilt incorporating large oval window to facilitate manipulating reins, bars pierced with circles and hearts. Deeply crossed bun shaped pommel. $247 £125

A good, scarce mid 18th century English basket-hilted trooper's backsword, single edge bi-fullered blade 32½in. Hilt of steel sheet and bars in squares and oblongs, twin trailing loops, bun shaped pommel. Brass wire bound shark-skin covered grip.   **$416 £210**

A good, late 18th century Scottish officer's backsword of the 116th Foot, single edged blade 32in., with narrow back fuller, swelling, basket guard pierced with thistles within scrolls and with central device of crowned, rayed star engraved '116' within belt bearing motto 'Nemo me Impune Lacessit', wire bound fish-skin covered grip, small fluted conical pommel.   **$514 £260**

A scarce Scottish 17th century basket-hilted backsword, single edged blade 35in., multi-fullered at forte, struck four times on each side with large cutler's marks within ovals. Ribbon beak hilt of scrolls, bars and panels, bulbous pommel.   **$643 £325**

An 1890 pattern Cavalry trooper's sword, slightly curved blade 33in., retaining nearly all original polish, stamped 'E.F.D.' at forte and '99' on backstrap, steel bowl guard, diced black leather grips, in its metal scabbard. $55 £28

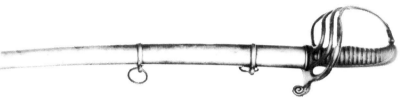

A 19th century French Cavalry sword, plain, slightly curved blade 34in., engraved on backstrap 'Manufacture De Klingenthal Coulaux Aines', triple bar steel guard, plain steel knucklebow, ribbed solid iron grip, in its metal scabbard $119 £60

A George VI 1912 pattern Cavalry officer's sword, slim, straight blade 35in., etched with crown, Royal Arms and cypher and foliage, plated scroll engraved bowl guard, plated mounts, wire bound fish-skin covered grip, in its leather covered field service scabbard, with leather dress knot. $119 £60

A 1788 pattern Light Cavalry officer's sword, slightly curved blade 35in., with one broad and one narrow fuller etched with mounted hussar, stylised figures, moon etc., steel stirrup hilt and langets, grooved polished wooden grip. $129 £65

A Prussian 1889 pattern Cavalry officer's sword, plated blade 32in., by Weyersberg, etched with officer's name 'Grossman' and 'Jager Regiment Zu Pferd No. 4', crossed cannon, foliage, Cavalry engagement, military trophies and floral patterns, plated hilt with folding guard, black composition covered grip, in a leather scabbard with plated mounts. $148 £75

An 1889 pattern Prussian Cavalry officer's sword, plated blade 31in., etched with foliage and regiment 'Hus Reg Kaiser Franz Joseph V. Oesterr Konig V Ungarn (Schlews-Holst) No 16', crowned 'FJ' cypher on blued panels, German silver guard, ribbed black composition grip, in its steel scabbard. $158 £80

A scarce, special pattern, late Victorian Cavalry trooper's sword as carried by The City of London Yeomanry, plain, straight blade 34in., by Hamburger Rogers & Co., London, retaining some original polish, plain sheet steel bowl guard, stamped on inside '2 C.L.Y. 207', steel mounts, ribbed wood grip, in its steel scabbard stamped at throat 'C.L.Y. 207', with two rings. $158 £80

A good 1821 pattern Light Cavalry officer's sword, slightly curved blade 35½in., by J. Davies, 340 Oxford Str., London, retaining nearly all original polish and finely etched with crown, 'VR', 'Uxbridge Yeomanry', foliate scrolls and officer's initials 'A.S.', triple bar steel guard, steel mounts, wire bound fish-skin covered grip, in its steel scabbard. $168 £85

An 1889 pattern Prussian Cavalry officer's sword, plated ,blade 32½in., etched with military trophies, foliate scrolls and Regt. 'Jaeger Zu Pferde XI A.K.', plated guard, ribbed black grip, in its plated scabbard.$168 £85

A scarce 1864 pattern Cavalry trooper's sword, slight curved blade 35in., ordnance stamp at forte, steel guard with markings of the 5th Dragoon Guards '5 D.G. 242', diced, black leather grips, in its steel scabbard stamped at top '5 D.G.116'. $188 £95

A good 1796 pattern Cavalry officer's heavy dress sword, double edged, tapered, fullered blade 32¼in., etched with foliate sprays, coat-of-arms, Georgian crown and 'GR' cypher, copper gilt boat shaped shellguard, plain copper gilt quillons and knucklebow, spherical double pommel and silver wire bound grip. $188 £95

A rare Light Cavalry trooper's sword, circa 1780, long, straight, single edged blade 35½in., with clipped back tip, ordnance crown stamp at forte, plain brass knucklebow, small langets and mounts, ribbed fish-skin covered grip.
                                                    $237 £120

A 1796 pattern Cavalry trooper's sword, single edged blade 35in., by 'A. Willans, Exeter Change, Strand, appointed cutler to the King', retaining some original polish and etched within scrolls 'G. T. Williams, Lieutenant in the Mudford (Somerset) Troop of Yeomanry Cavalry 1831', steel pierced guard, leather covered, ribbed grip, in its steel scabbard.

$396 £200

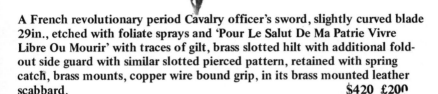

A French revolutionary period Cavalry officer's sword, slightly curved blade 29in., etched with foliate sprays and 'Pour Le Salut De Ma Patrie Vivre Libre Ou Mourir' with traces of gilt, brass slotted hilt with additional fold-out side guard with similar slotted pierced pattern, retained with spring catch, brass mounts, copper wire bound grip, in its brass mounted leather scabbard.

$420 £200

A 1796 pattern Cavalry trooper's heavy sword, straight, single edged blade 34½in., with hatchet point, stamped at forte with ordnance crown, pierced steel guard, plain steel mounts, knucklebow stamped with crown and 'CAST', markings below the guard of the 2nd Dragoons, leather covered ribbed grip, in its steel scabbard.

$483 £244

A scarce 1906 pattern (Mark 1) experimental Cavalry trooper's sword, slim blade 35in., by Wilkinson, Pall Mall, dated '06' on backstrap, steel bowl guard, steel mounts, diced wood grip, in a leather covered steel scabbard.

$554 £280

A Chinese double sword, double edged blades 17½in., brass crosspiece, pommel and mounts, decorated with traditional patterns, fluted wood grips, in its wooden scabbard with brass chapes similarly decorated.

$129 £65

An unusual Chinese sword, diamond section blade 22in., inlaid with brass dragons and symbols on one side with two shallow fullers to the other, cast white metal crossguard, engraved white metal mounted tape bound hilt, the triangular pommel similarly decorated, in its fish-skin covered white metal mounted scabbard, top and bottom mounts engraved with dragons and mythical scenes, the central suspension loop mounted with a lizard.

$158 £80

A fine Chinese sword, straight, double edged blade 27in. With plain, heavy German silver crossguard and pommel of traditional design, grip inlaid in brass wire. In its wooden scabbard with large, plain German silver mounts and some brass wire inlay to hilt. $200 £95

A good Chinese sword, curved blade 27in., with scrolled gilt sprays at forte, elaborately pierced oval gilt metal guard with designs of dragons within foliage, squared pommel and mounts similarly decorated, blue cord bound grip and blue tassel, in its vellum covered scabbard. $380 £190

A Victorian court sword, straight blade 30½in., by Wilcox & Son, Argyle St.
London, etched with crown, 'VR', furled standards and foliage, gilt hilt
with shellguard, knucklebow and urn pommel with beaded mounts, grip with
beaded edges, with original bullion dress knot, in its black patent leather scabbard with two gilt mounts. $40 £20

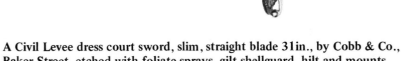

A Civil Levee dress court sword, slim, straight blade 31in., by Cobb & Co.,
Baker Street, etched with foliate sprays, gilt shellguard, hilt and mounts,
decorated with beaded pattern, urn pommel, in its leather scabbard with
gilt mounts, with bullion dress knot. $89 £45

A French, early 19th century, officer's dress court sword, straight, slim,
single edged blade 32½in., etched at forte 'Wester & Cie, Solingen' and with
military trophies, foliate sprays, etc., gilt brass, fluted, boat shaped guard,
single, plain knucklebow, armed head pommel, fluted wooden grip.$99 £50

An early 19th century Continental court sword, straight blade 33in., with
etched decoration of military trophies, foliage, with traces of gilt, gilt shellguard with oval panel with reclining Hercules, foliate borders, gilt Mont-
morency hilt, with knucklebow decorated with floral spray, fluted mother-
of-pearl grips. $119 £60

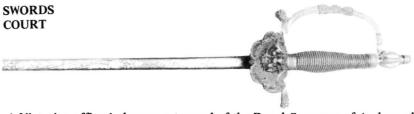

A Victorian officer's dress court sword of the Royal Company of Archers, slim blade 31in., by J. Stewart, 88 George Street, Edinburgh, etched with crown, 'VR', foliage and thistles, retaining nearly all original polish, gilt hilt with shellguard, knucklebow partly chiselled with foliage, fluted urn pommel, silver wire bound grip, in its patent leather scabbard. $129 £65

A fine cut steel hilted court sword, tapering, triangular, hollow ground blade 31½in., by Hill Brothers, London, etched with crossed halberd, lance and foliate sprays, steel hilt and shellguard decorated with facetted steel studs, knucklebow similarly decorated, urn pommel, patent black leather scabbard with two bright steel mounts and with original frog and silk shoulder belt.
                                                                $139 £70

A cut steel hilted court sword, plain, triangular, tapering blade 30½in., polished steel hilt, with shellguard, knucklebow and urn shaped pommel decorated with cut steel facetted studs, in its patent leather scabbard with two bright steel mounts and facetted frog stud button. $139 £70

A late 18th century Georgian officer's dress court sword, slim, plain, blade 30½in., of flattened diamond section, copper gilt hilt with double shellguard, single knucklebow, ovoid pommel, simple linear engraved pattern, copper wire bound grip, in its patent leather scabbard with three copper gilt mounts. $158 £80

A 19th century Dutch court sword, tapered, triangular section blade 30in.,
etched with scrolling foliage within panels on all sides, brass chiselled
shellguard, brass chiselled quillon, knucklebow and pommel, wooden grip
with mother-of-pearl panels, in its brass mounted, white vellum scabbard.

$168 £85

A good Victorian court sword, slim blade 31½in., by W. Buckmaster, New
Burlington St., London, retaining most original polish and etched with
crossed standard, crown, 'VR', foliate sprays etc., gilt hilt with shellguard,
crown pommel, rounded knucklebow, gilt wire bound grip, with original
bullion dress knot, in its gilt metal mounted patent leather scabbard.

$172 £87

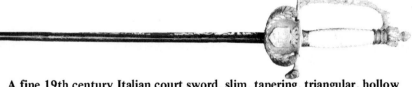

A fine 19th century Italian court sword, slim, tapering, triangular, hollow
ground blade 32in., retaining virtually all original polish and etched with
foliate sprays, gilt hilt with shellguard mounted with crown above shield
engraved with the Cross of Savoy, chiselled knucklebow decorated with
lion mask and foliage, similarly chiselled pommel, 'ram's head' back quillon, small back shellguard, fluted mother-of-pearl grips, in its patent
leather covered wooden scabbard. $277 £140

A good Victorian court sword, slim blade 31½in., by Marshall & Co., St.
James' St., London, retaining virtually all original polish and etched with
military trophies and foliage, gilt hilt with beaded edged shellguard with
crown, 'VR', laurel spray border, crown pommel, spiral panel to knucklebow, silver wire bound grip, in its gilt metal mounted leather scabbard.

$277 £140

A scarce Prussian 1854 pattern cuirassier trooper's sword, straight, double fullered blade 32½in., with spear tip, stamped at forte 'Clemen & Jung, Solingen', triple bar brass guard, brass mounts with regimental markings of the 2nd Kuirassier Regt. '2.K.4.52', beneath guard, brass wire bound leather covered grip. $198 £100

A French AN XI cuirassier trooper's sword, straight, double fullered single edged blade 38in., with hatchet tip, engraved on backstrap 'Manufre Rle du Klingenthal Fevrier 1812' triple bar brass guard, brass knucklebow and mounts, with arsenal stamps, ribbed, leather covered grip.
$208 £105

A French AN XI cuirassier sword single edged, double fullered blade 37½in., with hatchet point and with oblong ordnance stampe at forte of cap-of-liberty and fasces, triple bar guard, knucklebow stamped 'Versailles', brass mounts, brass wire bound, leather covered grip, in its metal scabbard. $218 £110

A French AN XI cuirassier sword, straight blade 37in., with spear point and double fuller. Triple bar brass guard and mounts. Brass wire bound leather covered grip. Stamps on knucklebow, in its steel scabbard. $317 £160

A Victorian dress sword of the Military Knights of Windsor, plain, straight
blade 28½in. of flattened diamond section, gilt Gothic cruciform metal
hilt with garter stars in central panel, flattened grip, in leather scabbard.
$59 £30

A 19th century Austrian diplomat's dress sword, straight fullered single
edged blade 30¼in. Brass hilt, lion's head pommel, knucklebow with oak
leaf entwining, shell guard overlaid with crowned Imperial eagle, plain
mother-of-pearl grips. $99 £50

A Georgian Naval officer's 1805 pattern dress sword, triangular, hollow
ground blade 25½in., with traces of etched decoration, copper gilt guard,
shield langets with crown, fouled anchor, round stirrup knucklebow engraved with oak leaves, wire bound black fish-skin covered grip. $99 £50

An Imperial German officer's dress sword of the State of Wurttemburg,
plain, single edged blade 30in., by Weyersberg, brass shellguard with State
Arms, plain brass knucklebow and mounts, diced wood grip. $109 £55

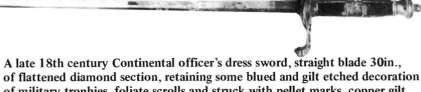

A late 18th century Continental officer's dress sword, straight blade 30in.,
of flattened diamond section, retaining some blued and gilt etched decoration
of military trophies, foliate scrolls and struck with pellet marks, copper gilt
sideloop, copper gilt mounts, single knucklebow, lion's head back quillon,
diced black grips. $194 £98

A Victorian 1st Life Guards officer's dress sword (1865/1978), straight,
single edged blade 36in., by 'Hawkes & Co. London, Manufacturers to the
Queen' etched at forte with foliate scrolls, steel pierced guard, wire bound
fish-skin covered grip, brass pommel, in its brass mounted steel scabbard.
                                                        $246 £125

A Georgian officer's mameluke dress sword, circa 1820, plain, curved, clipped
back blade 31in. Copper gilt crossguard and mounts, ivory grips secured by
two floral rosettes. In its leather covered wooden scabbard with three copper
gilt mounts engraved with foliate patterns. $257 £130

A Georgian Naval officer's dress sword, 1805, plain, straight, slim, single edged
blade 24½in., copper gilt hilt, shield langets with fouled anchor, rounded
stirrup guard, the pommel in the form of a crouching lion, diced ivory grip,
copper wire bound grip, in its leather scabbard with three plain copper gilt
mounts. $297 £150

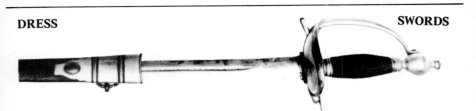

A good Georgian 1796 pattern Cavalry officer's heavy dress sword, tapering, double edged blade 31½in., retaining some original polish, signed in the fuller 'J. J. Runkel, Solingen', copper gilt guard retaining much original gilt, silver wire bound grip, in its leather scabbard with three copper gilt mounts.
$356 £180

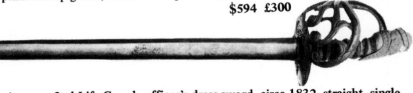

A Georgian Naval officer's fine dress sword, circa 1805, as worn by Commanders and above, slim, tapering, double edged blade 27½in., of flattened diamond section, etched at forte with foliate sprays and with unusual wavy line decoration extending nearly the entire length of the blade, the whole heightened in gilt, copper gilt hilt, fouled anchors engraved on shield langets, plain stirrup guard, 'lion's head' pommel, wire bound ribbed ivory grip.
$594 £300

A scarce 2nd Life Guards officer's dress sword, circa 1832, straight, single edged blade 39½in., by 'Prosser, Manufacturer to the King, London 1832', with Prosser proof stamp and etched within panel with crown, flaming grenade, 'L.G.2' and foliate spray, brass scrolled guard, grenade to back stool, pommel strap with winged lightning and grenade, wire bound fish-skin covered grip, hatchet point.
$614 £310

A rare 1796 pattern Cavalry officer's heavy dress sword, fitted with late 17th century multi-fullered broadsword blade, deeply struck at forte with four 'Turks' heads' marks and signed in the fullers '(S) A.H.A.G.U.M.', copper gilt hilt with boat shaped guard, rounded knucklebow, ovoid pommel and rounded quillons, silver wire bound fish-skin covered grip, in its black shagreen covered scabbard with three copper gilt mounts.
$792 £400

A Malayan jungle sword parang, broad, swollen, single edged blade 21in., engraved with flowers and scrolling foliage. White metal crosspiece with applied fruit finials. Octagonal horn grip with foliate embossed white metal mounts. In its wooden sheath with large white metal locket and chape. $79 £40

An interesting 17th century Central Indian two-handed sword, straight, double edged blade, swollen bi-fullered blade 26¾in. Tubular iron grip with three equally spaced hollow iron balls, lotus finial to pommel. $99 £50

A scarce Assam Khasi long sword dao (noklang), swollen, single edged blade 27in., with bi-furcated tip. Two brass mounted brass covered iron crosspieces, facetted integral iron grip. Long spike pommel with brass bands. $99 £50

An old Moorish sword, broad, straight, double edged blade 26in., iron hilt with plain, short down drooping quillons, iron grip and conical Moorish pattern pommel in its blind tooled leather covered wooden scabbard with iron mounts with some inlaid silver stud pattern, brass, decorated, openwork chape. $123 £62

An Indian sword, khandar, heavy, broad, spatulate, single edged blade 28in., with clipped back tip and decorated with applied brass strips and panels containing tigers, fighting elephants, human figures, floral patterns etc. Iron tulwar hilt with silver damascened floral patterns. $148 £75

A Nepalese executioner's heavy kora, plain, curved blade 23in., inlaid at top with brass geometric design, plain steel hilt, in its leather covered wooden scabbard.   **$178 £90**

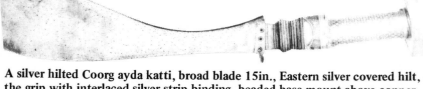

A silver hilted Coorg ayda katti, broad blade 15in., Eastern silver covered hilt, the grip with interlaced silver strip binding, beaded base mount above copper sheet panels, raised circular panels with toothed borders.   **$228 £115**

A silver mounted Singalese sword kastane, curved blade 17in., the hilt of low-grade Eastern silver with 'monster's head' pommel, with red-stone eye (one missing), down drooping quillons in form of monsters, in its wooden lined scabbard of Eastern sheet silver.   **$238 £120**

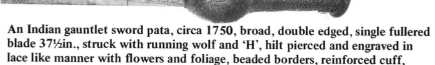

An Indian gauntlet sword pata, circa 1750, broad, double edged, single fullered blade 37½in., struck with running wolf and 'H', hilt pierced and engraved in lace like manner with flowers and foliage, beaded borders, reinforced cuff, hinged wrist strap plates.   **$277 £140**

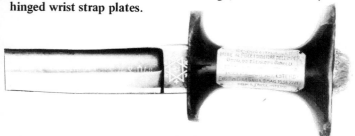

An Abyssinian sword shotel, presented to Mussolini, curved blade 30½in., by Henry Wilkinson, Pall Mall, retaining much original polish and etched with Royal Arms, foliage and inscription within panel, composition grip with domed pommel, in its velvet covered wooden scabbard.   **$436 £220**

SWORDS
EXHIBITION

A fine Spanish exhibition sword in the style of the 15th century, slightly tapering, double edged blade 34in., etched with foliate panels in gold and enamels, on blued background. Also etched within fuller 'Arta Faba de Toledo 1891', iron hilt with large down drooping flattened quillons finely chiselled with gold damascened patterns, the hilt and conical pommel similarly decorated, in its cloth covered metal scabbard with three iron mounts chiselled and decorated in gold.
$891 £450

FALCHION

A Saxon Artillery falchion, blade 24½in., with fuller on one side, horn grips, brass pommel, in its brass mounted leather scabbard with matching numbers to crossguard '12. A. 7 77'. $119 £60

A Russian 1827 brass hilted pioneer falchion, broad, saw-backed, curved blade 19in., Russian stamp at forte, dated '1833' on crosspiece, ribbed grip, in its brass mounted leather covered wooden scabbard. $238 £120

HAND-AND-A-HALF

A good, early 19th century copy of an early 16th century German hand-and-a half sword, tapering, broad, double edged blade 39½in., stamped at forte with imitation armourer's mark and 'Me Fecit en Solingen', iron crossguard of flattened form with acorn type terminals, double ring guard, wire bound grip, spiral fluted iron globular pommel. $139 £70

A 19th century European hunting sword, single edged blade 17in., with
broad and narrow fuller, etched at forte with crown above 'S.S.', traces
of gilt, small fluted gilt shellguard, plain brass crosspiece and mounts, stag
horn hilt, in its brass mounted leather sheath with provision for companion
knife.   **$99 £50**

A 19th century European hunting dress sword, plain, straight, single edged
blade 17½in., small white metal shellguard, hoof quillons and mounts, stag
horn grip well carved with hounds pursuing deer amidst forest.   **$109 £55**

A French 18th century silver mounted hunting sword, plain, slightly
curved blade 24½in., with back fuller, Continental silver crosspiece
embossed at centre with hound attacking deer, flattened ivory grips,
with three silver rosette mounts with traces of gilt, silver stirrups.
                                    $109 £55

A mid 18th century French hunting sword, slightly curved blade 21in.,
etched with hounds pursuing boar and stag, birds and scrolls, small brass
quillons, brass pommel, copper and brass wire spiral bound bone hilt,
in its brass mounted cloth covered wooden scabbard.   **$139 £70**

SWORDS
HUNTING

A late 19th century German hunting dress sword, single edged blade 15½in. Knight's head maker's stamp at forte. Retaining some original polish. Small, fluted, steel shellguard, steel mounts with reversed hoof quillons and chiselled 'lion's head' pommel. Stag horn grip. $139 £70

A mid 19th century European hunting sword, single edged, tapering blade 22in., etched at forte with stag within foliate panel, brass shellguard, brass knucklebow and mounts, pommel chiselled with huntsman, hounds etc., tortoiseshell grip. $208 £105

A late 19th century German hunting sword, single edged blade 16in., etched on backstrap 'W. Michovus Hoflieferant Gottbus', brass shellguard with stag design, reversed brass hoof quillons, brass mounted stag horn hilt mounted with three acorns, in its brass mounted leather sheath. $208 £105

A late 19th century German dress hunting sword, straight, single edged blade 16¼in., etched with huntsman, stags within forest, hounds hunting foxes, hunting trophies etc., gilt, fluted shellguard, reversed hoof quillon crossguard, stag horn grip mounted with three oval plaques, fluted pommel, in its leather sheath, with companion knife, blade 4in. $277 £140

A good mid 18th century Austrian hunting sword, tapering, single edged blade 23in., etched at forte with hound pursuing a stag and a boar, heightened with gilt, shellguard chiselled with huntsman bordered with animals, knucklebow and mounts chiselled with stags and boar amid foliage, fluted ivory grip, the pommel chiselled with hounds pursuing a stag, in its leather covered wooden scabbard. $307 £155

A good early 19th century Bavarian dress hunting sword, long, single edged blade 24½in., retaining approximately sixty per cent blued and gilt etched decoration of fox, hunting trophies and foliate sprays, copper gilt, fluted shellguard, reversed quillons and plain mounts, flattened horn grips, in its leather sheath with two plain copper gilt mounts. $346 £175

A good early 19th century German hunting sword, broad, single edged blade 15½in., etched with stag and boar, hunting trophies including horn, quiver etc., foliate scrolls, fluted steel shellguard, rectangular plain crossguard, steel mounts, stag horn grip carved in relief with a stag and two hinds, fluted iron pommel cap, in its steel mounted leather sheath. $455 £230

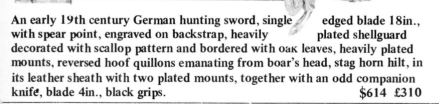

An early 19th century German hunting sword, single edged blade 18in., with spear point, engraved on backstrap, heavily plated shellguard decorated with scallop pattern and bordered with oak leaves, heavily plated mounts, reversed hoof quillons emanating from boar's head, stag horn hilt, in its leather sheath with two plated mounts, together with an odd companion knife, blade 4in., black grips. $614 £310

A sword of one of the German states, circa 1830, straight, single edged blade
34in.; brass guard with single plain knucklebow and double sideloop guard,
ribbed leather covered grip. $63 £32

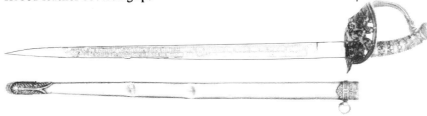

A miniature of the Imperial German sword, presented to Bismarck upon
the Unification and Founding of the German State, 1871, plated blade,
brass pierced guard with Germania crowning the German Eagle, solid brass,
oak leaf decorated grip, crowned pommel, in its brass scabbard. $109 £55

A Prussian 1889 pattern Cavalry officer's sword, plated blade 33in., etched
with floral and foliate patterns, Cavalry combat, military trophies and
Regt. '2 Westf Husaren Reg No. 11', white metal hilt, folding side guard,
ribbed composition grip, in its black painted scabbard. $119 £60

An Imperial German Artillery officer's sword, slightly curved, plated blade
31in., brass hilt with stirrup guard with oak leaf pattern, langets with
crossed cannon and grenade and armorial shield, 'lion's head' pommel,
ribbed black grip, in its black painted metal scabbard. $139 £70

A Nazi miniature Luftwaffe officer's sword, plated blade 6in., by Alcoso, plated mounts, wire bound, blue leather covered grip, in its leather covered metal scabbard with plated mounts, mounted on metal propellor paperweight.

$158 £80

A Nazi Police officer's sword, plain, straight blade 33in., by Herm Rath, Solingen, also stamped at forte with S.S. runes, plated knucklebow and mounts, wire bound, ribbed grip inset with police emblem, in its black painted metal scabbard with plated mounts and original dress knot, the pommel engraved with officer's initials.   **$178 £90**

A Nazi Army officer's sword, slightly curved, plated blade 33½in., by Eickhorn, gilt hilt with stirrup knucklebow and mounts decorated with oak leaves, Army Eagle on langet, 'lion's head' pommel, inset with red glass eyes, wire bound, black ribbed grip, in its black painted metal scabbard.   **$188 £95**

An Imperial German Naval officer's sword, slightly curved, pipe-back, clipped back blade 31in., by W.K.C., retaining some original polish, etched with crowned fouled anchor, Imperial Eagle etc., large and small folding brass guards, 'lion's head' pommel inset with green and red glass eyes, wire bound ivory grip, in its leather scabbard with brass mounts with traces of gilt.**$198 £100**

An Imperial German Naval officer's sword, slightly curved, pipe-back, clipped
back blade 30in., of watered steel, by W.K.C., etched with crown, fouled
anchor, sailing ships etc., gilt brass hilt, with large and small folding guards,
'lion's head' pommel inset with red and green glass eyes, ribbed ivory grip,
wire bound, in its brass mounted leather scabbard. $208 £105

A Nazi Luftwaffe officer's sword, plated blade 25½in., by SMF Solingen, light
metal mounts, wire bound blue leather covered grip in its blue leather covered
metal scabbard with bright metal mounts, with integral belt clip. $278 £110

A German mid 18th century brass hilted sword, double edged blade 31in., with
short fuller at forte engraved 'IHIN', solid heart-shaped guard, plain knucklebow
with sideloop to each side and thumb ring, twist spiral grip, ovoid pommel.
                                                        $218 £110

A Nazi Naval officer's sword, plain, pipe-back, clipped back blade 32in., by
A.C.S., with Nazi Eagle stamp above 'M', gilt hilt with folding guard and
small side guard stamped '0686', white ivorine gilt wire bound grip, 'lion's
head' pommel, in its brass mounted leather scabbard. $271 £140

A Nazi Luftwaffe officer's sword, plated blade 28½in., by F. & A. Helbig Gaefler Steinach, with small inspection stamp, plated mounts, wire bound, blue leather covered grip, in its blue leather covered scabbard with plated mounts. $337 £170

A Nazi Naval officer's sword, slightly curved blade 32½in., by A.C.S., retaining nearly all original polished finish and etched with naval trophies, foliage and battleships, gilt folding side shellguard, 'lion's head' pommel with green and red stone eyes, brass wire bound white grip, in its brass mounted, patent leather scabbard, with rare leather thong hanging straps and clips, hook and chain and with bullion dress knot. $396 £200

A Nazi Luftwaffe officer's sword, plated blade 30in., by SMF, with small inspection stamp, light metal mounts, wire bound, blue leather covered grip, in its blue leather covered metal scabbard with integral belt clip.
                                         $416 £210

A late 18th century German double-handed parade sword, broad, double edged flamboyant blade 47½in., shallow diamond section, squared forte deeply struck with armourer's mark and with integral upturned counterguard. Swollen bulbous pineapple pommel, swollen wooden grip bound with wound wire and with red tassel decoration. $535 £270

A Japanese sword ken, double edged blade 76cm., signed Tsuda Echizen Nokami Sukehiro, chiselled with five sanskrit characters as Bhuddistic invocation horimono. $356 £180

A pair of Japanese swords, daisho, katana blade 67¼cm. mumei, Doran Gunome Hamon, distinct nie clusters. Wakizashi blade 50½cm. mumei. Koshirae iron mokko tsubas with two sages in boat beneath moon with foliage inlaid in gilt, silver and shakudo. Tape bound same tsukas, shakudo menuki with gilt mounts, shakudo nanako fuchi kashiras with gilt foliage. $990 £500

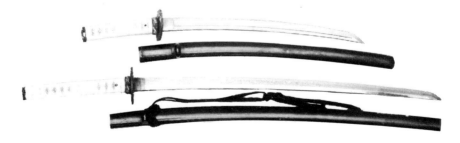

A pair of Japanese swords, daisho, comprising katana, blade 67cm., mumei, three mekugi ana, ko-choji hamon. Wakizashi, blade 44½cm., signed 'Bishu Osafune Morimitsu' and dated Oei 25th Year (1418). Gunome hamon, bo-hi ni tsure hi, three mekugi ana, distinct nie line. Koshirae, shakudo nanako mokko tsubas and with gilt gambolling lions and silver waterfalls. Black lacquered sayas. $2,673 £1,350

An interesting George V Infantry officer's sword, mounted with family blade, a Victorian 1822 pattern pipe back, clipped back blade 34in., by John Nicholls, 42 Jermyn St., St. James', London, and with family crest and crown, 'VR', laurel sprays within panel and oak leaf spray, wire bound fish-skin covered grip, in its leather field service scabbard. $51 £26

A Victorian 1827 pattern Rifle Volunteer officer's sword, slightly curved blade 32½in., etched with crown 'VR', foliate scrolls and '6th Lancashire Rifles' with strung bugle, steel guard and mounts, wire bound fish-skin covered grip, in its steel mounted leather scabbard. $55 £28

A U.S. 1840 pattern NCO's Civil War period sword, straight, plain blade 32in., brass double shellguard, plain knucklebow, simulated wire bound grip and mounts, in its brass mounted leather scabbard. $69 £35

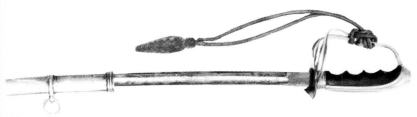

A late 19th century U.S. Army officer's sword, plated, curved blade 31½in., by 'The M. C. Lilley & Co., Columbus', etched with 'U.S.', U.S. Eagle, military trophies and foliage, white metal triple bar guard and plain mounts, shaped horn grip, in its plated metal scabbard with a bullion dress knot. $79 £40

A Bavarian Army officer's sword, plated, curved blade 31in., with early
Eickhorn trade mark, etched within panel with motto, Royal Arms and oak
trees, plain brass stirrup guard and mounts, ribbed black grip, in its steel
scabbard. $79 £40

A Spanish Infantry officer's sword of 1822 pattern, plain, slightly curved,
pipe-back, clipped backed blade 34½in., retaining some original polish, brass
hilt incorporating Spanish Royal Arms, wire bound fish-skin covered grip,
in its steel scabbard. $89 £45

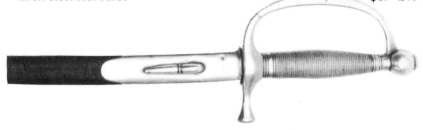

A U.S. Civil War period 1840 pattern musician's sword, blade 28in., by
'Ames, Chicopee' also stamped 'U.S. G.W.C. 1864' and retaining most
original polish. Plain brass, single knucklebow and mounts with simulated
wire bound grip, in its brass mounted leather scabbard. $89 £45

A post-1902 Naval officer's sword, blade 29½in., etched with Royal Arms,
crown, fouled anchor and foliate sprays, gilt brass hilt, 'lion's head' pommel
and mounts, wire bound white fish-skin covered grip, in its brass mounted
leather covered scabbard, with bullion dress knot. $89 £45

A Victorian 1827 pattern Rifle Volunteer officer's sword, slightly curved blade 32½in., retaining nearly all original polish and etched with crown, 'VR', foliage, strung bugle, blank scroll and the other scroll etched 'Rifles', steel hilt, wire bound fish-skin covered grip, in its steel scabbard. **$97 £50**

An 18th century Spanish Military sword, single edged blade 27in., marked 'B.Y. I.O. 1794', with crowned 'R' and 'CS IV', iron single loop side guard, single plain iron knucklebow, ovoid iron pommel, fluted spiral brass grip.
$99 £50

A Victorian drummer's Mark I pattern 1856 sword, spear pointed, straight, double edged blade, 19in., etched with scrolls, cast brass hilt with trefoil terminals to quillons and 'VR' cypher to central panel, ribbed grip struck with ordnance stamp, in its brass mounted black leather scabbard, with frog stud to top mount. $103 £52

A George V officer's sword of The Scots Guards, blade 32in., by Henry Wilkinson, Pall Mall, well etched with crown, regimental badge, royal cypher and arms, battle honours to South Africa 1902, steel guard and mounts, wire bound fish-skin covered grip, in its leather covered field service scabbard.
$109 £55

An 1889 pattern Prussian Infantry officer's sword, plain, plated, fullered blade 31½in., brass folding guard and mounts, crowned 'WRII' cypher to grip, brass wire bound fish-skin covered grip, in its black painted metal scabbard. $109 £55

A 19th century Spanish officer's sword, curved blade 33in., etched with foliate scrolls, with gilt backing and 'Artilleria Fabrica de Toledo 1889', steel bowl guard chiselled with Spanish Arms and foliage, also with gilt background, wire bound, fish-skin covered grip, in its steel scabbard.
$109 £55

A 1796 pattern Cavalry officer's heavy dress sword, straight, single edged blade 31½in., etched 'John Gill Warranted' within scroll, 1801-16 Royal Arms, military trophies, floral sprays, etc., copper gilt hilt, with boat-shaped guard and rounded crosspiece, ovoid pommel, silver wire bound grip, in its steel scabbard. $109 £55

A scarce World War II Italian Air Force officer's sword, slim blade 32in., by Horster, also stamped 'Lardoni Milano', retaining nearly all original polish and etched with Royal Arms, military trophies and foliage, gilt 'feathered' guard, 'eagle's head' pommel, wire bound horn grip, in its leather covered metal scabbard, with three gilt mounts. $119 £60

A Victorian 1822 pattern Infantry officer's sword, slightly curved blade
32½in., by Noel Edwards & Son, Hanover St., London, etched with crown,
'VR', foliate scrolls and 'Kilkenny Militia', copper gilt hilt with folding side
guard, copper wire bound fish-skin covered grip, in its leather scabbard.
                                                  $119 £60

A George V 1897 pattern Infantry officer's sword, blade 32in., retaining
most original polish and etched with Royal cypher, Arms and foliage.
Plated guard and mounts. Wire bound fish-skin covered grip, leather dress
knot, in its leather covered field service scabbard. $119 £60

A post-1902 Naval officer's sword, blade 31in., by Gieve, Mathews &
Seagrove, Portsmouth, retaining much original polish and etched with
Royal Arms, crown, fouled anchor and foliage, gilt hilt with 'lion's
head' pommel and folding side guard, gilt wire bound white fish-skin
covered grip, in its gilt mounted leather covered scabbard. $129 £65

An Imperial German cadet's sword, slightly curved, plated blade 25½in.,
etched with foliage, cornucopia, name 'Alfred Wolker', military trophies
and inscription 'Es Lebe Hoch das Regiment das Sich wir Stolz Die Wil-
den Nennt', brass hilt with foliate pierced side guard, knucklebow with
roped decoration, 'lion's head' pommel, wire bound fish-skin covered
grip, in its plated metal scabbard. $129 £65

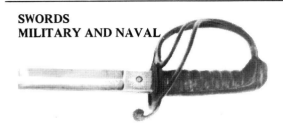

A Victorian 1821 pattern Light Cavalry officer's sword, slightly curved, fullered blade 35in., etched with 'VR' cypher within scrolled panels, triple bar steel hilt, wire bound fish-skin covered grips, in its steel scabbard.

$129 £65

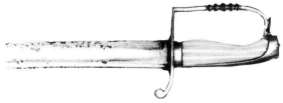

A late 18th century Georgian officer's 'five-ball' hilted sword of the type favoured by Naval officers, plain, curved blade 29½in., with narrow and broad fullers, stamped 'Harvey' on backstrap, copper gilt hilt with single knucklebow, incorporating 'five-ball' design, plain mounts, fluted ivory grip.

$133 £67

A Victorian mounted officer's sword, believed of the 2nd Life Guards, circa 1835, slim, straight blade 33in., with short fullers, brass crosspiece with flaming grenade badge in centre, 'eagle's head' pommel, wire bound wood grip, in its metal scabbard.

$139 £70

An Edward VII Scottish Field officer's sword, double fullered blade 32in., with Thurkle proof stamp, etched with Royal cypher, crown, thistles and foliage, plated foliate scrolled guard, plated mounts, red liner, wire bound fish-skin covered grip, in its leather covered field service scabbard, with plated tip.

$139 £70

A Czech Army officer's sword, slightly curved blade 32½in., stamped at forte 'Vlasziquit', Czech lion stamp etc., white metal triple bar hilt with bowl guard, decorated with ivy leaf pattern and Czech arms, wire bound, fish-skin covered grip, in its plated scabbard.   **$139 £70**

A George V Scottish officer's sword, 1897 pattern, blade 32in., by 'Sanderson Bros. and Newbould LD, Sheffield', etched with crown, Royal cypher, foliate sprays and with cruciform German silver crosspiece, fluted pommel and mounts, silver wire bound fish-skin grip, in a leather covered field service scabbard.   **$139 £70**

An interesting late 18th century European Military sword with Eastern re-curving blade 27in., with pronounced clipped back tip, half length back fuller, long central fuller, traces of plating overall, cast brass hilt with straight cross-piece, scaled grip, 'lion's head' pommel.   **$139 £70**

A Nazi Army officer's 'Prinz Eugen' pattern sword, curved, plated blade 32in., by Eickhorn, gilt hilt with Nazi eagle langet and with Nazi Eagle on pommel, stirrup guard with oak leaf pattern, black wire bound grip, in its black painted metal scabbard with Nazi dress knot. **$139 £70**

A Victorian R.E. 1857 pattern officer's sword, slightly curved blade 32in., retaining much original polish and etched with crown 'VR', 'Royal Engineers', winged lightning and foliate sprays and struck at forte and below guard with ordnance issue marks, brass guard, copper wire bound fish-skin covered grip, in its steel scabbard.   **$139 £70**

An interesting 1821 pattern sword, mounted with earlier French, single edged blade 36in., with narrow back fuller and clipped back point, triple bar pattern steel guard, steel mounts, wire bound fish-skin covered grip, in its metal scabbard.   **$139 £70**

An Edward VII 1897 pattern Infantry officer's sword, straight blade 32½in., etched with Royal cypher, winged lightning, 'West Riding, Royal Engineers' and officer's monogram 'CLP' and scrolls, plated guard, wire bound fish-skin grip with gold cord and acorn dress knot, in its plated scabbard. **$139 £70**

A scarce Imperial Italian Air Force officer's sword, straight blade of flattened oval section, 29½in., etched with 'wings', flying trophies, Royal Arms and foliage, solid bronze guard cast as spray of feathers, 'eagle's head' pommel and backstrap, composition grooved grip, in its bronze mounted leather scabbard.   **$139 £70**

A good Georgian sword of the type favoured by Naval officers, double fullered, curved, clipped back blade 25½in., divided steel knucklebow with single scroll side bar, twisted ball pommel, copper spirally bound wooden grip, retaining pleasing patina overall. **$139 £70**

A Nazi Army officer's sword, slightly curved, plated blade 33½in., by Robert Klaas, brass hilt, Nazi Eagle on langet, stirrup knucklebow and mounts decorated with oak leaves, 'lion's head' pommel with red glass eyes, wire bound, black ribbed grip, in its black painted metal scabbard. **$148 £75**

A special pattern George V Infantry officer's presentation sword, blade 32in., etched with 'GR', foliage and blank panel, steel guard pierced with scrolls and bordered with thistles, wire bound fish-skin covered grip, in its leather covered field service scabbard. **$148 £75**

A Victorian Naval officer's sword of The Royal Dockyard Battalion, slightly curved blade 31in., well etched with crown, 'VR', fouled anchor, foliage and 'Royal Dockyard Bttn', copper gilt guard, 'lion's head' pommel, wire bound fish-skin covered grip. **$148 £75**

SWORDS
MILITARY AND NAVAL

A late Victorian 1822 pattern Infantry officer's sword, blade 33in., by Henry Wilkinson, etched with Imperial crown, interlaced cypher, Royal Arms, foliage etc., brass guard, the cartouche with addition of a rose beneath the cypher, brass mounts, wire bound fish-skin covered grip, in its steel scabbard, with dress belt of Morocco leather with three bullion stripes. $158 £80

A George V Irish Guards officer's sword, blade 32in., retaining most original polish, etched with crown, regimental badge, crown, Royal cypher and scrolls, plated guard and mounts, wire bound fish-skin covered grip, leather dress knot, in its leather covered field service scabbard. $158 £80

An interesting EIC 1822 pattern Infantry field officer's sword, slightly curved, pipe-back blade 31in., retaining some original polish, frost etched with 'EIC' and lion amid leaf scrolls and the Company's motto 'Auspicio Regis et Senatus Angliae' in blued and gilt scrolls, copper gilt hilt, wire bound fish-skin covered grip, in its brass scabbard. $168 £85

An Irish Infantry officer's sword, straight blade 33in., etched with Celtic patterns and scrolls etc., brass triple bar guard, fluted brass pommel, wire bound fish-skin covered grip, in its plated scabbard. $168 £85

132

A French 1854 model cuirassier sword, double fullered, single edged blade 38in., with spear point, stamped at forte with ordnance marks, rounded backstrap, triple bar brass guard, brass mounts, brass wire bound leather covered grip. $178 £90

A Georgian Naval officer's fighting sword, circa 1785, plain, double fullered, single edged blade 25in., with long clipped back point, copper gilt hilt with slotted guard with anchor design, fluted knucklebow with openwork panel with fouled anchor, fluted pommel, fluted ivory grip with gilt band and cartouche. $178 £90

An 1822 pattern William IV Infantry officer's sword, slightly curved, pipe-back, clipped backed blade 32½in., retaining much original polish, copper gilt guard retaining much original gilding, wire bound, black, fish-skin covered grip, in its leather scabbard with three copper gilt mounts. $178 £90

An Austrian Cavalry officer's 1904 pattern sword, plated, slightly curved, pipe-backed, clipped back blade 30in., plated hilt and mounts with pierced honeysuckle guard, brass wire bound fish-skin covered grip, in its plated scabbard with original dress knot with 'K' cypher (of the Emperor Karl).
                                                              $188 £95

A Georgian Naval officer's sword as worn by Commanders and above, circa 1805-1825, slim, straight, single edged blade 26in., retaining some blued and gilt etched decoration of fouled anchors, Royal Arms, crown, 'GR', etc., copper gilt hilt with stirrup guard, 'lion's head' pommel, wire bound ivory grip, in its leather scabbard with three copper gilt mounts. $198 £100

A Georgian Naval officer's sword, blade 31in., retaining most original polish, etched with crown, fouled anchor, Royal cypher and foliage, brass guard with small folding side guard, copper wire bound white fish-skin covered grip, in its brass mounted leather scabbard with bullion dress knot and patent leather belt. $198 £100

A post 1902 Naval Warrant Officer's sword, blade 31in., by W. Cracknell, etched with fouled anchor, Royal Arms, and foliage within panels, solid guard, plain pommel, wire bound grip, in its gilt brass mounted leather scabbard, and original dress knot. $198 £100

A George VI Naval officer's sword, straight blade 31½in., with Gieves proof mark and etched with crown, Royal cypher, fouled anchor, blank panels and foliage, gilt guard, 'lion's head' pommel and mounts, folding side guard, copper wire bound white fish-skin covered grip, in its brass mounted leather scabbard with original bullion dress knot. $198 £100

A Victorian levee pattern officer's sword of The Scots Guards, slim, single edged blade 32in., retaining some original polish, well etched with crown, interlaced 'VR', regimental badge, thistle etc., plated guard and mounts, silver wire bound fish-skin covered grip, in its plated metal scabbard.

$198 £100

A Light Company officer's sword with hilt similar to 1788 Light Cavalry pattern, slender, curved, fullered blade 33in., etched sun, moon and trophy on each side with traces of original blued and gilt decoration. Iron stirrup hilt, facetted steel backstrap, woven copper wire bound leather covered grip, long rectangular langets, in its steel scabbard. $198 £100

A Victorian E.I.C. Naval officer's sword, slightly curved blade 30in., by Harman Calcutta, etched with E.I.C. lion and fouled anchor, brass guard, 'lion's head' pommel, wire bound fish-skin covered grip, in its brass mounted leather scabbard. $198 £100

A Georgian Naval officer's sword, as worn by Commanders and above, circa 1805, straight, single edged blade 32½in., engraved 'Solingen' on backstrap and retaining much original blued and gilt etched decoration of 1801-1816 Royal Arms, etc., copper gilt hilt with stirrup guard, 'lion's head' pommel, wire bound ivory grip, in a Georgian leather scabbard with two copper gilt mounts. $198 £100

An 1857 pattern Royal Engineer field officer's sword, slightly curved blade 32in., retaining much original polish and well etched with winged lightning, 'Royal Engineers', crown, 'VR', interlaced cypher, foliate scrolls, brass hilt and mounts, wire bound, fish-skin covered grip, in its brass scabbard.

$198 £100

A Georgian EIC 1822 pattern Infantry officer's sword, slightly curved, pipe-backed, clipped blade 32½in., etched with EIC lion and foliate scrolls, copper gilt guard and mounts, folding side guard, copper wire bound fish-skin covered grip, leather scabbard with three copper gilt mounts and two suspension rings, top mount with crossbelt frog stud. $208 £105

A good ERII Naval officer's sword; blade 31in., retaining all its original polish, etched with crowned, fouled anchor and roped, oak leaf panels, solid gilt turn-down guard, 'lion's head' pommel and backstrap, white shark-skin grip, bullion dress knot, in its leather scabbard with gilt mounts.

$208 £105

A late Victorian levee pattern Coldstream Guards officer's sword, slim blade 32½in., retaining most original polish and etched with crown, interlaced 'VR', regimental badge, foliage, battle honours to 'Suakin 1885' and officer's initials 'C.E.P.', plated guard and mounts, wire bound fish-skin covered grip, in its plated scabbard with original buff leather slings. $208 £105

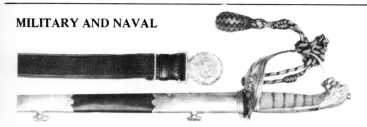

An Edward VII Royal Indian Marine Naval officer's sword, blade 31in., retaining much original polish and etched with crown, Royal cypher, Indian Star and fouled anchor, foliate sprays, gilt guard with Indian Navy cartouche and 'R.M.', gilt mounts, 'lion's head' pommel, wire bound white fish-skin covered grip, in its leather scabbard. $218 £110

A Victorian 1822 pattern Infantry field officer's sword, blade 32in., retaining much original polish and well etched with crown, 'VR', foliage, officer's coat-of-arms and crest and motto 'Toutjours Prest'. Fine gilt hilt, copper wire bound fish-skin covered grip, in its brass scabbard. $218 £110

A Georgian officer's sword, circa 1800, of the St. James' Loyal Volunteers, straight, single edged blade 32½in., retaining some blueing and gilt, copper gilt hilt, with plain knucklebow, small feathered langets, fluted black wood grip, inset with oval band and cartouche, in restored brass mounted cardboard scabbard. $218 £110

A William IV 1821 pattern Light Cavalry officer's sword, retaining virtually all original polish, etc., etched with crown 'W.R.IV' cypher and foliate spray within panel, triple bar steel guard, plain steel mounts, wire bound fish-skin covered grip, in its steel scabbard. $218 £110

An Imperial Russian Naval officer's sword, circa 1860, plain, curved blade 32½in., etched on backstrap with Russian script, gilt brass triple bar flattened guard, plain brass mounts and scrolled back quillon, flattened octagonal langets, copper wire bound leather covered grip, in its brass mounted leather scabbard. $228 £115

A Victorian special pattern Royal Scottish Fusilier officer's sword, slim, single edged blade 30in., retaining much original polish and etched with St. Andrew 'XXI Royal Scots Fusiliers', regimental badge and motto, crown, 'VR', foliage, battle honours to Crimea, brass guard pierced with thistles, brass mounts, wire bound fish-skin covered grip, in its steel scabbard.
                                                                                 $228 £115

A Victorian 1822 pattern Infantry Field officer's sword, blade 32in., officially sharpened and retaining some original polish and well etched with crown, 'VR' and foliate scrolls etc., also fitted with 'Patent Solid Hilt', wire bound diced grip, copper guard and mounts, in its brass scabbard. $238 £120

A Georgian Grenadier Company officer's 1803 pattern sword, curved blade 29½in., etched with military trophies, foliage, 'Warranted' etc., traces of blueing and gilt, copper gilt guard, 'lion's head' pommel, diced ivory grip, in its leather scabbard with two copper mounts. $238 £120

A rare Georgian 1805 Naval officer's sword as worn by a Master-of-the-Fleet, straight, single edged blade 32in., etched with crown, fouled anchor, Naval trophies, angel cherub, 1801-16 Royal Arms, copper gilt hilt, shield langets engraved with one large and two small anchors (for Master-of-the-Fleet), plain stirrup guard and pommel, wire bound black fish-skin covered grip.
$247 £125

A Georgian Dragoon officer's sword, circa 1790, broad, straight, single edged blade 33in., with narrow back fuller, etched with crown, 'GR' and foliate sprays, with traces of blueing and gilt, plain steel single knucklebow, mounts and single sideloop, finely diced black grip, in its iron mounted leather scabbard.
$257 £130

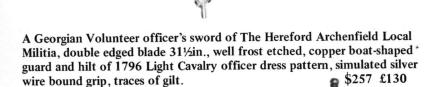

A Georgian Volunteer officer's sword of The Hereford Archenfield Local Militia, double edged blade 31½in., well frost etched, copper boat-shaped guard and hilt of 1796 Light Cavalry officer dress pattern, simulated silver wire bound grip, traces of gilt.
$257 £130

An Edward VII Indian Army general officer's 1831 pattern mameluke hilted sword, curved, clipped back blade 33in., retaining virtually all original polish, etched with 'ERI' cypher, copper gilt crossguard, ivory grips with rosette studs, in its plated scabbard.
$297 £150

A Royal Naval officer's World War I period sword, plain, sharpened blade
31in., standard gilt guard with 'lion's head' pommel, wire bound, white
fish-skin covered grip, leather dress knot, in its leather covered field service scabbard. $297 £150

A Georgian Naval officer's rare fighting sword, circa 1790, plain, tapering,
single edged blade 30in., copper gilt hilt with broad, oval guard engraved with
Naval trophies and foliate sprays, fluted knucklebow, plain ivory grip inset
with copper gilt fouled anchor, small back quillon. $297 £150

A Light Cavalry trooper's sword, circa 1780, long, plain, single edged blade
35in., with clipped back point, plain brass hilt with single knucklebow, ribbed,
fish-skin covered grip. $297 £150

An English Dragoon trooper's sword, circa 1740, plain, slightly curved blade
27in., with narrow back fuller and Shotley Bridge 'running fox' mark with
'SH' brass basket guard, with rayed pierced base, flattened circular pommel,
fish-skin covered grip, in leather scabbard with brass lug and chape.
                                                                 $307 £155

A George V mameluke levee sword of the 10th (Prince of Wales) Hussars, curved, flat blade 31½in., retaining much original polish, etched with Royal cypher, Prince of Wales' feather and wreath, amid scrolled panels, ivory grip with gilt rosettes, gilt ornamental crossguard and langets, silver and crimson sword knot, in its chromium plated scabbard. $307 £155

A fine 1822 pattern George IV general and staff officer's sword of Major General George Dick, slightly curved, pipe-backed blade 34½in., with clipped back tip, fine copper gilt hilt, wire bound fish-skin covered grip, in its leather scabbard with three fine copper gilt mounts. $376 £190

A 1796 pattern Cavalry officer's sword, broad, curved, single edged blade 32½in., blued and gilt for over half its length, etched with trophies of arms and floral tributes. Copper wire bound leather covered grip, regulation stirrup hilt and steel scabbard with two hanging rings. $376 £190

A fine Victorian 1831 pattern general officer's mameluke sword, curved, clipped back blade 31in., well etched with crown, 'VR', laurel sprays and general's insignia, Royal Arms etc., and retaining virtually all original polished finish, gilt metal crossguard decorated with foliate sprays, gilt straps, ivory grips with brass rosettes, in its brass scabbard. $376 £190

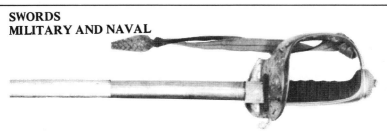

A Victorian HAC officer's sword, plated blade 33in., etched with crown, 'VR', regimental badge and crest, officer's initials 'J.W.P.F.' and foliage. Steel 1882 type hilt incorporating HAC grenade in oval panel, wire bound fish-skin covered grip, in its steel scabbard.   **$396 £200**

A late Victorian levee pattern Grenadier Guards officer's sword, slim blade 32½in., retaining much original polish and well etched with crown, interlaced 'VR' cypher, regimental device, battle honours to 'Suakin 1885', plated guard and mounts, wire bound fish-skin covered grip, in its plated scabbard.   **$410 £205**

A Georgian 1805 Naval officer's sword as worn by Lieutenants, single edged blade 32in., retaining much original polish and well etched with crown, fouled anchor, military trophies, 1801-16 Royal Arms, foliate sprays, copper gilt hilt, shield langets, plain pommel, copper wire bound black fish-skin covered grip, in its copper gilt mounted leather scabbard.   **$416 £210**

An Edward VII Indian Army general officer's 1831 pattern mameluke hilted sword, curved, clipped back blade 33in., retaining virtually all original polish, etched with 'ERI' cypher, general's insignia within scrolled panels, copper gilt crossguard, ivory grips with rosette studs, in its plated scabbard.
    $475 £240

A rare Georgian 1796 pattern officer's sword of the 1st The Royal Regiment of Foot (The Royal Scots), broad, tapering, double edged blade 32in., etched at forte 'Eginton's Warranted', and with blued and gilt etched panel of crowned' regimental device, copper gilt hilt with double shellguard, the upper panels affixed with pre 1812 regimental badges, plain knucklebow, urn pommel, simulated silver wire bound grip. $515 £260

A Georgian Naval officer's sword, circa 1815, straight, single edged blade 28in., with gilt etched decoration at forte, fine copper gilt hilt with Patriotic Fund style 'lion's head' pommel and mane backstrap, squared knucklebow with fluted pattern and floral chiselled back quillon, rectangular langets, diced black grip with base mount chiselled with laurel sprays, in its leather scabbard with three fine copper gilt mounts. $594 £300

A Georgian Naval officer's sword, 1805, straight, single edged blade 30in., double fullered and signed in the fullers 'Andria Farara' (probably a family blade), fine copper gilt hilt, with fouled anchors engraved on langets, 'lion's head' pommel, plain stirrup knucklebow, copper wire bound ribbed ivory grip, in its leather scabbard. $594 £300

A U.S. Naval officer's sword of the period of the war of 1812, slightly curved blade 30in., with pronounced clipped back tip, etched with fouled anchor, oak leaf spray and ring of thirteen stars, copper gilt stirrup knucklebow and mounts, acorn terminals to crosspiece, 'eagle's head' pommel and plumage backstrap, ivory grip carved with stylised feathers. $614 £310

SWORDS
MILITARY AND NAVAL

A rare Georgian 1803 pattern Flank Company field officer's sword of The 28th Foot (North Gloucestershire), curved, clipped back blade 31in., by Prosser, well frost etched with crown above '28', grenade, sphinx, military trophies and battle honours within panels 'Barrosa', 'Egypt' and 'Waterloo', copper gilt guard, copper wire bound fish-skin covered grip, in its copper scabbard. $693 £350

A Georgian officer's regimental pattern sword of The 23rd (Royal Welch Fusiliers) Regiment of Foot, curved, flat blade 31in., with spear point, double edged for last 11in., copper gilt stirrup shaped knucklebow, large oval langets, 'lion's head' pommel and backstrap, fish-skin covered grip, bound with copper wire, in its black leather scabbard. $792 £400

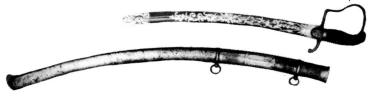

An interesting 1796 pattern Light Cavalry officer's sword, curved, fullered blade 32in., retaining most original polish and blued and gilt decoration of foliage and stylised trophies, steel stirrup knucklebow with pronounced bow, half round langets, plain backstrap, leather covered grip, in its steel scabbard with two hanging rings. The sword of Captain Mercer R.H.A. carried at Waterloo.
$1,109 £560

A fine 1796 pattern Georgian Infantry officer's presentation sword, tapering, double edged blade 32in. of flattened diamond section, retaining nearly all original blued and gilt for almost the entire length. Fine, copper gilt hilt, double shellguard chiselled at edges with foliate sprays, one guard folding urn pommel, flattened knucklebow, copper and gilt wire bound grip, in its patent leather covered metal scabbard. $1,683 £850

A 17th century mortuary sword, double edged blade 29in., with running wolf mark and spurious dated '1414', iron basket hilt, the guard with simple decoration, chiselled ovoid pommel, wire bound, leather covered grip.   **$198 £100**

A mid 17th century mortuary sword, single edged blade 34in., with double fullers with traces of signature, iron basket hilt, the bowl chiselled with masks and foliage, pommel chiselled with foliate pattern.   **$218 £110**

A 17th century mortuary sword, long, tapering, single edged blade 36½in., with narrow back fuller and with traces of etched decoration of nobleman, with traces of inscription, iron semi-basket guard, partly pierced and chiselled with masks and foliate sprays, the looped guard also incorporating masks, ovoid pommel, plain wood grip.   **$297 £150**

A 17th century mortuary sword, straight, single edged, multi-fullered blade 33in., signed in fullers 'Andrea Ferara', traces of armourer's mark at forte, iron basket guard with solid base, chiselled with foliate patterns, wire bound grip with 'Turk's head' finials, pommel chiselled with foliate patterns.
                                                    $470 £225

SWORDS
SCHIAVONA

A 17th century Venetian sword schiavona, double edged, tapering blade 33in., struck at ricasso with crowned mark and engraved with zig-zag pattern at forte. Good looped and rayed iron basket guard with thumb ring and curved back quillon, wire bound leather covered grip, eared pommel. **$198 £100**

A good Venetian sword schiavona, circa 1580, straight, single edged, fullered blade 40in., with contemporary repair. Multi-bar swept hilt, wrought from one piece, incorporating large thumb ring, integral square sectioned quillon with swollen finial. Brass pommel of eared form, wire bound grip with brass ferrules. **$574 £290**

SHORT SWORDS

An attractive Chinese short sword, straight double edged blade 16in., with spear tip, brass crosspiece, pommel and mounts decorated with traditional patterns including a bat, fluted wood grip, in its tortoiseshell covered wooden scabbard, with five brass mounts. **$109 £55**

An interesting 18th century Continental short sword, double edged, straight, fullered blade 26½in., etched with standing classical figure and two inscriptions in Latin, within profuse arabesque scrolls, inlaid with gold, plain steel hilt, crosspiece with gold washed line engraving. **$247 £125**

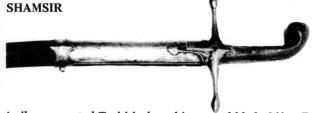

A silver mounted Turkish shamshir, curved blade 31in., Eastern silver cross-piece with simple pattern decoration, bulbous horn grips, fluted silver back-strap, in its leather covered wooden scabbard, with two large Eastern silver chapes, with some engraved foliate patterns.   **$210 £100**

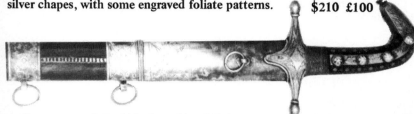

A silver mounted Turkish shamshir, slightly curved blade 28½in., with double back fullers, Eastern silver crossguard engraved with foliate pattern, horn hilt mounted with Eastern silver strip and pommel bound with silver wire at base and inset with silver and brass studs, leather covered wooden scabbard.

$297 £150

A 17th century Persian sword shamshir, curved, single edged blade 32in., watered with the pattern of the forty steps or 'Ladder of Mahommed'. Steel crosspiece well chiselled in low relief. Two-piece bone grips embossed silver pommel and rivet heads.   **$475 £240**

A Turkish sword shamshir, curved, ribbed back, clipped back blade 27in., engraved silver langets and quillons with swollen terminals, two-piece horn hilt with bulbous pommel, in its low grade Eastern silver mounted, leather covered scabbard.   **$535 £270**

SWORDS
SHAMSIR

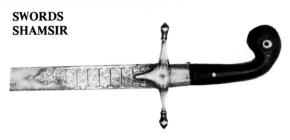

A Turkish sword shamshir, curved, watered steel, single edged blade 33in., silver nielloed crossguard and langets and backstrap, downturned horn grip pierced for lanyard.   **$535 £270**

A very fine Indo-Persian sword shamshir, finely watered, curved, single edged blade 31in., shallow single fullers, inscribed in gold with maker's cartouche 'Assad Ullah', one-piece ivory grip carved as a lion head with snarling face, copper gilt crosspiece and scabbard mounts. Large chape and locket, two suspension bands, in its wooden scabbard with later black leather covering.

$693 £350

SHASQUA

A Caucasian sword shasqua, curved, treble fullered, single edged blade 27½in., with some etched decoration at forte, one-piece wooden grip with downturned pommel, in its iron mounted leather covered scabbard.   **$36 £18**

A Russian officer's 1904 Caucasian pattern shasqua, curved, multi-fullered blade 29in., etched at forte with Imperial Eagle, crowned cypher of Nicholas II, plain eared horn hilt, in its leather covered wooden scabbard with brass bottom chape and with original leather belt with brass mounts.**$148 £75**

A silver hilted Russian sabre shasqua, curved, single edged, fullered blade 27in., silver hilt nielloed with scrolls, rosettes and borders. $148 £75

A scarce Soviet Military shasqua, plain, slightly curved blade 30in., retaining much original polish and '1930' at forte, with Soviet stamps, brass mounts, Soviet 'C.C.C.P.' emblem to 'bird's head' pommel, spiral wood grip, in its steel mounted leather covered wooden scabbard with provision for bayonet. $168 £85

A Caucasian shasqua, curved blade 30½in., with double back fuller, etched 'K.K.B.', within foliate panel at forte, plain eared horn grips, in its leather covered wooden scabbard with four white metal mounts decorated with foliate niello patterns. $200 £101

A Soviet Cavalry trooper's shasqua, curved, single edged blade 31½in., dated '1939' at forte, with Soviet stamps, brass mounted hilt, the pommel with 'C.C.C.P.' and state emblem, spiral wood grip, in its leather covered wooden scabbard with brass mounts. $208 £105

A late 18th century brass hilted small sword, tapering triangular, hollow ground blade 30in., etched with foliate patterns. Oval guard pierced with scrolled patterns and with beaded rim. Grip, knucklebow and pommel with stepped patterns, in its leather covered wooden scabbard with two steel mounts. $67 £34

A late 18th century pierced brass hilted small sword, tapering, triangular, hollow ground blade 31in., etched with foliate sprays etc. Oval pierced guard with facetted edge and beaded pattern. Knucklebow, grip and pommel of hollow form and painted black for mourning. In its vellum covered wooden scabbard with two steel mounts. $67 £34

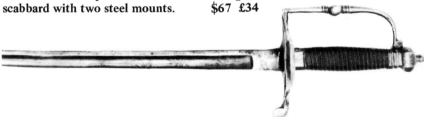

A Napoleonic era Continental officer's dress small sword, straight, single edged blade 33in., etched at forte 'S.H.', military trophies and foliage, brass guard, solid side shell with design of Pegasus, knucklebow incorporating single ball design, pommel engraved with foliate pattern, copper wire bound grip.
$97 £49

A late 17th century transitional rapier small sword, slim, straight blade 30in., of diamond section, iron, multi-pierced double shellguard, iron knucklebow and mounts with traces of decoration, fluted ovoid pommel, plain wood grip.
$107 £54

A late 18th century officer's small sword, slim, double edged, tapering blade 32in., with short fuller, copper gilt double shellguard, plain knucklebow, urn pommel and mounts, two loops to base of knucklebow, small crosspiece, copper wire bound grip with 'Turk's head' terminals, in its leather covered scabbard with two small copper gilt mounts. $109 £55

A mid 18th century mourning small sword, tapering, triangular, hollow ground blade 30in., plain iron hilt, wire bound grip with 'Turk's head' finials, double shellguard, blackened finish overall. $119 £60

A steel hilted small sword, circa 1725, black painted for mourning use, slender hollow ground, triangular sectioned blade 27½in. Double shellguards with swollen edges, large ricasso, rings, integral swollen knucklebow, bulbous pommel, finely woven black hair binding and 'Turks' heads'. $158 £80

A fine late 18th century European small sword, slim, straight blade 27¼in., of diamond section, with blued and gilt etched decoration at forte of foliate sprays, copper gilt hilt with double shellguard chiselled with foliate scrolls, the grip with foliate and floral patterns, the pommel and knucklebow decorated en suite with the shellguard. $218 £110

An officer's dress small sword, circa 1785, slim, tapering blade 33in., of diamond section, retaining approximately fifty per cent blued and gilt etched decoration of military trophies etc., fine fire-gilt double shellguard, knucklebow, urn pommel and mounts, silver gilt wire bound grip with 'Turk's head' terminals. $228 £115

An early 19th century Spanish silver hilted small sword, single edged blade 27½in., retaining some blueing and gilt and etched with Spanish Royal Arms, 'Viva Espana' and 'Vive Le Roy', bowl guard, pierced at back and fluted with foliate pattern, narrow, fluted knucklebow with hallmarks, spiral twist grip and pommel. $277 £140

A small sword, circa 1770, colichmarde blade 31in., etched with foliate patterns, oval steel guard with fretted edge and engraved with circular patterns. Plain steel knucklebow and facetted urn pommel, silver wire and band bound grip with 'Turk's head' finials in its vellum covered wooden scabbard, with steel top mounts. $307 £155

A Continental silver hilted small sword, circa 1770, blade 30in. of shallow flattened diamond section, etched with foliage at forte with ornamental fullering. Large guard with shell thumb piece, ribbed borders, pommel, grip and ricasso worked with swirling design. Ribbed knucklebow and quillon terminals. $317 £160

A French (hallmarked for Paris 1787) silver hilted small sword, slender, triangular sectioned blade 32½in. Silver hilt cut, pierced and facetted, dish-shaped guard, shallow ricasso rings, integral knucklebow. $356 £180

A Naval officer's small sword of Vice Admiral Sylverius Moriarty R.N., circa 1790, tapering, triangular, hollow ground blade 34in., retaining some blued and gilt etched decoration, oval copper gilt guard, urn pommel, knucklebow and mounts. Silver wire and strip bound grip with traces of gilt. $515 £260

An early 18th century English silver hilted small sword, colichmarde blade 30in., double shellguard chiselled with nobleman's head and masks, the ricasso also with nobleman's head, large arms, the knucklebow with standing figure and struck with hallmarks and maker's initials, silver wire bound grip with 'Turk's head' terminals. $535 £270

A good English silver hilted small sword, triangular, tapering, hollow ground blade 28in., plain shellguard, fluted knucklebow and mounts, fluted ovoid pommel, silver wire bound grip, the mounts clearly stamped with hallmarks, the knucklebow showing hallmark for 'London 1731'. $554 £280

A German mid 18th century silver hilted small sword, mounted with 17th
century rapier blade 33in., signed in the short fuller 'In Mene', boat-shaped
guard with German hallmark stamps, plain knucklebow, pommel and
mounts, silver wire bound grip, in its leather scabbard with top mount and
belt hook of hallmarked German silver. $554 £280

A fine French late 18th century silver gilt hilted small sword, slim, tapering,
triangular, hollow ground blade 30½in., retaining much original blued and
gilt decoration of military trophies and foliate sprays, the silver gilt hilt with
oval guard intricately chiselled with urns, foliate sprays, musical trophies
etc., the grip, knucklebow and ovoid pommel similarly decorated en suite,
Paris hallmarks on Pas d'Ane rings for 1786. $614 £310

A fine English silver hilted small sword, circa 1760, colichmarde blade 33in.,
with traces of foliate scroll etched decoration at forte, finely pierced and
chiselled double shellguard, the quillon block, arms and ovoid pommel similarly chiselled and pierced, the knucklebow chiselled with military trophies
and foliate scrolls, the grip bound with silver bands and wire. $733 £370

A U.S. society sword, blade 28in., retaining all original polish, etched with Masonic symbols and foliate scrolls with gilt wash background, plated Gothic hilt, shellguard with Masonic symbols, human head pommel, plain, rounded black grip, in its plated scabbard with two Gothic mounts.   **$51 £26**

A U.S. society sword, plated blade 27in., retaining some original polish and etched with Masonic symbols etc. Gothic hilt, plated crosspiece decorated with U.S. Eagle and stars, black grip mounted with cross. Plumed helmet pommel, in its leather scabbard with two plated mounts.   **$59 £30**

A U.S. society sword, blade 28in., retaining some original polish and etched with foliate scrolls, plated Gothic hilt, cruciform crosspiece, 'knight's helmet' pommel, black grip with Masonic symbol, in its black leather covered metal scabbard with two plated mounts, top mount with Masonic symbol. **$67 £34**

A U.S. society sword, straight, plated blade 27in., ornate Gothic gilt crosspiece marked 'G.U.O. O.F.' and Masonic emblems, ornate pommel, chain guard, rounded bone grip, in its gilt metal scabbard with Gothic mounts.   **$71 £36**

A U.S. society sword, blade 30in., by Ward, New London, etched with tournament scene, scrolls etc., with gilt wash background, retaining much original polish, plated Gothic crossguard, 'knight's helmet' pommel, ivory grip inset with cross in its plated scabbard with three Gothic mounts. $89 £45

A U.S. society sword, blade 30½in., by Lilley, Columbus, retaining all original polish and etched with tournament pavilion and foliate scrolls etc., reversed plated Gothic crossguard, classical pavilion tent pommel, wire bound leather covered grip, in its plated metal scabbard with three Gothic mounts. $89 £45

A U.S. society sword, blade 30in., by Ames Chicopee, retaining most original polish and etched with tournament, knights etc., 'knight's helmet' pommel, wooden grip mounted with Masonic symbol, in its plated scabbard with engraved decoration. $99 £50

A good U.S. society sword, blade 28in., by Wilson, Boston, etched with foliate sprays, gilt metal Gothic hilt, central panel with U.S. Eagle, eagle surmounting pommel, chain knucklebow, wire bound leather grip, in its gilt metal scabbard engraved with foliate sprays. $109 £55

A good U.S. society sword, blade 27in., by Ames Chicopee, retaining all original polish and etched with knights and foliate sprays, with gold wash background, fine gilt metal Gothic hilt, with pierced and enamelled crosspiece, with Masonic symbols, 'knight's helmet' pommel, chain knucklebow, ivory grip, in its gilt metal scabbard mounted with Gothic mounts of trophies etc.
$129 £65

A U.S. society sword, blade 25½in., retaining most original polish by Ames Chicopee, etched with tournament, knight and foliate scrolls with gilt wash background, plated Gothic hilt, 'knight's helmet' pommel, ivory grip, chain knucklebow, in its steel scabbard with three plated Gothic mounts.
$129 £65

A U.S. society sword, straight blade 28in., retaining all original polish by Virgil Price, New York, etched with knights in combat, castle, foliate scrolls, standard bearer etc., gilt Gothic hilt, cruciform crosspiece with Maltese cross in centre, 'knight's helmet' pommel, wooden grip inset with Masonic cross, in its gilt metal scabbard.
$129 £65

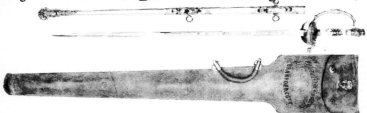

A fine U.S. society sword, straight blade 30in., of German manufacture, with knight's head stamp, etched with trophies, 'F.C.B.' on shield, foliage, initials etc. and 'Colonel R. F. Hosley Branford, Conn' upon gilt background, gilt double shellguard, one folding, gilt knucklebow, pommel with belt and oval panels, ivory grip, in its gilt metal Gothic scabbard, contained in its leather carrying case.
$247 £125

An Indian sword, straight, broad, single edged blade 31in., double fullered, iron tulwar hilt with gold foliate damascene decoration, in its brocade covered wooden scabbard.　　　　　　　　　　　　　　　　　　　　　$79　£40

A good 18th century silver inlaid Indian sword tulwar, single edged wootz blade 28in., struck with armourer's marks. Steel hilt of traditional form, inlaid overall with engraved silver flowers, thistles and foliage in geometric arrangement with silver borders, in its tooled red leather covered scabbard with silver chape.　　　　　　　　　　　　　　　　　　　　　　　　$89　£45

A good Indian solid silver hilted sword tulwar, slightly incurved, single edged, fullered blade 28½in., integral silver hilt, pierced foliate langet terminals, fluted grip, knucklebow incorporates three zoomorphic animals, pierced foliate plate on disc pommel.　　　　　　　　　　　　　　　　　$198　£100

An Indian tulwar, curved, multi-fullered, watered steel blade 28½in. Steel hilt decorated with gold damascened foliate patterns. Wheel pommel with oval panel beneath bearing an inscription. In its leather covered wooden scabbard.　　　　　　　　　　　　　　　　　　　　　　　　　　　$247　£125

An Indian good, old tulwar, curved, multi-fullered blade 34in., of heavy
form and of watered steel with pronounced clip back tip, the iron hilt overlaid with gold damascene patterns of geometric and other forms.$247 £125

An Indian tulwar, slightly curved blade 29in., of watered steel and decorated
with blue chevron panels, iron hilt and knucklebow chiselled with foliate
patterns, gold damascene overall. $317 £160

A fine Indian tulwar, curved, watered steel blade 31½in., inlaid at forte with
maker's mark, the hilt finely covered with gold damascene decorated with
foliate patterns and contained in an English made leather scabbard with three
copper gilt mounts. $495 £250

A very fine gold inlaid Indian sword tulwar, curved, single edged, wootz
blade 34in. Large hilt, chape and locket all inlaid with two colour gold repeat
pattern with flowers and foliage against a blued background. Large dished
pommel with pierced hinged ornamental top ring, large swollen quillon terminals, foliate langet terminals, pierced borders to chape and locket, in its
leather covered scabbard. $713 £360

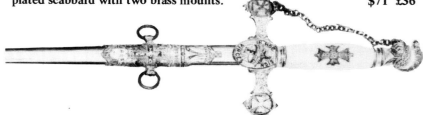

A U.S. Civil War period NCO's sword, plain, straight blade, 32½in., with central fuller, marked at forte 'J.S. J.H. 1864', plain brass double shellguard, plain brass knucklebow, mounts and simulated brass wire bound grip, in a plated scabbard with two brass mounts. $71 £36

A U.S. society sword, plated blade 28in., retaining most original polish and etched with medieval tournament, knights, foliage etc. Gold wash background, elaborate Gothic plated hilt with pierced crossguard, bone grip, plumed helmet pommel, chained knucklebow, in its plated scabbard. $89 £45

A U.S. society sword, plated blade 30in., retaining most original polish, etched with medieval tournament, foliage etc. Gothic hilt with plated mounts, pierced crosspiece with enamelled triangles. Plumed helmet pommel, black grip inset with cross, plated scabbard with three Gothic mounts. $119 £60

A U.S. society sword, plated blade 28in., retaining all original polish and etched with medieval battle, knights, Masonic symbols etc., with gilt wash background. Gothic hilt with plated cast crosspiece decorated with knights' heads etc. Black grip inset with cross. Visor helmet pommel and chain guard, in its plated scabbard. $139 £70

A Japanese sword wakizashi, blade 52cm. signed 'Kawachi No Daijo Kunisada', with two mekugi ana. Broad gunome hamon with distinct nie clusters. Iron mokko tsuba, tape bound same tsuka, toad menuki, chiselled shakudo fuchi kashira, in its black lacquered saya.$653 £330

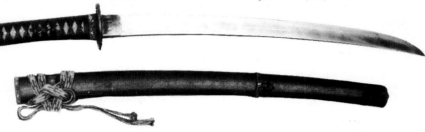

A Japanes short sword wakizashi, blade 18in., signed 'Idzuminokami Fujiwara No Kunisada'. Hira zukuri, bo-hi ni tsure-hi and gomobashi, ayasugi and mokume hada, sugumidare ha. Nekogake gin habaki, pierced iron tsuba of mokko form. Leather bound tsuka. Red lacquered saya with crinkled finish. $1,039 £525

YATAGHAN

A good Turkish yataghan, curved blade 24in., with double fuller and with wavy raised pattern to backstrap, silver copper mounts with some filigree pattern and mounted with coral plaques, large bone eared grips, in its leather covered wooden sheath with white metal top. $188 £95

A good Turkish sword yataghan, recurved, single edged blade 22in., inlaid with extensive silver script within scrolls and dog tooth borders. Two-piece eared walrus ivory grips, grip strap and blade mounting of ornamental silver. Silver scabbard with gilt top pierced and worked in relieved bands, integral stylised dragon chape. $1,327 £670

SWORDSTICKS

A Malacca swordstick, slim, single edged, plated blade 27in., with spring catch, rhino horn grip, silver ferrule band, engraved with foliate sprays (hallmarked Birmingham 1910), in its Malacca scabbard. $99 £50

A Georgian Malacca swordstick, slim, straight, single edged blade 26½in., etched with foliate sprays with traces of blueing and gilding, hilt with bulbous top, in its Malacca scabbard with long brass bottom ferrule. $123 £62

A hallmarked silver mounted sword cane, fullered, single edged blade 28½in., etched 'Defence Not Defiance', 'Peace With Honour' and scrolls. Hallmarked London 1896 'W.L.', silver top and ferrule, scroll embossed. Male Malacca cane, brass mounted steel tip. $158 £80

A Victorian sword cane, shallow diamond sectioned blade 27in., blued and gilt with scrolls for half its length. Foliate embossed silver top (not hallmarked) and ferrule engraved 'A.B.', white metal mounted steel tip. $158 £80

A good Victorian swordstick, slim blade 27½in., of diamond section, etched 'Toledo' with foliate scrolls, spring catch, horn, gnarled hilt with gilt, hatched band mount, in its Malacca scabbard. $178 £90

FLINTLOCK
WEAPONS

ALARM GUN

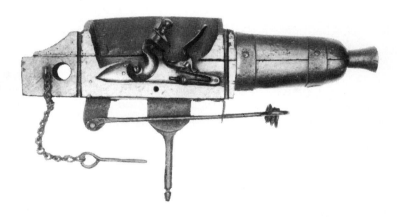

A classic flintlock alarm or trap gun, circa 1800, overall length 20in., iron barrel with swollen muzzle. Lock taken from Brown Bess musket, timber clad and iron bound with hinged stake and numerous loops for trip wires.

$733 £370

BLUNDERBUSS

A Turkish horseman's flintlock blunderbuss, 23in., half octagonal flared barrel, 12½in., inlaid with scrolling silver designs. Full-stocked, engraved lock. Engraved steel furniture, foliate finialled trigger guard, saddle bar and lanyard ring on sideplate, buttcap silver inlaid en suite with barrel. Foliate and basket weave design carved stock with a little white metal wire inlay. **$436 £230**

A rare and massive Spanish miquelet flintlock, bell mouthed blunderbuss, circa 1765, probably made in Ripoll, 44in., half octagonal, stepped barrel 26in., deeply engraved 'IINA' at breech. Bell muzzle and chevron engraved reinforcing band. Full-stocked, bridled striated frizzen, ring top jaw screw, bridled cock with stepped neck. **$535 £270**

A massive flintlock blunderbuss for wall defence, 44in., barrel 25in., with pronounced bell-shaped muzzle, diameter 3¾in., Birmingham proved, line engraved lock with ring neck cock, marked 'Cooper & Goodman'. Full-stocked, the fore-end drilled for swivel mounting, brass furniture, original heavy ramrod. **$792 £400**

A late 18th century brass barrelled flintlock blunderbuss, circa 1775, 31½in., bell mouthed barrel 16in., with London proofs and engraved 'Kingsland Road', flat lock with scroll engraved tail and signed 'Waters' in script, full-stocked with brass mounts including engraved sideplate and trigger guard with pineapple finial, brass tipped, wooden ramrod. **$851 £430**

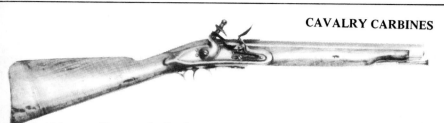

A 10-bore military style flintlock carbine by J. & W. Richards, 30in., barrel 14½in., London proved. Slightly convex lock line engraved. Full-stocked with Brown Bess type furniture except for flat sideplate, steel ramrod.
$198 £100

A late 16-bore flintlock colonial type cavalry carbine, 37in., barrel 21in., Birmingham proved. Full-stocked, military style lock and brass furniture with scrolled trigger guard, buttcap, ramrod pipe and throat pipe. Swivel ramrod and saddle bar with two lanyard rings. Stock stamped with maker's name 'W. Pike'.
$317 £160

A 20-bore Kurdish miquelet flintlock carbine, 41in., barrel 27½in., inlaid with silver arabesques at breech and muzzle in Persian taste. Full-stocked, covered with scroll engraved brass plates, steel trigger guard and lock with striated frizzen.
$346 £175

A 10-bore Elliot pattern Volunteer flintlock cavalry carbine, 40in., barrel 24½in., Tower proved. Full-stocked, lock engraved 'Brander'. Regulation brass mounts, steel saddle bar with lanyard ring, steel ramrod. $356 £180

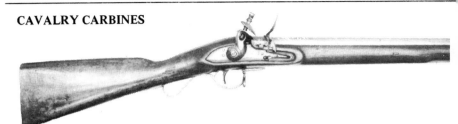

A 10-bore E.I.C. New Land pattern sergeant's flintlock carbine, 49in., barrel 33in, London proved. Full-stocked, lock engraved with E.I.C. lion. Regulation brass mounts, scrolled trigger guard, steel sling swivels and ramrod.
$396 £200

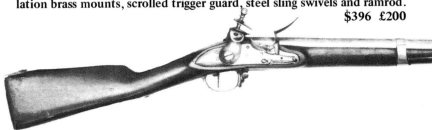

A 13-bore Belgian flintlock carbine, 45½in., barrel 30in., engraved Belgium with stamps. Full-stocked, regulation lock stamped with toughra mark, brass pan. Regulation brass mounts, steel sling swivels and ramrod, carved cheek-piece.
$475 £240

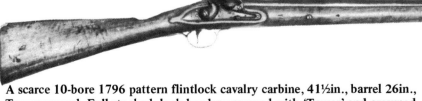

A scarce 10-bore 1796 pattern flintlock cavalry carbine, 41½in., barrel 26in., Tower proved. Full-stocked, lock border engraved with 'Tower' and crowned 'G.R.'. Regulation brass mounts, buttcap tang engraved 'E14. 4. D.G.' (4th Dragoon Guards), steel saddle bar, ring and ramrod. Stock struck with ordnance marks 'B.O.' and date '1833'.
$693 £350

A double barrelled 16-bore flintlock coaching carbine by Grierson, 25in., heavy twist barrels, 10in., inlaid in gold on top rib 'Grierson – Gun Maker to His Majesty', gold vents and breech lines, silver inlaid military trophies at breech, inlaid star shaped silver foresight. Stepped lockplates, rainproof pans, roller bearing frizzen springs.
$1,980 £1,000

A French boxlock flintlock powder tester eprouvette, 6½in., foliate engraved frame. Wheel engraved with scale graduations 1-10. Throathole cock, swollen wooden butt.
$515 £260

A Belgian boxlock flintlock powder tester eprouvette, 6in., sprung wheel graduated 1-11, linear engraved frame, throathole cock, tension sprung frizzen, slab walnut butt. $554 £280

A mid 18th century French flintlock powder tester eprouvette, 11in., graduated wheel 1-10. Small 'chimney pot' for powder, slightly banana shaped lock with stepped bevelled edges. Steel trigger guard with swollen finial, steel sideplate, butt carved as a bird's head.
$594 £300

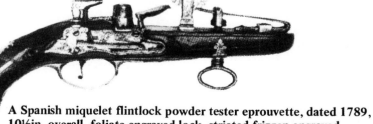

A Spanish miquelet flintlock powder tester eprouvette, dated 1789, 10½in. overall, foliate engraved lock, striated frizzen engraved '1789'. Foliate steel wheel with graduated 1-12 and ring screw puller for slackening spring tension. $990 £500

A scarce detached screwless flintlock by H. Nock, the pattern fitted to the 1796 Harcourt carbines, pan cover engraved with crown over 'G.R.', plate with ordnance stamps and 'H. Nock'. $95 £48

A detached lock from a large flintlock rampart gun, length 9¼in., border-line engraved and also with 'Tower', crowned 'G.R.' and crowned arrow ordnance stamp, large border line engraved throathole cock and teardrop frizzen. $247 £125

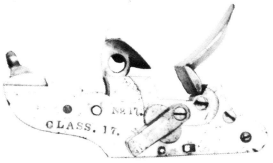

A good, brass boxlock ship's cannon lock, 6in., side stamped 'Class 17. No. 17'. Massive cock and frizzen, enclosed action, steel loop for lanyard trips the scear. Hinged windshield. $653 £330

A 24-bore Japanese matchlock gun, 36½in., octagonal barrel 23¾in., signed Funiu Chogen Suiju Saku. Block sights with swollen muzzle. Full-stocked in cherrywood. Brass back-action lock with external mainspring. Plain brass furniture and pin plates, carved butt, wooden ramrod. $693 £350

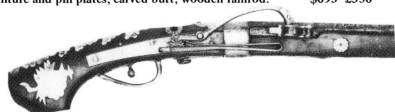

A good 20-bore Japanese matchlock gun, circa 1750, by Goshaku, 51in., tapered, octagonal barrel 39½in., with pierced block sights. Breech inlaid with brass and copper, hinged brass pan cover. Full-stocked in cherrywood with carved butt. Back-action brass lock, inlaid and engraved brass furniture. Button trigger, rounded trigger guard. $1,010 £510

A good 14-bore heavy Japanese matchlock temple gun, 108cm., heavy iron barrel 70cm., octagonal at breech, full length top flat, swollen muzzle, deeply chiselled with maker's signature and details. Barrel silver damascened with birds and foliage. Stoutly constructed brass lock and mounts, steel serpent, sliding pan cover. Stock impressed with temple seal. $1,584 £800

A good .22in. bore Japanese matchlock rifle, 35½in., 5-groove rifled barrel 23½in., silver damascened with butterflies, flowers and Buddhistic emblems, sighted flattened barrel top. Full-stocked in cherrywood. Back-action iron lock and serpent with brass head. Brass pan cover and silver inlaid flash guard. Brass furniture and pin plates, engraved throat guard. $1,722 £870

A 10-bore Sea Service flintlock musket, 53in., barrel 37in., Tower proved.
Full-stocked, lock with traces of crowned 'G.R.' and 'Brander' on tail.
Regulation brass mounts. Steel ramrod. $396 £200

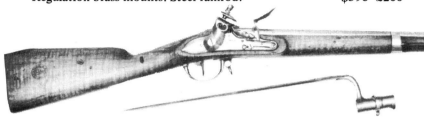

A 15-bore Belgian flintlock musket, 58in., barrel 42¾in., struck with unusual
proofs at breech. Full-stocked, lock stamped 'D.D. Ancion et Files a Liege',
brass pan, French military pattern. Regulation steel mounts, sling swivels and
ramrod. Carved cheek-piece. Complete with triangular socket bayonet.
                                                          $455 £230

A 10-bore India pattern flintlock musket, 54in., barrel 39in., Tower proved.
Full-stocked, lock engraved with 'Tower' and crowned 'G.R.'. Regulation brass
mounts, steel ramrod and sling swivels. $535 £270

An interesting 12-bore full-stocked Spanish military type miquelet musket,
59½in., round barrel, octagonal at breech 44in., stamped 'Ex' at breech,
walnut stock with brass mounts including buttcap with fretted spur, plain
trigger guard and three brass barrel bands the last doubling as ramrod
throat pipe. $584 £295

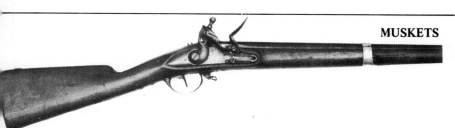

A 13-bore French flintlock musket, 56in., barrel 40½in., Liege proved with military stamps. Full-stocked, lock engraved 'Mre Rle St Etienne', brass pan, regulation brass trigger guard and barrel bands, steel buttcap, trigger plate and sideplate. Steel sling swivels and ramrod, carved cheek-piece. $594 £300

A scarce 10-bore 42in. Volunteer Brown Bess flintlock musket, 58in., barrel 42in., London proved with maker's mark, crowned 'R.W.'. Full-stocked, lock engraved 'R. Watkin', regulation brass mounts with broad flush escutcheon. Steel sling swivels, brass tipped wooden ramrod. Complete with triangular socket bayonet, blade 16in., stamped 'John Gill'. $634 £320

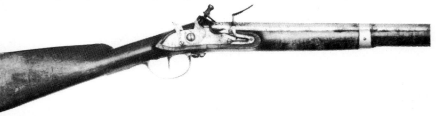

A scarce 9-bore Scandinavian flintlock doglock musket, 58½in., barrel 42in., stamped 'HQ-MOF', with crowned 'Ch'. Full-stocked, regulation flat lock with hinged dog safety. Regulation brass mounts, steel sling swivels and ramrod. $742 £375

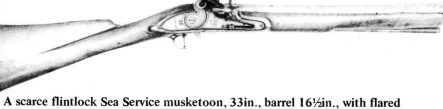

A scarce flintlock Sea Service musketoon, 33in., barrel 16½in., with flared muzzle, diameter 1½in., private Tower proofs, large flat bridleless lock, line engraved with crown and 'Tower' across tail, ring neck cock, brass furniture with flat serpentine sideplate and flat naval type buttplate, correct brass ended wooden ramrod. $772 £390

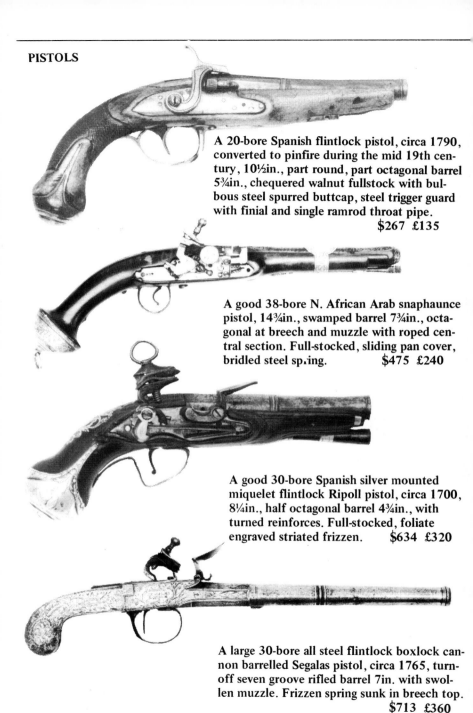

A 20-bore Spanish flintlock pistol, circa 1790, converted to pinfire during the mid 19th century, 10½in., part round, part octagonal barrel 5¾in., chequered walnut fullstock with bulbous steel spurred buttcap, steel trigger guard with finial and single ramrod throat pipe.

$267 £135

A good 38-bore N. African Arab snaphaunce pistol, 14¾in., swamped barrel 7¾in., octagonal at breech and muzzle with roped central section. Full-stocked, sliding pan cover, bridled steel sp.ing. $475 £240

A good 30-bore Spanish silver mounted miquelet flintlock Ripoll pistol, circa 1700, 8¼in., half octagonal barrel 4¾in., with turned reinforces. Full-stocked, foliate engraved striated frizzen. $634 £320

A large 30-bore all steel flintlock boxlock cannon barrelled Segalas pistol, circa 1765, turn-off seven groove rifled barrel 7in. with swollen muzzle. Frizzen spring sunk in breech top. $713 £360

A .56in. long Sea Service flintlock belt pistol, 19½in., barrel 12in., Tower proved. Full-stocked, border engraved lock struck 'Tower' with crowned 'G.R.'. Regulation brass mounts, steel belt hook, wooden ramrod with brass tip. $495 £250

A 30-bore flintlock brass barrelled belt pistol, circa 1780, 13½in., swamped barrel 8in., London proved, engraved London. Full-stocked, lockplate engraved 'W. Ketland & Co.', unbridled frizzen. Steel belt hook and wooden ramrod. $515 £260

A scarce 13-bore Spanish military miquelet flintlock belt pistol, 14½in., barrel 9in. octagonal at breech. Halfstock, regulation lock, brass pan, horizontally acting sear, ring top jaw screw. Regulation brass mounts, foliate finialled trigger guard, brass buttcap, forecap, backstrap, sheet sideplates, steel belt hook and ramrod. $554 £280

A .56in. Tower long Sea Service military flintlock belt pistol, 19¼in., barrel 12in., regulation walnut fullstock with brass mounts including buttcap, trigger guard and ramrod pipe, lockplate with crowned 'G.R.' and 'Tower' and ordnance crowned arrow. $594 £300

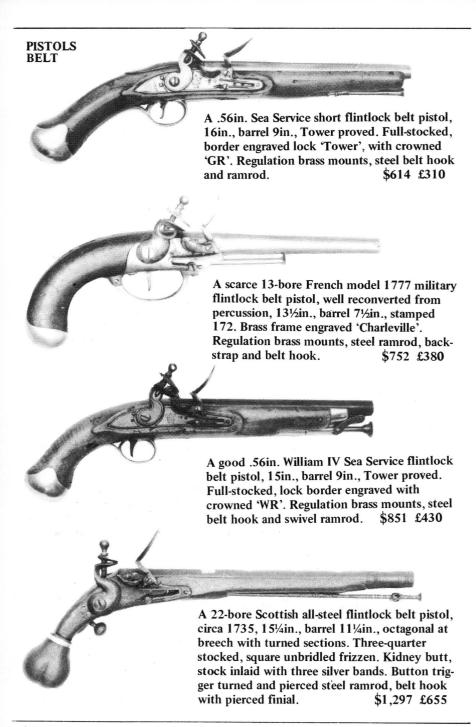

A .56in. Sea Service short flintlock belt pistol, 16in., barrel 9in., Tower proved. Full-stocked, border engraved lock 'Tower', with crowned 'GR'. Regulation brass mounts, steel belt hook and ramrod.   **$614 £310**

A scarce 13-bore French model 1777 military flintlock belt pistol, well reconverted from percussion, 13½in., barrel 7½in., stamped 172. Brass frame engraved 'Charleville'. Regulation brass mounts, steel ramrod, back-strap and belt hook.   **$752 £380**

A good .56in. William IV Sea Service flintlock belt pistol, 15in., barrel 9in., Tower proved. Full-stocked, lock border engraved with crowned 'WR'. Regulation brass mounts, steel belt hook and swivel ramrod.   **$851 £430**

A 22-bore Scottish all-steel flintlock belt pistol, circa 1735, 15¼in., barrel 11¼in., octagonal at breech with turned sections. Three-quarter stocked, square unbridled frizzen. Kidney butt, stock inlaid with three silver bands. Button trigger turned and pierced steel ramrod, belt hook with pierced finial.   **$1,297 £655**

A Spanish miquelet flintlock blunderbuss pistol, circa 1700, 17in., half octagonal, stepped barrel 10in. Full-stocked, traces of engraving to barrel and lock, striated bridled frizzen, bridled lock, ring top jaw. Barrel tang screw secured foot of ribbed brass trigger guard. Sprung steel belt hook.
$218 £110

A brass barrelled flintlock boxlock blunderbuss pistol, 7¼in., swollen barrel 3in., octagonal breech, turned muzzle, Birmingham proved. Integral brass frame engraved 'Wheeler & Son, London'. Sliding top thumb safety, tension sprung frizzen. Slab walnut butt. $376 £190

An attractive Turkish flintlock blunderbuss pistol 17½in., half octagonal Spanish barrel 8¾in., struck with crowned maker's marks of 'Domingo Mas (Ripoll, C. 1715)' and fleurs-de-lys. Full-stocked military type lock with brass pan. Brass furniture, saddle bar with sliding lanyard ring. Chequered and carved butt. $445 £220

One of a pair of English brass barrelled brass mounted flintlock blunderbuss pistols, by I. Yates, circa 1690, 12½in., half octagonal, stepped reinforced flared barrels 6½in. Three-quarter stocked, brass lockplates, iron long-spur buttcaps, scroll engraved foliated finialled trigger guards. $2,475 £1,250

A 16-bore flintlock duelling pistol by Holland, circa 1780, 17½in., octagonal barrel 12in., inlaid with large gold oval maker's poincon stamped 'Holland', full-stocked, stepped lockplate screwed directly to breech, ramp frizzen spring. Gold lined vent. Floral engraved acorn finialled trigger guard, horn forecap, flattened grip with chequered back. $614 £310

A good quality 22-bore full-stocked flintlock duelling pistol by P. Bond, 14in., octagonal swamped barrel, 9in., London proved, barrel signed 'Stubbs', chequered hooked grip with small line and floral engraved buttcap, steel spurred trigger guard with pineapple finial, steel ramrod pipes, fore-end with two cross keys, bolted stepped flat lockplate with line border and minor floral engraving, swan-necked cock, teardrop frizzen with roller to spring. $614 £310

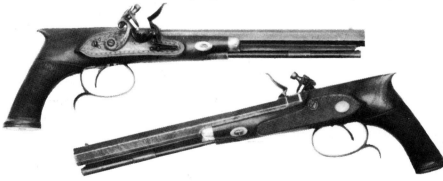

A pair of 34-bore saw-handled flintlock duelling pistols by H. W. Mortimer & Son, circa 1810, 16in., octagonal barrels 10in. Half-stocked detented bolted locks, French style cocks, rainproof pans, roller bearing frizzen springs, silver breech lines and vents, capstan screw set triggers.
$1,980 £1,000

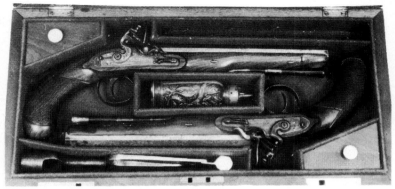

A good pair of 16-bore flintlock duelling pistols by Parsons of Salisbury, circa 1800, 14¾in., octagonal sighted barrels 9in., engraved on the top flat 'Salisbury' with silver foresights. Full-stocked in finely figured walnut, linear engraved stepped lockplates, sliding side safety bolts. Rainproof pans, friction rollers on frizzen spring. Blued pineapple finialled trigger guards.

$2,772 £1,480

MUFF

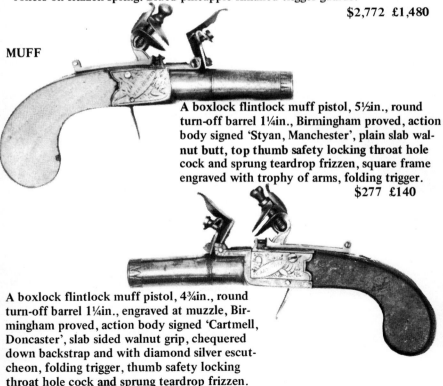

A boxlock flintlock muff pistol, 5½in., round turn-off barrel 1¼in., Birmingham proved, action body signed 'Styan, Manchester', plain slab walnut butt, top thumb safety locking throat hole cock and sprung teardrop frizzen, square frame engraved with trophy of arms, folding trigger.

$277 £140

A boxlock flintlock muff pistol, 4¾in., round turn-off barrel 1¼in., engraved at muzzle, Birmingham proved, action body signed 'Cartmell, Doncaster', slab sided walnut grip, chequered down backstrap and with diamond silver escutcheon, folding trigger, thumb safety locking throat hole cock and sprung teardrop frizzen.

$327 £165

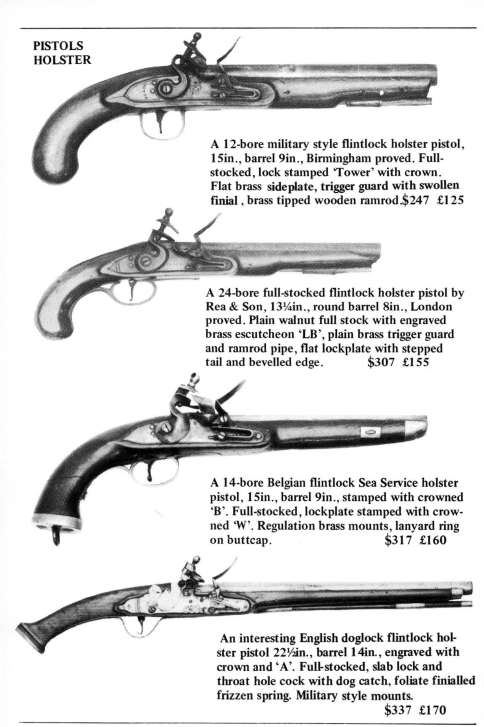

A 12-bore military style flintlock holster pistol, 15in., barrel 9in., Birmingham proved. Full-stocked, lock stamped 'Tower' with crown. Flat brass sideplate, trigger guard with swollen finial, brass tipped wooden ramrod. $247 £125

A 24-bore full-stocked flintlock holster pistol by Rea & Son, 13¼in., round barrel 8in., London proved. Plain walnut full stock with engraved brass escutcheon 'LB', plain brass trigger guard and ramrod pipe, flat lockplate with stepped tail and bevelled edge. $307 £155

A 14-bore Belgian flintlock Sea Service holster pistol, 15in., barrel 9in., stamped with crowned 'B'. Full-stocked, lockplate stamped with crowned 'W'. Regulation brass mounts, lanyard ring on buttcap. $317 £160

An interesting English doglock flintlock holster pistol 22½in., barrel 14in., engraved with crown and 'A'. Full-stocked, slab lock and throat hole cock with dog catch, foliate finialled frizzen spring. Military style mounts. $337 £170

A good Turkish 14-bore flintlock holster pistol, 19½in., barrel 12½in., with top rib and chiselled decoration at breech, full-stocked with foliate carving round barrel tang and brass fore-end cap, plain rounded lock with swan-neck cock, brass mounts including chiselled long-spurred buttcap.
$356 £180

A 65-bore Italian provincial flintlock holster pistol, circa 1780, 9in., barrel 4½in., engraved 'Antonio Magnani' on raised top sighting rib. Full-stocked, foliate engraved stepped lock with bevelled edges, squared pan and unbridled frizzen. Foliate finial-led trigger guard, long-spur buttcap with whirled boss, silhouette sideplate. $396 £200

A .56 American martial flintlock holster pistol, 14in., barrel 8½in., stamped 'US-JA-P'. Half-stocked, regulation lock stamped 'US-R. Johnson, Middn Conn 1838', brass pan. Regulation iron mounts, swivel ramrod, backstrap from barrel tang integral with buttcap. $396 £200

A 16-bore New Land pattern military flintlock holster pistol, 15in., barrel 9in., Tower proved. Full-stocked, stepped lockplate engraved with 'Tower' and crowned 'GR' cypher, regulation brass mounts, trigger guard bow engraved with rack number '26'. $396 £200

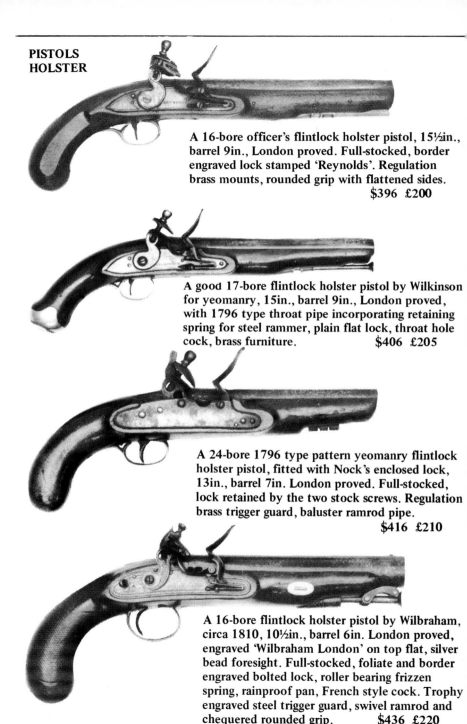

A 16-bore officer's flintlock holster pistol, 15½in.,
barrel 9in., London proved. Full-stocked, border
engraved lock stamped 'Reynolds'. Regulation
brass mounts, rounded grip with flattened sides.
$396 £200

A good 17-bore flintlock holster pistol by Wilkinson
for yeomanry, 15in., barrel 9in., London proved,
with 1796 type throat pipe incorporating retaining
spring for steel rammer, plain flat lock, throat hole
cock, brass furniture. $406 £205

A 24-bore 1796 type pattern yeomanry flintlock
holster pistol, fitted with Nock's enclosed lock,
13in., barrel 7in. London proved. Full-stocked,
lock retained by the two stock screws. Regulation
brass trigger guard, baluster ramrod pipe.
$416 £210

A 16-bore flintlock holster pistol by Wilbraham,
circa 1810, 10½in., barrel 6in. London proved,
engraved 'Wilbraham London' on top flat, silver
bead foresight. Full-stocked, foliate and border
engraved bolted lock, roller bearing frizzen
spring, rainproof pan, French style cock. Trophy
engraved steel trigger guard, swivel ramrod and
chequered rounded grip. $436 £220

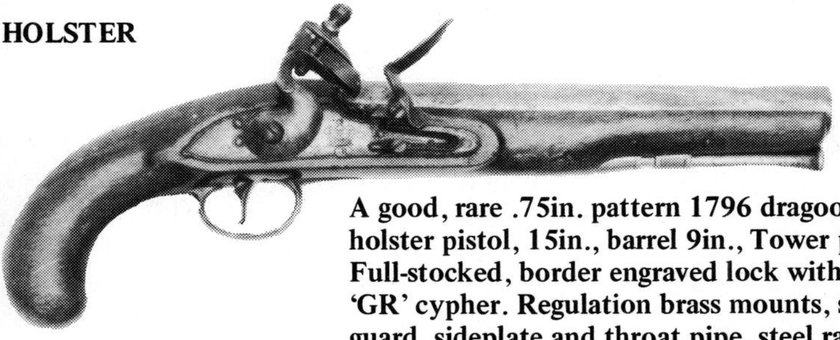

A good, rare .75in. pattern 1796 dragoon flintlock
holster pistol, 15in., barrel 9in., Tower proved.
Full-stocked, border engraved lock with crowned
'GR' cypher. Regulation brass mounts, short trigger
guard, sideplate and throat pipe, steel ramrod.

$437 £220

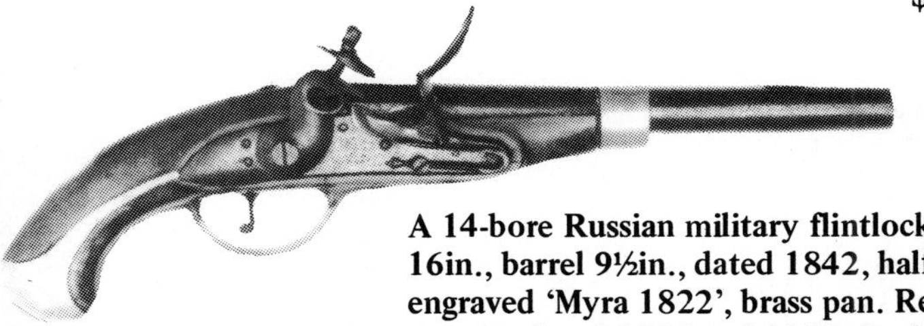

A 14-bore Russian military flintlock holster pistol,
16in., barrel 9½in., dated 1842, half-stocked, lock
engraved 'Myra 1822', brass pan. Regulation brass
mounts dated 1834 and 1842. Oval brass escutcheon
engraved with crowned cypher of Tzar Alexander 1st.

$455 £230

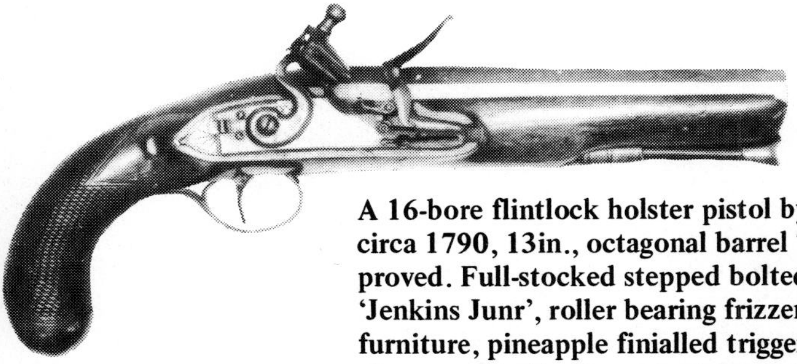

A 16-bore flintlock holster pistol by Jenkins Jnr.,
circa 1790, 13in., octagonal barrel 7¼in., London
proved. Full-stocked stepped bolted lock engraved
'Jenkins Junr', roller bearing frizzen spring. Steel
furniture, pineapple finialled trigger guard. Rounded
chequered butt, silver escutcheon, brass tipped ebony
ramrod with brass capped worm. $495 £250

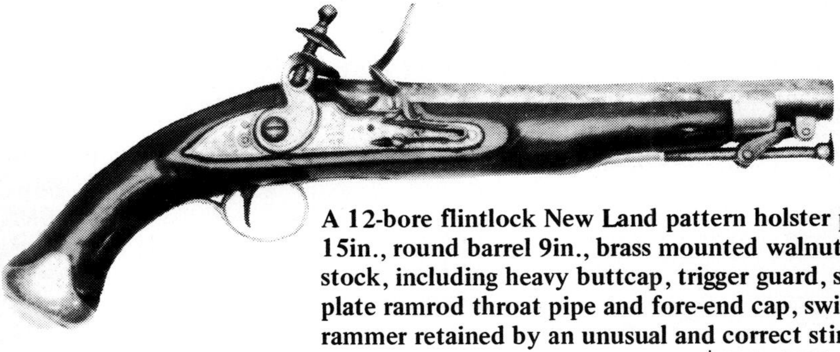

A 12-bore flintlock New Land pattern holster pistol,
15in., round barrel 9in., brass mounted walnut full
stock, including heavy buttcap, trigger guard, sideplate ramrod throat pipe and fore-end cap, swivel
rammer retained by an unusual and correct stirrup.

$495 £250

A rare French 14-bore revolutionary period flintlock
military holster pistol, 13¾in., blued barrel 7¼in.,
struck at breech with '93', brass mounted full stock
stamped opposite lock with letter 'AN', brass mounts
include heavy skull cracker buttcap, trigger guard and
fore-end cap combination barrel bands, plain flat lockplate with rounded tail, brass flashpan, throat hole cock.
$495 £250

A rare 12-bore French officer's rifled flintlock holster
pistol by Ringeisser, 13½in., round barrel grading to
flats at breech 8in., struck with a proof mark, walnut
full stock with brass mounts including buttplate, trigger guard and two ramrod pipes, flat lockplate Swan
necked cock. $515 £260

A 16-bore Dutch doglock military flintlock holster pistol,
circa 1735, 21in., half octagonal stepped barrel 14in.,
deeply engraved 'T.C. No 2/B.L.R.', slightly banana
shaped flattened lockplate, cock, dog and squared frizzen.
Regulation steel trigger guard, sideplate, barrel band with
two lanyard rings. $515 £260

A good 16-bore military type Volunteer flintlock holster pistol, 15½in., round browned twist barrel 9½in.,
with flat top impressed 'Dublin' and with single proof
mark of crowned 'P' in oval, plain flat lock, rainproof
pan, roller on frizzen spring, plain full stock with flattened butt, heavy military type brass mounts, swivel
ramrod. $515 £260

An 18-bore silver mounted Turkish flintlock holster pistol, 19in., half octagonal damascus twist barrel 13in., chiselled for half its length and at muzzle in relief with scrolls etc. Full-stocked, engraved lock with gold inlaid border. Engraved silver furniture struck with touch marks. Acorn finialled trigger guard, long-spurred butt-cap, escutcheon, sideplate and ramrod pipes. $554 £280

A 16-bore New Land pattern flintlock holster pistol, 15in., barrel 9in., Tower proved. Full-stocked, lock engraved 'Tower' with crowned 'GR'. Regulation brass mounts and swivel ramrod. $564 £285

A scarce 30-bore rifled German flintlock holster pistol, circa 1740, slotted for detachable shoulder stock, 17in., stepped swamped barrel 11½in. Full-stocked, stepped bevelled lock, unbridled frizzen, heart shaped frizzen spring finial. Steel trigger guard with swollen facetted spear finial. Swollen ribbed ramrod pipes.
      $594 £300

A 20-bore Montenegran silver stocked miquelet flintlock holster pistol, 20in., barrel 13½in. Full-stocked in Eastern silver, cast and chased with interlaced scrolls in relief overall. Trigger guard and muzzle band all en suite. $624 £315

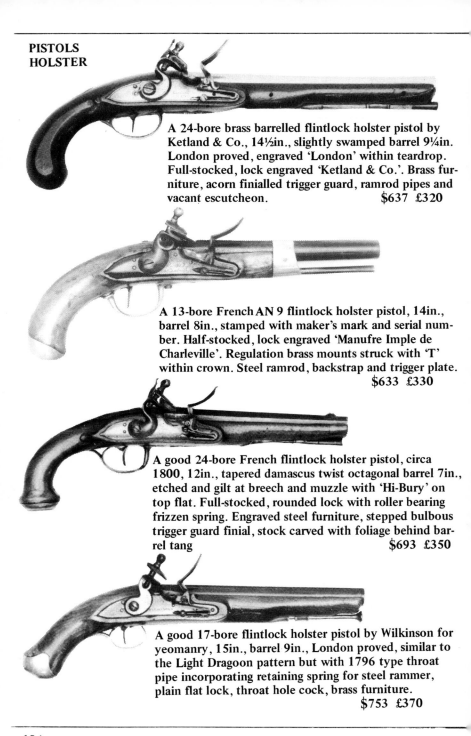

A 24-bore brass barrelled flintlock holster pistol by Ketland & Co., 14½in., slightly swamped barrel 9¼in. London proved, engraved 'London' within teardrop. Full-stocked, lock engraved 'Ketland & Co.'. Brass furniture, acorn finialled trigger guard, ramrod pipes and vacant escutcheon. $637 £320

A 13-bore French AN 9 flintlock holster pistol, 14in., barrel 8in., stamped with maker's mark and serial number. Half-stocked, lock engraved 'Manufre Imple de Charleville'. Regulation brass mounts struck with 'T' within crown. Steel ramrod, backstrap and trigger plate. $633 £330

A good 24-bore French flintlock holster pistol, circa 1800, 12in., tapered damascus twist octagonal barrel 7in., etched and gilt at breech and muzzle with 'Hi-Bury' on top flat. Full-stocked, rounded lock with roller bearing frizzen spring. Engraved steel furniture, stepped bulbous trigger guard finial, stock carved with foliage behind barrel tang $693 £350

A good 17-bore flintlock holster pistol by Wilkinson for yeomanry, 15in., barrel 9in., London proved, similar to the Light Dragoon pattern but with 1796 type throat pipe incorporating retaining spring for steel rammer, plain flat lock, throat hole cock, brass furniture. $753 £370

A good 13-bore French AN 9 flintlock holster pistol, 14in., barrel 8in., stamped 'B.C. 1810', barrel tang stamped 'Mle AN 9'. Half-stocked, lock engraved. Regulation brass mounts struck with crowned 'P', steel ramrod, backstrap and trigger plate. $752 £380

A 14-bore Saxony flintlock holster pistol, 17½in., barrel 10¾in. Full-stocked, rounded lockplate, raised lip to pan, re-faced frizzen. Regulation brass mounts, long-spur butt-cap with swollen integral boss, trigger guard bow engraved 'C.R. s.c. No 42' on inside. Swivel ranrod. $792 £400

A good 32-bore flintlock holster pistol by E. Bate, circa 1770, 14in., half octagonal barrel 9in., London proved with maker's mark, engraved 'Bate, London', silver spider foresight. Full-stocked, stepped lock with small foliate motifs. Gold lined pan and vent, roller bearing frizzen spring. Engraved acorn finialled steel trigger guard. Horn tipped wooden ramrod. $832 £420

A mid 18th century 20-bore officer's flintlock holster pistol, 15in., stepped barrel 9in., with London proofs, plain rounded lock signed 'Griffin'. Full-stocked with carved apron around barrel tang, brass mounts including plain military style trigger guard and long-spurred bul-bous buttcap, pierced foliate sideplate and baluster ram-rod pipe, brass tipped wooden ramrod. $851 £430

A good 32-bore flintlock holster pistol by W. Mills, 14in., heavy octagonal twist barrel 8in., engraved 'W. Mills, 120 Holborn, London', twin gold breech lines, silver foresight. Half-stocked, bolted detented lock. Roller bearing frizzen spring, rainproof pan, silver lined vent. French style cock. Engraved steel furniture, pineapple finialled trigger guard, serpent engraved on bow. Foliate engraved buttcap of unusual form. Silver forecap, barrel wedge plates and escutcheons.$881 £445

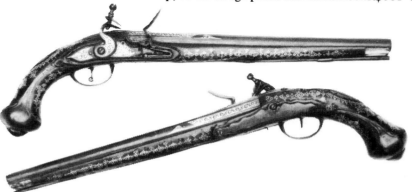

A pair of 16-bore Caucasian flintlock holster pistols, 19in., barrel 12¾in., damascened with silver scrolls at breech and along top flat. Full-stocked, locks damascened en suite with barrels. Steel furniture, long-spur butt-caps, foliate finialled trigger guards. Stocks inlaid overall with tri-sected brass nails geometrically arrayed. $950 £480

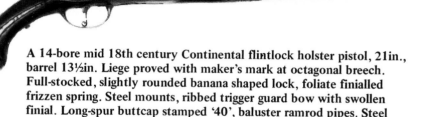

A 14-bore mid 18th century Continental flintlock holster pistol, 21in., barrel 13½in. Liege proved with maker's mark at octagonal breech. Full-stocked, slightly rounded banana shaped lock, foliate finialled frizzen spring. Steel mounts, ribbed trigger guard bow with swollen finial. Long-spur buttcap stamped '40', baluster ramrod pipes. Steel tipped wooden ramrod. $950 £480

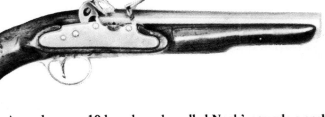

A 22-bore brass barrelled flintlock holster pistol by Louis Barbar, circa 1725, 15½in., stepped slightly swamped barrel 9¾in., London proved with maker's mark 'L.B.', engraved 'Barbar' with line of pellets. Full-stocked, slightly rounded border engraved brass lockplate with 'Barbar', foliate finialled frizzen spring. Brass furniture, ribbed trigger guard bow with foliate finial emanating from grotesque mask. Pellet engraved long-spur buttcap, grotesque mask boss. Pierced foliate sideplate, foliate bordered escutcheon, true baluster ramrod pipes. Stock carved with low relief cusps. Ebony ramrod with steel worm.   **$1,188 £600**

A scarce .56 British military dragoon pattern flintlock holster pistol by Jordan, dated 1739, 19in., barrel 12in. Full-stocked, slightly rounded banana shaped lockplate engraved with crowned 'GR' cypher and 'Jordan 1739' on tail. Border engraved en suite with cock and bridled frizzen. Regulation brass mounts, long-spur buttcap, swollen sideplate, flush escutcheon. Brass tipped wooden ramrod. Carved stock struck with crowned 'GR'.   **$1,237 £625**

A good, scarce 10-bore brass barrelled Nock's screwless enclosed lock volunteer flintlock holster pistol, 15in., brass barrel 9in. Tower proved stamped 'HN'. Full-stocked without provision for ramrod, lock script engraved 'H. Nock' with sunburst. Brass trigger guard, rounded butt.   **$1,386 £700**

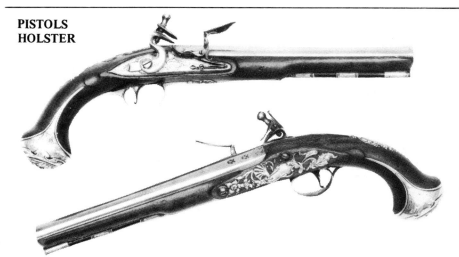

A good pair of hallmarked silver mounted brass barrelled flintlock
holster pistols by Spear, circa 1766, 15in., swamped barrels 9in.
Tower proved engraved 'London' within teardrops. Full-stocked,
border engraved bolted locks with 'Spear' within rocaille and foliate
frame. Rainproof pans. Shell finialled hallmarked silver trigger
guards (John King, London 1766), floral engraved bows. Grotesque
mask long-spur buttcap bosses, trophy engraved. $3,366 £1,700

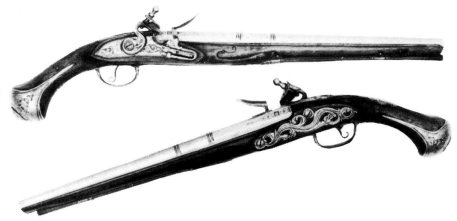

A good pair of 20-bore Silesian flintlock holster pistols, circa 1740, 20½in.,
half octagonal barrels 14in., each struck at foliate engraved breeches four
times with Oriental poincons. Full-stocked, locks chiselled with foliage in
low relief, bridled striated frizzens. Foliate chiselled steel furniture, long-
spur buttcaps, swollen trigger guard finials. Pierced foliate sideplates incorporating three monsters' heads. Floral chiselled escutcheons.$3,564 £1,800

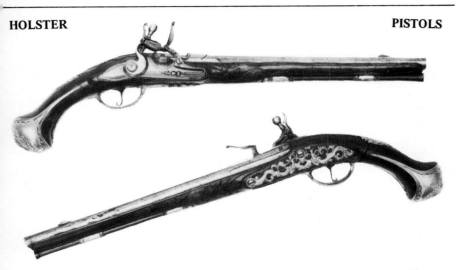

A pair of 18-bore Belgian flintlock holster pistols by F. Roland, probably
made in Liege, circa 1720, 20½in., barrels 13¾in., inlaid at octagonal
breeches with three crowned brass poincons and initials 'F.R.'. Full-
stocked, brass lockplates with stepped bevelled edges, foliate finialled
frizzen springs, bevelled cocks, chiselled frizzens. Gilt brass furntiure.
Trigger plates engraved 'F. Roland'. $5,148 £2,600

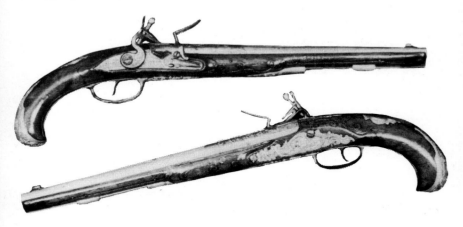

A good pair of 34-bore German flintlock holster pistols by J. J. Kuchenreuter,
circa 1760, 18in., tapered barrels 12in., foliate chiselled with 'Johann Jacob
Kuchenreuter' engraved on top rib, silver foresights, three leaf rearsight.
Full-stocked, stepped locks and scroll engraved cocks. Set triggers. Chiselled
gilt brass 'Carlsbad School' furniture. $6,534 £3,300

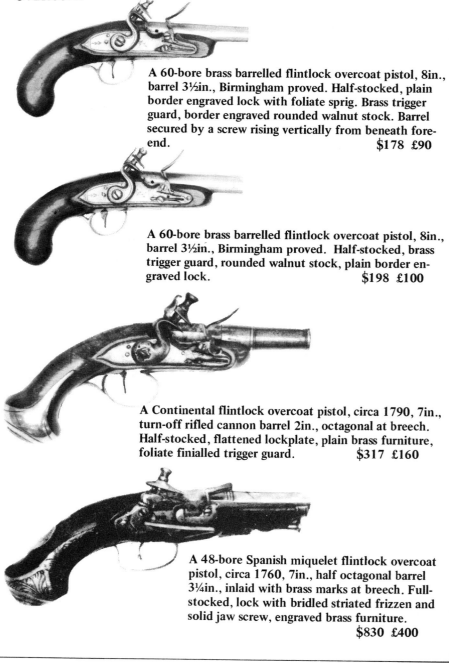

A 60-bore brass barrelled flintlock overcoat pistol, 8in., barrel 3½in., Birmingham proved. Half-stocked, plain border engraved lock with foliate sprig. Brass trigger guard, border engraved rounded walnut stock. Barrel secured by a screw rising vertically from beneath fore-end.   **$178 £90**

A 60-bore brass barrelled flintlock overcoat pistol, 8in., barrel 3½in., Birmingham proved. Half-stocked, brass trigger guard, rounded walnut stock, plain border engraved lock.   **$198 £100**

A Continental flintlock overcoat pistol, circa 1790, 7in., turn-off rifled cannon barrel 2in., octagonal at breech. Half-stocked, flattened lockplate, plain brass furniture, foliate finialled trigger guard.   **$317 £160**

A 48-bore Spanish miquelet flintlock overcoat pistol, circa 1760, 7in., half octagonal barrel 3¼in., inlaid with brass marks at breech. Full-stocked, lock with bridled striated frizzen and solid jaw screw, engraved brass furniture.
                                  $830 £400

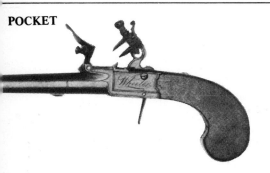

A flintlock boxlock pocket pistol, circa 1785, 6¾in., turn-off barrel 1¾in. Tower proved. Border engraved frame with 'Wheeler London' in script. Throat hole cock, tension, sprung frizzen, concealed trigger, slab walnut butt.

$178 £90

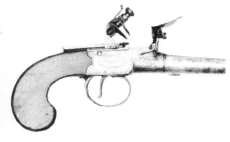

A flintlock boxlock pocket pistol by Edgson Stamford, 6in., round turn-off barrel 1¾in., London proof, slab sided walnut grip, top thumb safety locking throat hole cock and tear drop frizzen. $267 £135

A flintlock boxlock all-steel pocket pistol from Liege, circa 1760, 5½in., turn-off cannon barrel 1¼in., octagonal breech. Foliate and floral engraved frame and butt with 'London' in script. Sliding trigger guard safety through fence locking frizzen with spring sunk in breech. $287 £145

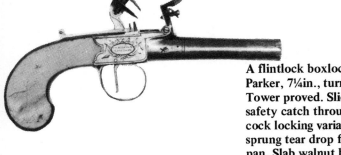

A flintlock boxlock pistol by W. Parker, 7¼in., turn-off barrel 2½in., Tower proved. Sliding top thumb safety catch through throat hole cock locking variable tension sprung tear drop frizzen to raised pan. Slab walnut butt with oval silver escutcheon. $287 £145

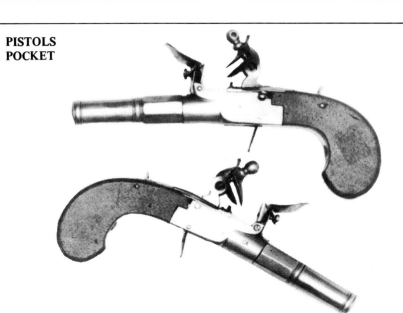

A pair of brass framed and barrelled boxlock flintlock Continental pocket
pistols, 7½in., part round, part octagonal cannon barrels 2½in., stamped
'EX' on right side, walnut slab grips, folding triggers, top thumb safety
locking throat hole cock and teardrop frizzens. $515 £260

A pair of Continental brass framed and barrelled flintlock boxlock pocket
pistols, 5½in., octagonal barrels 2in. with turned reinforced muzzles.
Frames engraved with four trophies. Sliding top thumb safety catches,
throat hole cocks, tension sprung frizzens. Slightly rounded wooden butts.
                                                                $594 £300

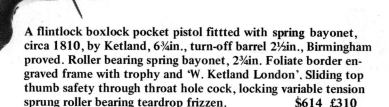

A flintlock boxlock pocket pistol fittted with spring bayonet, circa 1810, by Ketland, 6¾in., turn-off barrel 2½in., Birmingham proved. Roller bearing spring bayonet, 2¾in. Foliate border engraved frame with trophy and 'W. Ketland London'. Sliding top thumb safety through throat hole cock, locking variable tension sprung roller bearing teardrop frizzen.   **$614 £310**

A good quality flintlock boxlock, over and under, tap action pocket pistol, 7¼in., turn-off barrels 2½in., slotted for barrel key. The bottom barrel numbered 1, by Wallis, London proved. External spring to frizzen, sliding bar top safety, steel trigger guard and mounts. Plain slab sided wood butt inset with silver oval escutcheon engraved 'Presented by D. McK. to D.H.R., July 1797'. **$634 £310**

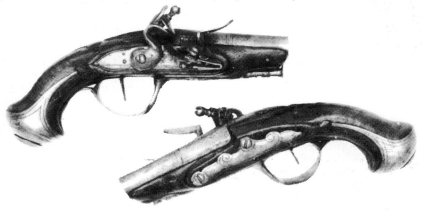

A pair of 65-bore French provincial flintlock pocket pistols, 6½in., barrels 2¾in. Full-stocked, border engraved rounded locks and steel furniture. Swollen trigger guard finials and sideplates. Some stock carving around trigger guards and barrel tangs. One steel ramrod.   **$841 £425**

A good and desirable pair of 60-bore flintlock target pistols by Boutet (Directeur Artiste) Manufacture a Versailles, 15in., hair groove rifled swamped, octagonal barrels 9½in., with top sighting channels. Breech plugs each inlaid with two bevelled rectangular gold maker's poincons 'Boutet'. Half-stocked, detented locks, chequered capstan, screw set triggers, ramp and roller bearing frizzens and springs. Plain steel furniture.

$9,108 £4,600

TRAVELLING

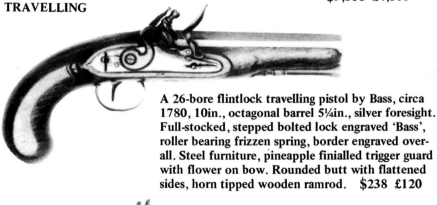

A 26-bore flintlock travelling pistol by Bass, circa 1780, 10in., octagonal barrel 5¼in., silver foresight. Full-stocked, stepped bolted lock engraved 'Bass', roller bearing frizzen spring, border engraved overall. Steel furniture, pineapple finialled trigger guard with flower on bow. Rounded butt with flattened sides, horn tipped wooden ramrod. $238 £120

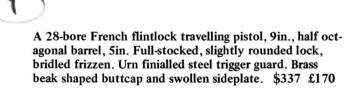

A 28-bore French flintlock travelling pistol, 9in., half octagonal barrel, 5in. Full-stocked, slightly rounded lock, bridled frizzen. Urn finialled steel trigger guard. Brass beak shaped buttcap and swollen sideplate. $337 £170

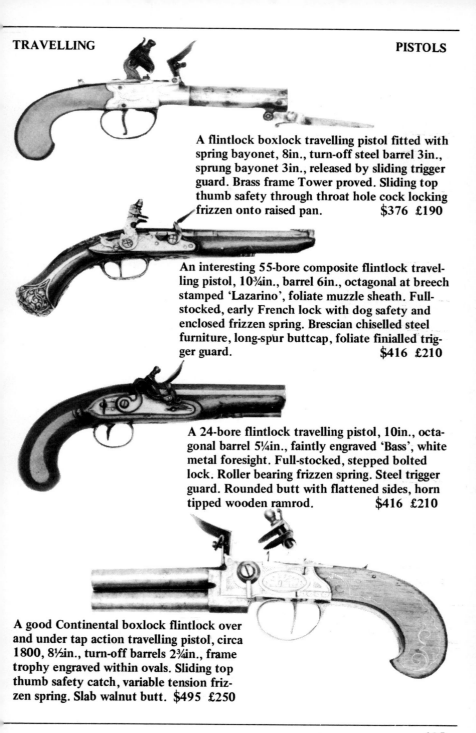

A flintlock boxlock travelling pistol fitted with spring bayonet, 8in., turn-off steel barrel 3in., sprung bayonet 3in., released by sliding trigger guard. Brass frame Tower proved. Sliding top thumb safety through throat hole cock locking frizzen onto raised pan.   **$376 £190**

An interesting 55-bore composite flintlock travelling pistol, 10¾in., barrel 6in., octagonal at breech stamped 'Lazarino', foliate muzzle sheath. Full-stocked, early French lock with dog safety and enclosed frizzen spring. Brescian chiselled steel furniture, long-spur buttcap, foliate finialled trigger guard.   **$416 £210**

A 24-bore flintlock travelling pistol, 10in., octagonal barrel 5¼in., faintly engraved 'Bass', white metal foresight. Full-stocked, stepped bolted lock. Roller bearing frizzen spring. Steel trigger guard. Rounded butt with flattened sides, horn tipped wooden ramrod.   **$416 £210**

A good Continental boxlock flintlock over and under tap action travelling pistol, circa 1800, 8½in., turn-off barrels 2¾in., frame trophy engraved within ovals. Sliding top thumb safety catch, variable tension frizzen spring. Slab walnut butt. **$495 £250**

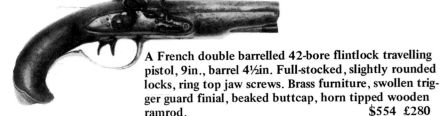

A French double barrelled 42-bore flintlock travelling pistol, 9in., barrel 4½in. Full-stocked, slightly rounded locks, ring top jaw screws. Brass furniture, swollen trigger guard finial, beaked buttcap, horn tipped wooden ramrod. **$554 £280**

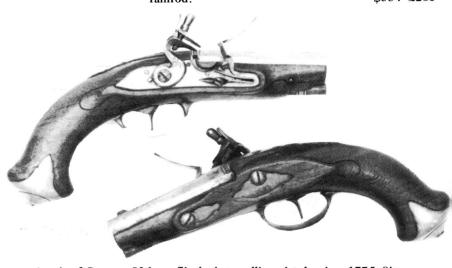

A pair of German 80-bore flintlock travelling pistols, circa 1775, 8in., slightly swamped barrels 3¼in., octagonal at breeches. Full-stocked, unbridled frizzens, foliate engraved cock necks. Brass furniture, flower and leaf carved behind barrel tangs. Wooden ramrods. **$940 £475**

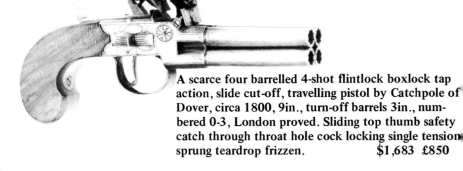

A scarce four barrelled 4-shot flintlock boxlock tap action, slide cut-off, travelling pistol by Catchpole of Dover, circa 1800, 9in., turn-off barrels 3in., numbered 0-3, London proved. Sliding top thumb safety catch through throat hole cock locking single tension sprung teardrop frizzen. **$1,683 £850**

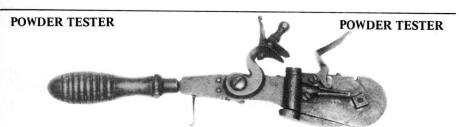

A mid 18th century all steel German flintlock Pulverprufer (powdertester). 9¼in., exterior action, vertical powder chamber propelling wheel flap downwards, frame side engraved with grades 1-12. Turned wooden handle.

$495 £250

RIFLES AND GUNS

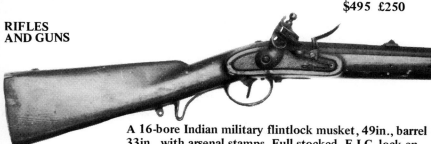

A 16-bore Indian military flintlock musket, 49in., barrel 33in., with arsenal stamps. Full-stocked, E.I.C. lock engraved 'Mortimer 1798' with heart mark. Regulation brass mounts, bayonet bar at muzzle, steel ramrod and sling swivel. $257 £130

A 34-bore Kentucky flintlock long gun from the Reading area of Pennsylvania, 61in., octagonal sighted barrel 44in. Full-stocked, stepped lock with fern tip engraved tail. Brass furniture, hinged patch box with scrolled border, scrolled trigger guard spur. Inlaid brass star to carved cheek-piece.

$693 £350

An attractive 40-bore Turkish miquelet flintlock rifle, circa 1780, 52in., watered steel barrel 38in., chiselled at breech and muzzle with foliage, inlaid with gold maker's poincon, raised top sighting rib, full-stocked, lock inlaid with gold, sher bacha rearsight, green stained ivory forecap.$772 £390

SPORTING GUNS

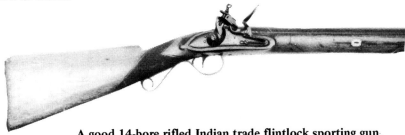

A good 14-bore rifled Indian trade flintlock sporting gun, 58½in., round twist barrel 42in., engraved 'Westley Richards, London', chequered full-stock with iron furniture comprising long-spurred buttplate, scroll backed trigger guard and three ramrod pipes. $436 £220

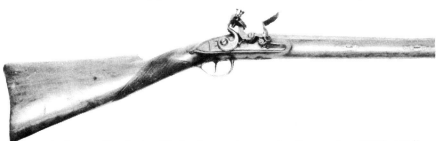

A 12-bore self-priming flintlock sporting gun by Jover, circa 1780, 54½in., half octagonal barrel 38½in., London proved, maker's mark 'W.T.'. Silver spider foresight, gold breech line and vent plug. Half-stocked, stepped lock foliate and floral engraved, roller bearing frizzen. Steel furniture, acorn finialled trigger guard. $693 £350

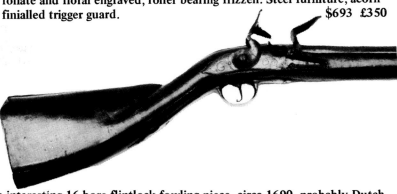

An interesting 16-bore flintlock fowling piece, circa 1690, probably Dutch, 66in., stepped barrel 50¼in., octagonal at breech. Full-stocked, rounded slightly banana shaped lock engraved with strawberry foliage. Swollen brass furniture, spear finialled trigger guard, buttcap heel formed as single blossom, pierced foliate sideplate. Downdrooping swollen butt. $792 £400

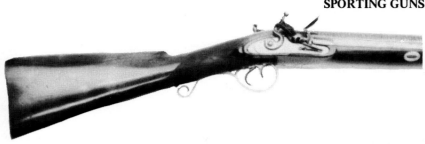

A rare 6-bore double barrelled big game flintlock sporting rifle by Jover, circa 1800, 51in., heavy browned twist nine groove rifled barrels 34in., gold inlaid 'Jover & Son, London', with twin gold breech lines, inlaid gold thunderburst at breech and gold bead foresight. Gold vents, ramped frizzen springs. Engraved steel furniture. $1,287 £650

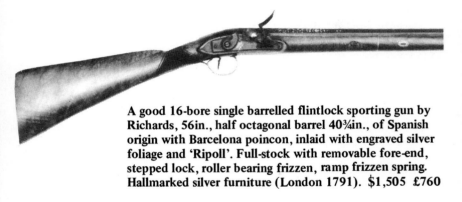

A good 16-bore single barrelled flintlock sporting gun by Richards, 56in., half octagonal barrel 40¾in., of Spanish origin with Barcelona poincon, inlaid with engraved silver foliage and 'Ripoll'. Full-stock with removable fore-end, stepped lock, roller bearing frizzen, ramp frizzen spring. Hallmarked silver furniture (London 1791). $1,505 £760

A hallmarked silver mounted double barrelled 20-bore flintlock sporting gun by H. Nock, circa 1781, 47in., browned twist barrels 30½in., inlaid with twin gold breech lines, vents and maker's poincons 'H. Nock London'. Half-stocked, locks border engraved. Rainproof pans, French style cocks, ramped frizzen springs, roller bearing frizzen feet. Hallmarked silver furniture. $1,782 £900

A very fine 12-bore Turkish miquelet flintlock sporting gun, dated A.H. 1231 (1816 A.D.), 50½in., half octagonal barrel 36in., inlaid with gold at breech and engraved London. Full-stocked, silver lockplate, silver cock elaborately chiselled as a lion and silver bridle. Military trophies on frizzen, gold lined vent. Squared section butt and engraved sheet silver buttcap with hinged trap, engraved sheet silver barrel tang surround. Four large silver gilt and nielloed barrel bands and silver tipped steel ramrod. $4,950 £2,500

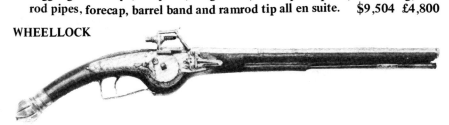

An exceedingly fine and most desirable 16-bore Austrian flintlock sporting gun by F. Heitzenperger, circa 1750, 57½in., half octagonal, half polygonal blued Spanish barrel 42in., gold inlaid 'Barzina Anod 1749 en Madrid', inlaid with eleven gold maker's poincons. Half-stocked, polished lock superbly chiselled in low relief military trophies and standards, rocaille, shells and foliage all upon an inlaid gold punctate ground. All the extensive steel furniture is made en suite and a magnificent urn trophy on the buttcap. Furniture comprises large buttcap, crowned vacant escutcheon and sideplate; trigger plate, trigger guard straps, toe plate, sling screw, cheek-piece plate, barrel tang, ramrod pipes, forecap, barrel band and ramrod tip all en suite. $9,504 £4,800

WHEELLOCK

A 28-bore early 17th century Continental, probably Swiss, wheellock holster pistol, 24in., half octagonal barrel 15¾in., foliate and floral engraved octagonal section, turned muzzle. Full-stocked, foliate engraved lock borders, external wheel with bird-shaped bridle, bridle cock, sliding pan cover. Foliate and floral engraved trigger guard and ramrod pipe. $6,000 £3,000

MILITARIA

ARMOUR

A Victorian miniature suit of armour in 16th century style, of pressed tin, partly articulated, with lance rest to breastplate, close helmet, sabatons, mitten gauntlets, holding sword, height 16½in., on round, wooden base. $119 £60

ARMOUR

A Victorian miniature copy of a German full suit of armour, circa 1530, 15½in. overall. Helmet with two-piece skull, fluted visor, articulated gorget. $198 £100

A Victorian miniature copy of an articulated German Maximillian full suit of fluted armour, circa 1510, 16in. overall. Fluted gorget plates, barred visor, two-piece skull. $228 £115

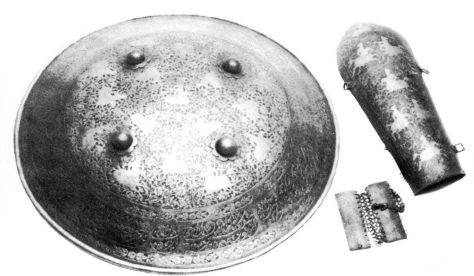

A matching part set of Indo-Persian armour, comprising kula khud, chiselled with mounted horsemen amidst flowers and foliage. Bazu band with mail linked wrist plates, brass rimmed dhal 18½in. Kula Khud not illustrated $366 £185

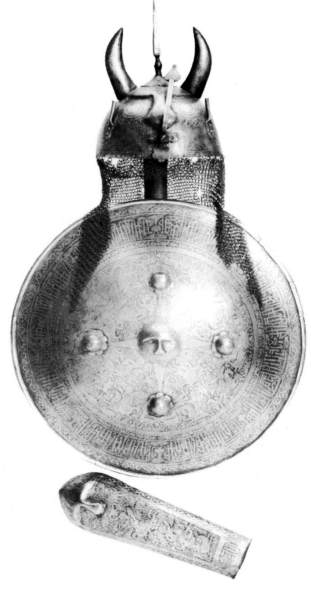

A matching part set of Indo-Persian armour, comprising kula khud,
embossed with devil's face, applied steel horns, top spike, plume
sockets and nasal bar. Etched overall with face, mounted hunters
and animals, traces of gold and silver damascene $396 £200
with Bazu Band and Dhal

A good pair of French 2nd Empire cuirassier trooper's breast and backplates, the heavy breastplate with brass lugs and studs, engraved inside 'Manufre Rle de Klingenthal Obre 1828. 2T. 1. Lrs. No. 3283'.　$356　£180

A rare 17th/18th century Moro armour, consisting of brass split links and plates of buffalo horn, hinged fastener at front and with rare companion matching helmet.　$376　£190

A good full length suit of 16th/17th century Turkish (Persian) horseman's chainmail armour, entirely composed of alternate rows of solid flat rings.　$436　£220

A good English Cromwellian trooper's breastplate, circa 1650, struck with Commonwealth four square mark, musket ball tested, pronounced medial ridge.　$436　£220

A good early 17th century Italian breastplate of peascod form, swivel hook fasteners for shoulder scales, simple line pattern, steel studded decoration. $455 £230

A set of Cromwellian half-armour for cuirassier, circa 1640, comprising 'lobster tail' helmet, breast and back-plate. Helmet of 'pot' with two-piece skull. Heavy gauge breastplate, musket ball tested, distinct medial ridge. Back-plate with line engraved turned over borders. $653 £330

A French 2nd Empire carabinier officer's brass covered breast and back-plate, breastplate skirt engraved 'Man-ufre Rall de Klingenthal, Avril 1833, 2T Llre No 400 M'. $675 £340

A good pair of Cromwellian breast and backplates circa 1640, breastplate with distinct medial ridge, two studs for fastening shoulder straps. Deeply struck with crowned 'I.R.' armourer's mark (James I). $911 £460

A composite half suit of 17th century armour, burgonet with one-piece
skull, tall comb, pierced ear-flaps. Breastplate with distinct medial ridge,
backplate from a black and white armour with added skirt. Two-piece
gorget riveted to five plate articulated shoulder pieces. $990 £500

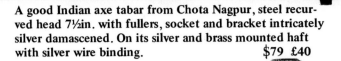

A good Indian axe tabar from Chota Nagpur, steel recurved head 7½in. with fullers, socket and bracket intricately silver damascened. On its silver and brass mounted haft with silver wire binding. $79 £40

An Indo-Persian all steel axe tabar, 26½in. double crescent head 5½in., etched with foliage and scrolls overall. Top spike of squared section, on its steel haft with bulbous terminal. $99 £50

An early 18th century Continental fighting axe, steel head 8¾in., etched with scrolls, integral side spurs. On its wooden haft covered with fabric and regular brass studs. $107 £54

A good Indian axe tabar from Chota Nagpur, steel recurved head 7½in. with fullers, socket and bracket intricately gold damascened. On its silver mounted haft with top spike. $129 £65

A rare Russian or Swiss axe berdiche, circa 1580, slender crescent shaped head 24½in., affixed through integral spur at base of blade to haft. Integral socket to head, on its original facetted wooden haft, with spiral twist painted decoration and iron hanging ring. $436 £220

A good and most unusual early 16th century double headed fighting axe, crescents 10½in., deeply struck with an armourer's mark. Long integral steel straps. Wooden haft 47in. $653 £330

BADGES

An other rank's 1878 pattern helmet plate of The 97th Regiment. $32 £16

An other rank's pre-1881 Glengarry badge of The 30th (Cambridgeshire) Regt. of Foot. $36 £18

An other rank's 1878 pattern helmet plate of The 97th Foot. $40 £20

A silvered and gilt officer's 1855 pattern shako badge of The 2nd Royal Tower Hamlets Militia (Queen's Own Light Infantry). $48 £24

A Victorian officer cadet's helmet plate of The Royal Military College. $51 £26

An other rank's pre-1881 Glengarry badge of The 7th (or Royal) Fusiliers. $51 £26

A Victorian other rank's Albert pattern helmet plate of The North Somerset Yeomanry. $55 £28

An other rank's pre-1881 Glengarry badge of The 8th (The King's) Regt. $63 £32

An other rank's shako badge of The 1st Regt. of Foot, 1869 pattern. $63 £32

A Victorian officer's gilt and enamel bonnet badge of The Queen's Body-guard of Scotland.
$69 £35

Belgium, Order of the Crown, large breast badge. $71 £36

An officer's silvered plaid brooch of The Gordon Highlanders, bearing the stag device and the regimental motto. $71 £36

A Victorian white metal helmet plate of The Welsh Regt. 2nd Glamorgan RVC. $79 £40

An other rank's pre-1881 Glengarry badge of The 78th Highland Regt. of Foot. $83 £42

An 1829 pattern Artillery Volunteer officer's silvered shako badge.
$89 £45

An other rank's pre-1881 Glengarry badge of The 106th Bombay Light Infantry Regt. $95 £48

A mid Victorian officer's gilt shako badge of The Royal Dock Yard Btn.
$99 £50

An other rank's pre-1881 Glengarry badge of The 47th Regt. of Foot. $99 £50

A Victorian officer's silvered helmet plate of The Lancashire Militia.
$99 £50

A Victorian officer's helmet plate of The Army Veterinary Department.
$109 £55

A Victorian officer's helmet plate of The Oxfordshire Light Infantry.
$119 £60

A Victorian officer's gilt and enamel bonnet badge of The Queen's Bodyguard of Scotland.
$119 £60

An officer's pre-1881 silvered Glengarry badge of the 93rd (Sutherland Highlanders) Regiment.
$119 £60

Poland, Cross for Silesia, Grand Cross breast star (78mm), eight pointed silvered star. $119 £60

An other rank's pre-1881 Glengarry badge of The 107th (Bengal Infantry) Regt. $119 £60

A Victorian white metal helmet plate of the 1st A.B. Elginshire Rifles.
$127 £64

A Victorian Volunteer Bn. officer's helmet plate of The Black Watch. $128 £65

A Victorian officer's helmet plate of The South Wales Borderers.
$139 £70

A Victorian officer's helmet plate of The North Staffordshire Regiment.
$139 £70

A Victorian officer's silvered helmet plate of The 6th Volunteer Btn. The Liverpool Regt.
$148 £75

A Victorian officer's helmet plate of The South Wales Borderers.
$148 £75

A Victorian officer's white metal helmet plate of The 5th (The Haytor) Vol. Btn. Devonshire Regt.$148 £75

A very rare original Nazi Spanish Cross with swords in bronze.
$168 £85

A Victorian officer's helmet plate of The 1st Devon Militia.
$168 £85

An officer's gilt Albert shako badge of The Royal Marines, 1845-55 pattern, silver globe.
$168 £85

A silvered plaid brooch of The Black Watch, in fitted velvet lined leather covered case.
$168 £85

BADGES

An officer's gilt, silver and enamel shako plate of The Nottingham Militia.$198 £100

A Victorian gilt, silvered and enamel helmet plate of The Royal Marine Light Infantry.
$198 £100

A Victorian officer's silvered helmet plate of The 3rd Royal Lancashire Militia.
$202 £102

An officer's gilt and silver Glengarry, 1872-1881, of The 91st Princess Louise's Argyllshire Highlanders.
$208 £105

A Victorian officer's silvered and green enamel helmet plate of The 5th Vol. Bn. The Royal Scots. $218 £110

A militia officer's gilt and silvered 1844 pattern shako badge of The Clare Regiment.
$218 £110

A senior NCO's gilt helmet plate of The Royal Marine Light Infantry Band, Portsmouth or Plymouth Division, 1878-1902 pattern. $228 £115

An other rank's 1844 Albert shako badge of The 89th Foot.
$228 £115

An officer's 1855 pattern shako badge of The 35th Regiment.
$257 £130

An officer's 1878 pattern helmet plate of The 55th Regiment.
$267 £135

An officer's gilt silver and enamel shako badge of The Royal Marine Light Infantry, 1866-78 pattern.
$356 £180

A post 1902 officer's silver shoulder belt badge of The King Edward's Own Gurkha Rifles.
$406 £205

An officer's bell-topped shako plate of the 82nd Prince of Wales' Volunteers, 1928-44 pattern.
$416 £210

An 1829 bell-topped pattern shako badge of The 46th South Devonshire Regiment. $416 £210

An officer's gilt shako badge of The Royal Marine Artillery, 1855-66 pattern.
$455 £230

An officer's gilt shako badge of The Royal Marine Light Infantry, 1855-66 pattern.
$485 £245

An officer's gilt shako plate of The Royal Marine Artillery, circa 1810. $594 £300

A rare, Officer's gilt helmet plate of the 26th (Cameronians) Regt. of Foot, 1878 pattern. $792 £400

CANNONS

A well made model of a naval coastal artillery cannon, stepped steel barrel, 17in., mounted on steel carriage with studded decoration, height of carriage 5½in. $75 £38

A Georgian bronze model mortar, barrel 4½in., bore 1¼in., elegantly turned reinforces, raised vent pan, integral trunnions. On later oak carriage with brass trunnion loops, pegged and chained, reinforcing bolts and wood elevating wedge. $198 £100

A good Malayan swivel cannon lantaka, the barrel cast with scrolled and other patterns, overall 31in., good patina overall. $317 £160

A fine Japanese brass hand cannon barrel, 10½cm., of swamped and waisted form, swollen muzzle, pierced rear and foresights of blocked form, raised figure of eight pan. Top of barrel well inlaid with two silver characters.

$594 £300

A Japanese bronze barrel from a hand cannon, 16½cm., turned reinforces at muzzle, block sights. Breech plug unscrews. Mounted on an old hardwood plinth base.

$673 £340

A good Malayan cannon lantaka, bronze barrel 44½in., swollen turned muzzle, tubular breech socket, on stepped wooden four-wheeled carriage with brass trunnion loops.

$812 £410

A good iron naval cannon barrel, circa 1800, bore approximately 1¾in., stepped barrel, marked above breech with 'P' and '1.1.15', length overall 37½in., trunnion width 9in.   **$990 £500**

A 19th century cast iron six pounder carronade, 46in., 16½in. across trunnions, breech cast with Imperial crown and '6pr'. Reinforcing rings at muzzle and breech with integral loop to cascabel.   **$1,188 £600**

An iron cannon, barrel 3ft.6in., bore 3¾in., breech stamped 'B. P. & Co.' and weight 3cwt.2qts.23lb. Trunnions stamped '45' and '4PO1'. Mounted on wooden garrison standing carriage with iron fittings.   **$1,584 £800**

A good Georgian naval cannon, 46in. overall, with 3in. bore and probably throwing 9lb. shot, 3-stage barrel with simple vent, 15in. across trunnions. On a later wheeled wooden carriage with elevating block. $1,584 £800

An early 19th century brass cannon barrel mounted on copper swivel, 28½in. overall with elegantly proportioned reinforces, swollen muzzle, integral cascabel and trunnions. Integral platform around vent drilled for cannon igniter. Mounted on a later stepped four-wheeled carriage. $1,683 £850

CAP DISPENSERS

A brass percussion cap dispenser of circular form, turned roped decoration to body stamped 'J. S. Improved'. Sprung delivery. **$107 £54**

A white metal percussion cap dispenser of circular form, turned roped decoration. Sprung delivery retaining leather suspension thong. **$119 £60**

A brass percussion cap dispenser of 'comma' form, turned roped decoration to body stamped 'Sykes'. Sprung delivery, brass suspension ring. **$123 £62**

A rare copper fulinate pill dispenser by Charles Moore, 5¼in., serrated wheel stamped 'C. Moore, London, 345'. **$217 £110**

CROSSBOWS

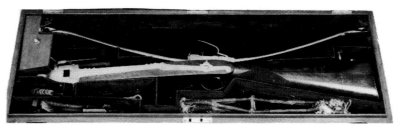

A fine early 19th century cased stonebow, span 32in., walnut stock 31½in., with steel mounts and side-plates, hinge-up mechanism finely chiselled with foliate sprays, spring-loaded rearsight, pin-hole apertures engraved with maker — 'Thos. Jackson, 29 Edward St., Portman Sqe., London', the top of stock inlaid with German silver urn and scrolled mount, contained in its fitted, blue velvet lined wooden case. **$3,366 £1,700**

A post 1902 officer's gilt bearskin grenade badge of The Royal Fusiliers.　$79　£40

A post 1902 officer's silvered bearskin grenade badge for Volunteer battalion.
$79　£40

An officer's gilt and silvered bearskin grenade badge of The Royal Inniskilling Fusiliers.　$89　£45

A Victorian officer's gilt bearskin grenade badge of The Northumberland Fusiliers.
$99　£50

A bandmaster's sealskin cap grenade badge in gilt and silver, 1876-78 pattern.　$267　£135

An officer's gilt, silver and enamel grenade helmet plate of The Royal Marine Artillery, 1879 pattern, eighteen flame points.　$376　£190

EPAULETTES

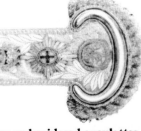

A fine pair of George IV officer's full dress embroidered epaulettes of The Coldstream Guards, silver bullion embroidery on yellow cloth, with gilt crown, garter star and George IV cypher, silver crescents and 3in. silver bullion tassels, scarlet leather, silk and velvet backings.　$267　£135

FIGURES

A solid brass figure of a private of The Rangers, in full marching order.
$109 £55

A white glazed china bust of Field Marshal Lord Roberts, overall height 21in., width 14in.
$277 £140

A standing bronze figure of the Prussian Emperor Wilhelm I, in full dress uniform of a field marshal.
$386 £195

A solid silver figure of a Captain, Royal Field Artillery, hallmarked London. Overall height 13½in. $634 £320

A bronzed brass equestrian figure of Napoleon Ist, mounted upon rearing horse. Overall height 18in., length of base 14½in.
$990 £500

A standing bronze figure of an Irish Dragoon, 1815, in full uniform, height 17in., base 22½in. overall. $990 £500

A Nazi D.A.F. district banner, red, with laid on D.A.F. symbol, the top left-hand corner with brown panel stitched with district 'Munster 7' within blue border, silver edge tassels, plated hanging rings, 47½ x 53in. $307 £155

FLASKS

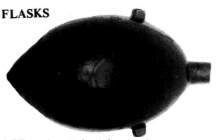

A Victorian Colonial carved coconut shell flask, 7in., pewter spout and suspension lugs. Body dated 1847. $34 £17

A late 18th century European horn bodied common topped gun sized powder flask, brass adjustable charger. $48 £24

A copper bodied common topped three-way pistol powder flask, unadjustable charger unit with two traps fitted to the bottom for caps and balls. $59 £30

An embossed copper powder flask with scarce plunger type, brass charger for fixed measure powder charges. $63 £32

A pistol sized copper powder flask, circa 1800, 3½in. overall, common brass top and charger, waisted body. $63 £32

A copper bodied common topped gun sized powder flask, brass adjustable charger unit. $69 £35

A patent topped copper bodied pistol powder flask, brass adjustable charger unit stamped 'AM Flack & Cap Co'. $71 £36

A copper bodied brass common topped pistol powder flask, unadjustable charger unit. $75 £38

A copper three-way pistol flask, 4½in. overall, circular brass cap unscrews for caps, common brass oval top with hinged ball trap. $79 £40

A good copper bodied common topped pistol powder flask, brass unadjustable charger unit. $79 £40

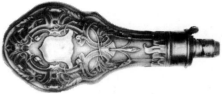

A good patent topped gun sized copper bodied powder flask, graduated brass charger unit. $89 £45

A good copper bodied patent topped gun sized powder flask, brass graduated charger unit, stamped 'Hawksley Sheffield'. $89 £45

A copper bodied brass screw topped pistol powder flask, brass graduated charger. $91 £46

A scarce copper bodied common topped pistol sized powder flask, brass unadjustable charger unit. $91 £46

An embossed copper French pistol flask, 5in., embossed with trophy of hunting arms and 'P.F.D.F. a Paris'. Common brass top. $95 £48

A good patent topped gun sized copper bodied powder flask, graduated brass charger unit. $99 £50

FLASKS

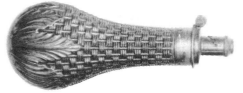

A good copper bodied patent topped gun sized powder flask, four position brass charger unit. $99 £50

A brass bodied common topped pistol sized powder flask, brass unadjustable charger unit. $99 £50

A copper powder flask, 6½in., body retains much original lacquered finish, lacquered brass common top by Hawksley. $103 £52

A good copper bodied French common topped gun sized powder flask, brass adjustable five-position charger unit, embossed copper body impressed 'B.A. Paris'. $110 £55

An embossed copper powder flask, 8in. body with four hanging rings, patent top stamped 'James Dixon & Sons, Sheffield'. $111 £56

A white metal, patent topped gun sized powder flask, white metal graduated charger unit. $111 £56

A copper bodied common topped three-way pistol powder flask, by J. Dixon & Sons, Sheffield, brass unadjustable charger unit. $119 £60

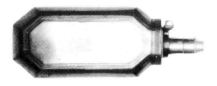

A good copper powder flask 'Shapes', brass charger unit, plain flutes to panel edge. $119 £60

A copper bodied three-way pistol powder flask, brass unadjustable charger unit incorporating compartment in top for balls. $119 £60

A good copper bodied screw topped three-way pistol powder flask, brass adjustable charger, the base with brass cap fitted with traps for ball and caps. $119 £60

A large copper powder flask of 'gunstock' form, 8in., copper body embossed with foliage and wrist chequering, registration mark for 1854. $123 £62

A scarce gun stock patent topped copper bodied gun sized powder flask, brass graduated charger unit stamped 'AM Flack & Cap Co'. $129 £65

A leather covered gun sized powder flask, 8in., body covered in sewn pigskin, lacquered brass charger by Dixon & Sons. $139 £70

A good copper bodied patent topped gun sized powder flask, brass adjustable charger unit stamped 'Hawksley'. $148 £75

A good copper bodied French patent plunger topped gun sized powder flask, brass five position graduated charger unit. $148 £75

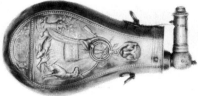

A copper bodied French gun sized powder flask, patent knee action graduated brass charger, body embossed 'T.N.N. a Paris'. $148 £75

225

FLASKS

A good copper bodied French gun sized common topped powder flask, brass five-position adjustable charger unit. $148 £75

A good copper bodied French common topped gun sized powder flask, brass adjustable charger unit, bag-shaped body. $148 £75

A copper bodied French common topped gun sized powder flask, brass graduated charger unit. $148 £75

A good patent topped pistol powder flask, 5¼in., brass graduated charger unit, copper body with hanging ring. $158 £80

A fine three-way pistol powder flask as cased with pairs of duelling pistols, by Sykes, brass charger unit, with swivel compartment lid, overall 4½in.
$166 £84

A copper bodied French gun sized powder flask, body part fluted, together with hanging rings. $168 £85

A patent topped pistol sized powder flask for a Colt pocket percussion revolver, brass adjustable charger unit, copper, bag shaped body with hanging ring. $228 £115

A 19th century Bohemian carved stag horn powder flask, 8½in., front carved in relief with stags and does. Screw cap acts as powder measure, twin horn suspension loops. $990 £500

A Spanish officer's small gilt brass gorget bearing the crowned cypher of 'Alfonso XIII' in silver, with original velvet lining with traces of maker. $49 £25

A mid 19th century French officer's brass gorget with silvered copper device of cockerel clutching lightning flashes and with one foot upon globe. $49 £25

A Georgian officer's copper gilt gorget, universal pattern, engraved with crowned 'GR' and wreath. $110 £55

A rare Nazi Kornett Der S.A. gorget (Brutschild) gilt central S.A. badge, white metal suspension chains. $170 £85

A rare Nazi political standard bearer's gorget, complete with suspension chain of square links alternating designs of Nazi Eagle and swastika. $297 £150

HELMETS

An R.A.F. officer's parade helmet, complete with bullion corded trim, gilt badge and feather plume. $69 £35

An other rank's post 1902 shako of The London Rifle Brigade. $99 £50

An other rank's post 1902 shako of The Highland Light Infantry. $109 £55

A French other rank's shako, circa 1855, height 8in., black beaver body with felt peak. $119 £60

An officer's pre-1888 pattern busby of The 4th (Queen's Own) Hussars. $158 £80

An other rank's post 1902 blue cloth ball-topped helmet of The Royal Army Medical Corps. $158 £80

A post 1902 other rank's shako of The Highland Light Infantry. $158 £80

A Victorian officer's spiked helmet of The 2nd Vol. Batt. The Yorkshire Regiment.

A good Prussian infantryman's Ersatz (pressed tin) pickelhaube, brass helmet plate. $168 £85

A Prussian infantry-
man's Ersatz pickel-
haube, brass helmet
plate and mounts.
$168 £85

A post 1902 shako of
The London Rifle
Brigade with black
feather plume.
$188 £95

An officer's shako of
The Cameronians
(Scottish Rifles) with
10in. black feather
plume. $188 £95

A Victorian blue cloth
ball-topped helmet,
complete with velvet
backed chinchain.
$198 £100

A cabasset, circa 1600,
formed in one-piece,
brass rosettes to rim.
$198 £100

A Prussian infantry-
man's pickelhaube,
gilt helmet plate,
brass mounts.
$198 £100

A helmet cabasset,
circa 1600, of one-
piece construction
with distinct medial
ridge. $198 £100

An officer's shako of
The Scottish Rifles,
complete with leather
chinstrap and feather
plume. $198 £100

A post 1902 officer's
blue cloth spiked hel-
met of The East Surrey
Regt., complete with
chinchain. $208 £105

An Indo-Persian spiked helmet, kula khud, two plume holders, adjustable nasal bar. $218 £110

A Victorian officer's peaked forage cap of The Duke of Wellington's (West Riding) Regt. $218 £110

A good cabasset, circa 1600, formed in one-piece, pear stalk finial to crown. $218 £110

A Saxony Jaeger shako, gilt cross and white metal arms and star helmet plate.$238 £120

A Victorian officer's blue cloth spiked helmet of The King's Own Royal Lancaster Regt. $238 £120

A Royal Artillery officer's busby with white horsehair plume on left. $238 £120

A post 1902 officer's green cloth helmet of a Volunteer Rifle Batt. $247 £125

A Prussian infantry reservist officer's pickelhaube, gilt helmet plate. $247 £125

A Victorian officer's blue cloth ball-topped helmet of The 1st Ayrshire & Galloway Artillery Volunteers. $247 £125

A Prussian officer's pickelhaube, believed Feld-Gendarmerie, gilt fluted spike and base mount. $253 £128

HELMETS

A Victorian officer's
peaked forage cap
of The 74th Regt.
$257 £130

A post 1902 officer's blue
cloth ball-topped helmet of
The Royal Artillery.
$257 £130

A late 16th century
cabasset, formed in
one-piece, tall crown,
with pear stalk finial.
$257 £130

A Victorian officer's
peaked forage cap of
The 2nd (North) Regt.,
Royal Guernsey Militia.
$267 £135

An Indo-Persian spiked
helmet, kula khud, the
skull chiselled with fol-
iate patterns. $227 £140

A Prussian infantry
officer's pickelhaube,
gilt helmet plate,
chinscales and mounts.
$277 £140

A post 1902 officer's
blue cloth ball-topped
helmet of The Aber-
deenshire Artillery
Volunteers.$287 £145

An officer's 1869
pattern shako of
The 96th Regt.
$287 £145

An officer's 1869
pattern shako of The
54th (West Norfolk)
Regt. of Foot.
$297 £150

232

A late 18th century Persian helmet, kula khud, one-piece steel skull.
$307 £155

HELMETS

A Continental dragoon type helmet, circa 1820, brass crown and ornamental crest. $297 £150

An officer's busby of The 3rd City of London Yeomanry (Sharpshooters). $297 £150

An other rank's busby of The Midlothian Rifle Volunteers. $297 £150

A pre-1888 officer's busby of The 14th Hussars. $307 £155

An Imperial Prussian infantryman's pickelhaube of the 9th Grenadier Regiment. $328 £165

A Cromwellian period 'lobster tail' helmet, three-bar visor, leather hinged ear-flaps, blackened overall. $337 £170

An officer's 1869 pattern shako of The First or North West Regt., Royal Jersey Militia. $337 £170

An early 17th century burgonet, plain comb with pointed peak, hinged ear-flaps, simple steel studded decoration. $337 £170

A 17th century German black and white morion of Town Guard type, formed in two-pieces, plume holder. $337 £170

An other rank's lance cap of The 9th Lancers, brass mounts, black horsehair plume in holder. $346 £175

A Victorian other rank's lance cap of The 17th Lancers, complete with horsehair plume. $358 £180

A post 1888 officer's busby of The 10th Hussars. $366 £185

A Victorian other rank's lance cap of the 12th Lancers. Date inside 1900. $376 £190

A Volunteer officer's 1869 pattern green cloth shako, possibly Oxfordshire Rifle Vols. $376 £190

A Victorian officer's white metal helmet of The Yorkshire Dragoons Yeomanry Cavalry. $376 £190

A Victorian officer's blue cloth ball-topped helmet of The 5th Lancashire Artillery Volunteers. $386 £195

A French mid 19th century cuirassier's helmet. $396 £200

A Victorian officer's blue cloth spiked helmet of an Inspector of Army Schools. $396 £200

A French model 1912 Mounted Gendarmerie helmet, brass skull and peaks with German silver mounts. $416 £210

A Prussian officer's pick-elhaube of The 91st Oldenburg Infantry Regiment. $406 £205

A trooper's 1847 Albert pattern helmet of The 6th Dragoon Guards. $416 £210

A 17th century bur-gonet, with hinged ear-flaps.$416 £210

An early 17th century burgonet, plain comb skull and pointed peak, hinged earflaps.
 $436 £220

A 17th century morion of classical shape, for-med in one-piece, steel studded brass rosettes around base.$436 £220

An early French other rank's Light Cavalry helmet, japanned skull and peak. $455 £230

An early 17th century helmet burgonet, two-piece skull with tall comb. $455 £230

An officer's 1869 pat-tern shako of The First or The Royal Scots Regt. of Foot.
 $475 £240

A trooper's brass hel-met of The 5th Dra-goon Guards.
 $515 £260

HELMETS

An officer's 1869 pattern shako of The 17th (Leicestershire) Regt.
$535
£270

A French shako of the type worn by The Gardes d'Honneur, 1811-14. $554 £280

An Indo-Persian gold damascened helmet, kula khud, one-piece skull. $614 £310

An other rank's white metal helmet of The Montgomeryshire Yeomanry. $554 £280

An officer's 1855 French pattern shako of The 4th West York Militia. $574 £290

An officer's 1878 pattern green cloth spiked helmet of The 60th (The King's Royal Rifle Corps). $634 £320

A French mid 19th century cuirassier's helmet, brass body peak and ornamental crest. $554 £280

A Victorian officer's lance cap of The 9th Lancers. $594 £300

An officer's 1855 pattern shako, possibly Rifle Brigade, black felt body. $634 £320

A Victorian officer's 1871 pattern helmet of The Lothian and Berwickshire
Yeomanry Cavalry.   **$614 £310**

A French shako of the pattern worn by The Gardes d'Honneur, 1811-14.
$634 £320

A Victorian officer's astrakhan busby of Hussar shape of The Royal Denbigh and Merioneth Militia. $792 £400

A post 1902 officer's helmet of The Household Cavalry.$792 £400

A Victorian blue velvet bonnet of The Royal Company of Archers. $792 £400

An officer's 1855 pattern shako of The Royal Dock Yard Battalion. $792 £400

An officer's Albert pattern helmet of The King's Dragoon Guards. $812 £410

A Victorian officer's silvered helmet of The Royal Dragoons. $812 £410

A bearskin cap of The 3rd Volunteer Batt. Royal Welsh Fusiliers.$851 £430

An other rank's white metal helmet of The Montgomeryshire Yeomanry. $871 £440

An Austrian officer's lance cap (Czapka) of The 1st Uhlan Regt., circa 1910.$871 £440

A Victorian officer's 1871 pattern
helmet of The King's Dragoon Guards.
$1,010 £510

An officer's 1844 Albert pattern shako
of The 39th Foot. $1,069 £540

An officer's shako, circa 1865, of The
Royal Buckinghamshire Yeomanry.
$1,089 £550

Blue cloth ball-topped helmet, silver
mounts and badge with scarlet backing,
bearing title 'First London Artillery
Volunteers'. $1,089 £550

A post 1902 officer's lance cap of The 12th Lancers, silver and gilt plate.
$1,160 £590

An Indian Army officer's 1829 bell-topped pattern shako. $1,118 £600

A Victorian mounted bandsman's blue cloth ball-topped helmet of The Royal Artillery.$1,118 £600

An early 17th century European horseman's close helmet of 'Savoyard' type, peaked hinged visor. $1,188 £600

A 1st Empire bell-top shako bearing large silvered crowned eagle badge of The 100th Regiment. Red tufted plume and red, white and blue cloth cockade. White metal bound peak. Ear bosses embossed with lyre and white metal chin-scales. $1,188 £600

An officer's 1829 bell-topped pattern shako of The Royal Fusiliers.
$1,327 £670

An officer's shako of The Royal Artillery as worn 1831-32. $1,584 £800

A Yeomanry officer's helmet, similar to the Dragoon helmet. $1,742 £880

An officer's 1829 bell-topped pattern shako of The 96th Regiment.
$1,762 £890

An officer's helmet, circa 1846, of The North Shropshire Yeomanry.
$2,772 £1,400

An officer's 1818 Roman pattern helmet of The 5th Dragoon Guards.
$2,970 £1,500

An officer's bell-topped shako, circa 1835, of The Buckinghamshire Yeomanry. $3,861 £1,950

An officer's 1812 pattern helmet of The 5th (Princess Charlotte of Wales's) Dragoon Guards. $3,960 £2,000

An officer's 1812 pattern shako of The 23rd (Royal Welch Fusiliers) Regt., knapped felt body, leather peak, black silk binding to headband and stand-up front, very fine gilt and silvered regimental badge. $4,356 £2,200

A Georgian officer's Tarleton helmet of The 23rd Dragoons, leather skull with black bear fur crest. $7,920 £4,000

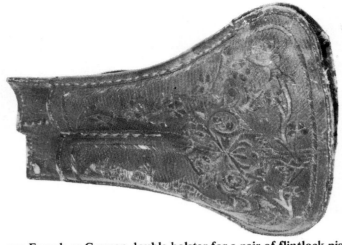

A rare French or German double holster for a pair of flintlock pistols, circa 1780, overall length of holster 11½in. with 10in. mouth. Red Morocco leather front, blind tooled leather back with suspension loop.
$158 £80

KNIFE HANDLES

A shakudo nanako kodzuka handle, with gilt abumi with ropes in low relief. $59 £30

A shakudo nanako kodzuka handle with dragon around Vajra hilted ken. $89 £45

A shakudo kodzuka handle, chased with tiger and dog worrying dragon, who guards the sacred jewel, gilt detail. $99 £50

A good iron kodzuka handle, signed 'Masamichi', carved in low relief with bow, arrows and two fans, inlaid with gold, silver and shakudo detail. $103 £52

A shakudo nanako kodzuka handle, with abumi, horse's bit and staff, gilt and silvered detail. $129 £65

A Japanese shibuichi kodzuka handle, signed 'Tomomitsu' and 'A Kakihan'. Carved in omori style. $198 £100

Crimea: 2 bars, Alma, Seb. (Impressed T. Maxwell, Ambulance Corps.)
$89 £45

China 1857: 1 bar Canton 1857. (Impressed C. Flynn, Ord, HMS Woodcock).
$129 £65

Pair: QSA, 1 bar Defence of Kimberley, Mayor of Kimberley's Star, (Pte. A. Nash, Kimberley town Guard) $148 £75

Trafalgar 1805. Mr. Boulton's white metal medal, contained in a glazed and silvered frame with ribbon attached.
$148 £75

Family Group of Three: Including East and West Africa 1887-1900: 2 bars Brass River 1895, Benin 1897. $158 £80

South Africa 1877-9, 1 bar 1879 (Rev. A. J. Law, Chaplain 4th Class.) $158 £80

Punjab 1849, 1 bar Goojerat. (Joseph Pierce, 53rd Foot.) $188 £95

Cape of Good Hope, 1 bar Basutoland (Tpr. H. Scrieber, CM Yeo.) $198 £100

Four: Natal, 1 bar 1906 (Natal Rangers), 1914-15 star (SAMR), BWM, Victory. (Pte. L. B. Levy, 4th SAH). $198 £100

Indian Mutiny: 2 bars Relief of Lucknow, (Sapper Geo. Cameron, Royal Engineers.) $208 £105

Seven: Natal 1906, QSA, 4 bars CC, Witte, Belfast, SA01, 1914-15 star, BWM, Victory Defence and SA War. $228 £115

MGS 1793, 1 bar Corunna, together with photocopies of recipients documents. $238 £120

MGS 1793, 1 bar
Talavera, together
with photocopies of
recipient's documents.
$247 £125

NGS 1915: 2 bars
Yangtze 1949,
Malaya. (B. C.
Jeffrey, Ord. Smn.
R.N.) $275 £139

NGS 1793, 1 bar Nava-
rino. (Wm. Bethell).
$356 £180

Nine: OBE, 2nd type, 1914 star, BWM, Victory (Sgt. 17th Lancers), 1939-45
star (Lancs. Fus.), Africa Star, Defence, War with oakleaf, USA Legion of
Merit (Col. E. A. Gordon, RPC), together with relevant miniatures. Complete
with citation for OBE (2), citation for Legion of Merit (2) and framed group
photograph of Lancashire Fusiliers 1934. $337 £170

NGS 1793, 1 bar
Syria. Lewis Hern
(Pte RM, HMS
Edinburgh).
$366 £185

MGS 1793, 6 bars,
Talavera, Busaco
Albuhera, Salamanca,
Vittoria, Toulouse.
$366 £185

NGS 1915, 1 bar Iraq
1919-20. $376 £190

Waterloo 1815.
(Richard Street,
2nd Btn. Grena-
dier Guards).
$376 £190

South Africa 1877-9,
1 bar 1879 (Lieut. C.
H. Gordon 2/3rd Foot.)
$386 £195

Army of India,
1 bar Ava.
$406 £205

Indian Mutiny: 1 bar Lucknow. (John Woodhead, A. B. Shannon) Naval Brigade. $406 £205

Four: Order of the Indian Empire, companion breast badge, second issue, Delhi Durbar 1903, in silver, Delhi Durbar 1911 Knight of Baluchistan Preceptory, hallmark silver gilt and enamelled neck badge awarded to Colonel A. McConaghey CIE, 1912-13. $436 £220

Pair: Egypt 1882, 5 bars, Tel-El-Kebir, Suakin 1884, El-Teb-Tamaai, The Nile 1884-85, Abu Klea, Khedives Star. (Pte. G. Phipps, 19th Hussars.) $436 £220

Four: AFC George V, 1914-15 star, BWM, Victory. (Flt. Lt. R. E. Dean, RNAS). $614 £310

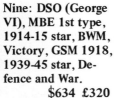

Nine: DSO (George VI), MBE 1st type, 1914-15 star, BWM, Victory, GSM 1918, 1939-45 star, Defence and War.
$634 £320

Three: DSO (Victoria), IGS 1895, 3 bars Punjab Frontier 1897-8, Samana 1897, Tirah 1897-8, Delhi Durbar 1903, in silver. (IGS - Lieut. J. B. Corry, RE 4th Coy. S. & M.). Mounted for wear, together with miniatures, cased.
$832 £420

Eight: Order of the Bath, companion's neck badge, BWM, Victory, GSM 1918, 1 bar Kurdistan, Defence, War, 1935 Jubilee, 1937 Coronation. (S/L R. P. Willcock, R.A.F.); together with embroidered R.A.F. 'wings' and recipient's details.
$832 £420

MISCELLANEOUS

Lead models of Army Medical Service, full dress, four bearers with stretchers, four staff officers, five nurses, eight wounded, round base figures issued from 1905.

$69 £35

A well constructed brass working scale model of a naval 7.5in. Mk.V deck gun, rifled barrel 14in., with breech opening to take a single cartridge of approximately 9mm., with hand-cocked striker, fired by lanyard. Mounted on circular base, overall. height 9in. $129 £65

A miniature painted on ivory of Napoleon 1st, half length, in uniform, in an oval metal mount with tortoiseshell and brass scrolled frame.

$218 £110

A large old iron man trap of gin type, set with two large springs, overall length 52in.

$198 £100

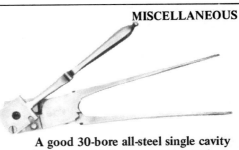

A Malayan painted carved wood kris stand in the form of a large seated frog with open mouth, seated on octagonal base with carved foliate patterns, height 18in. $208 £105

A good 30-bore all-steel single cavity bullet mould from a continental cased set, 6½in. overall, well formed arms and sprue cutter, with swollen shaped octagonal handle. $59 £30

A recruiting poster 'Remember Belgium Enlist Today', pictorial — Tommy with rifle. Poster No. 19, approx. 15 x 19½in. $40 £20

A recruiting poster 'Come Along Boys, Enlist Today', pictorial — Tommy marching. Poster No. 22, approx. 19½ x 29½in. $55 £28

Britain's lead models of Mountain Artillery Gun Detachment, four mules with gun parts, four dismounted gunners and mounted officer, no box. $97 £50

POWDER HORNS

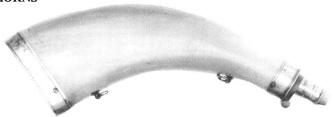

An early 19th century gun sized powder flask of flattened cow horn, brass screw topped graduated charger unit, brass capped base and mounted with two suspension rings. $59 £30

An 18th century military powder horn, 15in., sprung brass charger, turned brass nozzle cap for use as measure, turned ribbed brass base cap, brass hanging loops, red suspension cord. $69 £35

A late 18th century gunner's powder horn, brass nozzle and spring cut-off, two iron suspension rings, wooden base with screw-in plug, overall 13in. $89 £45

An Indian ivory topped recurved horn priming powder flask, 10in. overall, the ivory top carved in the form of an elephant's head with nozzle emanating from mouth, the body decorated with some silver pique work, complete with ivory stopper. $99 £50

An interesting late 18th century brass mounted powder horn, 9in., sprung brass charger of 'plunger' type, border engraved en suite with base.$103 £52

A large late 18th century cow horn powder flask, approximately 17in. overall, flanged charging nozzle to allow suspension cord attachment, wooden base plug pierced to admit coarsely threaded wooden filler bung, the body of the horn engraved 'Success to the British Arms' within scroll. $109 £55

A late 18th century military type cow horn powder flask, 11½in., sprung brass charger, two brass suspension rings, turned wooden base plug. $129 £65

An 18th century military powder horn, 15in., brass charger with wrap round spring, turned brass nozzle cap for use as measure, turned ribbed brass base cap, brass hanging loops, red suspension cord. $178 £90

A brass mounted cow horn powder flask of the type used with the Baker rifle, 10¼in. overall, brass charger and spring loaded cut-off, the brass base engraved 'C 29', with hanging loops and green cord. $317 £160

A brass mounted mid 17th century flattened cow horn powder flask, length overall 12in., the horn body decorated overall with engraved geometric circles, scallops, sun in splendour and foliate patterns.   **$416 £210**

A mid 17th century flattened cow horn powder flask, length overall 12in., the body engraved with medieval hunting scene, geometric designs and the letters 'SI', the iron top and bottom mounts restored and well aged.   **$495 £250**

A most attractive Bohemian carved stag horn powder flask, 7½in., carved with three deer moving through coniferous forest. Screw-off horn charger, silver hanging mounts, top mount made as oak leaves.   **$1,228 £620**

SABRETACHES

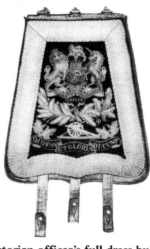

A Victorian officer's full dress bullion embroidered sabretache of The Royal Artillery, also three sabretache straps, complete with foul weather cover.
$158 £80

A Victorian officer's full dress bullion sabretache of The Edinburgh Artillery.
$317 £160

A Victorian officer's full dress embroidered sabretache of The Royal Artillery, 13in. x 10½in., blue cloth, gilt lace, embroidered Royal Arms, with its foul weather cover.$366 £185

A Victorian officer's full dress embroidered sabretache of The 19th (Princess of Wales') Hussars, in its foul weather cover. $396 £200

A Victorian officer's full dress embroidered sabretache of The 14th (King's) Hussars, scarlet cloth edged with gilt lace on yellow leather back. $396 £200

A Victorian officer's full dress embroidered sabretache of The Yorkshire Yeomanry Cavalry, scarlet cloth with broad silver lace border, complete with its scarlet leather foul weather case. $515 £260

A Victorian officer's full dress embroidered sabretache of The Queen's Own Royal Glasgow Yeomanry, 13½in. x 11½in. $594 £300

A Victorian officer's full dress embroidered sabretache of The Kent Yeomanry Cavalry, three attachment loops with scrolled white metal buckles. $752 £380

A Scottish highland shield targe or target, circa 1750, 16½in. diameter, wood covered with brown leather, with brass stud work in geometric rosettes and borders. Brass nail work forms owners initials T.A. and the name Clarinch around border. $416 £210

A good 18th century Scottish shield targe, 19½in. diameter of dished form, wood, covered with leather tooled with interlaced strapwork design, large brass central boss with four brass subsidiary bosses. Brass studded border. $554 £280

A bandsman's shoulder belt and pouch, probably French 3rd Empire, black patent leather, brass framed flaps with trophy of instruments device surmounted by Medusa head, wood liner, brass lyre badge on belt. $79 £40

A Victorian officer's full dress black patent leather pouch of The Life Guards, fine large, gilt, silver and enamel flap badge on crimson velvet backing, blind tooled inner pouch panel. $129 £65

A Victorian officer's full dress shoulder belt and pouch of The 10th (Prince of Wales's Own Royal) Hussars. $143 £72

A full dress embroidered shoulder belt and pouch of the Hampshire Artillery Volunteers, silvered mounts, silver embroidered flap device incorporating 'First Hants Artillery Volunteers'. $158 £80

A Victorian officer's black patent leather pouch of the Life Guards, large gilt, silvered and enamel flaps device on crimson backing, metal liner.
$158 £80

A Victorian officer's full dress pouch of The Dorset Artillery Volunteers, flap device incorporates the word 'Defence' over the cannon. White metal mounts.
$198 £100

A Victorian officer's full dress silver embroidered pouch of The Dorsetshire Volunteer Artillery, white metal mounts.
$198 £100

An officer's post 1902 full dress shoulder belt and patent leather pouch of The 1st Life Guards, gilt oak leaf lace belt with plain buckle, tip and slide and red flash cord.
$317 £160

An officer's shoulder belt plate of The Gordon Highlanders. $89 £45

An officer's shoulder belt plate of The Seaforth Highlanders. $110 £55

An officer's copper gilt rectangular shoulder belt plate of The Royal Marine Light Infantry, pre-1855. $119 £60

A Napoleonic brass shako plate of The 102nd Regt., diamond shaped, eagle with 'N' on central escutcheon. $139 £70

An officer's shoulder belt plate complete with its original buff leather shoulder belt and sword frog of The 20th (East Devonshire) Regt. $146 £74

A Georgian officer's silver rectangular shoulder belt plate, hallmarked (London) 1804. $158 £80

A Victorian officer's silver and gilt shoulder belt plate of The 1st (Renfrew) VB Argyll & Sutherland Highlanders. $158 £80

A Georgian pre-1801 brass oval shoulder belt plate of The Knole Volunteers, with 'GR' Royal Arms and title in scroll. $158 £80

An officer's rectangular shoulder belt plate of The 88th Regt., circa 1830-35. $168 £85

An officer's silvered and gilt rectangular shoulder belt plate of The 38th (1st Staffordshire) Regt. $168 £85

An officer's copper gilt shoulder belt plate of The 4th (King's Own) Regt., 1820/40.$178 £90

An officer's copper gilt rectangular shoulder belt plate of The 9th (The East Norfolk) Regt. of Foot, 1830-1855 pattern.$185 £90

A Victorian officer's copper silvered rectangular shoulder belt plate of The Donegal Militia. $195 £95

A Georgian officer's silver and gilt shoulder belt plate of The 54th (West Norfolk) Regt. $208 £105

An officer's silvered and gilt rectangular shoulder belt plate of The Royal Berkshire Militia. $238 £120

An officer's silver, oval shoulder belt plate of The Light Horse Volunteers of London and Westminster. $297 £150

An officer's copper gilt ornamental rococco design shoulder belt plate of The 59th (2nd Nottinghamshire) Regt. of Foot, pre-1855.$376 £190

A Georgian officer's silver (not HM) rectangular shoulder belt plate of The Royal Marines, circa 1780-1790. $515 £260

A male Malacca walking stick, 37in., turned, swollen, ivory top with good patina, foliate edged silver ferrule engraved 'Rogr Harling 1699'. Brass mounted steel tip. **$109 £55**

A Victorian toper's knotty walking stick, 36in., handle unscrews to reveal glass tube and glass. Silvered copper mounts, brass mounted steel tip. **$148 £75**

A Victorian toper's walking cane, 36in., handle unscrews to reveal glass tube and glass. Silvered copper mounts, steel tip. **$178 £90**

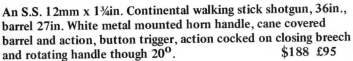

An S.S. 12mm x 1¾in. Continental walking stick shotgun, 36in., barrel 27in. White metal mounted horn handle, cane covered barrel and action, button trigger, action cocked on closing breech and rotating handle though 20°. **$188 £95**

A rare, late Victorian combined walking stick telescope, 35in., turned white metal top unscrews to reveal single drawer telescope. Rosewood shaft, white metal mounted steel tip. **$204 £103**

A good hallmarked (London 1831 'J.L.') silver topped walking stick, embossed with crowned 'WR' above union flowers and Royal motto, foliage and straps. Ebony shaft. **$396 £200**

TSUBAS

A pierced iron ko-umetada style tsuba, of circular form pierced and carved within the rim with a kiku-form design. $38 £19

A pierced iron tsuba of irregular form depicting a stylised kiku bloom in positive silhouette.
$51 £26

An iron ito-sukashi tsuba of mokko form, pierced in ito style with the slightly raised rim with two shuttlecocks and a bat, two ryu-hitsu. $55 £28

A circular iron tsuba, carved with a flowering prunus stump in relief, details in silver and gold. $55 £28

A Bushu School iron tsuba of oval form, decorated in kebori ito-sukashi and gold nunome, pierced with single hitsu-ana.
$57 £29

An iron yoshiro-zogan tsuba, of rounded rectangular form pierced with enlarged hitsu-ana.
$57 £29

An iron ito-sukashi tsuba of rounded rectangular form, pierced with a leafy bamboo tree and ryu-hitsu.
$59 £30

A pierced iron ito-sukashi tsuba of circular form, very finely pierced with stylised river, flowers and leaves. $59 £30

A thick, circular pierced iron sukashi tsuba, depicting formalised kiku, foliage and a bird, single ryu-hitsu. $61 £31

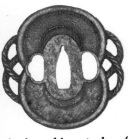

A pierced iron tsuba of irregular form, chiselled to represent a tsuzumi, pierced ryu-hitsu, raised rim with entwined ropes. $63 £32

A pierced iron Kinai style tsuba of circular form, carved in marubori with prunus and pines around two thatched buildings. $63 £32

An unusual iron tsuba of oval form, pierced with single hitsu-ana and applied in shakudo, shibuichi and gold. $67 £34

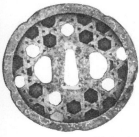

An iron tsuba of lobed circular form, decorated within raised rim with a design of hexagons, rim with traces of gold nunome decoration. $67 £34

A shire mono tsuba of mokko form, comprising two shakudo plates on a copper core, each plate stamped with Kirimon in gilt relief. $67 £34

A convex iron tsuba inside with dark green, black and gold guru lacquering, outside silver damascened. $69 £35

A pierced iron tanto tsuba, chiselled with two mushrooms and a piece of grass. $79 £40

A Nara style oval iron tsuba, carved with a Chinese sage and two boy attendants. Details in shakudo, gold and silver. $79 £40

An iron tsuba of mokko form, chiselled in relief with chokwaro sennin releasing the horse spirit from a gourd by waterfall. $83 £42

TSUBAS

A large pierced iron ito-sukashi tsuba, signed Muneyyuki, of circular form, single pierced riubutsu. $83 £42

A Nara style iron tsuba of mokko form, carved in relief with Gama Sennin and Tekkai Sennin. Details in shakudo and gold. $83 £42

A circular pierced iron sukashi tsuba, tri-sected with pierced riubutsu and three Soshu characters in positive silhouette. $89 £45

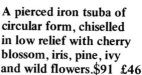

A pierced iron tsuba of circular form, chiselled in low relief with cherry blossom, iris, pine, ivy and wild flowers.$91 £46

An iron Nara School waki-zashi tsuba, inlaid with sha-kudo, copper, gilt and silver man punting down river past reedy banks. $99 £50

A pierced irom mokko wakizashi tsuba, chiselled with round lobes and leaves above, plugged with copper top and bottom. $110 £55

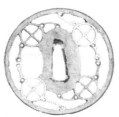

A pierced iron tsuba, of circular form, design incorporates two pierced horse bits in positive silhouette, inlaid with gold. $115 £58

An iron tsuba of mokko form, chiselled and inlaid with duck catcher by river. Pierced riubutsu, details inlaid with gold, silver, shakudo and shibuichi. $119 £60

A chiselled circular iron tsuba, 6½cm., with a child watering his bullock by a stream at moonrise. $119 £60

A shakudo oval tsuba, pierced with two riubutsu, inlaid with engraved silver toy duck, engraved gold and silver flowers. $119 £60

An interesting pierced circular iron tsuba, 6½cm., chiselled with a rabbit in relief inhabiting the moon above a wavy sea.
$119 £60

An iron Nara School wakizashi tsuba, inlaid with shakudo, copper, gilt and silver chrysanthemums and butterflies. $138 £70

A large iron tsuba, 8½cm., pierced with riubutsu and inlaid with shakudo chopper, gilt handle and gin gunome hamon.$139 £70

A pierced iron kyur-sukashi tsuba, delicate design incorporates two cherries, the design inverted in negative silhouette. $168 £85

A large iron tsuba of mokko form, inlaid in silver with Benkei and Tenguking by waterfall. $178 £90

A Japanese brass tsuba signed Hamano Hironao, carved, chiselled and engraved with Choki breathing out his spirit beneath pine tree by waterfall.
$208 £105

A large, squared iron tsuba, chiselled with waves and inlaid in silver and copper chidori and waves.
$218 £110

A darkly patinated shakudo tsuba, signed Shigemitsu, two pierced riubutsu. Details in gold, silver and shibuichi. $297 £150

273

A pre 1855 officer's coatee of The 42nd Native Infantry, scarlet buff facings, double-breasted, gilt buttons bearing 'XLII' within crowned wreath and circle, gilt embroidered loops to collar and slashed cuffs. $139 £70

An Indian Army officer's pre 1855 coatee of The 15th Native Infantry, scarlet and orange facings, gilt embroidered loops to collar, slashed cuffs and skirts, gilt buttons bearing 'XV' within a circle, inscribed 'Regiment' on a crowned star.$139 £70

An officer's short coatee, circa 1808, of The Aberdeenshire Volunteers, scarlet with yellow facings, high sloping collar, double-breasted with turn-back lapels, short skirts with white turn-backs and no ornaments. $158 £80

An officer's short coatee, 1808-16, of The 2nd Regt. Aberdeenshire Local Militia, scarlet with yellow facings, double-breasted with turn-back lapels, high sloping collar, silvered, slightly convex buttons. $188 £95

An officer's pre 1855 coatee of The 70th (The Surrey) Regt., black velvet facings, plain gilt buttons with '70' within circle, embroidered skirt ornaments.   **$218 £110**

An officer's coatee, circa 1808, of The Royal Edinburgh Volunteers, scarlet with blue facings, high sloping collar, turn-back front fastened with hooks and eyes, double row of buttons, gilt shoulder chain wings, gilt metal skirt ornaments, pockets at waist above skirts.   **$218 £110**

An officer's short coatee, 1812-16, of The West Renfrew Local Militia, scarlet with yellow facings, double-breasted with turn-back lapels, high sloping collar, gilt buttons.   **$218 £110**

A good pre 1881 bandsman's tunic of The 4th (The King's Own) Regt. of Foot, blue facings, pointed cuffs, blue and white braid trimmings and wings.   **$267 £135**

An officer's double-breasted coatee, circa 1808-1816, possibly staff or militia, scarlet with very dark blue facings, stand-up collar with turn-back lapels, two rows of eight buttons. $297 £150

A good pre 1881 bandsman's tunic of The 33rd (The Duke of Wellington's) Regt., scarlet facings, slashed cuffs, red and white braid trimmings and wings. $297 £150

An officer's coatee, 1806-16, probably Oldham Local Militia, scarlet with blue facings, double-breasted with turn-back lapels, high sloping collar, gilt, slightly convex buttons, plain gilt lace strap epaulettes. $307 £155

An officer's pre 1855 coatee of The North Durham Militia, scarlet with white facings, silver lace loops to collar and slashed cuffs, handsome silvered buttons bearing crowned 'NDM' in high relief within scalloped border. $327 £165

An early 19th century tunic of The Royal Archers, The King's Bodyguard, hard tartan cloth with green silk lining, edging and puffed shoulders with braid trim, heavy outer skirts and tails, silvered, open backed, slightly convex buttons. $346 £175

A good 1848-1855 officer's coatee of The Northumberland (Light Infantry) Militia, double-breasted, scarlet with white facings, silvered lace loops to collar, slashed cuffs, tails with embroidered stringed bugle, silvered buttons bearing motto title. $356 £180

An 1845-1855 officer's coatee of The 16th (Bedfordshire) Regt. of Foot, double-breasted, white facings, gilt lace loops to collar, slashed cuffs, tails embroidered '16' within title on star, gilt buttons. **$356 £180**

A scarce pre 1855 other rank's double-breasted coatee of The 83rd Regiment of Foot, scarlet with yellow facings, white cloth turn-backs, white lace loops to collar and cuffs, pewter buttons with crown over '83' within wreath.

$376 £190

An officer's coatee, circa 1812, scarlet with blue facings and front fastened by hooks and eyes with gilt embroidered loops in pairs with buttons bearing wreathed crossed baton and sword.
$416 £210

An officer's coatee, circa 1840, of The Hertfordshire Yeomanry Cavalry, rifle green with scarlet facings and plastron front, collar and cuffs with rifle regiment type black braided tracery, silvered closed back buttons.**$495 £250**

An officer's jacket, circa 1805, of The Berwickshire Yeomanry Cavalry, scarlet, single-breasted and cut almost straight at the waist, dark green facings, silver braid trimmings, three rows of silvered ball buttons. $550 £270

A Sergeant s coatee, circa 1808, of an unidentified infantry volunteer unit, single-breasted, scarlet with blue facings, silver lace trim, including eight loops to chest in pairs with buttons.$554 £280

A rare pre-1851 officer's coatee of The 6th Dragoon Guards (Carabiniers), scarlet single-breasted with nine convex, closed-back buttons to front, white cloth facings and turn-backs to skirts, two gold lace loops to collar.$594 £300

A Victorian uniform of The Royal Company of Archers, green tartan tunic with silver and pale blue cord and bead trimmings, loops to chest and cuffs, green velvet facings and shoulder wings with bullion tassels. $792 £400

A Light Company officer's short coatee, 1812-1816, of The North York Militia, scarlet with black velvet facings and front with silver lace loops, hooks and eyes fastenings, silver buttons bearing the rose within crowned garter and inscribed 'North York', silvered chain wings with silver bullion tassels and white metal disc bearing gilt stringed bugle. $1,010 £510

An interesting all steel African throwing weapon, 24½in., head with multiple spikes and crescent, etched with Khoranic inscriptions and inlaid with brass script and borders. Crocodile skin covered grip. $89 £45

A George IV painted Police truncheon of the City of Bath, 14in., painted with town arms. Turned wood grip. $103 £52

An Indo-Persian all steel war hammer zaghnal, 18¾in., head 8½in., chiselled with flowers, foliage and stags couchant, heightened with gold damascene, on its steel haft. $107 £54

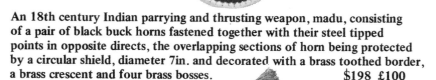

An 18th century Indian parrying and thrusting weapon, madu, consisting of a pair of black buck horns fastened together with their steel tipped points in opposite directs, the overlapping sections of horn being protected by a circular shield, diameter 7in. and decorated with a brass toothed border, a brass crescent and four brass bosses. $198 £100

A set of Japanese arrows in quiver with lacquered wooden support for mounting on bow, seven flighted arrows with steel heads, contained in leather quiver embossed with gilt mon. $317 £160

PERCUSSION
WEAPONS

ALARM GUN

A good, all steel Reuthe's patent double-barrelled percussion alarm gun, 8in., cast with 'F. Reuthe's Patent, May 12 1857', muzzle numbered '3122'. Cast fluted handle and tapering octagonal barrels. Bi-furcated spear pointed line slide for trip wires. $297 £150

BLUNDERBUSSES

A brass barrelled percussion blunderbuss, circa 1790, converted from flint-lock by drum and nipple method, 29in., swamped barrel 13¾in., full-stocked, stepped bolted lock engraved 'Sanders'. Brass mounts of regulation military type. $544 £275

A large steel barrelled Military pattern ship's percussion swivel blunderbuss, 39½in., barrel 23½in., with swamped muzzle and London proofs, slightly rounded lock of late flintlock form stamped 'Tower' and 'Gilks Wilson & Co. London', plain fullstock, the fore-end pierced for swivel mount, regulation pattern brass mounts with an Enfield pattern steel ramrod. $594 £300

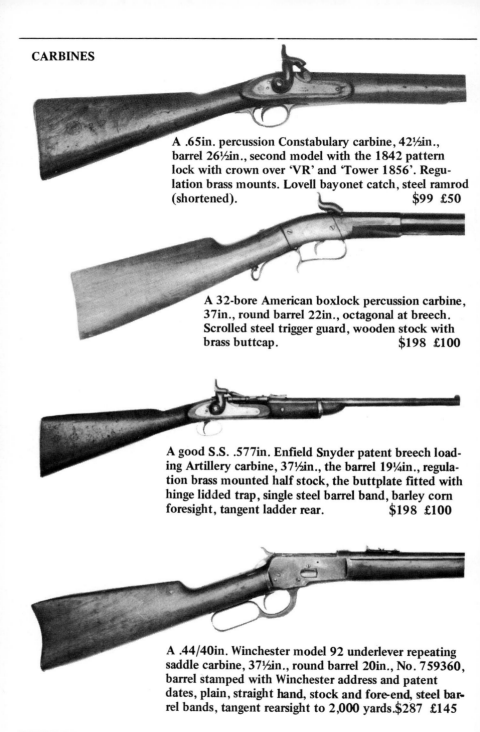

A .65in. percussion Constabulary carbine, 42½in., barrel 26½in., second model with the 1842 pattern lock with crown over 'VR' and 'Tower 1856'. Regulation brass mounts. Lovell bayonet catch, steel ramrod (shortened). **$99 £50**

A 32-bore American boxlock percussion carbine, 37in., round barrel 22in., octagonal at breech. Scrolled steel trigger guard, wooden stock with brass buttcap. **$198 £100**

A good S.S. .577in. Enfield Snyder patent breech loading Artillery carbine, 37½in., the barrel 19¼in., regulation brass mounted half stock, the buttplate fitted with hinge lidded trap, single steel barrel band, barley corn foresight, tangent ladder rear. **$198 £100**

A .44/40in. Winchester model 92 underlever repeating saddle carbine, 37½in., round barrel 20in., No. 759360, barrel stamped with Winchester address and patent dates, plain, straight hand, stock and fore-end, steel barrel bands, tangent rearsight to 2,000 yards. **$287 £145**

A scarce 45/70in. Winchester Hotchkiss first model bolt action repeating carbine, 44in., round barrel 24in., No 15921, receiver with address and patent dates to July 23 1878, one-piece walnut stock with steel buttplate, trigger guard, saddle rings and single spring retained barrel band, bolt lock and safety mounted on right side of stock. $297 £150

A .50 Maynard's patent breech loading percussion carbine, No 18287, 37in., rifled barrel 20in., hinged rearsight to 500 yards. Lanyard ring on saddle bar. Boxlock action, underlever fastening. Butt struck with inspector's initials 'J.M.' and 'G.W.S.'. $317 £160

A good 16-bore percussion Yeomanry carbine, 36in., barrel 20in., Tower proved, full-stocked, lock engraved 'Tower 1848' with crowned 'VR' cypher, regulation brass mounts, swivel ramrod, trigger guard bow engraved 'UYC. 12' (Uxbridge Yeomanry Cavalry), steel saddle bar and ring. $356 £180

A .577in. two band rifled percussion Cavalry carbine by Barnett, 37in., barrel 21in., London proved, leaf sights to 300 yards. Full-stocked, lock engraved 'Barnett London'. Regulation pattern brass mounts, steel barrel bands, swivel ramrod and saddle bar with lanyard ring.$356 £180

A scarce 44/40in. Winchester, model 1892, underlever repeating trapper carbine, 35¼in., barrel 18in., No. 321439, plain wooden stock with steel furniture, full length tube magazine secured to underside of barrel by two bands, pinned blade foresight, ladder rear to 900 yards, action with fitted saddle ring to left side, King's patent loading gate.
$436 £220

A 14-bore French Military percussion carbine, 38½in., barrel 23in., octagonal breech, ladder rearsight to 600 yards, bayonet bar at muzzle. Half-stocked, lock engraved 'Mfe Rle'. Regulation brass mounts, steel sling swivels and ramrod. $475 £240

A rare 6-shot 11mm. Continental double action revolving carbine, 41in., barrel 25½in., Birmingham black powder proof, straight hand chequered stock with blank white metal escutcheon, steel buttplate and scrolled trigger guard, gate loading and rod ejection, octagonal blued barrel with tangent rearsight.
$515 £260

A scarce 12-bore Victoria pattern percussion carbine by Lacy, 42in., barrel 26in., with most features of the first model except for side action lock and without break-off breech, brass furniture, swivel ramrod, block rearsight, side bar. $535 £270

A .577in. model 1853 Artillery percussion carbine, 40in., barrel 24in., Tower proved, sight to 300yards. Full-stocked, regulation brass mounts, buttcap tang engraved 'V. HA ll', steel barrel bands, sling swivels and ramrod, long experimental type bayonet lug at muzzle. $634 £320

A scarce .44in. rimfire Winchester model 1866 under-lever repeating carbine, 39½in., round barrel 20in., No. 78150, walnut stock with heavy brass crescent buttplate, plain fore-end with single barrel band and full length tube magazine, muzzle barrel band with integral foresight, flip-over aperture rear to 500 yards. $653 £330

A rare .44in. rimfire Winchester model 1866 third model underlever repeating carbine, 38½in., round barrel 20in., No. 120092, plain walnut stock and fore-end with brass buttplate, fitted with sliding trap cover, full length tube magazine, flip-over rearsight to 200 yards. $911 £460

A scarce 18-bore Norwegian percussion dog lock Military pistol carbine with detachable shoulder stock, 26½in. overall. Rifled barrel 9in., stamped 'R66. 900' with military and London proof marks. Full-stocked, regulation brass mounts, buttcap stamped 900. Sprung brass mounted detachable shoulder stock with lanyard ring under butt. $1,470 £700

DERRINGERS

An S.S. .41in. rimfire Brown 'Southerner' derringer, 4¾in., part octagonal barrel 2½in., No. 7036, bronze frame with spur trigger, polished wooden grips and side swing barrel, white metal foresight.
$40 £20

A scarce S.S. .41in. rimfire National derringer, 5¼in., barrel 2½in., No. 3107, chequered rosewood grips to bird's head butt, bronze frame with spur trigger, side swing barrel with thumb latch on right side.
$59 £30

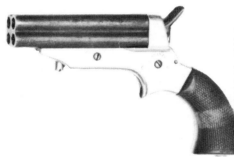

A four-barrelled .30in. rimfire Sharp's model 2 pepperbox derringer, 5½in., barrel 3in., No. 75, frame stamped, moulded diced hard rubber grips, plated bronze frame with spur trigger, hammer with rotating striker, fluted barrel group.
$59 £30

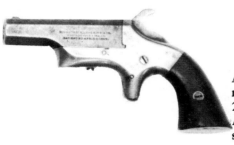

An S.S. .41in. rimfire 'Southerner' derringer, 4¾in., part octagonal barrel 2½in., No. 3851, stamped 'Merimark Arms & Mfg Co.', bronze frame with spur trigger, polished wooden grips and side swing barrel, white metal foresight.
$79 £40

A good .41in. rimfire Colt No. 3 Thuer single action derringer, 4¾in., barrel 2½in., No. 9536, polished rosewood grips to bird's head butt, nickel plated bronze frame, blued barrel with white metal foresight and stamped 'Colt' in large letters. $89 £45

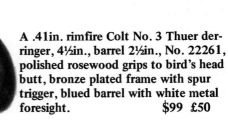

A scarce 4-shot .32in. rimfire Starr button trigger Derringer 5½in., fluted barrel group 2¼in., sideplate stamped 'Starr's Pat's May 10 1864', rosewood grips, bronze frame with circular sideplate, tip-up barrels fired alternatively by rotating striker, mounted in standing breech, unusual steel button trigger and side mounted hammer. $99 £50

A .41in. rimfire Colt No. 3 Thuer derringer, 4½in., barrel 2½in., No. 22261, polished rosewood grips to bird's head butt, bronze plated frame with spur trigger, blued barrel with white metal foresight. $99 £50

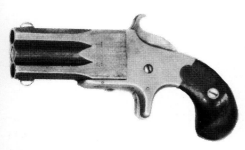

A 2-shot superimposed 32in,. rimfire Frank Wesson derringer, 5in., fluted barrel group 2½in., No. 396, rosewood grips to bird's head butt, bronze frame with spur trigger turn over barrels each with white metal blade foresight and located by spring latch at bottom strap. $99 £50

DERRINGERS

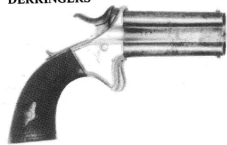

A scarce double barrelled superimposed .297in. rimfire Woodward patent derringer, 5in., barrels 2¼in., No. 779, chequered wooden grips to angular butt, silver plated steel frame with spur trigger, turn-over barrels with latch in front of trigger. $99 £50

An S.S. .41in. rimfire National derringer, 5¼in., barrel 2½., No. 8165, chequered wooden grips to bird's head butt, scroll engraved steel frame with spur trigger, side swing barrel and latched with sprung bolt on right side. $109 £55

A four-barrelled .30in. rimfire Sharp's pepperbox derringer pistol, No. 2493, wooden grips, bronze frame with spur trigger, fluted barrel group. $139 £70

A presentation .41in. rimfire Colt No 3 Thuer derringer, 4½in., barrel 2½., No. 26067, twopiece polished ivory grips to bird's head butt, plated bronze factory scroll engraved frame with spur trigger, the barrel sides and muzzle well scroll engraved and nickel plated overall. $238 £120

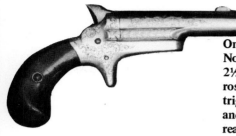

One of a pair of S.S. .41 in. rimfire Colt
No. 3 Thuer derringers, 4¾in., barrels
2½in., Nos. 41843 and 46505, polished
rosewood grips to bird's head butt, spur
trigger, swing out barrels for loading
and ejection, blade foresight hammer
rear. $307 £155

A good S.S. .41 in. rimfire Colt No. 1
all steel derringer, 4¾in., ribbed barrel
2½in., No. 2298, lightly curved grip
with three chequered panels, spur
trigger, body with floral spray engraving, chequered trigger, down
swinging barrel secured with button
latch on right side. $495 £250

A rare single shot .41 in. rimfire
Colt No. 1 National derringer,
4¾in., barrel 2½in., No. 1623,
all steel construction, sharply
curved butt with a small chequered panel to each side and
a large chequered panel to the
rear, ribbed ovoid barrel.
                    $693 £350

A rare .41 in. rimfire Colt No. 1 National derringer, 4¾in., barrel 2½in.,
No. 4066, all steel construction,
with sharply curved butt engraved
with chequered panels and integral
with action, ribbed ovoid barrel,
knife blade extractor. $713 £360

EPROUVETTES

An 18th century hand ignited brass powder tester eprouvette, 8¼in., overall, wheel engraved with graduations 1-5 marked off with quarter divisions. Turned wooden grip. $139 £70

A mid 18th century brass hand ignited powder tester eprouvette, 5½in., wheel engraved with 1-5 graduations. Bulbous wooden butt. $495 £250

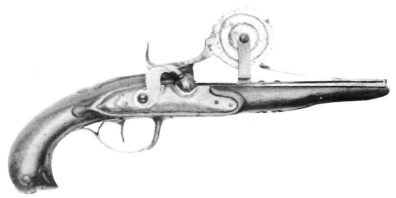

A good French percussion powder tester eprouvette, circa 1760, converted from flintlock, 10in., full-stocked, sprung graduated wheel engraved with graduations 1-14, border engraved lock, foliate finialled trigger guard.
$673 £340

A very rare barrel from a late 16th century English 14-bore matchlock musket, 46½in., octagonal breech section 17¾in., with raised ribs dividing sections. Inlaid with two raised stepped octagonal brass bands. $198 £100

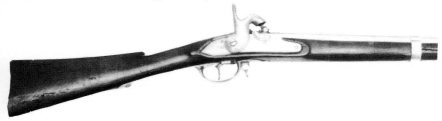

A 12-bore Russian Military percussion musket, 57in., barrel 41in., dated 1838, converted from flintlock, full-stocked, brass mounts including three barrel bands, sling swivels, the buttplate tang impressed with Imperial Eagle and cypher of Nicholas I in centre, all the mounts dated 1838. $257 £130

A good 14-bore German percussion musket, 57in., barrel 40in., Liege proved with inspector's marks. Full-stocked, regulation steel mounts, sling swivel and ramrod, barrel bands secured by sprung clips, carved cheek-piece. $297 £150

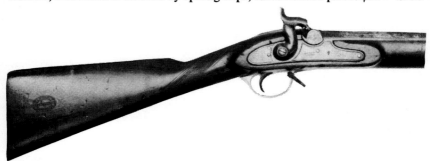

A massive 4-bore Military type percussion musket, 47in., barrel 30in., London proved, with bore size '4' stamped between proofs. Full-stocked, twin line border engraved lock stamped 'Barnett London'. Regulation brass mounts, steel swing swivels. $495 £250

A scarce 22-bore Austrian cadet's tubelock Military musket, 47in., barrel 33in., with military stamps. Full-stocked, captive anvil in hinged bolster facilitating insertion of tube. Regulation brass mounts.
$594 £300

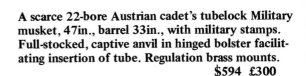

A 28-bore Austrian Military type percussion musket, possibly built for a child, 37¾in., round barrel 26½in., numbered 325 at breech. Full-stocked with brass mounts, including buttplate, trigger guard and three barrel bands. $634 £320

A good, scarce 11-bore Brown Bess Military musket converted to pellet lock by Hayward, 55in., barrel 39in., Tower proved. Full-stocked, lockplate engraved 'Tower Hayward', with crowned 'GR', converted with tube fed bolster and tangent slide feed system. Regulation brass mounts, two steel sling swivels and steel ramrod.
$840 £420

A good 20-bore Japanese matchlock musket, 35½in., tapered, heavy iron barrel 22½in., inlaid with large butterfly mons, octagonal swollen muzzle, block rearsight, Full-stocked in magnolia wood, back-action brass lock and serpent. $1,584 £800

A 50-bore Allen & Thurber boxlock percussion pistol, 11½in., half octagonal, turn-off barrel 8in., No. 5106, round frame, two-piece, bag-shaped wooden grips, hammer off-set for sighting. $148 £75

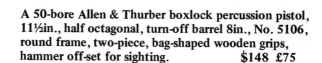

A double barrelled 12mm Continental underlever opening PF pistol, 8in, twist barrels 3¾in, No. 135, fluted grip with steel buttplate, spurred trigger guard, tip-down barrels. $168 £85

A good S.S. 8mm. French Flobert type Saloon pistol, 15½in., octagonal barrel 10in., finely chequered walnut grip with case colour hardened buttcap, scroll engraved trigger guard with finger spur. $198 £100

A double barrelled 20-bore percussion Howdah pistol by R. H. Bate, 13in., browned twist barrels 7in., Birmingham proved. Chequered walnut full-stock with horn buttplate, blank white metal escutcheon, large bow steel trigger guard. $396 £200

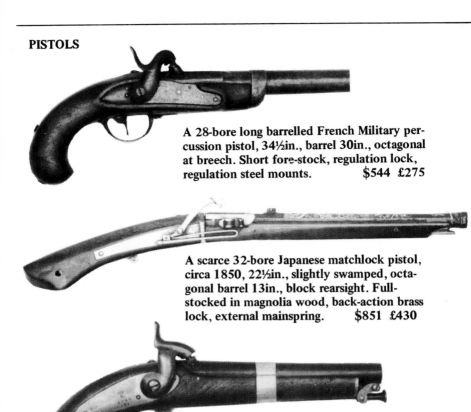

A 28-bore long barrelled French Military percussion pistol, 34½in., barrel 30in., octagonal at breech. Short fore-stock, regulation lock, regulation steel mounts. **$544 £275**

A scarce 32-bore Japanese matchlock pistol, circa 1850, 22½in., slightly swamped, octagonal barrel 13in., block rearsight. Full-stocked in magnolia wood, back-action brass lock, external mainspring. **$851 £430**

A Norwegian 19-bore, back-action, side hammer percussion Naval pistol, 11¾in., barrel 6½in. Full-stocked, single brass barrel band, strap, trigger guard and buttcap. Lanyard ring on butt, swivel ramrod. **$911 £460**

A very rare 6-shot double action 7mm. pinfire Continental harmonica pistol 5½in., barrel group 2¾in., No. 821, plain wooden grips to bird's head butt. **$1,782 £900**

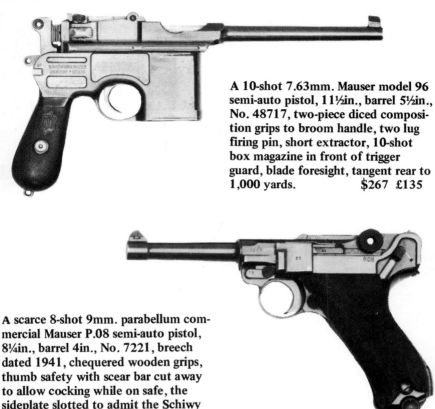

A 10-shot 7.63mm. Mauser model 96 semi-auto pistol, 11½in., barrel 5½in., No. 48717, two-piece diced composition grips to broom handle, two lug firing pin, short extractor, 10-shot box magazine in front of trigger guard, blade foresight, tangent rear to 1,000 yards. $267 £135

A scarce 8-shot 9mm. parabellum commercial Mauser P.08 semi-auto pistol, 8¼in., barrel 4in., No. 7221, breech dated 1941, chequered wooden grips, thumb safety with scear bar cut away to allow cocking while on safe, the sideplate slotted to admit the Schiwy scear safety which is rivetted to the receiver beside the cover plate.
$406 £205

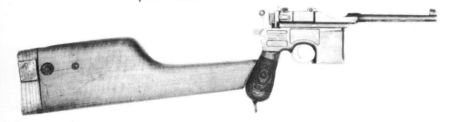

A good 10-shot 9mm. Oberndorf Mauser model 1896-1912 semi-auto Military pistol, 11¾in., barrel 5½in., No. 104259, ribbed wooden grips with impressed red '9', with fitted lanyard ring, thumb safety, tangent rearsight to 500 yards, short extractor and two lug firing pin.
$455 £230

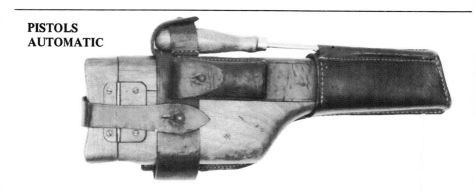

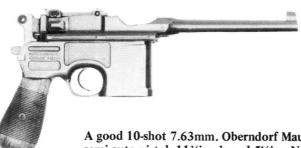

A good 10-shot 7.63mm. Oberndorf Mauser model 1896-1912 semi-auto pistol, 11¾in., barrel 5½in., No. 397878, ribbed wooden grip, second pattern safety, short extractor and two lug striker, small ring hammer and machined side panels, tangent rearsight to 1,000 metres contained in its wooden shoulder stock holster with leather harness and housing clearing rod and spare magazine spring. **$455 £230**

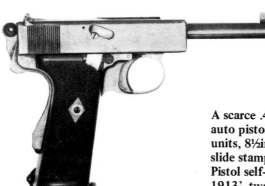

A scarce .455in. Webley Mark I semi-auto pistol as used by Royal Naval units, 8½in., barrel 5in., No. 769, slide stamped 'Webley & Scott Ltd., Pistol self-loading .455 Mark I N. 1913', two-piece diced composition grips with fitted lanyard ring and magazine release. **$475 £240**

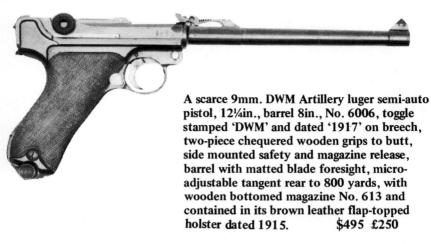

A scarce 9mm. DWM Artillery luger semi-auto pistol, 12¼in., barrel 8in., No. 6006, toggle stamped 'DWM' and dated '1917' on breech, two-piece chequered wooden grips to butt, side mounted safety and magazine release, barrel with matted blade foresight, micro-adjustable tangent rear to 800 yards, with wooden bottomed magazine No. 613 and contained in its brown leather flap-topped holster dated 1915. $495 £250

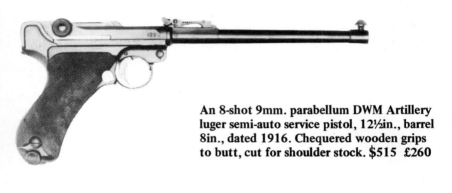

An 8-shot 9mm. parabellum DWM Artillery luger semi-auto service pistol, 12½in., barrel 8in., dated 1916. Chequered wooden grips to butt, cut for shoulder stock. $515 £260

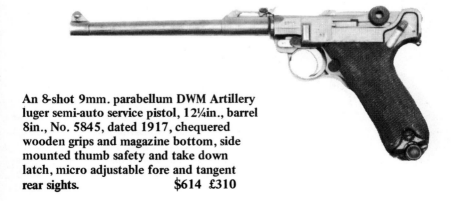

An 8-shot 9mm. parabellum DWM Artillery luger semi-auto service pistol, 12¼in., barrel 8in., No. 5845, dated 1917, chequered wooden grips and magazine bottom, side mounted thumb safety and take down latch, micro adjustable fore and tangent rear sights. $614 £310

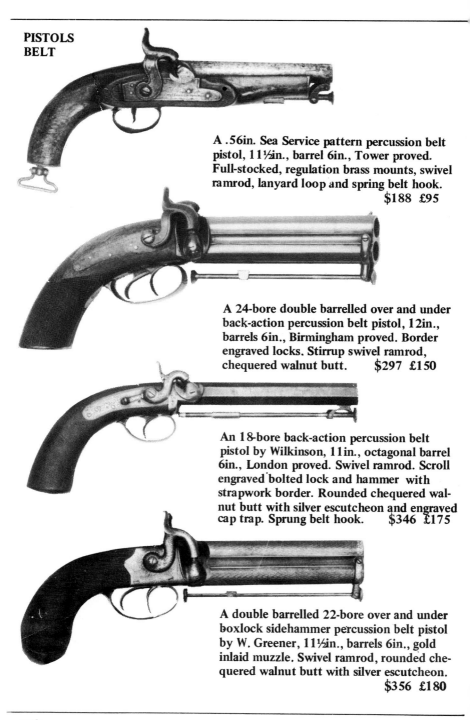

A .56in. Sea Service pattern percussion belt pistol, 11½in., barrel 6in., Tower proved. Full-stocked, regulation brass mounts, swivel ramrod, lanyard loop and spring belt hook.

$188 £95

A 24-bore double barrelled over and under back-action percussion belt pistol, 12in., barrels 6in., Birmingham proved. Border engraved locks. Stirrup swivel ramrod, chequered walnut butt. $297 £150

An 18-bore back-action percussion belt pistol by Wilkinson, 11in., octagonal barrel 6in., London proved. Swivel ramrod. Scroll engraved bolted lock and hammer with strapwork border. Rounded chequered walnut butt with silver escutcheon and engraved cap trap. Sprung belt hook. $346 £175

A double barrelled 22-bore over and under boxlock sidehammer percussion belt pistol by W. Greener, 11½in., barrels 6in., gold inlaid muzzle. Swivel ramrod, rounded chequered walnut butt with silver escutcheon.

$356 £180

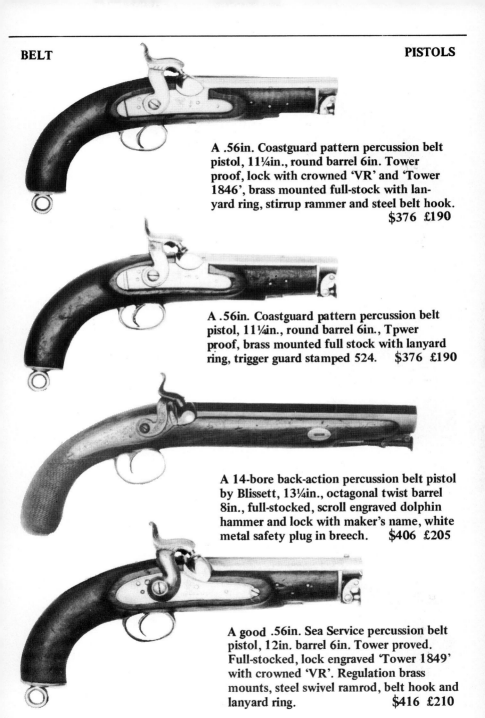

A .56in. Coastguard pattern percussion belt pistol, 11¼in., round barrel 6in. Tower proof, lock with crowned 'VR' and 'Tower 1846', brass mounted full-stock with lanyard ring, stirrup rammer and steel belt hook. $376 £190

A .56in. Coastguard pattern percussion belt pistol, 11¼in., round barrel 6in., Tpwer proof, brass mounted full stock with lanyard ring, trigger guard stamped 524. $376 £190

A 14-bore back-action percussion belt pistol by Blissett, 13¼in., octagonal twist barrel 8in., full-stocked, scroll engraved dolphin hammer and lock with maker's name, white metal safety plug in breech. $406 £205

A good .56in. Sea Service percussion belt pistol, 12in. barrel 6in. Tower proved. Full-stocked, lock engraved 'Tower 1849' with crowned 'VR'. Regulation brass mounts, steel swivel ramrod, belt hook and lanyard ring. $416 £210

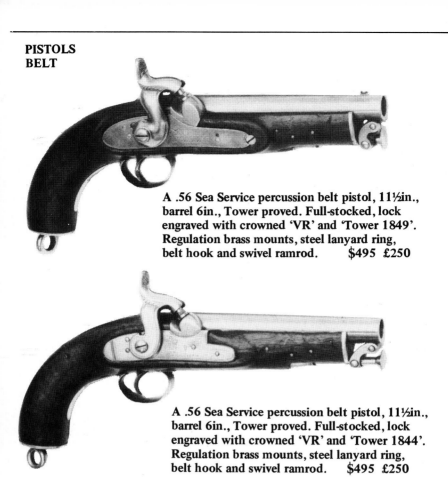

A .56 Sea Service percussion belt pistol, 11½in.,
barrel 6in., Tower proved. Full-stocked, lock
engraved with crowned 'VR' and 'Tower 1849'.
Regulation brass mounts, steel lanyard ring,
belt hook and swivel ramrod. $495 £250

A .56 Sea Service percussion belt pistol, 11½in.,
barrel 6in., Tower proved. Full-stocked, lock
engraved with crowned 'VR' and 'Tower 1844'.
Regulation brass mounts, steel lanyard ring,
belt hook and swivel ramrod. $495 £250

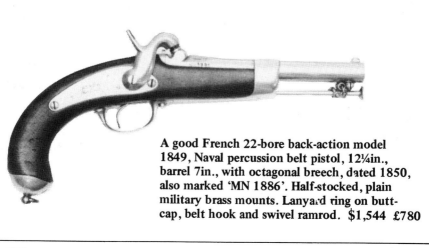

A good French 22-bore back-action model
1849, Naval percussion belt pistol, 12¼in.,
barrel 7in., with octagonal breech, dated 1850,
also marked 'MN 1886'. Half-stocked, plain
military brass mounts. Lanyard ring on buttcap, belt hook and swivel ramrod. $1,544 £780

A 13-bore model 1822 French military percussion Cavalry pistol, 13½in., barrel 8in., stamped 'Cie, 17-6-A, 1968', engraved '1822 bis' on barrel tang. Half-stocked, lock faintly engraved 'Mre de St Etienne'. Regulation brass mounts, stock stamped '1968', steel lanyard ring.   **$420 £200**

A 13-bore French model 1822 military percussion Cavalry pistol, 13¾in., rifled barrel 7¾in., stamped '1825, 2008c de C*M', barrel engraved 'Mle 1822 bis'. Halfstocked, lock engraved 'Mre Rle de Mutzig'. Regulation brass mounts struck with factory marks, anchor struck on buttcap denoting naval requisition, steel lanyard ring and shovel ended ramrod.   **$535 £270**

A fine .22-bore model 1851 Prussian percussion Cavalry holster pistol, 15in., round cannon mouth, comb sighted, barrel with octagonal breech 8¾in. and raised groove rearsight. Nipple protector operates on an external spring (as for frizzen), brass furniture, flat steel sideplate, bright blued trigger.   **$2,079 £1,050**

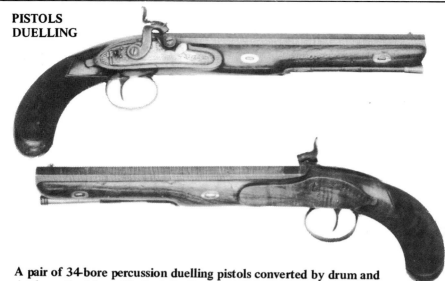

A pair of 34-bore percussion duelling pistols converted by drum and nipple method from flintlock by Dunderdale Mabson & Labron, 15in., heavy octagonal, browned twist barrels 10in., engraved 'London' at breech. Full-stocked, stepped bolted detented locks. Engraved pinapple finialled trigger guards. $1,188 £600

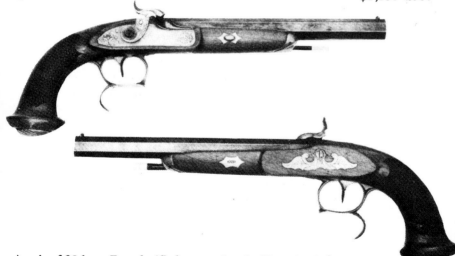

A pair of 32-bore French rifled percussion duelling pistols by Martiny of Marseilles, 15¾in., octagonal, heavy rifled barrels 8¼in., numbered 1 and 2 in gold. Half-stocked, locks silver inlaid 'Ma(r)tiny a Marseille'. Engraved white metal furniture, spurred trigger guards, foliate trigger guard finials. Hinged cap traps in butts with fluted lids. Ivory tipped whalebone ramrods with steel tips. Scale carved grips. $1,980 £1,000

A good pair of 34-bore percussion duelling pistols by Henry Probin, circa 1830, 15½in., octagonal twist barrels 10in., silver foresights and inlaid twin breech lines. Half-stocked, foliate engraved bolted detented locks with 'Probin' set triggers. Foliate engraved steel trigger guards. silver fore-end caps, barrel wedge plates, safety plug and escutcheons. Brass tipped wooden ramrods, rounded chequered butt. Contained in their green beize lined fitted mahogany case.

$2,970 £1,500

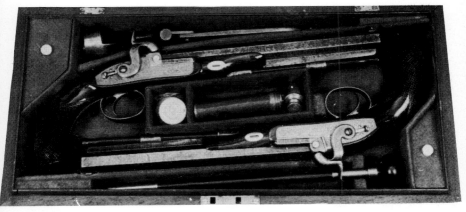

A fine pair of 38-bore percussion duelling pistols by Jno Manton, No. 9523, circa 1827, 14¼in., octagonal twist hair rifled barrels 9¼in., foliated engraved breeches with safety plug. Half-stocked, detented bolted locks. Foliate engraved trigger guards, pineapple finials, serial numbers on bow. Horn forecaps, silver barrel wedge plates and escutcheons, horn tipped wooden ramrods, rounded chequered butts. Contained in their green beize lined mahogany fitted case. $5,544 £2,800

A French 20-bore percussion back-action, sidehammer Gendarmerie pistol, 9¼in., barrel 5in. Threequarter-stocked, plain steel mounts, lockplate engraved 'Mre Nle De Mutzig' with crowned 'K' stamp, bird's head butt with plain steel buttcap. $287 £145

A 20-bore French model 1812 percussion Gendarmerie pistol officially converted from flintlock, 9½in., barrel 5in., stamped 'B 1812'. Full-stocked, lock with traces of manufactury engraving. Regulation steel mounts. $428 £215

A 20-bore French percussion Gendarmerie pistol, model 1812, converted from flintlock, 9½in., barrel 5in., stamped 'B 1812', model number engraved on barrel tang. Full-stocked, lock with traces of manufactury engraving. Regulation steel mounts. Stock struck with storekeeper's mark dated 1812. $445 £225

A 22-bore French percussion Gendarmerie pistol, 9½in., barrel 5in., threequarter-stocked, steel mounts, barrel dated 1848 and with other stamps at breech. Marked 'Mle 1842' on backstrap, back-action lock marked 'Mre Nle de Mutzig'. $585 £290

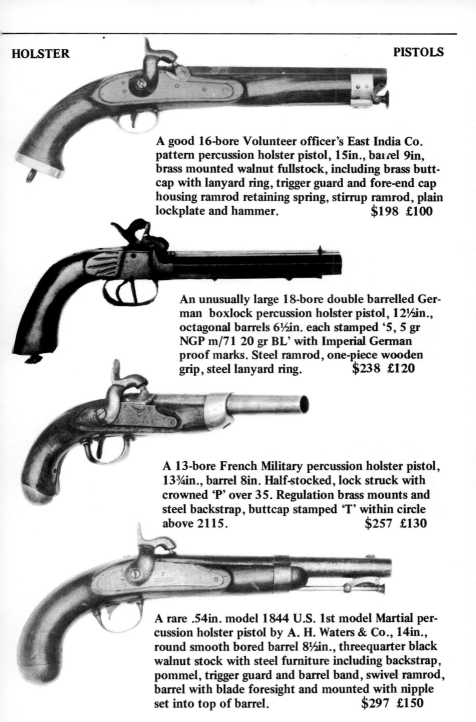

A good 16-bore Volunteer officer's East India Co. pattern percussion holster pistol, 15in., barrel 9in, brass mounted walnut fullstock, including brass butt-cap with lanyard ring, trigger guard and fore-end cap housing ramrod retaining spring, stirrup ramrod, plain lockplate and hammer.   **$198 £100**

An unusually large 18-bore double barrelled German boxlock percussion holster pistol, 12½in., octagonal barrels 6½in. each stamped '5, 5 gr NGP m/71 20 gr BL' with Imperial German proof marks. Steel ramrod, one-piece wooden grip, steel lanyard ring.   **$238 £120**

A 13-bore French Military percussion holster pistol, 13¾in., barrel 8in. Half-stocked, lock struck with crowned 'P' over 35. Regulation brass mounts and steel backstrap, buttcap stamped 'T' within circle above 2115.   **$257 £130**

A rare .54in. model 1844 U.S. 1st model Martial percussion holster pistol by A. H. Waters & Co., 14in., round smooth bored barrel 8½in., threequarter black walnut stock with steel furniture including backstrap, pommel, trigger guard and barrel band, swivel ramrod, barrel with blade foresight and mounted with nipple set into top of barrel.   **$297 £150**

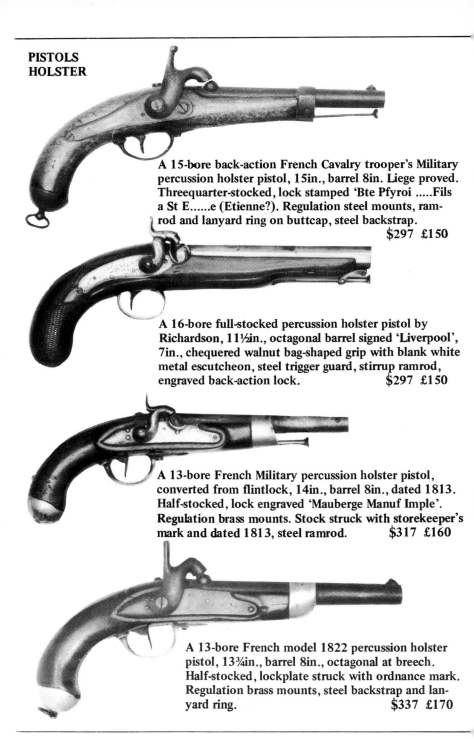

A 15-bore back-action French Cavalry trooper's Military percussion holster pistol, 15in., barrel 8in. Liege proved. Threequarter-stocked, lock stamped 'Bte Pfyroi .....Fils a St E......e (Etienne?). Regulation steel mounts, ramrod and lanyard ring on buttcap, steel backstrap.
$297 £150

A 16-bore full-stocked percussion holster pistol by Richardson, 11½in., octagonal barrel signed 'Liverpool', 7in., chequered walnut bag-shaped grip with blank white metal escutcheon, steel trigger guard, stirrup ramrod, engraved back-action lock.
$297 £150

A 13-bore French Military percussion holster pistol, converted from flintlock, 14in., barrel 8in., dated 1813. Half-stocked, lock engraved 'Mauberge Manuf Imple'. Regulation brass mounts. Stock struck with storekeeper's mark and dated 1813, steel ramrod.
$317 £160

A 13-bore French model 1822 percussion holster pistol, 13¾in., barrel 8in., octagonal at breech. Half-stocked, lockplate struck with ordnance mark. Regulation brass mounts, steel backstrap and lanyard ring.
$337 £170

A double barrelled 23-bore over and under box-lock sidehammer percussion holster pistol, 13½in., damascus barrels 7in. Scroll engraved frame and hammers, game engraved on trigger guard, hinged cap trap to chequered walnut ·butt. $337 £170

A 22-bore French brass barrelled percussion holster pistol converted from flintlock by drum method, 11in., swamped octagonal barrel 6¼in., foliate engraved at breech, struck with crowned 'M'. Brass lockplate, scroll engraved hammer, engraved brass furniture.
                                          $346 £175

An interesting 16-borė French percussion holster pistol, circa 1820, 12in., heavily swamped, octagonal barrel 6½in., chequered walnut halfstock with engraved domed buttcap, iron trigger guard with foliate finial, éngraved iron sideplate and ramrod throat pipe.
                                          $356 £180

A 16-bore Belgian Military type percussion holster pistol, 14½in., barrel 8in., Liege proved. Half-stocked, lock stamped 'Dresse Laloux & Cie, Liege'. Steel backstrap and trigger plate, brass mounts, steel lanyard ring and ramrod. $376 £190

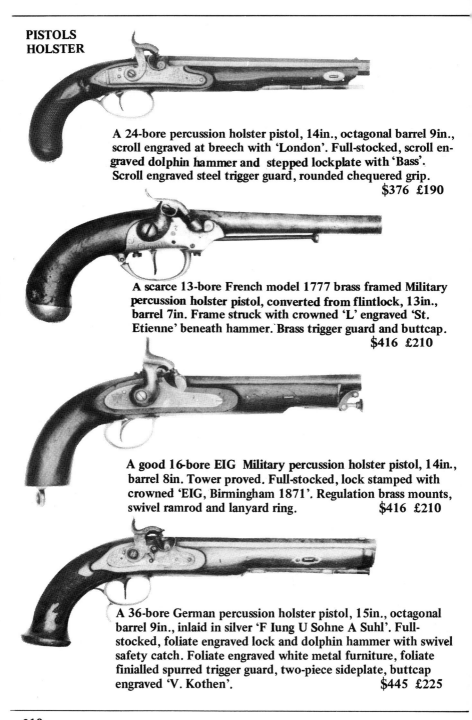

A 24-bore percussion holster pistol, 14in., octagonal barrel 9in., scroll engraved at breech with 'London'. Full-stocked, scroll engraved dolphin hammer and stepped lockplate with 'Bass'. Scroll engraved steel trigger guard, rounded chequered grip.

$376 £190

A scarce 13-bore French model 1777 brass framed Military percussion holster pistol, converted from flintlock, 13in., barrel 7in. Frame struck with crowned 'L' engraved 'St. Etienne' beneath hammer. Brass trigger guard and buttcap.

$416 £210

A good 16-bore EIG Military percussion holster pistol, 14in., barrel 8in. Tower proved. Full-stocked, lock stamped with crowned 'EIG, Birmingham 1871'. Regulation brass mounts, swivel ramrod and lanyard ring. $416 £210

A 36-bore German percussion holster pistol, 15in., octagonal barrel 9in., inlaid in silver 'F Iung U Sohne A Suhl'. Full-stocked, foliate engraved lock and dolphin hammer with swivel safety catch. Foliate engraved white metal furniture, foliate finialled spurred trigger guard, two-piece sideplate, buttcap engraved 'V. Kothen'. $445 £225

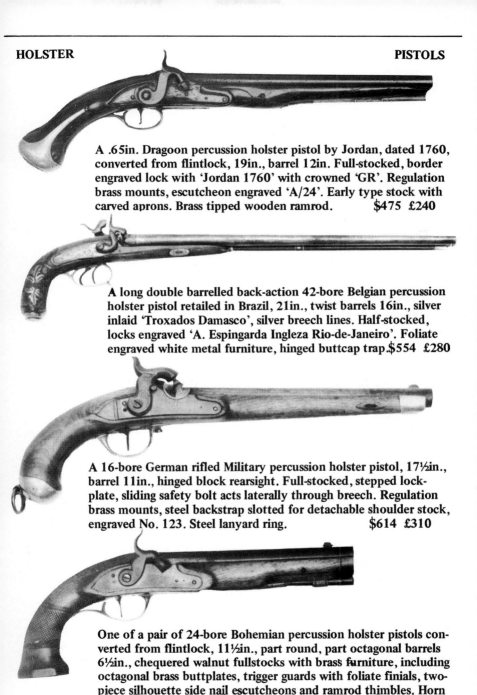

A .65in. Dragoon percussion holster pistol by Jordan, dated 1760, converted from flintlock, 19in., barrel 12in. Full-stocked, border engraved lock with 'Jordan 1760' with crowned 'GR'. Regulation brass mounts, escutcheon engraved 'A/24'. Early type stock with carved aprons. Brass tipped wooden ramrod. $475 £240

A long double barrelled back-action 42-bore Belgian percussion holster pistol retailed in Brazil, 21in., twist barrels 16in., silver inlaid 'Troxados Damasco', silver breech lines. Half-stocked, locks engraved 'A. Espingarda Ingleza Rio-de-Janeiro'. Foliate engraved white metal furniture, hinged buttcap trap.$554 £280

A 16-bore German rifled Military percussion holster pistol, 17½in., barrel 11in., hinged block rearsight. Full-stocked, stepped lock-plate, sliding safety bolt acts laterally through breech. Regulation brass mounts, steel backstrap slotted for detachable shoulder stock, engraved No. 123. Steel lanyard ring. $614 £310

One of a pair of 24-bore Bohemian percussion holster pistols converted from flintlock, 11½in., part round, part octagonal barrels 6½in., chequered walnut fullstocks with brass furniture, including octagonal brass buttplates, trigger guards with foliate finials, two-piece silhouette side nail escutcheons and ramrod thimbles. Horn capped fore-ends. $693 £350

A rare 16-bore French back-action 2-shot superimposed loading single barrelled rifled percussion holster pistol by Le Page of Paris, 13in., octagonal twist barrel 8in., deeply rifled, 14-groove. Panel etched 'Le Page . Moutier . Arger . Brevete . a . Paris', 'bis . in . idem'. Locks, breech, furniture and muzzle all etched en suite with fruiting grape vines. Locks etched 'Le Page Moutier Arger A Paris'. Single trigger, hinged butt trap, rounded wooden butt. $940 £475

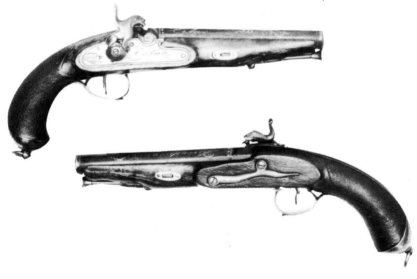

A pair of 16-bore Spanish percussion holster pistols dated 1841, 12in., barrels 6½in., turned at muzzles, silver inlaid 'Derraduras Por Jose Unzueta Eibar 1841', with scrolls. Full-stocked, hammers chiselled as seated lions, plates engraved 'Eibar' with foliate motifs on tails. Slightly foliate engraved steel furniture, foliate finialled trigger guards, backstraps integral with buttcaps bearing lanyard rings. Rounded chequered butts. $1,287 £650

An exceptionally good .451 Westley Richards 'Monkey Tail' breech loading Military percussion holster pistol, 14½in., barrel 9in., No. 638. Birmingham proved and stamped at breech '25 Grains', rifled barrel stamped 'Whitworth Patent'. Walnut full-stocked stamped with Continental crown and 'A.E. 1867' on side above trigger guard, brass mounts, lanyard ring on buttcap.

$1,782 £900

An attractive pair of 42-bore silver mounted German percussion holster pistols, converted from flintlock, circa 1770, 15½in., half fluted Italian barrels 9½in., engraved 'Lazarino Cominazo'. Full-stocked, foliate engraved stepped lockplates. Set triggers. Silver furniture, comprising foliate finialled trigger guards engraved on bows, pierced foliate finialled sideplates, longspur buttcaps. Octagonal silver ramrod pipes. Horn forecaps and horn tipped wooden ramrods.   **$1,980 £1,000**

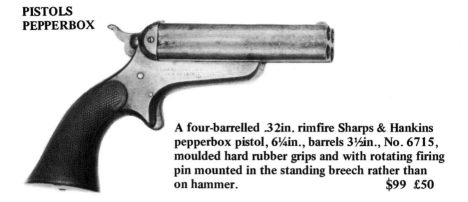

A four-barrelled .32in. rimfire Sharps & Hankins pepperbox pistol, 6¼in., barrels 3½in., No. 6715, moulded hard rubber grips and with rotating firing pin mounted in the standing breech rather than on hammer. **$99 £50**

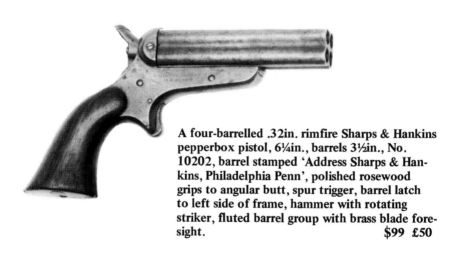

A four-barrelled .32in. rimfire Sharps & Hankins pepperbox pistol, 6¼in., barrels 3½in., No. 10202, barrel stamped 'Address Sharps & Hankins, Philadelphia Penn', polished rosewood grips to angular butt, spur trigger, barrel latch to left side of frame, hammer with rotating striker, fluted barrel group with brass blade foresight. **$99 £50**

A four-barrelled .32in. rimfire Sharps 3rd model pepperbox pistol, 4¼in., barrels 2½in., No. 2153, polished rosewood grips to tightly curved bird's head butt, case hardened steel frame with spur trigger, hammer rotating firing pin. **$158 £80**

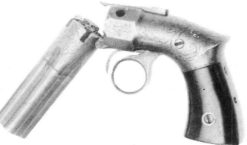

A scarce 5-shot .31in. Robbins & Lawrence breech loading ring trigger percussion pepperbox pistol, No. 2692, 7½in., fluted barrels 2¼in., to loading section stamped 'Robbins & Lawrence Co. Windsor VT Patent 1849'. Tipdown capping section, scroll engraved rounded breech and frame with thumb web spur. Hinged top locking lever, two-piece rosewood grips.
$356 £180

A good 5-shot .31in. Robbins & Lawrence self-cocking ring trigger breech loading percussion pepperbox pistol, No. 5649, 9¼in., fluted rifled barrel section 4½in., rifled section 3¼in. unscrews for loading. Tip-down breech for capping. Octagonal breech, scroll engraved round frame, ring cocking lever, separate trigger. Two-piece polished wooden grips. $495 £250

A scarce 5-shot .31in. Robbins & Lawrence breech loading ring trigger percussion pepperbox pistol, No. 3965, 9¼in., fluted barrel unit 4½in., unscrewing above breech for loading, tip-up at breech for capping. Rotating concealed hammer, ring trigger, two-piece polished wooden grips. Foliate engraved breech and rounded frame. $643 £325

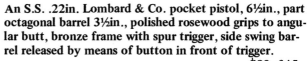

An S.S. .22in. Lombard & Co. pocket pistol, 6½in., part octagonal barrel 3½in., polished rosewood grips to angular butt, bronze frame with spur trigger, side swing barrel released by means of button in front of trigger.

$89 £45

An interesting S.S. .32in. rimfire Rollin White pocket pistol, 7¼in., ribbed octagonal barrel 3in., No. 479, swing out chamber, polished rosewood grip to angular butt, bronze frame with spur trigger, chamber locked by latch to left side of frame and fitted with a sprung hand ejector.

$109 £55

A boxlock percussion pocket pistol, 6in., turn-off barrel 1¾in., Birmingham proved. Foliate engraved frame with 'Johnson & Sons' within oval. Concealed trigger, sliding top thumb safety. Rounded chequered walnut butt with oval white metal escutcheon.

$119 £60

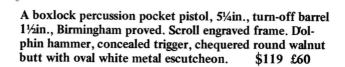

A boxlock percussion pocket pistol, 5¼in., turn-off barrel 1½in., Birmingham proved. Scroll engraved frame. Dolphin hammer, concealed trigger, chequered round walnut butt with oval white metal escutcheon.

$119 £60

A 45-bore Belgian boxlock percussion pocket pistol by Albert Francotte of Liege, 6in., turn-off twist barrel 2in., multi-groove rifled, Liege proved with crowned 'A.F.'. Scroll engraved frame, rounded walnut butt. $129 £65

A good 48-bore Belgian boxlock percussion pocket pistol, 5½in., turn-off barrel 1¾in. Liege proved. Foliate scroll and floral engraved frame, hammer off-set for sighting, concealed trigger. Rounded swollen walnut butt inlaid with shield shaped silver escutcheon. $139 £70

A Belgian boxlock percussion pocket pistol, 7½in., screw-off octagonal barrel 2¾in., with multi-groove rifling. Liege proved. Hammer off-set for sighting. Tiger wood butt inset with blank white metal shield escutcheon. $148 £75

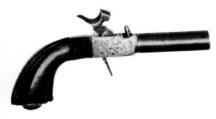

A sidehammer Continental boxlock percussion pocket pistol, 6¾in., turn-off twist barrel 3¼in., fluted walnut grip with engraved steel cap, folding trigger, square frame engraved with scrolled floral designs. $158 £80

One of a pair of 40-bore boxlock percussion pocket pistols, 7½in., turn-off barrels 3in., Birmingham proved. Scroll engraved frames, slab wooden butts.
$158 £80

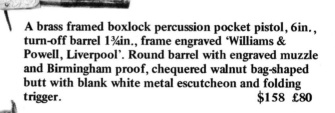

A brass framed boxlock percussion pocket pistol, 6in., turn-off barrel 1¾in., frame engraved 'Williams & Powell, Liverpool'. Round barrel with engraved muzzle and Birmingham proof, chequered walnut bag-shaped butt with blank white metal escutcheon and folding trigger.
$158 £80

A double barrelled 12mm. Continental, pinfire pocket pistol, 7¾in., barrels 3½in., fluted wooden grip with steel buttplate, folding trigger, underlever opening, tip-down barrels for loading, the frame and trigger engraved with scrolling ivy leaves.
$158 £80

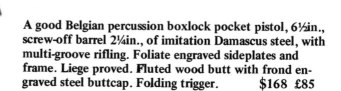

A good Belgian percussion boxlock pocket pistol, 6½in., screw-off barrel 2¼in., of imitation Damascus steel, with multi-groove rifling. Foliate engraved sideplates and frame. Liege proved. Fluted wood butt with frond engraved steel buttcap. Folding trigger.
$168 £85

A good Belgian percussion boxlock pocket pistol, 6in.,
screw-off barrel 2¼in., of imitation Damascus steel,
slotted for barrel key. Sideplates and frame engraved
with foliate scrolls. Liege proved, folding trigger, hammer partly off-set for sighting. Fluted ebony butt, with
foliate engraved steel buttcap.   **$168 £85**

A good round framed Continental boxlock percussion
pocket pistol, 5¾in., fine twist turn-off barrel 1¾in.,
Belgian proved, No. 2189, ebony bag-shaped grip carved on each side with foliage, white metal buttcap
with trap and folding trigger.   **$168 £85**

A 26-bore Belgian boxlock percussion
pocket pistol by Albert Francotte of
Liege, turn-off octagonal multi-groove
rifled barrel 2in. Liege proved. Foliate
scroll engraved frame, hammer off-set
for sighting, concealed trigger. Rounded ebony butt with later soft metal
cap.   **$168 £85**

A good Continental boxlock percussion pocket pistol,
9in., turn-off blued octagonal barrel 4in., inlaid with
silver scroll, foliate etched and engraved frame, fluted
wooden butt.   **$178 £90**

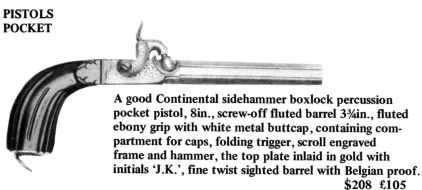

A good Continental sidehammer boxlock percussion pocket pistol, 8in., screw-off fluted barrel 3¾in., fluted ebony grip with white metal buttcap, containing compartment for caps, folding trigger, scroll engraved frame and hammer, the top plate inlaid in gold with initials 'J.K.', fine twist sighted barrel with Belgian proof.
$208 £105

An unusual four-barrelled .25in. centre fire Continental pocket pistol, 3¼in. barrels 1¾in., No. 3781, two-piece wooden grips to angular butt, side mounted safety and barrel release catch, the barrels slide vertically down into action body and are removed for loading or extraction. $218 £110

A good 5-shot .31in. E. Whitney's Patent, second model, percussion pocket revolver, No. 18798Y, 8½in. octagonal barrel 3½in. Underlever rammer, cylinder well roll engraved with Anglo-American shield, brass trigger guard, two-piece polished wooden grips. $238 £120

A Belgian double barrelled over and under boxlock percussion pocket pistol, 7¼in., turn-off rifled twist barrels 2½in. Frame scroll, shell and floral engraved, concealed single trigger, double hammers. Fluted walnut butt with foliate carved panels, steel buttcap. $287 £145

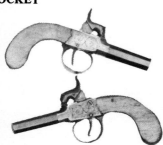

A pair of boxlock percussion pocket pistols, 5¼in., turn-off octagonal barrels 1¾in., Birmingham proved. Slab walnut butts with white metal escutcheons.   **$289 £146**

A double barrelled turn-over boxlock percussion pocket pistol, 7¼in., turn-off barrels 2¾in. Birmingham proved. Dolphin hammer, rounded chequered walnut butt with chamfered white metal escutcheon and oval white metal buttplate.   **$297 £150**

A good boxlock percussion pocket pistol by Dyball Norwich, 7½in., round turn-off barrel 3in., fitted with 2½in. spring bayonet. Birmingham proved. slab shaped butt, sliding trigger bayonet catch, scroll engraved frame. **$307 £155**

A rare 5-shot .31in. Nepperham Fire Arms Co. single action percussion pocket pistol, No. 2616, 9in. octagonal barrel 4¼in. Silver plated brass trigger guard, underlever rammer, removable sideplate, two-piece wooden grips.   **$346 £175**

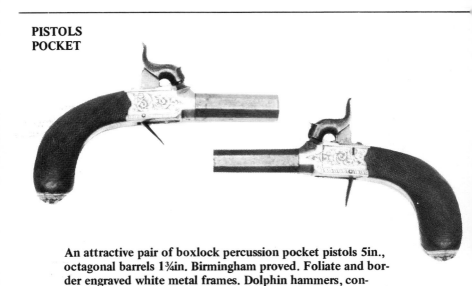

An attractive pair of boxlock percussion pocket pistols 5in., octagonal barrels 1¾in. Birmingham proved. Foliate and border engraved white metal frames. Dolphin hammers, concealed triggers. Rounded chequered walnut butts with lion's head buttcaps and oval escutcheons. $396 £200

A scarce .40in. superimposed loading Lindsay's Patent double hammer percussion pocket pistol, 6in., octagonal barrel 4in., roll engraved sides, brass frame, sheathed trigger, two-piece wooden grips. $495 £250

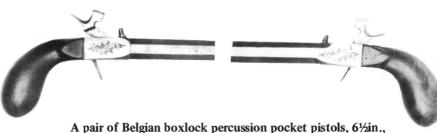

A pair of Belgian boxlock percussion pocket pistols, 6½in., turn-off octagonal barrels 2¾in., with false damascus pattern. Scroll engraved frames, concealed triggers, off-set hammers, rounded grips. $495 £250

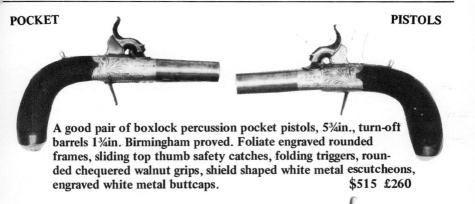

A good pair of boxlock percussion pocket pistols, 5¾in., turn-off barrels 1¾in. Birmingham proved. Foliate engraved rounded frames, sliding top thumb safety catches, folding triggers, rounded chequered walnut grips, shield shaped white metal escutcheons, engraved white metal buttcaps.   **$515 £260**

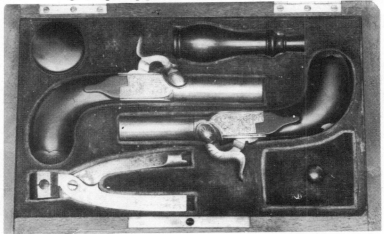

A scarce 5-shot .28in. Colt first model 1855 Roote sidehammer pocket pistol, 8in., octagonal barrel 3½in., No. 9397 (matching), polished one-piece wooden grip, spur trigger, left side fitted with circular sideplate, plain unfluted cylinder, underlever rammer and closed frame, brass bead foresight, top strap groove rear.**$554 £280**

A good pair of Continental boxlock percussion pocket pistols, 5in., round turn-off barrels 1½in. Belgian proved. Plain ebony bag-shaped grips with steel buttcap with fitted trap and shield shaped white metal escutcheon, square scroll engraved frame with folding trigger, off-set dolphin hammer to allow for sighting. Contained in their original purple beize lined and close fitted mahogany case.   **$812 £410**

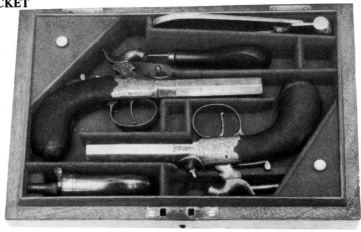

A pair of boxlock percussion pocket pistols by G. Green, 6¾in., turn-off octagonal barrels 2½in. Birmingham proved. Scroll engraved frames, dolphin hammers, rounded chequered walnut butts with diamond shaped white metal escutcheons, sliding top thumb safety catches. In an excellent green beize lined fitted mahogany case.   **$832 £420**

A scarce pair of four-barrelled Belgian boxlock percussion tap-action pocket pistols, circa 1835, 5in., turn-off rifled barrels 1¼in. Liege proved. Frames engraved with floral filled urns, foliate engraved selection taps. Chevron carved rounded walnut grips.   **$990 £500**

A rare S.S. .22in. long rifle Smith & Wesson first model 1891 target pistol, 11¼in., round ribbed barrel 8in., No. 15886, moulded hard rubber extension grips, tip-down barrel for loading and extraction, bead foresight adjustable square notch rear, carbon steel hammer and trigger guard. $237 £120

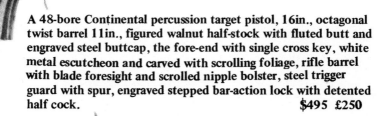

A 48-bore Continental percussion target pistol, 16in., octagonal twist barrel 11in., figured walnut half-stock with fluted butt and engraved steel buttcap, the fore-end with single cross key, white metal escutcheon and carved with scrolling foliage, rifle barrel with blade foresight and scrolled nipple bolster, steel trigger guard with spur, engraved stepped bar-action lock with detented half cock. $495 £250

A 34-bore Austrian percussion target pistol by Senger of Vienna, converted from flintlock, 14½in., slightly swamped octagonal barrel 9¼in., hairgroove rifled, silver inlaid at breech and muzzle with flowers and foliage. Full-stocked, rope border engraved, detented lock, silver inlaid with cornucopia. Adjustable set trigger. Silver flower inlaid steel furniture, foliate engraved trigger guard and throat pipe. $544 £275

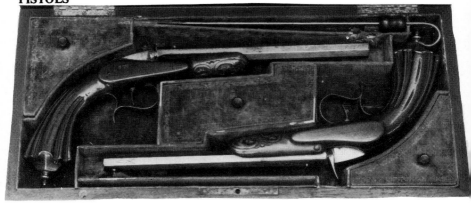

A good cased pair of .22in. Belgian boxlock Flobert saloon target pistols, 14½in., octagonal scroll engraved barrels 9in., fluted wooden grips with steel buttcaps, engraved spurred trigger guards, heavy hammers, bead foresight and dovetailed notch rear. Contained in their mauve velvet lined and fitted mahogany case with silver lid escutcheon, clearing rod and lidded compartments.   **$756 £380**

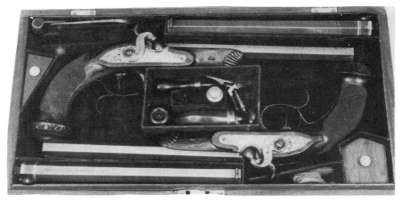

A pair of 38-bore French rifled percussion target pistols by Gosset of Paris, with an interchangeable pair of smoothbore barrels by Rigby of Dublin, 15¾in., slightly swamped octagonal twist barrels 9¾in. Half-stocked, detented locks with capstan screw, adjustable set triggers. Locks and steel furniture are finely engraved en suite with foliage, flowers and birds. Chequered grips, butts foliate carved, fore-ends shell carved. In their brass bound blue velvet lined fitted mahogany case.
$3,960 £2,000

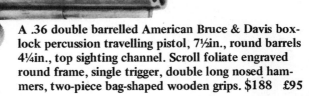

A .36 double barrelled American Bruce & Davis boxlock percussion travelling pistol, 7½in., round barrels
4¼in., top sighting channel. Scroll foliate engraved
round frame, single trigger, double long nosed hammers, two-piece bag-shaped wooden grips. $188 £95

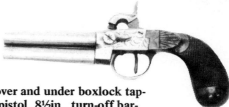

A Belgian double barrelled over and under boxlock tap-
action percussion travelling pistol, 8½in., turn-off barrels, 3½in. Liege proved, foliate engraved frame, rounded chequered walnut butt. $198 £100

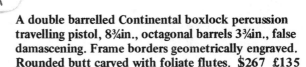

A double barrelled Continental boxlock percussion
travelling pistol, 8¾in., octagonal barrels 3¾in., false
damascening. Frame borders geometrically engraved.
Rounded butt carved with foliate flutes. $267 £135

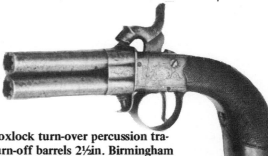

A double barrelled boxlock turn-over percussion travelling pistol, 7in., turn-off barrels 2½in. Birmingham
proved. Scroll engraved frame, dolphin hammer, rounded chequered walnut butt with engraved white metal
buttcap and oval escutcheon. $277 £140

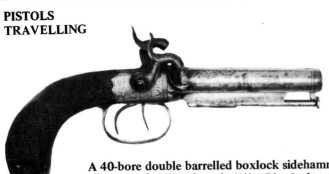

A 40-bore double barrelled boxlock sidehammer percussion travelling pistol, 8¾in., barrels 4¼in. Birmingham proved. Scroll engraved frame, hammers and barrel tops with 'Smith, London' on top rib, chequered walnut grip with silver escutcheon, original steel ramrod. $297 £150

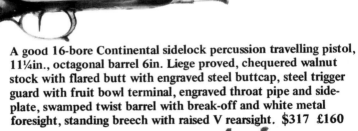

A good 16-bore Continental sidelock percussion travelling pistol, 11¼in., octagonal barrel 6in. Liege proved, chequered walnut stock with flared butt with engraved steel buttcap, steel trigger guard with fruit bowl terminal, engraved throat pipe and sideplate, swamped twist barrel with break-off and white metal foresight, standing breech with raised V rearsight. $317 £160

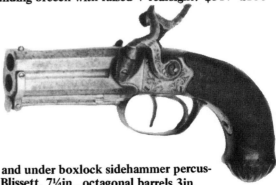

A double barrelled over and under boxlock sidehammer percussion travelling pistol by Blissett, 7¼in., octagonal barrels 3in. London proved. Foliate engraved frame, dolphin hammers and trigger guard. Underlever swivel ramrod. Rounded chequered ebony butt, engraved silver escutcheon and butt disc. $376 £190

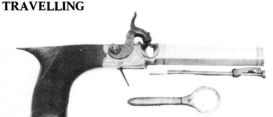

A boxlock percussion sidehammer travelling pistol by
W. Green, London, 8½in., octagonal white metal barrel
4in., Birmingham proof. Finely chequered walnut saw-
handle stock with engraved white metal buttplate containing cap trap, folding trigger, dolphin hammer, captive rammer in white metal mount beneath barrel.
$416 £210

A double barrelled 54-bore sidehammer boxlock percussion travelling pistol by Osborne & Jackson 8¼in.,
side by side barrels 3½in., with central rib and engraved muzzles, finely chequered walnut bag-shaped
grip with blank silver escutcheon scroll engraved
frame with bolted locks, dolphin hammers, swivel
rammer. $436 £220

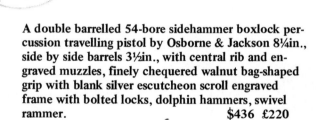

One of a pair of 26-bore micro-groove rifled French
percussion travelling pistols, 11in., octagonal sighted
twist barrels 5½in., well chequered walnut stocks
with engraved iron furniture, comprising domed buttcap, trigger guards with foliate husk finials, large ornate
sideplates and fore-end cap, blank silver grip, escutcheons and crosskey plates. $891 £450

A scarce S.S. .44in. rimfire Hammond bulldog single action pistol, 7¾in., octagonal barrel 4in., No. 6080, rotating breech block, wooden grips to rounded butt, steel frame with spur trigger, white metal foresight, spring loaded breech block lock rear. **$109 £55**

A scarce double barrelled over and under .22in. and .32in. rimfire American Arms Co. Wheeler's Patent pistol, 6in., barrels 3in., No. 1539, polished rosewood grips to angular butt, bronze frame with spur trigger, turn-over barrels with individual white metal foresights. **$198 £100**

An early model 4-shot .44in. rimfire Colt clover leaf model of 1871, single action house pistol, 6¾in., round barrel 3in., No. 933, polished rosewood grips to bird's head butt, bronze frame with spur trigger, side loading and rod ejection, high spurred upright hammer, barrel with integral foresight and ejector rod bush. **$436 £220**

A 5-shot .32in. breech loading Robbins & Lawrence Patent self-cocking percussion pistol, 9¼in., fluted cylinder 3¼in. to breech loading stage, 4½in. to hinged capping end. Scroll engraved rounded frame, concealed hammer, ring cocking with secondary trigger. Two-piece wooden grips. **$455 £230**

A 6-shot 12mm. Continental double action pinfire revolver, 10in., round barrel 4¾in., finely chequered angular walnut butt, folding trigger gate loading and rod ejection, unfluted scroll engraved cylinder.

$99 £50

A large 6-shot 11.4mm. Austrian Montenegrin gasser type open framed double action revolver, 15in., round barrel 9¼in., No. 164495. Polished ivory grips to bag-shaped butt, with lanyard ring, gate loading and rod ejection, unfluted rebated cylinder. $119 £60

A 6-shot .450in. Webley Pryse double action revolver, 10in., octagonal ribbed barrel 5½in., one-piece chequered walnut grip with fitted lanyard ring, tip-down barrel latching at bolster by means of double cross bolts. $123 £62

A 6-shot 12mm. Continental double action pinfire revolver, 10in., round barrel 5in., chequered ebony grips with fitted lanyard ring, gate loading and rod ejection, bead foresight hammer rear, the action body and cylinder floral scroll engraved against a stippled ground. $139 £70

A large 5-shot 11mm. Continental gasser double action revolver, 10in., barrel 5¼in., No. 8222, chequered wooden grips to bag-shaped butt with fitted lanyard ring, tip-down barrel for loading and ejection, latching to hammer bolster by finger actuated cross bolts. $158 £80

A 6-shot 10.6mm. German model 1883 single action service revolver made by Erfurt, 10in., part round, part octagonal barrel 4½in., No. 4283, dated 1894, plain walnut grip, with lanyard ring eye, side mounted thumb safety, semi-fluted cylinder gate loading. $168 £85

A 6-shot 11.3mm. German single action revolver by Erfurt, 10in., barrel part octagonal 4½in., No. 9170, dated 1894, plain walnut grips to bag-shaped butt with lanyard ring, sideplate with thumb safety to left side of frame, gate loading, church steeple fluted cylinder. $168 £85

A 6-shot 9mm. Continental double action pinfire revolver, 10¾in., round barrel 6¼in., No. 3408, carved ebony grips with lanyard ring, scroll and line engraved frame and cylinder, gate loading and rod ejection, blued barrel with wedge fore-sight. $178 £90

A 5-shot 120-bore Adam's Patent self-cocking percussion revolver of Continental manufacture, 7in.,
octagonal tapered barrel 3in., Belgian proof marked,
walnut grip carved with vines and foliage, scroll engraved blued frame with spring hammer safety to
left side, side lever rammer, plain border engraved
cylinder.   **$178 £90**

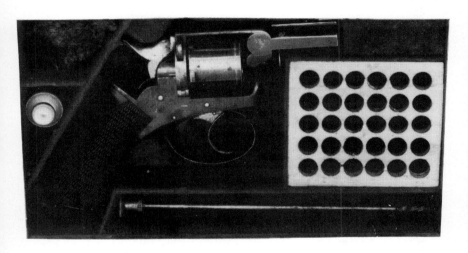

A 6-shot .442in. Webley bulldog type double action revolver, 7in., octagonal barrel 2¼in., No. 395, chequered walnut grip with lanyard eye, closed
frame, gate loading, blade foresight hammer bolster rear, in its fitted
leather covered case with oil bottle, cleaning rod and Deane & Son trade
label.   **$198 £100**

A scarce 6-shot 9mm. Continental ring trigger double
action pinfire transitional revolver, 10in., smooth
bore barrel 4½in., rifled cylinder 2¼in., No. 44 RU,
polished ebony grips to bag-shaped butt with lanyard
ring which screws out to double as an ejector rod,
gate loading, open frame, long fluted cylinder with
six chambers rifled.   **$228 £115**

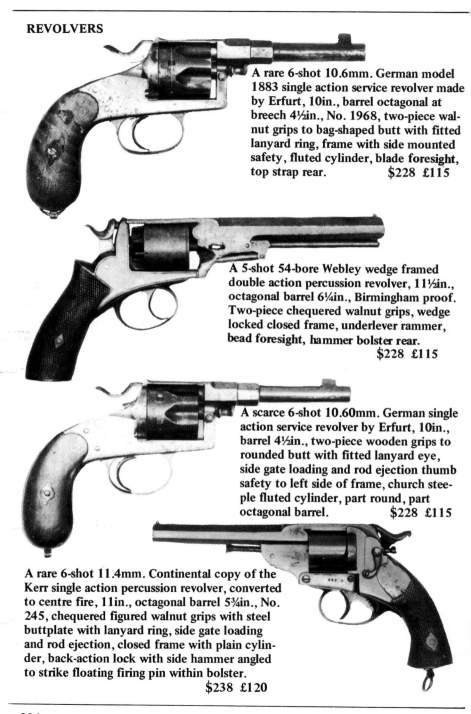

A rare 6-shot 10.6mm. German model 1883 single action service revolver made by Erfurt, 10in., barrel octagonal at breech 4½in., No. 1968, two-piece walnut grips to bag-shaped butt with fitted lanyard ring, frame with side mounted safety, fluted cylinder, blade foresight, top strap rear. $228 £115

A 5-shot 54-bore Webley wedge framed double action percussion revolver, 11½in., octagonal barrel 6¼in., Birmingham proof. Two-piece chequered walnut grips, wedge locked closed frame, underlever rammer, bead foresight, hammer bolster rear. $228 £115

A scarce 6-shot 10.60mm. German single action service revolver by Erfurt, 10in., barrel 4½in., two-piece wooden grips to rounded butt with fitted lanyard eye, side gate loading and rod ejection thumb safety to left side of frame, church steeple fluted cylinder, part round, part octagonal barrel. $228 £115

A rare 6-shot 11.4mm. Continental copy of the Kerr single action percussion revolver, converted to centre fire, 11in., octagonal barrel 5¾in., No. 245, chequered figured walnut grips with steel buttplate with lanyard ring, side gate loading and rod ejection, closed frame with plain cylinder, back-action lock with side hammer angled to strike floating firing pin within bolster. $238 £120

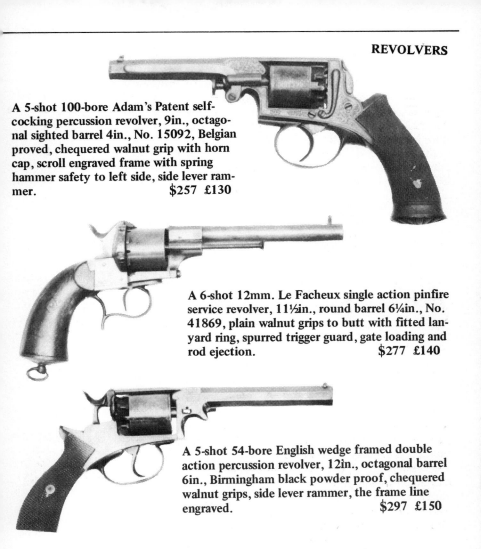

A 5-shot 100-bore Adam's Patent self-cocking percussion revolver, 9in., octagonal sighted barrel 4in., No. 15092, Belgian proved, chequered walnut grip with horn cap, scroll engraved frame with spring hammer safety to left side, side lever rammer.　　　　**$257 £130**

A 6-shot 12mm. Le Facheux single action pinfire service revolver, 11½in., round barrel 6¼in., No. 41869, plain walnut grips to butt with fitted lanyard ring, spurred trigger guard, gate loading and rod ejection.　　　　**$277 £140**

A 5-shot 54-bore English wedge framed double action percussion revolver, 12in., octagonal barrel 6in., Birmingham black powder proof, chequered walnut grips, side lever rammer, the frame line engraved.　　　　**$297 £150**

A 6-shot 60-bore self-cocking top snap percussion transitional revolver, 12in., octagonal rifled barrel 5¾in., Birmingham proved. Round frame foliate scroll engraved with chequered border. Strap work engraved bar hammer, two-piece chequered walnut grips with white metal cups.　　　　**$297 £150**

A 5-shot .36in. Continental Adam's type self-cocking percussion revolver, 9in., octagonal barrel 4½in., No. 2931, one-piece chequered walnut grip with horn buttcap, closed frame with scroll foliate engraving, side lever rammer, spring retained cylinder pin, spring hammer safety, brass blade foresight, hammer bolster rear..   **$297 £150**

A 6-shot 12mm. Dumonthier Military double action pinfire revolver, 10½in., round barrel 6in., No. 5182, burl walnut bag-shaped grip with fitted lanyard ring, gate loading and rod ejection.   **$297 £150**

A rare 5-shot 12mm. Continental copy of a Kerr side hammer single action revolver converted from percussion, 10¼in., octagonal barrel 5¾in., No. 864, barrel and cylinder struck with small anchor, one-piece chequered walnut grip with fitted buttcap and lanyard loop, back-action side lock, gate loading and rod ejection, spring loaded cylinder pin bolt to left side, plain unfluted cylinder.   **$317 £160**

A 5-shot 54-bore 1851 Adam's self-cocking percussion revolver, 11½in., octagonal barrel 6¼in., London proved. Scroll engraved frame, chequered one-piece walnut grip.   **$317 £160**

A 6-shot 12mm. Continental Military single action pinfire revolver, 11¼in., round barrel 6¼in., two-piece wooden grips to butt with fitted lanyard ring, spurred trigger guard, side gate loading and rod ejection, bead foresight, hammer rear. $337 £170

A 6-shot 12mm. Le Faucheux Military single action pinfire revolver, 11in., round barrel 6¼in., No. 12029, plain wooden grips to butt with fitted lanyard ring, spurred trigger guard, gate loading and rod ejection, bead foresight, hammer rear, the frame cylinder and back strap well foliate scroll engraved overall. $346 £175

An unusual long gripped 6-shot .42in. Webley open wedge framed self-cocking percussion revolver, 9¼in., octagonal barrel 4½in., Birmingham proved, long chequered walnut grip with buttplate containing trap with sprung lid for caps and blank white metal escutcheon, engraved rounded action body and spurless hammer, underlever rammer, plain unfluted cylinder which rotates from right to left. $356 £180

A scarce 6-shot .44in. Russian Smith & Wesson single action revolver, 11½in., round ribbed barrel 7in., No. 38315, plain walnut grips, blued trigger guard with second finger spur, irregular shaped sideplate, tip-down barrel latching to hammer bolster, rack and pinion auto extraction, pinned blade foresight. $356 £180

REVOLVERS

A 6-shot 80-bore English self-cocking transitional percussion revolver, 9½in., octagonal barrel 3¾in., Birmingham proved. Chequered walnut grips with steel buttcap with fitted trap, engraved rounded action body with bar hammer slotted for sighting, plain border engraved cylinder. $356 £180

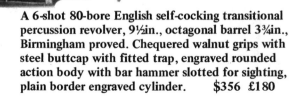

A 6-shot 120-bore model 1851 Adam's self-cocking percussion revolver, No. 9766R, 9in., octagonal barrel 4½in., London proved. Foliate engraved frame, chequered one-piece walnut grip with radial horn buttcap. $356 £180

A 6-shot 12mm. Le Faucheux military pinfire revolver 11½in., barrel 6¼in., barrel stamped on octagonal section 'Le Faucheux Invr Brevete', two-piece wooden grips to butt with fitted lanyard ring, spurred trigger guard. $376 £190

A good 5-shot .36in. Metropolitan Police single action percussion revolver, 9in., round barrel 4½in., No. 1177, polished walnut grips, brass trigger guard, backstrap, semi-fluted rebated cylinder, underlever rammer, brass bead foresight hammer rear. $396 £200

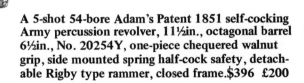

A 5-shot 54-bore Adam's Patent 1851 self-cocking Army percussion revolver, 11½in., octagonal barrel 6½in., No. 20254Y, one-piece chequered walnut grip, side mounted spring half-cock safety, detachable Rigby type rammer, closed frame. $396 £200

A 5-shot .45 Kerr's Patent back-action single action percussion revolver, 10½in., octagonal barrel 5½in., London proved. One-piece chequered wood grip, lanyard ring on buttcap, underlever rammer.
$410 £200

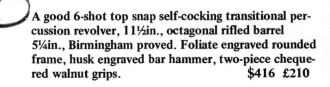

A good 6-shot top snap self-cocking transitional percussion revolver, 11½in., octagonal rifled barrel 5¼in., Birmingham proved. Foliate engraved rounded frame, husk engraved bar hammer, two-piece chequered walnut grips. $416 £210

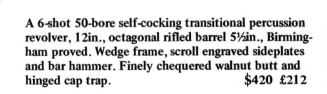

A 6-shot 50-bore self-cocking transitional percussion revolver, 12in., octagonal rifled barrel 5½in., Birmingham proved. Wedge frame, scroll engraved sideplates and bar hammer. Finely chequered walnut butt and hinged cap trap. $420 £212

A good 5-shot 120-bore Beaumont Adams double action percussion revolver, 9in., octagonal barrel 4¼in., No. 36152R, top strap engraved, one-piece chequered walnut grip with steel cap, plain line engraved frame with cylinder lock, side lever rammer, blade foresight, hammer bolster rear. $436 £220

A scarce 6-shot .455in. Webley Fosbery model 1901 automatic revolver, 10½in., barrel 6in., two-piece wooden grips to hinged butt with fitted lanyard ring, thumb safety with brass safety escutcheon, tip-down barrel for loading and extraction, cylinder with rear cut flutes.
$436 £220

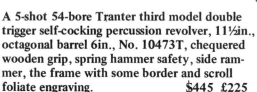

A 5-shot 54-bore Tranter third model double trigger self-cocking percussion revolver, 11½in., octagonal barrel 6in., No. 10473T, chequered wooden grip, spring hammer safety, side rammer, the frame with some border and scroll foliate engraving. $445 £225

An interesting 10-shot .34in superimposed loading double hammer single action Walch Patent percussion revolver, 8½in., octagonal barrel 3¼in., open brass wedge frame, sheathed trigger, two-piece polished wooden grips. $455 £230

A good 6-shot 54-bore Webley pattern long spur single action transitional revolver with reciprocating gas seal cylinder, 13in., octagonal barrel 6in. London proved. Finely chequered flared walnut grip with oval silver escutcheon and engraved steel buttcap housing trap for percussion caps.
$455 £230

A good 6-shot .36in. transitional self-cocking bar hammer percussion revolver, 11½in., octagonal barrel 5in., No. 6241, two-piece finely chequered walnut grips, fitted steel buttcap with trap, white metal rounded frame. $455 £230

A good 5-shot 54-bore Continental copy of the Adam's model 1851 self-cocking percussion revolver, 11½in., octagonal barrel 6¼in., No. 10382, chequered walnut grip with blank white metal escutcheon and engraved steel buttcap, scroll engraved closed frame. $455 £230

A good 6-shot 80-bore transitional bar hammer self-cocking percussion revolver by Blake & Co. London, 9¾in., octagonal barrel 4in., London proved. Two-piece chequered walnut grips and buttcap with small trap, round frame, bar hammer, fully fluted cylinder. $475 £240

REVOLVERS

A 6-shot .36in. Continental double action percussion sidehammer revolver, 11in., octagonal barrel 6¼in., No. 1356, chequered walnut grip with steel buttcap (restored), hinged frame secured at hammer bolster by cylinder pin screw.
$495 £250

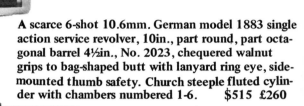

A scarce 6-shot 10.6mm. German model 1883 single action service revolver, 10in., part round, part octagonal barrel 4½in., No. 2023, chequered walnut grips to bag-shaped butt with lanyard ring eye, side-mounted thumb safety. Church steeple fluted cylinder with chambers numbered 1-6. $515 £260

A good 5-shot 54-bore Beaumont Adams double action percussion revolver, 11in., octagonal barrel 5¾in., No. 22773R, top strap engraved, 'Charles Nephew & Co. Calcutta'. London black powder proof, well chequered walnut grip with engraved steel cap, spurred trigger guard, side-mounted rammer, blade foresight, top strap rear. $515 £260

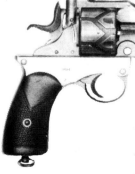

A scarce 6-shot .455in. Webley Fosbery model 1902 automatic target revolver, 11½in., barrel 7½in., two-piece chequered walnut grips with inlet brass 'safe' escutcheon to left side, thumb safety, tip-down barrel for loading and extraction, top strap button cylinder release, large blade foresight. $544 £275

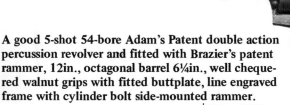

A good 5-shot 54-bore Adam's Patent double action percussion revolver and fitted with Brazier's patent rammer, 12in., octagonal barrel 6¼in., well chequered walnut grips with fitted buttplate, line engraved frame with cylinder bolt side-mounted rammer.

$535 £270

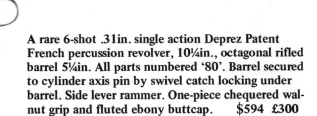

A rare 6-shot .31in. single action Deprez Patent French percussion revolver, 10¼in., octagonal rifled barrel 5¼in. All parts numbered '80'. Barrel secured to cylinder axis pin by swivel catch locking under barrel. Side lever rammer. One-piece chequered walnut grip and fluted ebony buttcap. $594 £300

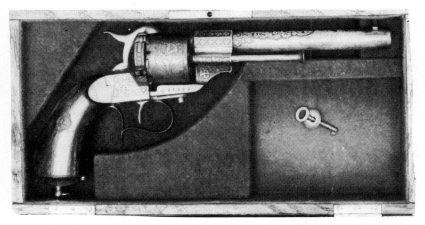

A 6-shot 12mm. Continental single action pinfire officer's revolver, 11½in., round barrel 6½in., No. 21064, plain walnut grips with fitted lanyard ring, spurred trigger guard, gate loading and rod ejection, bead foresight, hammer rear. The barrel, cylinder, frame, trigger guard, backstrap and buttcap all etched with flowers, foliage and geometric designs. Contained in a green beize lined and fitted oak carry case.

$634 £320

REVOLVERS

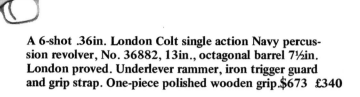

A 6-shot .36in. London Colt single action Navy percussion revolver, No. 36882, 13in., octagonal barrel 7½in. London proved. Underlever rammer, iron trigger guard and grip strap. One-piece polished wooden grip.$673 £340

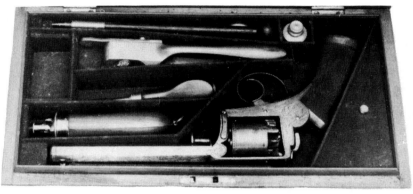

A good 5-shot 54-bore self-cocking Adams percussion revolver, 11in., barrel 6in., engraved on top strap, no provision for rammer, hammer stop on left, scroll engraved frame. Contained in its beize lined wooden case complete with bullet mould, Dixon powder flask, nipple wrench, cleaning rod, jag and oil bottle. $693 £350

A good 54-bore 5-shot Tranter's Patent double trigger percussion revolver, 11½in., octagonal barrel 6in., No. 10246T, finely chequered walnut grip with engraved buttcap, nice border and scroll foliate engraved frame with hammer spring, half-cock safety, side rammer, trigger guard pierced for trigger. $465 £350

A fine 5-shot 84-bore Tranter's Patent double trigger percussion revolver, No. 2110T, 10in., octagonal barrel 5in., London proved. Foliate engraved top strap, muzzle and frame. Early type detachable side rammer, sprung hammer safety, chequered one-piece walnut grip, foliate engraved buttcap.   **$713 £360**

A 5-shot 54-bore double trigger Tranter's Patent percussion revolver No. 9290T, 12in., octagonal barrel,6¼in., London proved. Foliate engraved frame, rammer and trigger both stamped 'W. Tranter's Patent''. One-piece chequered wood grip. Contained in its green beize lined fitted mahogany case.   **$792 £400**

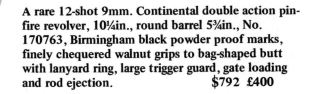

A rare 12-shot 9mm. Continental double action pinfire revolver, 10¼in., round barrel 5¾in., No. 170763, Birmingham black powder proof marks, finely chequered walnut grips to bag-shaped butt with lanyard ring, large trigger guard, gate loading and rod ejection.   **$792 £400**

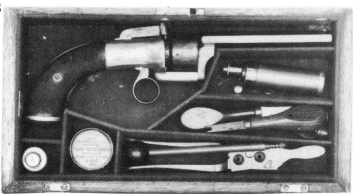

A good 6-shot .38in. English self-cocking bar hammer transitional percussion revolver, 11¼in., octagonal barrel 4¾in., Birmingham proved. Finely chequered walnut grips, steel buttcap with trap, German silver frame with integral cap flash shield. Contained in its original green beize lined and fitted mahogany case with brass lid escutcheon. **$871 £440**

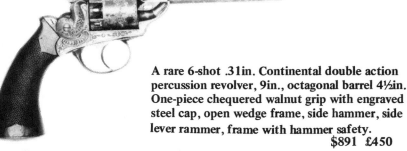

A rare 6-shot .31in. Continental double action percussion revolver, 9in., octagonal barrel 4½in. One-piece chequered walnut grip with engraved steel cap, open wedge frame, side hammer, side lever rammer, frame with hammer safety. **$891 £450**

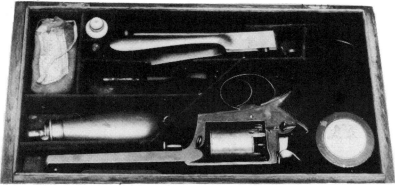

A good 5-shot 54-bore double action Adam's percussion revolver, 12in., barrel 6in., swing-up loading rammer and hammer stop on left, safety catch on right. Contained in its beize lined wooden case complete with bullet mould, powder flask, oil bottle, cleaning rod, nipple wrench, jag bag for Eley's caps. **$901 £455**

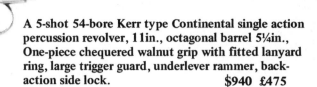

A 5-shot 54-bore Kerr type Continental single action percussion revolver, 11in., octagonal barrel 5¼in., One-piece chequered walnut grip with fitted lanyard ring, large trigger guard, underlever rammer, back-action side lock.   **$940 £475**

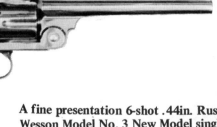

A fine presentation 6-shot .44in. Russian Smith & Wesson Model No. 3 New Model single action target revolver, 12¼in., ribbed barrel 6½in. Beautifully factory fitted mother-of-pearl grips with Smith & Wesson medallions, highly polished and nickel plated frame, bottom strap slotted to receive solid bow shaped trigger guard.
                                    $1,168 £590

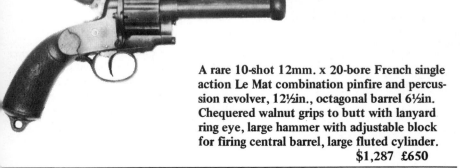

A rare 10-shot 12mm. x 20-bore French single action Le Mat combination pinfire and percussion revolver, 12½in., octagonal barrel 6½in. Chequered walnut grips to butt with lanyard ring eye, large hammer with adjustable block for firing central barrel, large fluted cylinder.
                                    $1,287 £650

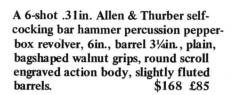

A 6-shot .31in. Allen & Thurber self-cocking bar hammer percussion pepperbox revolver, 6in., barrel 3¼in., plain, bagshaped walnut grips, round scroll engraved action body, slightly fluted barrels. $168 £85

A 6-shot .31in. Allen & Thurber top snap percussion pepperbox revolver, 7¼in., fluted cylinder 4in. Round frame foliate engraved, two-piece bag-shaped wooden grips. $198 £100

A good 6-shot 7mm. Continental pin-fire pepperbox revolver, 4½in., barrels 1¾in., two-piece ivory grips, open frame with blued fluted cylinder, micro-groove rifled bores, side gate loading to left hand side of frame, folding trigger, the frame and cylinder border inlaid with silver wire line work. $238 £120

A 6-shot .31in. Allen & Thurber self-cocking bar hammer percussion pepperbox revolver, 7¼in., barrels 3½in., walnut two-piece grips to bag-shaped butt, round scroll engraved action body.
                                $238 £120

A 6-shot .28in. Blunt & Syms Patent
ring trigger percussion pepperbox revolver, 7¾in., fluted cylinder 3½in.
Foliate engraved round frame, two-
piece bag-shaped wooden grips.
$247 £125

A 5-shot .31in. Allen & Thurber self-
cocking bar hammer percussion pocket
pepperbox revolver, 6¼in., semi-fluted
barrels 3in., walnut grips to bag-shaped
butt, rounded foliate engraved action
body with integral flash shield, rounded
hammer. $257 £130

A 6-shot .31in. Allen & Wheelock self-
cocking bar hammer percussion pepperbox revolver, 7in., fluted barrels
3½in., walnut grips to bag-shaped butt,
rounded scroll engraved action.
$257 £130

A 6-shot .31in. Allen & Thurber top
snap percussion pepperbox revolver,
7¼in., fluted cylinder 4in. Round frame
foliate engraved, two-piece bag-shaped
wooden grips. $257 £130

A good 5-shot 31in. self-cocking Allen & Thurber percussion pepperbox revolver, 6½in., fluted cylinder 3in. Bar hammer, scroll engraved rounded frame, two-piece bag-shaped walnut grips.
$257 £130

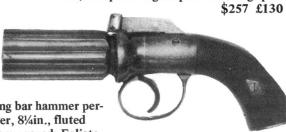

A 6-shot .31in. self-cocking bar hammer American percussion pepperbox revolver by Allen & Thurber, 7½in., fluted cylinder 4in. Scroll and foliate engraved rounded frame and nipple shield, two-piece bag-shaped wooden grips.
$257 £130

A 6-shot .36in. self-cocking bar hammer percussion pepperbox revolver, 8¼in., fluted cylinder 3¼in., Birmingham proved. Foliate engraved round steel frame, two-piece rounded chequered grips. $335 £130

A 6-shot top snap self-cocking percussion pepperbox revolver, 8in., fluted cylinder 3¼in. Birmingham proved. Foliate engraved rounded frame, nipple shield and bar hammer. Two-piece chequered walnut grips. $267 £135

A 6-shot .31in. American top snap self-cocking percussion pepperbox revolver by Allen & Thurber, 7¼in., fluted cylinder 4in. Round frame and nipple shield foliate scroll engraved. Bar hammer, two-piece bag-shaped wooden grips. $267 £135

A 6-shot 8mm. Continental self-cocking centre fire pepperbox revolver, 5¼in., barrels 2¼in., walnut grips to angular butt, folding trigger, hinged link supporting cylinder pin at forward end, long fluted cylinder with each barrel rifled. $267 £135

A 6-shot .31in. Allen & Thurber top snap self-cocking pepperbox percussion revolver, 7½in., barrel 3½in., polished walnut grips to bag-shaped butt, round action body with some foliate scroll engraving, bar hammer, cast steel barrels. $277 £140

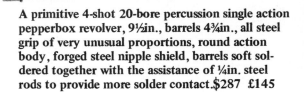

A primitive 4-shot 20-bore percussion single action pepperbox revolver, 9½in., barrels 4¾in., all steel grip of very unusual proportions, round action body, forged steel nipple shield, barrels soft soldered together with the assistance of ¼in. steel rods to provide more solder contact. $287 £145

A 5-shot .25in. self-cocking percussion pepperbox revolver by Blunt & Syms, 5in., fluted cylinder, 2in. Foliated engraved round steel frame,
ring trigger, two-piece bag-shaped walnut grips.
$297 £150

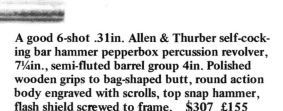

A good 6-shot .31in. Allen & Thurber self-cocking bar hammer pepperbox percussion revolver,
7¼in., semi-fluted barrel group 4in. Polished
wooden grips to bag-shaped butt, round action
body engraved with scrolls, top snap hammer,
flash shield screwed to frame. $307 £155

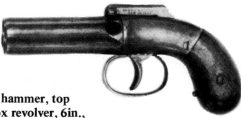

A four-barrelled Allen's Patent, bar hammer, top
striker, percussion pocket pepperbox revolver, 6in.,
barrels 2¾in. Plain steel rounded frame and mounts,
rounded wood grips. $337 £170

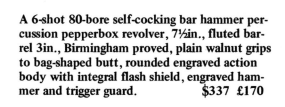

A 6-shot 80-bore self-cocking bar hammer percussion pepperbox revolver, 7½in., fluted barrel 3in., Birmingham proved, plain walnut grips
to bag-shaped butt, rounded engraved action
body with integral flash shield, engraved hammer and trigger guard. $337 £170

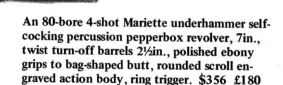

An 80-bore 4-shot Mariette underhammer self-cocking percussion pepperbox revolver, 7in., twist turn-off barrels 2½in., polished ebony grips to bag-shaped butt, rounded scroll engraved action body, ring trigger. $356 £180

A 6-shot 90-bore Mariette ring trigger self-cocking percussion pepperbox revolver, 8in., turn-off twist barrels 2¾in,, slotted for key. Liege proved. Rounded frame foliate scroll engraved en suite with integral grip strap and facetted buttcap. Two-piece ivory grips etched with scrolls. $354 £180

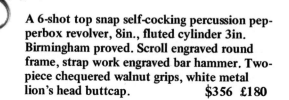

A 6-shot top snap self-cocking percussion pepperbox revolver, 8in., fluted cylinder 3in. Birmingham proved. Scroll engraved round frame, strap work engraved bar hammer. Two-piece chequered walnut grips, white metal lion's head buttcap. $356 £180

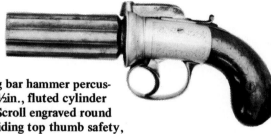

A 6-shot .36in. self-cocking bar hammer percussion pepperbox revolver, 8½in., fluted cylinder 4in., Birmingham proved. Scroll engraved round frame and nipple shield. Sliding top thumb safety, two-piece bag-shaped polished walnut grips.
$366 £185

A 6-shot .31in. Bacon's Patent single action underhammer percussion pepperbox revolver, 8½in., fluted cylinder 4½in. Foliate engraved rounded frame and nipple shield. Two-piece bag-shaped wooden grips. $396 £200

A rare 5-shot .32in. rimfire Mariette single action hand rotated pepperbox revolver, 7¼in., fluted barrel group 3in., chequered bag-shaped grip with vacant white metal shield shaped escutcheon, scroll engraved trigger guard, action body and top strap. $396 £200

A 6-shot .36in. Marston & Knox bar hammer self-cocking percussion pepperbox revolver, 7½in., barrels 3½in., walnut grips to bag-shaped butt, round scroll engraved frame, fluted barrel.
$396 £200

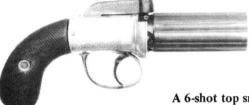

A 6-shot top snap self-cocking percussion pepperbox revolver, 7½in., fluted cylinder 3in. Birmingham proved. German silver round frame, scroll engraved. Two-piece chequered walnut grips. $396 £200

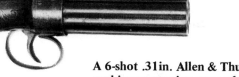

A 6-shot .31in. Allen & Thurber bar hammer self-cocking percussion pepperbox revolver, 7½in., barrels 3¾in. Polished walnut grips to bag-shaped butt, round action body with some foliate engraved decoration. $396 £200

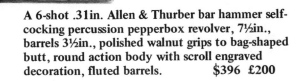

A 6-shot .31in. Allen & Thurber bar hammer self-cocking percussion pepperbox revolver, 7½in., barrels 3½in., polished walnut grips to bag-shaped butt, round action body with scroll engraved decoration, fluted barrels. $396 £200

A 6-shot .45in. English bar hammer self-cocking percussion pepperbox revolver, 9½in., fluted barrels 4in. Birmingham proved, chequered walnut grip, steel buttcap with trap, round action body and integral cap shield. $416 £210

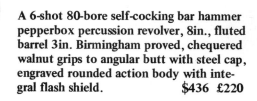

A 6-shot 80-bore self-cocking bar hammer pepperbox percussion revolver, 8in., fluted barrel 3in. Birmingham proved, chequered walnut grips to angular butt with steel cap, engraved rounded action body with integral flash shield. $436 £220

A 6-shot .36in. Allen's Patent self-cocking percussion pepperbox revolver, 10¼in., fluted cylinder 5½in. Foliate engraved round frame and nipple shield, spurred trigger guard, two-piece bag-shaped wooden grips. $455 £230

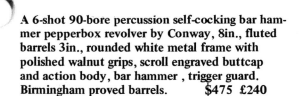

A 6-shot 90-bore percussion self-cocking bar hammer pepperbox revolver by Conway, 8in., fluted barrels 3in., rounded white metal frame with polished walnut grips, scroll engraved buttcap and action body, bar hammer, trigger guard. Birmingham proved barrels. $475 £240

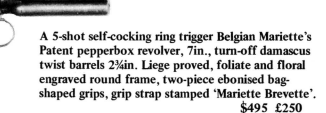

A 5-shot self-cocking ring trigger Belgian Mariette's Patent pepperbox revolver, 7in., turn-off damascus twist barrels 2¾in. Liege proved, foliate and floral engraved round frame, two-piece ebonised bag-shaped grips, grip strap stamped 'Mariette Brevette'. $495 £250

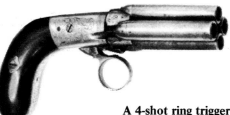

A 4-shot ring trigger self-cocking underhammer Mariette percussion pepperbox revolver, 6¾in., turn-off damascus barrels 2½in. Liege proved. Foliate engraved round frame and two-piece bag-shaped ebony grips. $495 £250

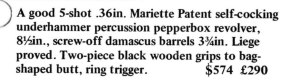

A good 5-shot .36in. Mariette Patent self-cocking underhammer percussion pepperbox revolver, 8½in., screw-off damascus barrels 3¾in. Liege proved. Two-piece black wooden grips to bag-shaped butt, ring trigger.   **$574 £290**

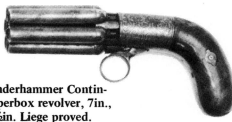

A scarce 6-shot .38in. Mariette underhammer Continental self-cocking percussion pepperbox revolver, 7in., turn-off browned twist barrels 2½in. Liege proved. Plain polished walnut grips to bag-shaped butt, ring trigger and underhammer.   **$614 £310**

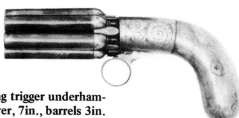

A good 6-shot .36in. Mariette ring trigger underhammer percussion pepperbox revolver, 7in., barrels 3in. Two-piece polished wooden grips, round frame with scrolling foliate engraving.   **$653 £330**

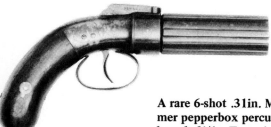

A rare 6-shot .31in. Marston self-cocking bar hammer pepperbox percussion revolver, 8in., fluted barrels 3¼in. Two-piece walnut grips to bag-shaped butt, round action body, rivetted nipple shield.
                    $673 £340

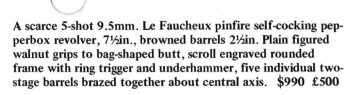

A scarce 5-shot 9.5mm. Le Faucheux pinfire self-cocking pepperbox revolver, 7½in., browned barrels 2½in. Plain figured walnut grips to bag-shaped butt, scroll engraved rounded frame with ring trigger and underhammer, five individual two-stage barrels brazed together about central axis. $990 £500

A good 6-shot 36-bore top snap percussion pepperbox revolver by J. Dickson & Son, 8½in., Birmingham proved fluted cylinder 3½in. to flash shield. Well scroll engraved frame, nicely engraved hammer top strap, blued trigger guard and butt trap, finely chequered walnut grip with chamfered rectangular silver escutcheon. Contained in its fitted brass bound oak case. $1,185 £600

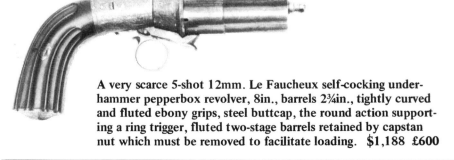

A very scarce 5-shot 12mm. Le Faucheux self-cocking underhammer pepperbox revolver, 8in., barrels 2¾in., tightly curved and fluted ebony grips, steel buttcap, the round action supporting a ring trigger, fluted two-stage barrels retained by capstan nut which must be removed to facilitate loading. $1,188 £600

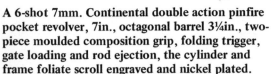

A 6-shot 7mm. Continental double action pinfire pocket revolver, 7in., octagonal barrel 3¼in., two-piece moulded composition grip, folding trigger, gate loading and rod ejection, the cylinder and frame foliate scroll engraved and nickel plated.

$51 £26

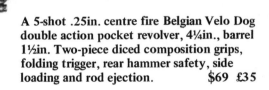

A 6-shot 7mm. English pinfire double action pocket revolver, 7¼in., round barrel 3¼in. Two-piece chequered walnut grips to bag-shaped butt, folding trigger, side gate loading and rod ejection, barrel octagonal at breech with dovetailed foresight hammer notch rear.

$65 £33

A 5-shot .25in. centre fire Belgian Velo Dog double action pocket revolver, 4¼in., barrel 1½in. Two-piece diced composition grips, folding trigger, rear hammer safety, side loading and rod ejection.

$69 £35

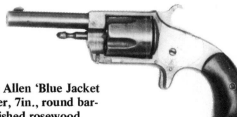

A 5-shot .32in. rimfire Hopkins & Allen 'Blue Jacket No. 2' single action pocket revolver, 7in., round barrel 2¾in. Birmingham proved. Polished rosewood grips to bird's head butt, spur trigger, side loading, closed frame, blade foresight, hammer bolster rear.

$71 £36

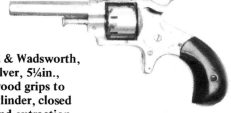

An early 5-shot .380in. rimfire Hopkins & Allen single
action pocket revolver, 6½in., octagonal blued barrel
2¼in. Polished rosewood grips to bird's head butt,
spur trigger, closed frame with cylinder pin extractor.
$99 £50

A scarce 7-shot .22in. short Forehand & Wadsworth,
sidehammer single action pocket revolver, 5¼in.,
octagonal barrel 2½in. Polished rosewood grips to
bird's head butt, spur trigger, plain cylinder, closed
frame, cylinder removes for loading and extraction.
$97 £50

A good 7-shot .230in. rimfire Webley No. 2 double
action pocket revolver, 4½in., round barrel with
top flat 2in. Polished ivory grips to bird's head
butt, fitted with screw-in ejector rod, ring trigger,
gate loading, unfluted cylinder. $99 £50

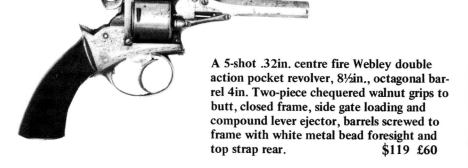

A 5-shot .32in. centre fire Webley double
action pocket revolver, 8½in., octagonal barrel 4in. Two-piece chequered walnut grips to
butt, closed frame, side gate loading and
compound lever ejector, barrels screwed to
frame with white metal bead foresight and
top strap rear. $119 £60

A 7-shot .27in. short Smith & Wesson first model second issue pocket revolver, 8in., octagonal ribbed barrel 3¼in. Polished rosewood grips to angular butt, spur trigger, silver plated bronze frame, tip-up barrel for loading and extraction, driven white metal blade foresight, cylinder stop notch rear.   **$119   £60**

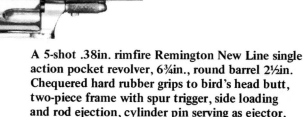

A 6-shot 7mm. Continental double action pin-fire pocket revolver, 6½in., round barrel 2½in. Carved and chequered walnut grips to angular butt, folding trigger, gate loading and rod ejection, the frame, cylinder and rear of the barrel well scroll foliate engraved. **$119   £60**

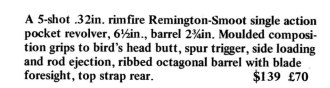

A 5-shot .38in. rimfire Remington New Line single action pocket revolver, 6¾in., round barrel 2½in. Chequered hard rubber grips to bird's head butt, two-piece frame with spur trigger, side loading and rod ejection, cylinder pin serving as ejector, barrel with white metal blade foresight.**$129   £65**

A 5-shot .32in. rimfire Remington-Smoot single action pocket revolver, 6½in., barrel 2¾in. Moulded composition grips to bird's head butt, spur trigger, side loading and rod ejection, ribbed octagonal barrel with blade foresight, top strap rear.   **$139   £70**

An unusual 7-shot .27in. short single action pocket revolver by Derringer, Philadelphia, 6in., round ribbed barrel 3in. Polished rosewood grips to bird's head butt, spur trigger, bronze frame, tip-up barrel for loading and extraction. **$139 £70**

A good 6-shot 7mm. E. Le Faucheux double action pinfire pocket revolver, 7½in., round barrel 4in. Polished wooden grips to angular butt, folding trigger, gate loading and rod ejection. **$161 £84**

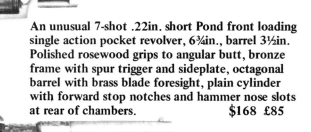

An unusual 7-shot .22in. short Pond front loading single action pocket revolver, 6¾in., barrel 3½in. Polished rosewood grips to angular butt, bronze frame with spur trigger and sideplate, octagonal barrel with brass blade foresight, plain cylinder with forward stop notches and hammer nose slots at rear of chambers. **$168 £85**

A good 6-shot 7mm. E. Le Faucheux double action pinfire pocket revolver, 7½in., round barrel 4in. Polished wooden grips to angular butt, folding trigger, gate loading and rod ejection. **$168 £85**

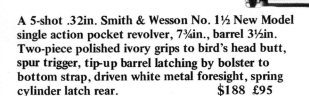

A 5-shot .32in. Smith & Wesson No. 1½ New Model single action pocket revolver, 7¾in., barrel 3½in. Two-piece polished ivory grips to bird's head butt, spur trigger, tip-up barrel latching by bolster to bottom strap, driven white metal foresight, spring cylinder latch rear.   **$188 £95**

A 5-shot .32in. rimfire Remington New Model single action pocket revolver, with a cylinder conversion from percussion, 7¾in., octagonal barrel 3½in. Polished rosewood grips, spur trigger, underlever rammer.   **$198 £100**

A good 7-shot .22in. short Smith & Wesson model No. 1 third issue single action pocket revolver, 6½in., barrel 3¼in., two-piece polished ivory grips to bird's head butt, spur trigger, tip-up barrel for loading and extraction, latching to bottom strap, ribbed barrel with driven white metal foresight, cylinder stop rear.   **$198 £100**

A scarce 6-shot .28in. Bliss & Goodyear single action percussion pocket revolver, 6¾in., octagonal barrel 3in. Two-piece wooden grips to angular butt, spur trigger, underlever rammer, plain cylinder, brass bead foresight, top strap rear.   **$218 £110**

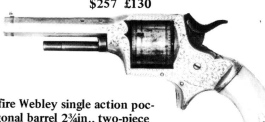

A 7-shot .22in. Smith & Wesson model No 1 single action pocket revolver, 6¾in., octagonal ribbed barrel 3¼in. Polished ivory grips, silver plated bronze frame with irregular sideplate and spur trigger, tip-up barrel for loading and extraction, driven foresight.
$257 £130

A good 6-shot .32in. rimfire Webley single action pocket revolver, 6½in., octagonal barrel 2¾in., two-piece ivory grips to angular butt, spur trigger, bronze frame and barrel with irregular shaped sideplate to left, cylinder dismounts for loading and extraction.
$257 £130

A 5-shot .31in. Remington Beal's first model single action pocket revolver, 6½in., octagonal barrel 3in. One-piece composition grip, white metal trigger guard, external acting cylinder indexing lever, closed frame, white metal bead foresight hammer bolster rear, plain cylinder.$257 £130

A 5-shot .31in. Colt model 1849 single action pocket percussion revolver, 8¾in., octagonal barrel 4in., polished walnut grip, silver plated brass trigger guard and backstrap, underlever rammer, brass bead foresight, hammer notch rear, roll engraved cylinder.
$287 £145

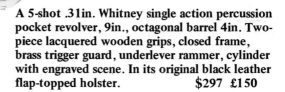

A 5-shot .31in. Whitney single action percussion pocket revolver, 9in., octagonal barrel 4in. Two-piece lacquered wooden grips, closed frame, brass trigger guard, underlever rammer, cylinder with engraved scene. In its original black leather flap-topped holster.   **$297 £150**

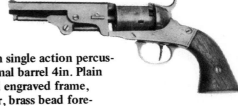

A scarce early 5-shot .31in. Bacon single action percussion pocket revolver, 9in., octagonal barrel 4in. Plain walnut grips to butt, foliate scroll engraved frame, plain cylinder, underlever rammer, brass bead foresight, hammer rear.   **$307 £155**

A 5-shot .31in. Colt pocket single action percussion revolver, No. 86842, 11in., octagonal barrel 6in. Underlever rammer, stagecoach scene on cylinder, brass trigger guard and grip strap, one-piece wooden grip.   **$317 £160**

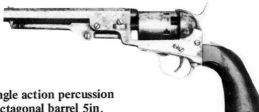

A 5-shot .31in. Colt pocket single action percussion revolver, No. 148389, 10in., octagonal barrel 5in. Underlever rammer, stagecoach scene on cylinder, brass trigger guard and grip strap, one-piece wooden grip.   **$317 £160**

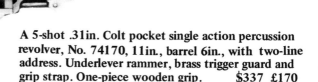

A good 5-shot .31in. Colt 1849 single action percussion pocket revolver, 8½in., octagonal barrel 4in., with two line address, brass trigger guard and backstrap, under-lever rammer, cylinder with traces of finish and crisp scene. $317 £160

A 5-shot .31in. Colt pocket single action percussion revolver, No. 74170, 11in., barrel 6in., with two-line address. Underlever rammer, brass trigger guard and grip strap. One-piece wooden grip. $337 £170

A 5-shot .31in. Whitney single action percussion pocket revolver, 9in., octagonal barrel 3¾in. Two-piece polished wooden grips, brass trigger guard, underlever rammer, closed frame. $337 £170

A 6-shot .31in. Colt pocket single action percussion revolver, 11in., octagonal barrel 6in. London black powder proof, one-piece walnut grip, steel trigger guard and backstrap, underlever rammer, unfluted cylinder with traces of stagecoach scene, white metal bead foresight, hammer notch rear.$337 £170

A 7-shot .32in. rimfire Tranter Patent single action closed frame pocket revolver, 8in., octagonal barrel 3½in., finely chequered walnut grips, spur trigger, gate loading and rod ejection, plain cylinder. In its burl walnut veneered blue beize lined and fitted case.   **$346 £175**

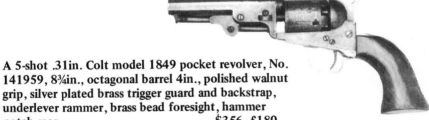

A 5-shot .31in. Colt model 1849 pocket revolver, No. 141959, 8¾in., octagonal barrel 4in., polished walnut grip, silver plated brass trigger guard and backstrap, underlever rammer, brass bead foresight, hammer notch rear.   **$356 £180**

A 5-shot .31in. Whitney single action percussion pocket revolver, 9in., octagonal barrel 4in. Two-piece lacquered wooden grips, closed frame, brass trigger guard, under-lever rammer, cylinder with engraved scene. **$376 £190**

A 5-shot .31in. Remington New Model single action percussion pocket revolver, 7¾in., octagonal barrel 3½in., white metal foresight, underlever rammer, sheathed trigger, two-piece polished wooden grips.
$386 £195

A 5-shot .31in. Colt pocket single action percussion pocket revolver, 9in., octagonal barrel 4in., underlever rammer, brass trigger guard and grip strap, one-piece wooden grip with eleven notches. Cylinder engraved with stagecoach hold-up scene. $396 £200

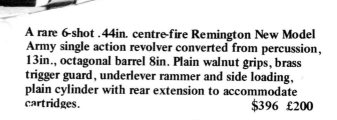

A rare 6-shot .44in. centre-fire Remington New Model Army single action revolver converted from percussion, 13in., octagonal barrel 8in. Plain walnut grips, brass trigger guard, underlever rammer and side loading, plain cylinder with rear extension to accommodate cartridges. $396 £200

A 6-shot .31in. Colt model 1849 pocket percussion single action revolver, 11in., octagonal barrel 6in. with single line address, polished wooden grip, brass trigger guard and backstrap, underlever rammer, white metal blade foresight. $396 £200

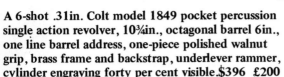

A 6-shot .31in. Colt model 1849 pocket percussion single action revolver, 10¾in., octagonal barrel 6in., one line barrel address, one-piece polished walnut grip, brass frame and backstrap, underlever rammer, cylinder engraving forty per cent visible.$396 £200

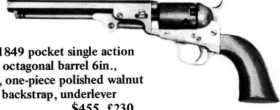

A 5-shot .31in. Remington New Model pocket single action percussion revolver, 7¾in., octagonal barrel 3½in. Two-piece polished wooden grip, spur trigger, underlever rammer, white metal blade foresight, top strap rear. $416 £210

A 5-shot .31in. Colt model 1849 pocket single action percussion revolver, 10¾in., octagonal barrel 6in., barrel with two line address, one-piece polished walnut grip, brass trigger guard and backstrap, underlever rammer, plain cylinder. $455 £230

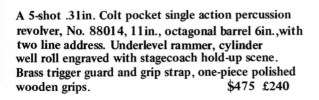

A 5-shot .31in. Colt pocket single action percussion revolver, No. 88014, 11in., octagonal barrel 6in.,with two line address. Underlevel rammer, cylinder well roll engraved with stagecoach hold-up scene. Brass trigger guard and grip strap, one-piece polished wooden grips. $475 £240

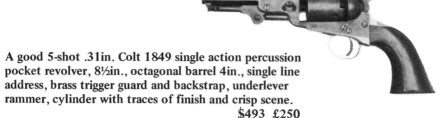

A good 5-shot .31in. Colt 1849 single action percussion
pocket revolver, 8½in., octagonal barrel 4in., single line
address, brass trigger guard and backstrap, underlever
rammer, cylinder with traces of finish and crisp scene.
$493 £250

A 5-shot .31in. Colt model 1849 single action pocket
percussion revolver, 11in., octagonal barrel 6in., barrel
with single line New York address, one-piece walnut
grip, brass trigger guard and backstrap, underlever
rammer, unfluted cylinder. $495 £250

A good 5-shot .31in. factory engraved Union Arms Co.
single action percussion pocket revolver, 8¾in., octagonal barrel 4¼in. Polished walnut grip, brass trigger
guard, underlever rammer, plain cylinder with closed
frame, brass bead foresight, top strap rear.$495 £250

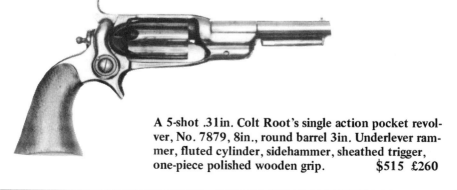

A 5-shot .31in. Colt Root's single action pocket revolver, No. 7879, 8in., round barrel 3in. Underlever rammer, fluted cylinder, sidehammer, sheathed trigger,
one-piece polished wooden grip. $515 £260

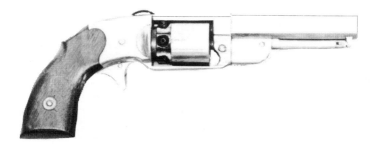

A rare 6-shot .31in. Alsop single action percussion pocket revolver, 9in., octagonal barrel 4in. Two-piece wooden grips, spur trigger, sideplate to left side of frame, underlever rammer, sidehammer, brass bead foresight, top strap rear. $594 £300

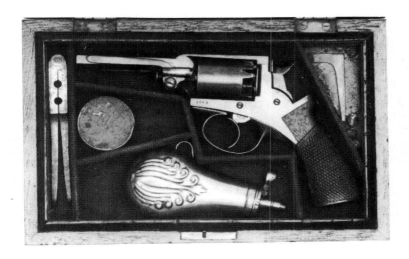

A 5-shot .31in. Adam's Patent double action percussion pocket revolver, 7½in., octagonal barrel 3¼in. Chequered walnut grip with steel cap, plain cylinder, side lever rammer. Contained in a contemporary red beize lined and fitted pistol case, containing mould, flask, cap tin, screw driver and a few bullets. $841 £425

A 6-shot .32in. rimfire Smith & Wesson model No. 2 old model single action revolver, 10½in., octagonal ribbed barrel 6in. Polished rosewood grips to angular butt, irregular sideplate, spur trigger, tip-up barrel for loading and ejection latching to bottom strap forward of trigger. $178 £90

A 6-shot .36in. Whitney single action percussion revolver, 13in., octagonal barrel 7½in. Plain walnut grips, brass trigger guard, underlever rammer, closed frame, plain cylinder, brass blade foresight, top strap groove rear. $247 £125

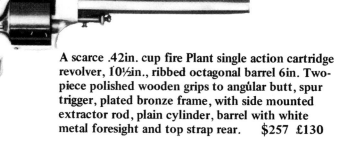

A scarce .42in. cup fire Plant single action cartridge revolver, 10½in., ribbed octagonal barrel 6in. Two-piece polished wooden grips to angular butt, spur trigger, plated bronze frame, with side mounted extractor rod, plain cylinder, barrel with white metal foresight and top strap rear. $257 £130

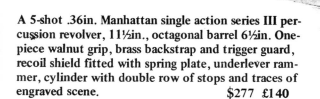

A 5-shot .36in. Manhattan single action series III percussion revolver, 11½in., octagonal barrel 6½in. One-piece walnut grip, brass backstrap and trigger guard, recoil shield fitted with spring plate, underlever rammer, cylinder with double row of stops and traces of engraved scene. $277 £140

A 5-shot .36in. rimfire Remington Police New Model single action cartridge revolver converted from percussion, 9in., barrel 4½in., octagonal barrel 4½in. Two-piece wooden grips to butt, brass trigger guard, underlever rammer, plain cylinder with backplate pierced for striker nose.   **$297 £150**

A 6-shot .36in. Manhattan series IV single action percussion revolver, 9¼in., octagonal barrel 4¼in. London black powder proof. One-piece wooden grip, brass trigger guard and backstrap, underlever rammer, unfluted roll engraved cylinder with double set of indexing notches, white metal foresight, hammer rear.   **$297 £150**

A 6-shot .36in. Colt Navy single action percussion revolver, 13in., octagonal barrel 7½in., London proved. Underlever rammer, brass trigger guard and grip strap.   **$297 £150**

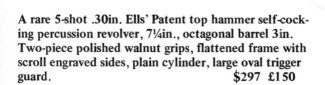

A rare 5-shot .30in. Ells' Patent top hammer self-cocking percussion revolver, 7¼in., octagonal barrel 3in. Two-piece polished walnut grips, flattened frame with scroll engraved sides, plain cylinder, large oval trigger guard.   **$297 £150**

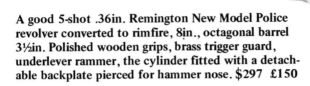

A good 5-shot .36in. Remington New Model Police
revolver converted to rimfire, 8in., octagonal barrel
3½in. Polished wooden grips, brass trigger guard,
underlever rammer, the cylinder fitted with a detachable backplate pierced for hammer nose. $297 £150

A rare 5-shot .31in. Colt Hartford single action percussion revolver, No. 185327, with iron trigger guard, 9in.,
octagonal barrel 4in., with two line address. Cylinder
with traces of stagecoach hold-up scene. Iron grip strap,
one-piece polished wooden grip. $297 £150

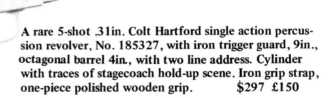

A 6-shot .31in. Allen's Patent top snap ring trigger self-
cocking pepperbox revolver, 7½in., fluted cylinder 3in.
Scroll engraved, round frame and nipple shield, bar
hammer, two-piece bag-shaped polished walnut grips.
                              $317 £160

A 5-shot .31in. Colt pocket single action percussion
revolver, No. 20949, 10in., barrel 5in. Underlever
rammer, traces of cylinder engraving, plated brass
trigger guard and grip strap, one-piece polished
wooden grip. $317 £160

A 6-shot .36in. Colt Navy single action percussion revolver, No. 37448, 13in., octagonal barrel 7½in. Underlever rammer, traces of navy scene to barrel. Plated trigger guard and grip strap, one-piece polished wooden grip. $327 £165

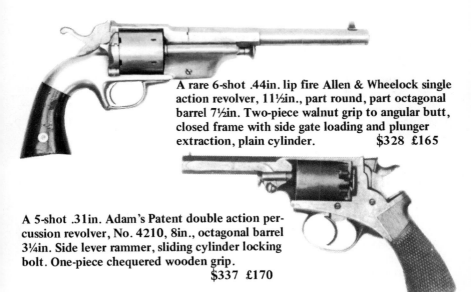

A rare 6-shot .44in. lip fire Allen & Wheelock single action revolver, 11½in., part round, part octagonal barrel 7½in. Two-piece walnut grip to angular butt, closed frame with side gate loading and plunger extraction, plain cylinder. $328 £165

A 5-shot .31in. Adam's Patent double action percussion revolver, No. 4210, 8in., octagonal barrel 3¼in. Side lever rammer, sliding cylinder locking bolt. One-piece chequered wooden grip.
$337 £170

A scarce 6-shot .36in. Remington Navy single action percussion revolver, 13½in., octagonal barrel 7½in. Wooden grips, brass trigger guard, underlever rammer, brass blade foresight, top strap rear. $337 £170

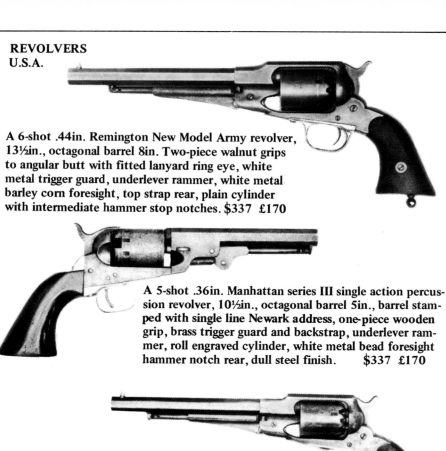

A 6-shot .44in. Remington New Model Army revolver, 13½in., octagonal barrel 8in. Two-piece walnut grips to angular butt with fitted lanyard ring eye, white metal trigger guard, underlever rammer, white metal barley corn foresight, top strap rear, plain cylinder with intermediate hammer stop notches. $337 £170

A 5-shot .36in. Manhattan series III single action percussion revolver, 10½in., octagonal barrel 5in., barrel stamped with single line Newark address, one-piece wooden grip, brass trigger guard and backstrap, underlever rammer, roll engraved cylinder, white metal bead foresight hammer notch rear, dull steel finish. $337 £170

A 6-shot .44in. Remington Army single action percussion revolver, No. 6174, 14in., octagonal barrel 8in. Top sighting channel, underlever rammer, brass trigger guard, two-piece wooden grips. $337 £170

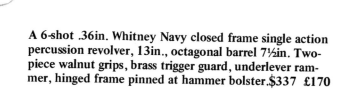

A 6-shot .36in. Whitney Navy closed frame single action percussion revolver, 13in., octagonal barrel 7½in. Two-piece walnut grips, brass trigger guard, underlever rammer, hinged frame pinned at hammer bolster. $337 £170

A scarce 6-shot .28in. Warner's Patent single action percussion revolver, 6½in., round barrel with integral top strap 2½in. Two-piece walnut grips to rounded butt, round frame with some scroll engraving, off-set hammer, small roll engraved cylinder. $337 £170

A rare 6-shot .44in. lip fire Allen & Wheelock single action revolver, 11½in., part round, part octagonal barrel 7½in., No. 90. Two-piece walnut grip to angular butt, closed frame with side gate loading and plunger extraction, plain cylinder with stops located at front, barrel screwed to frame with dovetailed brass foresight, hammer bolster rear. $346 £175

A 6-shot .44in. Remington Army single action percussion revolver, No. 289447, 14in., octagonal barrel 8in. Top sighting channel, underlever rammer, brass trigger guard, two-piece wooden grips. $356 £180

A 6-shot .36in. Whitney single action percussion revolver, 13in., octagonal barrel 7½in., No. 8826, two-piece wooden grips, latter underlever rammer latch, brass trigger guard, closed frame with plain cylinder.
                                                  $356 £180

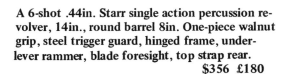

A 6-shot .44in. Starr single action percussion revolver, 14in., round barrel 8in. One-piece walnut
grip, steel trigger guard, hinged frame, underlever rammer, blade foresight, top strap rear.
$356 £180

A 6-shot .44in. Remington New Model Army single
action percussion revolver, 13½in., octagonal barrel
8in., plain wooden grips, brass trigger guard, underlever rammer, steel foresight, top strap rear.
$356 £180

A good 5-shot .36in. Manhattan series II single action
percussion revolver, 11in., octagonal barrel 6½in. One-
piece polished grip, brass trigger guard and backstrap,
underlever rammer, engraved cylinder with double
row of stops. $356 £180

A 6-shot .44in. Remington Army single action percussion revolver, No. 78460, 14in., octagonal barrel 8in.
Later blade foresight, top sighting channel, underlever
rammer, brass trigger guard, two-piece wooden grips.
$356 £180

A 6-shot .44in. Remington Army New Model single action percussion revolver, 13¾in., octagonal barrel 8in. Two-piece walnut grips, brass trigger guard, underlever rammer, white metal foresight, top strap rear, plain cylinder with intermediate recesses.

$366 £185

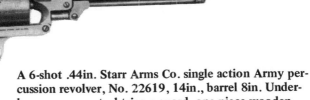

A 6-shot .44in. Starr Arms Co. single action Army percussion revolver, No. 22619, 14in., barrel 8in. Underlever rammer, steel trigger guard, one-piece wooden grips. $366 £185

A 6-shot .36in. Colt model 1851 Navy single action percussion revolver, 13in., barrel 7½in. Wooden grip with steel backstrap and trigger guard, underlever rammer, octagonal barrel, plain cylinder with traces of Naval engagement scene. $366 £185

A rare 6-shot .36in. Remington Navy model 1861 single action percussion revolver, 12¾in., octagonal barrel 7¼in. Two-piece walnut grips, brass oval trigger guard, plain cylinder with intermediate hammer recesses, underlever rammer slotted to allow removal of cylinder without dropping lever. $376 £190

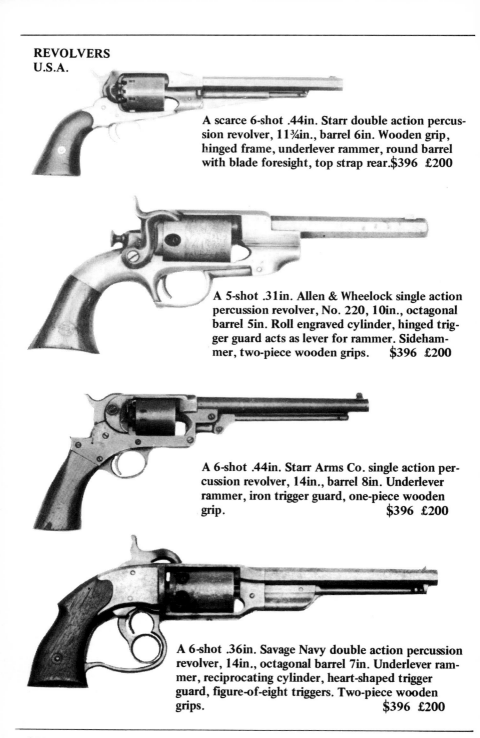

A scarce 6-shot .44in. Starr double action percussion revolver, 11¾in., barrel 6in. Wooden grip, hinged frame, underlever rammer, round barrel with blade foresight, top strap rear.$396 £200

A 5-shot .31in. Allen & Wheelock single action percussion revolver, No. 220, 10in., octagonal barrel 5in. Roll engraved cylinder, hinged trigger guard acts as lever for rammer. Sidehammer, two-piece wooden grips. $396 £200

A 6-shot .44in. Starr Arms Co. single action percussion revolver, 14in., barrel 8in. Underlever rammer, iron trigger guard, one-piece wooden grip. $396 £200

A 6-shot .36in. Savage Navy double action percussion revolver, 14in., octagonal barrel 7in. Underlever rammer, reciprocating cylinder, heart-shaped trigger guard, figure-of-eight triggers. Two-piece wooden grips. $396 £200

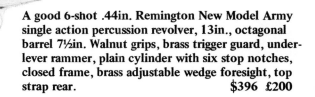

A good 6-shot .44in. Remington New Model Army single action percussion revolver, 13in., octagonal barrel 7½in. Walnut grips, brass trigger guard, under-lever rammer, plain cylinder with six stop notches, closed frame, brass adjustable wedge foresight, top strap rear.   **$396 £200**

A good 6-shot .44in. Rogers & Spencer single action Army percussion revolver, No. 983, 13in., octagonal barrel 7½in., top strap with channel sight. Under-lever rammer, steel trigger guard and grip strap, two-piece wooden grips with two small chips.**$396 £200**

A 6-shot .44in. Starr Arms Co. single action percussion revolver, No. 87065, 13½in., barrel 8in. Underlever rammer, one-piece wooden grip.   **$396 £200**

A good 6-shot .36in. Whitney single action percussion revolver, 13in., octagonal barrel 7½in. Polished wal-nut grips to angular butt, brass trigger guard, under-lever rammer, cylinder engraved with scene and cut with stop notches.   **$396 £200**

A 6-shot .36in. Colt Navy single action percussion revolver, No. 171354, 13in., octagonal barrel 7½in. Underlever rammer, brass trigger guard and grip strap, cylinder engraved with navy scene.   **$406 £205**

A good 5-shot .36in. Manhattan series III single action percussion revolver, 11½in., octagonal barrel 6½in., barrel with single line Newark address, polished walnut grip, plated brass trigger guard and backstrap, underlever rammer, the cylinder with twelve stop notches.
$416 £210

A 6-shot .44in. lip fire Allen & Wheelock single action revolver, 12½in., part round, part octagonal barrel 7½in., polished wooden grips, side gate loading and rod ejection activated by lowering the trigger guard, brass foresight, top strap rear.   **$416 £210**

A 6-shot .44in. Colt model 1861 Army single action percussion revolver, 13½in., barrel 8in. with New York address, one-piece walnut grip, brass trigger guard, underlever rammer, white metal blade foresight, hammer rear.   **$416 £210**

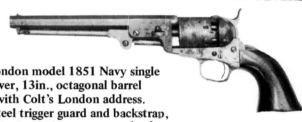

A 6-shot .36in. Colt London model 1851 Navy single
action percussion revolver, 13in., octagonal barrel
7½in., barrel stamped with Colt's London address.
Polished walnut grip, steel trigger guard and backstrap,
underlever rammer. Cylinder with some scene clearly
remaining. $416 £210

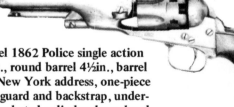

A 5-shot .36in. Manhattan Navy single action percussion revolver, No. 68591, 9in., barrel 4in., London
proved. Underlever rammer, roll engraved vignette
scenes on London proved cylinder. Plated brass trigger guard and grip strap. One-piece polished wooden
grip. $416 £210

A 5-shot .36in. Colt model 1862 Police single action
percussion revolver, 9¾in., round barrel 4½in., barrel
stamped with single line New York address, one-piece
walnut grip, brass trigger guard and backstrap, underlever rammer, half fluted rebated cylinder, brass bead
foresight, hammer notch rear. $416 £210

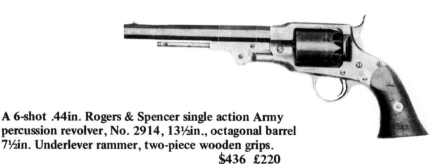

A 6-shot .44in. Rogers & Spencer single action Army
percussion revolver, No. 2914, 13½in., octagonal barrel
7½in. Underlever rammer, two-piece wooden grips.
                                        $436 £220

A 5-shot .36in. Colt Police single action percussion revolver, No. 8113, 9½in., octagonal barrel 4½in. Underlever rammer, brass trigger guard and grip strap, rebated cylinder, one-piece wooden grip.
$436 £220

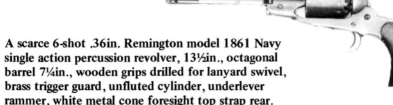

A 6-shot .44in. Remington New Model Army single action percussion revolver, No. 83924, 14in., octagonal barrel 8in. Two-piece walnut grip, brass trigger guard, underlever rammer, white metal cone foresight, top strap rear. $436 £220

A scarce 6-shot .36in. Remington model 1861 Navy single action percussion revolver, 13½in., octagonal barrel 7¼in., wooden grips drilled for lanyard swivel, brass trigger guard, unfluted cylinder, underlever rammer, white metal cone foresight top strap rear.
$445 £225

A good 5-shot .36in. Manhattan series IV Navy single action percussion revolver, 12in., octagonal barrel 6½in., two line barrel address, polished walnut grips, brass trigger guard and backstrap. New pattern underlever rammer with tapered square section, cylinder with double row of stop notches. $455 £230

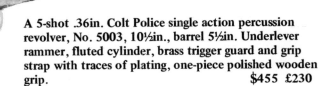

A 5-shot .36in. Colt Police single action percussion revolver, No. 5003, 10½in., barrel 5½in. Underlever rammer, fluted cylinder, brass trigger guard and grip strap with traces of plating, one-piece polished wooden grip. $455 £230

A 6-shot .44in. Remington New Model Army single action percussion revolver, 13½in., octagonal barrel 7¾in. Two-piece wooden grips, brass trigger guard, underlever rammer, closed frame, plain cylinder. $455 £230

A 6-shot .44in. Colt model 1860 Army single action percussion revolver, 13½in., round barrel 8in. One-piece wooden grips with crisp inspector's stamp, brass trigger guard, underlever creeping rammer, rebated cylinder with clear engraving. $455 £230

A 5-shot .31in. Allen & Wheelock sidehammer single action percussion revolver, 9in., rifled octagonal barrel 4in. White metal foresight, sighting channel top strap. Hinged trigger guard acts as lever rammer. Cylinder engraved, removeable sideplate, two-piece polished wooden grips. $465 £235

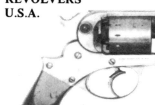

A scarce 6-shot .44in. Starr double action percussion revolver, 11¾in., barrel 6in., wooden grip with inspector's stamp, hinged frame, underlever rammer, round barrel with blade foresight, top strap rear. $475 £240

A 6-shot .36in. round barrelled Colt Navy single action percussion revolver, No. 4409, 13in., round barrel 7½in. Brass trigger guard and backstrap. Creeping rammer, one-piece wooden grip. $495 £250

A 6-shot .44in. Colt Army single action percussion revolver, No. 74159, 14in., round barrel 8in. Underlever rammer, roll engraved navy scene to rebated cylinder. Brass trigger guard, slotted for shoulder stock, one-piece wooden grip. $495 £250

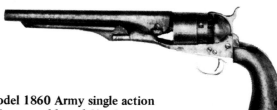

A 6-shot .44in. Colt model 1860 Army single action percussion revolver, 14in., round barrel 8in. Large walnut grip, brass trigger guard, underlever creeping rammer, white metal foresight, hammer notch rear, rebated cylinder. $495 £250

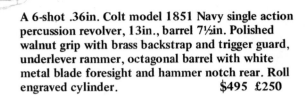

A 6-shot .36in. Colt model 1851 Navy single action percussion revolver, 13in., barrel 7½in. Polished walnut grip with brass backstrap and trigger guard, underlever rammer, octagonal barrel with white metal blade foresight and hammer notch rear. Roll engraved cylinder.   **$495 £250**

A 6-shot .44in. Remington single action Army percussion revolver, 14in., barrel 8in. Underlever rammer, brass trigger guard, two-piece wooden grips.   **$495 £250**

A 6-shot .36in. Remington model 1861 Navy single action percussion revolver, 13½in., octagonal barrel 7½in. Underlever rammer relieved for axis pin head travel. Brass trigger guard, steel frame, two-piece wooden grips.
$495 £250

A scarce 6-shot .44in. Allen & Wheelock Army single action percussion revolver, 13in., part round, part octagonal barrel 7½in. Two-piece wooden grip to angular butt, trigger guard, loading lever, closed frame, plain cylinder with central row of stop notches, under barrel mounted cylinder pin, brass foresight hammer notch rear.   **$495 £250**

A scarce 6-shot .44in. Pettengill self-cocking Army percussion revolver, 13¾in., octagonal barrel 7½in. Walnut grips to small butt, large trigger guard, closed frame, underlever rammer, white metal foresight, top strap rear. **$505 £255**

A good 6-shot .44in. Colt model 1860 Army single action percussion revolver, 13in., round barrel 8in. One-piece crisp walnut grip with clear inspector's stamps 'C.J.L.' and 'J.T.', brass trigger guard, underlever rammer, white metal blade foresight, hammer notch rear, rebated cylinder with crisp naval scene. **$515 £260**

A good 6-shot .44in. Remington New Model Army single action percussion revolver, 14in., octagonal barrel 8in., barrel stamped with Remington New York address. Two-piece wooden grips, brass trigger guard, underlever rammer, barrel with barley corn foresight, top strap rear, plain cylinder. **$515 £260**

A scarce 6-shot .44in. Freeman's Patent single action Army percussion revolver, 12½in., round barrel 7½in. Underlever rammer, steel trigger guard and grip strap, two-piece wooden grips. **$515 £260**

A 6-shot .44in. Colt model 1860 Army single action
percussion revolver, 13in., round sighted barrel 8in.,
barrel with New York address, plain walnut grip
cut for shoulder stock, underlever rammer, rebated
cylinder. $515 £260

A 5-shot .36in. Colt Police single action percussion
revolver, 11½in., round barrel 6½in., one line barrel
address. Underlever creeping rammer, fluted cylinder,
brass grip strap and trigger guard, one-piece wooden
grip. $515 £260

A 6-shot .44in. Remington New Model single action
Army percussion revolver, 14in., octagonal barrel 8in.
Underlever rammer, brass trigger guard, two-piece
wooden grips. $525 £265

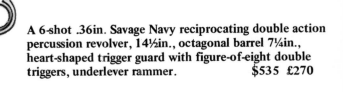

A 6-shot .36in. Savage Navy reciprocating double action
percussion revolver, 14½in., octagonal barrel 7¼in.,
heart-shaped trigger guard with figure-of-eight double
triggers, underlever rammer. $535 £270

A scarce 6-shot .44in. Starr double action percussion revolver, 11¾in., round barrel 6in. One-piece grip with inspector's stamp, jointed frame latching at hammer bolster, underlever rammer. **$535 £270**

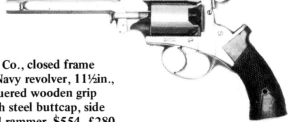

A 6-shot .44in Remington New Model Army single action percussion revolver, 14in., octagonal barrel 8in. Two-piece walnut grip, brass trigger guard, underlever rammer, white metal cone foresight, top strap rear. **$535 £270**

A 6-shot .36in. Mass Arms Co., closed frame double action percussion Navy revolver, 11½in., barrel 6in. One-piece chequered wooden grip drilled for lanyard and with steel buttcap, side mounted cylinder lock and rammer. **$554 £280**

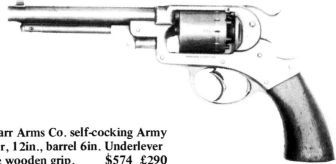

A 6-shot .44in. Starr Arms Co. self-cocking Army percussion revolver, 12in., barrel 6in. Underlever rammer, one-piece wooden grip. **$574 £290**

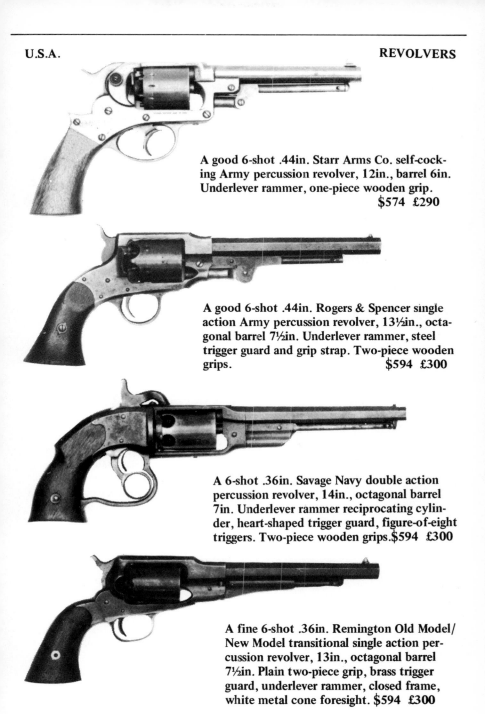

A good 6-shot .44in. Starr Arms Co. self-cocking Army percussion revolver, 12in., barrel 6in. Underlever rammer, one-piece wooden grip.
$574 £290

A good 6-shot .44in. Rogers & Spencer single action Army percussion revolver, 13½in., octagonal barrel 7½in. Underlever rammer, steel trigger guard and grip strap. Two-piece wooden grips. $594 £300

A 6-shot .36in. Savage Navy double action percussion revolver, 14in., octagonal barrel 7in. Underlever rammer reciprocating cylinder, heart-shaped trigger guard, figure-of-eight triggers. Two-piece wooden grips.$594 £300

A fine 6-shot .36in. Remington Old Model/ New Model transitional single action percussion revolver, 13in., octagonal barrel 7½in. Plain two-piece grip, brass trigger guard, underlever rammer, closed frame, white metal cone foresight. $594 £300

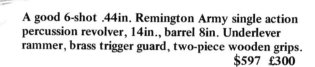

A good 6-shot .44in. Remington Army single action percussion revolver, 14in., barrel 8in. Underlever rammer, brass trigger guard, two-piece wooden grips.
$597 £300

A 6-shot .36in. Colt model 1851 Navy single action percussion revolver, 13in., octagonal barrel 7½in., barrel with New York address, one-piece wooden grip, brass backstrap and trigger guard, underlever rammer cylinder with naval scene.
$594 £300

A good .44in. Colt model 1860 Army percussion revolver, 14in., round barrel 8in., barrel stamped 'Address Col Saml Colt, New York, U.S. America'. One-piece walnut grip, brass trigger guard, underlever rammer, white metal blade foresight, hammer notch rear, plain rebated cylinder.
$594 £300

A 6-shot .36in. Colt model 1851 Navy single action percussion revolver, 13in., octagonal barrel 7½in. One-piece walnut grip, brass trigger guard and backstrap, underlever rammer, plain cylinder with traces of scene.
$594 £300

A 6-shot .44in. Remington New Model Army
single action percussion revolver, No. 111685,
14in., octagonal barrel 8in. Underlever rammer,
brass trigger guard, two-piece wooden grips.
$594 £300

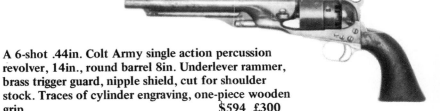

A 6-shot .44in. Colt Army single action percussion
revolver, 14in., round barrel 8in. Underlever rammer,
brass trigger guard, nipple shield, cut for shoulder
stock. Traces of cylinder engraving, one-piece wooden
grip. $594 £300

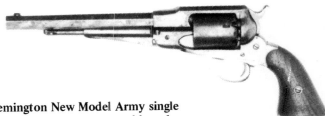

A 5-shot .28in. Colt Root's model single action percussion revolver, 7½in., octagonal barrel 3½in.,
barrel stamped with Colt's Hartford address, one-
piece polished rosewood grip, sidehammer, underlever rammer, closed frame, plain unfluted cylinder.
$614 £310

A 6-shot .44in. Remington New Model Army single
action percussion revolver, 14in., octagonal barrel
8in., two-piece walnut grip, brass trigger guard,
underlever rammer, white metal cone foresight,
top strap rear. $614 £310

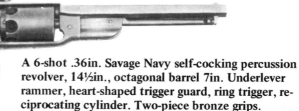

A 6-shot .44in. Colt model 1860 Army single action percussion revolver, 14in., round barrel 8in., barrel with New York address, large walnut grip, brass trigger guard, underlever creeping rammer, white metal foresight, hammer notch rear, rebated cylinder.

$614 £310

A 6-shot .36in. Savage Navy self-cocking percussion revolver, 14½in., octagonal barrel 7in. Underlever rammer, heart-shaped trigger guard, ring trigger, reciprocating cylinder. Two-piece bronze grips.

$614 £310

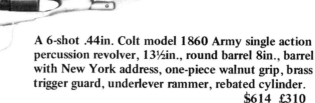

A 6-shot .44in. Colt model 1860 Army single action percussion revolver, 13½in., round barrel 8in., barrel with New York address, one-piece walnut grip, brass trigger guard, underlever rammer, rebated cylinder.

$614 £310

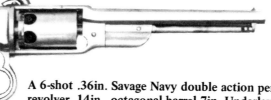

A 6-shot .36in. Savage Navy double action percussion revolver, 14in., octagonal barrel 7in. Underlever rammer, reciprocating cylinder, heart-shaped trigger guard, figure-of-eight triggers. Two-piece wooden grips.

$614 £310

A 6-shot .44in. model 1861 Remington Army
single action percussion revolver, 14in., octagonal barrel 8in. Top sighting channel, underlever rammer with cut-out section for sliding
cylinder axis pin. Brass trigger guard, two-
piece wooden grips. $614 £310

A scarce 6-shot .44in. Starr Arms Co. double
action percussion revolver, 11½in., round
barrel 6in. One-piece polished walnut grip,
hinged frame with top strap secured to hammer bolster by means of knurled screw, underlever rammer, round barrel with dovetailed
blade foresight and hammer 'v' rear.$653 £330

A good 6-shot .44in. Remington New Model Army
single action percussion revolver, 14in., octagonal
barrel 8in., barrel stamped with patent dates, address
and New Model, two-piece walnut grips, brass trigger
guard, underlever rammer, plain cylinder. $653 £330

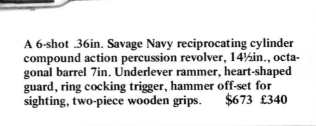

A 6-shot .36in. Savage Navy reciprocating cylinder
compound action percussion revolver, 14½in., octagonal barrel 7in. Underlever rammer, heart-shaped
guard, ring cocking trigger, hammer off-set for
sighting, two-piece wooden grips. $673 £340

A good 6-shot .44in. Remington New Model Army single action percussion revolver, 13in., octagonal barrel 8in., barrel stamped with 1858 patent date and address, plain wooden grips, brass trigger guard, underlever rammer, cylinder with intermediate hammer notches. $673 £340

A good 6-shot .36in. Savage Navy double action percussion revolver, 14in., octagonal barrel 7in. Underlever rammer, reciprocating cylinder, heart-shaped trigger guard, figure-of-eight triggers. Two-piece wooden grips. $693 £350

A scarce 6-shot .36in. Savage Revolving Firearms Co. Navy double action revolver, 14in., octagonal barrel 7in., walnut grips, heart-shaped trigger guard, reciprocating cylinder, underlever rammer, bead foresight, hammer bolster rear. $713 £360

A very scarce 6-shot .36in. Colt model 1851 Navy single action percussion revolver, 13in, octagonal barrel 7½in. One-piece walnut grip, brass trigger guard and backstrap, underlever rammer, brass bead foresight, hammer rear. $713 £360

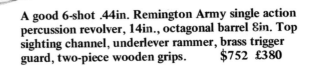

A good 6-shot .44in. Remington Army single action percussion revolver, 14in., octagonal barrel 8in. Top sighting channel, underlever rammer, brass trigger guard, two-piece wooden grips. **$752 £380**

A rare .44in. Colt model 1848 first model Dragoon single action percussion revolver, 13in., round and part octagonal barrel 6¾in. One-piece apparently old ivory grip, brass trigger guard and backstrap, v-shaped main spring, plain cylinder with oval stop notches.
          $891 £450

A very rare 6-shot .44in. Colt third model Dragoon single action percussion revolver, 14in., round barrel 6½in. Brass trigger guard, one-piece walnut grip, backstrap cut for shoulder stock, underlever rammer, white metal blade foresight, large plain cylinder with square stop notches.
          $1,237 £625

A fine 6-shot .36in. Colt Navy single action percussion revolver, 13in., octagonal barrel 7½in. The following parts are damascened with gold sheet : trigger guard, hammer, screw heads, trigger, ramrod latch, muzzle and capping groove. One-piece polished wood grip, in its original leather holster. **$3,366 £1,700**

RIFLES

An 11mm. Japanese converted chassepot rifle, 47in., part round, part octagonal barrel 30½in., plain half-stocked, one-piece fore-end, short butt section.　　$158　£80

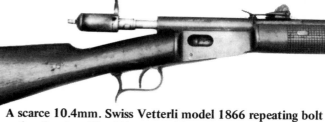

A scarce 10.4mm. Swiss Vetterli model 1866 repeating bolt action Service rifle, 51in., round barrel 33in., regulation walnut full stock with chequered fore-end, steel mounts.
　　　　　　　　　　　　　　　　　　　　$168　£85

A .577in. second model 1853 Enfield three-band Military percussion rifle, 55in., round barrel 38¾in., regulation walnut military full stock, brass mounts, steel sling swivels.
　　　　　　　　　　　　　　　　　　　$337　£170

A .451in. Westley Richards monkey tail breech loading percussion rifle, 52½in., barrel 34in., Birmingham proved, ladder rearsight. Full-stocked, regulation steel mounts and ramrod.　　　　　　　　　　　　　　　　$396　£200

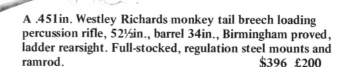

A .38in. WCF Winchester model 1873 underlever repeating rifle, 43in., round barrel 24¼in. Plain walnut stock with heavy crescent buttplate containing trap.　　$416　£210

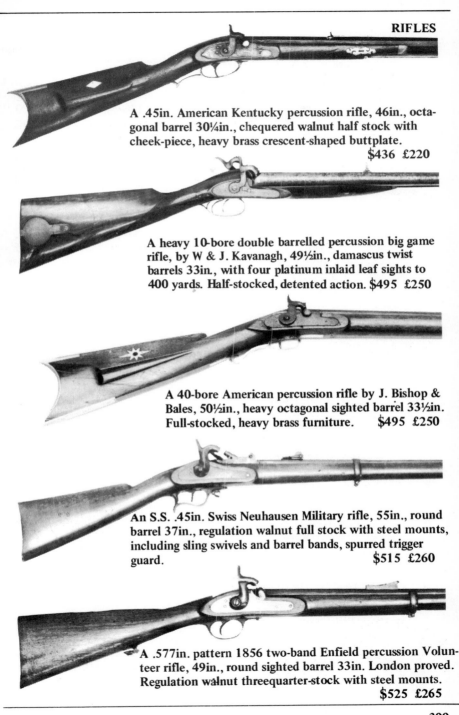

A .45in. American Kentucky percussion rifle, 46in., octagonal barrel 30¼in., chequered walnut half stock with cheek-piece, heavy brass crescent-shaped buttplate.

$436 £220

A heavy 10-bore double barrelled percussion big game rifle, by W & J. Kavanagh, 49½in., damascus twist barrels 33in., with four platinum inlaid leaf sights to 400 yards. Half-stocked, detented action. $495 £250

A 40-bore American percussion rifle by J. Bishop & Bales, 50½in., heavy octagonal sighted barrel 33½in. Full-stocked, heavy brass furniture. $495 £250

An S.S. .45in. Swiss Neuhausen Military rifle, 55in., round barrel 37in., regulation walnut full stock with steel mounts, including sling swivels and barrel bands, spurred trigger guard. $515 £260

A .577in. pattern 1856 two-band Enfield percussion Volunteer rifle, 49in., round sighted barrel 33in. London proved. Regulation walnut threequarter-stock with steel mounts.

$525 £265

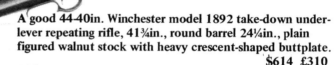

A good 44-40in. Winchester model 1892 take-down under-lever repeating rifle, 41¾in., round barrel 24¼in., plain figured walnut stock with heavy crescent-shaped buttplate.
$614 £310

An Indian percussion superimposed load Torador, 36½in., barrel 31½in., the muzzle in the form of a monster, fluted and decorated breech, eight silver barrel bands. $614 £310

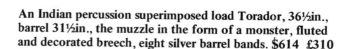

A good .577in. two-band Enfield Volunteer percussion rifle, 42¾in., barrel 28¾in., Ordnance and Birmingham proved. Full-stocked, regulation steel mounts, chequered small and fore of stock.
$653 £330

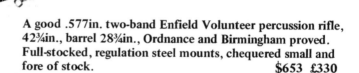

A good .32-40in. Winchester model 94, take-down underlever repeating rifle, 44in., barrel 26in., barrel part round, part octagonal, walnut stock with sling swivel and steel buttplate.
$713 £360

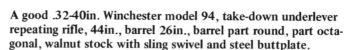

A Continental pump-up air rifle, circa 1800, 49½in., barrel 31¾in., external action slightly foliate engraved, iron screw on butt reservoir with wooden comb, associated stirrup pump.
$792 £400

A rare 70-bore 6-shot David Hn. Patent single action revolving percussion rifle, 40in., octagonal rifled barrel 23½in. Side lever rammer. Scrolled trigger guard, chequered small of stock. **$832 £420**

A .577in. Volunteer three-band Enfield percussion rifle, 55½in., barrel 39in., Birmingham proved, rearsight to 800 yards. Full-stocked, regulation steel mounts, with plaque engraved '1st Sussex Rifle Volunteers, 2nd prize won by Sergt. S. Russell.' **$990 £500**

A 5-shot 20-bore double trigger Tranter's Patent percussion revolving rifle, 48in., octagonal barrel 29¾in., London proved. **$1,039 £525**

A fine 60-bore Continental Military percussion rifle, 51in., browned twist barrel 33in., tangent rearsight. Liege proved. Double set triggers. **$1,089 £550**

A 16-bore Indian Enfield type percussion replica carbine, 42in., barrel 26in., threequarter-stock with iron mounts, steel barrel bands, bar action lock. **$1,386 £700**

A rare Webley Mark II air rifle, 41½in., barrels 25½in., chequered walnut
stock with composition buttplate, in its original canvas backed green
beize lined and fitted carrying case, with three barrels in .177in., 22in.
and 25in. bore sizes. $1,386 £700

A very rare .44in. rimfire model 1860 Henry underlever
repeating rifle, 44in., full octagonal barrel 24in. Walnut
stock with heavy brass second pattern crescent buttplate,
steel sling swivel screwed to left side. $2,277 £1,150

SPORTING GUNS

A 14-bore double barrelled percussion sporting gun,
44in., twist barrels 27¼in., with safety plugs. Half-
stocked, foliate engraved steel furniture.$257 £130

A good 5-shot 6.5mm. Mannlicher Schoenaver bolt
action repeating sporting carbine, 38½in., barrel 18in.
Chequered full length walnut stock with steel buttplate, double set triggers, bead foresight, bolt aperture rear, rotating spool type magazine. $267 £135

A double barrelled 12-bore x 2½in. top lever opening hammerless boxlock non-ejector sporting gun, 46¼in., barrels 30in. barrel rib engraved, chequered semi pistol grip walnut stock with horn buttcap and blank silver escutcheon. $297 £150

A good double barrelled 12-bore x 2½in. top lever opening hammer sporting gun by C. Pryse & Co., 44½in., browned damascus barrels 28½in. Chequered straight hand figured walnut stock. $297 £150

A good 14-bore Indian trade percussion sporting gun, 63in., round barrel 46½in., chequered walnut full stock with iron furniture, long spurred buttplate and trigger guard with acorn finial and scrolled finger rest. $297 £150

A double barrelled 15-bore percussion sporting gun by Manton, 48in., twist barrels 32in., with break-off breech and secured by flat key, stepped locks. $317 £160

A good double barrelled 12-bore x 2¾in. top lever opening boxlock ejector sporting gun by Webley & Scott, 43in. barrels 26in, straight hand chequered walnut stock with blank white metal escutcheon. $337 £170

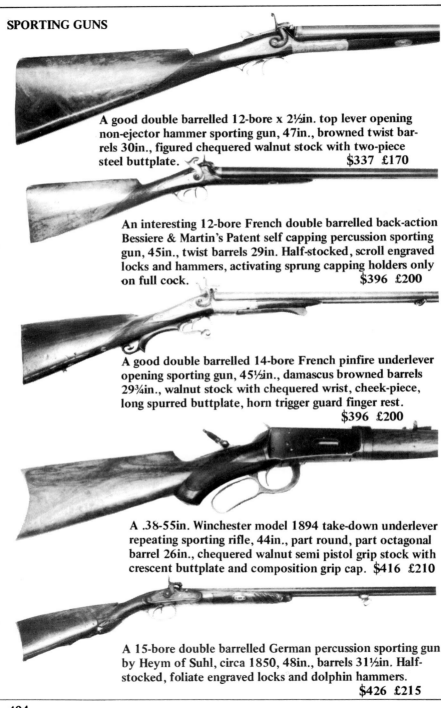

A good double barrelled 12-bore x 2½in. top lever opening non-ejector hammer sporting gun, 47in., browned twist barrels 30in., figured chequered walnut stock with two-piece steel buttplate.   **$337 £170**

An interesting 12-bore French double barrelled back-action Bessiere & Martin's Patent self capping percussion sporting gun, 45in., twist barrels 29in. Half-stocked, scroll engraved locks and hammers, activating sprung capping holders only on full cock.   **$396 £200**

A good double barrelled 14-bore French pinfire underlever opening sporting gun, 45½in., damascus browned barrels 29¾in., walnut stock with chequered wrist, cheek-piece, long spurred buttplate, horn trigger guard finger rest.   **$396 £200**

A .38-55in. Winchester model 1894 take-down underlever repeating sporting rifle, 44in., part round, part octagonal barrel 26in., chequered walnut semi pistol grip stock with crescent buttplate and composition grip cap. **$416 £210**

A 15-bore double barrelled German percussion sporting gun by Heym of Suhl, circa 1850, 48in., barrels 31½in. Half-stocked, foliate engraved locks and dolphin hammers.   **$426 £215**

A double barrelled 15-bore French back-action percussion sporting rifle, 44in., tightly twisted barrels 27in. Half-stocked, locks engraved, plain hardened steel furniture with swollen finials, steel ramrod with sling swivels.

$445 £225

A double barrelled 12-bore x 2½in. underlever opening back-action hammer sporting gun by Boss & Co., 46in., browned damascus barrels 30in., chequered straight hand figured walnut stock with steel buttplate and silver escutcheon. $495 £250

A good 5-shot .275in. Mauser bolt action sporting rifle, 43in., round barrel 21in. Half length chequered walnut pistol grip stock, sling eyes, down-turned small bolt handle, bead foresight, two folding leaf rear. In its brass mounted leather covered red beize lined and fitted case. $515 £260

A double barrelled 12-bore x 2½in. underlever opening back-action hammer sporting gun, by Boss & Co., 46in., browned damascus barrels 30in., chequered straight hand figured walnut stock with steel buttplate and silver escutcheon $544 £275

A scarce double barrelled 14-bore Needham bolt action needle fire sporting gun, 46in., barrels 27in. Chequered walnut stock with long spurred steel buttcap and integral bolted fore-end with white metal escutcheon.

$634 £320

SPORTING GUNS

A good double barrelled 12-bore x 2½in. top lever opening hammerless boxlock ejector sporting gun, 46½in., barrels 30in, chequered semi pistol grip, walnut stock with horn butt plate and white metal escutcheon. $634   £320

A good double barrelled 12-bore x 2½in. boxlock hammerless top lever opening ejector sporting gun, 42¼in., barrels 25in., chequered straight hand, walnut tear-drop stock and chequered Anson fore-end, auto safety. $693   £350

An 18-bore double barrelled percussion sporting gun, 46in., browned twist barrels 30in., London proved. Half-stocked, foliate engraved locks and hammers, most unusual sliding thumb safety on barrel tang spur locks triggers. Steel furniture, pineapple finialled trigger guard. Silver barrel wedge plates. Contained in its blue and velvet lined fitted mahogany case. $1,228   £620

A 24-bore double barrelled percussion sporting rifle, 47in., twist barrels 30in., five groove rifling, leaf sights to 300 yards. Half-stocked, bolted detented locks. Steel furniture, chequered small and fore of stock, silver escutcheon. Contained in its brass bound green beize lined fitted mahogany case. $1,485   £750

A good double barrelled 10- bore x 3¼in. top level opening boxlock non-ejector sporting gun, by J. Purdey & sons, 47¾in., barrels 31in. Chequered straight hand figured walnut tear-drop stock with rubber extension. $1,485 £750

A good double barrelled 12-bore x 2½in. thumbhole trigger guard opening back-action hammer non-ejector sporting gun, by J. Purdey, 47in., browned damascus barrels 30in. $1,600 £850

A good double barrelled 30-bore back-action German percussion sporting rifle by J. A. Kuchenreuter, circa 1840, 42½in., damascus twist barrels 27in., twin silver breech lines with silver safety plugs. Steel furniture. Carved cheek-piece and scrolled wooden trigger guard, chequered within scrolled borders at small of stock. $1,980
                                                                                 £1,000

A good double barrelled 12-bore x 2½in. top lever opening, hammerless side lock ejector sporting gun, 47in., fine twist barrel 30¼in. Walnut tear-drop stock with chequered wrist and butt, engraved silver escutcheon. In a leather covered red beize lined and fitted motor case, with brass corners and lock. $2,376 £1,200

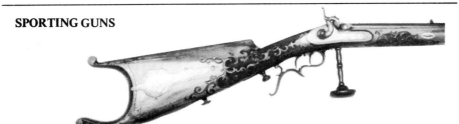

A good 60-bore Dutch percussion target or sporting rifle, circa 1840, 51in., octagonal rifled barrel 32in., scroll silver inlaid at breech, tube foresight, tangent midsight. Half-stocked, stepped detented lock, double set triggers. Scroll engraved steel furniture. Brass tipped whalebone ramrod.$2,376 £1,200

A .451in. percussion sporting rifle, 53in., octagonal twist barrel, adjustable rearsight to 1,300 yards, half-stocked, detented scroll engraved bolted lock. Scroll engraved steel furniture, chequered small and fore of stock. Contained in its leather lined fitted oak case. $2,376 £1,200

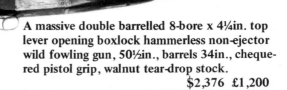

A massive double barrelled 8-bore x 4¼in. top lever opening boxlock hammerless non-ejector wild fowling gun, 50½in., barrels 34in., chequered pistol grip, walnut tear-drop stock.
$2,376 £1,200

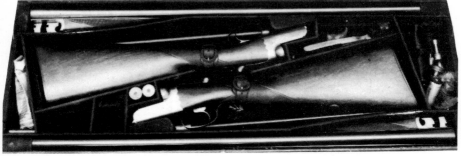

A pair of double barrelled 12-bore - 2½in. top lever opening boxlock ejector sporting guns, 44½in., barrels 28in., chequered straight hand, walnut stock with horn buttplate and silver escutcheons. Contained in their green beize lined and fitted leather blocked gun case. $4,554 £2,300

INDEX

BURNOUT:

**Strategies for Personal and Organizational Life
Speculations on Evolving Paradigms**

Michael Lauderdale
The University of Texas at Austin

Learning Concepts

Distributed by
University Associates

Burnout:
Strategies for Personal and Organizational Life
Speculations on Evolving Paradigms

© 1982 by Michael Lauderdale

Library of Congress Cataloguing in Publication Data

Lauderdale, Michael L.

   Burnout, strategies for personal and organizational life.

   Bibliography: p.
   Includes index.
   1. Fatigue. 2. Work—Psychological aspects. 3. Organizational
behavior. I. Title.
HD4904.5.L38   658.3′001′9   81-16298
                                                               AACR2
First Printing

ISBN 0-89384-063-7

Learning Concepts
Austin, Texas

Distributed by University Associates, Inc.
8517 Production Avenue
P.O. Box 26240
San Diego, California 92126

Permission Acknowledgments

Chapter epigraphs: Chapter 1, p. 3: From *Notes to Myself* by Hugh Prather. Reprinted by permission of Real People Press and the author. Chapter 2, p. 25: From *Of a Fire on the Moon* by Norman Mailer. © 1969, 1970 by Norman Mailer. Reprinted by permission of the author and the author's agents, Scott Meredith Literary Agency, Inc., 845 Third Avenue, New York, New York 10022. Also by permission of Little, Brown and Company. Chapter 3, p. 39: From *The Dynamics of Change* by Don Fabun. © 1966 by Kaiser Aluminum & Chemical Corporation. Reprinted by permission. Chapter 4, p. 51: From "The Me Decade and the Third Great Awakening" by Tom Wolfe, *New York Magazine*, August 1976, pp. 26-40. Copyright © 1976 by Tom Wolfe. Chapter 5, p. 65: From *People of the Lake: Mankind and Its Beginnings* by Richard Leakey and Roger Lewin. Reprinted by permission of Doubleday Communications Corporation. Chapter 6, p. 77: From *Scientific Management* by Frederick W. Taylor. Reprinted by permission of Harper and Row Publishers. Chapter 7, p. 89: From "Sellers Strikes Again," *Time*, March 3, 1980, p. 64. Reprinted by permission from *Time*, The Weekly Newsmagazine; Copyright Time Inc. 1980. Chapter 10, p. 145: From *Zen and the Art of Motorcycle Maintenance* by Robert M. Pirsig. Reprinted by permission of William Morrow & Company, Inc., Publishers. Chapter 12, p. 189: First selection from *Science and the Common Understanding* by J. Robert Oppenheimer. Reprinted by permission of Simon & Schuster, Inc., Publishers. Second selection reprinted from *The Structure of Scientific Revolutions* (2nd ed.) by Thomas S. Kuhn, by permission of The University of Chicago Press. © 1962, 1970 by The University of Chicago. Chapter 13, p. 205: From *The Awakening of Faith* by Ashvaghosha, translated by D.T. Suzuki (Illinois: Open Court Publishing Company, 1900). Third selection reprinted from *The Modern Temper* by Joseph W. Krutch. Reprinted by permission of Harcourt Brace Jovanovich, Inc. Chapter 14: p. 219: Second selection from *Demeter and Other Poems* by Alfred, Lord Tennyson (New York: Macmillan, 1889). Chapter 15, p. 241: First selection from *Modern*

To Camille, Gregory, and Marisa

Nautilus. Cephalopod mollusk belonging
to the sole surviving genus (*Nautilus*) of a
subclass that flourished 200 million years
ago, known as the nautiloids. The spirally
coiled shell consists of a series of chambers;
as the nautilus grows it secretes larger chambers, sealing off the old ones with thin
septa.

New Columbia Encyclopedia

Preface

This book began as an attempt to understand burnout and to provide some techniques for individuals, managers, human resource development personnel, and others who work with people to lessen the impact of burnout. For several years, I have worked as a manager and as a consultant to various organizations. During this time, I have watched organizations move toward what might be called a people-intensive quality. Few jobs today can be performed by a single individual with only a few tools and the raw materials needed to create a product. Rather, the tasks in organizations now involve complex relationships with several individuals as part of the nature of work. This seems almost as true today for the traditional products sector of the economy as for the services sector. Paralleling this movement toward people-intensive work has been an increased involvement of all persons in work and in formal organizations.*

Quotas are set and each step in achieving the quota is rationally determined to maximize output per unit of resources. Moreover, it seems that this obsession with achieving the most possible within formal organizations has spread to each individual's sense of what life should be. More than ever, people are intent on achieving something for themselves. Activities are judged for what they accomplish for the individual. Simultaneously, there is an increased awareness, both a cognition and an emotion, that what is achieved is less than what is anticipated.

Through my efforts to understand burnout, I found it pertinent to examine some other concepts in the literature of worker productivity—especially stress and alienation. It was also necessary to explore burnout beyond the work place. Satisfaction on the job cannot be simply explained in terms of the type of work, amount of pay, working

---

*By *formal organizations,* I refer to social groups that are consciously structured with detailed tasks to achieve specific goals.

conditions, and modes of supervision. How one perceives one's work and, consequently, one's self is also affected by what is happening at home and in the rest of the world. The task in understanding burnout would be far simpler if people could lead their lives in tight compartments. But people's lives do not exist as tight compartments.

Because of the interconnectedness of people's lives beyond work, I found that in examining burnout I was continually drawn into broader and deeper waters. These waters consist of many things, including the world view of our culture, the rate and type of social and technological change, and the logical structure of formal organizations, to name a few. Rather than attempt to exhaustively analyze the contributions such factors make to burnout, I dipped in and out of these areas to draw illustrations of the inherent implications. When I was finished, it seemed I had two books or perhaps two perspectives that if taken together give a more complete picture of the phenomenon. So, this book is divided into two parts. The first, some ten chapters, defines burnout, discusses how widespread it is, probes for its probable causes, and offers some suggestions for personal use and for managers and human resource developers to use in helping employees. The second part delves more deeply into social evolution in order to establish a larger context within which to view individual expectations and aspirations. It poses what I feel are the larger, more distal causes of burnout. In both parts, available data are less than what the tasks require and I have, in some cases, drawn inferences that test the rules of prudence. Nevertheless, I feel that such an exercise is useful in tying burnout, in a preliminary fashion, to changes in the culture and extending the current concern about burnout to what appear to me to be its deeper sources.

This book may be read for different purposes. Some may read it to understand what burnout is and what an individual may do to alleviate one's own personal case. It may be used similarly by one who works with or supervises others, to understand personal and social change. The intent is to describe and explain the feelings and problems associated with change and to suggest strategies that are restorative for the individual.

The first part of the book, chapters 1 through 10, are intended for individual use on how to deal personally with uncertainty, frustration, and unmet expectations. Chapter 10 arranges the tools specifically for use by managers and trainers within organizations. Chapters 11 through 16 locate historically and culturally the roots that give rise to the individual phenomena involved with change and relate them to broader organizational as well as psychological currents. That part may prove to be more laborious reading and of particular interest to the reader who wishes to dig more deeply into the general etiology of social change, the evolution of individual consciousness and, necessarily, burnout. But, an understanding of these chapters is not necessary for reaching more effective coping strategies for dealing with personal burnout.

Four themes are addressed in varying fashion in the following pages. One theme deals with defining burnout and relating the definition both to internal states of the individual and to the exterior content of the culture. The second theme is the preliminary examination of the consequences of mostly continuous rather than periodical ambiguity. The changing or evolving consciousness of the individual is the third theme, and viewing social change in terms of epochs or paradigms with the general characteristics of an emerging paradigm is the fourth.

Contents

List of Figures

List of Tables

Part I

Strategies for Personal
and Organizational Life

The following ten chapters focus on the symptoms, progression, and explanation of burnout. Case examples are presented to illustrate various personal manifestations of burnout which relate it to changes in roles and expectations.

Burnout is examined as a phenomenon appearing both at work and in one's personal life. The consequences of changes in the world of work are tied to the occurrence of burnout and an argument is presented that the changes are creating a different sense of personal identity. Solutions for dealing with burnout personally and as a manager are also included.

Chapter 1 illustrates personal perceptions about our times through a series of case histories. Chapters 2, 3, and 4 explore the meaning of the word *burnout*, provide a general explanation and an illustration of the factors that lead to it, and examine habitual responses that are developed for coping with burnout. These chapters are designed to encourage a self-assessment process and to provide an understanding of the different degrees of burnout and responses available for dealing with the problem.

Chapters 5 and 6 sketch the cultural and organizational changes which give rise to our current world and individual consciousness. Chapter 7 is an elaboration of organizational and personal themes that develop in response to the social reality described in the preceding chapters and asserts that individual reality becomes an attempt to construct a viable role. The eighth chapter illustrates personal accommodations to the times and returns to the concepts offered in the second, third, and fourth chapters. It presents a definition of the self that is more consistent with the times and, thus, less vulnerable to severe burnout. The ninth chapter offers specific procedures for developing a new sense of identity as a response to burnout. The tenth chapter is intended especially for managers and other personnel who must cope with burnout in others in work situations.

I have used a nautilus shell to symbolically depict the growth and maturation of the individual over time. Such symbolism is useful to remind ourselves that, in spite of change, memories and experiences provide continuity and both limits and potential for individual change.

1

Finding One's Self Through the Commodity Markets

Just when I think I have learned the way to live, life changes and I am left the same as I began. The more things change, the more I am the same. But there will never be means to ends, only means. And I am means. I am what I started with, and when it is all over I will be all that is left of me.

Hugh Prather, *Notes to Myself.*

Midway through the seventies, I got a touch of what might be called silver fever. I had ventured in and out of the stock market, mutual funds, and real estate. Like most people, I made some money and lost some money. One thing I learned was that you can't make money by just investing in something and holding it for the long run. The interest the bank pays in a savings account beats you every time. One summer I decided to get into the hottest game in town, the commodity markets and into the hottest commodity—silver futures. I quickly learned what a fast game was about as my investment in a few weeks rose from a few thousand dollars to over $100,000 and then, before I could cash in some of my winnings, my wealth plunged to where I had started.

Each morning I had to read the *Wall Street Journal* to see what the markets had closed with even before I had my coffee. I pored over the financial pages daily and devoured *Barron's*, the financial weekly, each Monday. I subscribed to commodity newsletters, drew charts, and kept a hot line to my broker during daily trading hours.

There was no rest even on the weekends as I analyzed commodity patterns, agricultural prices, world economies, weather patterns, and potential unrest across the world. In my quest for knowledge, I soon learned that the price of silver is complexly related to all these variables. West Texas farmers, as an example, were then converting dollars into silver as a way to hedge against the declining value of the dollar and the rising cost of petroleum-based fertilizer. World unrest encourages silver buying and hoarding, for it is the poor man's gold, a hedge against chaos. The hoarding restricts the supply driving the price up. India must be watched very closely as millions of Indian women have for years used silver jewelry rather than banks to store any savings and famine in India could cause the women to trade silver for food thus depressing the price of silver. The American government must also be watched because of the potential of unloading silver from government stockpiles to strengthen the dollar. And finally, there are the gnomes of Zurich, the sheiks of Saudi Arabia, and the Hunts of Dallas. The first are secretive and cunning; the second, wealthy beyond measure; the last, bold and daring. Each can change the rules of the game at a moment's notice because of their vast holdings of silver.

In a matter of weeks, I found that I had become a commodity junkie. Each day my worth could be calculated on the international markets—fluctuating by the minute during the day. Actually, I learned, as a consequence of modern communications, my worth changed around the clock because while I slept a commodity market was open in another part of the world. My identity, which had become so closely involved with my financial worth in silver futures, was continually changing. I checked the paper each morning to determine the state of my existence.

This daily transformation and trading of my self wearied me after several weeks. I closed out my contracts and left the silver markets to the gnomes and the Hunts. However, the experience left an indelible impression of how quickly our world changes and how changes throughout the world can come home to us very rapidly. I was also struck by the notion that each of us is a commodity whose worth is determined in the market each day and how we must plunge into this market every morning.

Commodity markets consist of unromantic, mundane things. Things like peanut oil, steers, scrap steel, cattle hides, old newspapers, heating oil, corn, broiler chickens, lumber, and pork bellies. They are bought and sold in markets around the world for same-day-delivery or delivery a few months in the future. They are the raw material—the food stuffs, fiber, and energy—that feed, clothe, house, and move us about.

As humans, our existence is a little different. Each morning we get up and check the newspaper or television for the weather to see what clothes to wear. The set of the television morning news program is constructed to resemble a living room so that our living room or breakfast area blends in unnoticed with the network world. News of world events and political commentary tells us what our emotions should be that day. Horror and sadness for the Far East; anger for the Middle East; bemusement for England; and of course, the French are having another national strike. The television provides timely advice like the farmer's almanac on exercises to combat middle-age bulge and how to replace a broken light bulb stuck in the socket. Ads with persons as familiar as our own family tell us how we should shave, bathe, and perfume every part of our body. Breakfast commercials remind us, with a patience that mother never had, what our nutrition should be or what our children's nutrition should not be.

Driving or commuting to work we follow a route like a rat in a maze or a widget moving down the assembly line. Traffic lights tell us to stop and go. Signs tell us when to turn and where to get off the freeway. The office, the factory, the school, the grocery store direct us, move us, channel us. Our co-workers assure us to get along, you must go along. And so goes the day until we are processed back home at day's end to be lulled by the evening television until the market opens in the morning.

ESTRANGEMENT AND CONTRADICTIONS

Commodities are raw products that are transformed by our economy into various consumable items. The extent to which this same process is changing each of us ranges far and wide. It has begun to change the definition of ourselves as individuals, the meaning of family and career, and started a transformation of several of the central institutions of our society. More and more people today do not feel fully a part of the world they live in. Every day they sense a growing estrangement from other people around them and from society. The world seems to be full of inconsistencies and contradictions. Each of us is expected—obliged—to have a career, to be something, to do something useful. Everyone is expected to accomplish something, to make something of himself. Yet, there has perhaps never been a time when it was so very difficult to decide what is worthwhile or laudable.

If we choose a career in business and the pursuit of personal wealth, is this a sure route to happiness or to respect? If we decide to be a teacher, can we really accomplish anything or are students indifferent to learning? If we choose to be an engineer or an architect or a carpenter, are we engaged in building things or only destroying our environment?

We proclaim the steadfastness of family and marriage. Everyone of age is either married, going to be married, or hastening to get unmarried. We may be more casual—less official—in sanctioning the act of marriage, but whether it be called marriage, cohabitation, or living together, it is the normal state for a person to be part of a couple. Yet, it is difficult to define exactly what a marriage is. One definition is that it is essentially an economic agreement with some separation of duties and the pooling of two incomes. For some, marriage is a sacred commitment sanctioned by a religion, a tie that can only be broken by death. In other cases, marriage is a transitory sexual bond—an open, revolving door for both partners. In our times, marriage is all of these things and yet for any individual it cannot be all of these things without great contradiction.

In economic life, we have many maxims of thrift and savings. We remember that "a penny saved is a penny earned," to "save for a rainy day," and to "waste not and want not." Our cultural heritage reminds us that consumption and indulgence are the root of all evil, and yet of all the nations on earth we consume the most in energy, food, travel, and entertainment. With less than 10 percent of the earth's population, we utilize 40 percent of the earth's extractable resources. Great wealth itself is made not through saving but by debt. In these years, apart from being lucky by birth or marriage, the key to wealth is to borrow a large sum of money at an interest rate less than the rate of inflation. If you have a 100 percent mortgage on your home at 7 percent interest and inflation is running at 10 percent, your wealth grows each year such that by the end of eight years your home is worth twice the mortgage. Most of home-owning America is now playing this game, yet few people question the source of the wealth. The key is simply the transfer from those who deposit their savings in banks to those who borrow for homes.

The size of our economy exerts its impact on the world through the utilization of natural resources or the degree of debt it has created in this turbulent period. In 1979, the United States used one-third of all the petroleum produced in the world and imported more than Japan and West Germany which have no domestic production to speak of.

It is very difficult to get a complete picture of the amount of wealth and debt within the United States. Some current estimates of the national debt exceed $9 trillion. That means that the debt is equal to nine years of our current gross national product of $1 trillion. The federal debt alone requires interest payments of over $1 billion each week. Thus, each of us must pay $5 each week for federal interest charges alone. Henry Kaufman, a general partner of the investment banking firm Salomon Brothers, estimated total corporate and private debt at $3.8 trillion in 1979 and rising to $10.2 trillion by the end of the 1980s (*Dow Theory Letters*, 1979).

The desire for riches contributed immeasurably to the development of both American continents. Spain, France, the Netherlands, and England all exploited the wealth of North America, and from one perspective the American Revolution was a consequence of an argument over wealth. Abundant natural resources and individual pursuit of riches have been a national norm.

Another fundamental value has been the freedom of religious expression. The United States is a land of churches. Our currency proclaims "In God We Trust" and we pledge ourselves as "one nation under God." The Constitution declares religious freedom and the importance of religious devotion. Yet, what is the definition of this God and of religion?

A hundred years ago it was a protestant God that emphasized abstinence, methodical study, and simple, austere places of worship. With the coming of large number of Irish and Eastern European Roman Catholics, a definition of God emerged that was more ornate. Today, every city offers over a hundred creeds, even advertising in the Saturday paper and on billboards along the streets, often with strikingly competing definitions of religious expression and proper devotion. In the sixties these treatises were expanded by streams of thought from Asia. No airport in the United States is without urban apostles pressing on weary travelers the writings of Asian mystics from three thousand years ago. Yet religion, by and large, does not engender for most of us the extreme supplication, obligation, or ecstasy of our forebears. The majority of Americans associate with one of the formal organized religions, but it is unlikely that anywhere near a majority is certain of the correctness of their choice of religious institution.

The proper roles for men and women are no longer drawn along strict lines, but are often the subject of heated debate. What is a man supposed to be and what is a woman supposed to be? Are they equal, should they be equal, and *can* they be equal is a national debate. There is little question about the anatomical differences. Biochemical differences seem well established and perhaps there are sex-related differences in psychological functioning. The debate is around the issues of social roles and whether most or all roles can and should be open without discrimination to both sexes and if patterns of courtesy, aggression, or dominance should be the same for both females and males.

Large questions have developed today around parenting as it relates to the sexual role. For example, should men care for infants and young children? In *Generation of Vipers* published in 1942, Philip Wylie coined a term "momism" wherein he explained the many problems of that generation as a consequence of the fact that boys had very little contact with older males. Mothers cared for the young boys at home, their schoolteachers and nurses were females, the boys were typically dealing with females in a female-dominated world until junior high or high school. Today many men and women are raising the question of how we might get more men involved as teachers in the early grades or in nursing. Moreover, men are declaring rights to be single parents.

Other questions are surfacing, such as should single males be permitted to adopt children, a young girl, most critically. Or, in the case of divorce, should a court award custody to the father and require the mother to pay child support or alimony?

Turning to the children themselves, should sex education be taught in school? Should children or teenagers be permitted or encouraged to engage in sexual activity? Much of the media seems to condone sexual freedom for all individuals and since many children today have unsupervised access to the media, we must conclude that in that way alone sexual activity is encouraged. Many children today have had primary sexual contact by the age of sixteen. Does that imply that birth control procedures should be made available at that age or earlier? Instruction about sex and procreation has been the responsibility of the family though the peer culture has been a strong influence in the last few generations. Does sex education in the school system weaken the authority of the family? Reserving such instruction to the family gave the family the authority to regulate premarital sexual intercourse. Does putting sex education in the schools dilute or alter this authority? Should any such authority remain with the family?

Appropriate sexual conduct has become increasingly an individual matter, perhaps largely because there is so little agreement within the larger society. Premarital and extramarital sexual activity is endorsed by experts and practiced by many. But it is also condemned by other experts and seen as a disgrace by some groups of people.

Relations with one's own sex is also a matter of popular inquiry. Gay liberation and anti-gay liberation have become a bitter public quarrel. Yet, as recently as ten years ago homosexuality was seen as a psychiatric illness and was discussed in whispered voices.

The rapid social change of the last few years that makes us as individuals seem to be commodities disturbs almost all sectors of modern life. And this disturbance seems to have set off hundreds of individual attempts to develop a better sense of the meaning of life. Daniel Yankelovich writing in *Psychology Today* (1981) about his recent survey of American attitudes about life says, ". . . the search for new meanings is an outpouring of popular sentiment and experimentation, an authentic grass-roots phenomenon, involving, in one way or another, perhaps as many as 80 percent of all adult Americans. It is as if tens of millions of people had decided simultaneously to conduct risky experiments in living, using the only materials that lay at hand—their own lives" (p. 39).

HEDONISM AND THE APOCALYPSE

For many of us the current hedonism seems most extreme among our youth. They often reflect with less guile the central emotional core of their parents. A recent study by David Manning (1980) finds that the most visible aspect of inflation's impact on the school age population is the increased presence of the part-time job. Working after school has become a pervasive part of the youth culture and is becoming a central focus in the lives of high school students.

In examining work study habits of juniors and seniors in a cross-sectional sample of schools in an eastern state, Manning found that the typical part-time job averages twenty hours a week and an inverse relationship exists between the number of hours spent on the part-time job relative to the hours devoted to homework. Interestingly, students who work after school average only one hour on homework per night, yet three out of four indicate an intention to attend college. This growing disparity between studying to achieve deferred benefits and working to earn immediate cash is predictive of very poor performance in college. According to the survey, only a quarter of the money is saved for college education and future needs and almost none is contributed to the family budget. Rather the money is spent to provide gasoline for personal autos, tickets for rock concerts, expensive jeans, exotic footwear, and fast foods.

Manning argues that the primary motive for the student is indulgent self-interest. There is little evidence of a sense of responsibility for the student's future needs or for the financial sacrifice of parents. He notes that increasing inflation requires even longer work hours to maintain this consumption schedule especially in the light of high peer pressure and that "money in the pocket of a young person has immediate value; the value of a high school education by contrast cannot be measured in such utilitarian terms."

The wealth, the mobility, the freedom, the hedonism are all based on a growing economy and an expanding base of material resources. The nineteenth century was an age of optimism for Western society. That optimism remained with us, slowly waning through the first half of the twentieth century. In the closing years of this century, we have become no less interested in the future and indeed are probably more future-oriented than ever. But the scenarios are no longer routinely optimistic. In the early seventies, a study commissioned by the Club of Rome issued a forecast of a coming dark age of poverty, overpopulation, and declining civilization (Lazlo and Bierman, 1977). Conservation groups decry the destruction of natural resources and warn of imminent depletion of the vital foodstuffs and raw materials necessary for modern society. Conversely, pressure from people living in poverty throughout the world necessitates the need for greater economic growth to raise standards of living. Modern governments continually watch economic indicators in an attempt to massage the economy, avoid recession, minimize inflation, and escape the specter of economic collapse. Such specters and our dependency on central economic production and distribution machinery have made millionaires of a few Cassandras who write books and newsletters forewarning of the collapse of this machinery and providing instructions on building and stocking a retreat for when the day of the apocalypse arrives. Such warnings indeed make one anxious and uneasy and, as our dollars shrink each year, the prophecies of doom seem less farfetched.

These turbulent crosscurrents—these inconsistencies—clearly take an ever larger toll on many people day in and day out. Testimony to this toll is the extent to which we regularly rely on chemicals to control the pressures and the effects of stress. Librium and Valium, the routine tranquilizers, are the most common medical prescriptions. Alcoholic beverages—an ancient means of meeting stress and lessening inhibitions—are a multi-billion dollar, recession-proof industry.

Our inadequacies and frustrations in meeting the terms of today's world have become very evident to us. Returning to the Yankelovich survey (1981), we see, "Acting in the name of self-fulfillment, many people are startled to wake up one day and find themselves with a broken marriage, a wrong-headed career change, or simply a muddled state of mind about what life choices to make. But despite many failures, the experiments persist. There is something about our times that stimulates Americans to take big risks in pursuit of new conceptions of the good life" (p. 39). Typically at least one self-improvement or self-assertion book is on the best seller lists. New psychotherapeutic regimens appear as regularly today as patented medicines did in the previous century.

The closing years of the twentieth century seem to bring the dawning of an Age of Malaise that vaguely anticipates a dozen different cataclysmic visions, from marauding sharks to oil blockades, nuclear accidents, and world economic collapse. We seem to stand on the edge of a final apocalypse—and the sharks are the least of our worries. The uncertainty, the contradiction, the ambiguity steeped with stress have an impact not only on our personal visions of what the world is and what is wrong with it, but this climate of change and turmoil comes to manifest itself as well in our social or public lives. Its impact and consequence for us is labeled many things: stress, job fatigue, burnout, future shock, work boredom, or alienation.

Among the labels, dimensions, and symptoms associated with our time, I have found burnout to be among the most frequent complaints. But while it is an oft cited complaint, it is not a condition of life that cannot be altered. Burnout occurs when we achieve less than our expectations. Sometimes the awareness of this discrepancy is not conscious. We are vaguely dissatisfied but not certain why. In other cases, we clearly see the discrepancy but are at a loss to know what to do about it.

If we think of life like a candle that is burning, we may burn through life rapidly with both ends ablaze or slowly with a dimly flickering flame. The choice, at one end, is to burn out quickly and, at the other extreme, to burn out slowly. Time passes. Opportunities come and go. The world goes on and we are left to make of it what we will. The interpretation we make of the world, about our lives and the lives about us, will dictate whether we suffer burnout. When we think of life like a candle that is being used up, burnout is inescapable. While many things about the world cannot be changed, our relationship to it can. Throughout this book, we will look at alternative definitions of our relationship to the world and the consequences for experiencing burnout.

In the course of this book, I have not tried to provide a solution to social change. On the other hand, there are some straws in the wind that let us judge the direction of the wind and its speed and can help us improve our ability to understand these times and maybe even become mildly successful. Happiness may or may not be in the cards for each of us individually, but we can gain some satisfaction from understanding these issues better and being less a straw before the winds.

SOME CASE STUDIES OF BURNOUT

Before we examine what the consequences of burnout are for the individual, let us take a look at some illustrations of the effects of the social climate on five successful people.

Emptiness in the Executive Suite

The first case is a man in the prime of his life and career. Rohrer & Company is one of the leading investment banking firms in the United States. It has offices in several major cities and underwrites millions of dollars of bond issues yearly. Originally, the company was characterized by strong entrepreneurial leadership that specialized in highly leveraged and risky financing and used largely the personal money of the original founders. However, today the company has become a solid part of the banking establishment and acts as a broker between large estates, pension funds, commercial banks, and municipalities seeking bond financing.

Harvey Eagleton is Vice President for Rohrer & Company and one of its brightest stars, but he seems to be starting to sputter and grow dim. By any standard, Harvey is a successful man with a base salary of fifty thousand dollars a year, which is often more than matched with incentive and bonus payments from total sales activities. Harvey joined Rohrer & Company after holding positions with two companies in the same field. In his twelve years with the company, total underwriting has grown at an average annual rate of over 20 percent. Harvey, a graduate of an eastern private school with a degree in the liberal arts, served two years in combat in the Korean War and has two grown children. Harvey's wife of twenty-seven years, Judith, is active in the Junior League and has returned to college to work on an advanced degree in European History.

In addition to Harvey's corporate and family responsibilities, he is extremely active in civic affairs and in the Republican party. In the 1968 presidential election, he served as the state finance chairman for the party and was a delegate to the Republican National Convention. A two-over-par golfer and always fit and tan, he prides himself on wearing the same suit size as he did when he concluded his army tour in the mid-50s.

Three years ago Harvey and Judith talked about getting a divorce as they began to realize that with the children gone they seemed to have fewer mutual concerns. However, after several months of discussions they each agreed to go somewhat their separate ways, but neither felt sufficiently angry to initiate a divorce. In Judith's words, the marriage has grown comfortable and casual. It is convenient and dependable, yet not exciting. Since Judith has returned to college, she has become much more enthusiastic about life and is usually gone a couple of evenings a week to the library or participating in a seminar. Harvey, however, has grown less and less enthusiastic about anything. A creative and thoughtful organizer, Harvey's sales division functions well with only an occasional touch from him. His investments are carefully structured so that they do not require day-to-day involvement.

Here's what Harvey has to say about himself: "I'm no complainer. Life's been very good to me. I've worked hard and achieved whatever I wanted. I'm proud to be known as an achiever—a self-starter. It's true I got off to a good start and didn't live as a kid in poverty, but I've still worked for everything I have.

"I guess life is what you make of it. It's also important who you know, but if you don't know someone there's always a way to meet him. Money's not the answer to everything but it makes important things possible. Money is simply a measure of what you have achieved and a man should have the right to do what he wants with the money he has made.

"Judith and the family are important to me—at least as important as my work. They are a part of me but they have their own lives. It's just as well I suppose. The kids today get to me after awhile. They've got answers for everything, but not always the questions. I suppose youth must have their day. But that's not my problem. It's a free country and the kids—my kids—have got to make their own way.

"I guess I really don't know if Judith and I are happy. She's changed, you know, the last two or three years. I can't really remember when it began. At first I thought it was just the change of life. I think I was jealous when she first started to take the courses at the university. I still can't see why she does that. She has everything anyone could want. And a couple of the faculty she's so impressed with. Kind of arty types. Hell of a poor competition if you ask me.

"That's funny, I guess I am jealous. You know she has a right to her life. I've had my good times.

"I don't know what to think about the future. I wonder about it quite a bit; where the country's going. Where I'm going. Maybe I'm just getting by. Going with the flow. I guess I really don't know."

The interview with Harvey Eagleton ends with him staring out the window with the city below him. It is a city that has been Harvey's world and he is a prince of that world. His heavy broad hands are finely manicured and that seems contradictory. His suit, tie, shirt, shoes are impeccable and manly. The office is decorated with Danish modern: steel, glass, and oiled woods. The lines are bold, clean, even austere. Harvey has helped build this world and it, in turn, has created him. Yet one is left with the impression that something is amiss.

Sexual affairs or romantic involvements once titillating for Harvey no longer command any attention. Though physically trim and fit, Harvey has complained of chronic tiredness for the last several months. His annual physical exams indicate no problems whatsoever. Harvey's secretary of fifteen years has noticed that he has begun to spend part of an afternoon each week compulsively strolling in a nearby park or visiting the library. He has become far less active in civic affairs and turned down an invitation to handle the fund raising for a prominent senator's re-election. He is also much more forgetful about his appointment calendar. Harvey has not discussed these problems with anyone, other than complaining about the weariness to his physician. At times he will push these thoughts aside and assign them to some form of midlife crisis that can easily be bested by analysis and forceful forgetting. Yet, Harvey notices he is increasingly beset by a feeling of malaise and immobility.

The Discontents of Liberation

Ann Schraeder graduated at the head of her class at Boston University in 1969. Raised in suburban Connecticut, Ann was a popular and attractive teenager who had finished high school a year ahead of many of her friends and enrolled in B.U. with a scholarship in the fall of 1966. Ann's father was a lawyer and her mother, a public school teacher. Both had urged Ann to prepare a career for herself and to delay marriage until after college graduation. When she was a small girl, Ann's father had begun to stress to her the importance of economic independence.

Ann participated in a limited way in the political activism that surged about her during those years. She joined a few marches but mostly limited her involvement to class and dorm discussions and was viewed by her friends as politically unaware. She finished her bachelor's degree in the spring of 1969 and got a second degree the next December in accounting. That spring, Ann joined a large national accounting firm and was assigned to their Washington office as a management trainee. By 1974 at twenty-six years of age, Ann had completed an MBA, held senior responsibility for a government contract, and was proving to be an aggressive account manager.

During high school and college, Ann dated regularly. She consciously avoided arrangements that might lead to marriage, although she would often have what she called a "steady friend" for a year or two. By the time Ann finished her MBA, she had fully adopted a new sexual standard. Vacation weekends with a man were considered proper and the costs were on an equal share basis. She tried living with a man but found the arrangement to be "too much hassle." By her thirtieth birthday, Ann had begun to doubt that she would marry and carefully avoided opportunities for office romances with associates.

Ann's group supervisor began to notice a gradual change in Ann. She had been with the company eight years, and the firm was her first and only employer. During her first few years, Ann impressed everyone as bright, energetic, and adaptable. Eager to show her male counterparts that she was their equal, she volunteered for travel and weekend assignments and enjoyed the image of female executive and jet set single.

For Ann, the age of thirty was symbolic and solidified a decision that had been made gradually over the years. Ann saw that her life would continue to be far different from that of her parents or of many of her high school and college friends. Before turning thirty Ann always considered being a mother and a housewife a possible though remote option. Most of her friends, it seemed, had married and, though a considerable number were single again, Ann saw this as an experience she had missed, sacrificed for her career. From the first, her job had been a fulfillment, a long sought-for goal. However, seeking the goal seemed different from achieving and maintaining it. Too often Ann perceived her efforts with clients as reinventing the wheel. The first three or four years were full of challenges as she applied concepts from her classes and had the opportunity to travel. However, the last two years had been frustrating. Her job remained much the same with only some added supervisory responsibilities. Though she did not feel threatened by newer and younger employees, she often wondered if her experience made her valuable enough to withstand their competition. She had received good salary increases and had a small portfolio of stocks in her retirement account that languished with the market. Two years ago she put her cash savings of eight thousand dollars into a condominium and inflation pushed her equity up by twice that. Yet, her income and prospects for increases often depressed Ann. She felt that no matter what she made, taxes and inflation always balanced it out. She thought at times of joining one of her client's firms to get closer to operational levels rather than staying in an advisory consultant's role, but her clients seemed to have no greater control over the events in their work than she did in hers.

Ann's most frequent complaint was that events seemed so much beyond her control. Ann's supervisor noted that her work had become cyclical; for periods of a couple of months she performed like her old self but then became distracted and uncommunicative. Supervisees complained that on these occasions she gave unclear and vague directions, and while she was always willing to listen to their problems, she could not find a helpful solution.

Ann describes her world with a sense of irony that seems inappropriate for a young woman who has had such success: "Yes, I suppose I should think I've got it made—no dirty diapers to change, no noses to wipe, no man to bore me with problems of the office. I wouldn't buy into that world on a bet, but I've got no bed of roses either. Harold (Ann's supervisor) thinks fannie patting is going to replace baseball as the national pastime. For every male client I have, I have a proposition to put up with. Keeping a house and a car going drives me crazy. Repairers can only come during working hours. And auto mechanics have this thing about women. They think we should be in bed or pregnant, not driving cars. They see you coming from a mile off and you never know what they've done to your car.

"Yeah, I'm successful. All my college friends wish they had my freedom—my opportunities. I surely don't want their world, but I'm not certain I want this one either. I don't know why. Things aren't what I thought they would be."

Ann's firm does not want to lose her but is concerned about her. She complains of vague depression, restlessness, and fatigue. Recently, she began to talk of going into an entirely different field or just traveling for a couple of years to find herself.

Blue-Collar Blues

The third case is a laborer and Vietnam veteran just beginning adult life. The most loyal, and indeed the most avid, fan of the Pittsburgh Steelers in all of Alabama—Larry Thomas. Larry is a steel worker in Birmingham and with his union wage, overtime, and wife's work as a secretary, their total income exceeds $20,000 in a good year.

Larry had several years of odd jobs before getting regular work with the steel mill. His father was a small farmer. He remembers his high school years fondly as football, beer, and girls. Vietnam was a boring and frightening experience laced with drugs and violence, and life since returning from Vietnam has been rough.

Larry speaks quickly and is surprisingly articulate about his life: "Yeah, I'm not happy with what I've got and feel I should have more. I served in 'Nam. I didn't burn a draft card, and I can tell you it was pure hell there. We could of won that war. We should have. But the draft dodgers back home and the fat ass brass over there queered it all. Those were years down the drain for me and my buddies. Some of them didn't come back. I was lucky.

"I guess I'm still sowing my wild oats. You know what I mean? And praying for crop failure. That's what weekends are for. I guess marriage is important. I get lonely without a woman. Even out of my head. By God, though, they love to nag—buy this, do that. Sometimes I think I'm back in the army, in basic again.

"The job sucks. Like the song that says 'take this job and shove it.' Most times I work hard and try to stay out of trouble but no one . . . no one screws me over. I've had that. I believe in the union for getting ahead. Stick it to them—to the man—before they stick it to you. If I could get a little ahead in a couple of years I'd like to get a place back out in the country where the folks come from—you know, ten acres or so. I've got a pickup. I could put my own house up, have a garden, get out of this town. I could see working here but living there. I guess that's about it. That's what I'm looking for."

Larry first married when he was eighteen. He continues to pay support for a child from that first marriage. He has a two-year-old boy from his second marriage. Larry's second marriage and his job with the steel firm were supposed to be a chance to get things together and settle down. It worked that way for a while, but six months ago Larry began to get very restless in his job and was charged by the foreman as reporting for work drunk on two occasions. Larry and several of his friends at work protested that this was not so, but came about as the result of a grudge the foreman held against him. The foreman is twenty-five years older than Larry and most of the newer workers. He criticizes their lifestyle and their politics. Larry, like his friends, feels that the steel company rips them off at every turn and was an active supporter of the election that resulted in union representation for the shop. Since the union election, Larry has become more belligerent on the job and is actively and openly hostile in his criticism of the company. Larry says that for the first couple of years, he was fooled by the company. He believed their promises that after he had gained experience he would be eligible for higher pay. Now, the foreman conspired to dismiss him on a trumped-up charge, rather than provide him with the increase in pay he felt he had earned. Though his net salary has not increased with union representation, he feels he now has a way to "stick it" to the company and says that he will do so every chance he gets.

Larry's life at home has its ups and downs. At least weekly he and his wife, Jean, have arguments about Larry's occasional beer with the boys after work and his wife's open admiration and attraction to her employer. Disagreement about money is a recurrent theme in their marriage. Weekends are the best times, when Larry and his wife go out. But when he has visitation rights with his son, jealousy appears with Jean expressing her hostility toward Larry's first wife and his still ambivalent feelings of affection and hostility.

Going with the Flow

Sue Torres is a social worker in a suburb of Chicago. She has lived in Chicago all her life and has two children in school whom she has supported since the death of her husband five years ago. Working for a state agency providing social services, Sue assists both younger and older people in dealing with a variety of problems. Many of her cases focus on inadequate income, but she also helps out in housing disputes, marital discord, and problems between parents and children.

Sue came to the agency ten years ago when her husband was still alive and working. She was pleased to get a job that would permit her to supplement the family income and work with people. Until her children got into high school four years ago, Sue's life was so busy she never paused to think about the future. Dance lessons for her daughter, baseball practice for her son, and other school events filled the holidays, evenings, and weekends. In addition, her job kept her busy much more than the forty hours she was in the office. The work pace helped Sue forget the death of her husband. Her major goal was to keep the family together and put the children through school.

Her son, Aaron, is a senior this year and plans to spend six months after graduation from high school traveling through Europe. He has a scholarship that will assist him when he enters college next year. Laura her daughter, has proved to be much more of a challenge than Aaron ever was. Entering her junior year in high school this fall, she has a steady boyfriend and Sue is certain that they are sleeping together in spite of Sue's admonitions to her daughter. Laura has also had a couple of bad experiences with drugs at all-night parties at a friend's house and drinks on weekend dates. Sue often finds herself thinking of her daughter when she works with single mothers who have children, a succession of boyfriends, and few employment prospects.

In the last two years, Sue feels that the bounce has gone from her life; now she tries to meet each day as best she can and finds herself jumping at every ring of the telephone. Alarmed at how her drinking increased when she began to have trouble with her daughter, Sue saw her physician. He prescribed a routine tranquilizer that Sue finds makes her days more bearable. She knows that her work has suffered. She frequently finds herself disgusted with her clients' failures to come to grips with their own lives. She often remarks to her co-workers that she lives for the weekend. But with Laura's problems, those too are filled with anxiety and it is a rare week that a family crisis does not occur.

Sue rarely goes out in the evening, though on occasion she, Aaron, and Laura will go shopping or to a movie. She feels that the streets, particularly after dark, are unsafe for a woman and usually finds herself at home watching TV in the evening, often too fatigued to stay awake beyond nine.

Sue Torres measures her words carefully, as if she is speaking to one of her clients: "I try to plan carefully for the future. Aaron's and Laura's education are assured. I know Aaron appreciates all that I try to do for him, but I just don't know about Laura. Aaron is a lot like his father. I'm very proud of him and he is always there when I need him. Laura's another matter. I pray a lot for her. You know I would never have thought it, but raising a girl is much more difficult than raising a boy. When Aaron was in junior high, I really needed his father then to sit down on him but he grew out of it. Laura is simply another matter. We have communication problems. I worry about what she could get into, if she will get pregnant, or if she will get a disease or something. She won't plan ahead. I don't know where she'll end up. All she says is 'just go with the flow.'

"My dreams are my children. I guess I know that. I've got to work at least ten more years to get them started off. Bill (her husband) had hoped to retire back in Texas near my folks. I don't think much about that. Chicago is home, but every year gets tougher.

"I don't think I'll marry again. Putting another family together just wouldn't work out. I'm afraid Aaron would be resentful and I don't know what Laura would do. Besides I get uneasy, nervous about adjusting to a man. You know, marriage requires compromises on both sides. Perhaps it's best that people marry when they are young before they know better.

"I guess I'm not very satisfied with my job. But it pays a living. I thought I would enjoy working with people, but the kind of people I deal with are the dregs of society. They truly are! Prostitutes and drug pushers—they bring it on themselves and then bring children into this world. It's the children I feel for. It's not right. They didn't ask for that.

There's not much more to say about work. My colleagues are okay. The pay is poor and benefits are much less than in industry. Still, it's a job and that's important now."

You notice as you talk with Sue that she continually wrings her hands and presses her skirt, palms down and outward in a nervous, sweeping motion. She seems tired and morose, as if a heavy burden rests on her shoulders.

There are days when Sue feels that home repairs, car trouble, and appliance failures are the only meaning to life.

Life on the Fast Track

Tim Ferris is thirty-eight, no longer young but not yet middle-aged. For four years he has been the large-scale systems sales manager for the Seattle area of the Pacific Telecommunications Corporation. Pacific Telecommunications specializes in providing applications of telephone and data transmission equipment for business use. Among the company's products are point-of-sale cash registers and order terminals that permit retail branch offices to transmit sales and inventory information immediately to the home office. Tim's early accomplishments with the company included being a part of a team of engineers and information systems analysts that developed the hardware and software procedures for the use of such technology in food franchise and convenience store applications.

Since the development of that technology, Tim has been involved in demonstrating its use for potential customers and in supervising and conducting the training of customer's employees when a Pacific Telecommunications package is sold.

Tim is successful in his job, but he doesn't plan to stay with the company more than one more year. Prior to joining Pacific, he held a succession of sales and management jobs with three other companies after finishing two years of college in California almost twenty years ago. Tim is uncertain what his goals in life are or whether he is in the right career. He explains his approach to life as moving to the top by moving around. Tim is critical of his colleagues who are as talented as he and, in some cases, better prepared but have advanced less because they were afraid to move. Tim sees himself on the fast track to the top and expects to move to another company in a year or two—probably to another state.

In conversation Tim is lively, spontaneous, quick to suggest ideas or adopt those of others. He has charm that can be turned on and off like a light switch and never seems at a loss for direction. Tim's wife, Beth, was a schoolteacher and taught for seven years before she married Tim when she was twenty-eight and he was thirty. They have one child who is six years old. Beth would either like to have another child or return to work. Tim seems to be less involved in family life than he is in his job and feels that Beth should make the decision about a second child.

When Tim answers questions about satisfactions or frustrations, he says: "I'm basically happy and pretty successful. When the job gets me down, Beth and I get away for a few days, usually where we can lie in the sun. Other times, I buy something for the house. I look forward to getting a new car every two years. I think you can buy happiness and I do that. I work hard and I have to keep moving, but I enjoy doing what I do and look forward to new places and new challenges. I don't think anyone can say what the future will be. It's like the turn of the roulette wheel. You just need to be prepared for whatever comes."

Tim feels prepared and has few doubts about himself. His supervisor at work says he is energetic, congenial, and success-oriented, but he doubts that advancement opportunities will come as quickly as Tim wants. He notes that people like Tim are valuable but difficult to retain.

SUCCESS, YET MALAISE

Each of these fairly typical and successful American lives rings with an emptiness—a hollowness. If we asked them, most would mention a vague uneasiness, a dissatisfaction, and yet would be hard put to pinpoint a specific problem that when corrected would make life rich and fulfilling.

For Harvey Eagleton, the system has provided material rewards and then some. He has gained financial independence, raised his children, and enjoys excellent health. Ann Schraeder is bright, young, and successful. She has made her childhood dreams a reality. Larry Thomas has had much less success than Ann or Harvey and, unlike them, he seems less able to set goals and work toward them. His life seems like a pendulum that swings far in one direction and then to the other extreme. Sue Torres does not appear to choose goals, nor does she react to frustrations with anger like Larry. She seems to meet the challenge of living by grudgingly giving in a little each day. Tim Ferris, among the five, has no doubts or misgivings. Yet, I am sure we each must wonder whether there isn't a surprise—a curve in the road—for Tim as well. None of these five can be called failures, but with the exception of Tim, none would call their lives fully successful. In fact, each would probably say that they feel they should be getting more from life.

This lack of completeness—nagging malaise—is symptomatic of the atmosphere of frustration, alienation, burning out. Though these feelings or perceptions have existed in earlier times for a few individuals, the pervasiveness of the phenomenon among all walks of American life is the remarkable dimension to the current situation. In all likelihood there has never been a time when all members of the society were productive, enthusiastic, and avidly pursuing goals. From the little we can be certain of such matters in past times, the securing of food and shelter and the avoiding of disease and war left little opportunity for questions about the meaning of life or one's degree of satisfaction with life. There are no comparable epochs in history where so much of the western industrialized world has been set free of the most fundamental exigencies of survival. But this freedom from deprivation, from endless hours of drudgery, and from crippling disease has not been matched by a sense of well-being, satisfaction, or eagerness for life that might seem a logical consequence of such beneficial conditions for life. Instead, these case studies represent individuals who are cautious, fatalistic, conscious of limits not potentialities, who possess an uneasiness about the all-too-fleeting fullness of life and the growing twilight—a transition from the bright noonday sun of ambition and unlimited potentials to the darkening evening of uncertainty and resignation.

Almost everyone feels and, after a second of introspection, knows that life is much better today than 100 years ago or 500 years before that. In the eighth and ninth and then again in the thirteenth century, almost half of Europe was eliminated by the plague. A few centuries ago, death in childhood was common. Thousands died of smallpox every year and, with the myriad of diseases and calamities waiting to cut life short, the aged were revered partially because so few people lived to old age. No one in America need suffer from hunger today and what is called poverty here would be affluence in the third world or at least a comfortable life in earlier times.

Why this paradox of weariness and helplessness occurs in this era of unparalleled human achievement derives from the institutions of traditional life, the newly emergent structures of the modern world and a dawning consciousness of a higher sort of individualism. Along our path in the coming chapters, we will examine the interplay of the traditional and new institutions and how this has promoted an increased consciousness. The next chapter turns to a more careful examination of the definition of these new feelings of weariness and helplessness, explores how they are experienced by different people, labels these feelings "burnout," and charts the characteristic sequence of events associated with burnout.

DOONESBURY
by GB Trudeau.

Symptoms of the Times

The mind of the WASP bears more resemblance to the laser than the mind of any other ethnic group. To wit, he can project himself extraordinary distances through a narrow path. He's disciplined, stoical, able to become the instrument of his own will, has extraordinary boldness and daring, together with a resolute lack of imagination. He's profoundly nihilistic. And this nihilism found its perfect expression in the odyssey to the moon—because we went there without knowing why we went.

Norman Mailer, *Of a Fire on the Moon.*

Our conscious imagery in our thoughts and our language are all metaphors. We can never know reality directly but only apprehend it, feel it through our senses. We know the red of the apple only through the mediation of our visual apparatus. A certain portion of the light spectrum strikes the retina and excites conelike structures into producing a chemical reaction. This reaction triggers a nerve impulse that runs along an optic roadway until it reaches a terminus in the brain. At that terminus, some form of decoding process occurs upon the impulse and it receives a verbal sign—the word *red*. The assigning of the word *red* to the perceived color and shape of the apple comes from associational learning. From a very young age, we are taught to pair certain words with certain visual images and, in this way, we gradually build our knowledge of the world.

All of the activity that goes on in the brain is a metaphoring, analogyzing process. We develop representations of reality, maps of reality, rather than directly being a part of external reality. As we mature, the imagery becomes ever more important and each new thought or experience is to some degree determined by what we have already learned.

This metaphoring process is greatly enhanced and expanded by language. The word *red* gives us a handle to put on the visual sensation of seeing an apple and helps us remember what seeing an apple is like. The process enlarges our internal, conceptual world and permits us to apply the concept of red to a girl's blush, the sunset, or to interact with an emotion—to see red is to be angry.

Our choice of metaphors tells us something about the way we feel and our general outlook on the world. Burnout is a simple metaphor that may have come from persons watching a fire slowly burn down or perhaps a candle burning out. When the fire or the candle goes out, the essence is used up. It is no longer useful for its intended purpose. A new candle must be found. A new fire must be started.

To use burnout in the same metaphorical sense to describe or depict feelings about life seems uniquely appropriate for these times. Now, if you will bear with me a bit, I would like to try to extend this metaphor into some new territory to use it to describe some feelings and to characterize the symptoms of the times.

WHAT BURNOUT MEANS

As a way of understanding and, in the case of medicine, treating an illness, modern medical practice and traditional scientific thinking emphasize the isolation and description of the state or condition followed by a recounting of the progression of events that lead up to that state. When a physician examines a patient's throat for redness, the lymph nodes for swelling, and the lungs for congestion, he is looking for information to describe the physical state that may be associated with the patient's complaint of having a sore throat. The physician asks when the discomfort started and whether the patient has had a fever, to attempt to develop the progression of events up to the present time. If the progression of events and the data about the patient's physical state fit a disease with which he is familiar, then the physician may hazard a prediction of where the condition may be headed and what interventions—such as antibiotics or rest—may be appropriate. The description of the patient's condition is called the symptoms and the progression of events leading to the condition is called the cause or causal sequence. A similar logical set will be used through the next two chapters in trying to pin down the phenomena of malaise, disaffection, and confusion—the symptoms of burnout mentioned in the first chapter.

Burnout may be defined in terms of its symptoms, the stages through which one can pass when affected by burnout, or the role conflict that is fundamental to all instances of burnout. Let's look first at role conflict and how that produces burnout.

At its most fundamental level, *burnout means there is a disparity between what is expected from a role and what is achieved.* A role is a set of behaviors that an individual conforms to. It is a social reality and exists relative to and in interaction with other roles. Being a parent is a role. Its set of behaviors involve caring for a dependent younger person, protecting the younger person, and giving guidance. A student, a spouse, a citizen, a friend are all sets of behaviors and are examples of roles. All social life is built and maintained through roles.

Each role involves a set of behaviors and a set of expectations. Some roles, such as mother and physician, generate high esteem; others are held in low esteem like used car salesman, criminal, or beggar.

Roles also vary in the degree of choice permitted for changing the role. The role of friend leaves one with considerable choice in continuing the role, but the role of a criminal, particularly an imprisoned criminal, provides less choice about the role.

OPTIONS AND BURNOUT

The presence of burnout is related closely to the role options. When options are few, burnout is less likely. Options are generated by social change.

Central to this explanation of burnout is that it is a relatively new phenomenon. The slave in the Roman galley, the serf of the Middle Ages, the colonial farmer in the eighteenth century, the industrial worker of the thirties all may have worked fourteen hours a day, suffered chronic malnourishment, and lived with exploitation, abuse, and ignorance. There would clearly have been stress and perhaps alienation. Some of them probably had hopes and aspirations for a better life, but they were wishes—not expectations. The galley slave, serf, and colonial farmer *expected* much less from life than the average American today. Thanks to the advancements of science and labor laws, our lives are much easier. But with each advancement our expectations are raised higher. What we accept as bare existence, the galley slave would welcome as luxury. We saw what happens when you try to lower expectations to a previous level when speed limits were reduced to fifty-five miles an hour. "But our cars can go eighty miles an hour. We've been driving at seventy for years." What is one day a new blessing is tomorrow a right or privilege.

Unfulfilled expectations are the key to the start of the burnout process. But burnout is more like freedom or literacy—it doesn't come on line. It doesn't become a concern until a certain level of development is reached within a culture.

Burnout is intensified by alienation and stress and is most common in rapidly changing times, especially when people feel trapped and unable to control events about them. When societies change rapidly, traditional expectations cease to be met, thus burnout begins. It appears through a growing separation—an estrangement—between the individual and his family; between the worker and his work; between the professional and his profession; between the person and the community. The person may maintain the role and the expectations, but the level of performance declines and enthusiasm wanes. Often the complaint is voiced that the fire has gone out—burned out—that the person is still there but the role seems hollow. In fact, the dominant emotion of burnout is not anger, but loss—empty, unfulfilled sensation—rather than simply a negative feeling toward work or life.

STAGES OF BURNOUT

Burnout does not happen suddenly, but occurs as a gradual deterioration. There are three stages that can occur in the burnout progression. The first stage is puzzlement, confusion, and the appearance of frustration. The second stage is characterized by intense frustration and anger. The third stage is apathy, withdrawal, and despair.

Stage 1: Confusion

The individual begins to feel that something is not quite right. There is an occasional feeling of anxiety—a nagging worry that something is amiss. Somehow what was expected is not what is happening, but it's difficult to identify just what is wrong. Low level health complaints start to appear. These include headaches, tension, sleeplessness, lack of energy, and so on. Let me use an example to illustrate this state. Ron Copeland grew up on a farm in western Kansas during the sixties with one recurrent thought and that was to get off the farm and not spend his life on a tractor. Ron attended college at the state university and continued through to get an MBA. On graduation he took a job as a management intern with a West Coast firm in their Los Angeles headquarters. By the end of the third year, Ron found himself thinking that driving the freeways was in some ways worse than plowing with the tractor. While he knew he would never return to Kansas, Los Angeles had some flaws too.

Stage 2: Frustration

At the second stage, confusion turns toward frustration and anger. The individual begins to feel somehow that he has been taken. He may lash out at friends or coworkers, quit his job, or in some other way show his frustration through anger and hostility. For Ron, the freeways became a rat race. They were a sixty-minute endurance test each morning and each evening. Work consisted of sixty-hour weeks and too many meetings. Ron says, "You do this for twenty years to get to the top and still you may not make it. This is not how I expected it would be." Ron is beginning to conclude that mid-management is not what he thought it would be. There is no status, no recognition, and he has no hope of moving farther ahead.

In this stage, confusion gives way to frustration. The person takes action motivated by anger. He thinks that what he should receive is in some way being denied him. He feels cheated, deceived.

Physical symptoms now become more pronounced. Tension-related illnesses such as backaches or migraine headaches occur. Tranquilizers or alcohol are often required for the individual to relax.

Stage 3: Despair

In time, these feelings of anger and frustration may shade toward a feeling of inadequacy. At the third stage, the individual feels that he and his efforts have no meaning or value. The activity—the role—loses its meaning, its consequence. At this juncture, burnout is at its extreme and the individual feels like an object used by others.

Now Ron's anger toward others is directed toward himself. The drive on the freeway becomes a courtroom with Ron putting himself on trial about his career and his life. Ron stays in the job and in Los Angeles, but he grows more cautious and more cynical about his job and himself. He learns to follow the rules carefully to protect himself. The rules, in time, become what meaning he can draw from the job. More than anything else, in the final stage of burnout, the person experiences a well-defined weariness with work, responsibility, family, or the world. "Life is no damn good" sums up the feeling. The individual becomes apathetic and withdrawn and feels inadequate.

At none of these stages does the person necessarily conclude that he or she is burned out. You do not have to be aware of burnout to suffer from it. Though the condition may not progress through to the third stage, everyone is vulnerable to burnout. In fact, most of us reach various stages of burnout (in various roles) several times in our lives. In many instances, we are able to change the role or the expectations to lessen the burnout.

ROLES, REALITY, AND EXPECTATIONS

Burnout is contingent on the degree of disparity among the expectations of a role, the reality of a role, and the presence of role alternatives. As long as role expectations and reality fit or are fairly close, the individual will not burn out in that role. However, if either role expectations change or reality changes, burnout will commence. The level of burnout with a role will intensify if the disparity develops and an alternative appears. Burnout, then, is an interaction between what one expects and what one experiences. It is intensified with role alternatives.

Our social experiences are the source of our role expectations—our family, friends, the media, the culture. These expectations are what we feel we should receive or deserve from life and its roles. Marriage, parenthood, employment are among the roles in life. We are taught what to expect from these roles and burnout does not occur if we achieve our expectations.

Change in the relationship of roles and reality may come in three possible ways. One way is for the environment to change so that our expectations become less likely, for example, recession can bring the loss of a job, thus disparity between role expectation and experience.

Another way for the role expectations to change is for the social norms that define role expectations to change. Here social change produces ambiguity. Instead of role achievement being more difficult, the value of the role is changed. Women's roles provide a good example of changing values. Women have been taught for several generations to expect to marry, raise children, and stay at home. Particularly in the current generation of young women, the validity of that role has been challenged. Women now have role alternatives and role conflicts around family and career.

Role expectations also change when aspirations start to become expectations—an example of rising expectations. Aspirations are hopes, wishes, the individual's fantasy world. However, aspirations may become expectations. Once a thought becomes an expectation, the person expects to achieve a particular outcome.

When the person realizes that there is an option, continuing in the current role may become even more frustrating. Using marriage as an example, when divorce remained comparatively rare, there was not much of a feasible or realistic alternative once one was married. Thus, feelings of burnout had a low likelihood of occurring. However, when in any given group a few persons divorce and remain single or remarry and appear to be the better for it, divorce will then become a reality for more and more couples. Those who once saw marriage as lasting for a lifetime, now have a plausible option. The fact that the alternative now exists, impresses upon the person that a choice was made in the current partner and a choice must be made to maintain that partner or separate. The development of an alternative follows this process:

1. Steady state—no known alternatives exist. "My work is farming; everyone I know earns a living by farming, and I can't think of an alternative."

2. Options appearing—known alternatives exist. "Yes, I am aware that some people make a living by getting a job at a factory. I could do that."

3. Options become attractive—known alternative seems preferable to the current situation. "I want to change what I do. I want to get a job at the factory."

As long as the person is in the steady state or aware of options appearing, there is a low likelihood of burnout occurring. Burnout, to some degree, depends on options becoming attractive.

Assuming the responsibility for one's choice enlarges the psychological burden of making right and wrong decisions. Thus, the existence of alternatives and the freedom to choose alternatives are part of the equation that can produce burnout. Faced with a multitude of choices, we may find it difficult to choose . . . since selecting one alternative usually means losing the other.

Because people choose their jobs as well as their careers, each of us may feel that we have chosen wrongly. The same is true in the choice of a marriage partner. Since marriages are no longer arranged by tradition, making the wrong decision in marriage is a possibility. Similar observations hold about having children, choosing friends, even buying a house or a car. As that doubt about the right choice occurs and grows, so does the potential for burnout.

DIFFERENCES IN VULNERABILITY TO BURNOUT

Burnout is a relationship between the expectations we have developed internally and the opportunities and rewards we achieve from the environment. It is a consequence of disparity between what our expectations are and what our environment provides. Environments differ substantially in bringing about the possibility of burnout. The literature today is only suggestive. But, we can begin to examine some situations that contribute differentially to burnout and compare the incidence of burnout among different groups.

Table 1 summarizes the available literature on relative vulnerability or incidence of burnout.

Table 1
Some Incidence Characteristics of Burnout

	High Risk	Low Risk
Jobs	high complexity or redundancy in work low autonomy jobs that have declined in status poor working conditions	variability in job tasks with worker controls high autonomy, high status jobs good working conditions
Groups	young, highly educated lower and middle organizational levels	older, less educated upper levels of management
Regions	urban, high density east and west coasts bedroom communities	rural, low density middle of the country neighborhoods frequent friendly interaction

High- and Low-Risk Jobs

Jobs vary in their likelihood to cause burnout. In general, those positions associated with high pressure for performance and repetitious or ambiguous tasks lead to higher-than-average rates of burnout. Jobs that are low in social prestige are high-risk jobs and even more so are those jobs where social prestige has dropped sharply. Among the highest-risk jobs are school teachers and full-time housewives with children at home. At similar risk are emergency medical workers, crisis social workers, and physicians. In factory settings, foremen appear to have the highest burnout rates, and in white-collar jobs the first supervisory level has a high rate of burnout.

Individuals who climb to a high rung on a career ladder, but because of structural factors can go no higher, are high-risk candidates for burnout. The enlisted man who moves through the ranks to master sergeant or warrant officer and cannot enter the commissioned officer grades, but can only wait for retirement, is a familiar burned out person.

As a general observation, positions that provide low worker autonomy and do not permit innovation, especially when coupled with poor or inadequate supervision, prove to have high burnout rates. Assembly line jobs, particularly in the older industries (e.g., steel, auto industry, shipbuilding) are characteristic of these kinds of situations and have fairly high and consistent levels of worker discontent.

The more unpredictable and crisis-oriented the job, the higher the burnout rate appears to be. Air traffic controllers and emergency medical personnel are illustrative of this type of job.

Usually jobs with low or poor quality interaction and low prestige will have high burnout rates. Garbage workers and day laborers are representative of this group. And, even though garbage workers receive excellent pay in many areas, burnout rates appear high. However, the situation can be changed, as was demonstrated in San Francisco where garbage workers—or sanitation workers as they are known—have a responsibility for contracting with the companies for waste removal and therefore add an entrepreneurial dimension to their activities. Consequently, the sanitation worker in San Francisco may be much more stable than the garbage worker in New York City.

Large organizations appear to have higher rates than small and medium-size organizations, but what is more important is that the more highly centralized the organization and the fewer opportunities workers have to participate in decision making, the greater the rate of burnout. The higher rate of burnout in large organizations is probably more a consequence of the latter issue, because effective communication and opportunity for workers to participate in decision making is much more problematic in a large organization and thus leads to a greater rate of worker burnout. Small organizations (those with less than 100 employees) and medium-size organizations (with fewer than 5,000 employees) require less formalized communication and permit more workers to participate in the full range of activities in the organization.

Jerome Rosow, a former assistant secretary of labor, in a recent article (1981) underscored the problems associated with large organizations in producing burnout conditions. Citing a variety of data he argues that today's workers differ sharply from those of twenty years ago concerning attitudes toward work. Today's workers, for example, feel they have a *right* to take part in decisions affecting their jobs, and almost half of those surveyed feel they do not receive enough information to do their jobs well. Involvement and communication are the key variables here, and they are far more difficult to achieve with workers when organizations are large. Involvement is made difficult because the typical worker often does only one part of a process involving thousands of other workers. For one worker to change the way something is done could have implications for dozens of others; thus, the opportunity for an individual to make a change in work routines is limited. Communication to higher levels is thwarted by the same conditions. Large corporations usually involve many levels and offer little opportunity for communication to the top.

High job complexity, if coupled with inadequate communication and poor supervision, leads to high burnout rates. This is demonstrated in assembly line jobs when a production change is made without adequate orientation and training of employees. The result is high levels of worker frustration, work slowdowns, and even strikes.

Finally, strict rigid rules that are applied without consideration of situational variables contribute to worker alienation and burnout. Often employees will protest rigid work rules by applying them in a correspondingly exact and rigid fashion, resulting in work slowdown or work stoppage. In most work sites, rules can only operate as guidelines and when implemented in a strict form only generate a decline or cessation in work activity.

Low-risk jobs are those that permit independence, knowledge of work conditions, control over work conditions, and other factors that maximize the relationship of the job to the worker. When a worker feels in control of the job and is permitted and encouraged to introduce improvements and modifications, burnout should be lessened.

Small business entrepreneurs and farmers are not high in social prestige, but they are among the lower-risk jobs for burnout. Federal judges have no higher prestige than surgeons and considerably less earning power, yet they should suffer much lower rates of burnout because they are under less time pressure in their jobs than the surgeon.

Artists and crafts workers should have relatively low rates of burnout because they maintain a close relationship with their work. Important in all of these low-risk jobs is the degree of opportunity to adjust personal expectations and the degree of control over the day-to-day activity on the job.

High- and Low-Risk Groups

Burnout appears at different rates according to age and rural or urban surroundings. People who reside in rural areas, as opposed to urban dwellers, experience less burnout perhaps because the pace of life is slower. By having a slower pace of life, there is less physical stress from the environment, thus less fatigue and less susceptibility to burnout. We often find more jobs in rural areas that permit worker autonomy and thus both the type of work as well as level of stress varies from urban to rural areas. The most salient factor in making burnout less frequent in rural areas is the slower rate of social change and the lower probability of encountering role alternatives. If this is so, increased travel and advances in telecommunications should spur disenchantment and burnout in rural regions.

Younger workers—especially those under thirty—are far more likely to burn out as are workers with less experience. This may be explained by the fact that age and experience seem to encourage tolerance and more measured expectations from life and probably a longer time orientation to compensate for immediate frustrations.

High levels of burnout in relation to high levels of education seems to be a contradictory observation. However, higher education often serves to sharpen the disenchantment and frustration with boring and uninteresting work. We have a far greater number of bright and well-educated people working in uninteresting jobs than vice versa. Also, the higher one progresses in education, the more socialized the person may well be in the routines and rituals of this society. Achievement and instilling in each individual restlessness and guilt over inadequate achievement is one of the prime rituals of our society. Aimlessness, satisfaction with the status quo, or just drifting through life is not regarded highly in our society. To be able at times to pursue nothing, to feel no anxiety about accomplishing something would be an excellent antidote for burnout. Even when we speak of recreation, we use the term *leisure pursuits*. We pursue or strive for leisure. Again, a paradox.

Generally, the higher the person is in an organization, the lower the burnout. This seems to be related both to higher status and to greater autonomy in controlling the nature and rate of work activity. Also, the more freedom a worker has to express and analyze his or her feelings, to intellectualize frustration and irritation associated with the job, the lower the level of burnout experienced.

High- and Low-Risk Regions and Neighborhoods

The rates of burnout experienced among people may vary with geographical locations. The east and west coasts—being more densely populated—seem to have higher rates in urban areas than in rural regions.

Bedroom communities where schools, employment, shopping, and recreational areas are located elsewhere are high-risk neighborhoods. Large apartment complexes with high anonymity and mobility are high-risk areas *and* magnets that draw people who are burning out. Anonymity may increase burnout because the situation generates fewer social supports for one's expectations. In most instances, one's roles and their expectations are maintained through the presence and interaction with like-minded others. Communities and regions where neighbors are known, where one sees friends and associates at the grocery, the theater, schools, and other places are lower-risk areas.

Challenge and stress are part of the fun and variety of life, but when too much is encountered, burnout can be produced. Paradoxically—but importantly—too little challenge as well can be frustrating and lead to burnout. The key is the degree of fit between what we expect and what we get.

THE SIGNIFICANCE OF THE SYMPTOMS

The term *burnout* began to appear frequently in the scientific literature around 1975. By the end of 1980, there were about fifty research articles and four books dealing with burnout and innumerable articles in the popular media describing burnout. In many cases, *burnout* appears as a synonym for low job satisfaction. In other cases, the symptoms described are characteristic of those associated with alienation. One inescapable conclusion that comes from a review of the literature is that the concept is new and ambiguous and that definitions vary from author to author. One consistent thread across the literature is that burnout is most likely to appear or will be highest where expectations and experiences are most divergent.

Workers in human service fields have been the subjects of study more often than factory workers or self-employed individuals. This may be because human service workers are more introspective, but it is more likely because the success of their efforts is less dependable. When products are being manufactured, though the process may be boring or tedious, the outcomes are predictable. Trying to help people manage their lives, or even to communicate with them clearly and effectively, is much less predictable or dependable.

Finally, the significance of the appearance of the term in 1975 should not be ignored—though it may be coincidental. In the seventies, for the first time since the Great Depression, American culture began to doubt itself. The youth revolt of the late sixties, riots in the cities, the assassination of leading political figures, the Vietnam debacle, runaway inflation, and the moral bankruptcy of the political process signaled by Watergate sharply contrasted our expectations and our reality. In almost every aspect of our lives, the level of success was less than our expectations. This was a painful period and the concerns have not grown smaller. It may be that burnout can pervade a culture and be the symptom of the times.

Explaining Burnout

When man began to travel in vehicles—
whether on horseback, raft, or dugout canoe—
he began a process of separation which
amplified over the centuries by advances in
vehicular technology, broke society into little pieces, and made strangers of us all.

In recent years, this fragmentation has been
attributed to the invention of printing, with
its formalized breaking down of human experience into standard bits and pieces that
can be arranged into linear sequences. This,
it is said, was later transplanted by advanc-
ing technology into the standardization of
parts (pieces of type), the assembly line for
mass production (sentences on a page), and
the specialized and repetitive actions of
workers, which has reflected in the separation of our arts and sciences; in the compartmentalization of our formal education,

and the over-specialization of our economic lives. The result was the breaking between organisms, each other, and their environment, into static, standardized bits and pieces. Our intellectual, emotional, social, and economic lives had been reduced to a series of "still" pictures which, if sequenced properly and run through the machine at the "right" speed gave us the illusion of life, but not the feeling of it.

Don Fabun, *Dynamics of Change.*

One may conveniently divide the factors that produce burnout into two broad categories. One group of factors are those that are external to the individual and may be simply called stress-producing events. These are events that occur to the individual and demand a response from the individual. The second group of factors leading to burnout are those internal experiences or changes within the individual that cause the individual to perceive the environment differently. Physical changes within the individual are an example. When a child moves from childhood into adolescence, internal changes result that require the person to react differently to the world than he or she did as a child. The individual's motivation changes during life and those changes in motivation are an important factor in understanding burnout.

ILLUSTRATIONS OF EXTERNAL FACTORS

Frequent external changes can lead to or contribute to burnout. A job that continually changes in an unpredictable or uncontrollable fashion will produce or can produce burnout. As an example, in investment circles, markets that tend neither to rise nor decline but move erratically within a range called trading markets produce high levels of frustration and failure among investors, because the market's nature is contrary and unpredictable.

Also related to changing situations are jobs with high complexity and ambiguity; for example, an air traffic controller must consider many factors in order to make a correct decision. But often not all of the pertinent factors can be known.

Ambiguous jobs which provide little feedback to the individual about his or her performance are high burnout situations. Such jobs are typical of civil service and middle-management positions in large corporations. Imagine the engineer in the automobile firm who designs cars making it almost impossible to change spark plugs without removing the engine. He has little knowledge of who will buy the product and what owner or mechanic must try to repair the device. The lack of feedback to the engineer produces his burnout and his product kindles the frustration of the anonymous consumer.

Indeed, the lack of communication between a worker and the final user of a product occasionally produces a macabre humor. An example is the new car dealer who had an automobile with a thump that was only heard when the car was driven with the windows rolled down. When the inner door panel was removed, a beer bottle was found tied to a string which, in turn, was tied to the window crank and swung freely only when the window was rolled down. Inside the bottle was a message from a Detroit automobile worker that he was being held prisoner at the factory.

Positions that are far removed from the final product also tend to be burnout-producing as well as jobs with a high level of monotony and tedium. The worker on the assembly line who installs a circuit in a television set sixty steps before the final product rolls off the assembly line has little personal investment in the product and receives little gratification in seeing the set in a department store window. He may not even recognize it. Compare this position to the typesetter who sees the magazine she set last week on the newsstand today.

INTERNAL FACTORS CAUSING BURNOUT

The second group of factors are those experiences that internally throw the individual off balance. Young people are less anchored, less certain of themselves, and have a less well-developed sense of self-identity than people thirty years and older. Consequently, they are more susceptible to burnout. Testing expectations is part of the maturation process. Children often have fantasies of omnipotence and immortality. Comic book heroes like Superman and Wonder Woman reflect these fantasies. Later, as teenagers and young adults, while the fantasies may be more realistic, the likelihood of improbable expectations remains high.

Education has a far greater impact on the individual than just assisting in the accumulation of facts. It provides interpretations about the world, about how things come to be and what causes changes. It also opens new horizons and liberates the student from traditional modes of thinking. It encourages people to compare themselves with others and often suggests greater expectations for oneself and for the future. Therefore, increased education may translate into a greater likelihood for burnout.

Changes in the social meaning of a role, especially negative changes, increase the likelihood of burnout. Soldiers in Vietnam burned out because of the stresses associated with battle, but also because the social value of the soldier's role in that war was extremely low. Historically, the soldier has been honored as a hero, greeted by ticker tape parades and grateful civilians. It's not surprising that the Vietnam veteran who has watched movies and newsreels of the reception World War II and Korean War veterans received would expect the same. But because of the unpopularity of the war, these expectations were not met.

Life challenges to the individual that are stress producing increase the susceptibility to burnout. Thomas H. Holmes and colleagues at the University of Washington School of Medicine have developed a life-events scale that is used to measure psychological stress and identify those events that are strong stressors. It also permits an identification of cumulative events over a period of time that lead to burnout. Holmes's work indicates that if two hundred or more life-change units in a single year are accumulated the individual will be vulnerable to illness (Holmes and Rahe, 1967).

A life-change unit is an event that precipitates change in an individual's life. Sample events are: death of a close friend, change in jobs, son or daughter leaving home, minor law violation. Holmes found that such events could be ranked in terms of their stressfulness, with death of a close friend being several times more stressful than a minor traffic violation for the average person.

Passing through stages in life suggests certain points of high vulnerability to burnout because life stages are accompanied by certain social expectations which the individual has usually internalized. For example, in American society, it is expected that by the age of thirty a person will have established a marriage and a career. If an individual has not met these expectations, turning thirty may become a crisis. Turning sixty-five and facing retirement is another such crisis.

Eric Erikson (1963) and D.J. Levinson et al. (1978) have begun to identify the critical stages of psychological development during the life cycle. Levinson identifies four major eras. The first is childhood and adolescence, from birth to seventeen years; the second is early adult, extending from the end of childhood to forty; the third is middle adult from the forties through the sixties; and the fourth is the late adult era. Each of these eras have challenges and particular motivational needs. The end of each era is a critical point for the appearance of burnout because it signals a change in roles and expectations.

Childhood and adolescence is the era where most of clinical and academic study has been directed. From age seventeen to twenty-two is the first of three transition stages—a period of early adult transition. It is when the adolescent typically begins to leave home and starts to develop routines of life as an independent person rather than a child within the family.

From age twenty-three through twenty-eight is the time of entering the adult world, when the individual begins to learn what these roles are. From age twenty-nine through thirty-three the individual begins to establish adult roles like starting a family and establishing a career. These transition stages, which often lead to changing expectations, are critical times for burnout.

At forty, the middle adult era begins with a period known as the mid-life transition from forty to forty-five. These can be tumultuous times for men and women alike as they review the forty years of life behind them—particularly the twenties and the thirties—contemplating whether they have achieved success and whether they have met the expectations that were laid down for them as children and that they formed in early adulthood.

This can often be a period of sharp changes as marriages are put under pressure—sometimes breaking apart—and sudden career shifts may be made. It is also a threatening time for the woman who has borne children, since her children are no longer in need of as much attention and she is forced to consider roles other than motherhood as it loses its all-consuming character.

After sixty is the beginning of the late adult era—the final era. Once again a transition period occurs that can be highly traumatic for the individual. Facing retirement, declining family responsibilities, and often deteriorating health, the succession of changes may seem overwhelming. Whatever adjustments are made in the sixty to sixty-five period largely prefigure the degree of happiness and satisfaction that the individual will experience for the duration of life.

PERSONAL SYMPTOMS OF BURNOUT

When one has a nagging cold or recurrent bout with a virus, there may be more to it than just a simple infection. The same can be true as well with chronic backaches or headaches. In some cases, the symptoms are indicative of a general susceptibility that apparently arises from stress. Another similar physical complaint is a feeling of tiredness or exhaustion much of the day, especially when there is no physical reason to account for the condition. When the stress brings ringing in the ears, flushing of the face, a tightness of the chest, this is hypertension. It means simply that the body is in a chronic-alert condition.

As long as one is enthusiastic about work or family life, there's a built-in psychological resistance to fatigue and stress. But an interactive deterioration can set in when an individual becomes frustrated with the task or social role—suffering more fatigue which then causes more frustration and then more fatigue. The fatigue/frustration process is an early sign of burnout.

Burnout is especially noticeable in orientation to one's work. It becomes more and more difficult to get out of bed and go to work every day. The familiar burnout syndrome also includes more frequent-than-usual daydreaming, continual fantasies about getting away from it all, and chronic clock watching. Resistance to work may take the form of postponing business appointments, resisting phone calls and meetings, avoiding travel necessary to make client contacts or using travel to avoid office decisions, walking through department stores or the park during working hours or for extended lunch hours, and unusual absenteeism and tardiness. When one begins to count the days every week until Friday and feels anxiety each Sunday about Monday morning, a work burnout syndrome is beginning to emerge.

The syndrome may intensify, reducing the effectiveness of work and consequently requiring more and more time to complete tasks. Routine work begins to pile up and creates excessive anxiety. Unopened mail and unanswered memos begin to mount, while a stack of unreturned phone calls accumulates at the end of each week. As the quantity of work performance declines, quality also suffers and a marked change in working style may appear.

The individual may begin to stereotype customers and clients or associates and lose the ability to respond to people in terms of their individual needs and characteristics. Complaints may be met with intolerance and an inability to understand or empathize. Cynicism regarding colleagues, customers, and clients may appear with an emerging blaming attitude of "they create their own problems." Rather than attempting to understand others, more and more reliance is placed on rigid rules to deal with issues and demands.

Usually this behavior is then coupled with increased irritability and arguing with friends, family, or co-workers. The person has difficulty concentrating or listening to what clients or colleagues are saying. During conversations, the individual is distracted and forgetful. Eye contact is difficult to maintain and the burned out individual will repeat himself frequently as a way of re-establishing where the conversation is. Co-workers may begin to note that the person will avoid casual conversation with them and may be rude and unpredictable in responding.

Feeling alone and isolated at work, but emerging from the "chrysalis behavior" at the end of the workday, burnout will begin to affect the individual's personal life. Chrysalis behavior is characterized by lassitude, noncreative and unemotional responses during the working day with the individual doing just enough work to get by, and low commitment or enthusiasm for tasks or co-workers. However, at the end of the day, the individual then exhibits a great burst of energy much like a moth or a butterfly emerging from the dormant period of the chrysalis as a bright, active creature. However, if burnout continues, the enthusiasm for after-work activity begins to wane. The isolation intrudes into leisure pursuits and usually involves marital discord and an abandonment of contact with friends.

By now, increased consumption of alcohol, coffee, or tobacco as well as sleeplessness occur. A nightcap or sedative is required for a good night's rest. The person may find, particularly on the job, that he is immobilized and overwhelmed by responsibility.

At this time, the indicators include a high level of interpersonal incompetence. The individual is unable to make himself clear in giving directions or engaging in casual social conversation. Sexual functioning may change and may manifest itself either as impotence, lack of interest in sex, a sharp decrease in sexual activity, or it may conversely appear as an adolescent fixation with sex.

The slow, self-destructive behavior that occurs under burnout begins with a life-style—often sedentary—that increases problems of hypertension, ulceration, and maintaining general physical well-being. The human body has tremendous resiliency. It can suffer from physical and chemical abuse, inadequate nutrition, and then, with care, can rebound. However, when the abuse is unceasing, real costs are incurred. General resistance levels are lowered and the abilities of the body's natural defenses are impaired through alterations within the autoimmune system.

Not just one of these signs taken by itself means burnout, but when several—or even one—occurs in an intensive fashion, the syndrome is established. Accompanied by a growing frustration with work, friends, family, then life, it represents what is meant by burnout.

INDIVIDUAL DIMENSIONS OF BURNOUT

The various personal signs of burnout may be grouped into five identifiable dimensions as burnout is manifested in the individual. The dimensions may not appear at the same time in one person, but can be seen when one abstracts from several individuals. The five dimensions are: physiological, social, task, emotional, and value. These dimensions illustrate the many faces which burnout can assume, mirroring the complex physical, psychological dimensions of the individual. Health and psychological well-being are two sides of the same coin. Burnout may be manifested either through physical symptoms or through changes in psychological processes.

Physiological Dimensions of Burnout

The physiological dimension of burnout is manifested through fatigue and tiredness, as well as hypertensive features such as flushing of the face, a sallow washed-out countenance, rapid heartbeat, high blood pressure, loss of appetite or overindulgence in food, alcohol, coffee, and tobacco. A report in *The Austin-American Statesman* (Peterson, 1979) indicates that such physical symptoms may take the form of group hysteria among assembly line workers. The article describes a group of women assembling aluminum lawn furniture in a small Midwestern factory. First one and then others saw a blue mist hovering over them. Many of the women began to complain of headaches, bad taste in the mouth, dizziness and weakness. The symptoms spread among the workers until the plant had to be closed. Afterward, industrial hygienists took air samples and discovered no toxic chemicals in the atmosphere to account for the physical symptoms.

Most of the outbreaks reported to the Occupational Safety and Health Administration have occurred on assembly lines when workers were performing highly repetitious tasks, but have even occurred in schools under conditions where organized activity is underway. More than 90 percent of the typical victims are women. It appears that in addition to the womens' being in highly repetitious jobs, they were on the average less educated than unaffected co-workers and holding jobs under conditions where they were the sole or important economic support of the family.

Table 2
Indicators of Burnout Grouped by Five Dimensions

Physiological	Social
fatigue, tiredness	irritability with friends
overindulgence	and family
hypertensive	no time for small talk
weight control problems	or humor
chronic illnesses	search for more interesting
	friends, mates, etc.
Task	**Emotional**
boredom	rigid thinking
lack of creativity	combative or paranoid
inability to handle complex	stance
tasks	abrupt mood shifts
disorganization	chronic criticism of others
procrastinating behavior	

Value
other people exist only to exploit you
life has no meaning
existential despair
suicidal thoughts

Social Dimensions of Burnout

Changes in social behavior are a second dimension of burnout. Here burnout is manifested in terms of irritability and unseemly criticism of burnout is manifested in terms of irritability and unseemly criticism of co-workers, family, and friends. The person assumes a harsh and brittle stance in social interaction, behaving in abrupt fashion and refusing to compromise on the most petty of issues. With no time for informal talk, the person has an alternatively weary and then distracted style of dealing with others. The person begins to disrupt his or her traditional family, friendship, and work/social ties. Sometimes the individual will launch a hurried search for more satisfying social relationships or engage in prolonged examinations of interpersonal relationships.

Task Dimensions of Burnout

The third dimension of burnout is the task dimension, where work and intellectual activities are interrupted by boredom and a loss of creativity. In this dimension, missing deadlines and complaining accelerate to an inability to accomplish complex tasks and then generalize to an inability to handle more routine work. Both quality and quantity of work suffer with a tendency to start but not complete efforts, and the organization of materials or tools becomes haphazard.

Emotional Dimensions of Burnout

The fourth dimension of burnout is emotional. It involves a tendency to view differences narrowly in a black-and-white manner, "us" versus "them." A defensive, pessimistic posture toward life and work appears and often includes a suspicion of others' intentions. Mood shifts are more frequent and more profound. A person may burst into tears without being able to explain or understand why.

Value Dimensions of Burnout

The fifth dimension of burnout is value. Others' needs are first perceived as threats to oneself and—in time—life, truth, and happiness begin to seem meaningless. In this dimension, personal value or being is questioned. The person has great difficulty in seeing anything in life as being worthwhile. Chronic depression appears in this dimension, frequently with a high level of intellectual sophistication in denying and negating the meaning of all things.

CONCLUSION

Levels or stages of burnout vary for each individual and the personal symptoms and associated dimensions vary as well. While I have emphasized the role expectations play in burnout, the impact is more than psychological. The causes of burnout are woven complexly into the individual and his physical and social environment. The consequences of burnout are complex, as well, and have critical implications for all aspects of the individual's life.

4

The Response Matrix

Most people, historically, have *not* lived their lives as if thinking, "I have only one life to live." Instead they have lived as if they are living their ancestors' lives and their offsprings' lives.

> Tom Wolfe, "The 'Me' Decade and the
> Third Great Awakening."
> *New York Magazine.*

Burnout involves the abandonment, alteration, or collapse of a role. The teenager who runs away from home rather than remain as a child, the salesperson who quits the sales position and becomes a truck driver, and the family who sells their suburban home to move to a farm to escape a consumerist culture and high technology environment are all examples of abandoning a role.

Rather than abandoning a role, a person may attempt to modify it. An individual unhappy with a marriage may seek counseling or plan to have a child as a way to change the marriage. An unhappy employee may discuss dissatisfactions with his or her supervisor and try to reach a better accommodation.

Burnout may also lead to the collapse of a role. Burnout in the third stage (despair and withdrawal) may mean that the person stops responding. A formerly vivacious person suddenly seems withdrawn, the person exists in name only. It's the colleague or neighbor you are only aware of when they are gone.

RESPONSES IN DEALING WITH BURNOUT

Many of us today seem to stay at a low level of burnout, at times gaining little satisfaction from our jobs, our families, or our friends. We use a number of minor distractions as one strategy to achieve some form of equilibrium, but sometimes we require responses that are more dramatic, involving significant changes in our lives.

Response I—"A Quick Break": Small External and Internal Changes

On occasions when the situation does deteriorate, we initially try to change external events to bolster internal feelings. We use a number of minor distractions as a strategy to achieve some form of equilibrium. We take vacations, purchase a new car or stereo equipment, or take a trip to the Caribbean or Las Vegas when our spirits begin to plunge. By making a small purchase or getting away for a few days, we do not change the expectations in the role but just take a short vacation from the expectations. Typically, external events are changed by small diversions such as taking a three-day weekend or making a small purchase of a shirt or blouse. Alcohol and other drugs are also typically used as diversions for this response. Other examples are going to a movie, watching television, or having a party. This is Response I, "A Quick Break."

Response II—"The Compromise":
Moderate External and Internal Changes

Sometimes, we try to change some of the external circumstances and some of the expectations as well. If job success or earning power is less than what we expect, we will compromise by putting more energy into that role and seeking more support or understanding from our supervisor and colleagues. We may change our expectations as well and try to accept the current level of success or income. The response I refer to as "The Compromise" is achieved by an increase along both the external and internal change dimensions.

Response III—"The Fresh Start"
Large Changes on the External Dimension

If Response II is not effective, we may then take a larger step—changing jobs within the organization, for example, or using the riskier strategy of changing to another organization. These larger, external changes are termed Response III, "The Fresh Start." Response III keeps the expectations the same but changes the external situation. We may expect as much success in our career or in our marriage, but to achieve the success make large-scale external changes—moving to a new company or a new mate. There is internal change as well, but the preponderant focus of the change is on external factors.

Response IV—"The Inner Journey"
Large Changes on the Internal Dimension

When the change of external events does not prove to be effective, we may then embark on a strategy of seeking to change internal factors. We choose to stay with the external factors of the role, but work to revise our expectations. The meaning of work may be changed from a search for self-fulfillment to a dependable source of income. Being a parent may become hanging in there until the kids grow up. We may refocus some expectations in the role. Marriage, for example, can change from excitement to dependable companionship. Whatever the change, the emphasis is on keeping external factors the same and changing expectations.

Response V—"New Beginnings":
Large External and Internal Changes

Some individuals may make large-scale external and internal changes. Such abrupt changes are rare but dramatic. They require a high degree of risk-taking behavior and a large investment of personal energy and time. In this case, we may change jobs and then, psychologically, restructure the personal meaning of the work. We may radically change both our social and our family life. As an example, an executive in New York may leave his corporate position and become the owner of a hardware store in Vermont. The bohemian cultures that flourish in most large cities today are a testimony to the large number of Americans who seek to change both their way of economically caring for themselves and the psychological meaning of life itself. The growth of these counter-cultures reached popular awareness in the late fifties and earned the label "the beat generation." In many ways beatnik culture provided the norms for the youth revolution of the sixties and the "dropout culture" in the seventies. These countercultures now consist of people of all ages and, in some areas, traditional culture has become the minority culture. Combining high external and internal changes yields Response V.

Table 3
A Summary of the Major Change Responses

The Quick Break

Examples of this response include: change of routine, minor change of work surroundings, vacation, new car, new clothes, getting away for a movie or a weekend, having some friends over, and going to a concert or football game. This response is the least risky of all and the most frequently used. Environment and expectations are adjusted slightly.

The Compromise

You change your expectations of the job and your supervisor changes his or her expectations of you. You and the environment, including other people, do some negotiating. Both external and internal factors are changed to a greater degree than in the "Quick Break."

The Fresh Start

With this response, the person's expectations stay much the same; but he or she moves to a new environment. Examples are: different job and different organization, move to another city or another state complete with new circle of friends, and divorce and marry again.

The Inner Journey

This response involves major psychological changes—lower expectations of work, redefining the meaning of work, adopting different expectations of marriage. This is the "Inner Journey" response. Don't try to change the world. Change yourself.

New Beginnings

This is the response of starting completely over as a different person in a different environment. Both the person and the situation are new. Sharp change in life's meaning, movement toward solitary pursuits (Thoreau's Walden Pond), changing careers, developing a new life-style, self-exploration and analysis may result in transcendental outcomes.

THE RESPONSE MATRIX

The five responses to burnout (table 3) can be arranged in a grid according to the level of internal change to external change involved. This grid is displayed as the Response Matrix in figure 1. Low levels of internal and external change provide "The Quick Break"—Response I, the approach most of us use most of the time. It is an incremental or gradualist approach where one changes the environment a bit and changes one's self a bit. Most of the time this response works for most people.

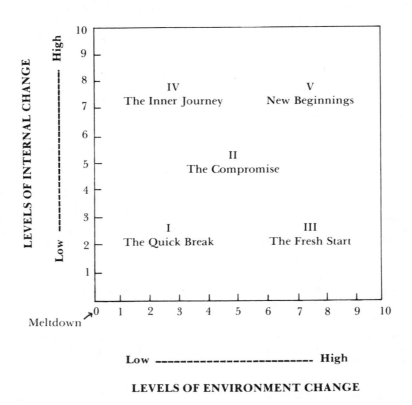

Figure 1
The Response Matrix

When both internal and external change are increased, "The Compromise" is being created. This response is usually the step beyond "The Quick Break."

"The Fresh Start" is achieved by increasing external change. As a response, it is usually dependent on available external alternatives and resources. It is a move from one state to another or from one job to another.

"The Inner Journey" accomplishes change by adapting to a situation, not through changing the situation. It is learning to live with a role. When resources are scarce, when opportunities are limited, Response IV is the typical approach.

Maximizing external and internal change produces the "New Beginnings" response. Such large-scale change happens rarely but time does produce some situations that require Response V approaches. Marriage and retirement are examples of such situations. Of all strategies, it is the most extreme and most demanding. Of course it produces large dislocations in the individual's life and often in those around him.

MELTDOWN

There are, of course, other alternatives within the response matrix. Not uncommon is a tendency to change neither expectations nor the environment. In this case the person is using minimal change on both dimensions and is moving toward entropy or "Meltdown." This is a response of no action; yet it does have consequences. By taking no action, pressures become generated within the person and a chronic sense of failure and inadequacy results.

The "Meltdown" response coincides with, and in fact is, the third stage in the burnout progression. The person still feels he should be more than what he is yet is unable to change the reality or give up the expectations. Apathy, futility, bitterness, depression are among the symptoms. Often, the individual will take no responsibility for his actions and may become very dependent on others. The "Meltdown" response in other individuals may take the form of social isolation, sometimes including efforts to avoid social contact or difficulty in maintaining social relations.

OTHER ROLE RELATIONS

A person may experience burnout in one role but not in all roles. Indeed, the usual situation is to encounter burnout in a role but initially not be able to localize which role is in conflict. Because we all participate in so many roles, it is easy to suffer frustration in one role yet be unable to pinpoint it. For example, a man may enjoy the role of husband, wage earner, home handyman, and father to his youngest child but be highly frustrated with being the parent of a teenager.

The conscious identification of which role is initially the source of burnout may not occur at all; and the burnout may eventually spread to other roles. How so? Your performance is impaired in your other roles because of exhaustion. You want to be left alone. Your interaction is lessened with others. The degradation of your performance means that others' expectations of you are not met, and they suffer burnout. Thus, burnout can be passed from one person to the next as well as from role to role.

Burnout is relative to a set of expectations; yet, when a response is used it may affect other roles. Indeed Response I, "Quick Break," is the use of internal and external change to shift into a different role. Having a party, going to a movie, going camping for the weekend shifts one internally and changes the external environment. Going home in the evening or on the weekend are role shifts as well.

The more extreme the movement along the external change dimension of the response matrix, the greater the likelihood that the person's other roles will be affected. Maximum movement on the external change dimension generates "The Fresh Start" response. Now if the response is generated in terms of the work role and the person moves to a new town as an aspect of taking a new job, many other roles are forced to change as well. New neighbors and new friends will enter one's life. If the move is far enough—say from the midwest to the coast or from the city to the country—a whole series of roles may change.

On the other hand, maximum movement on the internal change dimension seems to result in greater role compartmentalization. The individual lessens expectations of a role and seeks to survive or simply put up with the role. That is what causes what I have termed chrysalis behavior. The person is drab or colorless in one role while being creative and exciting in another. The habitual response of lowering expectations in the face of challenges, however, may mean a lessened expectation in role after role. If many people in a community use such responses, social change could be slowed. Such a change, if it persisted for any length of time, would be at variance with the history of the recent past since rising expectations have largely characterized Western civilization in the industrial era.

We may take the response matrix and add a third dimension to it by drawing a vertical line and thus stacking roles upon each other like stories or levels in a building. Now we can see that much movement by one role can disturb or shift adjoining roles or possibly all roles. A person, for example, may be fed up with his job and decide to move a thousand miles away and start over again. This "Fresh Start," however, means a new climate, a new neighborhood, a new house, and maybe a new family. Your spouse or your children may not agree to your "Fresh Start" since it involves changes for them also. Figure 2 illustrates how roles may be seen as contingent upon each other.

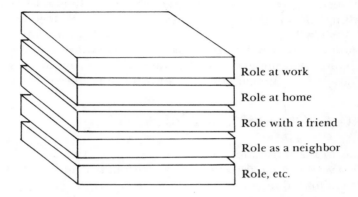

Figure 2
Relationship of Multiple Roles

Again, a singularly important dimension of the way an individual's mental state leads to burnout is the associated expectations that the individual holds with a given role. For example, if a sales agent's expectation is that he or she will become the best in the company, and if in due time that expectation is not met, burnout will begin. Re-evaluation of the role may occur as well as alternatives and burnout may intensify. If a parent hopes that a child will be outstanding in school achievement and the child does not excel, the parent may then begin to question his or her adequacy as a parent and burnout may commence.

The essential relationship in burnout is between the expectations and the actual reality that is perceived. Indeed whole nations can burn out. In the United States today, expectations around the quality of life, the amount of leisure time, personal safety, the availability of material goods, and national prestige are being revised downward. In the process, the nation loses, collectively, its sense of security and direction and experiences burnout. The ultimate and final levels of burnout are not a predetermined course that every individual, institution, or society must run, eventually reaching the final stage. Rather, the several stages earlier identified are degrees or gradations that can be reached, but there is no ultimate eventuality of reaching the final levels of burnout for any person or organization.

The response an individual chooses relative to the level of burnout may be mismatched. For example, if an individual is at an extreme level of burnout and yet continues to depend on Response I styles of coping—using consumer purchases to restore energy and direction—the use of this response typically proves futile. On the other hand, some individuals have such high personal expectations of life, every minute should be exciting and fulfilling, that just the slightest frustration causes them to plunge into a new life-style, a Response V. Apparently, many of the groups drawn to the rapidly proliferating psychotherapy techniques are filled with just such extreme plungers or gamblers who rush frantically from one therapy fad to another in search of ultimate and everlasting pleasure and enlightenment.

FACING A PLAUSIBLE ALTERNATIVE

Returning to the illustrations in the first chapter, Ann Schraeder has, though not yet thirty, faced a series of role decisions in her life that have led her back and forth through the burnout stages. Early in her college years, Ann was forced to make a decision to be a traditional student or an activist.

As Ann expressed it, "Many nights during my sophomore year, I would leave rap sessions in the dorm to go to my room or the library to study. I had to break up with my boyfriend, Brad, because he said I was part of 'the establishment,' part of the war and racism he and his friends were fighting to bring down. I fought with him every day and seemed to cry all the time. I felt like a Ping Pong ball being bounced between Brad and my own fear of not making it through college. Finally, I decided to accept social isolation and pursue my studies. Though I said I would not look back on that decision, I have—lots of times."

It was in that sophomore year that Ann began to realize alternative roles or choices for herself that she, alone, could make. She also learned that she had to bear the responsibility for the choice, bittersweet though it might be.

The student activism environment and her boyfriend made her face a plausible alternative. She could have become an activist, chosen the "relevant" over the academic. Ann chose to reject the alternative role and intensify her commitment to the role she had grown up with, the diligent and dedicated student. She employed Response I, Response II, and Response III in avoiding her activist friends, their hangouts, and breaking with her activist boyfriend. Ann then "locked in," using these tactics until the present time. There is, however, a hint that she may be considering a more risky shift to Response V by moving to a different line of work and a different definition of herself.

Harvey Eagleton chose to make a much different change for himself, Response V, "New Beginning." As Harvey relates it, "All my life I thought

I knew what I wanted to be. Money, a family, and prestige were my goals. I chased the bitch goddess, Success, till I caught her and then *I* was caught. Two-thirds of my life were gone before I saw that.

"When Judith entered college, it made me realize I could do something like that. I sat down with her one evening and told her I was cashing everything in—my stocks, my job, my retirement. I said I wanted to sell the house; to my surprise, and maybe not to my surprise, she agreed. The kids were shocked and tried to talk us back to our senses. My parents asked an old friend, a psychiatrist, to talk with me. His advice was if that's what you want to do, then do it.

"After the dust settled, I came out of the marriage with $300,000. I spent $5,000 on a trip to Australia thinking I would settle there, but Australia seemed too slow and backward. So, after two months I moved to Santa Fe. I grew a beard, lost twenty-five pounds, and had six affairs in four months.

"I've slowed down now and am starting to get it together in a different way. I run a welding shop, something I've always wanted to do, and peddle a little land. Judith calls every few weeks and seems happy. My parents are still stunned, but they're coming around. It's the kids I'm really surprised about. They think I've gone crazy. Funny, how hard it is for them to see my path."

Perhaps more today than ever before, life is filled with options and alternatives. The fact that so many options exist makes burnout possible. When a plausible alternative occurs, several things happen. We may become filled with anxiety and vacillate between our present situation and the alternative. We may, like Ann Schraeder, make some environmental changes and recommit ourselves to our present situation—our current role. We may, on the other hand, activate the third or fourth response and move to the new alternative.

Or, we may neither increase our commitment to the old role nor move to a new one. That is the saddest choice, the one that ensures burnout. We slowly or rapidly collapse upon ourselves, extinguishing our dreams, mocking ourselves with criticism, and looking to the world with bitterness.

Sue Torres was never able to increase her commitment to her current role or move to another. Each year Sue grows more cautious, feebly using Response I efforts. Yet, more extreme changes are needed. Today, both Sue's children are grown and have left home. Sue observes, "Aaron and Laura have their own lives now. I seldom see them and, even with the problems with Laura, I didn't realize how much I would miss them when they were gone.

"The office? Not much to say. Nothing really changes. I do wonder what life would have been like if I had moved from Chicago when the children were still with me. I believe I could have made it then, but I wouldn't want to try it now that I'm alone."

It has now been more than a decade since Larry returned from Vietnam, yet he remains an angry young man. Larry's approach to burnout is to make radical changes whenever frustration builds, a Response III. He is now separated from his second wife and has changed jobs several times. His life has become a series of "Fresh Starts." Larry has moved into an apartment and has found a world where there are many other single unattached persons. Larry doesn't speculate much about life now. He says he takes it as it comes.

Tim Ferris shows few symptoms of burnout and apparently, when he does, his responses are adequate. One cannot say what the future will hold for Tim.

I have had several friends who have used all the responses two or three times. One of them, Jerry, was a promising artist and high school teacher when I met him. In Jerry's words, "I've always wanted to do my own thing and that is to paint, but I have to have public notice and approval for what I do. Painting is communicating and someone out there has to listen, has to respond. Teaching is how I make a living, but painting is life."

The art critics said that Jerry had potential, but he never seemed to bring it off. For a couple of years, Jerry worked Response I frantically. He would change his mode of dress or his painting style frequently. He moved his painting loft twice. He grew a beard.

Finally Jerry decided that to become a successful painter he must devote himself to painting. Teaching got in the way. It was a distraction. He quit his teaching job and moved to a small town. His wife got a job as a teacher to support the two of them and their child. This was a much more dramatic move—Response III. Originally two roles appeared as conflicting to Jerry, teaching and painting. His decision was to eliminate the teaching role and concentrate on the painting.

Still, Jerry's paintings did not sell. His work did not achieve enough critical acclaim. At this point Jerry began to use a mixture of Response IV and Response V. He began to drink heavily and took a part-time teaching job at a community college two hundred miles away. He would be there three days a week and at home, four. In the college town, he lived with a young art teacher and tried to persuade his wife to come and join them. Jerry's wife finally filed for divorce.

Three years ago I visited Jerry in the city of Guadalajara in northern Mexico. He was part of an American free college that taught art and pottery. Jerry said he got by on fifty dollars a month. He observed, "I think I'm finally becoming whole. All that pressure in the States to 'do this, be that,' was shredding me apart. It warped my head. I did the mushroom thing here for months before I saw my way. Now I have all that I need and am whole."

Last year I was in San Diego and saw Jerry again. He was running a travel agency and enjoying life with a new wife. He had met her in Guadalajara and decided to return to the States with her. Apparently, Jerry had tried a variety of responses in seeking success in the artistic role and had ended by de-emphasizing that particular role.

Another friend, a few years older than Jerry, has slowly burned out while basically using a "Meltdown" response. When I met Art fifteen years ago, he was a promising young banker on his way to the top. Somewhere along the way, Art was passed over for promotion to senior vice-president of the bank twice. Since then, Art has had several chances to leave and start his own bank or become an officer in another. Each time he turned the opportunity down. For several years, he got a lift out of life with a new car or a vacation. Now that all his children are grown, all there is to his life is the job. His wife and friends shake their heads sadly. Art maintained his role but seems to have given up with it. Burnout in his case comes from having stood still.

I have known Carol since college. In college she excelled at everything: looks, popularity, grades. She graduated at the top of her class and married the man most likely to succeed, and then worked to put him through law school. After two children, Carol started her own business, a tax preparation agency, and now makes much more than her husband.

When I asked Carol the secret of her success and happiness, she said, "Part of my philosophy is don't look back, something could be gaining on you. You know, what happens for me is there is always a timer in my head that goes off when things are going well, getting smooth. I don't expect life to be that way, and I don't fool myself. I think a lot about what I want out of life, almost every week. I then sit down and write those things out. I find I can use the same thing to identify those things that are starting to get to me. That way I think I can always keep ahead."

Carol intuitively understands burnout and how one must respond to life. I've often wondered if there were any problem she couldn't handle. I don't think there is.

SUMMARY

Burnout is a relationship between events in life and the meaning and understanding the individual draws from life. Burnout is occasioned or precipitated by stress and alienation, but it will not occur until the individual experiences dissatisfaction with a given situation. As long as the situation is seen as a given, a condition of life, the individual may struggle, may feel pain, but not burn out.

Typically, the response is limited. "My wardrobe is dated. I need a new suit or dress. I'll feel better about things after I've been away for a few days." Most of the time, small changes or adjustments eliminate the feelings of burnout.

At other times, small changes do not remedy the situation and more consequential changes may be attempted—large purchases, such as a new auto or different house, or maybe a move to a large city or a new job. When resources for making external changes are limited, expectations may be revised. Finally, when these responses do not relieve the burnout feelings, the environment and its related goals and internal meanings may be altered.

The responses discussed in this chapter are approaches that we each pick up during our lifetime. By arranging the responses along dimensions, one for external change and one for internal change, the response matrix is produced. Various responses can now be seen as mixtures of levels of internal and external change. Usually the responses a person uses are habits that become ingrained over time and may or may not be effective in reducing burnout. In many cases, the responses are not effective or are not matched well to the stage of burnout. They may provide a temporary relief to the symptoms, but without a clear identification of the role causing the burnout and a suitable response, the burnout will reappear. With each reappearance the burnout may be more severe and relief more elusive.

An intent of this book is to clarify the habituated responses to burnout and permit the reader to determine if his or her usual response in a given role is effective. Chapter 9 returns to this problem and introduces a technique, Designing Expectations, to reduce the floundering from response to response as well as the tendency to use ineffective approaches.

A significant aspect of our species is its ability to accommodate to change and to create its own environment. Considerable research supports the psychological need for change and the tendency of humans to produce change just for novelty's sake. The resolution is not, however, in terms of change being good or evil, but rather the extent to which an individual or a total society has effective strategies for coping with change and has some control in the rate and direction of change.

To understand how well prepared we are to do this today, and especially during the next couple of decades, we must step back a bit and look at some of the changes in our world, how they contribute to burnout, and the prospects for achieving understanding of these changes and effective strategies to deal with them.

5

Changing Times and Changing Motives

What kind of society is it, then, where working life begins at fifteen years at the earliest, and finishes at sixty, with an average of about two and a half hours of labor each day in between?

Richard Leakey and Roger Lewin, *People of the Lake: Mankind and Its Beginnings.*

The key to understanding burnout is to understand what external changes have occurred in our world, changes that have both expanded the number of roles we maintain and also made many of these roles so fluid. Salient among all internal and external changes is the increased involvement today of men and women in formal positions of employment. Working, being employed, has become the single most important indicator of status—the major anchor of being. Though people have always worked, only in this century has formal employment—work at a job where a direct salary is paid—been so pervasive and so central to personal identity. The distinction between work (anything that requires the expenditure of energy) and formal employment (involving a specific job, a place where that job is done, and a fixed wage) is important for our purposes.

The growth of this phenomenon of formal employment, the appearance of the complex corporate organization, and the relation of each of these to traditional institutions and self-concept are the next set of hurdles on the path to understanding burnout.

The industrialization process is the driving force producing the proliferation of roles for the individual and simultaneously creating a dominant ethic of utilitarianism that makes every role highly tenuous. Utilitarianism implies that something should only be retained as long as it is useful or productive. If a thing or a role loses its usefulness, it should be abandoned. The utilitarian ethic demands the use of a means/ends test. Every activity must be related as a means that leads to some end, some goal. It requires that all activities—all processes—be useful, functional, productive. When something or someone is not useful, then the person or the thing becomes a problem to be corrected or eliminated. This is the root of the tenuous quality of all roles under this ethic.

PATTERNS OF LIFE IN THE PAST

Though we may frequently think of today as a time of luxury and leisure, there are reasons to suggest that we live in one of the most work-intensive eras of history. Preliterate and pretechnological people probably worked far fewer hours daily or weekly than their modern counterparts. The anthropologist Richard Leakey (1978) has estimated that prehistorical people probably averaged only two and a half hours per day to provide food, clothing, and shelter. Aborigines, in settings undamaged by today's technological intrusions of intensive farming or mining, perhaps work double that daily estimate. The farmer of the Middle

Ages experienced days of long hard labor around the harvest, but much of the time during the year he was relatively unencumbered by onerous work demands. Many things which we think of as work, such as food preparation, repair of clothing, and care of children, were defined as personal responsibilities and not *work* in the current sense of the word. Efforts around these responsibilities were imbued with a sense of ritual, rhythmically performed, so that they were a way of life, not requiring the postponement of the enjoyment of life.

The technique and procedures of farming grow from an ancient tradition stretching back as long as twenty thousand years and antedating all civilization. All remains of ancient cities, the oldest of which date back approximately ten millennia, show evidence of farming. Indeed, farming was probably a necessary prerequisite for the high-density dwellings and barter markets that characterized early cities. Throughout history, farmwork has been organized not by the clock or by the first-line supervisor's instructions in a factory, but by the sun, the season, and the weather.

The movements and thoughts of the individual in a life of farming had a gradual and recurrent tempo of caring for animals, planting, harvesting, storing foodstuffs, and preparing the soil for the next growing season. Though crises occurred, they were infrequent and most often associated with birthing of animals and changes in the weather. There were no daily crises like those experienced by the physician or nurse in emergency receiving rooms or the police officer in the large city. The continual bustle and tension-filled world of the office worker in the large city and the persistent buzz of human interaction for the clerk in a department store were nonexistent too.

Rather than being divided into seconds and minutes, the farmer's time perspective was relatively long. Work was often planned and carried out over several months, according to a season. A farmer spent several years clearing a section of land, changing the rotation of crops, or establishing a new strain of animals in a beef or dairy herd. In this world, the pace of innovation was slow, and generations were required for a new invention to be accepted and spread among a group of farmers.

Tradition governed technique. Procedures for knowing when to plant, what to plant, how to make farm implements, the construction of harnesses, tools, fences, and buildings were not learned through a formal school process, but rather through oral tradition passed from generation to generation. The farm belonged to the family, or at least some share of the products did. These products were partially, and in some cases totally, used for consumption by the farm family. Some items were bartered for other goods or sold for cash. Money was an incidental part of the farming enterprise, and the activities of the farm family were not oriented toward maximizing cash return. Labor was shared mutually by all family members. Neighbors traded help, especially at harvest time or when barns or other buildings needed to be built. No ledgers or books were kept on the amount of work done by each family member or on work owed to neighbors.

Even the land was part of the family and passed down to the children. For an individual to be without land, or for a family to lose their land, was to lose the essentials of life. Fathers ensured the obligations of sons to them through the fear of the loss of inheritance. Daughters were also bound to families through the use of the dowry. The choice of husband was as much predicated upon the amount of land the young man had available as any other attributes. Indeed, separating the land from the people that reside on it and trading the land for money is a relatively recent development. By way of illustration, it was not until the sixteenth century that land in England was surveyed and then exchanged on an open market for money.

All in all, traditional farming was a slow-paced life graded or broken into very large units. Daily stress from crises and high-frequency social interaction was missing. The things that were produced were mostly for home consumption. Almost every item that a person used was made partially or totally at home. In traditional farming communities, most of the people were farmers. Only a small fraction of the total population was engaged in nonfarm pursuits. Working hours were very long, tedious, and physically exhausting. However, verbal activity and complex analytical and conceptual skills were not demanded. Change came less than occasionally, only rarely, and the entire culture was conservative. The extended family and neighbors were the major, often only, social referent. Individual identity was centered or anchored in these groups; the individual maintained this single group membership for a lifetime.

The other major work form in the traditional era preceding the industrial period was craft work. Craft work required special skills and special tools and could support only a small percentage of the population in most communities. In the main, craftsmen were stonemasons, watchmakers, printers, tailors, cabinetmakers, boot makers, chemists, potters, weavers, goldsmiths, shipwrights, and carriage makers. All craft workers accounted for a minority—hardly more than 10 percent—of the population in most communities. By the Middle Ages, these artisans began to associate in guilds to control the quality and the amount of work, the prices they charged, and the apprenticeship of new workers.

The knowledge of how to practice a craft was not available through books or teachers, but could only be obtained through a lengthy apprenticeship where the novice worker traded time to a master artisan in return for the opportunity to learn a craft. Apprenticeships could stretch into years as the younger worker struggled not only to obtain the requisite knowledge, but also to accumulate sufficient capital for tools and then initial raw materials to begin a trade. The learning and admission process was slow, conservative, and powerful. It was almost impossible to challenge such a system, and entering an apprenticeship meant more than acquiring an economic skill. Choosing a craft became a way of life and an outlook on life. Needless to say, through this process, crafts remained in families for generations with relatively low involvement from outside individuals. The craftsman's product was more art than commodity and was an extension of the artisan's view and understanding of the world. The most skilled craftsmen were known through their work, and special marks—logos—were placed on their products to identify them. In fact, modern corporate symbols are a simple continuation of the craftsman's mark, one of the few remnants in the modern technological world of that ancient mode of organizing production.

The countryside was the domain and possession of the farmer, but the craft and trade guilds created and controlled the villages and towns. Large cities were unusual and only occurred near seaports and major trade routes, such as navigable rivers. The countryside and village were the social world; the nation was only dimly perceived.

The meaning of life and the merits of an alternative occupation would have been rare and improbable questions for these folk. In this era, literacy was not far advanced. Few craftsmen could read and even fewer farmers. Communication about alternative ways of life occurred infrequently and was largely a curiosity, not a challenge to existing ways. The tales of Marco Polo were just that, tales. They were for entertainment; the far wood or the opposite ocean shore represented a frightening unknown zone across which scarcely a soul ventured. The government and the Church controlled access to outside societies and thus alternatives to cultural patterns. Printed material was hard to come by and expensive. The freedom to write and publish one's own thoughts remained unconceived.

For the individual farmer or tradesman, there were no alternative roles. For this era, as for almost the entire history of civilization, the means of earning one's livelihood provided the definition of life. Earning a livelihood was often secondary to the pattern and ritual which held the core meaning for the individual. Tradition authorized one's actions and bound one to a cycle of life like the spokes of a wheel bind the rim to the hub. Individuals were not responsible for their own fate, but received it through the family and the capriciousness of fortune. Men and women alike were motivated by tradition, duty, and obligation. Change moved as does the snail. Alternative thoughts were few.

BREAKING THE PATTERNS OF THE PAST

In the late Middle Ages, a number of events began to slowly stir this slumbering world that would alter the social fabric in culture after culture and shake profoundly the mentality of the peasant farmer. These movements provided the seedbed for industrialism and the resulting mechanisms that produced alienation and burnout. Among the changes was the ebbing strength of tradition's grip on society and individual mentality. No single event or idea was responsible for this ebbing, but rather a number of forces inimical to traditional life were gathering strength like darkening clouds growing turbulent before the storm.

Increased land and sea trade with other cultures—primarily the Orient—introduced Europe to products and patterns of life that contrasted sharply with its own and often proved more desirable. Wandering seafarers followed by merchant seamen began to exploit the lucrative spice routes to India, and the finite limits of the known world dissolved. Merchants began to create trade empires that challenged the orthodox powers of feudal times, and common people began to see alternatives never dreamed of before.

The weakening of the grip of the Church of Rome in the more northern regions of Europe gave rise to governments in Great Britain, Germany, and Switzerland that were hostile to Catholic influence. Technological improvements in warfare—especially the use of steel and gunpowder—began to change the ancient power relationship in the established fiefdoms and estates of the Middle Ages, rendering the fortified stone castles of the older order obsolete.

The invention of the printing press by Guttenberg and the Copernican Revolution—accelerated by the telescope—changed man's knowledge of the earth and the universe, exposing tradition and dogma to question. The opening of the New World spurred trade and entrepreneurial activity. Concomitant with this trade was the development of religious and personal philosophies that emphasized individual responsibility in determining one's fortune on earth and one's fate after death.

Coupled with these philosophies was the rise of science as an increasingly salient and competitive explanation for life and physical existence, paralleled by a shrinking of the importance and authority of the world's more ancient institutions, especially the Church and royalty. Accelerating during the Renaissance, the appearance of machines such as power looms, pulleys and levers, and other incipient mechanical technologies multiplied human power immeasurably. Finally, by the eighteenth century, an unimaginably immense storm broke that loosened a wave of wars and social upheavals, dissolving the bonds of farmers and peasants to the land, to the feudal lord, and to tradition.

Now throughout Europe and North America, tradition was on the retreat in almost all areas of religion, art, technology, farming, industry, and man's definition of himself. Charles Darwin, Sigmund Freud, Albert Einstein, Karl Marx, Frederick W. Taylor, the English and American industrialists and militant Protestants, each in different domains, proffered competing and eventually successful new versions of reality.

NEW TIMES AND NEW MOTIVES

In the work place, factory employment proved to be very different from farming or craft work. First of all, work was organized around central precepts of specialization and division of labor. The dawning of the industrial era ended the craft worker's dominance in nonagricultural work and accelerated the flow of farm labor into highly organized work sites that became factories. In these sites, the workers did not proceed to tasks that they chose but rather were assigned tasks, materials, tools, and stations by foremen and owners. Though in the first years of the industrial revolution, men, women, and children alike were pressed into industrial employment, they did not enter as families but as individuals and worked as individuals at their tasks. The workers did not own the materials, tools, or products, but rather exchanged their time for a wage. The consequence of this approach to the work place was that life became organized around units of work or discrete tasks in the factory. More than ever before, the worker was now controlled not by body cycles of energy and fatigue, or by the weather or the season, but by the clock. Under the discipline of the factory, production per unit of an individual's work could increase a thousandfold or more. This excess productivity surpassed the needs of local consumption and required the owners of the factory to develop national, and ultimately international, markets to handle the cheap yet quality goods produced by this radically new way of organizing work.

Under the new factory organization, the strings of tradition were weakened as a control of individual behavior, and a stronger need for internal motivation was occasioned. Part of this motivation came as a consequence of the large numbers of landless and unemployed men, women, and children driven from the land by war, famine, and social disorder, much as in the newly industrializing countries of today in Asia and Central America. Such individuals, because of their subsistence needs, were willing—often desperate—to trade their time for cash and to use the cash to purchase housing, food, and clothing. Thus, the social disorder that accompanied the industrial revolution helped provide the motivational impetus for individuals to abandon the weakened tradition and seek work within the new social organization.

The intensive concern with questions about human motivation and work did not appear until the industrial era with the harnessing of abundant but untrained farm and peasant labor to factory tasks. Within the factory, men had to be motivated not out of tradition to do a certain kind of work, as in the former era, but out of a tradition to be diligent, to be useful, to be involved in work and to seek self-gratification in terms of things which could be purchased through money. The rich and transcendental gratification associated with craft work or farming of the earlier era was soon to become taboo. Work became separate from the rest of life, with the quality of work recognized through the amount of pay provided to the individual.

The male in the household became an "economic man," and the cash income encouraged the development of an authoritarian family structure for some homes since the family grew more dependent on the single adult male wage earner. On the traditional farm, no single person was the sole support, so power and authority in the domestic household could be more diffuse. Life prior to industrialization was rural or small town and was the first romantic era of family life. Families included children, grandparents, and often cousins, aunts, and uncles—all drawn together in a daily tempo of shared activity. Young children helped draw water and bring wood or coal indoors for the morning cooking, while older children cared for the family cow, pigs, and chickens. Parents and grandparents taught children gardening, canning, sewing, cooking, farming, animal care, carpentry, and so forth at an early age. The formal education period for most persons was only six to eight years, and people learned as much from their families about how to conduct themselves in life as from formal schooling.

Children were valued for the joy they brought but also for the help they provided. The family without strong boys to work the fields and healthy girls to run the household was a family that soon disappeared. The work roles of both sexes overlapped greatly, since the demands of work and the absence of hired help or machines required men and women alike to be able to perform many of the same tasks. These were the times that the Currier and Ives prints portray at Christmas time or the Waltons present on evening television. The family, at least in the romantic notion, was a large organic group that required cooperation and participation of all family members.

The first accommodation of the family to industrialization was for the male to enter the wage economy labor force while in many cases maintaining a small farm operation. In time, though, cash income from the male's efforts decreased dependence on homegrown products and women began to specialize in the household activities, especially the care of children remaining at home. Thus, in the United States by the 1950s, the rural farm family had been replaced as the typical social unit by the wage economy family, with the male as the external income provider. Usually the male was also the most influential family member in setting goals for the family, such as the choices for major expenditures, and in disciplining children. The female, on the other hand, had the responsibility of running the household and nurturing the young child.

Television of the 1950s concisely summarized and parodied that family ideal in Ozzie and Harriet Nelson and their two sons, David and Ricky. Here was not the large extended family of the Waltons, with several boys and girls and grandparents all engaged in farming, cooking, and sewing. Instead, here was a family basically centered around the children. Ozzie would disappear early each morning to a job somewhere—what he did few knew and none seemed to care. Harriet, often preparing breakfast by pouring milk on the cornflakes, would then likewise disappear for eight hours until the boys and Ozzie returned home. What they did during the day is one of the mysteries of the twentieth century but, suffice it to say, family life began again around five o'clock in the evening.

By the sixties, the women's movement urged women to put aside their aprons and to seek their destiny and fortune in the compelling and exciting world of work. Institutional arrangements were quickly patched together to take care of children through kindergarten and day care, and marriage changed from an economic proposition to an arrangement for shared quarters and companion affections. Now, women too were fully economic beings, freed from the chains of households and children.

One might ask which arrangement—the extended family with arranged marriages or the nuclear family with romantic attachment—is better or more just. It seems the answer, like the definition of beauty, is in the eyes of the beholder. The traditional family as it existed prior to the technological era was a productive social unit that seems to have been based on a minimum of choices in social roles. Women had their roles and men had theirs, and questions were not asked. Variation and romantic love occurred in the upper classes, but these classes were an exceedingly small proportion of the population. Men and women were not equal but rather had separate domains, and usually the men were dominant. According to Edward Shorter (1977), almost all of the man's work was out-of-doors with the exception of the lighting of the oven in the morning. Men did heavier muscle labor, but both sexes spent much time in heavy, tiring tasks. It is also Shorter's (1977) contention, incidentally, that such labor coupled with poor nutrition and lack of private rooms sharply curtailed sexual expression. For the laboring classes of the traditional era, sexual relations were infrequent and not romanticized.

THE CONSEQUENCES OF CHANGE

In the traditional work setting, clear social anchorages existed for peasant farmers and village artisans. For both, one major anchor was the family. The peasant farmed as a member of a family and chores were divided among men and women, sons and daughters. For the village craftsman, the craft was passed usually from father to son and the family name became associated with the craft. In both of these cases, one's concept of self, of duty, of obligation, and of the future was inextricably bound up within this social or reference group. Work meant far more than simply earning one's way or earning a wage. The work—the product—was the expression and affirmation of the self.

Historically, the major life anchors have been the family, one's chosen way of life, the neighbors, and religion. With the factory era and industrialization, the anchorages of the self changed. Life's station became something that the individual did not inherit but rather strived to achieve. Whatever station one reached, one felt responsible for the success achieved and, most importantly, the failure endured.

Technology and industrialization changed work and the meaning of life. Through the act of employment, the person, and the person's self-concept, is merchandized on a daily basis as a commodity and exchanged for money. Motivation or energy to work is reduced to a simple monetary exchange. Other basic human motives—affiliation, friendship, dependability, loyalty, and fidelity—are banished from the work place. Only energy to do work, and thus the amount of work accomplished, remains as a legitimate human attribute. The long-cherished motives become worthless within the work place. Through the process of industrialization, one sees oneself as an extension of the machinery in the factory and, as such, begins the gradual process of alienation from work, associates, and ultimately one's self.

Thus, the economic man has his roots in the change of the value definitions of work which were formerly individualistic and sacred but became utilitarian and common. To fully understand this individual, we must understand how work came to be redefined. The new social systems that replaced the former organic whole within which work was embedded and the new, valid source of motivation in the factory era—the exchange of time for money—were the duality that redefined the meaning of work.

Industrialization changed the meaning of work and the way work was done. While making work more efficient, it also made the work place an alienating environment, an environment where the individual has little control.

Burnout is produced by holding expectations that are beyond what reality brings. If we expect a job to be challenging and to offer a variety of experiences, we may encounter burnout if the job proves to be routine and colorless. We may respond to the burnout either by lowering our expectations or by trying to bring reality into line with our expectations.

When there is little or no social change, new and different expectations for the individual are unlikely to occur. There is, as well, a dependable matching of an individual's expectations to reality. What we expect to be and what we turn out to be has high congruence, is a good match.

Social change, however, brings forth alternative roles and makes possible new expectations. It may, as well, encourage one role and lessen the value of another. This seems to have been the case for women's roles in the last two or three decades, particularly. The existence of role alternatives, the change in social valuation of housework, and the disparity between what a woman may have expected from being at home and what it seems to be can cause burnout.

These changes in role choices for women are examples of the process of creating role alternatives and changing social valuation that comes as a consequence of social change. Another part of the process is the development of new expectations and the failure of old expectations to be fulfilled. The large-scale changes that characterized the movement of societies to the industrial era bring the potential of burnout to dozens of roles in contemporary society. Expectations and roles concerning work, marriage, leisure, retirement, dating, church—all aspects of where we live, how we live, and how we relate to others—have felt and continue to feel the impact of this social change. In the next two chapters, I will focus more narrowly on the consequences of change and burnout on formal employment.

6

Employment Becomes the Meaning of Life

"He merely happened to be a man of the
type of the ox,—no rare specimen of humanity . . . on the contrary, he was a man
so stupid that he was unfitted to do most
kinds of laboring work, even."

Frederick W. Taylor, *Scientific Management.*

From the beginnings of the factory era to the present, there have been two major accommodations between the changing nature of the organization and the changing motivational needs of the worker. The initial accommodation was the worker to the job. The second accommodation—and what came to be an opposing viewpoint—focused on the feelings of the worker and the requirement that the manager in the work place strive to meet the motivational needs of the worker.

Four main ideas made the industrial revolution possible. Perhaps the most important was the emphasis in the factory on the product rather than the means of creating the product. Activities in the factory were designed to maximize the production of large quantities of uniform, quality-controlled goods, unlike the craft guilds which were oriented toward the creation of stylistic, almost one-of-a-kind products. A second idea was to develop complex products that had interchangeable parts. Each product was to be made of parts so consistently machined that it was unnecessary to assemble and fit each part uniquely in a given product. As an example, every piece of the sewing machine was intended to be so uniform that a bobbin taken from the assembly line at any time would always fit in any sewing machine produced by the factory. A third major idea was to use machines and to develop new machines that lessened the need for human labor, particularly heavy or monotonous labor. The fourth major idea was using money as a way of translating the worth of land, machines, products, and most importantly, people's labor into a universal commodity. In this way, no particular portion of the equation (i.e., labor, land, machines, or raw material) became exclusive, but all were exchangeable through the medium of money. Thus, nothing remained special, unique, or irreplaceable.

MANAGEMENT AS SCIENCE

As the twentieth century emerged, organizations developed more and more around the specialization of labor, the individualization of each worker, and complex assembly lines. Frederick W. Taylor (1911) used the term "scientific" to refer to the management of this form of organization. Like many of the pioneers and chroniclers of the method, Taylor heightened a paternalistic dimension in the work situation for one particular role, the manager. He conceived a form of structural authority somewhat reminiscent of the social forms of the traditional era. The business owner and manager achieved a power over workers similar to the feudal lord's power over serfs and peasants.

The essential nature of scientific management was to operate by these principles:

1. Develop a science for each element of a job. (This principle replaced the old rule-of-thumb method that characterized the oral tradition of the craftsman.)
2. Select, train, and develop the best worker for each particular task. (This principle supplanted the traditional practice of allowing the worker to select tasks and take responsibility for learning the task.)
3. Develop hardy cooperation between management and workers in carrying on the activities; discourage individualistic efforts of workers. (Using this principle the manager's role was made paramount in planning and directing work activity.)
4. Plan and divide the work so that there is specialization among the workers. (The intent of this principle was for a minimum of responsibility to be placed with the worker and maximum responsibility to be placed with management.)
5. Develop the concept of reward in terms of payment for each unit of work so that there can be a maximum relationship between units of work and units of reward.

Management was directed to accumulate knowledge about tasks rather than permitting each group of workers to pass the knowledge haphazardly from generation to generation. The principles stressed the responsibility of management in controlling work, thus removing control from the worker and centralizing it with the organization and the manager. Under this system, the manager was to plan out in advance each day what was to be done by each worker and then provide that worker with written, detailed instructions. Management was the management of tasks, and productivity was increased through the elimination of waste, work simplification, time-and-motion studies, standardization of procedures, removal of duplication, specialization of workers, and the development of labor-saving machines.

Scientific management sought to construct the world of work along rational, predictable, and efficient lines and was largely successful. Through a painstakingly thorough analysis, the artistic routine of the craftsman was broken down into simple, easy-to-learn, repetitious tasks. With the concepts of scientific management, large numbers of unskilled farm laborers, who truly had just tumbled off the turnip wagon, were then taught a few of the repetitious tasks. By linking groups of tasks to workers along the assembly line, the complex performance of the artisan could then be replicated by the unskilled laborer. Additionally, through the use of machines, the laborer's efforts were multiplied and output was sharply increased. In field after field, factory organizations based on scientific management replaced the craftsman with the unskilled laborer and increased productivity per worker by factors of ten, a hundred, or more.

Scientific management assumed workers would be motivated by wages alone, and was dramatically successful creating corporations that drew millions of workers from small farms and apprenticeships into the factory. Scientific management became the wedge that broke the traditional base of family farms and family trades. The factory provided a new thought pattern that dissolved the old mentality of family obligation and ascribed status. It replaced that mentality with a new one of greater mobility, more individualism, and status achieved through individual striving. Rank and pride were no longer a consequence of family birth, but rather positions reached and maintained through individual effort.

Scientific management explained human motivation through a cause/effect approach. The organization set goals and dictated the method to achieve these goals. Then untrained workers were hired who had needs that could be satisfied through purchases. For example, an unemployed worker may have needed money for food or housing, but if the worker's hunger was for status or recognition, the money may have been used to purchase attractive clothing to provide the status. In actuality, the scientific management model assumed that there were few, if any, human needs that could not be met through the use of the marketplace and that as one need was satiated, a new one emerged. The organization traded money for the workers' efforts to help the organization reach its goals, and the workers used the wages to purchase goods or services to meet their needs.

However, there were certain unanticipated ends or consequences that came from scientific management. Among these consequences was a tremendous withering of traditional social ties that left large numbers of workers feeling at loose ends, alone, and alienated. Because of moves from the countryside to urban settings, family, church, and neighborhood began to decline in meaning. At first, some workers shifted their psychological anchor to the work place, but the factory or the corporation proved to be an unresponsive anchorage. In time, workers formed their own social ties within the factories, and these social ties became powerful challenges to management. Soon management began to actively oppose the informal social ties, often pushing the informal work groups into organized unions that would openly vie for worker loyalty and challenge the authority of management. As time passed, the wages lost some of their former power to motivate the employee. Individuals quickly learned that the ratio of wages to work was heavily controlled by management and always subject to a new ratio more favorable to management.

Among the unfortunate aspects of scientific management was the centralization of power in terms of knowledge and the concentration of tools and capital in the hands of the company, causing harsh, manipulative, and authoritarian practices in many situations. Such practices began to engender feelings of anger and a sense of injustice in employees. Such feelings led to worker-organized countermovements, unions, that, in many ways, were an attempt to reestablish a parity of power between workers and the organization. A new phenomenon in the traditional world of work began to appear under scientific management in the factory. A broad, deep gulf developed between the individual and his work. As the gulf widened, production slowed and conflict arose within organizations, often culminating in violence. In response to unionization, strikes, riots, and lockouts then became a part of the legacy that scientific management established.

The final blow, and perhaps the heaviest, to the uncritical acceptance of scientific management in the industrial era was the world-wide economic collapse of the 1930s. Whereas unionization was on the decline in the booming twenties, the Great Depression was perceived to be an indictment of the values and social order built on scientific management and the authority of the manager and the organization. The depression demolished the sense of inevitability and unquestioned validity of scientific management, restored the vigor of the union movement, and accelerated the second accommodation of organization and worker.

THE HUMAN RELATIONS REVOLUTION

Declining productivity after application of the techniques of scientific management, coupled with frequent open hostilities between labor and management, precipitated a frantic search for better management tools. Whereas the focus of scientific management had been on the organization of the essential tasks to manufacture the product, a new school of thought arose that focused on interpersonal relations among workers and the feelings of the individual worker. In a rare instance of serendipity in science, a group of university researchers in an assembly plant of Bell Telephone's manufacturing arm, Western Electric, found that productivity gains were enhanced more by recognition given employees by management than by pay increases or improvements in physical working conditions (Roethlisberger and Dickson, 1939). From this study, followed a series of inquiries and industrial experiments throughout the

United States that within twenty years established the human relations school of management. This school focused on the concept that formal organizational structures and positions designed by management were often very different from and tended to ignore the actual relations among workers and the resulting informal groups that workers formed.

These informal or natural worker groups and their impact on the workers are summarized in the classic findings drawn from the work of human relations research. Critical to this school of study was the recognition that social relations—the attitudes and expectations of and among employees—were more important in setting the rate of production than the actual ability of the individual. These social relations could, and regularly did, override the amount of pay in establishing the level of work output. Workers would set their rate of work in spite of pay rewards or penalties to maintain their friendship and respect of associates. Moreover, it was found again and again that individuals preferred not to work alone, but in small groups that developed their own procedures and work rates and selected their own informal leaders. More often than not, this leadership was different from the organization's and was very potent in its impact on production. Finally, it was concluded that effective communication and participation through democratic processes—otherwise known as participatory leadership—are the most important prerequisites for effective management and, consequently, high productivity.

Human relations, like scientific management, was a social movement. It occurred not only because of serendipitous and provocative findings, but also because of the mounting failures of scientific management to fully explain worker behavior and the growing union movement that challenged the former complete hegemony of management over workers.

The human relations movement had two messages: first, wages tended to be inadequate over time for motivating employees; and second, unions would grow in their challenge to the power of management, therefore management must make accommodations to employees.

There are a number of different interpretations of the meaning of the human relations movement. One interpretation is that the movement represents a return to the highly affective nature of work organizations that were imbued with concern and acceptance, not the brutal "how are you useful to us?" orientation of the factory. The movement emphasizes participatory decision making and acceptance of the worker complete with idiosyncrasies and merits. This truly intrinsic acceptance is the same as the ascriptive acceptance of the family member in the pretechnological society. Relations are warm and diffuse, and work flows incidentally out of the human relationships. This state of affairs is a frequent description of the way good human relations should occur in management.

A slightly different interpretation of human relations comes from humanistic psychology. It sees work and management, if properly understood and utilized, as a way of developing unknown potentials in the employee. This human potential side of the human relations movement sees the work site more as a place for human growth and less as a locus of simple economic exchange.

A third interpretation by some of the more radical critics of the human relations movement is that it is nothing more than a sophisticated and devious tool for management to restore the former power that older, less sophisticated management lost to the union movement. These critics assert that human relations maintains for management the paternalistic and ultimately exploitative control over the employee that was originally achieved via scientific management.

Finally, a fourth interpretation is that the movement is an indicator of a dramatically different way of viewing work. It is a revolt against the instrumental, striving characteristics of the employment site and of the conversion process that requires individuals to be solely economic creatures. It is this latter interpretation that makes the human relations movement seem more a revolution.

The human relations explanation of worker motivation is more complex than the scientific management explanation. According to human relations, management must help workers come to know their own needs; by assisting them to meet their needs, organizational goals will be met as well. In scientific management, the focus is on the task and the manager. In human relations, it is on the worker, his or her motivational needs, and the working climate, especially the climate of the work group.

BURNOUT AND WORK

In the work place, burnout derives from the loss of the sense of self, continuity, and control over one's life that came from industrialization and working in the factories. While escape from the life of a peasant brought expectations of independence, work in a factory began to make the worker a commodity—a being that existed solely for utilitarian purposes. As it enhanced the physical and economic well-being of the worker, the meaning of the worker as a social being—not simply a physical object—was chewed up in the maw of entrepreneurial capitalism.

Human relations is and has been the managerial approach to meet that problem of a sense of loss of self and personal worth. But human relations has not proven to be a fully adequate answer. Many managers believe that the emphasis on the worker seriously impairs the ability of the manager to do future planning and lessens the efficient arrangement of tasks and personnel to accomplish organizational goals. It is charged that communication and participative management are excessively time-consuming, that the time spent on these concerns distracts management from other concerns that can spell the final success or failure of the enterprise. It is also often asserted that no matter how employee-centered an organization is, if market conditions are not favorable, the organization will fail.

In labor-intensive industries, such as clothing or shoe manufacturing, international competition from cheap labor markets has made the case for this criticism. Most factories and many service institutions are established for economic purposes first and foremost. Limited capital is available and the outputs must usually compete with alternative outputs, either similar products or services or for a specific allocation of capital relative to other expenditures. Steel from a mill, for example, must compete with steel from other mills and alternative materials such as aluminum and plastics. It is, moreover, a product that can see a lessening demand in economic downturns. Such factors assert themselves over the concerns of the employee from time to time. The future of the organization itself, relative to other organizations and the environment, must enter into the equation of human motivation. When there is a declining need for a product, such as mechanical adding machines, or for a service, such as railroads, organizations and employees both suffer.

Frequently, human relations is a management strategy that is only applied at certain times in the economic cycle or at a certain point in the life cycle of an industry. When the economy is running at full speed and unemployment is low, employers are eager to keep employees and more liberal forms of management are utilized. In mature industries that have monopolistic or cartel arrangements, employee groups can achieve considerable power within the organization and the organization, rather than arbitrating with employee demands, can pass increased labor costs on to the consumer. In these cases, human relations management is more likely to flourish. In economic downturns, when labor is abundant, traditional scientific management is more dominant. Thus, rather than being a higher, more enlightened and successful form of management, human relations appears to be an alternative that occurs with general economic highs or at certain stable points in the life cycle of a given industry.

The factory and its theory of human behavior changed more than simply the world of work. Factory employment changed the social institutions of the family and the neighborhood, the definition of work, and indeed the definition of the individual. By boosting the productivity of the male wage earner, and later the female as women joined the work force, individuals became liberated from the family, the farm, from traditional society and from traditional roles. Factory employment loosened these anchors and gave the individual expectations of more freedom, more autonomy. Industrialization made the individual responsible for any failure as well. One's fate in life was no longer ascribed or decreed, but rather achieved or earned by the efforts of the individual. This freedom, which also involved a subsequent loss of social anchors and the placement of the responsibility for one's fate on the individual, gave rise to stress and frustration as well as change and modernization. Stress and frustration at high levels led to alienation and burnout. Human relations was a response to the tremendous social and psychological changes deriving from factory times, but it has proven, when used as a management tool, to be a temporizing, not a total, solution.

THE ORGANIZATION OF WORK AND INDIVIDUAL AUTONOMY

Work in a factory or an office is a highly structured experience. In most instances the worker does only a small portion of the work on a product. In a sewing machine factory, one person may run a machine press that stamps out the same part day after day. The worker is aware of the final product, the sewing machine, but cannot claim to be the maker of the sewing machine. Rather, the worker is a cog in a larger machine, the factory, which is the maker of the sewing machine.

The same is true for the clerk or secretary in a bureaucracy. Pieces of paper are created, passed to another office or filed in a metal box. The movement of these pieces of paper is the work, and the clerk is one step in a vast sorting process.

This slotting and arranging of people undeniably has brought much greater material happiness. Without factories, machines, and complex organizations, most of the items of our daily existence would be unavailable or far more costly. But the consequence of scientific management is that each employee becomes part of a larger machine and has less control over his or her life. This establishes a conflict for the individual when he first understands that he is responsible for his station in life, but simultaneously discovers he is only a participant in a larger corporate process. The development of the industrial era led to a greater individual consciousness of independence and autonomy. Rather than being tied to the land, an individual could choose for whom and where he wished to work. But these expectations of choice, of independence, were thwarted by the controls of the factory and the worker's sense of being a part but not a willing participant.

The advent of human relations served to alleviate these feelings but did not change the basic facts of modern institutions. Giving a person a sense of greater participation is hedged by the reality that work is still conducted in the organization. Consequently, participatory management techniques result in spelling out just the degree and sense of frustration of one's expectations that may come from the modern world of work.

There is far more to theories and research on life and work in formal organizations, and about the organizations themselves, than is covered in these few pages or could, indeed, be covered in hundreds of pages. Among the central themes of that literature are employee satisfaction and motivation, decision-making models, the role of compensation and work place factors, human-machine relationships and the design of structures, work and information flows, and the allocation of power within the organization. Yet, apart from the sheer size of this literature, we must recognize that organizations as we know them are mostly creations of the last hundred and fifty years. They have only lately become our natural habitat. And among the consequences of this new habitat is the appearance of burnout.

The industrial model began in factories but has spread to most areas of modern life. Almost everyone works or is expected to work, and tasks and schedules are defined by the organization. Personal life and family life are defined by the industrial model, with an emphasis on working outside the home. Individuals are evaluated through their occupations; they are dependent, as well, on industries and institutions for a livelihood. The restructuring and control of the world by formal organizations can prove to be alienating and the demands stress-producing. One end result is that both the private dimension and the working dimension of our lives generate burnout for us. Burnout is as likely to occur at home as on the job.

Roles for a Temporary World

"Just relax and be yourself."
"No," replies the nervous thespian,
"that would be altogether impossible. I
could never be myself."
"Never yourself?"
"No, you see, there is no me. I
do not exist."
The actor draws conspiratorially close
to the anthropomorphic amphibian and,
with many a wary
glance over both shoulders, whispers:
"There used to be a me. But I
had it surgically removed."

"Sellers Strikes Again." *Time.*
(A bit of dialogue between the actor Peter Sellers
and Kermit the Frog on "The Muppet Show")

But I was thinking of a plan
To dye one's whiskers green,
And always use so large a fan
that they could not be seen.

Lewis Carroll, *Through the Looking-Glass
and What Alice Found There.*

Conditions of high social change charge our world with debates on questions such as energy use versus conservation, growth versus quality of life, male and female roles, the meaning of life and death, parenthood or a single life-style, career or family. High and continuous conditions of labor unrest, dissatisfaction with life, and a general deterioration of personal well-being and of the United States' leadership in the world seem to be constant companions. In response to these complexities and ambiguities, a number of attempts are surfacing toward rebuilding traditional anchorages.

The late sixties were remarkable in the extent to which a generational cleavage occurred when some of the youth of the country sought to build a world and reality apart from the rest of the country. Woodstock was the high-water mark of that movement, which, in its decline, broke into many separate groups. Since the end of that decade, religious cults and separatist movements have multiplied, springing from roots that vary from traditional evangelical Protestantism to Buddhist and Hindu transplants from the Orient.

In all cases, these communitarian movements call for strong and unswerving commitment of the individual to the group. They require the person to relocate, change habits, adopt a certain clothing style and diet, and often truncate relations with former associates, friends, and family. The psychological import of these movements is the degree to which they are characteristic of social forms existing prior to the industrialized era—forms that establish a full and total anchoring of the individual, his identity, his world view in an all-inclusive group. In one way, the apparent unconventionality of these movements is a testimony to the degree to which the modern world has been successful in uprooting the traditional anchorages of the individual and achieving the dissolution of traditional, ascriptive institutions.

THE ORGANIZATION AS THE ANCHOR

In Europe, more so than in the United States, a model of industrial democracy has been developed that can be seen as a somewhat distinctive attempt to achieve the re-anchoring of the individual in a corporate social group. Worker representation on corporate boards has occurred in large European industrial concerns such as Volkswagen and Fiat. The intent of this movement is to make workers a part of the management and the ownership process, thereby reversing the trend of alienation between worker, product, and organization. A similar occurrence has appeared with the growth of industrialization in Japan, where there has been a melding of the ancient fraternal kin structures of traditional Japanese society with industrial concerns, encompassing the individual worker and his family, the business concern, and even the state itself.

Indeed, the extent of the vertical integration of the individual and his family into the firm and into a prominent place within the apparatus of the state makes the Japanese version of public and private enterprise the extreme extrapolation of industrial democracy among the world's societies at this time. There the family firm becomes the corporate empire and then subtly begins to merge with the state.

Whether or not these industrial models will produce lower levels of worker alienation is not known. Nor is it possible to say whether there will be commensurate productivity and efficiency returns to offset the competitive advantage of countries with lower standards of living and lower labor costs. Such are the critical economic and social questions that must be met by the older industrialized societies in the next two decades.

Within the United States, a similar device of employee ownership and participation has occurred through stock option plans of both public and privately owned companies. There are a number of mechanisms to achieve this. One is the employee stock ownership plan (ESOP), a relatively new corporate device. A block of stock is placed in a trust from which employees can purchase shares through their retirement plan. In time, employees and retired employees can own and achieve control of a company. To a lesser degree this has happened in some of the older, publicly owned companies such as Sears, where employees own large percentages of the corporations. A related process is also occurring within the public sector where employee retirement trusts have become perhaps the single largest ownership block in the publicly held company.

These devices may, as well, be seen as strategies to enhance the anchorage of the individual worker in the economic production unit. However, the extent to which employees may achieve the ownership of a sizeable percentage of big companies is debatable and certainly varies greatly from company to company. However, ownership may not mean control or the feeling of control. There are not sufficient data to date to determine whether employees who participate in these types of companies suffer less alienation and less burnout. The key issue may be that the more remote the relationship between ownership and employment, the less effective are employee ownership plans in mediating alienation.

Expectations of control over one's work are probably more difficult to achieve in large, complex organizations because the rules governing work are developed elsewhere in the organization. Thus the strategy of employee ownership may have considerable success in small companies where the total number of employees is small and management is known to the individual employee, but the technique may be highly diluted and not effective in larger firms which characterize the U.S. industrial scene today.

THE WORK PLACE AS A TOTAL INSTITUTION

For some, these developments may suggest that the dominant management strategy in this temporary and changing world should be that the work place should become a total institution—more than simply the place where wages are exchanged for time in the tradition of scientific management. When the work place becomes a total institution, it anchors the individual to it in the way that the family or the church did in medieval times. Close approximations of this exist in Japan, where a person joins a company, spends his entire working life as its employee, and expects his sons and daughters to work in the company after him. Under such conditions, the company may develop an obligation toward the employee that goes beyond a simple economic exchange of labor for salary and may provide lifetime employment, health benefits, housing, recreation, and food subsidies through canteens and discount company grocery stores.

In the total institution, labor is no longer free in the sense of the liberal process of the last five hundred years. And this could well represent a reversion to the social and economic forms of medieval serfdom. It is perhaps unfortunate and sorely narrow that the characterization of serfdom typically has negative connotations. More than likely, during the Middle Ages, serfdom was a more secure and dependable sort of existence than that available without feudal attachments. Serfdom provided a secure place on the land, the protection of the liege lord, and a pattern of activities that ensured economic survival. Apart from this world, a man had no community and had to live by his wits. Without community supports, life was probably neither enjoyable nor long.

Certainly the development of the total institution is a response to the anomie and rapid change of our times. But, the secure psychological anchorings that the total institution provides must be contrasted against the conservative and ultimately stifling social arrangement that it can represent.

One of the most provocative indicators of the psychological content of the human mind in any era has been the theater. Julian Jayne's work (1976), which elaborates the concept of the bicameral mind and evolution of consciousness, brings our attention to the possibility that social evolution is paralleled by a psychological process. For example, contrasting the almost simpleminded narration of Homer's *Odyssey* with the vivid subplots and internal mental machinations of Shakespeare's *King Lear* and *Macbeth* seems to hint that psychological complexity increased immensely in the two millennia from early Greece to sixteenth century England. The awareness of multiple roles and the arbitrary quality of social roles emerged in the theater in the late nineteenth century through the works of Ionesco, Pirandello, and Genet. These authors, especially Pirandello, whose works form the core of the theater of the absurd, focus on the role of the character and the differences between the role as the character perceives it and the way other characters perceive the role.

Among the modern observers of social interaction at the one-to-one level, none has been more acute than Erving Goffman. Goffman (1956) has brought to our attention how the development of the person's social role constructs reality and molds the person's emotions and cognition of events and other persons.

Role fantasies have emerged as a form of play for youth with the works of Tolkien leading into the elaborate fantasy game "Dungeons and Dragons." Players assume complex roles and play a medieval game of conquest and survival that may last for days. But perhaps most significantly has life as a role appeared in the world of work.

ROLE ALTERNATIVES IN THE CORPORATE WORLD

Michael Maccoby* has suggested an easy way to contrast the survival styles among the types of workers in the corporate world today. Essentially Maccoby (1976) suggests that workers develop styles or, as I am using the term, *roles* to relate to work.

---

*Maccoby's work was derived from a series of interviews with corporate managers. Only 4 percent of those interviewed were women. Consequently, the terminology used in describing these roles could easily be interpreted as ignoring women's roles in the corporate world. The changing roles of women in formal organizations has only recently received much attention. This is, in part, due to women's lesser participation in formal organizations and, in part, to an assumption that such participation is transitory or even epiphenomenal. Events of the last two decades, though, suggest that these reasons for the lack of attention to women's participation are without substance.

As we have observed earlier, a role is a set of expectations that are bundled together. Any organization can be viewed as a network of roles, of bundles of expectations.

For Maccoby, the oldest type of worker is the Craftsman, a worker whose anchorage is essentially within the work itself and the pleasure derived from doing the work. The expectations of the Craftsman are tied to the work product. His or her expectations include quality materials, appropriate tools, and an opportunity to practice the craft. In the organization, this person's emphasis is upon problem solving and personal contribution to the quality of work, while holding social ties to others to a minimum in the organization. The Craftsman sees the organization as a place to practice a craft, but loyalty to the organization is only through the opportunity to perform the craft. Other social affiliations with the organization and others in the organization are minimized. The Craftsman may typically be seen as a perfectionist and represents a continuation from the village artisan of ancient times with his or her identity anchored in work and the family. Maccoby notes that the Craftsman, while a vanishing breed, is also a much sought-after worker in the new high-technology corporations which depend on these dedicated and innovative individuals as sources of technological change.

The second type of person in the corporate world is the Jungle Fighter. In opposition to the Craftsman's traditional ways, the Jungle Fighter seeks to change events to meet his own prescription—his definition of how things should be. The Jungle Fighter thrives on conflict within the organization and sees the career ladder as a struggle against nature. The focus and reward is not on the work itself but rather on the acts of conquest over contending personalities and divisions within the organization. The Jungle Fighter anchors within himself and his conquests, but not within the work and the quality of work. Expectations are for change and thus personal opportunities. Stability, uniformity, regulations are the Jungle Fighter's undoing.

The third type of worker is the Company Man—the worker who is anchored in the organization through and through. William F. Whyte (1956) and David Riesman (1950) directed our attention to those individuals as the dominant personality types of the fifties with an orientation to work which is a consequence of the dominance of organizations in American life. The Company Man acts to adapt and change his coloration to fit the current dictates and needs of the organization. These workers provide the necessary binding or glue to hold the organization together and provide continuity over time. The Company Man's expectations are vested in the organization. He or she expects the organization to always be there to provide employment, and he or she, in turn, will be loyal to it. They are the living repository of the organizational aims and goals and of the folkways and procedures of the organization. They describe themselves in terms of their position; the Craftsman, in terms of the work; and the Jungle Fighter, in terms of personal successes and major competitors.

The fourth and recently emergent type is the Gamesman. Though the Gamesman is a character long identified in our culture, only in the last decade has he become a dominant figure in the organizational world. The Gamesman is inventive, quick, fascinated by complexities and paradoxes, and plays the organizational world with verve and zest. As the name denotes, work is a game of chance—a gamble—with rewards going to the quick, the bright, the innovative. With expectations anchored in himself, personal abilities, and an ever-changing world, the Gamesman loves change and wants to influence its course. In many ways the Gamesman is the perpetual adolescent, always testing a personal value of omnipotence against the challenges in the world. Buck Rogers in the trackless regions of deep space or Odysseus sailing in uncharted waters, the Gamesman is always prepared for the risks in the gamble, knowing its terms, never basking in successes for long, but rather continually preparing for a new quest.

We can take Maccoby's corporate players and illustrate the roles in terms of contemporary Western movie idols. The craftsman is John Wayne, solid, dependable, not quick or cunning but able with sure resolve and thoroughness. He represents the traditions of the past—the integrity, solidity, unchangeableness—in the face of swirling currents and shifting light. The Jungle Fighter is portrayed by a Clint Eastwood or Charles Bronson. He is cunning, ruthless, and plays the game utterly to eliminate the opposition. He travels alone and is unable to develop close interpersonal relationships or participate in teams; he seeks challenges that largely permit only individual expression. The Company Man is the ever-present deputy to the sheriff or marshal in the Western town. He is Matt Dillon's Chester or Festus, dependable but dependent. His capability grows from his role, and he represents the community's expression of order and continuity through its offices. He is always the supporting actor, never the star. The Gamesman is illustrated by a couple of roles played by the Robert Redford-Paul Newman team in movies like *The Sting* or *Butch Cassidy and the Sundance Kid*. The goal is in the excitement of the play, the game. These are essentially role resolutions that avoid dealing with issues of continuity or stabilization, but with each accomplishment the person quickly moves from any sense of permanence to the interstitial, fluid areas of the world and begins the game anew.

The Gamesman is a recurrent figure in American culture. Horatio Alger, the Hardy Boys, the heroes of Edgar Rice Burroughs, so much of the popular science fiction and comic book literature have heroes defined in the Gamesman mode. Recent versions of this theme are the characters of Luke Skywalker and Han Solo of the *Star Wars* saga. Again and again the duo encounters overwhelming odds but with courage and playful disregard of the dangers, they best the enemy, escape from predicaments, and rescue the princess. There is a mystical dimension to these exploits that George Lucas, creator of the films, calls "The Force." The Force is the ultimate reservoir of energy or power that can be tamed, directed by the Gamesman to extend his power far beyond his personal resources. The universe of *Star Wars* is unfolding, unknown, full of challenges and full of the optimism, of the limitless good luck of youthful thinking. Interestingly, both good and evil appear to have their roots at the same locus in The Force, and there are suggestions of one being transformed into the other. Evil can be conquered and made good, and good can be corrupted and made evil.

Maccoby's leadership types all represent personal adaptations to our temporary and changing world. The roles remain male-oriented, though their exclusivity and certainty as solely male roles is contested today as women remain in the background in the formal organization.* Whether any of these social roles or leadership types are adequate accommodations to the new social reality and the institutions of the time is too early to tell.

The Craftsman is a very old role and one that grew out of antiquity. The Jungle Fighter is the warrior role that in antiquity belonged to the military. The Jungle Fighter's corporate heyday was during the age of young industries and the individual entrepreneur; but no role is more anachronistic today than the Jungle Fighter. The Company Man was the response in the fifties that most fully recognized the hegemony of the corporate world. It may become the most predominant type if the total institution as described earlier in this chapter prevails as the new order

---

*I have used male roles consciously in this chapter since I feel that accurately reflects the male dominance of formal organizations in our culture. This situation is, without a doubt, changing and I suspect that females will fill Maccoby's role types as readily as males may appear to. My central thesis, however, is not concerned with female or male roles per se but instead with the roles occasioned by bureaucratic existence.

within society. However, the role lacks the incentive for innovation and adaptability and seems especially inadequate when high competition and social change demand individuals who can adapt to new technologies or new work groups as events dictate.

Of all types, the Craftsman is perhaps least alienated and suffers less from burnout. As long as he or she is permitted to practice the craft and maintain a home, even though employers may change, the Craftsman's self-definition remains secure. Of all types, the Craftsman's expectations seem most under personal control though technological change can make the craft obsolete.

Many Jungle Fighters burn out. Declining strength and vigor cause them to come up short again and again when challenged, and they eventually find that the competitive marketplace forces them to admit their deficiency and inadequacies. Aging ensures in time that they can no longer fulfill their expectations of conquest. The Jungle Fighter also faces another sort of threat and that is from organizational attempts to end chaos and achieve stability. Like a warrior, if peace comes, his expectations of conflict and thus of meaning end. As long as the definition of self remains that of the Jungle Fighter, burnout is always the ultimate fate. There is no alternative.

The Company Man does not suffer from burnout as long as the organization does not change more rapidly than his or her ability to adapt to new rules and new norms. As long as there is a clear role, the Company Man has direction and purpose. Expectations and existence rest with the organization.

The Gamesman is uniquely susceptible to burnout. Like the Jungle Fighter, the thrill of life is in the struggle, the competition, but the struggle is not with another individual but with a challenge within the company. The Gamesman is most adept in developing teams and instilling enthusiasm and teamwork in a group of new individuals. Like the Jungle Fighter, the Gamesman is never able to be satisfied or at one with himself or through personal accomplishments. However, the Gamesman too will suffer from declining health and vigor and perhaps even a declining desire for the game. And, of course, the greater the change within the game and the rules of the game, the greater toll it exacts on the successful performance of the Gamesman.

Both the organizational attempts and the personal strategies presented in this chapter are continuing efforts, some ancient and others of more recent vintage, to reconcile people to social change and to accommodate to the consequences of the modern world. The Craftsman's role is drawn from the remaining shreds of the traditional world. Work is an art form, and the family and family life, is a refuge, a "haven in a heartless world," that beckons each evening. The Jungle Fighter is not of a paradigm but between paradigms. Born from disorder and anomie, the Jungle Fighter, as entrepreneur or politician, ushers in the modern world with its attendant bureaucracies that are so threatening. The Jungle Fighter sows the seeds of his own demise. As the Craftsman is the perfect creature of the traditional world, so the Company Man is the proper human form for the technocratic world. Eager to draw identity from external social roles, anxious, compliant and obedient to authority, the Company Man is a plastic being waiting to be molded by the organization.

Probably, the Gamesman is a more transitional form than the Jungle Fighter. As for the Jungle Fighter, the temporary world is his natural habitat. The Gamesman, who appears to be the characteristic strategist of our time, shifts the meaning of life to a series of passing roles, performed with verve and enthusiasm, but also with the expectation that the role will soon end. Such a dominant role exemplifies the sharp temporary quality of our times. The Gamesman is the final expression of the economic man occasioned by the paradigm of our times. Like money, the Gamesman is transmutable and transferable from group to group, task to task, role to role. Like the airline slogan "we're only as good as our last flight," the Gamesman is only as good as his last successful challenge. There is no enduring quality, no revered role This is the quintessence of the economic man, but in its occasional, quixotic nature it is a transition to something different.

The demands of social change require that we accommodate through devising some workable role for ourselves. Being able to shift roles quickly is perhaps the most adaptive response. Organizational life, moreover, defines roles for us and demands that we adapt to them. Being required to meet organizational expectations that frequently change means that to survive we must be able to change roles readily. Changing roles readily seems to mean as well that we suffer burnout just as readily. The next chapter examines why role change seems to bring about burnout.

Developing a New Sense of Identity

Your journey is toward homeland. Remember that you are traveling from the World of Appearances to the World of Reality. Solitude in the crowd. In all your outward activity remain inwardly free. Learn not to identify yourself with anything whatsoever.

Abdulhalik Gujdavani, *Essense of the Teaching of the Masters.*

"Under the conditions of today's world, a person will find fewer long-term involvements with any group but rather will be immersed intensively with a task group for short periods of time that may not exceed a couple of years. During that time, one must engage in intense personal ties, while operating with a general orientation that, in a matter of months, a new set of associations will be formed." Such a statement in some variation or another has appeared innumerable times in the last decade to describe future society. If the statement is accurate, then what does it mean for the individual's sense of identity?

TRANSITORY ROLES FOR A TEMPORARY WORLD

Because we are living in a temporary world, we may be less likely to develop unique and stable qualities of our personalities. Uniqueness comes from specialization, and specialization requires some permanency, a continuation of activity over time. Narrow specialization, though, carries personal risk. An individual who is highly specialized can become obsolete if times and market conditions change. Buggy whip makers, switchboard and elevator operators, carhops, cowboys, and vaudeville troupers are specialties in little demand today. Thus, specialization seems unlikely to occur under high change conditions. While we face the threat of the risk to specialize, because we are so similar to others, we will seek to develop unique, distinct qualities as a recourse to alienation, loss of self, and loss of identity.

The solution for persons will be to become much more alike. Change will mandate a similarity in fashions, accent, values, and orientation. Yet, in a complex social and technocratic society, high specialization is mandatory. This will be achieved through a personal ability to specialize quickly and intensely, to identify highly and fully, yet to rapidly drop the specialization when it is no longer needed. Multiple roles will be replaced by a process of creating and discarding roles.

It is important to emphasize that both specialization and uniformity will occur in a far different fashion that we are accustomed to. Individuals will be much more adaptable and able to move and fit in from one section of the country to the next, while regionalism and ethnic orientations will disappear. Intense personal relationships with strangers will be achieved very quickly. Individuals will be capable of understanding profuse amounts of information, while being able to relate with a great deal of intellectual specialization. There will be differentiation and specialization yet uniformity across the population.

Achieving these skills will be a challenge even though other kinds of specialization have occurred under other cultural norms. For example, individual identity was not well advanced in traditional cultures. A person had only a vague consciousness of himself as an individual, separate from the group. In such societies, individuals were moved through collective action, and consciousness of the individual as a person with independent judgment and self-determining qualities was minimal.

With the development of industrialization, individuals specialized in skills, talents, avocations, and even emotions. Bankers dealt with money and were conservative, predictable, controlled, and unemotional. Teachers dealt with children and were dependable, gregarious, and spontaneous. Salesmen dealt with fancy while moving mundane wares and were talkative, extroverted, and manipulative. Men were strong, independent, and unemotional. Women were weak, loving, and warm. These were learned roles, but they were more or less permanent, lasting a lifetime.

Stereotyped characteristics based on occupation and social class had considerable truth in the past but will have little dependability in the future. Rather, each person will be far more capable of portraying all of these characteristics and at the appropriate instance. Such individuals will be highly flexible and unpredictable but not in a sense of volatile or temperamental.

This new type of high flexibility and yet uniformity is apparent in the material culture where even moderate-sized cities offer a choice of perhaps a dozen different motel and food chains that appear consistently across the country. Such uniformity with complexity is also evident in our telephone system, with area codes and direct dialing procedures being standardized across the country. But while there is horizontal uniformity in the telephone system, increased potential for specialization and variety is also permitted. As an example, a local telephone installation can be used to transmit photo facsimiles of printed materials. It can be used to transmit digital data between computers. It offers self-dialing numbers and alternate cost routing of long-distance calls. Soon, it will be able to receive long-distance commands to perform household chores such as paying bills, changing the thermostat, checking physical security of the house, and turning the television set, stereo, or oven on and off. It will routinely receive and store messages. All these illustrate the vertical specialization dimension while horizontal uniformity is maintained.

Sexual, social, and racial stereotyping already have much less truth to support them today. In the near future, each of us will feel at home in almost any social situation; yet for almost everyone in this first generation of the temporary world, there will remain a feeling of incompleteness, of standing outside the action.

The most popular diversions will be those which can produce a feeling of oneness or unity. Films, television, and books will depend on themes that permit alienated individuals to merge with central characters and the story, rather than being observers of the events which heightens feelings of isolation. Music and drugs, both of which involve parts of the brain separate from the consciousness centers of the frontal lobe and the planfulness of the left hemisphere, will also be used to achieve feelings of oneness and unity.

SOCIAL ANCHORS AND INDIVIDUAL DEFINITION

Much of the individuality and freedom that is held dear today was brought about in the nineteenth century—an Age of Optimism. In those years, the individual was breaking free of many of the claims associated with the family and place of birth. However, many of these central social anchors were maintained—though weakened—and provided the individual a constant reference point from which to grow and extend.

The first part of the twentieth century became, however, an Age of Anxiety as individuals saw conflict between old values and new, and were unable to reconcile the two. By then, a person was a member of several groups, and the values of one often contradicted the values of another. Work became highly segregated from the home. Each reference point had somewhat different codes of conduct, producing conflict for the individual at points of transition. This, of course, explains much of the awkwardness when one's spouse and children come to the office or when business associates are invited to the home. Historically, relations with one's family require acceptance in spite of conduct, while the world of business permits acceptance only when earned by correct conduct. In one world, status is assigned; in the other, achieved and maintained through daily struggle. However, achieved status is now becoming mandated for the home as well. Children and parents are trying to please each other; husband and wife now judge each other in terms of one's performance toward the other.

Our current Age of Anxiety, of competing values, is now giving way to a third age—an Age of Malaise. The third age replaces the competing values of city versus country, male versus female, career versus family, local versus cosmopolitan with transitory or situational values. Rather than enduring, universal codes of conduct, there are contingencies for a given situation. For example, one does not swipe fruit in the grocery store because that is a lower class behavior, but one cheats on a college exam because it is routinely done. One does not pilfer from the church collection box, but one overstates travel expenses because "everyone does." In fact, travel reimbursement forms are known as swindle sheets in many firms. Honesty or dishonesty is relative to the situation, rather than a virture or a standard across situations.

Figure 3 displays the relationship between alternative social anchors and the individual's personal outlook.

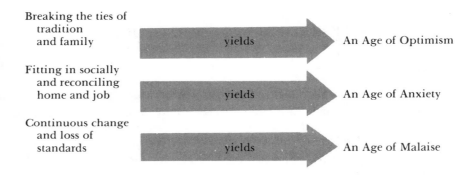

Figure 3
Social Anchors and Personal Outlook

The movement of individuals from the ties of tradition with family and community to ties of occupation and profession was characteristic of more optimistic times. New opportunities opened for individuals, and one could escape from having been born into insignificant families by personal striving. In the United States, these were the times of self-made men—Andrew Carnegie, John Rockefeller, Abraham Lincoln—individuals who came from humble backgrounds but through personal initiative rose to high rank in society. Individually achieved status came to be far more admired than inherited status. Yet this important change in the way one achieved status—how one developed recognition—lays the foundation for burnout.

When there is little social change, individual status does not change. When social change occurs and brings with it individual responsibility for one's status, a person develops expectations of what should be achieved. When the reality is less than the expectations, burnout begins.

Social change has extended and elaborated the use of achievement to define status in all spheres of life. Our jobs require that we achieve. Leisure and recreation demand better performance. We seek to improve our golf game, increase the number of miles we jog, or lead a more active social life. We strive to improve our appearance, maintain a youthful look, and avoid signs of physical deterioration. In all areas of life—private as well as public—we are expected to improve, and we learn to expect more of ourselves.

As times have changed, our social roles have become more numerous. Each of us belongs to many groups and has one or more roles in every group. At work, we often have the roles of employee, colleague, supervisor, and supervisee. We are a son or daughter, a spouse, a mother or father. We are a consumer, a neighbor, a friend, a member of civic clubs, political parties, a bridge club, or a bowling league. The average individual today has fifteen or more roles each with a set of expectations, and typically the roles and expectations are fairly changeable.

For many years, multiple roles have been encouraged as a healthy thing for individuals. Through multiple roles, an individual is exposed to different outlooks or viewpoints and may be more likely to change. One of the major goals of economic development in underdeveloped regions of the world is to break the hold of tradition by expanding individual ties beyond family and community. Modern communications, newspapers, television, and radio widen horizons, make the individual more progressive, more inclined to participate in cultural change.

Participating in multiple roles is also seen as a step toward more positive mental health. By participating with many others, the individual is enriched and not dependent on a single relationship. Therapists and developmental psychologists often explain this relationship as growing beyond the initial child-parent or infant-mother dependency.

Through this multiple role membership, we become far more conscious of ourselves as members of several separate groups and of multiple and often conflicting demands. These demands, which develop a greater sense of individual self-consciousness or awareness, increase the likelihood of burnout. We are aware of belonging to many groups, thus having to participate in many roles. The expectations that the roles require, and that we in time come to think of as our own, bring about multiple conditions for burnout.

The sheer energy required to maintain all these roles lessens our ability to keep reality at the level of our expectations. And, as a role evaporates, for many of us some of the expectations are left behind. The expectations that remain often haunt us. We find ourselves reliving roles and wondering how things would have turned out had we done this or that differently. This is why multiple roles and changing roles can produce burnout. Unable to put the roles and especially the expectations behind us, we keep them in our memories, as ghosts reminding us of what we could have done, what could have been . . . .

In one way, multiple role membership is too much of a good thing. Having more than one or two roles permits us to spread our bets, to avoid putting all our eggs in one basket. By having multiple roles, the probabilities of success or recognition are increased in at least one role. But, as roles multiply, each role becomes more temporary. Old roles are dropped and new roles are added. Social reality becomes a will-o'-the-wisp, intangible, passing, here today and gone tomorrow. There is no firm ground, no anchors.

COPING WITH THE LOSS OF ANCHORS

Standards shift from situation to situation, and many of us will notice this and long for more stability. Yet, when stability is encountered—like stopping over in a small town in Iowa—we will quickly experience tedium and boredom. However, no one is required to adapt to boredom. Travel and communications are always available to return the person to the exciting, ever-changing temporary culture. Each of us will make occasional, nostalgic visits to the small town in Iowa, but none of us can stay there. Like the fish that first breathed air, we too may look back to the sea but cannot truly return. Because of this nostalgia, this age will be an Age of Malaise, of vague discomfort. There will be no values to revolt against, there will only be a feeling of emptiness, of incompleteness.

Remember, if you will, the feelings you have had when you moved to a new city. The die is cast and you cannot go back, yet there are feelings of unease, worry, and fitful anticipation.

Apart from this melancholy of the Age of Malaise, though, each of us will become more and more sensitive, and aware of the attitudes and feelings of others. Private, internal existence, being shut off from others, cannot be maintained. The individual will recognize that norms vary from group to group and will, moreover, be aware of the fundamental, arbitrary nature of all group norms. A person will apply, with flexibility and dexterity, a relativism that will permit adaptation to the norms of the immediate group in a full, enthusiastic fashion rather than in a mechanical, artificial way. Such individuals may seem shallow to many of us today, yet this adaptability is only a continuation of a trend over the last several generations. It does not, however, imply anarchism or nihilism. The human tendency is to structure experience and social interaction, and the emerging individual will be able to do so quickly and adapt to new structures readily. Such characteristics will require the fullest development of the person and will militate against new group norms that would narrow and distort the human spirit. Because of the temporariness of the society and social groupings, individuals will appear hedonistic, narcissistic, and selfish to us today, but not tomorrow. This is simply the end result of a higher level of individualism that we have yet to experience.

The lack of attachment to one's parents, to family, to church, or to the job is the natural consequence of this fully-permeating sense of the temporary. Social causes, loyalty to the party or the company, are replaced by narrow self-interest groups. It is difficult to build broad-based groupings or maintain an organization over time because of the high rate of change which generates the high level of personal self-interest. The self-interest is logical; it is all that endures.

Nativistic revivals will continue to occur as anxieties periodically arise. Such revivals are social movements that attempt to bring back, to reestablish, a bygone era. These vacations of nostalgia serve to ease a period of transition.

The ethnicity of the seventies, with the peasant fashions and back-to-the-earth life-styles, was a nativistic phenomenon that attempted to resurrect and revitalize an old reference group as a way of adding meaning, structure, and authorization to individuals' lives. But the narrowness of the old ethnicity relegates it to nothing more than an occasional nostalgic nod from the individual.

One of the more colorful nativistic movements near to the current time was the Ghost Dance that appeared during the collapse of various American Indian cultures under the white onslaught. The first cult came into existence through a Paiute prophet, Wodziwob, who foretold in 1869 of the end of the existing world, the ousting of the white man, the restoration of the Indian way of life, and the return of dead relatives. The belief incorporated rituals, costumes, and a ceremonial dance intended to achieve the restoration. The costumes included a shirt with special designs—the Ghost Shirt—that was said to make the wearer impervious to the bullets of the white man. A second Ghost Dance appeared in 1890 that spread even more broadly than the first throughout many of the Plains tribes and into the eastern woodlands.

Accompanying the Ghost Dance was the appearance of the peyote cult, which apparently arose from an ancient reservoir of mysticism and the use of trance inducing substances common among the Indians of Mexico since pre-Columbian times. The Huichol, Tarahumare, and the Mescalero Apache introduced the cult to the Comanche and the Kiowa, from whom it spread to the Shawnee, Delaware, Cheyenne, Arapahoe, and numerous other tribes. With the peyote cult, even more Indian prophets arose, including great visionaries like the Comanche Quanah Parker and the Caddo-Delaware John Wilson. One branch of the cult, especially the Sioux, counseled violent uprisings which culminated in the death of the prophet warrior Sitting Bull and hundreds of Indians when the Ghost Shirts failed to stop the white man's bullets. The final act of the uprising came to an end with the massacre of more than two hundred Indians in 1890 at Wounded Knee in South Dakota.

Another branch of the Indians took a route of separation from the dominant culture and the ways of the world to follow a strategy presented in a vision to Quanah Parker. He was told by the Great Spirit: "Lay down your arms, Quanah Parker. Your solution, as is the solution of all creatures, is personal. Turn your energies toward conquering the self. Only through this will you and your people have a freedom that exceeds the white man's. The white civilizations will destroy themselves and the Indian will return to his lands, master over himself and at peace with all."

Using the scheme of response options introduced in chapter 4, the American Indian was made to choose either responses of high internal or external change. Neither the culture nor the individual Indian could ignore the onslaught of white civilization. The tale of Quanah Parker is one of shifting abruptly from Response II to Response IV, substituting high internal change when high external change is not possible.

Some nativistic movements assume a malignant and terrifying quality—individual identities and individual consciousness careen into an apocalypse. The Manson family in California or the Jonestown settlement in Guyana give testimony to the potential of brutality under the regimen of togetherness. While nihilism and hedonistic pursuits give pause for concern, so must the call for a return to a simple tribal consciousness.

Such movements, while rarely predicting the future, are excellent signals of individual and social transition. While they may not foretell the direction the new wind will blow, they are warnings and reminders of the change.

THE CONSTRUCTION OF SELF

Traditionally, identity was intertwined with family, land, and community. Individual life outside the community was very rare, as were individual reflections on purpose, goals, career, satisfaction, or aloneness. The individual was highly social—social in the sense of embeddedness—like a single molecule in a crystal formation. The molecule is not distinct; the unit is the crystal. Family and community were the more visible units.

Social change in the last two generations fractured that crystal and rebuilt the linkages of the self-concept more like a network or web of social roles, with the individual self-consciously playing several roles. Within the individual's consciousness has occurred another sort of differentiation. This differentiation, starting about four centuries ago, was the divorcing of the mind from the body.

An intellectual giant of the Renaissance, Rene Descartes, established the concept of self that has proved eventful for the modern world and established the mind-body divorce. Descartes's version of the self required a new and different sort of relationship between individual consciousness and the body. Under Descartes's version, all individuals localized a sense of consciousness within the mind. The mind became distinct from the rest of the body, which was a machine within which the mind and consciousness resided. The result of Descartes's efforts was a scientific understanding of the body that involved regarding the mind as an entity wholly separate from the body. This was the first step in divorcing the mind and the body.

The second step was reflected in the attempts by Sigmund Freud to describe the mental process in terms of three constructs. The Freudian definition of identity relating body and mind posed a division of three parts—the id, the ego, and the superego—which are in conflict and competition with each other so that identity becomes a moving compromise among three parts. As Freud used the constructs they develop a life of their own, become reified, and, only by accident, happen to be stuck in a body. These three entities quarrel among themselves for control of the body in which they are bound.

Descartes and Freud are but two signposts along a road that leads to an explanation of identity as a mind imprisoned in a body. Little concern is given for the impact of the condition of the body on the mind or of the relationship between thoughts and emotions and the condition of the body. Yet, the weight of scientific evidence today shows a shift of thinking toward a complex interrelation between mind and body. To conceive of mind and body as separable risks damage to each. Among the signs of burnout are many physical symptoms, such as exhaustion, headaches, ringing of the ears, tenseness. Failure to achieve one's expectations can have an impact on physical health, and health is related to mental outlook. The degree and extent of the relationship is not known, though some would suggest that even diseases such as cancer or cerebral and cardiovascular disease may be related to mental states.

During a transition period, like the present, the social environment will not support a concept of self linked to stable social groups. If the psychological process is toward some kind of stabilization and the environment is unstable, the search for stability and continuity will turn inward. Individuals will become more introspective, more aware of past experiences and memories and more concerned with developing personal abilities. Rather than seeking to serve others like the family or being loyal to the company, the individual's devotion will be to himself or herself. I see this as the explanation for the apparent rise in self-interest, in hedonism.

This trend indicates an internal anchoring of self and would include far greater awareness of the body as part of the self rather than viewing the body simply as the vehicle or container. Such a change involves greater emphasis on self-development activities such as personal improvement courses. It also involves greater interest in consumable personal items, such as personal autos rather than family autos, radios or sound equipment (especially with headphones), personal computers, personal video equipment—all technological items that permit personal use and personal creation of entertainment and elaboration of the person. The movement of technology seems to mirror and support this greater individualization: individuals and, of course, self-concepts that are very adaptable to many social circumstances yet are separately deep, complex, and uniquely composed. The growth of the individual shifts toward an internal locus with less dependence on others, involved with others quickly but peripherally.

SHIFTING THE BASE OF EXPECTATIONS

Burnout comes from unfulfilled expectations. In the past, these expectations were often based on other people, expectations about our supervisors, our colleagues, our family, our friends. I suspect the failure of many of these expectations forces the individual to base expectations on internal reference points. Rather than trying to please my supervisor, I will please myself. I will develop my own expectations of myself and less willingly adopt others' expectations. This is a subtle change since we learn to accept others' expectations of us through a socialization process that begins when we are children. The subtle shift is toward a much greater awareness of where expectations originate and what their implications are. Expectations will be weighed and sorted more carefully, with greater scrutiny.

A culture can either support or oppose this growth process in the individual. Most institutions in the modern world seem to oppose this process; yet I believe that the opposition shows signs of wear. Chapters 13 and 15 in Part II elaborate this point.

If expectations are more carefully developed and more under the control of the individual, burnout is less likely. Therefore, the solution for burnout is not in the environment but within the individual. The ultimate is a change in the self-concept.

The current temporary world has stretched the individual, each of us, into too many roles, making it difficult to handle them all and move abruptly from one to another several times each day. In the same way, the divorcing of the mind from the body has reached damaging levels. The consequences of this separation based on a cultural artifact dating back to Descartes are seen in the dimensions of burnout where physical stress symptoms appear. However, this breaking point of too many roles and too much mind-body separation begins, for many, a process of redefining one's sense of identity.

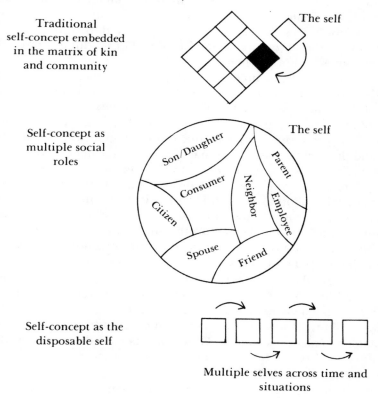

Figure 4
Alternate Self-Concept Structures

CULTURAL PARADIGMS AND PERSONAL IDENTITY

A useful way of understanding social change is through the use of a framework or a paradigm.* Our current sense of identity is heavily influenced by a social paradigm of an industrial society that stresses high achievement, continuous pursuit of new and larger goals, the attempt to remain youthful, and the accumulation of wealth. However, if our achievements are less than our goals, we do suffer burnout. The degree of suffering, of frustration, varies from person to person and from time to time. The roots of burnout, of personal identity, are very much implanted in the paradigm of our modern temporary world; any complete solution means that the individual must find a new paradigm for his or her identity.

Continually setting new goals for achievement is a style of living central to our culture. Yet this outlook in an untempered or unrealistic form creates candidates for burnout. We simply cannot achieve every goal we set, not as individuals or as a society. The pursuit of any goal without thorough examination of the likelihood of reaching it or of all the consequences leads to burnout.

The speed of social change in recent generations has made individuals painfully aware of their identity and isolation. Thus, the very success of the modern world establishes the conditions that usher in the waning of this world. The temporary world is already creating individuals who are beginning to reject the transient gratifications of the culture and the high intensity, external achievement demands. More and more people are pursuing a goal of central and enduring importance, a fuller awareness and development of themselves. Initially, this turning away is narcissistic but, as the child must first love himself in order to express love for parents, so does this narcissism provide the base for an expansion of identity and being to other individuals, to the external world. This expansion of identity though is not to conquer or control the world, but to be a part of it and, consequently, beyond it.

At this point, the new culture has an ancient aspect that draws from both Oriental and American Indian philosophies. Certain egos of the Orient have a much greater diffusion of the sense of self throughout the entire body. Many of the so-called autonomic processes have proven to be amenable to conscious control. Hindu adepts have demonstrated the ability to control respiration rate, blood pressure, and vulnerability to

---

*The concept of *paradigm* as I use the word is critical to understanding much of the material of this chapter. For further elaboration, see chapter 15.

pain. Asian cultures, Taoism and Buddhism, for example, also teach that the individual is an entity not separate from the world about, but rather is in continual action with the environment.

While the cultures of people on the North American continent prior to white settlements were very diverse, many shared an orientation that closely related the individual to both a sensory and spiritual world. For many Indian tribes, animals possessed a spiritual significance like humans. Even rocks, trees, and streams were alive with the same spiritual energy. In the world of the Navaho, the individual exists in an eternal and unchanging universe. Their ritual acts are designed to strengthen and reinforce this universe, to be at harmony and at balance with the forces of the universe. Their neighbors, the Hopi, view time as a circle. One continually passes through the same moment again and again, with past and future always there in the present.

The manner in which our self-concept is constructed is the most important clue to understanding burnout and preventing its intensification. By having a self-concept that must be rebuilt or merchandized each day, the likelihood of burnout is increased. As the demands on us change and as we either give up in the face of those demands or frantically search for the appropriate version of ourself, we become, in each case, more susceptible to higher degrees of burnout.

A rapidly changing world and a culture that emphasizes youthfulness and the importance of newness has created a self-concept that may be seen as the disposable self. Individuals shed one concept of self and take on another as the situation demands. The more situations we encounter, the more we create new versions of ourselves. But a time comes when a sense of memory appears, of deja vu, we've been here before. As the world changes, we realize that each of us as individuals has memories, a past beyond the present, and, as that awareness grows, the usefulness of the disposable self declines. Now the disposable self becomes the problem: requiring continuous change of ourselves heightens burnout.

The solution rests in a sense of identity that enlarges and evolves over time rather than a new identity that replaces the old. When living and experience are seen as personal growth rather than a sign of wearing out, then you have made the initial step to developing a new sense of identity. Taking the first step and the next may not prove easy. The next chapter provides some tools to assist you in such an action.

A Personal Strategy for Meeting Burnout

I do not know where to find any literature, whether ancient or modern, any adequate account of that nature with which I am acquainted. Mythology comes nearest to it of any.

Henry David Thoreau, *The Journal.*

In the previous chapters, I have tried to draw a picture that has one overriding theme and that theme is change. Returning to the concepts of the first chapters you will see, if this picture is correct, the conditions are set for producing high and continuous levels of burnout. What might be the result if one remains unmindful of these factors and without potential coping strategies?

Each person varies in how much change he or she experiences. Each one of us has, as well, a different tolerance level for change and the confusion and contradictions that often accompany change. There is very little that an individual can do to alter the amount of change in his or her life except move to more stable and tranquil environments; but even that move entails some initial change.

I am *not* suggesting in these chapters that change is inherently bad or good. It is simply a given in our environment. Much of the character of the consequences we encounter from dealing with the environment is a function of our personal ability to understand it. I am advocating an activist orientation to change, but advocating as well a consistent and thorough evaluation process as a prelude to action. Most of the time each of us has considerable resources to effect change in our expectations and our external world. Which route we take or the combination of the two routes is the key to successfully reaching our expectations and avoiding burnout. Burnout is most likely to occur when our responses become habitual—when we act or fail to act without thought.

To do what I am talking about will not be easy. It will take some time and some practice. It will probably require you to break some old habits and that is never easy. It will require you to take a long and thorough look at yourself and to examine who you are and how you came to be that way. You will need to review your relationships with others and place a value on what you get from those relationships. Last and most important, you will need to become more aware of yourself and less a person of habit.

None of this can be achieved in one reading on some rainy afternoon. Take this chapter a little at a time. Work the exercises on a few roles and then set it aside. In time, you will be able to assess all roles and monitor your experiences in each. I believe you may find that just doing that, without making any changes, will prove very useful.

A MODEL OF AMBIGUITY

Here is an interesting piece of work that seems to shed some light on the question. Many years ago, N. R. F. Maier (1949) was studying learning using various animals. One adaptation of his work was with the common house cat, by all accounts not the world's brightest animal. Maier was trying to determine how animals learned to recognize and cope with change.

Briefly, his design involved placing the cat on a small stand on top of a pole. Across an open space were two doors side by side, each painted with a different geometric symbol. One of the doors opened; the other was latched. An experimenter squirted the cat's backside with a blast of air, frightening it and causing it to jump. If the cat chose the correct door, it opened and the cat escaped the unpleasant situation. If it chose the wrong door, the cat dropped into a net, irritated and angry, and was put back on the stand to get another blast of air and try to escape again. The more the cat made mistakes, the more angry and nervous the cat became. In time, perhaps fifteen or more trials, the cat learned to match the appropriate symbol for the door that opened. The cat would learn to expect to escape the situation by making a particular response.

Once the cat learned to pick the door with the correct symbol, a circle or a triangle, the experimenter then switched symbols to see how long it took the cat to learn to make the switch. The cat had to change its expectations and its responses.

The final step—and this is the critical one for our purposes here—was to randomly vary the correct symbol for the open door for each trial. In this case, it was absolutely impossible for the cat to learn an effective, a workable strategy. Any expectation for escape was undependable. Surprisingly, many cats jumped at the post directly between the two doors. Evidently, the cat, in its fashion, knew that there was no escape and that dependable failure was better than ambiguity.

Complete or high ambiguity makes expectations impossible. One is neither able to read a given situation to understand it nor able to develop the internal models of reality that permit prediction or explanation. With ambiguity, the world loses its meaning, its coherence. Without some structure to develop expectations, the cats seemed to choose self-punishment. Expectations must be based on predictability and the only certainty was failure. It might be said Maier experimentally demonstrated how we learn to beat our heads against the wall.

AMBIGUITY, CHANGE, AND BURNOUT

This model of ambiguity leading to self-destruction is a major clue in building personal strategies to deal with burnout since the conditions of the temporary world continually induce ambiguity for each of us. An important element of a successful strategy for dealing with burnout is both to reduce the degree of ambiguity that each of us faces and to alter the meaning ambiguity has to us. Change means ambiguity and ambiguity means roles and expectations get shuffled and disoriented. And, if you will recall from the early chapters of this book (chapters 3 and 4 particularly), change can come from within the person or from the environment.

There are several ways that change in the meaning of a role may come about. One way is through your own maturing. Things that at one time were meaningful, were needed by you, can lose their meaning. You simply outgrow them. Most teenagers seem to need friends with them as much of the time as possible or they feel lonely and ill at ease. Yet, in time, they outgrow this need, becoming more independent of their peers. Adolescence is a period of destabilization and ambiguity, both physically and socially. Physical changes and the development of secondary sexual characteristics create new roles and expectations for the adolescent. In response to these changes and the accompanying ambiguity, the adolescent will often gravitate to other adolescents who, of course, are facing the same situation. Shared feelings develop into shared expectations.

Another way for a role to change its meaning is through an alteration in the social norms relative to that role. Norms are the standards that develop in a culture that define reality, appropriate conduct, and social roles. The age at which people can legally marry or the general social expectation that adults should have a job are examples of norms. Anomie and ambiguity are used to describe a society where norms are weak or collapsing. Roles themselves are norms, and learning and adopting a social role means that one is learning a norm. A role is a series of actions or behaviors that one follows, usually through interaction with other people. The role means that we have certain expectations of ourselves and of others and they, in turn, have expectations of us. Society is, in fact, built of such interlocking expectations. When a social norm changes, it may mean that a specific role is changing. The consequence is that now old expectations may be far afield from a new reality.

Motherhood is an apt example. While many of the role activities such as nurturance and childbearing have remained constant, the social norms in the United States concerning this social role have changed dramatically. No longer is every woman expected to be a mother. While it formerly was a full-time role, new norms and new institutions—such as day care— are changing it to a part-time role. Apparently, it is also not as highly valued a role as more young women seek to postpone or avoid motherhood and as some question the quality of fulfillment derived from the role. This may mean that the social value attributed to the role is lessened. The role may be ridiculed or belittled. Other role alternatives may be seen as preferred. Thus, the old expectations of respect for motherhood may not meet reality and female parents may consider role alternatives. An interesting sign that such thoughts lurk is when someone says, "I'm just a housewife."

People today anchor themselves in many groups and take on many roles: employee, friend, church member, parent, son or daughter, neighbor, committee member, consumer, taxpayer, commuter. Burnout begins when a person starts to encounter a reality that is less than the expectations with one or more of such roles. In many instances, the individual will begin to experience burnout but will not consciously know which role is producing the dissatisfaction. If the condition of burnout increases, more and more roles get caught in the disaffection process and the burned-out feelings and behavior spread from one role to another.

A number of processes appear when burnout gets started that increase the level of burnout and hasten its spread to other roles. One process is physical energy depletion. If our achievements fall below our expectations, we work a little harder, concentrate a bit more. More effort means edging closer to exhaustion, especially when positive results are not forthcoming. Weariness then degrades performance more and the gap between expectations and achievements widens. Burnout deepens.

Because of the exhaustion produced by burnout in one role, our efforts in other roles may be affected adversely. Burnout on the job may mean we have less energy at home and begin to burn out there as well. As we grow more tired and irritable, our efforts disappoint others and if they have expectations built around our efforts, they will suffer from burnout also.

SEEKING HELP THROUGH INSIGHT

Change may make our expectations untenable. At a minimum, change requires us to change our expectations. The question now becomes how can we come to understand our expectations and our reality. The implication is that each of us must understand ourself better and learn when and what expectations are feasible. To achieve personal change, it is useful to see what we know about the science and practice of personal change.

There are dozens of psychotherapies offered today to provide individual change; but their effectiveness is neither too substantial nor very predictable. This is not to say that individuals cannot change because they certainly do. The individual change process, however, is complex and in the case of psychotherapy is as dependent on the individual therapist as the techniques the therapist uses.

In a general sense, although there are many brands of psychotherapy, there are only two basic types. One type depends on the individual's achieving an insight into what is the cause of his or her problem. With that insight the individual may then take some action to solve the problem. Whether the therapy is classical psychoanalysis with years spent unraveling the personality or a therapy group with the expectation of achieving results in a few sessions, the intent is the same: to reach some insight into what the person does and why.

Individual, group, Gestalt, Jungian, Freudian, neo-Freudian, rational emotive, conjugal, transactional, the list is really very long and new approaches appear each year. By and large, though, these approaches differ in the methods used, the length of time, and the depth of insight. In all cases, though, insight is the goal and through insight comes change.

The other type of psychotherapy ignores trying to get the individual first to achieve insight. It presumes that all behavior is based on immediate rewards in the environment that cause behavior. The therapeutic approach concentrates on changing the environment to change the behavior. For example, if a teacher observes that a child creates a disturbance to get attention, insight therapy advocates bringing this to the child's awareness. Noninsight therapy—behavior modification is the best known—concentrates on not rewarding the child by ignoring the disturbances. The teacher would remove the child from the situation or give the child attention for acts that the teacher deems are positive.

The behavior therapies are not as old as the nonbehavioral approaches and are fewer in number. Behavior modification, aversive conditioning, behavioral therapy, and token economies are among the familiar and widely used procedures. The appeal of the behavior therapies is that the therapist begins to work immediately on the objectionable behavior rather than circuiting through establishing insight or why the person does what he does. Consequently, the behavioral approach may produce results more rapidly.

However, noninsight therapies are dependent either on having a therapist around to change the reward patterns to ensure the individual's appropriate behavior or on enabling the individual to learn to do that alone. In the latter case, then, the noninsight therapy becomes an insight therapy. Thus, for change to occur and be maintained, the individual must arrive at some insight in the present situation.

Early in the book, we saw how people use external and internal change to develop responses to burnout. All responses either bring reality to meet expectations or revise expectations. Quite often, a response contains a bit of each. The middle chapters of Part I have presented, among other things, an argument for an increased consciousness or awareness of expectations, achievements, and the demands of the world. Curiously enough, this increased awareness contributes significantly to burnout because increased awareness without action serves to intensify expectations. For example, you might expect to be financially independent by the age of forty. If the expectation is weak and you seldom think about it, insufficient progress to achieve such an expectation may have minimal effect on you. However, if you become more aware of the expectation and the inadequate progress, burnout will increase. Actually the value assigned to the expectation is rising, and the failure of expectations in relatively important roles is more critical than failure in less important roles.

This chapter stresses that successful coping with burnout calls for more awareness. In a nutshell, I will suggest that while awareness and options are necessary for burnout, more awareness and options can control it. The next several pages offer some techniques for increasing one's awareness, and some of this material has enough structure to suggest that we are still in the social paradigm of the industrial society (more about that in Part II). However, there are two important things to keep in mind about structure and techniques. Without structure and techniques, we have no freedom. We are awash in a sea of ambiguity. Freedom is based on structure in the form of understanding. The second thing about structure are the questions: whose structure and for what? If it's someone else's structure, then it may not offer freedom. But if the structure is ours, of our own devising and for our use, then, it is a key to freedom. The perception of personal freedom comes from feeling that we are doing things of our own choosing. Making choices means having values and that is a form of structure. The loss of values is represented by the Meltdown position, the third stage of burnout, despair. The second stage, anger, occurs when we feel that our expectations are blocked by someone else's values, by structure controlled by others but impinging on us.

These are the steps in the process of increasing our awareness about burnout and freeing ourselves from much of its debilitating consequences. This process is Designing Expectations.

DESIGNING EXPECTATIONS

The following is a summary of the steps in Designing Expectations. A thorough explanation of each step occurs later in the chapter, but first a quick run-through to get a glimpse of what the process involves.

Step 1: "Cooling Out"—If you're burned out but have neither the energy nor the peace of mind to begin your design efforts, this step is to provide you the appropriate perspective to begin Designing Expectations. It should be used throughout the process to help you maintain a broad perspective.

Step 2: "Role Mapping"—In this step you identify all your roles and determine which are sources of burnout by establishing the degree of satisfaction with each role.

Step 3: "Fitting the Map"—Once you have found the role or roles where the burnout is, you are ready to examine your expectations in the role. In this step, you try to determine if your expectations are realistic. You explore your options generating options in terms of the Response Matrix.

Step 4: "Choosing the Option"—When you have identified your options, one of them must be chosen with the new expectations. Once more, you reexamine the new expectations and see if they are plausible.

Step 5: "Final Plan"—You've mapped your role, identified the role where burnout is, critiqued your expectations, and generated an option. Now you develop the plan.

Step 6: "Action"—This is the hardest step. You follow through on your plan.

To handle burnout is to be able to recognize the symptoms at the early stages and choose appropriate responses. Let me again, however, offer a word of caution. For many people the tasks involved in these six steps may prove to be discomforting. So many of the expectations that we acquire are defined to us as imperative. Let's call them "shoulds." You *should* get an education. You *should* get married. You *should* get a good job. You *should* be polite, dependable, loyal, and so on. There will prove to be good reasons for most of these "shoulds," but their precise meanings and implications for us must be carefully evaluated. Simply examining long-held expectations means judging how well the expectations are being met and how appropriate the expectations are. If one has not done this recently it can be an uncomfortable experience. Examining expectations is like opening a closet that has been closed many years. We may get some unpleasant surprises and the task may involve a bit of effort.

Going through the steps in Designing Expectations should prove to be a challenging effort. In effect you are making a critique of the way you live your life and self-examination is not easy. However, it is important to recognize that you will only get as much out of this effort as you put into it. Just laying out the roles and the related expectations gives you a better sense of control over yourself and a changing environment.

You may wish to use the "Cooling Out" step several times. It serves as a "Quick Break" from an emotionally-involved activity and helps you keep a broader perspective for reviewing your roles. "Cooling Out" is learning to step back from your expectations and the physical and emotional involvement they usually imply.

Now, let's go through each of these steps.

Step 1—"Cooling Out"

To prepare for change, it may be necessary to develop specific psychological strategies for cooling yourself out. Self-hypnosis, meditation, progressive relaxation, and intensive physical exercise all achieve one meaningful change and that is an altered psychological reality. In one way or another, these techniques lessen the grip of ordinary consciousness, quiet the chatter of the mind, and decrease habitual levels of nervous anxiety. You reduce the feelings of frustration by developing abilities to alter consciousness. Many books on techniques for cooling out are available and are very useful as a "Quick Break" to support the resorting and pruning process described here. Table 4 contains a useful and simple self-assessment scale, to help you determine if you may first need to cool yourself out. It is intended to help you inventory both your health states and stress-producing events. The bibliography for this chapter lists several books that discuss techniques for helping you put things in perspective.

NOTE: The items on this scale and their values are drawn from work by Holmes and Rahe (1967). Reviews and analyses of this and related work are available in Sarason and Spielberger (1978, 1979). A very readable compendium is the work *Understanding and Managing Stress: A Workbook in Changing Life Styles* (1980) by John D. Adams, which is available from University Associates, San Diego, California.

An accumulation of 200 or more "life-change units" in a single year may be more disruption than an individual can withstand and make him vulnerable to illness.

Table 4
How Different Events Cause Stress

Event	Scale of Impact
Death of spouse	100
Divorce	73
Marital separation	65
Jail term	63
Death of close family member	63
Personal injury or illness	53
Marriage	50
Fired at work	47
Marital reconciliation	45
Retirement	45
Change in health of family member	44
Pregnancy	40
Sex difficulties	39
Gain of new family member	39
Business readjustment	39
Change in financial state	38
Death of close friend	37
Change to different line of work	36
Change in number of arguments with spouse	35
Mortgage over $10,000	31
Foreclosure of mortgage or loan	30
Change in responsibilities at work	29
Son or daughter leaving home	39
Trouble with in-laws	29
Outstanding personal achievement	28
Wife begins or stops work	26
Begin or end school	26
Change in living conditions	25
Revision of personal habits	24
Trouble with boss	23
Change in work hours or conditions	20
Change in residence	20
Change in schools	20
Change in recreation	19
Change in church activities	19
Change in social activities	18
Mortgage or loan less than $10,000	17
Change in sleeping habits	16
Change in number of family get-togethers	15
Change in eating habits	15
Vacation	13
Christmas	12
Minor violation of the law	11

"Cooling Out" is a "Quick Break" response that is useful not by forgetting about a role and expectations that are causing problems but by backing away from the immediate situation and its expectations. Moderate exercise at least three times a week for no less than twenty minutes is a good example. Walking, jogging, and swimming are among the best since they require minimal equipment and, importantly, can be done alone. Don't choose competitive sports for "Cooling Out" since they often produce just the reverse effect.

Step 2—"Role Mapping"

Role mapping is a simple technique to assist one in reaching some insight about expectations. Through insight about expectations, each of us may find which situations are sources of burnout.

The most effective first effort you can make to change the situation is to picture all of your roles at one time. Try to imagine yourself suspended on a net in midair. You are suspended by a network of lines radiating from you, each line representing one social role. These lines compose your social existence, direct your actions, and provide you with support and meaning. Burnout occurs when one or more of these lines begins to tug at you in a way that makes you uncomfortable rather than providing support. The expectations and the reality are in conflict.

When you visualize all your roles, then you should identify the total number of roles and review and evaluate the levels of frustration and satisfaction associated with each role. This maneuver permits you to see from a fuller perspective where you are fragmented and caught between contending roles or spread thinly across too many roles. After inventorying each role, you can then re-evaluate the meaning of certain roles and work to improve the roles or lessen their meaning or eliminate them entirely. This pruning process is rarely consciously done. Typically a person does not re-evaluate or change a role until a crisis is reached.

All too often we underestimate the number of roles and, thus, the sets of expectations that we have. For example, if your job requires you to supervise others, there is a role and set of expectations involved for you for each person you supervise. Though we may think of ourselves as behaving in a uniform way with each person, rarely is that true. All people, and that means those we supervise, are different. Some are brighter, some more energetic, others more dependable, and others more demanding. For each of these a role is developed for us, and we have other roles in the organization as well. We will probably have one or more colleagues and perhaps one or more supervisors. Each means another role.

There are many roles that we have that do not include a specific other person. If you live alone, you have a role as a housekeeper that probably will not involve any other person. When you travel, go to a movie or a concert, you assume roles that do not necessarily include a specific other person or persons. Consumer roles may imply concrete expectations for us yet not through interaction with a particular other person. Advertising is often based on selling us new expectations. When driving a particular car defines success, or when a cologne or perfume promises to enhance our sex appeal, or when a soap or toothpaste assures youthful vitality, we are being taught expectations. Typically what is being conveyed is that we are less than what we should be and to achieve those expectations, we should purchase a particular product.

In all instances, what is needed is an early look at what is happening in the role relationship. One needs to be conscious of the relationship of role expectations to current reality more quickly and, if that relationship is slipping out of place, decide how it might be changed gradually and more creatively.

By conceptualizing and inventorying each of your social roles, you may then establish which roles have the greatest priority and which you regard as less significant. Sometimes an insignificant role is the source of your frustration. You may be at peace with most everything, finding success and happiness in all phases of your life, but perhaps find you're frustrated by a nosy landlord. Once you achieve this understanding of which role is the source of irritation, you can quickly generate several options. You may make peace with your landlord. You may threaten him into avoiding you. You may learn to ignore him. You may pick another place to rent. Or, you may wish to buy your own house.

When you set priorities for your roles, you are actually spelling out your values. Your most important values are represented by your highest-priority roles. Things that are of minimal value to you are represented as low-priority roles. Values are the most abstract form of your beliefs, those things most cherished by you. Roles represent the social operation of values, and expectations are the psychological content of a role.

At any rate, by prioritizing your roles, frustration is reduced. You will see which roles are satisfying, which are mostly neutral, and which are sources of irritation. Once you have completed this exercise, you should find that some of the tension and stress is reduced. But before long you will find yourself wondering, now that I've identified a source of burnout, what am I going to do about it? Returning to the Response Matrix ask the question whether the environment or your expectations can or should change. Table 5 provides the details of the "Role Mapping Process."

Table 5
The Role Mapping Process

A. Visualize all your roles:

Mother or father
Employee*
Friend
Church member
Voter
Neighbor
Member of the car pool
Concerned citizen of your city, county, state and country
Member of some special interest group with special concerns (e.g., Sierra Club,
    League of Women Voters, or the Moral Majority)
Son or daughter
Spouse
Consumer

*Remember that some of your general roles, such as employee, may have several separate subroles. You may have a role with your immediate supervisor, another with those you supervise, another with your colleagues, perhaps one on a company or organization task force, and so on. Your first step is to list all of these roles.

B. Next, rate each role from 1 to 5 using the following scale on the degree of satisfaction you find with each role.

Highly Dissatisfied	Dissatisfied	Ambivalent	Satisfied	Highly Satisfied
1	2	3	4	5

C. Rank each role from most important to least important to you. Now see if there are low-ranking or high-ranking roles that produce dissatisfaction.

Rank Order	Role	Satisfaction
1	Employee	1 (Highly Dissatisfied)
2	Spouse	3 (Ambivalent)
3	Father	4 (Satisfied)

and so on through all your roles.

Through this process, you begin to reduce ambiguity and thus lessen stress and frustration. The personal meaning of frustration and ambiguity can be altered. One important step in changing is accepting that you cannot escape by denying. Running from ambiguity does not eliminate it and may increase the potential severity of burnout.

To illustrate the process, let's take one last look at one of our illustrations from the first chapter. What would Harvey Eagleton's Role Map have looked like? The following pages portray the Role Map Harvey could have used before he launched his "New Beginnings" odyssey.

Table 6
Harvey's Roles and Degree of Satisfaction

Role	Satisfaction Level				
	Highly Dissatisfied 1	Dissatisfied 2	Ambivalent 3	Satisfied 4	Highly Satisfied 5
Husband to Judith	X				
Neighbor					
to Staples			X		
to Harris				X	
to Ringes			X		
Church member					
Worshipper		X			
Sunday school teacher			X		
Homeowner				X	
Voter			X		
County Republican party chairman	X				
Friend to					
Anne				X	
Bill			X		
Stuart			X		
W.C.		X			
Corky		X			
Dean				X	
Employee—general role as business executive				X	
Employee—with subroles					
Supervisor for Williams			X		
Supervisor for Todd				X	
Supervisor for Kratz			X		
Supervisee of John Rohrer (President)	X				
Colleague to					
Bob Collins	X				
Tony Benediti				X	
Carl Irwin			X		
Sue Myers			X		
Neils Harrison			X		
Son					X
Father to					
Pete				X	
Elizabeth				X	

In table 6 Harvey visualizes his roles and rates them by degree of satisfaction. As you can see, Harvey has a large number of roles, with much variability from role to role in the level of satisfaction drawn from the role.

Table 7
Harvey's Roles Ranked by Priority

Priority	Role	Level of Satisfaction
1	Employee role as supervisee to company president, John Roh	1
2	Husband to Judith	1
3	Employee role as colleague to:	
	Bob Collins	1
	Tony Benediti	4
	Carl Irwin	3
	Sue Myers	3
	Neils Harrison	3
4	Father to:	
	Pete	4
	Elizabeth	4
5	County Republican party chairman	1
6	Friend to:	
	Anne	4
	Bill	3
	Stuart	3
	W.C.	2
	Corky	2
	Dean	4
7	Son	5
8	Voter	3
9	Employee—role as supervisor to:	
	Williams	3
	Todd	4
	Kratz	3
10	Employee—general role as business executive	4
11	Church member role as:	
	Worshipper	2
	Sunday school teacher	3
12	Homeowner	4
13	Neighbor to:	
	Staples	3
	Harris	4
	Ringes	3

Each of Harvey's roles is ranked with its satisfaction value from most important to least important (table 7). By listing the roles in a ranked order, it is clear that many of Harvey's high-priority roles are providing little satisfaction.

Step 3—"Fitting the Map."

Once you have mapped your roles and seen which are contributing to burnout, you must list and examine expectations for high-priority but low-satisfaction roles. It is important to examine the expectations in those roles that have a high priority.

Often our perception of what others expect of us does not match closely with others' actual expectations. For a variety of reasons others' expectations may diverge. Sometimes communication is simply lacking. We infrequently or never ask others what their expectations of us are. Often we do not ask because we fear the expectations are beyond what we can deliver or that disagreements will ensue as expectations are compared. In other cases, we become too busy to find out what another's expectations are or we feel uncomfortable in engaging in such tasks.

In all these cases, though, we soon find ourselves engaging in actions based on what we suspect other people think. We may be correct. But by never checking someone else's perceptions we build a large margin for error.

In Harvey Eagleton's case, his role as supervisee was a high-priority role that was producing considerable dissatisfaction. Harvey might have wished to examine the expectations he held and his perception of his supervisor's expectations. It would have been useful to have obtained his supervisor's expectations of him as well. Had he gathered that information it might have looked like this:

Role Expectations for H. Eagleton

Harvey's Expectations	Harvey's Perception of His Boss's Expectations	Harvey's Boss's Expectations
To have reached the position of president by now	To work hard but not challenge the boss or threaten his hold on the presidency	Harvey needs about five more years experience before he could be considered as a successor
That his boss would be more aware of Harvey's expectations for advancement	That his boss does not want to hear about or have to discuss with Harvey, Harvey's expectations	That Harvey should be more direct and open in discussing his career expectations
To be treated as a colleague	That he is an employee, a hired hand	That Harvey is a colleague

Two of these expectations are, of course, known to Harvey. The third expectation must be obtained from his supervisor. To do so will clarify the situation and generate issues.

Several questions must be asked. What are my expectations and the expectations of others? Do I have the energy to change my expectations or to affect the environment? Is change in the environment possible or likely? Do I want to make a commitment and do I want to do it now? How realistic are my expectations? How realistic are others' expectations? Do my expectations for myself in the role and those that others' hold for me match?

As you examine expectations, refer back to the Response Matrix and try to generate some of the responses for the role in question. Table 8 is an example of Harvey Eagleton's five major change responses for his work role as supervisee.

Table 8
Harvey's Five Major Change Responses for the Work Role

Response I—"The Quick Break"

Harvey decides to get a better perspective on his position at Rohrer & Company. He goes on a three-week vacation to the Caribbean, leaving his briefcase and all thoughts of the office behind.

Response II—"The Compromise"

Harvey acknowledges his expectations of being the company president and suspects he may be passed over. He schedules a long appointment with the president, airs his expectations, and finds that he is still in the running. He learns that the current president will shortly announce a plan to retire in two years and so Harvey rededicates himself to his work.

Response III—"The Fresh Start"

Harvey examines his opportunities at Rohrer & Company and concludes the prospects for advancement are no longer favorable. He realizes his feelings of burnout come from the lack of opportunity in his work and decides to make applications to similar companies in Philadelphia and other cities. He soon secures a position with a larger firm in Chicago where there are several opportunities for advancement.

Response IV—"The Inner Journey"

Harvey reviews his experience at Rohrer & Company, then checks with some other firms and finds that his age may work against him. A move would appear that he is being eased out, and he fears bringing his dissatisfaction to his superiors would imply disloyalty. Harvey decides to derive different meaning, satisfaction from his position in the company. He begins to read books about the development of the business and takes a larger role in training and developing up and coming employees.

Response V—"New Beginnings"

This was essentially the option Harvey picked, though his case suggests that it came more as a roll of the dice. Harvey changed his expectations of himself, his job, and his external environment and, in changing one role, changed many others.

It is fair to ask whether this process, this step in designing expectations, would have made a difference to Harvey. Would Harvey have selected Response V if he had looked at other alternatives? I don't know. But, a map can be helpful even if it does not tell you where you want to go. It does remind you where you are, where you came from, and where you have been.

Step 4—"Choosing the Option."

Now, as a result of role mapping, you may begin to think about changing a role and its expectations. Gather some data about your new terrain and see how well the new role map fits. Consider the stockbroker who wants to leave Chicago and run a ski shop in Aspen. Now this may have been a fantasy for several years, and the broker may be completely burned out in his current occupation. However, before making a change, one more step is a good idea.

Now, put yourself in the broker's shoes. First, go to a library and find out what the population of Aspen is, how many ski shops there are already, and how many tourists visit each year. Make a trip to Aspen and talk with the owners of existing shops. Find out how quickly their inventories turn over, how long their working hours are, and what their net profits are each year. Find out who might be willing to sell their shop or whether others are for sale. Ask around and see if people feel another ski shop is needed.

If the idea still looks good, then offer to work for free during your next vacation at a ski shop. Or, see if you can arrange a leave from your current job to spend two or three months. You may find that you have found a perfect role, or at least one far superior to your current role.

You may find that the wages are too low and the hours too long. You may miss the restaurants, the shows, the stores of the city. You may find you have to give up too many other things in the change. The loss of friends, family, or financial security may outweigh the benefits of working in Aspen.

Either way, this important step is to try out your new role map. For most things we do, it is best if we can try them out first. Don't burn the bridges behind you unless you're concerned about what might be following you.

Generate these data for at least two responses for a given role. I've done one here in figure 5 to illustrate the process.

One, with the role you want to change in mind, refer to the Response Matrix. We'll use our stockbroker example.

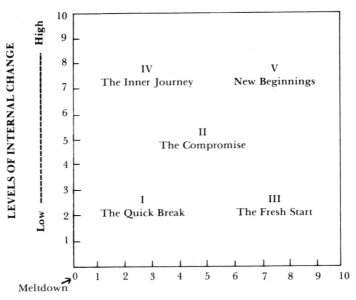

Two, outline your response options.

0, 0	Do nothing and melt down.
3, 3	Take a three-day weekend to Aspen for a "Quick Break."
5, 5	Change your expectations and reality by learning to cross-country ski in Wisconsin and thus achieving a "Compromise."
10, 1	Change to a brokerage firm in Florida and take up scuba diving to get a "Fresh Start."
1, 10	Stay with the job in Chicago but change your expectations by going on an "Inner Journey." Give up skiing.
10, 10	Leave Chicago and the brokerage business to start a "New Beginning" in Aspen.

Three, take the responses that seem the most appealing and gather some data on them. Gather data on internal and environmental change dimensions of the response and examine the pros and cons of other responses. This is *"Fitting the Map."*

Figure 5
Using the Response Matrix for Fitting the Map

After you have generated several options and examined them through the Response Matrix, you must make the best choice. And as the matrix indicates, making no decision will still yield a response. No one can tell you which is the correct option.

In order to make a good choice you need to get some distance between yourself and the immediate situation. You need to see the forest and not just the individual trees. The techniques of this chapter, the understanding of the various concepts of self and recognizing the habituated responses of the Response Matrix, are all tools for learning to see the forest. After looking at options and expectations you have to decide if you can commit yourself to a given option. A halfhearted commitment is really a "Meltdown Response." Yet because the world is so changeable, what may be a good option now may look different in a year. That is, of course, what we see when we look at the forest, the big picture.

But that in no way changes the big picture, or the need to select an option. You may indeed choose to keep your current option. Remember, if you do not select an option, you still make a response.

Step 5—"Final Plan."

Roles are mapped, you've cooled yourself out if necessary, you've fitted your map to the terrain, and you've finally selected an option. The next step is to circle back through your role map, looking at your roles and expectations one more time. Ask yourself whether the option chosen still looks the best. Rethink your resources for internal and external change and recheck the opportunities in the environment.

You might ask yourself as well, particularly if you are thinking about considerable change in a high-priority role, how often should I go through a process like this? That is a very good question. Making large scale changes in high-priority roles is not a matter to be taken lightly. Such changes are stressful for ourselves and for others. At the same time, social change is altering our external reality and, thus, our expectations may lose their fit, their congruence. The most important benefit of designing your own expectations is that more of the process of developing expectations is put under your control.

Now here is the way you develop your plan.

1. Put your response and the new expectations in writing. Try to think of every contingency.
2. Inventory your resources. What will the response cost in dollars and in energy from other roles? Accumulate the resources you

will need before making the change. And, keep in mind the life-events scale. Don't overload yourself. If you find you're planning to make a large-scale change and are in the midst of other changes, you may find you are going to strain physical and psychological resources.

3. Your inventory will suggest a timetable. Regardless of the response, set a timetable. Decide when you are going to put a decision in effect.

4. Select some objectives or milestones that you will pass along the way. In this way, you will have a better feel for your progress.

A final plan for Harvey Eagleton might look like this:

Response: "New Beginning"

Objective	Timetable	Resources
Find a new career	One Year	Myself and friends in other careers
List options	First three months	Myself, counselor
Gather data	Second three months	Library, phone calls
Visit potential sites	Third three months	Other persons in the career area
Try out	Fourth three months	Accumulated vacation and sick leave. Savings and home equity
Revise expectations with Judith	In the same year	Each other
Discuss mutual expectations	First month	Each other
Identify conflicts	Next three months	Each other, friends, counselor, minister
Establish new relationship	Next eight months	Each other, friends—old and new

Step 6—"Action."

This is the sixth and final step. You have the big picture. You know your expectations. You have looked at alternatives and chosen one. You've developed a plan. Now you put the plan into action.

SUMMING UP

Living life successfully is learning to assess expectations, identify options, and then make satisfactory decisions. Realizing that one must face options generates anxiety, yet psychological growth is a process of facing more options and more complex options. The options for the infant are ones of separating himself from his environment and recognizing that he is an entity distinct from his mother. The young child faces more options, to control body functions, to obey parents' wishes (both when parents are around and when they are not), to have friends or play alone. The adolescent faces the options of emerging from the family and developing a separate identity, of dealing with loneliness, and with social friendship. The young adult faces options around marriage, career, and adult identity. The adult in the middle years deals with the potential of changing careers, changing personal roles, and achieving financial security and independence. In old age, the options around retirement and how to approach death must be met.

To deny that options exist is to hide from the world. Psychological growth requires meeting options, options that become more complex and challenging the more one is successful. Mental illness is the result of failure to meet options adequately. Alcohol and the tranquilizing drugs are simply chemical means for mediating the awareness of options.

Decreased awareness of alternatives may also emanate from certain thinking styles. Chronic pessimism or denial that postpones decisions until external events bring about a decision is such a thinking style. This causes contingencies or crises to dictate much of the decision. The student who procrastinates studying until the night before the exam, the auto driver who checks the spare tire after the flat, the homeowner who decides to have the leak repaired in the roof when it begins to rain, the office worker who despairs of telling the boss that he cannot make the deadline until the deadline has passed, the nation that worries about energy supplies only when shortages occur are all examples of pessimism or denial as an approach to avoiding the reality of alternatives.

In the same way, daydreaming can be used to mask or avoid reality, as can a continuous indulgence in television watching, gambling, any number of leisure pursuits. Or, like Maier's cats, we may through anxiety or a rigid stubbornness engage in behavior this is blatantly self-destructive.

Indeed our world can set us up for burnout. As our society grows more and more complex, it begins to be filled with mechanical things that are our creation and responsibility. Cars, radios, stereos, cameras, refrigerators, washing machines, hair dryers, typewriters, clothes dryers, electric shavers, electronic games, calculators, personal computers, hobby equipment, watches, lawn mowers, kitchen mixers, processors, blenders, electric toothbrushes, auto tapedecks—the list goes on. When natural things do not behave as we intend, we feel no responsibility for them. We do not see natural things like snow or rain as something that should be commanded or under our control. But human creations, human technology, should be responsive to commands, to us. Thus, we set conditions for greater frustration from our web of complex technology. When the technology goes awry, someone should be able to do something about that.

If there is an escape from burnout, part of the escape is from certain dimensions of the modern world. At the individual level, it means lessening one's dependence on technology but not seeking to destroy technology. In and of itself, technology is neither good nor bad. The roles we choose for it, the way it operates in our lives, is where the value lies.

Using technology is not a neutral act. It involves us with someone else's world and often requires that we serve another's vision. It is the vision of the engineer who designs the car, of the manufacturer that produced it, of the advertising agency that persuaded us we should subscribe to its view of what success, prestige, or enjoyment should be.

The social system itself can be tuned to deny the existence of options. In our society, inflation and the emphasis on high consumption produced through advertising mask for many people the options of other lifestyles as well as the long-term social and economic consequence of high consumption and inflation for the society. Government interventions that seek to remedy unemployment, poor housing, or other ills at the same time may hide options from people. The minimum wage, for example, prevents people from being paid less than a specific wage but also removes the option of employment for many, especially teenagers. Government action to remove options may serve to stunt the psychological growth of its citizens and, in time, can constrict creativity and productivity.

Remember, if you will, some of the people we looked at early in the book: Ann Schraeder, the young career woman; Harvey Eagleton, the middle-aged successful executive; Larry Thomas, the angry steelworker; Sue Torres, the despairing social worker; Tim Ferris, a man on the fast track. The thing they all had in common was change in roles of which they were only slightly aware. Their styles of thinking denied for them available options. Some lacked the courage to analyze their roles, others rigidly ignored the changes, but none of them were consciously trying to evaluate their identities through their roles.

This simple thinking through and ordering of your affairs at the personal level is the single most important step in a strategy of coping with burnout. By stopping to identify all of your roles, you momentarily stop trying to meet all of the demands imposed on you by them. By taking this pause, you disengage the driving, achieving side of the brain for a few moments and give other parts of the brain an opportunity to size up the total situation. Once you stop the action, you can see how your own efforts become captured, the properties of others' intentions.

Living under today's conditions is becoming increasingly and continuously stressful. Resources are scarce and become scarcer. Maintaining one's standard of living, and especially increasing one's standard of living, demands more and more effort. More and more, each of us may think why should we do this. If I moved a thousand miles away, I can make ten thousand more dollars, but what is gained and what is lost in the trade-off? Ten thousand dollars is indeed more money, but is that money necessary for survival? Where are the hidden costs of establishing a new home, making new friends?

How often do you have to buy a new car to get serviceable transportation? Each year? Not really. Every five years? Not necessarily. In fact, if a car is necessary, and frequently it is, why not wait to buy a new one until the repair bills on the old one equal monthly payments for a new car? If life can have meaning to each of us beyond the possession of material objects, then a new car is never mandatory.

How many outfits can a person wear in a week? Not too many. Buy as many outfits as you think you need, but ask the question what you need them for. If you are at one with yourself, if you become your own anchor, then you have less need to merchandize yourself daily. You no longer need to sell yourself to someone.

Now you can engage in creative problem solving. What do you really want from life? When you get those things, what will they really mean? What will you have to give up to get those things? Where do you want to be in a year, in five years? As you understand and clarify your goals, the need for enhancing some roles and pruning others becomes evident.

The remaining step is to take action. The action, though, is best taken not by announcing the grand plan, the new strategy, the new self. The best steps into action are to quietly withdraw energy and participation from the roles due to be pruned.

One of the main reasons for quiet withdrawal is that most roles are reciprocal. There is both a driving force in us to engage the role and, as well, a pulling force from others that draws our energies into the role. In announcing your intention to abandon a given role or to scale down your involvement, you may well intensify the other party's efforts to keep you in your former mode. To initiate the role-changing process, especially the first few times, you are going to need all the help you can get, and intensifying the other party's efforts to keep you in place is no help. It's stacking the cards against you.

Indeed, many of us often engage in a neurotic pattern to intensify the bonding in a role. We become the child who announces he is going to run away so his parents will become more closely involved with him. We are the employee whose threats of quitting are really a cry for assurance that she is needed.

As your energy is drawn silently from a role, two things happen. First, it provides encouragement to you that you can change your life situation; second, from the other party's perspective, that person will begin to depend on you less because you are less visible. Remember that for the most part each of us is in a web of roles. As the strands that you represent in others' webs weaken, those people will intensify their remaining strands, their roles with others. Alienating environments and high social change are situations that minimize our control of events that affect us, but we always have two choices. We can alter the factors in our immediate environment or change environments. Returning to the Response Matrix, we must choose the mix of internal and external change that is available to us in each situation. In some cases, ample resources are available to make external changes. In other situations, we must simply internally shift our expectations.

Remember burnout comes from a discrepancy between what we expect from our roles and what actually occurs. Stress increases our susceptibility to burnout, as does working in alienating environments. Dealing with burnout requires that we develop methods to lessen the impact of stress as well as avoid continuously stressful situations.

SELF-ANCHORING

Here's a short experiment to illustrate the relationship between your version of what you feel you should be, your self-concept, and the world about you. You need a pocket compass and several small magnets. First, set the compass down and let the needle swing around and stabilize to magnetic north. Think of the needle as being your self-concept and the condition of stability, with the needle pointing toward magnetic north, as the self-concept under traditional times, largely constant, unvarying, controlled by powerful unchanging forces.

Now, place one of the small magnets a few inches from the compass at the three o'clock position. The needle will first destabilize, swinging widely, but then will come to rest at some balance between magnetic north and the small magnet. This condition represents the situation of the self-concept as tradition wanes and employment begins to occur. The self is balanced between tradition and the job.

Now, position several more magnets around the compass. It again becomes destabilized and the needle swings widely and erratically. This is a representation of the self-concept under multiple roles. In time, a balance can be achieved, but it is a much more sensitive balance, tenuous and volatile.

Next, begin to move some of the magnets about, two or more at the same time. Now we see the self in the temporary world, first anchoring in one direction then another. Movement is quick and unpredictable. The self becomes disposable.

Self-anchoring is the final step in this experiment and would be represented by demagnetizing the compass needle. Now the needle would no longer be moved through discernible external forces but rather responds to some other field of forces.

Demagnetization or self-anchoring is a process that is increased through expanding individual consciousness. The act of understanding the expectations you hold and then of designing your expectations is the process of self-anchoring.

Coping with Burnout in the Organization

To speak of certain government and establishment institutions as "the system" is to speak correctly, since these organizations are founded upon the same structural conceptual relationships as a motorcycle. They are sustained by structural relationships even when they have lost all other meaning and purpose. People arrive at a factory and perform a totally meaningless task from eight to five without question because the structure demands that it be that way.

Robert Pirsig, *Zen and the Art of Motorcycle Maintenance.*

Burnout results from holding expectations that are not met. In jobs where there is a heavy emphasis on achievement and a sense of personal responsibility for failure or success, falling short of expectations is a continual threat. Organizations that place high pressure for achievement risk, as well, high likelihood for burnout. As long as progress toward goals occurs, burnout will be at low levels among employees. However, if competition increases or the public loses interest in the services or products of the organization, success will lessen and burnout will increase. Declining industries may encounter more burnout than vigorous ones, and less successful companies may have more burnout than more successful organizations.

One of the more critical challenges of our times is learning how to develop organizations that are productive, efficient, responsive to change and can compel the loyalty and involvement of their members. The family farm and the family company had loyalty and involvement but were often inefficient and resistant to change. The scientifically managed corporation could offer productivity and efficiency yet employee loyalty and involvement were elusive.

It is important to recognize that social forms like the family farm or the assembly line factory are dependent on particular mentalities, consciousness or, as I have elaborated, self-concepts. When self-concepts and social organization fail to match, burnout occurs. It may well be that social change now requires a different sort of self-concept and different forms of social organizations.

HOW ORGANIZATIONS CAN CAUSE BURNOUT

If reality and achievement fall below what a person expects, burnout will begin. The goals and objectives of an organization are essentially the organization's expectations and to some degree these expectations become internalized by the organization's employees. In setting expectations, the organization may contribute to burnout. There are three ways in which this may occur:

The organization sets expectations too high.

The organization does not set clear expectations or changes them frequently.

The organization fails to provide environmental conditions for employees to achieve expectations.

Organizations set expectations too high when they set goals that are not achievable or appear to be unachievable. Several years ago, I worked for a large retail chain that did a high-volume business selling appliances that required home installation such as washers, refrigerators, air conditioners, and the like. One spring, the company initiated an incentive project for personnel who handled the installations. All employees were paid a minimum rate but had to make a certain number of installations to earn that rate and keep their jobs. Each particular appliance had a rate value so that an item like an air conditioner which was difficult to install would earn more points than a refrigerator which was usually easy to install. Employees whose rate of installation was above the minimum earned incentive income and could potentially double their base salary.

However, within a month, installers began to find that they had their hands full meeting the minimum. As the weeks went by, no one beat minimums and confusion turned to frustration and anger. Retail store outlet after retail store outlet was flooded by complaints about sloppy installations and surly personnel.

The company held an early Saturday morning meeting at each store to set weekly sales goals and to go over problems. Local store managers found themselves besieged by angry questions about how the minimum rates were set and for names of anyone in the country who could beat minimums. In three months, the incentive plan was cancelled but the damage was done. Sales declined by 15 percent during that period and customer complaints tripled.

Organizations may fail to set clear expectations or change expectations too frequently. A friend of mine loves to tell the story of the conglomerate that took a dozen financially sound and profitable businesses and combined them into a single failure. How was it done? By changing goals to achieve synergistic feedback. So much time was spent in involving top personnel in each concern to develop new goals that the old goals were lost.

Organizations may fail to provide environmental conditions for employees to achieve expectations. A colleague of mine spent a year in Japan in the mid-seventies studying the ingredients of success in Japanese corporations. I was particularly impressed by his description of the plant that produced Nikon cameras. Expecting to find a modern facility with surgical-like controls for a clean, dust-free environment, he found instead an old building with work spaces often cluttered and dusty. However, he found as well what others have reported about some Japanese corporations. Every worker maintained high involvement in the tasks of making camera bodies and lenses and felt a personal responsibility for the quality of the product. Though the work areas had many environmental shortcomings, each worker was able to handle the tasks without the environment acting as interference. The important dimension my friend saw for workers in this environment was the control they exercised over their particular tasks. If, for example, any part appeared defective or if the worker discovered a better way of making an element, the worker felt free, actually rewarded, in bringing this to the attention of his supervisor. While quality of working conditions seemed less than adequate, the important dimension to the worker was the environmental freedom to invest himself in his task and the control he held in the task.

Too often organizations today still do not go beyond the industrial revolution's formula of material, tools, and workers in the definition of organizational production. Successful enterprise requires a market, raw materials, and two forms of capital: technology and people. For many years, technology has been seen as a people-substitute rather than viewing both items as areas of capital investment. Technology is not an alternative to trained, dedicated, and capable people.

It is important to realize that the source of burnout may not be related to the job. The literature on job satisfaction and productivity is largely directed to on-the-job factors; yet many of the challenges to management are issues that come from the other parts of the employee's life. While the contemporary view of individuals emphasizes multiple roles, with persons playing the work role during business hours and setting aside other roles until the appropriate social setting, I feel that that arrangement is inherently unstable and is now beginning to fall by the wayside. Absenteeism, alcoholism on the job, and a general malaise among employees about the meaning of work are the negative indicators of a management approach that ignores the full individual and focuses solely on the work role.

As individual self-concepts move from a plastic skill in playing one role and then the next to a demand for personal continuity and authenticity, organizations must respond by developing procedures to permit employees greater involvement in designing and defining work tasks. This will mean a much greater emphasis on involving employees in understanding what the organization's goals are and how those goals are dependent on the efforts of each specific individual.

WORK FACTORS AND BURNOUT

Work and conditions associated with the job may or may not contribute to burnout. There are five general categories of factors associated with work and job conditions that can lead to burnout. These five categories are: work conditions, performance standards, feedback and control, type of task, and human interaction.

Work conditions refers to the physical setting. Is it quiet or noisy? Is there adequate heat, ventilation, cooling, and lighting? Are dangerous machinery or chemicals in the setting?

Performance standards relates to the goals of the organization and how they are interpreted in each work task and job. Are standards clear, meaningful, and realistic? Do workers have an opportunity to participate in setting standards?

Feedback and control are defined by what kind of information workers are receiving about their work and its quality. How do workers know or judge the quality of their work? What kind of control do they have over their work? Are they permitted to stop the work process to investigate what they are doing and redesign tasks? How willing is management to accept worker innovations?

Type of task refers to factors associated with complexity, predictability, boredom, and importance. Is the task simple or complex? Is it done repeatedly or is there high variation from day to day or week to week? How predictable is the task? Does one know what usually will happen or is every event unique? Can the worker vary the task or is repetition required and, thus, boredom likely? How critical is the task? What other things hinge on it? What is the consequence of a mistake?

Human interaction is a measure of how the worker relates to peers and supervisors. How are workers perceived? Are workers seen as replaceable parts that inevitably wear out? Can workers discuss jobs, techniques, seek assistance from each other? Are workers viewed as necessary but potential problems to be anticipated? Is just keeping workers happy or quiet a major concern? How great is the distance between management levels? Do employees at various levels have separate facilities such as parking spots, cafeterias, recreation areas? What is the level of social distance between people?

These factors can contribute to burnout in two general ways. One way is through conditions and tasks that are physically and mentally exhausting. Exhaustion leads to performance decline and thus failure of expectations. The other way these factors promote burnout is through conditions where the worker cannot develop and check expectations.

Ambiguity and loss of control cause burnout since expectations cannot be reached. The factors can be adjusted by the organization to lessen the likelihood of burnout.

High Potential for Burnout	Low Potential for Burnout
High pressure work conditions, demands for perfect performance	Performance standards are set more by employee than organization
Frequent deadline pressure with rescheduling difficult	Little deadline pressure or rescheduling is readily possible
Tasks are dangerous, potentially harmful to employee or others	Tasks are not dangerous, no threats in work environment
Work environment is noisy, filled with interruptions, e.g., phones ringing, unexpected visitors	Tranquil, relaxed atmosphere
Work is monotonous, little opportunity to do other tasks or vary work speed	Work is variable with many different types of tasks and employee may vary task selection
Work seems meaningless, little feedback to worker or quality of effort	Work has good feedback quality, employee knows when a good job is done
Little or poor human interaction, person must work alone or interaction with others is incidental to work	Much work is in a team with others, good opportunities for involvement around work
Task is low status in the organization or in the outside world	Tasks have high prestige either in the organization or in the outside world
Job has been devalued, is seen as less critical or important than two or three years ago	Job has grown in prestige in the last two or three years
Job has unpredictable characteristics, it is difficult to achieve or predict high performance, chance plays a large role in success	Employee has considerable control over the likelihood of success, hard work will bring rewards
Job is dead-end, increases in responsibility, pay, or esteem are unlikely	Job has built-in features for earned increases in responsibility, pay, or esteem

Figure 6
Job Design Factors in Burnout

These five categories are listed in a series of design factors in figure 6 according to high- and low-potential for burnout. Every work setting and every job should be assessed in terms of these factors and vulnerable jobs and settings identified that have high likelihood for producing burnout.

After assessing each job, supervisors should take steps to redesign jobs to lessen the potential for creating burnout. Feedback, for instance, can be increased in many jobs through the effort of a supervisor in stating what constitutes good quality work. Group critique sessions are helpful by having teams that perform the same or related tasks look at all the tasks to see how quality can be improved and the work climate made more responsive.

The assessment effort is worthwhile even if one is not a supervisor or with jobs with aspects that are difficult to change (the social value or prestige of a job). Knowing what one can and cannot change about a job builds realistic expectations.

BURNOUT CONTAGION

Most people are highly social creatures and are affected by the moods and attitudes of friends and colleagues. Consequently, individuals may be influenced by others experiencing burnout. When a person becomes highly disillusioned, he or she may express this disillusionment to another person and both will find comfort in the other's misery. Most supervisors are familiar with the situation of an unhappy and disgruntled person causing a rise in the general level of discontent among other workers. Indeed the only initiative such a burned-out individual will show is the desire to convince others that they, too, should be burned-out.

Managers must be aware quickly when one of their supervisees begins to burn out. Particularly at Stage II, anger and frustration, the feeling is likely to spread to other employees. At this stage, the individual may feel that because he is not meeting his expectations he has been misled and deceived. A manager must, at all costs, not avoid this matter hoping it will go away. If ignored, the disgruntled employee will perceive that his feelings of anger and frustration are justified. The employer is seen as a manipulator and the individual may quickly rally others to the cause. Where unionization is possible, it will flourish under these conditions. A union is, after all, an instrument employees may use to try to ensure their expectations.

If such social mobilization through unionization or other employee collective efforts does not succeed, the contagion moves to the third stage of burnout, despair. Workers who are able to find other jobs quietly move on. The workers who must stay behind grow cautious and, though often resentful, become wary of expressing their feelings. The organization may take on a quality of a doomed ship sailing to oblivion.

Of course, no manager can anticipate burnout in every employee and the source of burnout for a given employee may not be job-related; but, to the extent that work and organizational factors that promote burnout are present, one affected employee may become like a spark in dry tinder.

WHAT MANAGERS CAN DO

Perhaps the most important thing managers can do in dealing with burnout in the organization is to avoid burnout for themselves. This means managers must be aware of their own roles and the expectations in the roles. They must develop skills in appraising how realistic their expectations are and assessing resources in the environment. They must develop a sense of their own limits and know when they need to get away, to cool out. The preceding chapter suggests a number of procedures for cooling out and provides some tools to help managers cope with their own burnout.

Now, let's look at an individual in the role of a manager. From the perspective of the role of a manager, what can be done to help others cope with burnout?

There are, in actuality, three separate dimensions to the tasks of management today. Dimension One is the maintenance of the work effort. Does work meet the standards of quality and quantity? Dimension Two is the design of the work environment and task procedures. This is a collaborative activity between supervisor and supervisee. The checklist in figure 6 illustrates an aspect of this dimension. Dimension Three is coaching the employee on his expectations—assisting the employee in setting high yet feasible expectations. Often one comes to expect too much from one's work. Work should be able to provide satisfaction but not necessarily total fulfillment. Sometimes a manager has to get that message across.

At Dimension One these are the responsibilities of the manager in lessening burnout:

- Translate organizational goals and objectives into personal expectations and expectations for those supervised.

- Clarify expectations for employees and actively advocate for them when clear expectations are lacking or change too quickly.
- Review expectations to see how realistic they are. Managers have as much responsibility to the organization to interpret unlikely or impossible goals as to those they supervise.

Dimension Two is concerned with the efforts of the manager in changing the work environment and in the layout of job tasks. There are several activities available to managers to lessen burnout-producing conditions in the design of jobs. Here are some readily available steps.

1. Use figure 6 as a checklist and rate every job for which you are responsible.
2. Rank order jobs from most likely to produce burnout to least likely.
3. Take those jobs most likely to produce burnout and see which factors you may be able to change. For example, look at a job's performance standards. Try to commit to writing what constitutes a good effort. Try to relate the quality of that effort to the goals of the organization.
4. Begin to use these efforts as part of your management practices with those you supervise. Schedule regular conferences with each person you supervise to involve that person in examining each job by these design factors. Make mutual efforts to improve the design of each job a part of these conferences.

Managers, and each person they supervise, should always be alert to ways of revising tasks to make work more efficient and more pleasing. This must be a continual concern and the annual conference is a way of taking stock to remind each other of the process and review the year's accomplishments.

Dimension Three in the tasks of management is coaching the employee on expectations. Among the various responsibilities of management perhaps the least understood is how the manager is involved in the design of the employee's expectations. For the employee, the manager is the immediate human embodiment of the organization's purposes and goals. How these purposes and goals are reflected plays the largest single part in determining how an employee's job expectations develop.

Less competent managers are typically unaware of the process and may opt either to let the employee set expectations independently or narrowly focus on the work task. Either approach is an abdication of management's larger responsibility to the employee and to the organization. This larger responsibility is helping each employee set appropriate expectations and then assisting the employee in raising expectations as his or her ability grows.

The two elements that govern the degree of burnout are the external reality and the individual's expectations. A manager can and must serve as a reality check on both dimensions. A new employee may want to rise to the top in three years, earn twice as much salary in four years, or receive a total sense of fulfillment from the job. Part of a manager's job is to help an employee understand how realistic and how feasible these expectations are.

How do you as a manager participate in the design of expectations? Use the Designing Expectations tools and steps in the previous chapter. Focus the effort around job expectations and spell out the mutual expectations between yourself and each person you supervise. Suggest that the employee use the process personally for his or her other roles. Keep in mind that the goal is to increase each worker's awareness of his or her expectations, how they can be reached, and how feasible they are. The process should be done with each employee whenever you notice indicators of burnout.

The next step the manager should take is to work with the employee and assess what his or her expectations are. The employee's sense of failed expectations must be taken head-on. Often a few days off or a temporary new assignment is helpful. This breaks the communication cycle with other workers that may lead to their burnout though communication off the job cannot be controlled and should not be attempted.

If this "Quick Break" response does not work, then the manager and the employee must achieve some form of the "Compromise Response." A "Compromise Response" requires the manager to schedule a conference with the employee and then to spell out mutual expectations. Often a manager and an employee's expectations of each other resemble those of Harvey Eagleton and his boss that we looked at in the previous chapter. After both the manager and the employee arrive at mutual expectations then the manager must set some short-term objectives to see if the expectations can be met.

Finally, when neither is effective, and the employee is not producing up to standard, the manager often has no alternative but to take steps to effect the employee's termination. Remember that an important element in dealing with burnout and in achieving effective supervision is to attain an appropriate match between the manager's expectations and the employee's expectations. Forcing a "Fresh Start" response is the manager's last resort.

It is useful to keep in mind that the source of burnout can be other than job roles. All too often the work role appears as a noninvolved bystander in an individual's burnout. However, burnout in one role may lead to problems in other roles. Going through the steps of Designing Expectations can help an employee see that the sources of dissatisfaction are localized in roles other than work.

The first line of defense in dealing with burnout in the organization is the manager. Management failure can set ripe conditions for burnout contagion. When, as a supervisor or as a colleague, you see your team or co-workers start to exhibit burnout's early symptoms, there are measures that can be taken to stop the burnout. The first step is to make the person aware of the syndrome. Remember the three-step sequence: confusion, frustration, despair. Burnout is easiest to deal with at the confusion level. The person may need help in articulating goals and examining how realistic those goals are. Keep in mind that an organization's unrealistic goals can develop unintentionally. Sometimes goals are left over from an earlier period when conditions were different or inadequate attention was given to goal formulation. Finally, it is important for the manager to encourage the participation of supervisees in organizational training programs. Programs such as those that deal with job stress, burnout, and work planning and review can help the employee learn to clarify expectations and select realistic ones.

ROLES IN THE DESIGN OF EXPECTATIONS FOR TRAINERS AND HUMAN RESOURCE DEVELOPMENT STAFF

Building staff competence in an organization is an important emphasis in personnel relations that has grown in this country for the last two decades. The importance of this change can be seen through the increased prominence of human resource development or training functions in organizations.

The roles for trainers and human resource development personnel in preventing burnout and lessening its effect can be divided into three categories of activity.

Organizational diagnosis. Using questionnaires and observations as well as personnel records to determine level of burnout through absenteeism, illnesses, job turnover, employee attitudes, and rating job sites with high burnout level. An important aspect of the diagnosis is to ascertain the management competence of supervisors and their general awareness of the burnout process.

Training programs. Activities that increase the manager's and employee's awareness of what burnout is and techniques for dealing with burnout. In addition to direct efforts for dealing with burnout, attention should be paid to other training programs that indirectly lessen burnout (programs dealing with improving management practices, employee coaching, performance feedback, and so on).

Providing consultation to employees and managers. A very useful process is a three-way consultation between manager, employee, and trainer. The trainer can assist managers and employees in learning a mutual process of clarifying and adjusting expectations.

A crucial role that human resource development personnel can play is in early diagnosis of burnout. Typically supervisors, as well as employees, fail to see burnout in themselves or others until the syndrome is at the level of frustration or despair. Human resource specialists offer the best perspective for early detection of such problems, especially when many employees in a working unit or team are involved. The training or human resource development office can assist in diagnosing burnout and leading conferences between managers and employees in understanding its causes.

Training personnel should be active as well in assessing the expectations of workers in the organization. Since managers must be involved in coaching employees to set appropriate expectations, there is a continuing need for information about worker expectations. Training personnel can meet the important function of developing such information and are needed to work with managers in assessing realistic expectations.

Adjusting expectations, like redesigning jobs, will be a new task for many managers. Learning how to adjust expectations can be a demanding challenge for a manager and teaching these techniques is an appropriate and necessary training role. A number of the materials in this book can be used by trainers to help managers and employees alike assess personal levels of burnout and develop more effective coping strategies. It is important to remember vulnerability to burnout cannot be eliminated, so these efforts must be seen as ongoing responsibilities.

An extension of the "Role Mapping Process" is a helpful tool for trainers when working with employees and supervisors. Ask employees to write down their expectations for their jobs and at the same time have the supervisor write his or her expectations for each employee. This quickly identifies the gaps or lack of fit between the two roles and provides a basis of negotiation for mutual resolution. In many cases, it may be necessary to include the map of expectations from co-workers or other units in complex work settings. The critical role for the trainer is to make manifest the implicit expectations of the various parties. Unrealistic expectations from others, like unrealistic expectations of one's self, increase the likelihood of burnout.

Trainers and human resource development personnel are the second line of defense against burnout contagion. By the time burnout comes to the trainers' attention, usually several people are involved and managers are demoralized. Training at a site away from the employment setting for a two- to three-day period is useful. Don't overschedule the day. Build in some time for recreation and relaxation. To begin to deal with burnout you need to get people to think introspectively, in other words to cool out. Introduce the Response Matrix and take people through "Designing Expectations." Training, of course, must include the supervisor with the work team.

Understanding the relation between job factors and burnout means that every employee must begin to assume much greater responsibility for his or her job and ways in which it can be done better. Getting the employee to assume such responsibility is both a supervision and a training effort.

NEW CHALLENGES FOR THE MANAGER AND THE TRAINER

Bringing people together and getting their creative participation in the work place will be needed more in the future than ever before. Organizations will require staff who can deal effectively with forming new work groups and enhancing each member's involvement. Accommodating to new goals and being able to realistically appraise feasible goals may prove to be the most important competencies any employee can bring to the job.

As a partial consequence of social change and the parallel change in personal identity, employees today have a much greater awareness of the world and want to know how a given role fits into the world. Two short phrases can sum this up: relevant work and meaningful work.

A couple of generations ago, having money to buy basic necessities was enough return from a job for it to be meaningful. At times, having a job was sufficient meaning in itself. Today, however, many people ask for a sense of meaning, actually coherence, that requires a fuller answer. Such demands require management to relate company goals to the world and to the employee as well. The insurance company or the bank has to be able to explain to the employee what its goals are and how those goals fit in a coherent world view.

Management must, moreover, translate broad organizational goals to each local work unit. When workers see their jobs as meaningless, as dead-ends, management has failed. When rules and procedures lose their relationship to goals, when individual tasks appear discrete and unrelated, when work consists of "going through the motions," when management resorts to motivating workers solely with pay and benefits, work loses its coherence. Making and keeping work coherent is perhaps the greatest of the tasks of management.

Finally, every manager, every supervisor, each employee must understand the difference between a condition and a problem. A condition is a situation that, though it may be undesirable, is beyond individual, or perhaps human, control. A problem is, on the other hand, a situation that is inherently available to human control, that has a solution. The manager who feels the existence of staff disagreements is a problem that can be eliminated has mistaken a condition for a problem. Whenever people work together, some level of disagreement will be there. To set a goal of no disagreement is to set an impossible goal. There are many human problems that, at least for the individual, are better understood as human conditions. When a person or a group misunderstands a condition for a problem and sets a goal to solve or eliminate the problem, burnout will result.

As a culture, we are particularly fond of our myth that anything is achievable. No problem too complex. The difficult takes just a while; the impossible, a bit longer. No distance is too far; no challenge, too great. But, such statements are simply adolescent fantasies. There are challenges too great, distances too far. While it is necessary to believe something is possible before it may be accomplished, there are many things that, even with belief, remain impossible. While it may be said that nothing is lost in trying, that is often not true. The opportunity is lost and usually other resources as well.

The effective manager understands which goals are feasible, which are far-fetched, and which are in the realm of the impossible. Avoiding burnout means setting realistic goals and keeping them realistic.

The modern organization has much more complex technology but fewer jobs where people do machinelike work. In early factories, most tasks required people to work like machines. Indeed, workers and machines were seen as appendages of each other. Workers today are becoming more involved in complex decisional tasks and less in routine work which is easily shifted to a machine mode. As a consequence, the human side of the organizational equation of people, capital, and equipment begins to assume a different meaning. People change from being a replaceable part in the machinery to a part of the decision-making structure. Their involvement is needed in determining how to manufacture a given product or to deliver a given service. Employees become resources to be carefully developed and appropriately involved.

A Final Word

The previous pages have assumed that it is possible for people to change their lives, their surroundings, and how they relate to others. This concept of the individual having control over his or her life was greatly boosted over two hundred years ago in the Age of Reason, when philosophers argued that men could control their own destiny. Democracy and the American Republic grew from the seeds of these thoughts put forth many years ago and the individualism of today has its origin there.

The independence of the individual, though, seems to produce a considerable burden. The burden, in its sparest form, is that our condition in life is our own responsibility. While we may construct various social supports, either through voluntary action or government efforts, it is assumed that, as adults, we should be independent, self-supporting, and self-determining. However, when our expectations of ourselves, of what we do with our independence, are greater than our actual achievements, burnout may begin. To resolve this burnout, we may try to either change the external environment, including the expectations of others, or we can try to alter our own expectations.

It may prove helpful to visualize our environment as composed of spheres. There are different levels for each sphere based on the amount of influence we have in implementing change in that sphere. Each person may be seen as existing in a series of ever-larger spheres. Our most immediate sphere, and the one we have the greatest control over, is the self-system. The self-system includes our expectations, our past experiences, our abilities, our physical body.

The next larger sphere is the family system. It may vary from memories of mother, to children, cousins, aunts, and uncles, and family friends. We have no choice about the family in which we are born, but we do have considerable choices about family roles in adulthood. For example, a person born in a family with seven children where just getting food on the table was a continual struggle may choose, as an adult, not to have children rather than make the sacrifices a family requires.

The third sphere might be called the ecological system. It includes our place of work and our neighborhood, our type of job, religion and social class. For some of us, our ecologies are the cities; for others, the suburbs; for others, small towns and rural areas. Each choice has its opportunities and its drawbacks.

The fourth sphere is the cultural system. It includes the country in which we live, the language we speak, our government and available technology.

The fifth sphere is the earth and our universe. At this level, individuals become insignificant. The earth, the sun, the countless stars are not moved much by our expectations.

The first three spheres are areas in which one might achieve some change. Each of us can choose to lead a more healthy life, or read more, or worry less, and have a fair chance of reaching success. In the same fashion, a person can make some changes in the family system. Better relations with children or parents can be reached. Each of us can find interesting persons to be with who respect and enjoy our company.

We can have impact, as well, in our immediate ecology. However, we cannot *readily* bring change to our companies, our professions, or our neighborhoods. For change to occur in the ecological sphere others, far beyond ourselves and our immediate circle, must change. That may occur, but chances are we will not be the original cause of the change—only a step along the way. Change in the whole country usually requires change within many individuals. If we direct our energies for change in those spheres closest to us, our likelihood of success will be greatest.

Part II

Speculations on Evolving Paradigms

Part I of this book has been directed to an examination of the immediate sensations and causes associated with burnout. While most of the literature about burnout, and stress and job satisfaction as well, focuses on the work place, the job, and the organization as the important points of consideration for lessening burnout, it is my contention that such efforts are restricted only to the most proximate factors that produce burnout. There are often factors, more distant and yet more powerful and pervasive, that account for the proximate causes—expectations that exceed what is achieved. Moreover, feelings of burnout are not restricted to work. Some individuals experience burnout in school, in family life, and with life in general.

To attempt to explain burnout solely with reference to work place factors is either to assert that the work place is the sum total of life or to miss completely the connection between expectations and the larger culture. Complete reliance on proximate factors is akin to explaining a murder in terms of the effect the bullet has on striking the heart. At least as important to the explanation is the presence of a gun, someone's finger on the trigger, and the relationship between the person holding the gun and the person who is shot.

Part II is devoted to the larger contextual pattern of individual expectations and striving. The first chapter of the section is historical and examines some characteristics of early societies and the types of consciousness found in historical periods. The changes in awareness and the accelerating rate of change itself are related to burnout.

Chapter 12 casts alternative cultural realities into an individual world perspective or paradigm. The definition of work and theories of management are seen as rooted in a given paradigm. A case is constructed in this chapter for a definition of individual reality which is paradigm-based and the change in reality is related to the shift from one paradigm to the next.

Chapter 13 examines how a paradigm builds a personal consciousness for the individual and how the Technocratic Paradigm controls that consciousness through bureaucratic structures. In this chapter, burnout is viewed as a peculiar symptom of the paradigm governing our times and a warning as well to the inherent instability of the paradigm.

Chapter 14 is an enlargement of the paradigm conditions introduced in the previous chapter. The role of scientific advancement is considered as well as cultural modes of adapting to change. The chapter reviews the motive forces behind the paradigm and explores some of the many paradoxes that begin to loom large.

Chapter 15 compares current conditions to the reality demanded by the Technocratic Paradigm. These conditions pose paradoxes that the paradigm seems unable to resolve and an origin for the paradoxes is identified.

The final chapter of the section, chapter 16, is mostly conjectural. It attempts to anticipate the future and suggests an alternate paradigm if the current one is truly passing. For this chapter, and throughout Part II, burnout is interpreted not as an individual problem but as the consequence of a society dominated by an external achievement orientation. It is argued that the success, not the failure, of this orientation produces burnout and that the solution to burnout will result in a more internally-oriented personal perspective.

11

The Chambered Nautilus

Then Zeus, far seeing, made another race of man, the fifth, who live upon the fruitful earth. Would that I had no share in this fifth race of men, would that I had died before or afterwards been born. This is the race of iron. Not for a day do they cease from toil and labor, not for a night does their corruption cease. The gods will give them bitter sorrow to endure. Yet still some good things shall be mingled with the bad.

Hesiod, *Works and Days.* As quoted in *An Introduction to Early Greek Philosophy.*

To see a world in a grain of sand
And a heaven in a wild flower
Held infinity in the palm of your hand
An eternity in an hour.

William Blake, "Auguries of Innocence."

The glories of our blood and state
  Are shadows, not substantial things,
There is no armor against fate,
  Death lays his icy hand on kings,
  Scepter and crown
  Must tumble down
And in the dust be made
  With the poor crooked scythe and spade.

James Shirley, "The Contention of Ajax
  and Ulysses for the Armor of Achilles."

The world is very old, perhaps four or five billion years, the universe three times that. Life too is ancient, more than three billion years. Humanlike creatures appeared on earth no less than two million years ago; remnants of civilization date back to the last Ice Age.

There are millions of forms of life on earth: two million species of insects, two hundred thousand species of deciduous trees, and twenty thousand kinds of fish. Life is found at elevations above twenty thousand feet and in deep undersea trenches.

Earth itself, along with eight other planets and broken hunks of rock, some as large as mountains, orbits the sun—a nondescript young to middle-aged star of medium size in a small backwater region of the Milky Way galaxy. There are perhaps 100 billion stars in our galaxy alone. Five to ten times as many stars as there have been people that have ever lived. And this is only our local galaxy. There are billions of other such galaxies out there in that vast universe.

What was here before the universe was here and what will be here after it is gone? If stars are contained in galaxies and galaxies in universes, what is the universe contained within?

Men, women, the genus is *Homo*; the species is *sapiens*. We exist far from the center of the universe and are not the oldest form of social being. In fact, we don't even have a particularly long life span. There are some bristlecone pine trees in the mountains east of Los Angeles that were sturdy saplings when Christ lived, preached, and died.

From all available evidence, our form of life has never been too abundant. After thousands of years of existence, the species probably did not exceed 10 million members, living and dead, until the end of the Stone Age. When recorded time began, perhaps there were 5 million people, maybe 300 million in A.D. 1, and the billion mark was not reached until 1800. It took 130 years to reach the second billion in 1930. The third billion was reached in 1960 and the fourth in 1975. However, this geometric progression of growth appears to have peaked and is now ascending at a slower rate.

At birth, the human is one of the most helpless forms of infant life. Humans come into the world with very few wired-in instructions. A baby can distinguish heat from cold and dark from light. It can nurse and cry but not a great deal more. Compare it to a newly hatched baby turtle which can immediately fend for itself, and one wonders why the operating instructions were left out.

A TIME OF TRANSFORMATION

In spite of being very recent inhabitants of Earth, formerly few in number and relatively fragile, humans have become the most predominant life form on the planet and even locally in the solar system during the last decade. In a sense, in the past hundred years, we have transformed ourselves from creatures at the mercy of disease, famine, and weather to beings with only one real enemy—ourselves.

Recently, we have begun to depart the cradle of our creation, Earth, and to pry apart the molecular nature of our being. We have started to gather the keys that unlock the puzzles of many of our greatest mysteries and may properly suspect that we are at a watershed in human existence. Several potential paths lead from this point and none are clear or certain. What many have suspected may prove to be true: that humans are a transitional species. Unlike the shark that swims in a form similar to its ancestor of the Devonian seas of 200 million years ago or the cockroach which, like the shark, is an unchanging form of life, humans are in a constant state of change. Lacking high specialization, endowed with a marvelously plastic intelligence, and thus possessing a purely dangerous opportunity, we shall either transform ourselves or extinguish ourselves. That is the unique potentiality within our species.

The following pages address the events that brought us up to this time of transformation. Within them, there is an attempt to examine not so much the current human condition but the individual mood at this launching point. Considerable attention is devoted to surveying this mood, its relation to social life, and to sketching the outlines of a general framework of what has led up to this transition point and what may lie beyond.

Even at our greatest moments, in our most sublime accomplishments, we humans are made of flesh, composed of the minerals of the earth itself. To capture the meaning of the potential of transformation, to arrive at the launching point, we must first look to some of our most humble, day-to-day thoughts. From the content of these thoughts, from their direction and flow, we can plumb the murky depths of social existence and then rise to the surface. At the surface, we must test the speed and direction of the wind. Having done this, then perhaps we might venture to guess how close we are to the transition time and what that time may be or how that time may appear.

The thoughts of everyday life—our hopes, our satisfactions, our fantasies, our dreams—these are what we must assay. We must know their meaning and their origin. We must look at how we view the world, how we explain it, and how we think it operates. Ground must always be prepared before change may come. New ingredients must be sought. Unsuspected combinations will occur. It will seem the best of times and the worst of times. This is the stuff of which change is made or permanence composed. Change will come when thoughts change, but awareness of the change may occur only long after movement is begun.

ECHOES FROM ANTIQUITY

The form of the human being, *Homo sapiens*, common to the world today emerged only recently in geological history, perhaps no more than one to two hundred thousand years ago. If a lifetime is judged from Biblical accounts to be three score and ten or seventy years, the length of existence of modern human beings is, at most, about three thousand lifetimes. Carl Sagan (1977) has illustrated the length of time since the origin of the universe (perhaps fifteen billion years) by compressing that time into a single Cosmic Year which makes a billion of our years equal to twenty-four days of Cosmic Time. He uses a Cosmic Calendar (figure 7) to represent the events of that Cosmic Year. One second in this Cosmic Calendar is equal to 475 of our own years.

January 1st on this Cosmic Calendar is the Big Bang, when the universe was created. The present moment is the first second in Cosmic Year number two. By this calendar, the origin of life on Earth did not occur until September 25th of the Cosmic Year and the first fish did not appear until December 19th. The mammals began to inhabit the wetlands of the Triassic period on the 26th of December, and *Homo sapiens* stood erect for the first time at 11:00 p.m. on the last day of the year, December 31st. Such a reckoning of history minimizes somewhat the significance of humans and indicates we are much less central to the scheme of things than we might wish to think.

Using this Cosmic Calendar device, it was less than a second ago in 1650 when Archbishop Ussher declared to the Christian world that God, by the account of Genesis, created the world on the night preceding Sunday, October 23, 4004 B.C. However, the geological record, carbon 14 dating, and data acquired from radio telescopes have permitted modern theorizing to push the age of the universe back far earlier than this theological account. Indeed, some freewheeling thinkers suggest that the Big Bang, which occurred some fifteen billion years ago by their calculations, was preceded by another universe that collapsed into some highly dense, primordial molecule and then exploded and created the current universe.

Big Bang	January 1
Origin of the Milky Way Galaxy	May 1
Origin of the solar system	September 9
Formation of the Earth	September 14
Origin of life on Earth	~ September 25
Formation of the oldest rocks known on Earth	October 2
Date of oldest fossils (bacteria and blue-green algae)	October 9
Invention of sex (by microorganisms)	~ November 1
Oldest fossil photosynthetic plants	November 12
Eukaryotes (first cells with nuclei) flourish	November 15

COSMIC CALENDAR   ~ = *approximately*

DECEMBER

SUNDAY	MONDAY	TUESDAY	WEDNESDAY	THURSDAY	FRIDAY	SATURDAY
	1 Significant oxygen atmosphere begins to develop on Earth.				**5** Extensive vulcanism and channel formation on Mars.	
		16 First worms.	**17** Precambrian ends. Paleozoic Era and Cambrian Period begin. Invertebrates flourish.	**18** First oceanic plankton. Trilobites flourish.	**19** Ordovician Period. First fish, first vertebrates.	**20** Silurian Period. First vascular plants. Plants begin colonization of land.
21 Devonian Period begins. First insects. Animals begin colonization of land.	**22** First amphibians. First winged insects.	**23** Carboniferous Period. First trees. First reptiles.	**24** Permian Period begins. First dinosaurs.	**25** Paleozoic Era ends. Mesozoic Era begins.	**26** Triassic Period. First mammals.	**27** Jurassic Period. First birds.
28 Cretaceous Period. First flowers. Dinosaurs become extinct.	**29** Mesozoic Era ends. Cenozoic Era and Tertiary Period begin. First cetaceans. First primates.	**30** Early evolution of frontal lobes in the brains of primates. First hominids. Giant mammals flourish.	**31** End of the Pliocene Period. Quaternary (Pleistocene and Holocene Period. First humans.			

Figure 7
The Cosmic Calendar

From *The Dragons of Eden: Speculations On the Evolution of Human Intelligence*, by Carl Sagan. Copyright © 1977 by Carl Sagan. Reprinted by permission of the author and the author's agents, Scott Meredith Literary Agency, Inc., 845 Third Avenue, New York, New York 10022. Also reprinted by permission of Random House, Inc.

By looking at time and the universe in this fashion, human affairs are reduced to a different perspective. But even then, the worries and fears of people perhaps two hundred thousand years ago, when our specific life form apparently first appeared, are surely qualitatively different from the thoughts and concerns of individuals in the closing years of the twentieth century. For humans, the fifteen billion years leading up to *Homo sapiens'* emergence some three thousand lifetimes ago, or one hour ago by the Cosmic Calendar, were only a prologue to the beginning of a highly unspecialized species of life.

Humans, more than any other living creature, lack genetic specialization. We do not have the strength, claws, or large canine teeth of the great cats to make us hunters. We do not have the immense size or strength of the mountain gorilla to protect ourselves from predators. We lack the hooves and multiple stomachs of the ungulates (cattle, deer, antelope) that provide speed and the ability to draw nutrition from leaves and grasses.

Lewis Thomas (1979) reminds us how highly specialized life may become by recounting the mutual adaptations of a snail and a jellyfish that appear in the Bay of Naples off Italy. While both forms of life are very different in their evolutionary history and appear to be capable of existing alone, that is not the case for this particular type of snail and jellyfish. Each, at different stages of life, is a parasite on the other and both are so greatly specialized and adapted that neither can survive without the other. In fact, for many forms of life, evolutionary change has meant higher specialization to a specific environmental condition.

Human beings, unlike most species of life, specialize not for a certain ecological niche but rather concentrate on general adaptability. Lacking thick coats of hair, humans can live in the sweltering heat of the tropics or, by wearing the skins of other animals, exist in cold latitudes and at high elevations. Though unable to store much water internally like the camel, we can transport water in containers to permit existence in desert areas. Binocular vision, the opposable thumb, and the upright gait are all specializations that permit more generalizable adaptability. The human being's most striking specialization of this kind is a large, complex brain and the parallel lack of many genetically controlled behavioral patterns. In other words, most of what we do is not wired in but acquired through learning.

Forms of life lower on the phylogenetic scale have lower complexity. Reptiles, for example, are more complex than insects in general organization and in the amount of DNA material carried in a gene. Additionally, in higher forms of life, a larger brain is available for learning that increases the organism's adaptability to the environment.

Within the functioning of the brain itself, organisms vary by the degree to which behavior can be molded or shaped. For example, a cat at an early age has some behavioral responses that seem rigid or quite fixed as they appear. The sucking response of the kitten, for example, appears shortly after birth and is a specific, inflexible behavior. On the other hand, the cat is capable of other more complex, variable, and adaptable behaviors. Stalking is an example of such behavior. Even a cat raised in isolation will display some of this activity, but raised in the presence of other cats, the behavior will become more complex and involved. When raised with an adult cat who is a mouser, a kitten will model that behavior. On the other hand, the behaviors of stalking and killing mice have a considerable learned component and do not unfold simply as a cat grows older. The dog, which is evolutionarily more complex than the cat, is capable of much more involved learned behavior. Dogs can be taught commands and sequences of activity that go beyond the cat's ability.

Moving up the scale to primates, the impact of learning and the necessity of learning grow far more important. For example, though we often speak of sexual behavior as occurring naturally, that is far from the truth. Sexual behavior and maternal care for the primate has a very large learned component. Harry Harlow (1965) demonstrated this dramatically some two decades ago by raising rhesus monkeys in isolation. One of his early findings was that such monkeys had a low survival rate even though adequate food and temperature were maintained. Such infants, when they reached adulthood, often did not know how to perform primary sexual activity. Males were particularly deficient since their requisite performance is more complex. However, when females raised in isolation gave birth to their own offspring, they showed critical deficiencies as well by often walking away from their newborn and permitting them to die.

BISECTING THE NAUTILUS

The chambered nautilus is a deep-sea dwelling shellfish that grows by adding a spiral of shell around a central axis so that, as it grows, it slowly revolves about the axis. It grows by becoming different and yet remaining the same. What it once was is a part of what it is now, and what it will become will be, in part, what now is.

If we were to superimpose on a bisected nautilus shell the time in years of humans' evolving consciousness, which like the nautilus is based on the past with the future incorporating the present, we would have a visual representation of this process. Figure 8 and table 9 together provide a visual model and overview of the pattern of individual psychological and cultural evolution.

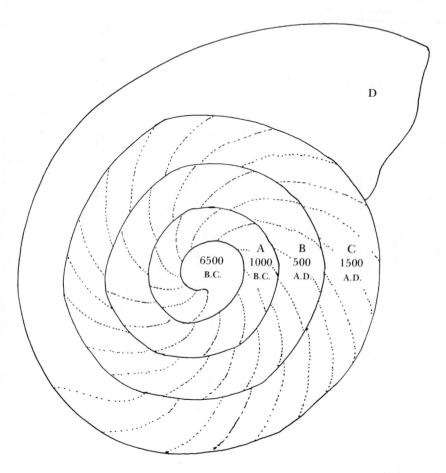

Stage
Axis: Tribal consciousness for hundreds of thousands of years
  A: Theocratic consciousness
  B: Appositional consciousness
  C: Feudal consciousness
  D: Technocratic consciousness

Figure 8
The Stages of Consciousness

Table 9
Major Events in Human Existence

Individual Consciousness	Historical Period	Events	Date	Level on Chart
	Stone Age	First use of tools	2,000,000 years ago	Axis
Tribal		Use of fire	1,350,000	Axis
	Late Stone Age	Development of abstract speech	40,000	Axis
		First agriculture	17,000	Axis
		Domestication of animals	10,000	Axis
				Dawning of Civilization
		First cities (e.g., Jericho)	6000 B.C.	A
Theocratic		Great cities of Mesopotamia, Sumer, Babylon First settlers in the Aegean Invention of writing	5000 B.C.	A
		First Egyptian kingdom Megalithic religion in Western Europe (Stonehenge in England)	3500 B.C.	A
		Great Pyramid of Cheops	2500 B.C.	A
		Invention of the alphabet Golden Age of Minoan culture	2000 B.C.	A
		Hammarabic legal codes in Babylon Middle kingdom in Egypt Indus valley culture Explosion of volcano at Thera	1500 B.C.	A
		Bronze cultures, Mycenaen kingdom, Trojan War, Olmec culture	1000 B.C.	B

Table 9 (continued)

Individual Consciousness	Historical Period	Events	Date	Level on Chart
Appositional				
		Iron metallurgy, Israelites escape from Egypt, Phoenician culture, Greek philsophy— Socrates, Plato, Aristotle, Euclid, Mayan culture	500 B.C.	B
		Asokan India, Chin dynasty, Buddha, Lao Tzu, Confucius, Zoroaster, Athens at its height	200 B.C.	B
		Jesus Christ Roman influence spread throughout known world	A.D. 1	B
		Archimedes, Ptolemy	A.D. 200	B
Feudal				
	Middle Ages, Dark Ages	End of Roman Empire Middle Ages begin	A.D. 500	B
	High Middle Ages	Reign of Charlemagne pre-Aztec Empire,	A.D. 800	C
		Norman Conquest, Crusades begin,	A.D. 1100	C
		Magna Charta	A.D 1200	C
		Hundred Years War, Fall of Constantinople, Gutenberg Bible,	A.D 1400	C
		Columbus, Cortez, awareness of the New World	A.D 1500	C

Table 9 (continued)

Individual Consciousness	Historical Period	Events	Date	Level on Chart
Technocratic				
	Renaissance	Religious turmoil and birth of Protestantism— Luther, Calvin, The Reformation, Shakespeare		
	Scientific Revolution	Copernicus, Galileo, Kepler, Descartes Creation of calculus and classical physics, Newton, beginning of mercantilism and heightened nationalism in Europe	A.D 1600	D
	End of Renaissance		A.D 1700	D
	Enlightenment	Beginning of industrial revolution in England— Adam Smith, inventors of spinning wheel, cotton gin, steam engine, Mill and Bentham's utilitarianism, American and French Revolutions, Age of Reason— Rousseau, Jefferson, Bill of Rights		
Technocratic		Napoleon's conquest of Europe, British Empire at its height, Bismark begins to construct the German republic. U.S. linked by railroads, telegraph, telephone, light bulb, steamships,	A.D 1800	D

Table 9 (continued)

Individual Consciousness	Historical Period	Events	Date	Level on Chart
		John Stuart Mill, Charles Darwin, Karl Marx, James Clark Maxwell, Faraday, use of electricity, discovery of radio waves, microscope.		
		Industrial revolution in United States. Bolshevik revolution in Russia. World War I, II, The Great Depression, nuclear energy, radio, television, the Pill, moon landing, world-wide telecommunications, commercial jet travel, Asian independence and opening of the Orient, collapse of European colonial empire, computers, silicon chip, laser, video recordings, urbanization of America, recombinant DNA, antibiotics, cybernetics in the factory, service economy, both sexes in paid wage-labor force	A.D 1900	D

Lack of specialization in the human race has made possible a series of striking transitions in the species especially within the past 50,000 years. From the best that can be determined today, some 700 lifetimes ago there were no cities, no farming, and no domestic animals. Fire and stone tools were present among our prehuman ancestors, even before *Homo sapiens*, but evidence indicates that their use and design had not advanced greatly for several hundreds of thousands of years. Although writing did not exist either, perhaps the beginnings of representational drawing had occurred. But somewhere between 25,000 and 40,000 years ago a rapid acceleration began both in the number and quality of tools that humans used, and, one might surmise, an abrupt increase in language facility and complexity. By 15,000 years ago, domesticated animals began to appear as did some cultivated crops. By 8,000 years ago or almost 6000 B.C., the prehistorical city appeared and the basis for the cradle of civilization in Mesopotamia was laid.

There is available evidence of a type of human physically somewhat similar to modern humans that is dated to approximately 2 million years ago. These creatures are usually called *Homo erectus* and their remains have been found in China as well as East Africa. Succeeded by our present form, *Homo erectus* differs from *Homo sapiens* in that current humans have a larger brain and a more favorable brain to body mass ratio by perhaps 30 percent. No such physical change seems to have occurred, though, between humans of 100,000 years ago and of 10,000 years ago. Yet, it is clear that their lives were much different. Humans, modern in physical form, roamed Africa, Asia, and Europe 100,000 years ago. Maybe 50,000 years later, they began to migrate across the Bering Strait into North America and into the islands off China and India to Australia, New Zealand, and Borneo. But in all these cases, these humans were hunters and, more than likely, scavengers. They were dependent on available animals, fishes, fruits, berries, and edible roots and competed with carnivores such as wolves, bears, the great cats as well as with birds for seeds and berries.

What made the change possible for humans to become herdsmen or farmers is not known. Maybe there were slight changes in the anatomy or the biochemical function of the brain. Or maybe it was just the quick accumulation of one social invention after another: animal domestication, farming, abstract language, numbers. That is not known. However, there was a transformation from a migratory, quick-learning hunter to a more settled dweller in houses and then in villages.

EARLY CIVILIZATIONS AND CONSCIOUSNESS

Up to this point noticeable change did not happen except every five to ten thousand years. Now the rate of change began to accelerate much more sharply, with significant changes in each millenia. Intensive farming appeared along the Nile in Egypt, and a priestly caste emerged whose apparent concerns were to interpret the meaning of life and to maintain a newly hierarchical society. Such a society would then insure proper successors to the various social ranks. Similarly ordered societies appeared along the Euphrates and Tigres rivers east of the Mediterranean and on the islands along the shores of Greece.

In these new societies, many more specific roles were developed for persons than occurred under the migratory hunting and gathering bands that preceded them. The newly specialized roles of priests, civil servants, and soldiers were made possible by the improved productivity yielded by the domestication of animals and the spread of agriculture. The great majority of individuals were farmers or laborers; yet, individuals began to be regarded in a different fashion. Rather than activities being dispersed and shared by all, there appeared specialized assignments and then, in time, definite classes. Probably the first social classes were priest-kings with leadership being merged in divine status. This was the initial level of civilization, the theocratic kingdoms. The king or queen was believed to be a descendant or continuous with a god. Also, during this time period, captured persons from enemy societies were forced into labor rather than being killed; thus, the institution of slavery came into being.

With the development of animal domestication, agriculture, slavery, and formal social structures, the pace of change in human civilizations began to accelerate even more, and discernable historical changes occurred every five hundred years. By 3500 B.C. the first Egyptian kingdom rose along the banks of the Nile, and in another thousand years pyramids were built. The year 2000 B.C. marked the invention of the alphabet and the beginning of the Golden Age of the Minoan culture on Crete and Thera off the Greek shores. By 1500 B.C. legal codes were established in Babylon. The Middle Kingdom was in full flower in Egypt, and culture began to blossom in India along the Indus valley.

Apparently, at the height of the flowering of the first of these theocratic kingdoms, there was a geological event of unimaginable proportions that caused great turmoil in the civilizations around the

Mediterranean. This was the eruption of the volcano at Thera leading to the collapse of the Minoan culture on the island of Crete and probably caused severe dislocation of other early Greek or proto-Greek kingdoms as well as in the Egyptian cultures to the south. This may be as well the source of the legend of Plato's Lost Atlantis. But apart from this cataclysmic event, in a scant five thousand years humans changed from wandering herdsmen to builders of empires. What, may be asked, were the psychological developments that accompanied the social change?

A compelling issue to address is the question of the level of human consciousness in these early societies as well as those societies that preceded the first cities and civilizations. From what we might surmise, the individual human consciousness prior to these first civilizations must have been similar to that which occurs in small, closely knit tribes. Here, individual awareness is elaborated very, very slightly, and the major personal reality is membership in the tribe. However, with the development of these first kingdoms with leaders who held godlike positions, individual consciousness must surely have become more ritualized, a theocratic consciousness.

Because populations were often composed of more than a thousand individuals, individuals came into daily or perhaps weekly contact with strangers. Religion was apparently used as a binding material to hold together these greater-than-tribe societies and to make comfortable the now frequent contacts in the city between nonkinsmen. This must have been a momentous change, requiring the invention and subsequent learning of a constellation of new social behaviors since urban life requires much greater use of abstractions in social relations. Individual-istic patterns between associates who know each other well become inadequate as more strangers are encountered. Ritualized social codes of conduct are demanded in urban life.

EARLY AWARENESS OF INDIVIDUALISM

The classical civilization of Greece that began to reach maturity around 200 B.C. was much more than an elaboration of the urban life built on the domestication of animals and plants. Greek civilization prompted a much greater awakening of the inner life of the individual. Competing assemblies of scholars developed, and attempts to explain and understand the world, the individual, and social life gushed forth: Archimedes in physics, Euclid in geometry, Hippocrates in medicine, Homer and Hesiod in ancient history, Ptolemy in astronomy, Plato in social organi-zation, Socrates in the art of inquiry, and Aristotle in scientific analysis.

So many of the roots of science, philosophy, and rational understanding trace to this brilliant period of the awakening of subjective contemplation and the abandonment of the rigid, hierarchical obedience of the antecedent god kingdoms.

Theology was changing too toward an individual god, a god knowable to each person but not residing in various animal spirits or in the temple. Beginning most importantly with Greece, a greater sense of the individual and of the internal and external qualities of the world began to appear.

The span of time between 6000 B.C. and A.D. 200 saw the elaboration of the new invention of cities and hierarchical societies in many parts of the ancient world. While the intellectual achievements of Greece were perhaps the greatest, Rome developed the hierarchical society most thoroughly and, through its military legions, extended its influence over the entire Mediterranean and north to the British Isles and to Scandinavia.

Through the proliferation of cultures in these preclassical and classical periods, humans became aware of other peoples and other cultures. We might suppose that prior to this time generation after generation could pass with little or no contact with any other being except kinsmen. Now trade and travel changed that isolation and must have given rise to what may be termed *appositional consciousness*. Individuals were able to see their culture, their folkways, their dress, their norms alongside those of a different people. This must have proven to be a truly significant change and one that at least made some people think of cultural alternatives.

THE COLLAPSE OF THE CLASSICAL WORLD

As the influence of Rome waned under internal dissension and from attack by external enemies, tribes in Europe and societies in North Africa and the Middle East broke free. The centralization of authority and order of Roman rule and classical enlightenment dissolved, especially in Europe, into hundreds of small worlds of peasants and serfs, all owing allegiance to a separate lord. The years then following the eclipse of Roman dominion produced decentralized communities rarely larger than a few score persons. The remaining influence of Rome was largely passed through the Catholic Church, and this influence served to thwart and deny change while encouraging the acceptance of things as they were.

Whereas the imperial Romans were social activists, warriors, and builders, Christianity transformed these energies to an acceptance of the world and a concern for individual salvation after death. Thus, the collapse of the Roman order produced greater individualism, but bound this individualism to loyalty, to established traditions of the Church, to the community, and to one's inherited role in life. The sense of the individual was increased, but quickly anchored to religious tradition. The emergent sense of individualism, albeit limited to a few and sustained by slave economies in the Greek and Roman states, was ensnared now in a dogma of individual communion with a redemptive God.

Further change and enlightenment were delayed until Jewish traders, irreligious merchants, and medieval soldiers of fortune induced disturbances in this slumbering world some centuries later. Now, for perhaps eight hundred or more years, the growth of knowledge and technology slowed perceptibly in Europe though in the Far East and Arab cultures the enlightenment of the Greek Age did not dim. But Greece, as the crossroads of the world, and Rome, as the network of civilizations, passed from time into memory. Now, more than ever, the world of the East, the Orient, was sundered from the Western world and the two were not rejoined for two thousand years.

Through the Dark Ages, that subperiod of the Middle Ages, a different social form appeared to provide the foundation for the society. In Greece and Rome, the economies were based on slaves. In both societies, there was a fundamental division between citizens and slaves. The labor of the slaves created the economic base, the surplus on which the citizen existed. Only by this surplus of slaves—producing more than they consumed—could the free citizen exist.

Slavery became modified as the Middle Ages passed. In time, former slaves—laborers—became attached to the land. Farmland and the peasant's home became inseparable, and responsibility and control over both were transferred by hereditary right from master to master. In Europe, the hereditary title was reserved to the king, but the king, unable to control the land alone, awarded stewardship to nobles who pledged themselves to the king and agreed to make payments for the lease of the land.

Nobles and lords then made similar contractual agreements with the peasants or serfs residing on the land. Nobility was composed of free men who could terminate their agreements with the landowner, the king, and move on. The serf had no such freedom but was required to remain with the land just as a tree remains where it is rooted.

From region to region, serfs were the majority and, though there was a much greater measure of reciprocity between lord and serf than between master and slave, the serf could not terminate his end of the agreement with his lord. Lords could terminate their agreement with the king and lords could come and go; serfs remained with the land. Women and children had even fewer rights than the men. Women were required to gain their lord's assent for marriage and, in some areas, the lord would claim the right to the bride on the marriage night. Though this system was rigid with little freedom and clearly exploitative of the serf, the alternative was to drift into the world of anarchy in the open forest between the feudal lands or estates. There, life was far more brutal and dangerous. The feudal social system was little better than slavery, but sufficiently better to be preferable for the serf.

By the second century of the second millenium, change began to quicken once again in Europe. The Magna Charta brought the separation of church and state and the written guarantee of certain individual rights. For the next two hundred years there began a slow shift in governance of the world from religious dogma to independent human thinking.

An important contribution of the feudal system was that it reorganized the world after the collapse of Rome and made the world more peaceful, and orderly and thus safer. From these feudal havens then, individualism began to grow again.

PARALLELS FROM BIOLOGICAL TO SOCIAL EVOLUTION

In one sense, parallels can be drawn from biological to social evolution; but not in the sense of Herbert Spencer and William Graham Sumner, who understood Darwin simply as survival of the fittest and thus attempted to give intellectual justification to poverty, exploitation, and the grossest accumulations and abuses of wealth. A small, but appropriate, parallel is that the most successful form of life, the most powerful, does not provide the ancestral base for the next dominant form. For example, the great carnivorous dinosaurs did not give rise to mammals or the carnivorous cats. Neither did birds come from the massive herbivorous brontosaurus. Rather, both mammals and birds evolved from separate ancestors who were small, insignificant dinosaurs. In evolution, the next great star comes not from the current stars, but from the bit players, those who have the small, insignificant roles. Now this does not mean that failures become successes or that a dominant form does not improve itself by more evolutionary advances. That happens as well. But startling new advances, great leaps, come out of the margin. They come from highly stressed populations that are often the fringes of the ecological niche. A similar thing seems to happen in social evolution.

Apparently, the most marginal roles in feudal society were the artisan and the merchant. Royalty, nobility, clerics, and serfs were the central functionaries in the hierarchical order. Because artisans produced goods, they were not self-sufficient but had to barter for foodstuffs and other goods. However, through bartering they had a chance to make profits and gain a freedom that bordered on the illegitimate in feudal society. Because of bartering and its rewards, some artisans became merchants and often moved to the village or traveled from point to point to trade their wares. In time, some gave up making their own wares and became middlemen, buying wares from other artisans and specializing in selling the various wares. Thus, through this mechanism, markets were revived and trade and travel were expanded. Especially important in this process were the Jewish merchants whose religion did not prohibit money lending. Thus, in the Catholic-dominated world, the expansion of trade through credit markets was dependent upon a small religious minority. Trading, mobility, and credit—things that were crass, marginal and often despised by the dominant forces—began the change process.

Then, in the sixteenth century, a number of catalytic events occurred that began to bring down the curtain on the feudal world and the linking of the individual to the land, the community, and religious dogma. The increased expansion of world trade fueled by profits from colonial holdings; the discovery of and immigration to the New World; and the beginning of the Reformation developing out of Luther and Calvin giving rise to Protestantism and religious legitimacy to markets, businessmen, and merchants—all contributed to the significant change in the way societies functioned. Another seminal event was the scientific revolution begun by Copernicus, who abruptly shifted the center of the world away from the earth and away from the human race.

CHANGE IN THE HEAVENS

What Copernicus did was to completely revise the concept of the earth as the center of the universe—an outlook that had been unquestioned for over two thousand years. Since the time of the Greek astronomer Ptolemy, the movement of the stars in the heavens was explained by assuming that all stars rotated about the earth. The irregularity and reversal of the patterns of some of these stars, especially those which we know now as planets in the solar system, worried Copernicus. He found that by assuming that the earth is not motionless but rotates on its own axis and at the same time orbits the sun would permit astronomers to predict celestial movements much better. Copernicus's efforts later were expanded by Kepler and Galileo, especially the latter who, using the newly invented telescope, found mountains on the moon and spots on the sun which destroyed the medieval beliefs that all of the heavenly bodies were perfect.

This new explanation of the heavens which threatened to change the understanding of the universe was quickly denounced by the Roman Catholic Church. And though for his own safety Galileo recanted his writings, the seventeenth century saw broader and broader acceptance not just of Copernicus's new paradigm of the universe, but also of a revised and largely diminished definition of humans and our importance in the world.

In the next two generations, two additional thought systems ushered in the scientific revolution and brought the Renaissance to its peak. The first thought system is attributed to Rene Descartes, who became entranced by the fantastic growth of machines such as clocks, water-wheels, levers, pulley systems, and others that were appearing in the everyday world. Descartes offered the notion that the human body could be explained in terms of machine principles. He also introduced the concept of a mind-body dualism, with the body being operated by the machine principles and the mind being something spiritual that resided like a spirit or ghost in the machine. In this way, Descartes sought to resolve the increasingly mechanistic explanations of the natural world and the waning spiritual notions of human's existence. By assuring the world that there was spiritual existence apart from the material world, but, importantly, that the material world yielded to mechanical explanations, Descartes extended mechanical explanations to the human body.

The final full development of the machinelike description of the world was provided by Isaac Newton in the latter part of the seventeenth century and the first quarter of the eighteenth. Newton formulated the law of gravitation which states that forces of attraction and repulsion keep bodies in space in motion and in balance. These same forces act like the giant mainspring in a clocklike universe.

Newton also began to develop the concept of scientific determinism, postulating that every event had an antecedent cause. He created the mathematical notion of the calculus to divide motion into many fine small units and demonstrated how a few of these units could then be measured to predict the future course over time of a given body. The two elements of calculus—differential and integral—are used, first, to differentiate or divide fluid motion into an infinite number of small units of movement and, then, to combine them back into the whole. Thus, the concept of bodies moving through space following laws that were determinant and that could be disassembled and then reassembled produced an outlook on the world that stressed the analytical division of the world into small units which could be studied, the processes understood, and then the future predicted for any subsequent point in time. Reality now became not an ineffable mystery but a complex puzzle. But, as a puzzle, it could yield to rational thought. It could be taken apart and put together again at will.

The great conceptual leap that Newton provided became a view of the world that saw human beings not as the center of the universe but rather as participants in a complex but finely tuned mechanical cosmos, a cosmos thoroughly determined, with no superfluous parts. The creation ran according to laws decreed by a divine being who, having constructed this immensely complicated but reliable piece of machinery, had retired to leave it running on its own. Thus, in a space of perhaps a hundred years, the philosophical definition of the world changed from an unchanging existence arrayed around humans in which earth and humans were the center of all things. Existence had been the strict adherence to fate, as decreed by birth, with the afterlife providing great rewards to those who honored the traditions of the ancient world with fidelity and loyalty. The new world that grew out of the seventeenth century was vastly more complex and, though human beings were no longer the center of the universe, our ancestors played a noble role within a predictable, and because of its predictability, benevolent universe. Humanity's role became a responsibility to discover the laws of this universe and thus be worthy of its creator.

Through the eighteenth and the nineteenth century, this view of reality extended itself from astronomy, physics, and philosophy into geology through Lyell, biology through Charles Darwin, philosophy through Herbert Spencer, economics through Adam Smith, and the human organizations through Max Weber and Karl Marx. The last vestiges of community life, life as a member of the tribe, were wiped first from England, then France, Germany, Holland, and then the United States, as industrialism spread from country to country and the world became filled with inventions and machines of human origin.

As the traditions of agrarian feudal society faded away, a consciousness developed for the individual that was not rooted in tradition or community, but rather in an external world of newly created social organizations and technology. There were essentially two new organizations. One was that of business empires in which men were employed—the source of their livelihood. The other organization was the nation-state which was able to transfer the loyalty of individuals from the feudal lord to a more abstract entity, that of the nation. With this nation-building, great and continuous conflicts between nations occurred. In the seventeenth century from 1600 to 1677, there was peace in Europe for only one year.

The eighteenth century opened in a burst of optimism and is remembered as the Age of Reason, the Enlightenment, when rational processes would perfect humanity and its world. The century ended with the great revolutions of America and France. The start of the nineteenth century saw the Napoleonic conquest of Europe, Napoleon's final defeat, and the extension of the British colonial empire with native wars throughout the globe. This nation-building and competition among nations continued at a fevered pitch in the twentieth century with the Russian Revolution, the Chinese Revolution, numerous revolutions in Central and South America, and two World Wars. All this social strife in one way is a product of the continuing collapse of the traditional world and the erection of modern states and corporate empires that have realigned individual loyalties from family and community to the new entities.

TIME AND REALITY

Consider time in two ways. First think of it as a long hallway. Look back down the hallway. It stretches straight to the horizon. That is the past. You can see the last moment or even yesterday clearly, just behind you. Last year is farther away, and ten years is far enough that the lines are a little fuzzy. Persons and things seem to stand against a misty background. Now look ahead into the future. You cannot see very far; a moment ahead, yes; a day ahead, maybe; but a year ahead or even fifty years; that is much more difficult.

Now think of time in another way. You're still standing in a hallway but one side is a partition just above eye level, rather than a wall that reaches to the ceiling. Stand on your tiptoes and peer over the partition. There is another hallway and there you see life of a hundred or five hundred years ago just next to you. Look down that adjacent hallway and see that it turns, it spirals around to the hallway where you stand. You now see that the hallway, because it is so long, only appears straight. But, by looking over the partition, you can see that it curves. It is like the earth; because we cannot see the curvature, it appears flat. Now, what has happened is that time, in this way, has changed; it has become curvilinear, not linear. By looking at time this way, the past of long ago seems as close as yesterday. You can visualize these two concepts of time by imagining time as a thread. Using the first way of thinking about time, the thread is stretched out in a never ending continuum. Using the second way, the thread is wound around a spool, with the past just adjacent to the present.

Now which is the true reality, time as thread stretched out or time as thread wound about a spool? In terms of subjective time, reading about history, conceptual awareness makes time fit a spool. In terms of watches and calendars, time fits the stretched out thread. Which is the reality? It may depend on the metaphor we use.

12

Revising the Paradigms

These two ways of thinking, the way of
time and history and the way of eternity
and of timelessness, are both part of man's
effort to comprehend the world in which he
lives. Neither is comprehended in the other
nor reducible to it.

> J. Robert Oppenheimer, *Science and the
> Common Understanding.*

In a sense that I am unable to explicate further, the proponents of competing paradigms practice their trades in different worlds.

Thomas S. Kuhn, *The Structure of Scientific Revolutions (2nd ed.)*.

The modern world and the world of the distant past differ by many dimensions. People were formerly fewer in number, lived shorter lives, and often had only limited personal possessions. Cities were smaller and less grand. Arts and the sciences were shared by a smaller proportion of the populace. The far woods, the mountains, the oceans were more distant and more mysterious.

Perhaps, though, the degree of difference between these two worlds is most remarkable along the dimensions of social organization and technology. In this chapter and the next, we see how these two dimensions in combination have created a new environment for the individual and have produced an individual suited for these times.

The use of the term *paradigm*, now widely established in the scientific and professional literature, owes much of its popularity to a treatment of how change occurs in science by Thomas Kuhn. In his monograph *The Structure of Scientific Revolutions*, a paradigm consists of a set of assumptions and rules that permit an individual to relate to the world. The concept of a paradigm often incorporates a philosophy or world view that guides the individual, the community, and the total society in their statements of their grandest aims and in the conduct of many of their day-to-day activities. For example, a part of the paradigm of the ancient Egyptian royalty was that there was a reality, a life, after death that was basically a continuation of day-to-day life. What was important for the pharaoh was to have the material items that were used in life available to him in the afterlife. Consequently, much of the building of the pyramids was concerned with developing a storage vault to hold and protect goods so that they could pass with the pharaoh into the afterlife.

In Kuhn's (1970) use of the word *paradigm*, he sought to distinguish two types of activity in science. The first was termed "normal" science. Most scientists are engaged in normal science, a routine which consists of conducting many small, orderly studies and experiments that collectively develop the general edifice of science. The work of normal science is much like building a vast brick wall, with each scientist engaged in using a trowel and mortar to place his or her particular brick in the wall. However, at times in the normal science process, anomalies, unexplained issues, arise and if they are particularly important, or if anomalies begin to mount, questioning of the normal science process begins to break out. Many scientists start to speculate about the appropriateness or correctness of the venture. Basically, using the brick wall analogy, what occurs is that individual scientists begin to ask whether a wall should be built instead of a patio or a building, even whether brick and mortar are the best building materials. This point, when the general design comes into question, Kuhn identified as the second type of activity in science, the paradigm-changing process.

The paradigm is the framework or design within which the scientist operates and serves to guide and direct his or her actions. Today, the concept of paradigm is often used to look at many forms of human endeavor, such as literature and art. It is used in ways very similar to statements about a person's general philosophy or world view.

A simplified way to understand scientific management (see chapter 6) and much of the engineering and organizational aspects of our lives and the suggestions inherent within human relations is to view each of them as representatives of distinctly different paradigms that explain and relate work, life and reality to the individual and to society.

THE TWO PARADIGMS

Scientific management exists within what I will call the Technocratic Paradigm. Through this window on the world, all things are understandable through analysis and experimentation. All things may be placed into one category or another and all categories are discrete, they do not blend into one another. A thing cannot be in two categories at the same time. In the Technocratic Paradigm, the direction of the arrow of time is forward only and takes the form of a line which can be easily divided into discrete, regular units: seconds, minutes, hours, days, weeks, and years. The future is always an extrapolation from the present and, consequently, is predictable from the present.

Human beings have progressed regularly over the centuries and manipulated and created their own environment. Our minds have analytical processes to think and behave in rational terms, but these processes, these abilities, are more developed and more available in some people. These people are the leaders and organizers. All individuals are motivated to seek pleasure and avoid pain, but individuals can be sorted in terms of how far they see ahead, how much vision they have. The simple person sees only for the moment or the day. The advanced person, the higher person, the leader, looks further into both the past and the future.

You can visualize this concept by imagining yourself standing on a path, with the present being the place on the path where you are standing now. You can move in only one direction, the future, and you come from only one direction, the past, but you can see in both directions.

The higher person, the one more fully in possession of his or her cognitive capabilities, seeks fuller strategies for meeting the pleasure-pain principle and comes to use control of the present and the future as the superior strategy.

In the Technocratic Paradigm, individualism, and thus nihilism, is prominent and the logical conclusion. If the sense of time and reality is Newtonian, the answer to fate is Darwinian. Life is a struggle that sorts the better from the lesser, the wise from the foolish. Individual consciousness and individualistic pursuits are glorified. The social organization should exist only to assist or expedite individualism. The goal or vision of the Technocratic Paradigm is to free the individual from backward organizations, the pettiness of the family, the parochialism of the neighborhood, those organizations that thwart progress and modernization, and to maximize the control of individuals over their environment.

Human relations may be representative of a much different outlook that could be called the Emergent Paradigm. In this paradigm, the world and its events are not fully knowable, but maintain a mystery and profundity that go beyond our analytical skills. Knowing emphasizes relations and processes. The knowing of things and facts is emphasized less. The development of basic elements and categories is greeted without enthusiasm. Aristotle is a minor Greek. Heraclitus is a revered figure. Time and the passage of time are less important. The emphasis is knowing and being with the present. If the present is well known and understood, future events will not jar or destroy equilibrium. In this paradigm, humans are emergent beings who harmonize more with their environment rather than achieving control over it. The rational processes are important, but the commonalities among people are emphasized, not the differences. Human motivation is seen as complex and variable, resistant to being reduced to one or even a few variables. Individual differences and individual attainments are seen either as singular expressions or as accidental occurrences.

Past and future are part of the present, and time is a position, a point in a field, not a point along a path. We may foresee rearrangements of the field, but the future is, in the main, emergent and thus unknowable. Knowing and understanding can be separated. Knowing is awareness of the facts—the apple is red. Understanding is coming to grips with consequences—to live is to experience happiness and sorrow. It is an ability that can be increased, a facility to adapt to an unknown.

In the Emergent Paradigm, individualism is an abstraction, not a reality. Gestalt or system relations are the reality. To focus on the manager or the worker is not seen as useful. The sense of time and reality is Einsteinian, perhaps post-Einsteinian, real but relative to the moment. Fate is a changing balance in a complex field. It is not control but accommodation and integration that should be sought. Organization and increasing integration, being a part, is the goal. Individual awareness is authentic but weak. The goal is greater unity and adaptation of the total system.

If the Technocratic Paradigm were a painting, it would have bold strokes, polychromatic brilliance, and predictable lines. The Emergent Paradigm would have muted hues and harmonies. Lines would be complex, curving, bending back on themselves. The Technocratic Paradigm tries to free the thread from the worn and tangled fabric. The Emergent Paradigm tries to reweave the thread into the fabric thus enhancing the tapestry.

Paradigms are not proven true or false, but rather are systems of belief laced with observable facts, world views embraced for a period of time. Both of these paradigms are operative today, though the Technocratic is older in the West, and dominant, but the Emergent is new and challenging.

NEW TECHNOLOGY
FOR THE TECHNOCRATIC PARADIGM

Breaking down an involved process, such as making an automobile, into its various component tasks is a tedious procedure, an operation of great complexity when completed. Every automobile consists of thousands of parts, and thousands of operations are necessary to make and assemble the parts. Keeping track of the process and monitoring its efficiency are difficult when change or innovation is introduced. Such tasks characterize the factory and the manufacture of most products. But further extensions of the technique of scientific management have often been blocked by tasks whose complexity exceeded that of most manufactured items.

However, in the last twenty years the development of the computer has permitted and aided the extension of scientific management to more functions in industry as well as to government and public service organizations. These are the sort of endeavors that, because of their involved and fluid nature, eluded the simplistic mechanistic nature of the traditional factory mentality. Elaborations of scientific management's time-and-motion studies, critical path method, program evaluation review techniques, and systems budgeting represent the extension of the linear logic of scientific management to complex organizations. Common to all of these tools is the division of work flow into small measurable units and the construction of flow systems that permit the manager to know the condition of the work process at a given time. Since such systems handle great quantities of data, the use of the computer has been a necessary occurrence.

The advent of computers and information systems has increased the knowledge and thus the power workers have over their tasks and relieved them of many of the more tedious and repetitious routines. Greater information to reduce ambiguity and mechanization to relieve boredom have been the fruits of these advances toward more satisfied and more productive employees. Yet, these systems and technologies are themselves stressors and contributors to burnout. The frustrations of dealing with rigid computer languages, systems that crash inexplicably, reams of computer printouts containing trivial data are chronic complaints of employees in complex organizations.

Scarcely a dozen shots had been fired in the human relations revolution when the complaint surfaced that managers were becoming psychotherapists rather than leaders, and that managers should manage people in terms of tasks, not in terms of motivation. Such admonishments form a restatement of scientific management's focus on the design of tasks and the hierarchical ordering of small tasks into larger ones to achieve the final product or service. The genius of scientific management was the division of complex tasks into small incremental ones that could be performed by uneducated and relatively untrained workers and that required little attention to the complexities of human performance. By breaking work into many small steps and managing in terms of the steps or the increments in the process, we are managing through small outcomes or objectives.

MAKING MANAGEMENT AN ASSEMBLY LINE PROCESS: MBO

It was Peter Drucker's restatement of scientific management in *The Practice of Management* (1954) that led to the term *management by objectives* (MBO). Under management by objectives, the manager, much like following the scientific management dictum, meets with the worker to jointly arrive at the objectives involved in completing a complex task and to decide which activities will lead to the objectives.

Both manager and worker reach an agreement that frequently is committed to paper and signed, leaving the management task then essentially to confer with the worker and review activities to date against agreed on objectives. When exceptions to the planned work activity occur, the manager can take corrective action with the employee in a nonambiguous situation and avoid questions of the employee's internal motivation and attitudes relative to the organization or the manager. When work does not meet specifications, the manager focuses on providing the employee with new or improved tools, an extension of time to complete objectives, training for the employee, or perhaps a reclassification of the objectives. Management becomes largely an impersonal task focusing on the activities rather than on the internal state of the employee; in fact, the internal state or feeling of the employee is viewed as something that belongs outside of the work place and the work role.

MBO approaches call for certain managerial and worker personality characteristics. Adaptable team members must submerge their own idiosyncracies, and managers must be comfortable with acknowledgment through their subordinates' accomplishments. Use of management by objectives tends to diminish colorful individual personalities of managers and thus there is no definable executive personality. Managers will be jacks-of-all-trades rather than specialists in a particular area. They will draw personal meaning and sustenance from the tasks and results of their work groups. Clearly, the prescription for management by objectives is that managers will anchor or center themselves in the organization and be useful and adaptive to the organization's changing demands.

Overall, management by objectives offers to clarify ambiguities in the task, to sharpen supervisory responsibility, and to structure the relationship between the worker and the supervisor. It represses individual differences and emphasizes the adaptation of the individual to the organization's goals and norms. Typically, the MBO format is tied into a functional budgeting scheme and a computer-based information system, which combine funding, work activity, and output in a cybernetic organization where all parts and processes are finely meshed in tune. In reality, management by objectives usually requires three or more years to implement fully and demands a high level of meeting and planning time to divide work into objectives, then subobjectives, then sub-subobjectives.

Research data on the application of management by objectives, although the concept sounds promising and reasonable, do not indicate any discernible increases in productivity. However, it clearly provides management with more information about work processes, permits earlier intervention, and lends itself to more rapid response time when problems occur.

Among the more frequent complaints about MBO is the overwhelming amount of paperwork required to divide work into objectives and subobjectives and to establish the detailed contract between worker and supervisor at every level. This necessity for paperwork leads to the related complaints that meaningful work is displaced by paperwork and that objectives created through paperwork lend a rigidity to the system, resulting in the pursuit of goals and objectives that eventually become artificial or no longer relevant to current conditions. While management by objectives does reduce ambiguity and clarify supervision, it makes manifest the complexity of the organization and repetitive nature of most tasks while increasing the number of forms that must be prepared to document progress toward goals.

In organizations where tasks are new to employees and among less experienced members of the work force, the MBO procedure provides positive benefit through the reduction of ambiguity, but it is not a new science or procedure of management. It is mostly a restatement of the dicta of scientific management, and its use serves to reduce the random as well as intentional variability of efforts by workers to uniform goals and procedures of the organization. Not surprisingly, the achievement of this intent acts to further the feelings of alienation of the workers in the sense of their being used for organizational purposes rather than being recognized as intrinsically valuable individuals.

SOFTENING THE PARADIGM—JOB ENRICHMENT

An important element of scientific management is work simplification which provides the following benefits to the organization:

1. Complex tasks are reduced to relatively simple steps, permitting untrained workers to learn to perform effectively one or two steps in a short period of time.
2. Factories are able to use common laborers rather than skilled craftspersons, thus increasing the labor supply and decreasing the costs of labor.
3. The factory organization can control the entire work production process.

However, in time, as employees outgrow the novelty of the job, the work simplification routine promotes boredom for most workers, leading to decline in worker satisfaction. The decline in worker satisfaction leads to higher rates of worker turnover, reduced productivity, and lower quality of work.

A number of theorists, especially Frederick Herzberg (1966), have suggested *job enrichment* as a countermeasure to the boredom occasioned by the simple and repetitive tasks generated through the use of scientific management. Job enrichment consists of reaggregating the simple and repetitive tasks of the assembly line process into larger pieces of activity, to permit greater responsibility in performing the job and create greater interest and opportunity for the worker in deciding how tasks should be carried out.

Hersey and Blanchard (1969) give an example of job enrichment by reciting an experience of a plant superintendent with a group of janitors. Soon after he was assigned to a new plant, the superintendent found that housekeeping practices had garnered many complaints and that the janitors appeared lazy and unmotivated. The superintendent set about to change the job description of the janitors by holding meetings with them and asking them for their suggestions about housekeeping practices. There was no reaction to such suggestions initially, but in time the janitors began to respond to the opportunity. The superintendent jotted the ideas down at regular meetings and agreed to accept the suggestions as an agreement between him and the janitors.

As time passed, the superintendent began to refer larger housekeeping problems to the janitors. They were provided an office where they could meet with cleaning equipment and supply sales reps. Decisions about cleaning supplies and equipment were delegated to the janitors and, in a few weeks, the performance of the men and even their personal appearance changed. They began to appear in clean, well-pressed work clothes, and comments started coming in from all over the plant about the remarkable change in the janitors' appearance and the improved quality of housekeeping.

Such an example illustrates how a job can be enriched by increasing the responsibility and scope of decisions permitted in the job. The job enrichment process works in a direction opposite to the task simplification demand of scientific management and encourages the employee to undertake greater areas of responsibility and to assume more complex tasks that require delegation and individual judgment. However, such opportunities for enlarged responsibility do not appear to work in all situations; they seem to work best when the work force is drawn from small communities that are not highly industrialized. As long as traditional middle class values of hard work, achievement, and upward mobility are present, job enrichment seems to have a favorable impact on productivity and employee morale. But, in highly industrialized urban areas, the response to job enrichment has not been nearly as favorable.

Job enrichment is really a reconsideration of the motivational assumptions about the worker: it looks at tasks that, because of their simplicity, appear not to be motivating and argues for the creation of tasks that have intrinsically greater appeal to the worker. Job enrichment, while basically coming out of the scientific management school, leads us from the Technocratic to the Emergent Paradigm. It is especially the Emergent Paradigm that has had a high rate of innovation and writing concerning employee motivation, disaffection, and burnout.

THE SOUNDS OF ANOTHER DRUMMER

Important in the development of the human relations approach to management were concepts far afield from the factory and business. Among the earliest were the field psychology theories of Kurt Lewin in the 1930s that were in bold contrast to the stimulus-response learning theories of the day. Lewin argued that behavior was not a simple function of first stimulus and then response, but rather a complex set of actions that developed out of an interaction of a field of stimulus objects and the person.

Lewin often used analogies from topography and the physics of electricity to elucidate his concept of the field and argued that the psychology of the thirties incorporated too few variables and improperly utilized a simple linear model. For Lewin, A did not cause B, but B was a consequence of many factors in the environment. He argued the explanation of human behavior would never be reached through stimulus-response reductionistic themes. The most prominent use of Lewin's work in the management literature is his experiment with group atmospheres or climates that compared authoritarian, laissez-faire, and democratic leadership styles in terms of productivity and the generation of aggression.

In the experiment, Lewin (1939) arranged students in three separate classrooms. In one classroom, the teacher was instructed to use highly directive or authoritarian procedures in teaching the class. For example, the teacher would explain that the first hour would be devoted to arithmetic and there would be no discussion or consideration of doing reading first or some other activity. The teacher would decide when the next activity was to start and what it would be. The students were given no opportunity to ask for more time to work on a given area or permitted any choice in what subject they should study at a given time.

In the second classroom, the teacher was told to use a very non-directive approach in teaching the class. Essentially the teacher told the students that he would be a resource to help them in their learning and then basically let them do whatever they wanted to during the day.

The third teacher was told to use a democratic style in that the teacher would discuss with the students the various areas which they would need to work on during the day and during the week. He would then involve them in a discussion about how they should study for a given area, which item they should study first, and what would be the best way of going about it.

Lewin then maintained these three teaching or leadership approaches in the experiment for several weeks and made measures of two dimensions. One dimension was the productivity of each group. Productivity was defined in terms of the amount of learning that occurred, homework accomplished, and so on. The other measure was the degree of aggression manifested among the students. Aggression consisted of fights, pushing, and other boisterous conduct.

The study indicated that initially the authoritarian model produced greater productivity, but over several weeks it also generated the greatest level of aggressive behavior which began to detract from high-level productivity. Democratic leadership, on the other hand, was more time-consuming but, as time passed, it proved to be the most productive form of leadership and produced the least amount of aggressive behavior. Laissez-faire leadership had the lowest productivity results and produced levels of aggressive behavior almost as high as those under authoritarian leadership. The experiment indicated the superiority of democratic leadership with an emphasis on participation and communication. Lewin's findings stressed the importance of grounding or anchoring the individual within the work group as the most important means of meeting motivational needs and ensuring high productivity and low frustration among group members.

In the fifties, Abraham Maslow, another psychologist, refined thinking about human motivation and argued that it was hierarchical and ascending in character. Maslow's model of human motivation (1954) was represented by a triangle or pyramid, with a broad base composed of physiological needs such as those associated with hunger, thirst, sex, and protection from the elements. The second level in this hierarchy was safety or security needs that dealt with the continuity of meeting the basic physiological needs over time and freedom from fear of physical danger. The third level of needs in the hierarchical model was affiliation needs associated with group belonging. These were needs arising out of the individual's seeking to be with others whom he or she found to be enjoyable and supportive. The fourth level of motivation was esteem needs associated with social recognition and approbation. The fifth and final level was self-actualization where the individual responded to goal states or motivational needs. These needs were defined within the individual's own conscious experience and were neither physiological in nature, like those at the lower motivational levels, nor related to the social approval or recognition needs representative of the two preceding levels. Maslow characterized people at the self-actualization level as highly creative individuals, such as artists or scientists, who act out of an internalized, very private view of what they should be doing and often disregard rewards of fame and riches that are available in the marketplace.

Maslow used a pyramid shape to describe his view of human needs for two reasons. One reason was to present the concept of the hierarchical nature of needs, with a lower need level necessarily having to be met before an individual begins to operate at a motivationally higher level. The other reason for the pyramid was to illustrate the proposition that the majority of the population is at the lower need levels, with decreasingly smaller percentages of the population operating at the successive higher need levels.

In terms of the consequences for burnout, Maslow's ideas would suggest that as long as the rewards from the organization fit the individual's motivational level, burnout would not occur. Thus, if an employee is at the social affiliation level, burnout would occur when work only provided responses to basic needs and security. On the other hand, if the work situation permits adequate social interaction and provides a warm and accepting climate, the employee should remain satisfied.

The theory seems to suggest that burnout would be more likely to occur when work tends to provide motivational values below the motivational needs of the employee. This particular model also would imply that the wealthier a society becomes and the greater its ability to provide a higher foundation of general welfare to its members, the more motivational rewards for work must come at the higher levels. It would seem to follow then that higher rates of burnout should occur when a society becomes wealthier if the bulk of work remains repetitious, uninspiring and limiting in opportunty for individual autonomy and creativity.

Some theorists, especially Chris Argyris (1962) and Rensis Likert (1961), have compared scientific management to the motivational theories of Lewin and Maslow and have argued that the organization designed through scientific management principles provides rewards only at the lowest motivational levels, thus requiring workers who operate at low motivational or immature levels. By emphasizing that reward should be through pay, and with the work simplification process removing opportunity for worker autonomy and creativity, workers are kept in a continuously immature state. By providing only the most fundamental levels of reward and using authoritarian management practices which heighten feelings of aggression, the use of scientific management should lead to worker unrest, alienation, burnout, and inability to perform complex and creative tasks. The traditional organization that demands rationality, control, predictability, clear division of duty, authority and responsibility requires people that function with the simple levels of cognition and motivational needs at the bottom of Maslow's hierarchy, thus insuring and promoting worker immaturity. This is referred to as the immature organization. Argyris, Likert, and others call for the design of organizations that permit the development of mature behavior.

Such organizations would have low status hierarchies with minimal divisions of authority and responsibility between management and workers, few levels of management, high opportunity for worker authority and responsibility (including the opportunity for workers to redesign the way tasks are done), and encouragement of the full participation of all workers in management decisions. Such a mature organization should provide democratic leadership and thus, in terms of Lewin's outlook, yield high productivity and low levels of tension and aggression and permit workers to participate in tasks that provide the appropriate level of motivational return. Under the operation of such organizations, workers should center or anchor their identity highly within the organization. High rates of worker burnout would not be anticipated.

How to redesign the many American industries that are heavily devoted to the traditional bureaucratic model while maintaining the efficiencies produced through scientific management has been one of the major stumbling blocks of the development of the mature organizational model. Much of the success of scientific management has been tools and technologies for implementing the idea of work simplification and the hierarchical control systems, but the corresponding tools and techniques for the human relations school have been less available. In fact, there is perhaps reason to think that the tool and technique incremental process for changing into the Emergent Paradigm may not be the method to use at all. We shall examine this idea more fully in chapter 15.

The two management schools and the paradigms in which the management schools are imbedded are sharpened through a reading of the work of Douglas McGregor (1960). In *The Human Side of Enterprise*, McGregor visualizes a situation through two polar approaches to management. The first, Theory X, is a management theory that assumes a highly hedonistic state of affairs for individual motivation and suggests an elitist view of human potential—that most people operate at a very fundamental need level with short time horizons and little ability to defer gratification, thus requiring very close and thorough-going supervision.

Theory Y draws from the humanistic psychological theories of Lewin and Maslow among others and views human potential as emergent. Thus, human potential is much greater than is apparent at a given time for a given individual. This is essentially an optimistic liberal viewpoint and suggests that human behavior is a consequence of the assumptions the manager makes about the workers rather than a reality residing within the workers themselves.

McGregor endorses Theory Y as the approach to management that is used by the mature and intelligent manager, while characterizing Theory X as the more primitive and less well-developed understanding of human nature. This outlook would indeed suggest that worker burnout is a consequence of the utilization of Theory X management—inadequate and constraining management practices—and that burnout can be prevented by moving to more modern management theories.

13

The Roots of Burnout

When the mind is disturbed, the multi-plicity of things is produced, but then the mind is quieted, the multiplicity of things disappears.

Ashvaghosha, *The Awakening of Faith.*
Translated by D.T. Suzuki.

He who knows does not speak
He who speaks does not know

Lao Tzu

...But gradually he comes to suspect that rationality is an attribute of himself alone and that there is no reason to suppose that his own life has any more meaning than the life of the humblest insect that crawls from one annihilation to another...As long as life is regarded as having been created, creating may be held to imply a purpose, but merely to have come into being is, in all likelihood, merely to go out of it also.

Joseph W. Krutch, *Measures of Man: On Freedom, Human Values, Survival & The Modern Temper.*

The growth of industry, modernization, and knowledge since the late Middle Ages has resulted in vast changes in social institutions. The traditional, ascriptive institutions where one's status and position came from birth, from family and neighborhood are an aspect of the paradigm of antiquity. It has withered though, and modernization with achievement-based institutions has replaced these original anchors.

Industrialization has played a particularly important role in redefining the way in which the individual thinks of himself, the present and the future, and in the degree of satisfaction that is gained from life. Democracies and representative governments have replaced monarchies and the theological dominance of government. In most Western nations, both government and the private sector are characterized by large, complex organizations that emphasize centralization of control, rationality, division of labor, specialization and, unfortunately, the bending of the individual will and identity to a larger organizational purpose.

As the industrial era intensifies, factories become transformed into corporate institutions and the individual is reduced to a small ship that scuttles from institution to institution, with each individual more and more defined and shaped by the institution. Unlike the factory, which began as a challenge to traditional institutions and proved to be a liberating force for the peasant farmer and the urban slum dweller, the modern institution (corporate or governmental) follows a conserving and controlling tack. Division of labor, uniformity, and specialization are maximized. As this internal dimension reaches its maximum, the institution moves to achieve greater control over its environment. If competition exists, it seeks to eliminate it or forms cartels that divide markets and restrain competition. Manufacturing institutions submit to regulations and then merge symbiotically with the regulators.

The institution grows from the factory but successfully extends the factory mentality beyond the standardization of products and seeks to mold and standardize people. While no longer simply responding to its environment, it acts to control the environment. The institution imposes strict rationality among people and on their activities to insure that each act builds toward a specific institutional goal. For the institution, people do not exist. The reality is roles and positions. People are viewed as exchangeable commodities that are replaced when they wear out. The institution does not recognize informal social obligations between individuals and excludes its employees from other social or institutional networks, at least during working hours.

General knowledge and informal procedures are replaced by operating manuals. Oral tradition is replaced by company policy and the self is continually delineated and processed by the formal bureaucracy. One's job is a position on a career ladder and one's future is regulated by the steps and grades developed by the personnel office. Success is a superior grade granted by one's supervisor. Identity becomes colored by not only where one works, but the particular office or part of the factory where one is assigned. The U.S. Department of Labor's *Dictionary of Occupational Titles* lists over 20,000 entries. Each is designed to describe, bind, and maintain a small piece of reality in the industrialized bureaucratic machine. This piece of reality exists independently of the person and is a station to which the person is assigned. When the person receives the assignment, only then does he or she become a real object in society.

More and more activities in society have come under the institutional aegis. Today most products—clothing, housing, food, energy, appliances, education, health care, justice, transportation, and communications—are the province of the institution. This is the full and final evolutionary stage begun by the small factories that began to appear two hundred years ago.

Those societies (the United States, Great Britain, Germany) more steeped in the Technocratic Paradigm characteristically exhibit mature and declining manufacturing industries, particularly basic ones such as steel, extractive mining, and heavy transportation, which are replaced by high technology industries as rising labor costs make imported goods cheaper than domestic items. In these societies, service institutions replace companies that manufacture products. Some blue-collar work that was formerly disparaged develops an artistic value and the wage differential between white- and blue-collar jobs disappears. The growth rate of the gross national product of the society slows, fertility declines, and the median age increases.

CONSCIOUSNESS IN THE PARADIGM

A new type of human consciousness is called forth in this technological society and it might well be called a technological consciousness. Max Weber first noted the appearance of a shift of consciousness in his work *The Protestant Ethic and the Spirit of Capitalism* (1958), wherein he argued that the Protestant ethic with its emphasis on self-assertion, striving, and the responsibility that each individual must assume for his station in life was a consciousness necessary for the subsequent development of capitalism.

Peter Berger, et al. (1974) describe this consciousness as an awareness that a particular individual has a small unit of knowledge necessary to do a job, but that this unit of knowledge comes from a vast body of scientific and technical knowledge of which the individual holds only one small part. Though the individual cannot know all of this knowledge, he or she thinks that it is potentially available and that he or she is like a cog in a large machine, an element that plays a role within a larger, highly ordered, and finely operating totality. An additional dimension of this consciousness is the worker's thought that there is a hierarchy of experts. The worker is one expert among many with greater and perhaps lesser expertise.

Important within this machine-like consciousness is a cognitive style that Berger refers to as componentiality. This is a way of thinking about reality as being divided up into units or components so that all reality and all thought then consists of a building block or tinker toy-like matrix. From this logical outlook then, the world is there to change, to tinker with, and from this develops a deep-rooted problem-solving outlook on not just work but life as well. Finally and importantly, by viewing reality as a tinker toy matrix, all parts are replaceable and thus the individual as a part becomes replaceable or truly anonymous.

This consciousness renders the world in a condition of order, predictability, and stability, but when individual life becomes stable, predictable, and orderly, uniqueness disappears and is replaced by individual anonymity. Finally, it is very apparent that this vein of thinking soon penetrates into off-work life. Relationships at home or with friends then, too, begin to yield to a technological consciousness so that all efforts have a means-ends quality to them. In other words, all activities are seen as a means that leads up to some end; there can be no aimless or idle activity.

Family life exists, now, for a purpose: to satisfy and fulfill family members. Family members must work at making the family a success. Togetherness and enjoyment are required, and churches and civic clubs start programs to improve family functioning. Fathers are taught how to be a friend to their sons; mothers, how to be a confidante to their daughters. Home economics teaches high schoolers how to run the family like a good business and, in colleges, courses with titles like Marriage and the Family are designed to make the courtship routine scientific and thus more effective. Even that most intimate of acts, sexual intercourse, succumbs to management. Manuals are available on how to improve your performance and your mate's performance.

REALITY VIA BUREAUCRACY

Technology is responsible for one aspect of the consciousness characteristic of the modern world, a consciousness of discrete causes and effects where each event causes another like one domino striking the next in a chain. Bureaucracy is another important aspect of modern consciousness. What is bureaucracy? It is a peculiar social construction that is based on roles, but roles that an individual must achieve not inherit. It is a cultural institution that deals with a limited area of responsibility yet seeks to maximize its competency in that limited area.

For example, the police force is a bureaucracy and is usually more narrowly defined as a political bureaucracy as opposed to a technological bureaucracy. IBM is a technological bureaucracy, a bureaucracy designed to administer a high-technology production process—producing computers among other things. A political bureaucracy, on the other hand, processes people and administers rules.

To illustrate the role of bureaucracy in modern consciousness, examining political bureaucracy, which is a more advanced form than the technological bureaucracy, is very helpful. A political bureaucracy can be a more extreme bureaucracy than a technological bureaucracy because that technology, the engineering process, provides some sense of limits.

For example, in a bureaucratic organization that produces watches there is a limit to how many workers can be involved in assembling a watch. After a certain number, a very visible decline in efficiency occurs. The workers get in each other's way.

On the other hand, the number of police officers involved in apprehending criminal activity has much greater room for expansion. We may, for example, expand the pursuit of criminals from capital murder, assault, and crimes of property theft to crimes of intimidation and crossing streets against the light. By expanding our list of criminal offenses, we greatly expand the number of police officers involved and permit exotic new specialties. We may have officers who specialize in detecting the theft of ideas. Perhaps at a gasoline station an attendant detects a customer who has learned to drive more efficiently so that more miles are gained from each gallon of gasoline. Now, more than likely, that customer copied that idea from another person and also, more than likely, did not compensate the inventor for that worthwhile service. Now, that would clearly be theft, and we could use a special police force that could track down such thievery.

This, of course, is the special genius of political bureaucracy. It permits almost unlimited expansion, but still within the finite area of enforcing the law.

Another dimension of bureaucracy is limited competence. A bureaucracy does not operate like a good utility player for a football team. A utility player can play several positions with some finesse. A bureaucracy has a specialized domain of competence. The police do not answer fire calls or turn on the water. They are not available for hire to take you to the airport. They may, however, serve as a referral source and send the fire department to you or refer you to the telephone number of a taxicab company. Referral is another part of the bureaucratic process.

There is, in the bureaucratic consciousness, an overweening compulsion for coverage and order. In terms of coverage, there must be a rule, preferably a written rule, for every event in its specialized domain of competence. When a new event occurs, that is the occasion for a new rule to handle that event. Though rules always require some discretion in handling a typical situation, the general tendency is to w.ite a new rule for every event.

In addition to rules, bureaucracies have specialized tools. After all, what would a bureaucracy be without paper and somewhere to keep all the paper? The most common and critical tools for the bureaucracy are memo pads and file cabinets.

A bureaucracy also demands order and predictability. Everything has a place and everything is in its place. Much of the work of the bureaucracy is simply sorting things out, putting them in their correct order.

Finally, bureaucratic consciousness demands proper procedure and review. There is a procedural manner, a prescribed route, for handling activities, for making decisions, and a specified route for protests or review. If an individual feels that his or her property taxes are unjustly high, there is an appeals board and a specific procedure for filing an appeal. Guarding against corruption is critical to proper procedure and appeal. A corrupt act is using an avenue of appeal that is not the specified one. Buying a drink for the tax assessor may have been shrewd in the past, but in a political bureaucracy it is corrupt.

The consciousness that emerges in the Technocratic Paradigm is one of a world that is to be finite, knowable, predictable, orderly, and bound by clear, fair, and apparent rules. Because of the rules and the vigilance against corruption, the individual must be anonymous. Otherwise, the individual risks asserting a personal dimension, a personal relation, that is unfair and ultimately corrupting. The consciousness of the Technocratic Paradigm is awareness yet denial of awareness, a waking comatose state.

The Technocratic Paradigm applies the clockwork determinancy of Newtonian physics to all knowledge. All things are subject to analytical, componential dissection. When wholes are broken into parts, replaceable parts can be used as a part wears out. In time, this logic is applied to homes and organizations; the modern bureaucracy is the result. The bureaucracy is intended to operate like a factory-built watch. Each watch is the same, operating in predictable limits. The same is true for the bureaucracy. The roles in the bureaucracy are analogous to the parts of a watch and, in the way that a part wears out and can be replaced, when a person wears out in a role the person can be replaced.

By the time we arrive at the postindustrial society, large changes in the social network have ensued. The old traditional relationships of work within the kin group have been replaced by an atomistic society with an emphasis on individualism and work performed in an institutional setting.

The individual scuttles among many institutions and develops several social selves, several social roles, and becomes a socially multi-faceted being. But the organizations limit the individual to cognitive involvement. The affective ties for the individual are systematically precluded by the rational demands of the organization, leaving the individual with fewer and fewer places to locate intrinsic association relationships where you are accepted for what you are rather than what you have done or can do. The person's self-concept itself fractures into many pieces which are related to each other only through the individual's efforts, not through some larger social network. The individual has one unit of self-concept tied into the work place, another to social and recreational gathering spots, another to neighborhood, and another to the marriage. Yet formal social organizations do not exist to bind the individual together and make him or her feel whole.

By breaking the ties of the individual to tradition and by developing looser ties to the proliferation of organizations, the individual becomes more and more free but, simultaneously and paradoxically, more and more alienated from society and eventually, from himself. Initially the collapse of the traditional society left individuals without anchors. In the U.S., many of these men and women drifted to the western frontier and built a new tradition of individualism, free land, the right to migrate freely, and nurtured a progressive optimism. In Europe and

Latin America, land was less available to absorb these rootless people so they became the fuel for political revolution. In Mexico, Egypt, China, France, and Russia, peasants and workers shorn from traditional moorings caused empires to collapse and either industrial capitalistic or monolithic socialistic states to rise.

In either instance, an immensely social creature was ushered in. The social person whose identity grows from affiliation in multiple groups. In the capitalistic society, the individual is given a choice of many groups. In the socialistic state, the bureaucracy reserves the appearance of choice. In both cases though, the individual belongs to multiple groups and must strive to maintain membership in the groups. Under both systems he or she must be a producer and a consumer. The consumer and the demands of the consumer state occupy central roles in the West and in the Soviet world. In both, the individual is the economic person.

The nineteenth century was especially a time of boundless promise, but the twentieth century edged into a world of uncertainty. The remaining two decades of this century seem destined to be an Age of Malaise. The many and complex institutions of the modern world have reduced the individual to a puny creature. Individual lives are played out among and between these institutional behemoths much like the mice that scurry around feeding cattle subsisting on the leavings of the more important and powerful creatures. This modern world of science and organization can be characterized by a belief system that I have labeled the Technocratic Paradigm.

But throughout the latter portion of the twentieth century, the Technocratic Paradigm has begun to be challenged by a world view of considerable difference. The human relations management approach which represents the Emergent Paradigm seemed, in the earlier years, to be largely an attempt to restore some of the affective properties of the traditional organization, the family, to the work place. The new paradigm has recently received buttressing from such disparate fields as elementary particle physics, neuroanatomy and continuing developments in humanistic and social psychology that are suggestive of a clear, viable and alternative world view. It interestingly enough has overtones that seem somewhat concordant with oriental religious and philosophical themes. We shall return in chapter 16 especially to the implications of this new paradigm for the individual and for society after we have surveyed more thoroughly the conditions of life and working in the post-industrial society brought about largely through the successes of the Technocratic Paradigm.

THE PARADIGMS AND THEIR RELATIONSHIP
TO BURNOUT

A paradigm is a shared outlook or world view that a group of people hold in common. It is not testable in the ordinary sense that a hypothesis, model, or theory is, but rather is a set of assumptions about the way the world really is from which hypotheses, models, and theories grow. Paradigms reflect not only the common sense, the ordinary reality of the layperson, but the untestable assumptions of the scientist as well and are inextricably bound-up within the language itself. For example, when we talk about things and processes in English, we are expressing some assumptions: that reality is divisible into concrete, separable entities like trees, persons, atoms and into fluid flows like moving water, social dialogue, photosynthesis. When we talk of the past, the present and the future, we are talking through a paradigm.

In our current paradigm, time is like an endless ribbon that rolls out before us with the past extending backward some great distance and the future stretching forward to perhaps infinity. The present is the small strip of time that we are standing on at the moment. Each of us trods along this path of time always moving from the present into the future. We are only capable of reminiscing about the past or reading evidence such as old newspapers of its existence. We have absolutely no data about the existence of the future; we only assume it is there.

Prior to the Technocratic Paradigm was the paradigm of antiquity, the Traditional Paradigm. This was the world of the peasant, the farmer, the craftsperson. It was a world where existence and status were given, not earned. It was a world, comparatively, of limited consciousness. Neighborhood and family tended to be the boundaries of one's private world. The awareness of each person as an actor determining his or her own fate and setting personal rewards was negligible. The social structure, families, neighborhoods, the church, royalty were givens, not organizations rationally conceived, planned or brought into existence for some specific purpose. Under this paradigm, it is doubtful that people suffered burnout. Surely they grew tired, weary, and older. Stress occurred from fright, frustration, or physical threat. Some jobs, some tasks were more pleasant than others and maybe some persons were seen as having received a better break from life. Alienation and burnout, though, must have been very rare. Both appear to require a higher degree of role choice, of more role alternatives, than would appear under the Traditional Paradigm. Burnout also requires the appearance of time slipping away, of time not used well, and the appearance of individual responsibility for making something of one's self. Such feelings would have been atypical under the Traditional Paradigm.

The Technocratic Paradigm formed slowly, rising gradually from the dissolution, decay, and collapse of the old world. The Paradigm did not emerge full blown one morning but grew erratically over the decades. Critical to the difference of the Technocratic Paradigm, as compared to the Traditional, is how certain events and processes that were restricted to a small fraction of the population in earlier times have expanded to almost the total population. One example is romantic love, an idea as old as the Trojan War and Helen of Troy. The Romans, Greeks, the ruling castes of India, all celebrated romantic love and an avowed sensuality. Yet, the individuals involved were a small fraction of the total population. The same is true for leisure time and introspective thought. Since city-building began, that has been more the special province of the higher classes. Tied particularly to introspective thought, literacy and education were opportunities historically limited to the very few. The same is true for the opportunity to travel, possession of material goods, and the freedom to do something from choice, not obligation. These things arise by degree. But these things were, more often than not, to no degree for the masses throughout historical time.

The Technocratic Paradigm changed individual existence from a given to a right that must be earned. It brought about a world of relatively greater individual consciousness. It resulted in new motivations, new urges for individuals. Now under these terms, life and work must provide more than the simple basics of existence. There must be excitement, meaning, fulfillment. Jobs must lead somewhere. A marriage must mean something. Each of us has the right to get something out of life.

As more options became available, life became a quest, a challenge, for each individual. Because of the social changes and the changes in individual consciousness, it was possible to see that you may be getting less out of life than you deserved. It was possible to make a mistake in one's choice in marriage. A job could be experienced as boring, tedious, a dead-end. Thus, with these changes came the likelihood of experiencing burnout. Role alternatives became more visible, more possible. There came a greater sense of time running out for each individual and the need to make the right decision, to make the best of each situation. This making the best of each situation extended itself from the job to family life. Family life was expected to be satisfying and rewarding. Family members were expected to perform for each other.

The social structures, social institutions, were now no longer givens that were there when you were born and continued after you died. Organizations came to be thought of as having been set up, constructed for a purpose such as to provide education, to produce automobiles, or to cure illnesses.

At the edges of each paradigm are the outlines of a potentially new one and this has been true of the Technocratic Paradigm. New alternative paradigms remain in the shadows until sufficient puzzles develop that the dominant paradigm cannot solve. As long as the dominant paradigm provides solutions to the puzzles that arise from life with the paradigm, alternative world views are ignored. The Traditional Paradigm remained dominant as long as social change and the growth of technology moved slowly. But, as these things began to move more quickly, alternative world views began to appear and the Technocratic Paradigm came into being.

One of the more profound accomplishments of the Technocratic Paradigm has been its impact on the social structure and individual consciousness. The impact on the social structure has been to move people from the small village and rural homesteads into large, urban centers leaving dying villages and abandoned farms. Extended families wither as nuclear families and individuals living alone become the typical social unit. Large social structures become not clans or villages but formally created organizations like corporations and governmental bureaucracies. The consequences of this paradigm for individual consciousness has been similarly profound. Under the Traditional Paradigm, the individual appears to have assumed that his or her station in life was decreed, given by the gods. The Technocratic Paradigm made the gods remote and replaced the decree of gods with individual responsibility. Individual responsibility means a choice of alternatives— of being in one role and envisioning another. The potential of alternative roles is made possible by this modern paradigm and, in the same way, so is burnout.

PROLOGUE FOR THE EMERGENT PARADIGM

Over the eight millennia or so of civilization, individual consciousness has changed to make the person more aware of alternatives and contingencies. The human environment is far different, now filled with our artifacts, a human-created environment. The paradigms have changed. The Traditional Paradigms of feudalism or theocratic kingdoms or tribalism are passing. For brevity and convenience, I have compressed several world views into a single paradigm, the Traditional. Remnants of these older world views still grasp the majority of earth's population. The Middle East has strong representation in theocratic kingdoms and feudalism. Iran, Saudi Arabia, Lebanon are more feudal or theocratic kingdoms than technocratic worlds. Much of Africa is beset with tribalism and the wars of tribalism.

Yet in all these examples, there are mixtures of the Technocratic Paradigm. But because the Technocratic Paradigm now appears to have its own inherent contradictions and weaknesses, emerging orders, unexpected alternatives, sprout up.

And finally, ambiguity may prove to be more continuous, more a companion for humanity than has ever occurred before. Life is a crucible and the test of any species is continuous. Our species is a paradox. We no more than learn how to adapt to a given ecological order than through our own actions we change the old order, the old environment.

The occurrence of burnout is a symptom of change in individual consciousness and signals a shift in the way the world is now organized. It is a sign that says important changes have begun. It is an aspect of the transformation process from the Technocratic Paradigm to a new reality. Where emergence is concerned, some things will not be hurried. There is a leavening process. When that process is concluded, the new paradigm, the structures, the reality will be manifest.

We cannot, though, know at this time whether a given movement, a prescribed intervention, a preferred therapy is of the new paradigm, of the old, or wholly incidental. The desire to declare the new, map it, and explain it is more than crass commercial hucksterism; it is also a human response to the ambiguity, to the frustration of the unknowing.

Our best hope for now is to be a survivor. Rush not headlong into any solution. Reserve judgment. Wait for the smoke to clear. For the wind to show its direction. Be open to the new. Thoughtful of its meaning, yet cautious not to judge solely in terms of the past. At this moment, this is all one can do.

The consciousness of the Traditional Paradigm is one wherein the world is viewed as a web and each action is felt throughout the web. At the center of the web is the individual and the universe centers on each individual. The world, the universe, is small and immediately known, and little analytical activity on the part of the individual occurs. The present time is an aspect of the past. Activity is directed to unquestioning duty and fidelity to tradition. The world is largely closed, yet there is little attention paid to cause and effect.

The consciousness of the Technocratic Paradigm has an emphasis on local times and local events. The world is seen to be filled with discrete, almost mechanical, causal sequences, and the person is one of the elements in just such a causal sequence. And though the world is more complex than that of the Traditional Paradigm, it is nevertheless finite and ultimately slowly runs down, becomes disorganized. It tends toward entropy.

The emergent consciousness is one of even greater felt limitations on human action, and yet, the individual is seen as more important, more noteworthy. Unlike the two previous paradigms, the system is open, emergent, and increases in complexities rather than running down into entropy. This is a time of solemn contemplation but not despair or melancholy.

14

The Map of the Temporary World

There is no remembrance of former things;
neither shall there be any remembrance of
things that are to come with those that shall
come after.

Ecclesiastes.

I have climbed to the snows of Age,
    and I gaze at a field in the Past,
Where I sank with the body at times
    in the sloughs of a low desire,
But I hear no yelp of the beast,
    and the Man is quiet at last
As he stands on the heights of his life
    with a glimpse of a height that is higher.

Alfred, Lord Tennyson, "By An Evolutionist." *Demeter and Other Poems.*

All cultures of the world can be seen as systems of values and personal conduct that develop over long periods of time extending far beyond the life of a single person. Many, many generations are involved, with each new generation adding a dimension or two to the culture and embellishing some older roles and norms, with each era reaffirming the sanctity of the tradition. This accumulation of tradition is what produces a culture, and the creation of a culture is the defining of reality. It explains what the world is, what we are to do within the world, how our hours are numbered, and how our days are spent.

Driving through your neighborhood in a large city or in a small community some night imagine what the world would be like the next morning if all the rules were forgotten? There would be no rush hour traffic in the morning because people would not know how to drive an automobile, much less the rules of driving and the meaning of signs and traffic lights. What would be the meaning of your home or personal property, for that matter, if not that dictated by culture? If you were to wake up in the morning without culture, you could choose just as easily to walk into the house next door and eat from that refrigerator as to eat breakfast in your own kitchen. Television and the newspaper, morning coffee, and breakfast could not occur without culture. The plans for the day, the routine of other members of the family are only realities insofar as we agree they are reality. So much of life and what fills the content of ordinary consciousness is this kind of stuff, inherited in bits and pieces but, by and large, coherent and well-organized as a pattern. Yet, so seldom do we realize how arbitrary it truly is. All cultures are temporary and ours may be more so than most.

THE CREATION OF CULTURES

The inheritance of most cultures is long. Modern England has had a basis in written law evolving for hundreds of years; Japanese and Chinese societies can be traced back through time for two millenia; the French have been a discernible, unified people since the Middle Ages. In all these cases, each generation has added to the fabric of the nation. These cultures, other societies of the past, and the majority of societies today evolved gradually with occasional sharp breaks and dislocations but, nevertheless, over years measured in the hundreds. Through such great periods of time, social systems acquire an expansive, collective memory that provides rules for all manner of situations, real and imaginary. These social systems can be termed tradition-rooted societies.

Tradition-rooted means that the past is the source of answers for questions in the present. The occupations of men and women are handed down by tradition. The length of childhood is prescribed by tradition. The structure of the society, its chief industries, religions and government are rooted in processes that evolve over hundreds of years. Individual freedom and responsibility with the promise of the future as bright or bleak and the tendency to meet challenges or avoid challenges are all governed by rules first, handed down mouth-to-mouth and then, set into writing. Such a gradual and time-involving pattern is followed in the development of most societies. It is a pattern that has worked countless times during humanity's existence and it is the only pattern that humans have known. There is an occasional Plato's *Republic* of what the world should be, but preordained utopian descriptions of a society do not succeed because the requirements of a fully functioning culture far exceed the conceptual grasp of the single, individual mind.

Societies may disappear in a similar fashion. Climates change and a forced migration is made. During the migration, encounters with new territories and new peoples cause the old system gradually to break into smaller units that grow anew or become assimilated into other societies. The population and culture of modern England is an example of this conglomerating process that builds a culture. England apparently began over three thousand years ago with the Druids who were mixed with Romans from invasions and colonization near the time of Christ. The country then experienced periodic invasion and intermingling with Celts from the Irish region, the Danish, and the Teutons from Viking incursions, and Norman conquests from France for the next fifteen hundred years. By the reign of Queen Elizabeth I in 1558, these influences were successfully melded into a uniform culture that then played a role of conquest on the world stage for three centuries.

In other situations, changes are more sharp and discontinuous; for example, when a plague, war, or earthquake decimates a people, the survivors depart more abruptly from tradition. The collapse of the ancient Minoan civilization with the volcanic explosion of Thera in the second millenium B.C. or, in recent times, the destruction of the American Indian cultures in North America illustrate cultural collapse and disappearance.

These society-building processes produce individuals who look strongly to the past to meet the present and create an individual psychology that does not dwell on the future. To a very large degree, most people of the world have in common such culture-building experiences.

In its history, however, American society has moved from this tradition-centered mode of culture development. Because the United States was not successfully colonized by a single society, a uniform cultural tradition was not transplanted from a single European country to this area of North America. Instead, the society has grown from a synthesis of several Western cultures and the Indians native to North America. Unlike Euroupe or Asia, American society has developed far fewer traditional rules to direct and govern the conduct of life, business, and employment. In frontier America, land was free, not governed by hereditary fiefdoms that prevented persons from developing and owning independent farms. Trades and occupations were less effectively controlled by the guild structures that had developed over several hundreds of years in Europe. Thus, the potential of the individual for beginning private enterprise was much greater. Because of free land, or perhaps more accurately because of land freed from Indians who were the original and rightful owners, capital was not accumulated in the hands of a few but open to the masses.

What occurred in the opening of the New World was an acceleration of a trend that had moved far more slowly in Europe—the separation of people from the land; thus permitting people to move freely across the countryside and develop new social forms with less constraint or direction from tradition. Such conditions, coupled with European immigrants, all of whom were to some degree fleeing from the strictures of tradition, shaped the American society toward solutions developed from contingencies or factors of the immediate present rather than dependence on tradition or time-honored solutions. Thus, the American culture acquired a highly adaptive style with an emphasis on contemporaneousness, individualism, optimism, social fluidity, and planning for the immediate future. It is a society that prides itself in defining and solving problems rather than coexisting with conditions or teaching individuals to endure oppressive or discomforting conditions.

All cultures are adaptive by degrees, but American culture is more than most. The American Revolution was the fullest expression of the Western enlightenment that came out of the European Renaissance and quickly spread its seeds of revolution back to the continent, especially France, then Germany and on to other colonial holdings in the New World and Asia. It is important to note, though, that it spread this revolutionary character through its experiences, its ideas and merchants, not through religious missionaries or colonial conquest, though the country was to enter a messianic phase with its participation in the First World War.

In the American culture, the adaptive style was further encouraged by the significant availability of natural resources from the largely unsettled and undeveloped continent and through the continued infusion of new human capital via immigration through the eighteenth, nineteenth, and twentieth centuries. The efforts to exploit and develop the natural resources and to assimilate diverse immigrant stock produced a cultural bias wherein human resources were viewed in much the same way as physical resources. They were resources to be measured, improved, and used. Because of the immigrant nature of its population, society had to quickly evolve value structures that reshaped and redefined the human character in order to maintain some level of cohesive national state.

The Morrell Act of the 1870s, intended to apply science to agriculture and industry through the land grant university, was one of the earliest expressions of the culture to develop human resources hand in hand with physical resources. By the twentieth century, the culture had produced a consumer society with extraordinary industrial productivity and agricultural enterprises that had become world standards and, in some cases, world dominant. Probably the most important key to American productivity, high standards of living, and social mobility has been the American commitment to the development of human and physical resources and the free, adaptive entrepreneurial spirit fostered by the notion of applied knowledge.

MODES OF CULTURAL ADAPTATION

Every culture represents an adaptation to the immediate environment in which a people find themselves. Human beings are the most adaptive of the primates and, unlike other highly adaptive species such as the insects, humans use intelligence rather than genetic change to permit life to flourish at most points on the globe and even, for brief periods of time, beneath the sea and in outer space. We humans, unlike all other forms of life, are able to externalize our intelligence through our tools, the material culture. Both the invention of the wheel and the discovery of fire are early examples of the externalization of intelligence, with numbers and letters becoming a most powerful illustration of the external intelligence of which humans are capable. These two particular inventions, letters and numbers, have expanded so greatly that the external intelligence now far exceeds the capability of any single individual. Machine technology is the third significant category of external human intelligence. This category has grown especially swiftly since the mid-nineteenth century. The automobile, the airplane, electronic communication, cybernetic machine systems on the assembly line, and the computer, all represent human thought and logic created and bound in an external device that is the cumulative result of hundreds of individual human intelligences. This is a very recent phenomenon since, as late as the Renaissance, individuals were presumably able to come to grips with the whole of human knowledge. The human brain for all its marvelous capacities has now been exceeded by its own creation, external intelligence.

However, all groups of people are not the same in their adaptability. Among the Indians of the American Southwest, two polar extremes exist in the degree to which the culture changes to meet new conditions. At the highly adaptive end of the continuum are the Navajo. Their culture over the last three hundred years has gathered religion from the Pueblo, an economy using sheep and horses from the Spaniards, and a technology and initial industrialization from modern America. Of all Indian groups on the North American continent, the Navajo have suffered as much from dislocation and forced encampment as other Indian groups; yet they are the largest intact tribe on the North American continent today with a population of over 100,000 members and controlling tribal lands in New Mexico, Arizona, Utah, and Colorado.

The Zuni represent the opposite polarity in adaptability with a style of life that has remained very resistant to change, retaining many of its structures and forms in their original intent to a far greater degree than have the Navajo. The Zuni remain in isolated village compounds, carefully controlling contact with outsiders, including other Indians, and avoiding as much as possible the introduction of other cultures from the outside world.

Neither high adaptability nor low adaptability are, in themselves, virtues. In the case of these two distinctly separate Indian peoples, both have survived over the centuries with one remaining relatively changeless and the other continually transmuting itself through contact with other cultures and environmental change. In a way, survival is the measure of whether high adaptability or low adaptability is the preferred mode.

There are circumstances where high adaptability is not necessarily useful. High adaptability in a world that changes slowly may mean a loose ordering of the code of life, resulting in confusion and conflict among members in the society and leading to a dissipation of energy. The original culture under these conditions will quickly disappear and the members of the society will die out or find themselves members of other societies. In a rapidly changing world, though, high adaptability seems more a virtue as long as some common thread of continuity for society can be maintained.

Tradition-Rooted Reality

The tradition-rooted society, while low on adaptability, has two distinct advantages. One is that tradition, like a habit, conserves energy. Tradition provides answers to questions and minimizes the amount of debate or thought needed before action can be taken. Second, tradition orders society and makes life predictable. Tradition makes today like yesterday; the present, a mirror of the past. Tradition acts to homogenize the members of a society over time so that shared outlooks become more and more alike, the level of satisfaction for members of the society increases, and harmony is more readily achieved.

The negative side of tradition-rootedness means that tomorrow will be much like today. Perhaps this is not a problem if there is nothing wrong today. But there is an implication that tomorrow can be like today only if other things remain mostly the same—they may not. Tradition imposes old solutions on new problems and, thus, may not be able to make tomorrow as intended or necessarily maintain the continuity of existence.

A tradition-rooted society depends on internalized codes of behavior for members of a society which make certain the individual does the proper thing under a given circumstance. The internalized code is taught in childhood, and usually there is no alternative to cause the individual to think differently. Internalized codes are, of course, designed to handle all situations and when a new phenomenon does occur, tradition develops a routine way of dealing with the new phenomenon. As these alternatives appear and ripple through the entire society, a choice must be made quickly or the society can collapse.

Imposed Bureaucracy

An alternative way of organizing social behavior is not through internalized codes of behavior, but rather through imposing a bureaucracy over individuals and achieving individual compliance with organizational authority. The imposed bureaucracy is a common approach when a conquering society imposes its will on another. Over several generations, the society may move from forced acceptance of the conditions of an imposed bureaucracy to an internalization of the codes of behavior.

The caste system of India is illustrative of this movement; each caste represents a succeeding wave of conquerors that swept the Indian subcontinent and imposed a bureaucracy over the existing people. The conquerors separated themselves by tradition and marriage from the conquered peoples, yet resided in the same general space and time. Thus, like sediment laid down on the surface of the earth to form geological strata, waves of conquerors gave rise to layers of bureaucracy which, in time, formed the caste society of India.

The imposed bureaucracy is costly to society in terms of energy because a large number of individuals must be provided with special power to enforce procedures on others, and considerable numbers of related individuals must be involved in the surveillance of other members of the culture. In addition, there exists a general level of tension within the society because the threat of revolution or overthrow of the existing government is omnipresent. Many members of the society see the culture and institutions not as their own but as a yoke imposed on them; that awareness and conflict within the society imposes a burden of suspicion on the conquerors. Considerable energy must also be devoted by the conquering class to justify their exalted position to the conquered class, convincing them of their inadequacies. The imposed bureaucracy, though, may be somewhat more adaptable than the tradition-centered society since people are given orders to follow and will follow new orders if they are given. The adaptability, however, rests on a small number of individuals in the controlling bureaucracy making the correct decisions and, of course, being aware of new contingencies that develop in the environment that demand change.

In the imposed bureaucracy, the Technocratic Paradigm has utilized scientific management as its major tool of socialization in controlling the anomie that occurs through modernization and industrialization. The modern organization fits well with an imposed bureaucracy orientation since both are elitist in orientation, emphasize control and order, and assume that the future can be predicted and achieved through goal setting and establishing methods to achieve these goals determined by the elite. Within the Technocratic Paradigm, public and corporate bureaucracies are substituted for tradition as means of providing authorization or anchors for individuals.

Contingency-Centered Consciousness

A third mode of organizing behavior is that descriptive of the contingency-centered society. The contingency-centered society places a heavy emphasis on a high degree of preparedness for each individual adult member to make independent decisions for the good of the individual. It is assumed that such decisions will also collectively contribute to the common good. Such a society must invest heavily in resources for education to prepare individuals for this responsibility and, then, additional resources to provide on-going information to the individual to improve his or her understanding of the contingencies and increase the likelihood of right rather than wrong decisions.

Such societies exhibit high decentralization of decision making and operate in terms reminiscent of the market in traditional economics. Rather than have a central group plan for the needs of all members of society and then handle distribution through a central bureaucracy, each individual is assumed to be sovereign and able to make decisions for his or her own good. Through the decentralization created by the market mechanism, a balance is achieved that protects all members. In a contingency-centered society there is a general domain assumption that people should be prepared to make positive decisions about life instead of using the authority of tradition or the control of governmental bureaucracy to prevent mistakes. In a contingency-centered society, the individual is then permitted to engage in chosen behavior and, when it is deemed wrong, the individual must suffer some adverse consequences as a result of that decision. Consciousness, awareness, is centered on contingencies.

The contingency-centered society is highly individualistic and places large responsibility on the individual to care for himself, make appropriate decisions, set goals, and use available resources. This freedom to use resources requires teaching people to limit their use. But the knowledge of this condition is especially critical for this form of society. It is especially important in the contingency-centered society that resources be understood to be scarce, not infinite, nor relying perpetually on ingenuity to replace any finite resource.

Such an adaptive society tends toward pluralism rather than a single culture model and builds in a fair degree of internal conflict. Market mechanisms sort and diffuse the conflict, and because of the indeterminancy of the present, there is a considerable future orientation. The contingency-centeredness means that the individual must routinely read the contingencies, make a projection for a desired future state, and then achieve in terms of that future state.

The contingency-centered society has a tremendous need for information because decisions are made based on information, facts about situations. The more information an individual has, the more the individual may maximize the correctness of the decision. Thus, a society will make considerable investments in creating and distributing information.

Because of its nature, information is difficult to hoard and easy to replicate and distribute. This quality promotes decentralization of power and acts as a brake to the growth and authority of bureaucratic forms in the society. Understanding and using information itself is the inverse of the tradition-centered society where precedent, rather than the information in the present situation, is the source of answers. It is the development of the contingency-centered society and its close relationship to the development and dissemination of information that provides a high emphasis on training, the creation of knowledge technology, and the knowledge industry. The free press and freedom of access to information are beliefs that must be cherished and protected by the contingency-centered society to insure the open market of information and avoid the control of information by elites and special interest groups.

Contingency-centered societies are a cultural form different in organization from either the tradition-centered culture or the bureaucratic culture. The tradition-centered culture looks to the past; the present is viewed as a representation of the past. The important concern is not information about the present, but faithful replication of the rules laid down in the past. The individual in a traditional society is a group member, not an individualist. Individual consciousness exists at a low and rudimentary level. Life and reality do not exist beyond the confines of the primary group. Consciousness has not yet dawned since that society is organized by rituals that are deeply internalized by every member. Because of the high level of internalization of rules that can be achieved through the traditional culture, the individual of that culture, when alone, may seem a willful and proud individualist. However, the strength of the behavior should not be judged in terms of the strength of the individual, but rather the degree to which traditional cultures can imprint their will on the mind of the individual and ensure certain conditioned responses even in the absence of other members of the society.

Bureaucratic culture is a response to the chaos prompted by social change that gives rise as well to higher levels of consciousness for the individual. Bureaucratic culture imposes rationally planned and designed organizations over the increasingly conscious people created from the decline of tradition-centered culture. The more culture moves into the contingency mode, the greater will be the cultural investment in information systems and structures designed to create and distribute data. Universities, public schools, and educational programs will proliferate. The print media will be varied and intensive.

Whereas information is sacrosanct in a tradition-centered culture, conserved and controlled in bureaucratic culture, it becomes a public utility in the contingency culture. Freedom of information becomes a high value, and the denial of public access to information, a capital crime. Electronic media for storing and disseminating information further increase the availability to all members. This variable, the availability of information, then initiates a reorganization of society that further loosens the strength of cultural forms that are holdovers from bureaucratic and tradition-centered cultures. The kinship system becomes even less a means for control of behavior, and bureaucracies find it more difficult to assure compliance among employees even during regular working hours. Large-scale intrusive government, a companion process to the bureaucratic society, begins to wither in the contingency culture. Codes of behavior, which were internalized in the tradition-centered culture or enforced in the bureaucratic culture, are choices that grow out of free individuals assessing contingencies and operating in terms of the contingencies in the new order.

In the United States, instruments of media communication and education are some of the more characteristic aspects of our culture. The U.S. is a media-intensive society and an education-intensive society. More of the total productivity of this society is devoted to these activities than in any other major society. It is not because the media or education are high values in and of themselves, rather a contingency-centered society requires information and the structures to process it in the same way that a tradition-centered society requires belief in a deity and devotes a significant proportion of its resources to temples and shrines of worship. The bureaucratic culture requires compliance and the use of fear to maintain the culture, and thus must invest heavily in instruments of control and surveillance and a police force to maintain compliance.

The operating equation for the creation of the contingency-centered culture is a rise of consciousness in the tradition-centered society which leads to its decline and social chaos. Table 10 summarizes the paradigms, their characteristic social structure, and the mechanism or process central to the maintenance of the system.

Table 10

Paradigms, Social Structures, and Maintaining Mechanisms

	Traditional Paradigm	Technocratic Paradigm	Emergent Paradigm
Social Structure	Tradition-rooted society	Imposed bureaucratic society	Contingency-centered society
Mechanism	Maintaining structure—religion	Controlling institution—internal military and police structures	Decision making, information creating and processing structures

Chaos is then resolved through a bureaucratic culture that exacts compliance but is unable to achieve the stronger internalization of the tradition-centered culture. Finally, as social change continues, the bureaucratic culture is unable to maintain its required level of compliance and increasingly must use force against its own members, thus leading to civil revolt. A new bureaucratic structure may be imposed resulting in another civil revolt and again new bureaucratic structures are imposed until gradually there may be an assertion of smaller, informal groupings which leads to the emergence of the contingency-centered culture.

As its members learn to use information to make decisions rather than depending on bureaucratic edict or on tradition, the contingency-centered culture grows. The growth of information and the mechanisms to create and disseminate information then must be understood as a requirement of this culture rather than values in their own right. In time, all the pre-existing institutions of the two former cultures are modified and stripped of much of their power by the growth of the contingency-centered culture. This is the culture of the temporary world.

THE KNOWLEDGE EXPLOSION

It has perhaps become a bromide to speak of the knowledge explosion, yet the accuracy of this statement is why the statement appears to be a bromide. Today we are each participants in the greatest burst of knowledge development since the Renaissance. Bursts of knowledge have been much like a supernova that explodes in the heavens and for a time dominates all other stars. Comparable past explosions mark the heights of the dawn of civilizations of Mesopotamia and the first and second Egyptian kingdoms. A critical difference that grows with each supernova is the shorter amount of time separating each knowledge burst and the increasingly vast amount of prior knowledge associated with each explosion. Indeed, in our time, we may have witnessed the achievement of a critical mass of knowledge wherein there is a continuing explosion like a plasma. The base of knowledge is such that it can achieve and sustain a continuing explosion that generates enough energy to be self-maintaining, rather than exhausting itself and then slowly stockpiling energy over the centuries for a new burst. This present condition contrasts with previous enlightenments that have been a brief period of illumination with a gradual ebbing of light over a thousand years until the next enlightenment.

The knowledge explosion of the nineteenth and twentieth centuries is surely not linear but grows in a geometric progression. In other words, each increment to the total base provides a larger base for the next addition which is larger in size than the preceding increment. Knowledge growth today is no longer Euclidean but occupies a multi-dimensional space. As a segment of the field grows and unfolds, it may be influenced and directed not just by the field from which it emanates but from unsuspected directions and often unrelated areas. For example, radical improvements in modern surgery have come from advancements in the adhesion industry with glues beginning to replace pins in bone fractures or from advances in engineering, telemetry, and optics for surgery in central body cavities that does not require cutting through the skin.

The knowledge explosion has made knowledge a valuable and much sought after resource that determines the fate of nations. This definition of knowledge is not the alchemist's secret incantation or a vial of heavy water to build a great bomb, but rather a total system or culture of trained persons, supportive institutions, and a special core of managers. National stature is increasingly measured in terms of this yardstick, and one need only glance at world history since the thirties to grasp the significance of this development. The German developments in chemistry, nuclear physics, and rocketry; the brief hegemony of the United States in nuclear weaponry; Russian space successes and the near panic of the United States in developing its own space program; the impact of American computer companies and the organizational breakthroughs of modern international corporations are all products and producers of the new knowledge economy.

Ninety percent of the scientists who have ever lived are living today. More than half of every high school graduating class in the United States enters college, and yet the knowledge base they acquire suffers obsolescence within five years after graduation. Today, the knowledge segment of the national economy accounts for over half the gross national product, though we do have a condition of educational inflation today whereby more schooling is required to do the same jobs, not to do them better, but just to be permitted to do them. Increasingly, we find individuals educated to very high levels who are performing jobs independent of their educational attainment. The lawyer who drives a taxi, the chemist working as a garbage collector, or the stockbroker who runs a bookstore are examples known to us all.

KNOWLEDGE AS CAPITAL

Moving a minute from the description of this force in social change, let us examine more closely what the force is. Knowledge can be viewed as a form of capital. For early humans and most nontechnological societies, capital was a function of the land, animals and humans' physical labor. The accumulation of capital was expressed as an excess of land, animals, or slaves. With development of money economies and through the classic store of wealth—gold—capital could be accumulated in a more transportable and less perishable nature through the development of money. In the eighteenth century in Western Europe and England, machines appeared as a form of capital and as a great producer of excess capital. This era coincided with the tremendous redirecting of human labor, all combining into what is today the world's most productive form of human organization: the industrial society.

Let us illustrate how knowledge can produce a capital resource. Take oil, for example. For thousands of years it lay at or beneath the surface of the ground but existed as a liability that lessened the land's worth. The very presence of oil on land made it unproductive for farming or cattle grazing. Such property was hard to give away, much less sell. Yet suddenly in the 1920s and thirties this basic fact changed. A section of oil-bearing land became worth far more than the finest Iowa farmland and once worthless pieces of real estate, such as the arid plains of West Texas, the swamps of Louisiana, or the deserts of the Middle East, became the sources of personal and corporate fortunes far beyond any that had ever existed before. In the late twentieth century, no other form of wealth is more secure or dependable than oil. The greatest empire of modern times, England, sees its luxury products and country estates now being purchased by its former colonial peoples of the Middle East.

This rapid shift in meaning of substance from a bane to an eagerly sought commodity illustrates the elusive and perplexing quality of capital. Capital, or at least what capital is producing, is socially and culturally defined. For the breeder, cattle or sheep are the prime source of capital. For the farmer, fertile land and favorable climate are the sources of capital. The advent of the machine enlarged the formula. Machines represent knowledge capitalized and secured in an external device created by humans, not a naturally occurring substance. Even the simplest of machines, like a hand tool or a hunting weapon, represent knowledge converted to an external state. Verbal language, writing, and mathematics are highly complex elaborations of this principle. These tools then turn and interact with the minds of people to change individual mentality. Through writing, language, and mathematics, the human mind is able to act more and more as a central processor and has less call to be a data storage unit. The data can be stored externally and accessed on demand through reading or recorded sound. These tools also make the individual far more conceptual and offer alternatives to conscious existence in immediate environmental stimuli. The ability to think of the past and speculate about the future is clearly tied to this development of external intelligence.

Machines provide an alteration in the relationship of humans to the natural environment; and although they do not make humans unessential, they radically redefine our role in the world of work. Machines in the first order make the individual much more productive; yet in an even more profound way, call for a different kind of person. With machines, not any sort of person will do. A technician, an engineer, or an industrial worker is called forth. The craftsperson and the physical laborer quickly see their work and their place in the world disappear.

Nations which formerly boasted a large population, a vast store of human resources, now bemoan this condition as a severe ill if their work forces are not technologically trained. Today, untrained workers are a plague on the economy of the nation. The powerful nation counts its strength in trained workers and in machines, not in population alone. Clearly, India or China, though perhaps fascinating in sheer human number, are both an anomaly in an industrial age and exceedingly weak in terms of productivity. The sheer size of the population alone mitigates against increases in individual or collective productivity.

This condition of vast numbers of untrained workers is the plague of the underdeveloped world. It is also a prime source of today's major international tensions. As the Israeli-Arab conflicts have shown, the well-equipped but clearly unsophisticated Egyptians cannot, through the possession of technology alone, overturn a highly technological society, though they may be a continual source of concern. These sources of tension will increase, not decrease, as technology itself amplifies and emphasizes a growing disparity between technological and under-developed countries. Yet, the simple importation of new technology does not simultaneously change the minds of the people. Rather, technology itself and the knowledgeable workers who accompany it usually appear as severe discomforts to the local population. This may, as in Iran, cause a nativistic movement, resurgent Islamic nationalism, which seeks to dispel the knowledge with its attendant cultural patterns.

In reality, the twentieth century has only lately seen a break from a further refinement of the basic formula of humans, machines, and natural resources established in England, the first of the industrialized societies. In the new stages of the knowledge explosion, knowledge itself becomes a capital item that must be added to the basic equation of humans, machines, and natural resources. As an item in that equation, knowledge changes the meaning of the other three components of the equation.

The impact of knowledge on items in the equation can be seen in the case of machines. The most radically new machine of our time is the computer. Nothing excites the imagination as does this machine. Basically, the computer is a knowledge storing, processing, and retriev-ing machine. It does not make cloth, it does not move earth, it does not fly through the air or ply the seas. It does, however, process information and information is a component of knowledge. Because the computer, like the book, is a pure knowledge technology, it proves to be a powerful tool indeed. It changes the equation by changing people who work with the computer and makes computer knowledge a new natural resource.

Knowledge itself is a strange form of capital. It cannot be depleted nor can it in the usual sense be hidden away or stored. It is an extremely elusive form of capital as its only source is humanity, and the people who work with knowledge are special people. As knowledge makers, they do not respond to the characteristic and familiar organizations of earlier people. Yet, increasingly, they carry with them the key to success or failure for communities, institutions, and even societies. We know little yet of this new element, or what effect it will have on human societies. What we do know is what profound changes may be in order, and what was predictable today may be chaos tomorrow. Once again, the basic categories, the core elements in humanity and our social order, are undergoing radical change. Through this development of knowledge as capital, the worker of today increasingly becomes the knowledge broker rather than the technician or even the craftsperson with fixed sets of skills to apply.

Information Technology

Among the prime generative technologies of change is information technology. Information technology is the systems, machines, and institutions that develop information, store it, and make access to it possible. Information technology refers to those institutions that serve as repositories of knowledge, such as libraries and schools; those institutions charged with the development of knowledge, such as universities, medical research centers, R&D labs in industry, and governmental research groups; organizations that serve as distributors of information, including telephone systems, newspapers and periodicals, publishers, the electronic media of television, radio, the emerging industries of videotapes and discs, and other facsimile transmission.

For 100,000 years information technology depended solely on the spoken word and visual gestures. Perhaps six to eight thousand years ago it expanded when writing was invented and expanded again with the invention of the printing press but, in the twentieth century, it has found a proliferating technology. Today, information is routinely transmitted on paper and in written form, through voice linkages over wires, through electromagnetic radiation via television and radio waves, through storage on videotapes and discs. It is now no longer necessary to go to the library to find a research report or a book. Such information can be acquired through a telephone coupler into a video screen, teleprinter, or a facsimile printer at home or in the office. The modern researcher no longer goes to the library and laboriously wades through journals and books to find information on a given topic, but rather has access to data banks where scientific reports are stored and then uses key descriptors to have the machine search through all known literature and provide literature which contains the descriptor words. As this process grows, information will become more and more a common utility available to individuals throughout the world and accessible at one's fingertips, requiring only a telephone and some form of terminal.

Electronics and Information

A second important generative technology is electronics. Electronics came into being only toward the end of the last century with the works of James Clerk Maxwell and Michael Faraday. Faraday, the experimentalist, found that by moving a magnet near a copper coil, the physical movement could be transformed into an electrical current in the coil. Maxwell theorized the concept of a field that linked the magnet to the copper coil though the two did not touch each other. Electrical field theory became a wholly separate area of physics which accounted for phenomena that could not be explained by the classic mechanical physics of Newton. Initial applications of electrical theory were modest, indeed, with its application to the internal combustion engine as a sparking mechanism to ignite fuel and as a source of light in the incandescent bulb. Then, simple electric motors began to be utilized in a variety of industrial applications; teamed with the compressor, home refrigeration was made available in the 1920s. It was, however, with the discoveries of Ferme, when electronics were found to be susceptible to application for the transmission of information through the regularities of electromagnetic radiation, that electronics began to grow as a generative technology.

In the fifties, the University of Illinois and Univac Corporation wedded electronics to information, producing the computer. In a twenty year span, electronics rapidly transformed information storage, dissemination, and even the control of many assembly line processes. Several generations of computers have now come and gone with the original house-sized Univac computer now exceeded in speed, size and reliability with versions that sit on a desk. Computer-generated displays guide aircraft, remote probes to outer space, and the micro probe of the brain surgeon. Memory chips growing out of computer development have replaced the mechanical moving parts of the watch and the carburetor metering system in the automobile. Computers now control temperature settings in large buildings, electrical power grid distribution for large utilities, the routing of telephone calls, the scheduling of airlines and railroads, and countless research applications where quantities of data must be rapidly and accurately recorded and summarized.

Both the growth of information and the electronic technology are important in another way. They both depart significantly from the linear, mechanistic tradition of science and the Technocratic Paradigm that gave birth to them. Electrical field theory could never be explained adequately by the mechanics of Newton. The generation and transmission of information in a linear and controlled sense ended with the printing press. The idea has been thoroughly abandoned with the introduction of the photocopier. Both technologies emphasize the immediate and make discrimination of the past and future very difficult. Videotapes are not discernible from live telecasts and television is increasingly independent of the clock.

Two More Important Technologies

While it is one of the most linear of the generative technologies, transportation has nevertheless played an extremely important role in ending the traditional communities of the world and hastening the arrival of the temporary world. Air travel more than land travel changed the topography of the nation and the world from large airport to large airport. From these points, population fans out in a 360 degree arc, unlike surface highways and transportation systems where populations tend to parallel route paths. The airline produces both a more urban and at the same time a more rural world. The urban centers become more highly concentrated and more in contact with each other, but the countrysides and the small villages will become progressively isolated particularly as long as general purpose individual vehicular traffic grows more restricted. The wandering and traveling that began with the horse and then the automobile is a passing era. Long distance individual travel will be replaced by the collective travel of the airlines. Human-powered travel will reappear in cities and communities. This is already appearing in the suburban malls, in the shopping, living, and working centers, that are developing in the inner city. At the same time, the countryside is becoming more and more rural, including the return of forested lands to the East and the reestablishment of species of life, such as the fox and the coyote, that had almost vanished east of the Mississippi.

Bioengineering will be among the greatest of the generative technologies for the remainder of the century and into the first decade of the twenty-first century. Already, enhanced nutrition and hygiene have lengthened the lifespan by twenty years in this century and will contribute to far greater levels of health for the first seventy to eighty years of the individual's existence. Entrepreneurial medical care oriented toward illness will be replaced by health maintenance organizations, with the individual assuming far greater responsibility for understanding bodily functions and recognizing problems when they occur, rather than delegating that responsibility to health professionals. Organ substitution technology is already becoming routine for arterial bypasses. More and more chemical interventions will be used to regulate the homeopathic processes of the body and mood states. The body is no longer sacred but becomes a part of the environment of the mind to alter, improve, and maintain. The great battles that will be fought will not be over whether to do it, but what role the state will have in certain situations, such as decisions about the unborn fetus.

This is a brief sketch, a rough reading, of the map of the temporary World. It is a terrain dominated by information more useful and more available than ever before. Communication will conquer space and knowledge will be immediately available. Time will lose much of its current meaning. Video storage technologies will make immediate events continuously available; the night and day cycles of our primate ancestors will be shelved. The development of knowledge will promote the contingency-centered culture. The culture, in turn, will direct resources for greater understanding of all events. The external world will grow more replete with new technologies, and the vehicle of the internal world, the body, will be shaped, modified, and repaired by technology.

15

The Foundering of the Technocratic Vision

It is the healer and builder and the propagator of untold suffering and death. Is it any wonder that science, the strong, the promising, the unforeseeable, the anarchical force in our modern world, should be cause of acute anxiety.

William S. Beck, *Modern Science and the Nature of Life.*

Nature is a part of our humanity, and without some awareness and experience of that divine mystery man ceases to be man. When the Pleiades and the wind in the grass are no longer a part of the human spirit, a part of the very flesh and bone, man becomes, as it were, a kind of cosmic outlaw, having neither the completeness and integrity of the animal nor the birthright of a true humanity.

Henry Beston, *Outermost House.*

It belongs to a highly developed race to become, in a true sense, aristocratic—a treasury of its best in practical and spiritual types—and then to disappear in the surrounding tides of men. So Athens dissolved like a pearl in the cup of the Mediterranean and Rome in the cup of Europe...

George E. Woodberry, *The Torch.*

The Technocratic Paradigm ultimately produces the temporary world which weakens and begins the dissolution of the massive bureaucracy that the Paradigm has required to produce its products and its wonders and to control the masses loosened by the collapse of the traditional world. Several paradoxes occur in the late stages of the Technocratic Paradigm that contribute to its demise.

Immense energies have created and sustained the Technocratic Paradigm and the controlling bureaucratic structure with its utilization of technology in an authoritarian mode. These energies now appear to be producing the collapse of the Paradigm, its dominant social structure, the bureaucracy, and hastening the demise of its characteristic personality, the Company Man. The Gamesman is a transitory style in the same way that the Jungle Fighter was between the traditional and technocratic. The Gamesman is the transitional figure from Technocratic to Emergent.

The Technocratic Paradigm is a world of high and over-production which mandates high-consumption and obsolescence to maintain full productivity. The population is taught multiple and high material needs. Relative deprivation is a continuous motivation achieved via advertising to prevent satiation leading to high energy consumption, depletion of natural resources and degradation of the environment. The Technocratic Paradigm assumes infinite resources, boundless horizons, and is in reality the adolescent's world view of power, dominance, and aggression. This is the culture of a new car each year, a new spring wardrobe, and colognes and facelifts that create and restore the person. It is a culture where aging does not occur, hair doesn't turn grey and wrinkles do not appear. Women remold their bodies with silicone and pantyhose. Hair transplants and massage parlors maintain male virility. Homes are redecorated and modernized before they become dated, and toothpaste isn't just a mundane cleanser for the teeth, but the sure route to a new popularity.

There are several boundary conditions that lead to the twilight of this world view. One is that the energy available to sustain this Paradigm would need to be infinite and it isn't. Fossil fuels have been the basic source of energy and they are finite and thus becoming more costly. Agriculture and the green revolution are turning brown.

Another boundary condition of the Paradigm is a failure of the hypothesis of human flexibility or plasticity necessary for extreme utilitarianism. The behavioral and social sciences of this Paradigm have long argued that behavior was plastic, amenable to the dictates of the social structure; yet the failure of these people-processing technologies is apparent from education, to management, to psychiatry. For the past decade, standardized scores in the schools have declined, a failure of education; productivity has stood still, a failure of management; and alcoholism, depression, and suicide have risen, a failure of the mental health professions.

THE PROCESS OF PARADIGM SHIFT

Both observations and speculations are included in this chapter. To a degree, observation and speculation tend to blend as a paradigm fades or as one approaches the edge of a paradigm. What constitutes an observable fact is contingent on what beliefs are operative at a given time. When the physicist looks at a trace of a line in a bubble chamber or on a photographic plate and then declares the evidence for an electron or a mu meson, certain beliefs must be operative for the statement to be accepted. Without a paradigm, the marks are a curiosity; they have no meaning. With a certain kind of paradigm, they have significant meaning.

Paradigms are world views, cultural orientations, epistemological assumptions. To emphasize the individual or the social group, to believe that destiny can be controlled or is to be met, to anticipate another life, to look for a mathematical harmony beneath the rough surface of apparent existence, to divide experience into things or view it as fluid are beyond empirical inquiry and thus are alternative positions that are taken, assumed but never proven. As the assumptions congeal, they form a paradigm, a generalized world outlook much of which is beneath the threshold of everyday consciousness. Paradigms are the product of social interaction, of experience and inquiry into the world. They are a foundation and basic structure upon which great elaborations are built as time passes.

But paradigms do not last forever though often their life span is measured in hundreds of years. Neither do they pass from existence sharply but rather tend to wane and gradually be abandoned as new assumptions grow in favor. At any given time, alternative world views exist and in a Hegelian sense a paradigm carries the seeds of its antithesis. The seeds of an alternative, though, will not grow until sufficient puzzles are developed that the dominant paradigm is unable to solve. For a while, the puzzle may assume the status of Zeno's paradoxes—intellectual curiosities that have no bearing on important issues in life. An example of a Zeno's paradox would be: how long does it take for a man to reach a given doorway if he first takes one step halfway and then each next step is only half the remaining distance? Logically, the man will continue to move toward the doorway yet cannot ever reach the doorway.

If, in time, the puzzles build or a given puzzle grows in importance, a crisis develops. Either the puzzle must be solved or a new paradigm is required. The search for a new paradigm and the competition among alternatives creates a chaotic period. In the course of this book, three general paradigms have been identified: Traditional, Technocratic, and Emergent. The shape and consequences of the third paradigm, the Emergent, is, by the nature of this process, unclear and tentative.

A PROLIFERATION OF PARADOXES

If sheer number and complexity of paradoxes is a measure of the challenge to a paradigm, then the challenge to our current paradigm has grown larger. I have enumerated and described some of the major issues that appear to go beyond our tried and true approaches to solution. But unlike Zeno's puzzles, these issues are rooted in the very substance of our current institutions and cultural processes.

The Education Paradox

The development and preservation of knowledge was originally handled by priestly castes of ancient civilizations, such as those of the Egyptians or Babylonians or in the Catholic Church of the Middle Ages. Within the church, specialization occurred to promote knowledge development in the priestly orders like the Jesuits. Such specialization provided the foundation for universities both in Europe and the United States. In Protestantism, Harvard was founded for theological purposes and then Yale, when Harvard was felt to have grown too liberal.

As recently as the early twentieth century, only the children of the wealthy and students of the ministry routinely attended college. Apart from the ministry, the attendance in college by the wealthy was a special socialization routine designed to provide them with the necessary social graces before assuming the command of family empires and to provide a larger pool than the immediate neighborhood for the selection of marriage partners. In the mind of the American academic, though, the college tradition is the embodiment of liberal notions that release a young mind from its parochialism and ethnocentrism through exposure to the great ideas and cultures of the past, thereby to assume a more responsible role as a citizen.

The tradition of the professional school (law, medicine, engineering, and business) is similar to trade guilds which preserved and maintained prescribed uniform traditions and ensured that they, the traditions, were passed to each new entrant. They serve as well as mechanisms to restrict the numbers of practitioners entering the field and, in some cases, ensure higher economic standing for the guild members.

Since the mid-sixties, the educational system in the United States has expanded vertically and horizontally. The American experience with the university has been both a necessity for the sustaining of the contingency-centered culture and a paradox of so many of the creations of the Technocratic Paradigm; the creation cannot inherently produce what it was intended to. The vertical expansion has been downward into the early childhood years, so that many children, beginning at the age of three, are in some form of organized educational experience. The upward vertical expansion has occurred in that many individuals in later life and in retirement maintain an involvement with the educational system. In some cases, corporations with a heavy research and development emphasis now offer their own advanced degrees; and the professions, particularly medicine, have begun to embrace required continuing education for practicing physicians to maintain their licenses.

The horizontal expansion has been from the uniform mandatory twelve years of education for all citizens to an increased number of private schools. These have appeared both in response to mandatory desegregation and to satisfy those who feel that alternative patterns of schooling are preferable to the public schools. Post-high school institutions have been the fastest growing sector, especially the community college. Almost every community today offers an additional two years of educational instruction beyond high school. In some cases, the instruction is trade and vocationally oriented, taking over for industry the preparation of automobile mechanics, refrigeration repairers, bookkeepers, and computer programmers. In other cases, the community college continues to teach what the high school failed to do; the basic curriculum of math, sciences, and literature is now spread over fourteen years rather than twelve.

Like the community college, the state college is a new institution lacking the norms that long existence provides. Often, such colleges attempt to imitate the characteristics of the private, liberal arts tradition, but available faculty and students fail to support that tradition. The private college tradition of socializing young men and women seems viable only for persons with inherited wealth and status. The typical middle class youngster must achieve some vocational preparation, or both the youngster and the community complain of the impractical nature of the college education. In other instances, the four-year college tends in the direction of the large research university and tries to duplicate the advanced degree and professional programs found in those universities. This, too, has been largely an unsuccessful venture because the same scarcity of resources is faced.

In many ways, the large research university is a perfect expression of the Technocratic Paradigm. Its driving vision is that all things can be known, all problems solved, all goals met through the application of resources in complex organizational systems. These research universities articulate goals of research, teaching, scholarship, and public service. They view themselves as entities that exist on the cutting edge of knowledge, moving that edge forward, applying that edge to technical problems within the society, training novices in the knowledge development and application process, and disseminating findings to an international society of modernists.

The funding of these behemoths is the fascinating world of the Byzantine. State appropriations, student fees, private donations, federal grants, and business research contracts are channeled in with each unit of funding directed toward goals that are largely incompatible with each other. Though the institutions are increasingly run not by scholars but by trained technocrats of the bureaucracy, the institutions are truly ungovernable in the bureaucratic tradition.

Arriving at the appropriate social form for the research university proves elusive. The bureaucracy devises measures and units of productivity that bear little relationship to the actual process of knowledge creation. The case of the scholarly journal is a pertinent example where the proliferation of journals is largely a consequence of a push phenomenon. This phenomenon is the result of requirements in most universities that scholars publish regularly to maintain a position and as justification for promotion and salary increases. Consequently, scholars are urged to perform in the same way that the worker on the assembly line does. One's success is known through the production of accountable items, articles accepted for publication in a journal. The journals then, and their articles, are not demanded or pulled into existence by a reading audience, but rather are pushed into existence by scholars who must have vehicles that will print their products.

This produces situations where high levels of information are available in a field, but the information is not organized into adequate frames of reference and often is of a vexing sort. Empirical inquiry in terms of the limitations of human spirit is infinite. Most of the activity of scientific research is directed toward the accumulation of empirical information and reviewing of data from experimental studies. Only the smallest part of the effort deals with the development of general models and theories that direct research and relate findings to general frameworks. This activity, though, the general frameworks, cannot be neglected or empirical findings pile up without systematic relationships being established among them. The accumulation of empirical findings is established well within the technocratic paradigm, but these mechanistic assembly line norms are not the fertile seedbed for the development of general frameworks.

The Production Paradox

Throughout this century the United States has been considered among the most productive societies of the world. During the First and Second World Wars, U.S. factories and farms provided the food, the combat equipment, and the industrial strength to achieve victory in two of history's greatest logistical undertakings. By the 1950s, the country had recovered from the effects of the Great Depression and the war to become the world's only economic superpower. Standards of living and median income in the United States were marvels to behold and much of the basis for the marvels was the notable productivity of the society. In fact, the productivity had become so great that a surplus crisis became a concern. To contain the crisis, the government began to stockpile wheat, peanuts, orange juice, butter, meat, silver, copper, all manner of agricultural and industrial commodities. Farmers were paid not to farm by idling land and putting it aside into native grasses or forests.

To deal with the surplus production, increased consumption was urged. Cattlemen put bumper stickers on their pickups exhorting everyone to "eat more beef." Families were told they should have two cars and certain truths were communicated to children and teenagers about how their own room, a car, and a stereo were inalienable rights.

Through radio, television, newspapers, and news magazines everyone learned, often to their surprise, that they were deprived, in a relative way. If you did not have your own home, you deserved one. If you had a home, you deserved a newer and larger one. One bath was not enough. Each member of a family deserved a separate bath. If you drove an older car, you must surely realize that you deserved better than that. You really deserved a new car each year as well as travel and entertainment. You worked hard and you have the right to pursue leisure. Under the belief that superhighways were national defense, giant subsidies were given to the automobile, petroleum, construction, and hotel concerns and their affiliated industries and unions so that a vast network of interstate highways could be built. The highways accelerated the demand for travel, for vacation, for autos, and for more highways.

Planned obsolescence was discovered. Unions and industries both found that goods could be produced so readily but so inexpensively that even advertising could not successfully keep people buying. After all, there is a limit to the number of bathrooms you can use at one time. We may have one car to commute in, another for highway travel, and another for recreation; but even Californians might grow weary of owning as many as seven or ten cars. However, if the cars could wear out or, even better, if they could appear outdated, out of fashion, a way could be found out of the box of the satiated consumer. When the buyer says, "No thanks, I have one," we can reply, "But not the latest, not a shiny one."

With planned obsolescence, things began to wear out, were discarded and demand rose. High demand led to increased production and full employment. However, demand always got out of control and shortages were created. The shortages yielded hoarding and inflation. To correct the inflation, government restrictured the money supply and production dropped. Production drops meant unemployment and unhappy unions and businesses. New government programs were funded to stimulate demand. The insatiable consumer came back to life and another whirlwind of consumption, increased production, shortages, and then surplus began.

Today, most Western economies exist in some overheated state of excess demand and inflation or sagging demand, unemployment, and idle industrial capacity. Government intervention through credit controls, unemployment compensation, and public sector purchasing is typical. Most national economies are planned economies; yet, the success of the planning seems to be lessening. The future of a planned consumer economy of no unemployment, full health and social benefits, and a thirty-hour work week seems faded and tattered.

The Ethic Paradox

Any group of people will, in time, evolve several shared beliefs or ethics that abstractly say how life should be led and what existence means. A central ethic of the Technocratic Paradigm is utilitarianism. John Stuart

Mill (1897) defined utilitarian ethics thusly: "Actions are right in proportion as they tend to promote happiness, wrong as they tend to produce the reverse of happiness. By happiness is intended pleasure, and the absence of pain; by unhappiness, pain, and the privation of pleasure." The happiness to which Mill refers is not individual happiness, but the collective feelings of a society. Thus, the individual may be used as a means to the end of a general good, a social good. The implication of utilitarianism is that an act or an individual cannot be judged good or worthwhile in itself but only in how it contributes to the general good, the average well-being. This philosophy has led us to put an estimated value, a money's worth valuation, to all things. We then begin to calculate our time in terms of money and what our time brings us in terms of money. Gradually, all things become part of the wage-cash economy. In a crude fashion, all things must be valued in terms of how they contribute to the Gross National Product. All acts of commerce, all labor, become valued in terms of money. Personal obligations and family obligations are replaced by economic considerations and a bookkeeping balance sheet. Children are not obliged to care for their parents but rather parents as working citizens earn their retirement by credits placed in the social security system. Each person is not expected to help the poor or the unfortunate. They should get a job and earn their own way.

As the ethic of utilitarianism grows, volunteerism, charity, social responsibility, and other acts that cannot find a place in the wage economy recede and become shrunken, odd symbols of the past. Beauty is defined through function. Truth is replaced by credibility. Justice becomes a plea bargaining process. Utilitarianism defines things in terms of money and using money and calculated worth as the basis for exchange rather than obligation. By looking at one's time in terms of money that is earned or could be earned, each person is encouraged to specialize in those things that he or she does best and for which he or she commands the highest wage. This leads to greater specialization and professionalization of all functions in life. As the individual becomes more and more specialized, generalized competence to perform the functions that are called living decline. This is further extended by professionalization that elaborates and mystifies procedures, and restricts access to tools and instruments to discourage and prevent individuals from recapturing areas of lost competence or developing new competencies. Utilitarianism thus leads to a declining individual competence, and a greater dependence on specialists in every phase of living. It promotes a sense of helplessness, an anxiety about living, about making decisions.

Energy Paradox

The acquisition of energy and the conversion of energy resources into a useable state becomes more demanding as the temporary world grows more complex. A hundred years ago, there was a problem of what to do with the approximately twenty pounds of manure produced by a horse each day. On the farm or prairie this was no problem; horse manure was an important part of the fertilization cycle and it was a valued substance. However, in the city, on the sidewalks and cobblestone streets, it became a problem offensive to pedestrians. The horse-drawn carriage, buggies, drays, and the riding horse required an ever-larger service industry to clean up after them.

The horseless carriage, the forerunner to the automobile, became a useful substitute. By substituting capital for the labor of the horse a more efficient means of transportation was found. By substituting capital and technology for animal labor, productivity increased. Cheap energy was required, though, to run these machines and natural resources were rapidly exploited for their cheap energy potential. Initially, forests were cut down for fuel for the steam-driven machines. As the forests disappeared, coal and petroleum were discovered in vast quantities and the machines were adapted for use with these fuels. Both fuels, particularly petroleum, were found to be compact and convenient energy sources. Soon wind-driven ships were replaced by oil-fired steamers; coal- and oil-fired locomotives supplanted the wood-burning engines; electricity became largely generated by coal or oil; and gasoline-propelled autos crawled across the landscape. The wood stove for cooking and heating became a junked relic.

Yet each step of the exploitation of these natural resources created a long-term debt on the books for society. Deforestation produced land erosion, flooding, and silting of harbors and rivers. Coal mining, particularly strip and open pit mining, rendered the land useless for generations. The burning of coal, oil, and even wood befoul the water and the air, damaging life and threatening the current and future generations through the release of carcinogens and hydrocarbons that filter and reduce the sun's radiation.

To clean up the environment damaged by these capital-intensive, laborsaving machines, requires more capital. Many of the benefits gained are short-lived because the hidden costs soon proved to exceed the visible benefits. What seems to be occurring is pirating of the future to the advantage of the present.

Farming Paradox

As recently as the early years of the current century, most Americans lived on the farm. Today each farmer feeds over a hundred people and less than ten million people reside on farms. Agriculture is America's most bountiful industry and our greatest source of exports. The initial push to high farming productivity was the replacement of human and animal labor by machines: the tractor, the reaper, the combine, the corn picker, and the cotton picker are a few. Fewer hands were required to farm the land, and animal labor was completely eliminated. High yield strains of plants, grains, and livestock replaced less productive varieties. Farmers began to view farming as a business, a commercial venture, not a way of life.

To acquire the machines, the highly productive strains of seeds, and livestock was not an inexpensive endeavor. Farmers had to go into debt to do this. Some were luckier and better capitalists than others. Because the machines were so efficient, those farmers found they could get more work done and thus could farm more land. By farming more land, more cash could be generated to help pay for the increasing cost of farm implements, seeds, and livestock. Thus, farm consolidation occurred.

The small family farm was a diversified, though small-scale, enterprise. Eggs, chickens, hogs, beef, milk, butter, wheat, rye, potatoes, cotton, mutton, wool, corn, and often small grains, fruit and fresh produce could come from a single farm. By having a variety of products, many needs of the farm family could be satisfied, and cash income would not be totally dependent on a single crop or product.

However, as the agribusiness approach replaces the family farm, there is a related move to income maximization and shift to a single-crop strategy. More farming decisions are influenced by prices in national and international commodity markets, and a single-crop strategy permits full exploitation of a good price for a given commodity. The single-crop strategy also permits specialization in much farm equipment, farming methods, and marketing. Income maximization also increases farmer interest in chemical technologies to enhance production, and greater use is made of synthetic fertilizers, insecticides, and herbicides.

By the 1960s, through this process, farming became a large-scale business enterprise, heavily utilizing mechanical and chemical technologies, with most farms using a single or limited crop strategy and using debt financing to cover the cost of the new technology and newly acquired land.

This farming strategy, highly specialized and highly technological, is vulnerable to increased energy costs and energy availability. Because it is so dependent on machines, farmers have few options that do not include the use of the machines. Highly dependent on fertilizer to achieve crop yields, they find these materials, being petroleum related, rising in price. Through single-crop strategy, fields become much more susceptible to specialized insect predation, and farmers must rely even more on insecticides. However, genetic resistances of insects are increasing, as well as public concern about insecticides. Moreover, the single-crop strategy, while maximizing income potential sharply, exposes the farm to unpredictable changes in commodity prices. Thus, if corn prices are high, everyone specializes in corn. If the weather is good, the harvest is bountiful, prices fall, and the farm suffers.

One final aspect in the farming paradox is the resultant land erosion and declining fertility that appear to be a derivative of the agribusiness approach to farming. By use of chemical fertilizer, quickly maturing crop strains and mechanization, more than one crop may be grown on a piece of land in a single year. Rather than restoring the fertility to the land by planting a cover crop, such as a legume that will naturally add nitrogen and organic matter, fertility is maintained by chemicals. Two problems arise. First, by having the soil bare for longer periods of time, more wind and rain erosion occur. Secondly, by not using plant or animal residues to provide fertilizer, an important organic component, plant cellulose, is not available to the soil. Plant cellulose, the leaves, stem, and roots, is an important element in building humus, the mixture of organic and inorganic materials that make a soil tillable and able to retain moisture. Gradually the soil of the agribusiness farm becomes hard packed to a depth of several inches. The hard-packed soil, hardpan, requires more effort and thus more expense to plow and plant. It is even more susceptible to erosion and since it retains less water and makes less efficient use of available rainfall, it is more susceptible to drought and various artificial irrigation practices are needed to maintain its former productivity. Thus, farming appears more and more as an extractive industry, like mining, with the current bountiful returns sure to decline. The decline, of course, is accelerated by further use of the technology that began the increase in the productivity cycle some years ago.

Employment Paradox

As the Technocratic Paradigm grows, more of the labor that was traditionally done by humans is done by machines. While this frees workers from labor that is heavy, dangerous and monotonous, it does not necessarily create new roles for them when new jobs occur, the workers displaced by the machine may not be the workers prepared to do the new job.

As more and more jobs disappear because of automation, unions and professions respond by restricting job entry via union rules, the minimum wage, licensing, and training requirements. Additionally, the size of the labor force is constricted by a pincers effect of using extended education to postpone entry into the job market until the twenties or even later and then, through early retirement, to hasten departure from the labor force. However, since the utilitarian culture requires that dignity and meaning can only be achieved by usefulness, and usefulness can come only by employment, more and more individuals seek employment. The youth and the aged, alike, are affected by the feeling of meaninglessness that comes from unemployment, and the labor force quickly becomes bloated.

In response to these pressures, job growth can be little achieved in the production sector without featherbedding; so jobs become expanded in the services sector. Since so much of work is simply a definition, the definitional game can be played to a high pitch with service jobs. Thus, someone who checks an application that someone else has checked has a job solely by definition; or, the bank employee who reviews a statement that is prepared by a computer that is incalculably more accurate than the human, performs a job that is necessary because someone thought someone should check the machine. Private disputes that were originally settled informally by the parties involved now require justice under law and conveniently more jobs are created: lawyers, judges, and court clerks. Yet, as more and more work is created in the service area, more and more of it seems to have a meaningless, ephemeral quality, so job satisfaction is low. Moreover, service jobs are largely not susceptible to capital intensive efforts to increase productivity; consequently, work output per person remains flat.

In the Technocratic Paradigm, everyone is a consumer and subject to the feelings of relative deprivation achieved through advertising. Each day, everyone has increased expectations of what should be achieved from life and thus, wage increase demands rise. However, since productivity is not growing, or growing only very slowly, the growth of material wealth cannot increase either. An inflationary syndrome is then generated as each group attempts to increase its relative affluence by increasing the cost of its products or services in the general market. These increases yield more dollars that chase a constant amount of goods and services, thus inflation. Finally the inflation lends a degrading and futile dimension to work and the achievement ethic. No matter how hard the donkey plods, the carrot moves farther ahead and economic life seems to be a cruel trick.

Motivational Paradox

Motivation under the Technocratic Paradigm is thought to be a consequence of the individual seeking to maximize profits and pleasure, and minimize loss and pain. Psychological research, though, indicates that, in effect, there are layers or levels of motivation and though initially, the individual is motivated to meet needs of hunger, food, sex, and power, when these needs are met, new motivations arise such as needs for security, affiliation, esteem, and perhaps self-actualization. The impact of the rising affluence possible by the Technocratic Paradigm is that everyone receives a higher standard of living, much of it as a guarantee from the society and not simply as a consequence of the job. This higher standard of living, in effect, raises motivational levels of workers from the needs that can be easily satisfied through purchases such as the need for food, housing, clothing. More and more workers then arrive at a need level that demands more interesting and more autonomous work. However, as the economic growth stagnates, there is a lower level of total job creation and both fewer and less interesting jobs are created. This constriction of jobs worsens motivational problems, and the more complete the success of the Technocratic Paradigm the more dissatisfied workers become.

Population Paradox

When the Technocratic Paradigm first came to life one to two hundred years ago, the total population of the world was less than five hundred million. In 1850, the entire North American continent had scarcely twenty-five million people. Today, it has over fifteen times as many. Better nutrition and hygiene across the world have increased longevity and lowered child mortality. One dread disease of children and adults, smallpox, has been eliminated.

Across the world, but particularly in the poorer lands, high population growth has occurred. Record population levels are reached in country after country. These population pressures have overwhelmed the ability of the countryside to absorb the people and lead to an increasingly intense concentration of population in urban areas. This population concentration in the cities and the inability of the government or industries in the cities to meaningfully involve the population in roles that provide employment, basic necessities, and dignity have led to urban violence, terrorism, governmental instability, and war. Thus, the various successes in protecting and prolonging human life lead now to its degradation and to violence that originates not with disease and starvation but with humans.

These eight paradoxes, there are many more, are fundamental problems that the Technocratic Paradigm cannot solve. They are a challenge that cannot be successfully met and, as a consequence, set in motion a process that gives us a different set of beliefs, assumptions, and expectations of the world. The temporary world is created by the Technocratic Paradigm, but it is a transitional world.

The Technocratic Paradigm's roots are really at the world view of Sir Isaac Newton, a mechanical world slowly evolving in a smooth and predictable way. It is a world with a known future. The temporary world is a world with alternate futures. It is a world of unpredictability, of the unforeseen, simply because the rate of knowledge development continuously changes the horizon.

THE ORIGIN OF THE PARADOXES

Again and again with the Technocratic Paradigm, we have met the spirit of utilitarianism, of judging things not on intrinsic merit but by their usefulness. Through these and other such paradoxes, a deeper, more profound ethic manifests itself, of which utilitarianism is only an aspect, a derivative. This deeper, more profound ethic is science, itself. For it is science that is the driving force of the West. It is not a force that shall succumb to the East. The destiny of East and West, in turn, rests with science but not through science. Science is an outlook on the world, but it is not a plan for the world. It is knowledge for knowledge's sake. It is simply a tool and simply the most powerful tool to come humanity's way since language. It is science that makes things obsolete and renders its practitioners nameless. The more a science advances, the less it has room for individual personalities. Newton or Darwin, two of its greatest practitioners, are little read or known by modern scientists. Their accomplishments have been far surpassed because science is additive, and the current sum is what is important. What is important to the modern physicist are the latest findings of the CERN lab in Switzerland or the linear accelerator in Berkeley; to the biologist, the latest DNA advance at Harvard. In the humanities, religion, and philosophy, personal anonymity is not the rule. Findings, teachings, thoughts of the past have current validity and meaning. Such is not so with science. The ethic of science is the ultimate root for burnout.

Science is a genie that has escaped from the lamp in the same fashion that capitalism escaped from national mercantilism. It is unrivaled in its power to change, shape, destroy the environment, and to create the dominant metaphor for our internal consciousness. It first escaped from the priesthoods of the Church, worked for and then against humanism, and then defeated it in the eighteenth century. Today, it is the ethical base of all dominant beliefs of the West but it is only an instrumental thing. It leads nowhere, only searches. Its practitioners are consumed by it. Since they can never attain wisdom, only secure accomplishments that are soon surpassed, their only fate is to be footnotes in history—a history that is seldom read. For the individual, science yields only anonymity.

The challenge of the new paradigm is to contain the tool, the instrument, which is science. Science has tremendous melting, or corrosive, powers. Through expanding knowledge, things that were earlier assumptions become subject to scientific examination and through this process science has demolished earlier ethical systems. When Galileo saw imperfections through the telescope on the heavenly bodies, he did more than add facts to the store of knowledge about celestial bodies. By finding imperfections in heavenly bodies, he opened to scientific examination the prevailing value assumption that such objects were made by God and were perfect. Soon, some began to suspect that there was no God or that His works were imperfect. This illustrates how science can profoundly disturb a general ethical system.

We seem to be left with two alternatives. Either we must construct successive ethical systems which, in time, must be abandoned as an outgrown shell. Or, we must develop an ethical system somewhat like the magnetic bottle used to contain the temperatures of nuclear fusion. Because those temperatures exceed the melting point of any metal or ceramic, no material bottle is possible, but the bottle concept is used through the application of the magnetic field.

Because of its tool-like nature, science is lost without a meaning in a larger value system. It has, in the past, been a servant of broad ethical systems. Under the Friar Mendicants, particularly the Franciscans and Dominicans during the Dark Ages, it served the Church and, during the Age of Reason, the humanists. But, like a genie, it escapes now and again from the magic lamp. It outgrows the lamp and becomes a wild thing until a new and better lamp is found. The search for the new paradigm is the search for that lamp.

The Outline of a New Paradigm

Only to a magician is the world forever
fluid, infinitely mutable and eternally new.
Only he knows the secret of change, only he
knows truly that all things are crouched in
eagerness to become something else, and it
is from this universal tension that he draws
his power.

Peter Beagle, *The Last Unicorn.*

We would win, I thought steadily, if not in human guise then in another, for love was something that life in its infinite prodigality could afford. It was the failures who had always won, but by the time they won they had come to be called successes. This is the final paradox, which men call evolution.

Loren S. Eiseley, *The Unexpected Universe*.

In terms of mobility, the map of the temporary world is not the fixed neighborhood of the farmer or the villager nor is it the wandering of migratory people of the past. All past migratory groups moved with immediate family so there was a stability of social ties even though the terrain changed. For most groups, mobility was through a narrow geographical corridor. During the four seasons, the group would pass up and then down the corridor with its familiy territorial markings that had been known to the band or the tribe over generations.

In the temporary world, mobility is restricted to the nuclear family or the individual. Most persons will pass through settings that they will never return to. When one rents a house and moves, it is very unusual, on a subsequent return to that area, to rent the same house. For those people who remain in a neighborhood for many years, their neighbors' mobility will give the surroundings a transient edge. Thus, whether an individual moves or the neighbors move, the environment is changed; the physical and social ecology will be very transitory. Whether the observer moves or the surroundings move, the effect is the same to the observer.

THE DISPOSABLE SELF

The collapse of the Traditional Paradigm wrought by social change cut the individual loose from all anchorages and ushered in the economic person. The economic person functioned simply to maximize his or her own immediate interest. Working for personal benefits, not from duty or obligation, the economic person became a free commodity drawn to markets that would pay the higher wage. It was freedom; and then again it was not freedom. It was freedom from tradition, but bondage to the pulls of the market.

A consequence of the Technocratic Paradigm is that people are known for what they do rather than who they are or who they were. Status is conferred not through birth, but through achievement. All things are examined and valued in terms of their immediate use; consequently, one dimension of the general philosophy of the Paradigm is extreme utilitarianism. Increasingly, all things are possessed less for the things themselves and more in terms of what their immediate use is. Because of increased costs of home ownership, more people rent today; those who buy, buy with long-term mortgages. However, before the mortgage is paid off, the house is sold or remortgaged. The home that is fully paid for and is a homestead, an abode, for two or three generations of a family is becoming unusual. Yet it is still called "buying" a home—

a case of the linguistic form remaining after the social meaning has changed. In reality, we are engaged in a renting, saving, tax shelter transaction, not fully paying up a debt on a home.

Many items of personal property are becoming disposable: razors, paperback books, clothing, records, tapes. Items are used a few times and then discarded. The values of durability, long use, and the kind of psychological investment that people traditionally have made in material objects such as articles of furniture or items of their private and personal possession grow less today. The consequence of this is that the boundary of the self continues to constrict; no longer do inanimate objects become part of the individual's identity. In times past, a person had a good watch and, occasionally, a good fountain pen that would serve for a lifetime and be handed down as an heirloom to a child. But, today watches are bought with the idea that they will last two or three years and be discarded. In fact, the best-selling ballpoint pens are designed to be disposable.

We translate the value of things into monetary terms and use money to make things more transferable, more transmutable. We compute the worth of our time in hours, not in proud accomplishments; we know the cost and the worth of a college education but not the liberating or transcending experience that education may provide. Increasingly today, when we think of having children, we think in terms of the cost that the child represents, even questioning whether or not we should have children, rather than seeing the child as a form of social insurance for our old age and an obligation to perpetuate the family. The transitory, temporary world, increasingly, produces a person who is alienated from the world because the world seems changeable, impermanent, transitory. The only thing that seems permanent is the person and because of the change in surroundings, the individual feels apart and separate from the surroundings. Other people and an individual's relations with them are shallow and superficial. We become sensitive to how few long-term, enduring relationships we have. An old friend is one you have known since your last move, your last job. Maintaining friendships throughout moves in residence and jobs is, at first, difficult and then meaningless as the degree of common interest and experiences with friends of longer duration and previous moves grows smaller.

This leads the individual to begin to see his or her identity as a current identity. You are defined by the current situation or role that is being played. You may be conscious of a feeling of both playing a role and seeing a part of yourself watching the other part play the role. You may be a manager, but in addition to being a manager, you can observe, critique, applaud, or criticize your own performance in that role. You may play the role of a competent, attractive person but you can watch yourself and see your weaknesses and insecurities.

This consciousness of oneself appeared in the early years of the Technocratic Paradigm and manifested itself as a person composed of several social roles. But, though the roles were several, and even though they created conflict, they typically lasted for many years. In the late years of the Paradigm in the temporary world, the roles do not last so very long. The mutating quality of work, leisure, or marriage focuses on the role played intensely, here and now, and then discarded. The self has a disposable quality. Life is a series of one-night stands.

In the temporary world, one of the greatest of all fears is aging and death. As the future and the past recede, time becomes the present only, passing from this scene becomes an unimaginable horror. Aging, the perceptible change and deterioration of the individual, is the warning of the process of passing from the scene. Already vast sums are spent to deny or slow the aging process. The cosmetic industry, including plastic surgery, is a multi-billion dollar industry. The motivation for the expenditures may well be not as much out of the pursuit of beauty as out of a wish to hide from the reality of aging. Perpetual youth, the Peter Pan syndrome, has great urgency, and yet there is also considerable interest in sign of any life where the great majority resides—in the land of shades beyond the river Styx. The phenomenal success of the works of Elizabeth Ross and her genre betray more than a simple interest in the psychological process of dying, but reflect as well a powerful urge by many to escape from the finality of the materialism of the Technocratic Paradigm.

CHANGING PARADIGMS

Societies vary, as do regions of a given country, in their involvement with the three paradigms described. Today, many countries of the third and fourth world reside largely in the Traditional Paradigm with the extended kin system being the dominant institution and individual consciousness residing in the differentiated web of that world. The most powerful countries of the world, such as Japan and the Soviet Union, are at various points in the Technocratic Paradigm, though in a large country like the Soviet Union much of the countryside, particularly in the Asiatic regions, exists largely within the Traditional Paradigm.

A country that is experiencing the greatest amount of paradigm shift toward the Emergent Paradigm is the United States, and that movement is most pronounced on the West Coast. The heartland remains largely in the Technocratic Paradigm, but because of modern communications, the likelihood of any region maintaining the Traditional Paradigm within the continental United States is quite low.

Social changes within the United States have, for the last twenty years, begun on the West Coast and then leapfrogged to the East Coast and then moved slowly from the West and East into the interior of the country. This process may continue or the present shift of population into the Sun Belt may alter the historical flow of social change in the United States.

Across the world, the growth of the Technocratic Paradigm occurred first in the countries of Western Europe and then Japan and the small island societies of Hong Kong, Singapore, and Taiwan. The historical development of the market economy that made the Technocratic Paradigm possible in Western Europe never occurred in the Soviet Union but rather, through the Bolshevik Revolution, an advanced form of state socialism was imposed on the peasant society early. During the Stalinist era, a series of bloody purges was utilized in an attempt to wrench that society rapidly into the technocratic world under the special vision of Marxism developed by Lenin and his associates.

What the Soviet Union seems to represent today is an extreme form of the bureaucratic-centered society that maintains a highly visible reign of surveillance and terror to hold the population in check and actively suppress the free flow of information and potential social change that would lead to the demise of the Technocratic Paradigm in that society. The third and the fourth worlds, like China, Mexico, Guatemala, and the emerging African nations, most surely are not going through the paradigm developmental process in a fashion similar to that which occurred for Western Europe. And Western Europe itself may look back to the traditional world with great longing and nostalgia far in excess of that reminiscing that will occur in the United States or the fourth world.

An interesting illustration of this point is a recent survey completed by Donald Kanter (Blundell, 1980), which examines differences in national character and attitudes in 1978 in several countries of the European community. Surveying middle class women between twenty-one and forty-two years of age, he found strikingly high levels of cynicism and alienation. Seventy-six percent of the French sample felt that most people were dishonest by nature, and eighty-three percent felt that people disliked inconveniencing themselves to help others. Kanter notes, "most respondents are saying that people are liars, reality is money, and those few who are unselfish are pathetic figures."

The British, Dutch, and Germans among the countries surveyed appeared the least alienated; the French, Italians, and Belgians were the most alienated. The study found that many Europeans believed that they had little control over their lives and displayed strong feelings of alienation and fear of the future. Over half of the Italians sampled believed it would be unfair to bring children into the world, so bleak was its outlook. Seventy-five percent of the French felt that the lot of the average man was getting worse, though only seventeen percent of the Germans agreed. Perhaps within France, where modernism in the West had some of its earliest roots, the malaise of the current paradigm is most advanced.

Table 11 is an outline of the paradigms and the roles associated with them. Though throughout this discussion three major paradigms have been identified—Traditional, Technocratic, and Emergent—the Traditional Paradigm could be divided into additional categories, but for our purposes it is useful to think of it as one paradigm. Between paradigms are times of social turmoil and revolution; when the paradigm disintegrates, so does society.

Table 11
The Relationship of Paradigms to Roles

Paradigm	Normative Ideal	Typical Role	Anchoring Institution	Chronology in the United States
Traditional	Priest	Peasant	Community-tribe	16th, 17th, to mid-18th century
Collapsing	Revolutionary Explorer	Rabble Entrepreneur	Extended family	18th to mid-19th century
Technocratic (Ages: Optimism Anxiety Malaise)	Physician Engineer Politician	Worker Manager Bureaucrat	Nuclear family and corporate bureaucracy	1850-1930 1930-1965 1965-current time
Collapsing (Appearance of Temporary World)	Television personality Media star	Consumer	Ad hoc group	Current time
Emergent	Transcendent being Guru	Learner acolyte	Self	Current time

It is possible to identify for each paradigm a normative ideal, a typical role, and an anchoring institution. The *normative ideal* represents the social role that most fully expresses the main thrust of the paradigm. For example, in the Traditional Paradigm, the priest was the representative of god among men and typified much of the central organizing activity of society. The *typical role* refers to that role in which most of the population exists. Today, in a collapsing Paradigm, almost everyone identifies as a consumer. The *anchoring institution* is the social grouping that is most prevalent for achieving or meeting individual affective needs. It is the social unit that provides ascriptive, nonconditional meaning for the person. In some cases, however, there is less than full affective acceptance as is the case with the corporate bureaucracy. In one way, it was this tension produced by life defined through bureaucratic roles that initiated the migration of identity from this institution.

Exactly where the temporary world leads and what the Emergent Paradigm will look like and what its consequences will be is difficult to predict. Some predictions, though, are interesting if for no other purpose than to loosen some of the verity quality of structures and states of mind constructed under the Technocratic Paradigm.

IMPLICATIONS OF THE EMERGENT PARADIGM FOR ORGANIZATIONS

The institution or complex organization reached its zenith in the past decades at the fullest power of the Technocratic Paradigm. As the temporary world grows and as individual loyalties to organizations are lessened, they, like the family and church before them, will wane in influence and authority. Even the bureaucracy of the state will weaken in the fluidity of the times. It has been people and their resistance to uniformity and plasticity that has been the long, painful, vexing thorn in the side of the institution. Indeed, the modern bureaucrat is in a position much like the builder of the 1880s before the advent of structural steel. Any older, large city—Paris is a good example—had an architectural discontinuity around 1880. Prior to that time, wood, stone, and mortar columns rather than steel were used as the frame or skeleton of buildings. The outer limits of vertical size and strength to support floors was about thirty feet or three stories. Except for the vaulted cathedrals, buildings could be built no taller than that. The basic materials of construction limited the height of buildings; so block after block of older buildings in Paris will be no more than about three stories tall. Buildings built using structural steel can and do rise many stories high. Thus, increasing building size, density, and complexity, one of the central technologies that made possible the skyscrapers—the steel and glass canyons of modern cities—were the creation of structural steel.

The strength of the bureaucratic structures within the Technocratic Paradigm is diminishing but in no way is the strength gone. The structures will continue to exert themselves, to maintain their existence, just as the Luddites did in the nineteenth century to maintain the traditional world through destroying machinery. The Soviet Union today is a complete illustration of the shift from the Traditional to the Technocratic Paradigm with its control structures at highest strength. And, while the progress of modernization appears now to be weakening such societies and structures over the world, they are not without power and resources. Indeed, those who would openly protest against the current paradigm may be in the situation of the first small mammal, probably a rodent-like creature, that appeared in the Mesozoic era some many millions of years ago. Though mammals would ultimately come to dominate the dinosaurs that were the reigning land life form in that era, it would have been foolhardy, indeed, for the individual mouse to challenge *Tyrannosaurus rex*. If he did and whenever he did, he would have illustrated very quickly that biological competition and survival is not simply at the individual level but at the species level as well. The individual mammal would have succumbed, but through millions of years mammalian species displaced the dinosaurs.

Evolution is built on a gradualist outlook on time with an assumption of incremental changes. The gene pool is thought to experience many random mutations in every generation, but only a fraction prove to be adaptive. The larger number are negative and thus drop out. Darwin was a student of Lyell who explained geological evolution in this fashion, and both Lyell's geology and Darwin's biology are imbued with the slow-evolving mechanical change concept of Newton's.

Biological change is a slow adaptive process of matching random mutations to environmental pressures and opportunities so that, through trial and error, organisms gradually become more successful relative to a specific environment. Thus, Darwin found that if nuts were plentiful, in time, birds would develop heavier beaks since the beak would be functional in cracking nuts. If seeds were a more plentiful and available food, longer, less heavy beaks would be developed that would be more agile in pecking at seeds. Yet, gaps in the evolutionary record are a continual frustration for the general theory of biological evolution. Instead of a smooth continuous line of gradual adaptations in some life forms, there are sudden breaks and sharp changes. It is as if pressure for change gradually builds and then, somewhat suddenly, rapid and discontinuous modifications occur. Thus, evolution may seem to have an emergent aspect—somewhat unpredictable, unintended. At one time there is balance between an organism and its environment. But as change and challenge build, stress increases on the organism and sudden evolutionary change may occur. Jay Gould (1977) has called this event *punctuated equilibrium* and notes that small peripheral isolates are those individual organisms in a species most likely to show rapid evolutionary change. If the study of biological evolution offers any implications for organizations, it may be that gradual growth and increases in complexity may not be the only pattern in evolution. Sharp changes and the collapse of some organizations may be in the offing as well.

BEYOND EINSTEINIAN PHYSICS

The term *paradigm* has been used in these pages in the sense of a very large world view. As a world view, it emerges from the vast complex potpourri of science, art, industry, and daily life in the society.

From the forces, experiences, and structures of our world is slowly emerging a new paradigm. To understand, to know, the shape that is beginning to appear, it is useful to look at some of the changes that are going on in science today. Since so much of the Technocratic Paradigm was rooted in the physics of Copernicus and Newton, it is useful and fascinating to look first at the state of physics today.

Through the seventies, physics has moved into a post-Einsteinian phase that promises to be as different from the physics of the atomic era as that era was from Newton's world. And, in all reality, the physics of Einstein, the world of relativity, was not of the Technocratic Paradigm but of a new paradigm—the Emergent Paradigm. Thus, the new paradigm has in it both the relativity theories of Einstein and subsequent developments that have come since his and his contemporaries' contributions.

The physics of Newton explained the universe through the presence of smoothly revolving bodies, the planets, involved in machinelike processes and controlled by one basic force, gravity. Gravity was the force; objects possessed size and density, best stated as mass, and once a body was set in motion through force, it continued in that movement until friction caused a dissipation of that energy. One of the conclusions that came out of Newtonian physics was that, in reality, the universe was slowly running down, moving into entropy. It suggested that time in our universe would slowly come to an end.

Einstein's contribution was severalfold. One thing that he saw was that the appearance of speed and movement were not absolute but rather were a consequence of the frame of reference of the observer. Thus, the speed of the movement of an arrow in flight was not invariant but was relative to the frame of reference of an observer standing at some point watching the arrow. Furthermore, Einstein stated that time, itself, was not an absolute as Newton had thought, but rather was variable and that instead, the speed of light was the absolute. Einstein's mathematics indicated that the faster a body moved, the slower time would be for the body. And, if a person or a thing could arrive at a speed approaching the speed of light, that time would slow and finally stand still.

Another contribution of Einstein's thinking was the famous equation $E = MC^2$ which demonstrated that energy and matter were ultimately one and the same, and the separate states were only points on an energy to matter continuum. Einstein suggested that all matter was ultimately convertible to energy and that the matter in the universe was, in essence, only frozen or solidified energy.

Classical physics and the Western analytical tradition have always assumed that explanation can be arrived at by analytically breaking units down into less complex subparts. The physics of the Greeks emphasized that there were four basic elements—fire, earth, air, and water—and that all reality could be analytically divided into those items. The science of the Middle Ages and of the scientific revolution expanded the list and, essentially, viewed chemical compounds such as water, wood, and sand as the fundamental units. The development of a periodical chart broke these chemical compounds into molecules such as oxygen, nitrogen, chlorine, sodium. And these, in this century, were subdivided again into atoms, which themselves consist of electrons, protons, and neutrons. Then later in this century, more particles were found beyond the electron, proton, and neutron. Today it is felt that the proton and the neutron are composed of more elementary particles than these and the term used to refer to these most elemental particles is *quarks*. Now, it is not known whether or not quarks exist; none have ever been seen, but to continue the analytical tradition, we must think that they do exist. Whether they are the final particle or whether there is another particle that composes quarks is part of the current scientific ferment in physics.

There is, at this time, considerable excitement within physics about the likelihood of definitive proof of the existence of quarks. If quarks can be proven to exist, if a relationship between quarks and the apparently ultimate light particle, the electron, can be developed, and if the new theories of forces—the gauge theories—can successfully relate the four basic forces (gravity, electromagnetism, and the nuclear weak and nuclear strong forces), then a great revolution will have occurred in physics. The search for the basic elements and process of matter will have ended. Now what would remain would be an infinitely large task of understanding all the permutations of the elements and forces, but one critical aspect would be changed. That aspect is that we would have reached the end of the path in one area of scientific explanation. To reach the end of the path in such a large part of the field of science could well have great philosophical or metatheoretical implications. It could mean that there is at least on one side an end to knowing via science and the conclusion could change science itself.

At the other end of physics are fascinating, new cosmological discoveries that make the universe far larger and much more complex than was even supposed in the 1950s. It is generally assumed today that the universe began in a vast explosion fifteen billion years ago and continues to expand at an unchecked rate today, in effect growing larger and larger. In addition to planetary bodies and stars which are continuous thermonuclear fusion explosions, there are starlike anomalies that pose gigantic problems for explanation. Among these puzzling objects, are objects called quasars. Quasars do not, in fact, seem to be stars at all though they give off tremendous amounts of electromagnetic waves. These objects appear to be perched at the very edge of the known universe and to be radiating energy a hundred times brighter than an entire galaxy of billions of stars as are common throughout the universe. How an object which apparently is no larger than the solar system can give off this kind of energy is an unexplained puzzle.

A second puzzle that is yielding to solution is the pulsar, which is now thought to be the body of a star older and larger than our sun that has collapsed and generates light waves in a pulsating fashion, hence the name. The idea of a star that has collapsed under its own gravity or weight, so to speak, gives rise to the third mystery, the black hole. Basically, a black hole is a star that has sufficiently collapsed and become so compact that its gravitational field permits nothing to escape, not even light. It appears to be a bottomless pit that swallows any object or any energy that passes in its vicinity. Indeed, there is some reason to think that the black holes represent an ultimate form of energy for an advanced civilization as well as the final end of the universe which could someday itself pass into a black hole.

Even bolder speculation by John Wheeler (1975) has suggested that the universe we live in, millions of light years across and fifteen billion years old, is but one of many such universes. Wheeler uses the term *hyperspace*, to describe the stage on which our current universe exists and suggests that black holes may be tunnels to another universe and the quasars may represent the other end of a black hole—tunnels that are pouring out energy from other universes into ours. Now, most of this fact and speculation is post-Einstein and yet, to a great degree, most people in the world today have not conceptually left Newtonian physics. So how these facts and frameworks will contribute to the new paradigm will come in hardly imaginable ways; yet most assuredly the new paradigm will not be congenial to our current world of organizations. A world neatly composed of boxes and lines, hierarchies of authority, and great specialization seem to harken more to the past than as a beacon to the future. A view of physical nature as being far more fluid and probabilistic than earlier thought may contribute to a more fluid and elastic concept of society.

IDENTITY THROUGH SELF-ANCHORING

The ability of the individual to change anchors from institutions of tradition to multiple social groups makes the corporation and the concept of nationality possible. The role strategy of the company man is the furthest extrapolation of the individual in the direction of the dictates of the institution. However, the fluidity that comes from social changes makes that strategy hollow. The corporation, the institution, is a conditional friend, a conditional lover. As long as the individual serves a useful and needed purpose for the bureaucracy, then existence is acknowledged. But when times change, when the person ages, when the individual cannot serve a purpose, then the individual is forgotten. It is this conditional quality that is bringing the demise not of the individual but of the institution.

The sense of identity developing for the individual under the Emergent Paradigm will not be indifference to the institution, but a growing caution toward working within the institution, to meeting goals set by institutions, and to control by institutions. Dozens of separate trends, hundreds of separate actions, are actively diluting institutional control. An underground economy that runs in the tens of billions of dollars each year is evidence of economic transactions that thwart tax authorities. Proof of this economy surfaces in interesting ways from the service barter organization, where a barber can trade haircuts to a lawyer for assistance in a title search, to the large amount of cash being held in an economy that was predicted to operate largely through credit cards and electronic transfers by the end of the seventies. The desire and ability of individuals to establish and control their own retirement account through the IRA mechanism and the development of cottage industries in the home are other indicators. The focus on health and the move by individuals to take responsibility for their own health rather than delegating that to the physician is another sign of the loosening of the authority of institutional aegis. Also the demystification of law, like medicine, through do-it-yourself divorce and legal clinics in shopping centers, is illustrative. The growth of do-it-yourself industries that provide tools and materials to assist one in home repair, auto maintenance, gardening, and the like are indicative as well. The desire for greater energy independence in the home, through more efficient structures, by more prudent use of energy, and by final achievement of an effective photo voltaic cell for utilization of the sun's energy will sharply lessen dependence on the institution.

One's self-identity in the past has largely come from roles imposed by tradition or organizations. In a sense, roles made the individual. Social change now makes roles disposable and, by implication, individuals as well. At the same time, technological advances offer the promise of making the individual far more independent of organization. As energy and information become available more directly to individuals and less through institutions, the way is opened for the individual to anchor himself internally rather than to roles prescribed by institutions.

Men and women will continue to extend their definition of identity through the occupational structure. Individuals will be known by present accomplishments. Friendships will grow out of current occupational involvement, although the individual will have several occupations in a lifetime and, in many cases, two or more major career shifts. Sexual expression will, of course, be greatly broadened and totally and finally separated from procreation. Sexual identity will become even more a matter of personal choice than has occurred in recent years, with many of the taboos attached to certain sexual acts and sexual orientation withering. Marriage will likely remain monogamous, but long-term marriages may not be normative, although they will occur with considerable frequency. There may indeed be a trend toward divorce being a mark of development. We may well hear someone remark, "Yes, it's sad. They've been married to each other for twenty years. Each is so dependent that they've been unable to grow beyond each other." In such an event serial monogamy, for example, would become normative and marriage without divorce, deviant.

STANDING LEADERSHIP ON ITS HEAD

The society will have national goals, but private profit and non-profit organizations will be used more and more as the method to achieve these goals. The giant bureaucratic structures of government and private industry will be seen as authoritarian throwbacks that contort and rigidly crystallize patterns long after the original purpose for the organization has ended. The disappearance of these large organizations, though, will be occasioned more by their inability to win the hearts and affiliation of their own membership than any national effort to legislate the monolithic organization away.

In fact, the legislative process is due for changes that will shatter its present structure and power. State and national initiatives and referendums will become increasingly popular, because both education and communication have eliminated many of the justifications for the representative democracy. Representative democracy was always justified on two major principles. One principle was that to act as a representative required specialized training, and suffrage has always been to an extent controlled by elitist social classes that held property, were literate, male, or in some way had, putatively, a better grasp of the totality of the environment. Such an argument will hold very little water in the latter part of the century, little at all in the coming century.

The other pillar of representative government has been the argument that transportation and communication difficulties effectively precluded the participation of all adult citizens in the way of the original town government structures of the early colonists. Neither will this argument be viable as a consequence of the communication and transportation structures available in the future. Indeed, Congress and state legislatures will be reduced in authority not much different than that of the national electoral college in presidential elections. Whereas the electoral college was originally a mechanism to control populist movements in the early years of the American political system, today, in spite of its potential authority to obviate or ignore the popular vote, it has become simply a rubber stamp in the same way that royalty and the House of Lords exist relative to the House of Commons in the British Parliament.

An interesting consequence of the temporary world and the appearance of the Emergent Paradigm is the lessened individual motivation to participate in war. Much of the soldier's motivation to hazard military service and risk life or injury in war is caused by the loyalty to others, to national honor, ideals or commitment to other members of the combat unit. Much of the willingness of a man to risk death is dependent on the honor that such valor will bestow on his family, his combat unit, and the rewards assured him in an afterlife. In the temporary world there is precious little family to bask in the reflected valor of another member, and in a society growing indifferent to religion, there is no thought of afterlife. Death, like decay and wearing down, must be avoided at all costs. The only meaning is current existence and thus the motivation for war is weakened.

War, though, may not necessarily disappear. Machines, however, will assume more and more of the soldier's role in the war. Indeed, combat beyond the earth's atmosphere appears likely to be largely one machine against another, and each step in the evolution of weaponry will be for one machine to nullify the advantage of another. Though the specter of nuclear war will remain, it has proven to be a much less satisfactory form of war since combat is largely an event of the systematic theft of one group from another. Nuclear war usually so damages the land, factories, or mineral resources that it defeats much of the purpose, thus rewards, of war. The neutron bomb and biological war do, however, offer technologies that fit into the design of the traditional intents of war. And it seems likely that wars, especially local wars, will continue. The natural resources required by technocratic societies grow ever scarcer and competition for the resources will lead to tension and conflict. Food, energy, chemicals, and minerals will be withheld from markets as means of economic war by less developed societies. Such conditions, such uncertainty and turmoil, will maintain critically high conditions of stress for individuals everywhere. Indeed, wars are much the expression of chaos that results from changing paradigms.

The most significant blow to nationalism will be the collapse of nations to control the marketplace through the issuance of currency. As long as a bureaucratic structure can define what money is, it can control the transactions of subunits down to the individual. However, as country after country moves into high degrees of individualism, and international trade results in commodity flows of many kinds across national borders, the sovereignty of a given currency will be weakened. In the final stage, currencies may well become secured by ratios to specific commodities; and international concerns like American Express or the Japanese banking and investment companies will have greater control of currencies than individual nations.

Government, as we know it today, will lose much of its mystery and much of its purpose since so much of the control of modern government is the result of elitist access to information. As technology makes the information more available and education makes individuals aware of it, the mystery of government is largely a priority-setting mechanism for goals among a group of people. Representative government arose in this country largely because of the inability of all members to participate in deliberations as they had in the small communities of New England. Now, technology is reversing this process and makes information available to all individuals and opens the possibility of a referendum on all items. In fact, a referendum on leadership goes on continuously now through polls of leadership preference, especially for presidential leadership. More and more traditional governmental forms will be supplanted by initiative and referendum processes, and polling assessments of voter preferences will begin to usher out the era of representative government and bring in a new era of democratic participation.

In a day when there is a call for strong leadership and political parties asking where the strong leaders of old are, we should stop and question what such calls mean. As much as anything, they are a nostalgic longing, an American nativism, for a god figure to resolve complexity and ambiguity. We should look with surprise and misgiving toward anyone who promises us strong leadership, uncompromising goals, or heroic stature. The strong, authoritarian leader is an anachronism in this world. Thoughtfulness, intelligence, patience, energy, sensitivity are much more important qualities for this social system than Napoleonic postures or people with dreams of empire.

The pursuit of individuals for high levels of income and high levels of consumption may begin to level out. The rapacious devouring of natural resources of the nineteenth and twentieth century will be lessened by a more mature population that will realize one's identity is not enhanced by cars, power boats, private airplanes, and other large mechanical toys. Architecture will revert to a more human scale, and the massive harbors, buildings, and highway projects of this century will continue only in the most unadvanced corners of the globe and will be seen as the humorous unsophistication of newly arrived people. Rather than growing larger, cities will grow smaller and will become far more self-contained, utilizing natural sunlight for many power needs, and waste and food cycles will become closed loops for many cities. The urban and suburban sprawl will retract as nuclear families raising children become much less a part of the physical and social landscape, and the countryside will become more rural, wild, and bucolic than it was during the entire twentieth century. Far greater efficiencies of farming will actually reduce the amount of land needed to feed the population, and during the first half of the twenty-first century, the general unavailability of independent, mechanized transportation associated with the automobile in its heyday will be the salvation of the child countryside. The entrepreneurial capitalistic energies of the West and the largely equivalent colonial energies of the Communist East will be increasingly directed toward the exploration and exploitation of the resources of the solar system, permitting the possibility of the earth becoming a special garden as the cradle of humanity. The incentives associated with income will be lessened, and the incentive structure will be much more directed toward recognition and the opportunity for creative outlets.

The major task of the first half of the twenty-first century will be teaching. The teaching will be directed toward bringing the bulk of humanity into that century. Keep in mind that the cutting edge and formative group that comprises the temporary world is a minority of the earth's population, perhaps 500 million out of 4 billion, about 12 percent. This 12 percent must be engaged in assuring that cultural leaps rather than simple progressions occur as the population moves from an orientation of excess consumption to appropriate trends and technologies and to direct the acquisitive and achievement energies that will come out of the breaking of the bonds of traditional cultures toward restoring the garden qualities on earth and exploring the solar system.

One of the tragic consequences of the collapse of the Traditional Paradigm was the demise of the ancient folkways of caring for others who were too young, too old, infirm or crippled. Family, charity, mutual help obligations of neighbors all declined and in their place were created state systems to provide such care and assistance. The replacement of private charity by public welfare, though not an unalloyed blessing, has on balance been highly positive. Yet, the administration of this justice through bureaucratic structure detracts from the justice.

To some degree, the tone of the times calls forth certain ideal personality types. For the Technocratic Paradigm bureaucrats and the politicians were prototypical personalities. Neither can be accused of suffering from an overburden of sensitivity of their impact on others. Indeed, some of humanity's worst times under the Technocratic Paradigm were brought about by the attempt of these personalities to recast all humans in such a person's private view of the future. Whether it be the sweatshops of the early capitalists or the grandiose visions of the bureaucratic elitists, the individual was simply a thing to be manipulated by some elite group or another. So much of the nature of the wars and upheavals was to determine whom the ascendent elite would be.

As each individual grows in his or her sense of security in living in this world of options, the person who would impose a personal view of reality on others, the great person of vision, will come to be seen as a lunatic. One measure of insanity will be the extent to which one seeks to gain control over others. Each person will have enough to do to understand his or her own contingencies. Help between others will be forthcoming but offered gingerly.

Neither history nor the social sciences can give us a clear description of how the self will appear with a new paradigm. If consciousness, interior reality, mirrors or derives from the external world, it must, for many people, be changing, contradictory, chaotic. Our physical world is in continuous change. Much of the success of technology is its ability to alter the world; to restructure the physical landscape with highways, buildings, bridges, factories. No point on the globe is out of reach of radio, television, and, with satellite transmission, the telephone. Dozens of airplane flights daily cross over the North Pole and there is apparently no spot on the North American continent undisturbed by high altitude passes of commercial jet traffic. The detritus of modern civilization is found in the most remote canyons, the deepest forests, the most arid deserts, the highest mountains. It is a residue of aluminum cans, styrofoam cups, and paper wrappers. More ominously, it is industrial wastes of toxic chemicals, heavy metals, and decaying radioactive particles. For better and for worse, science and technology have changed the world and like the hand of the mother that rocks the cradle, science, the mother of humanity is never away from us, not for a moment.

The sense of self, of social and individual reality, is much the product of the physical and social world. While physical change may seem to come much more quickly than social change, now that, too, is rapid and continuous. International political alliances change in two or three decades. The allies of one war become the enemy in the next. The social norms and the social hierarchy are not dependable. In one decade the "in" thing is to be antiestablishment and in the next decade the "in" thing is to become part of the establishment. Today, it is important to be "for" things but hard to define what those things are. Pundits and commentators stress the importance of the family but a common definition of the family is elusive; what may be one person's definition is an outrage to another. For example, are unmarried adults and children who live together for a while, then dissolve and move on, a family or, more critically put, a family ideal? For some, the situation is an ideal, for others, highly deviant.

What should be the goals for the individual? Should one strive for material achievement, or professional acclaim, or personal satisfaction, or public recognition, or individual competence? Should one view each situation in life as a challenge to best, as an opportunity for success? Should one reflect, seek to be at harmony with the world, to blend into its rhythms? Or should one strive for ecstasy beyond the world, become not part of the world but apart from it? Now, in these times, not just the physical world is changing. Sharp, discontinuous change stalks the social world.

How meaning can be made from this world is simply not apparent. There is a peculiar need in these times for individuals able to reside in ambiguity and yet derive meaning from the world. There is an urgent need for a concept of self that grows beyond immediate hedonism, one that can connect altruism and rationality. A system, open or closed, at the level of a clock or a culture, can either slowly run down into disorder or an open system may run up into a higher state of order. Biological growth is an example of the transformation of energy in an open system into high tension and higher complexity. The human being, in its ontogeny, evolves from a simple combination of two incomplete cells, an ovum and a sperm, into an organism composed of billions of cells complexly structured and specialized, that, in turn, interact in a culture of equivalent complexity. Now, at this dangerous and critical period in the evolution of individual consciousness, a higher level of consciousness, of order, is needed. This is why there must be a transformation to greater complexity, to higher order in internal consciousness or to a collapsing of the social edifice. Complex organizations and complex technologies must find a more complex human or the technologies and the organizations will fail. And more than likely if the complex being emerges, it will be on terms that will force changes in the organizations and the technologies.

Several psychological properties are imperative for the current environment. One property is the ability to handle large inputs of new information. Arousal of the brain is controlled within the limbic formation and is an ancient brain function that has important adaptive significance. Awareness of subtle environmental changes promotes the survival of an organism, yet in today's world continuous environmental changes may overload the limbic structure promoting such continuous states of vigilancy that the individual suffers fatigue and high irritability.

Once the brain is aroused, the cerebral cortex becomes involved in evaluating information and directing any forthcoming action. Two important properties are needed. One is the ability to quickly process large amounts of data and make multiple comparisons. For example, organizational tasks require an employee to segregate information about work from other information such as data referring to home, commuting, and recreation. Pertinent organizational data must then be recalled and often shared and exchanged with other colleagues. The exchange of data must be done in terms of knowledge about one's own role and knowledge of the roles of other colleagues. In the process, two older psychological tendencies must be kept under appropriate control. One tendency is territoriality. Some organisms, human beings appear to be one, establish domains which they tend to defend against other members of the species. While role is an application of the concept of territoriality, in the organization the individual must see roles as an attribute of the organization and not a personal property. The organization must depend on the individual understanding a role in this manner and be willing, when called on, to yield a role. A second ancient psychological property is dominance. Like territoriality, there is reason to suspect that this behavior stems from the evolutionary older areas of the brain and has a function in intra-species competition for mates, food, and living space. While organizations require hierarchical control, modern organizations with complex and changing tasks require that positions of power be passed frequently to different individuals. If a single individual is successful in holding power independent of his or her expertise on tasks, then the organization's capability is reduced.

Creativity is a much needed property. Much of the innovation that occurred under the Technocratic Paradigm was linear extrapolation. Large cities grew from small towns. Organizational skills developed in the military were applied to industry, industrial concepts were applied to human service bureaucracy. Linear extrapolation too often means more is better and larger is preferable. In meeting social challenges, some alternatives to such simple thinking must be developed.

Finally, what must be required and is implied through these pages is a form of psychological anchoring to social reality, social groups and institutions, where there is high involvement and commitment but the same willingness and flexibility to change, when appropriate, to a different social reality that happens with change in the physical or material culture. Modern people with, of course, some discomfort make the change from vacuum tubes to transistors, from woods to plastics, really quite readily. By and large, such changes do not assume highly involved or emotional proportions. In some way, this outlook must be generalized to many of our social institutions. We must learn to move our identity from them as readily. This means that social concepts like race or occupation or neighborhood must be as readily set aside as the tube for the transistor.

It seems anonymity can be conquered by each person becoming aware of his or her own uniqueness and life history—rather than the social role providing individuality, self-knowledge can.

In Retrospect

For several thousands of words, I have sought to sketch what appear to me to be some of the general outlines of present day human consciousness as well as what I feel to be critical aspects of the social order and of our cultural systems. Returning to where I began, I feel that the malaise, the burnout, of our times is particularly significant. Beyond seeking personal resolution for these feelings, which has been one of the book's themes, is the assertion that the times are changing. The change is discontinuous, not simply evolutionary.

This assertion and much of the material of Part II go beyond the facts. Indeed, if one looks at the bulk of the facts, the Technocratic Paradigm has grown stronger, more secure, in the last two decades. Yet I suspect that this security of paradigm, this firmness of outlook, is that highest point on a curve just before the line turns down. When a system is at its greatest strength is when worlds remain to be conquered. When the worlds are conquered, all foes vanquished, then the strength is more apparent than real.

"In the expansive phase of a culture, people are sensitive to the deep, unconscious, latent forces of history and are humble in their presence," observes Kenneth Boulding. "In the later stages, they develop pride, the *hubris* of the Greeks, and it is this which brings about their downfall." And so it is as well for a paradigm.

Acknowledgments

This book stems from experiences and opportunities which involve more people than I can adequately acknowledge for their contributions. Especially important are the many individuals I have worked with personally, in conferences and seminars, on the topics covered in Part I of this book—to them I owe an immense debt. A second, far smaller group of individuals was closely involved with me in various stages of the development of the manuscript. Most noteworthy and helpful were the comments received early on from John Bruhn, Richard W. Hendrickson, Ira Iscoe, Janey Mouton, James Peterson, Al Valiunas, Richard Grinnell, Pat Lauderdale, Carolyn Sherif, Brit Hall, Larry Davis, and Martha Williams. My colleagues Stephen Anderson and Michael Kelly contributed substantially to the application of many of these ideas to diverse populations, and I am pleased to be permitted to use the literature analysis provided by Michael Kelly and Katie O'Shinsky in the appendix. A special thanks is due Rosalie Anderson both for her conceptual contributions and her willingness to assume many administrative tasks during the preparation of the manuscript.

Ray Bard contributed much of the formulation of this effort and the constant focusing necessary to get the ideas into print. Without his time and enthusiasm the task would not have been completed; I am pleased to renew a collaboration with him that extends back more than twenty years. Leslie Stephen, my editor, and Martha Brown, my copy editor, showed extreme patience and marvelously honed skills in pruning my rambling prose while being mindful of the continuity of several key ideas. The most tedious burden of all was borne by Julie Cunniff, who typed innumerable revisions, remembered where I mislaid my notes, and remained good-humored and unflaggingly optimistic each step along the way.

There remain to be noted as well many colleagues whose various critical discussions helped me formulate these ideas and the resources of the University of Texas at Austin which made possible the synthesis of numerous personal experiences.

To each and all of these I extend my appreciation and assure the reader that the inevitable errors of fact and inference are my sole responsibility.

Appendix

Burnout: A Chart of the Literature

Burnout is a relatively new term in both the scientific and popular literature as the following work by Michael Kelly and Katie O'Shinsky indicates. Their work extracts, from hundreds of sources, just over fifty articles in a six-year period that focus on or closely relate to burnout. Most of the articles concern either workers or managers in human service fields; however, some of the most recent material concerns the appearance of the phenomenon in the private sector.

It is interesting to compare the relative amount of interest in burnout in the last two decades to the attention paid to job satisfaction and stress. Research on job satisfaction goes back several decades and there are dozens of studies yearly on the issue. Research on stress became very significant in the mid-sixties, especially through efforts of individuals such as Hans Selye and Thomas Holmes. Today, that topic generates as much and perhaps more, inquiry as job satisfaction.

Burnout is conceptually related to both job satisfaction and stress as well as alienation. Unlike these concepts, though, it tends to tie factors from all three into a single symptom experienced by the individual. It seems to offer, as such, a more integrated perspective for examining individual experiences across social settings and through social change.

Author	Field(s)	Source	Symptoms and Indicators
Adams, J.D.	Business	Guidelines for stress management and life style changes. *Personnel Administration 24* (1979): 35-81.	Detachment; unrealistic expectations of self; emotional exhaustion
Armstrong, K.L.	Social Work	How to avoid burnout: a study of the relationship between burnout and worker, organizational and management characteristics in eleven child abuse and neglect projects. *Child Abuse and Neglect 3* (1979): 145-149.	Alienation from job, apathy; detachment, dehumanization; disillusionment; anger; cynicism regarding clients; ill health; defensive behavior; highly anxious; insomnia
Bardo, P.	Education	The pain of teacher burnout: a case history. *Phi Delta Kappan 61*(4) (1979): 252-255.	Frustration, dissatisfaction; lowered self-esteem; despair
Benson, H. Allen, R.L.	Business	How much stress is too much? *Harvard Business Review 58* (1980): 86-92.	Anger; depressed; highly anxious
Bies, F. Molle, B.	Business	Career burnout. *Glamour 78* (1980): 32.	Alienation from job, apathy; detachment; frustration; fatigue; depressed
(no author)	Business	Burnout: beyond executive stress. *Management Review 70* (1981): 4-5.	Alienation from job, apathy; dehumanization; disillusionment; ill health

Personality Factors	Characteristics of Organizations	Job Characteristics	Task Related
None	None	Time demands and personal choices	High emotional involvement
People who have difficulty persevering and acting aggressively burn out faster	High turnover rate; absenteeism; job design; span of supervisory control; centralization of authority; accountability and support	Personal growth blocked. Tasks too difficult for immature leader who is unable to handle authority, and makes excessive demands on staff	Caseload size; high emotional involvement; noncreative work; repetitive work
None	High turnover rate; absenteeism	Increased responsibility without adequate compensation in pay	None
None	None	Time and performance stress	Noncreative work; high emotional involvement
Ambitious person	None	None	High emotional involvement
High aspirations; achievement oriented	Competitive	None	High emotional involvement

Author	Field(s)	Source	Symptoms and Indicators
Carroll, J.F.X.	Health	Staff burnout as a form of ecological dysfunction. *Contemporary Drug Problems 8*(2) (1979): 207-227.	Decreased effectiveness/increased effort; excessive overtime; disorganized performance; disillusionment; anger; cynicism regarding clients; ill health; fatigue; drug or alcohol abuse; depressed; emotional exhaustion; marital conflict; feels empty like automaton; bored; isolated; rigidity; takes unnecessary risks
Carrongton, P. et al.	Business	Use of meditation-relaxation techniques for the management of stress in a working population. *Journal of Occupational Medicine 22* (1980): 221-231.	Frustration; ill health; highly anxious; insomnia; irritable
Cherniss, C.	Business	Job burnout: growing worry for workers, bosses. *U.S. News and World Report 88* (1980): 71-72.	Alienation from job, apathy; detachment; frustration; fatigue; depressed; highly anxious; insomnia
Daley, M.R.	Social Work	Preventing worker burnout in child welfare. *Child Welfare 58*(7) (1979): 443-450.	Alienation from job, apathy; detachment; dehumanization; decreased effectiveness/increased effort; excessive overtime; disorganized performance; frustration; ill health; fatigue; no longer allows family to participate in work; highly anxious; fails to make eye contact with clients; physical distancing; shortens interviews with clients; derogatory labeling of clients

Personality Factors	Characteristics of Organizations	Job Characteristics	Task Related
None	Job design; centralization of authority; span of supervisory control; inflexible rules; high turnover rate; formalization of rules	Increased responsibility without adequate compensation in pay. Inadequate funding source	High emotional involvement; caseload size
None	None	None	High emotional involvement; repetitive work
Dedicated workers, demanding bosses	Competitive, striving	Complex, repetitive	None
None	High turnover rate; formalization of rules; centralization of authority; span of supervisory control; job design; inflexible rules	This article reviews other studies listed in this appendix	Caseload size; high emotional involvement

Author	Field(s)	Source	Symptoms and Indicators
Daley, M.R.	Social Work	Burnout: smouldering problem in protective services. *Social Work 24*(5) (1979): 375-379.	Alienation from job, apathy; detachment; dehumanization; decreased effectiveness/increased effort; disorganized performance; cynicism regarding clients; ill health; fatigue; no longer allows family to participate in work; highly anxious; fails to make eye contact with clients, physical distancing; emotional exhaustion; feels subjected to tremendous stress
Drews, K. Hare, I.	Social Work	*Worker Burnout in Child Protective Services.* Paper presented at the meeting of the National Professional Resource Center on Child Abuse and Neglect, Washington, D.C., 1979, 1-8.	Alienation from job, apathy; ill health; fatigue; emotional exhaustion; inappropriate attitude toward client
Emener, W.G.	Health	Professional burnout: rehabilitation's hidden handicap. *Journal of Rehabilitation 45*(1) (1979): 55-58.	Detachment; cynicism regarding clients; ill health; fatigue; unrealistic expectations of self; paranoid behavior toward self; insomnia; overreacts or underreacts in serious situations; bored; withdrawn; resists viable suggestions for improvement; derogatory labeling of clients

Personality Factors	Characteristics of Organizations	Job Characteristics	Task Related
None	High turnover rate; absentee- ism; accounta- bility and support	Role conflict; isolation. Unable to manage stress. Low morale	Caseload size; high emotional involvement
None	High turnover rate; absentee- ism; accounta- bility and support	Inappropriate training for job	High emotional involvement; caseload size; repetitive work
Over commitment, idealistic expecta- tions, noble aspira- tions, and an unreal- istic dedication to helping disabled people	Alienation; absenteeism	Ungratifying identity factor	High emotional involvement; caseload size

Author	Field(s)	Source	Symptoms and Indicators
Freudenberger, H.J.	Business	Speaking from experience. Burn-out: the organizational menace. *Training and Development Journal 31*(7) (1977): 26-27.	Decreased effectiveness/increased effort; excessive overtime; anger; cynicism regarding clients; ill health; fatigue; depressed; projects problems on others; paranoid behavior toward self; insomnia; bored
Freudenberger, H.J.	Education	Burn-out: occupational hazard of the child care worker. *Child Care Quarterly 6*(2) (1977): 90-99.	Cynicism regarding clients; ill health; feels helpless; depressed; shortens interviews with clients; paranoid behavior toward self; emotional exhaustion; marital conflict; emphasis on technical care; bored; withdrawn; staff uses every opportunity to socialize with staff; derogatory labeling of clients; rigidity
Freudenberger, H.J.	Health; Psychology	Freudenberger on staff burnout. *Journal of Drug and Alcohol Abuse 3*(1) (1976): 49.	Frustration; anger

Personality Factors	Characteristics of Organizations	Job Characteristics	Task Related
Dedicated, accomplishing staff members can be prone to burnout	Formalization of rules	Resistance to change	High emotional involvement; repetitive work
Workers dedicated to their work can burn out	Absenteeism; accountability and support; alienation; centralization of authority; span of supervisory control	Lower educational level. No follow-up of clients. Tasks that are too difficult for worker	High emotional involvement; repetitive work
The overly dedicated and excessively committed people are prone to burnout	Alienation; centralization of authority; span of supervisory control; job design; inflexible rules	Work overload. Isolation	None

Author	Field(s)	Source	Symptoms and Indicators
Freudenberger, H.J.	Health; Psychology; Administration	The staff burn-out syndrome. *Psychotherapy 12* (1975): 1-24.	Decreased effectiveness/increased effort; excessive overtime; disorganized performance; anger; ill health; fatigue; drug or alcohol abuse; depressed; paranoid behavior toward self; emotional exhaustion; insomnia; bored; withdrawn; rigidity; loss of charisma; takes unnecessary risks
Freudenberger, H.J.	Health; Psychology	The staff burn-out syndrome in alternative institutions. *Psychotherapy: Theory, Research and Practice 12*(1) (1975): 73-82.	Decreased effectiveness/increased effort; excessive overtime; disorganized performance; anger; ill health; fatigue; drug or alcohol abuse; depressed; paranoid behavior toward self; emotional exhaustion; insomnia; bored; withdrawn; rigidity; loss of charisma; takes unnecessary risks
Freudenberger, H.J.	Mental Health; Psychology; Administration	Staff burn-out. *Journal of Social Issues 30*(1) (1974): 159-165.	Decreased effectiveness/increased effort; ill health; fatigue; drug or alcohol abuse; paranoid behavior toward self; emotional exhaustion; insomnia; bored; rigidity; takes unnecessary risks

Personality Factors	Characteristics of Organizations	Job Characteristics	Task Related
The overly dedicated and excessively committed workers burn out. The staff member whose outside life is subsatisfactory. The authoritarian individual tends to burn out. This is the person who needs to be in control and feels no one can do any job as well as he can.	Alienation; centralization of authority; span of supervisory control; job design; inflexible rules; accountability and support	Administrator who wears too many hats. Overworked	High emotional involvement; caseload size; repetitive work
The overly dedicated and excessively committed workers burn out. The staff member whose outside life is subsatisfactory. The authoritarian individual tends to burn out. This is the person who needs to be in control and feels no one can do any job as well as he can.	Alienation; centralization of authority; span of supervisory control; job design; inflexible rules; accountability and support	Administrator who wears too many hats. Overworked	High emotional involvement; caseload size; repetitive work
The dedicated and the committed are prone to burnout. The individual who has a need to give is likely to burn out.	Accountability and support; alienation	None	High emotional involvement; caseload size; repetitive work

Author	Field(s)	Source	Symptoms and Indicators
Gaudinsky, M.A.	Health	Coping with expanding nursing practice, knowledge, and technology. *Aviation, Space and Environmental Medicine* 50(10) (1979): 1073-1975.	Alienation from job, apathy; dehumanization; anger; cynicism regarding clients; ill health; lowered self-esteem; emotional exhaustion; insomnia; withdrawn; inappropriate attitude toward client; irritable
Gillespie, D.F.	Social Work	*Protective Service Workers Study*, mimeographed, n.d., The George Warren Brown School of Social Work, Washington University.	Alienation from job, apathy; detachment; dehumanization; anger; ill health; lowered self-esteem; emotional exhaustion; withdrawn; isolated; takes unnecessary risks; powerless
Hall, R.C.W., et al.	Health; Psychology	The professional burnout syndrome. *Psychiatric Opinion* (1979): 12-17.	Decreased effectiveness/increased effort; frustration; anger; cynicism regarding clients; ill health; fatigue; drug or alcohol abuse; feels helpless; paranoid behavior toward self; emotional exhaustion; marital conflict; insomnia; isolated; rigidity; takes unnecessary risks; irritable
Harrison, D.W.	Social Work	Role strain and burnout in child protective service workers. *The Social Service Review* 54(1) (1980): 34-44.	Dehumanization; cynicism regarding clients; anger; emotional exhaustion

Personality Factors	Characteristics of Organizations	Job Characteristics	Task Related
None	High turnover rate; centralization of authority; span of supervisory control; accountability and support	Stressed from workload shift. Lack of training for position	High emotional involvement; repetitive work; caseload size
None	Absenteeism; high turnover rate	Preference for working in office as opposed to field. Status conflict. Low job satisfaction. Inability to deal successfully with client's anger	Noncreative work
Overly-committed people tend to burn out	Absenteeism; high turnover rate; accountability and support	Scapegoating. Dependency mode which results in anger at supervisor	High emotional involvement; caseload size
None	High turnover rate; job design; span of supervisory control	Role conflict. Low job satisfaction. Lack of clarity about job role.	Noncreative work

Author	Field(s)	Source	Symptoms and Indicators
Kahn, R.	Not specified	Job burnout—prevention and remedies. *Public Welfare* 36(2) (1978): 60-63.	Decreased effectiveness/ increased effort; ill health; emotional exhaustion; insomnia; inappropriate attitude toward client
Kaleina, G.	Not specified	Burnout: snuffing the productive. *The Pittsburgh Press*, April 20, 1980.	Alienation from job, apathy; dissatisfaction; anger, cynicism regarding clients; feels subjected to tremendous stress; bored; withdrawn
Kramer, M.	Business	Hysteria on the assembly line knocks them over like flies. *The Pittsburgh Press*, June 18, 1979.	Ill health; feels subjected to tremendous stress; bored
Larson, C.C. Gilbertson, D.L. Powell, J.	Health; Psychology	Therapist burnout: perspectives on a critical issue. *Social Casework* 59(9) (1978): 563-565.	Excessive overtime; lowered self-esteem; depressed; highly anxious; emotional exhaustion; withdrawn; isolated
Lee, D.S.	Social Work	Staying alive in child protective services: survival skills for worker and supervisor, part I—a preliminary examination of worker trauma. *Arete* 5(4) (1979): 195-208.	Detachment; anger; ill health; drug or alcohol abuse; feels helpless; fear of losing control; projects problems on others; reluctant to share information with co-workers; envy and resentment of the living; unrealistic expectations of self; emotional exhaustion; overreacts or underreacts in serious situations; takes unncessary risks

Personality Factors	Characteristics of Organizations	Job Characteristics	Task Related
Rigid personalities suffer less from role conflict	Centralization of authority; span of supervisory control; job design; inflexible rules	Role conflict. Overload	High emotional involvement
The person who wants to give 100% to his job or his life	High turnover rate; absenteeism	Increase in errors. Low morale	Repetitive work
Women tend to be more inclined to show emotion and may feel guilty about working rather than being home with their families	Absenteeism; accountability and support	Increased pressure to produce. Little promotion opportunities	Repetitive work
None	Alienation; person/job/fit; job design; accountability and support	Constant demands without rewards	High emotional involvement; caseload size
None	Accountability and support; alienation; job design; span of supervisory control; inflexible rules	Isolated. Overworked. Tasks too difficult for worker	Repetitive work; high emotional involvement; caseload size

Author	Field(s)	Source	Symptoms and Indicators
Levinson, H.	Business	When executives burn out. *Harvard Business Review 59* (1981): 72-81.	Alienation from job, apathy; detachment; frustration; ill health; fatigue; depressed; highly anxious; insomnia
Maslach, C. Jackson, S.E.	Law Enforcement	Burned-out cops and their families. *Psychology Today 12*(12) (1979): 58-62.	Alienation from job, apathy; detachment; excessive overtime; frustration; anger; cynicism regarding clients; ill health; lowered self-esteem; drug or alcohol abuse; projects problems on others; unrealistic expectations of self; paranoid behavior toward self; emotional exhaustion; marital conflict; feels subjected to tremendous stress; isolated; fear; despair; rigidity
Maslach, C.	Health; Psychology	Job burnout—how people cope. *Public Welfare 36*(2) (1978): 56-58.	Dehumanization; hostility; cynicism regarding clients; lowered self-esteem; morale; drug or alcohol abuse; marital conflict; bored

Personality Factors	Characteristics of Organizations	Job Characteristics	Task Related
High achievers	None	None	High emotional involvement
None	Absenteeism; alienation; formalization of rules; centralization of authority; job design; person/job/fit; accountability and support; span of supervisory control; high turnover rate	Ambiguity and conflicting values. Responsibility for other lives. Unpredictable crisis. Physical dangers	High emotional involvement; caseload size; repetitive work; noncreative work
Situational	High turnover rate; absenteeism; accountability and support	Lack of feedback	High emotional involvement; caseload size

Author	Field(s)	Source	Symptoms and Indicators
Maslach, C.	Health; Psychology	The client role in staff burn-out. *Journal of Social Issues 34*(4) (1978): 111-124.	Detachment; dehumanization; cynicism regarding clients; ill health; lowered self-esteem; drug or alcohol abuse; emotional exhaustion; marital conflict; staff feels patients deserve problems
Maslach, C.	Social Work; Health	Burned-out. *Human Behavior* (1976): 16-22.	Detachment; dehumanization; excessive overtime; cynicism regarding clients; ill health; drug or alcohol abuse; marital conflict; insomnia; emphasis on technical care; staff feels patients deserve problems
Mattingly, M.A. (ed.)	Education	Stress and burn-out in child care. *Child Care Quarterly 6*(2) (1977): 88-89.	Frustration; dissatisfaction; ill health; fatigue; high resistance to going to work every day; lowered self-esteem; feels helpless; fear of losing control; emotional exhaustion; withdrawn
Mattingly, M.A.	Education	Sources of stress and burnout in professional child care work. *Child Care Quarterly 6*(2) (1977): 127-137.	Dehumanization; ill health; fatigue; insomnia

Personality Factors	Characteristics of Organizations	Job Characteristics	Task Related
Situational	High turnover rate; absenteeism; accountability and support	Poor communication. Negative feedback feelings from client, therapist, and staff	High emotional involvement; caseload size; repetitive work
Situational	High turnover rate; accountability and support; inflexible rules; alienation; job design	Goes by book like a petty bureaucrat. Work overload. Burdened with responsibility. No respite from other staff members. Needs special training and special preparation	High emotional involvement; repetitive work; caseload size
Trained and dedicated workers	None	Excessive demands on energy, strength, resources	
None	None	None	High emotional involvement; caseload size

Author	Field(s)	Source	Symptoms and Indicators
Melhuish, A. Cooper, C.	Business	Stresses that make managers ill. *International Management 35* (1980): 51-54.	Detachment; frustration; disillusionment; ill health; fatigue
Minahan, A.	Social Work	Burnout and organizational change. *Social Work 2* (1980): 87.	Cynicism regarding clients; rigidity
Muldoon, J.F.	Health	The burnout syndrome: caring for yourself. *Journal of Visual Impairment and Blindness 3* (1980): 112.	Alienation from job; apathy; fatigue; bored; nothing satisfies them; inappropriate attitude toward client; isolated; irritable
Munro, J.D.	Health	Preventing front-line collapse in institutional settings. *Hospital and Community Psychiatry 31*(3) (1980): 179-182.	Dehumanization; disorganized performance; cynicism regarding clients; ill health; high resistance to going to work every day; drug or alcohol abuse; reluctant to share information with co-workers; fails to make eye contact with clients, physical distancing; marital conflict; insomnia; medications as opposed to behavioral management; staff feels patients deserve problems; staff uses every opportunity to socialize with staff; verbal/physical abuse of clients; resists viable suggestions for improvement

Personality Factors	Characteristics of Organizations	Job Characteristics	Task Related
High achievers	Complex	High performance	None
None	Absenteeism; accountability and support; inflexible rules	Work overload. Work relationships	Caseload size
A dedicated and devoted person who is devoid of a sound program of self-care	Centralization of authority; span of supervisory control; job design	An increase in productivity with a lack of concern for perceptions of worker	Repetitive work; high emotional involvement; caseload size
Dedicated and committed staff are the most prone to burnout	High turnover rate; absenteeism; centralization of authority; span of supervisory control; job design	Role conflict and role ambiguity. Line worker as opposed to staff. Poor communication, lack of cooperation between administrator and front line	Caseload size; high emotional involvement; repetitive work

Author	Field(s)	Source	Symptoms and Indicators
Nelson, J.G.	Business	Burn-out—business's most costly expense. *Personnel Administration 25* (1980): 81-87.	Alienation from job, apathy; detachment; frustration; disillusionment; fatigue; depressed; highly anxious
Patrick, P.K.S.	Health	Burnout: job hazard for health workers. *Hospital 53*(22) (1979): 87-90.	Anger; ill health; fatigue; insomnia; inappropriate attitude toward client; derogatory labeling of clients
Pilette, P.D. Olio, K.M.	Health	Burnout victims feel powerless. *American Journal of Nursing 3* (1980): 413-414.	Isolated; powerless
Pines, A. Maslach, C.	Education	Combatting staff burnout in a day-care center: a case study. *Child Care Quarterly 9*(1) (1980): 5-16.	Dehumanization; dissatisfaction; cynicism regarding clients; ill health; fatigue; emotional exhaustion; feels subjected to tremendous stress
Resener, M.	Business	Burnout: the new stress disease. *Harper's Bazaar 112* (1979): 92-93.	Frustration; disillusionment; ill health; depressed
Shubin, S.	Health	Burnout: The professional hazard you face in nursing. *Nursing 8*(7) (1978): 22-27.	Dehumanization; decreased effectiveness/increased effort; excessive overtime; cynicism regarding clients; ill health; fatigue; lowered self-esteem; drug or alcohol abuse; emotional exhaustion; insomnia; emphasis on technical care; bored; inappropriate attitude toward client

Personality Factors	Characteristics of Organizations	Job Characteristics	Task Related
Ambitious, dedicated managers	Large, rigid	None	None
None	Absenteeism; centralization of authority; span of supervisory control; job design; accountability and support	Employee feels both misunderstood and unacknowledged	Repetitive work; high emotional involvement; caseload size
None	Job design; span of supervisory control; accountability and support; centralization of authority	Isolation. Powerlessness	None
Situational	High turnover rate; absenteeism	Overload. Lack of feedback. Estranged from work	High emotional involvement; caseload size
None	None	None	High emotional involvement
People who want to help humanity	High turnover rate; centralization of authority; span of supervisory control; accountability and support; job design	Work overload. Alienation of staff members	High emotional involvement; repetitive work; caseload size

Author	Field(s)	Source	Symptoms and Indicators
Solomon, J.R.	Psychology; Social Work	Additional perspectives on therapist burnout. *Social Casework: Journal of Contemporary Social Work 60*(3) (1979): 177-178.	None
Storlie, F.J.	Health	Burnout: the elaboration of a concept. *American Journal of Nursing 12* (1979): 2108-2111.	Alienation from job, apathy; disillusionment; defensive behavior; paranoid behavior toward self; feels empty like automaton; emphasis on technical care; stagnant; ineffective; bitter; visionless; resigned; inappropriate attitude toward client
Sullivan, R.C.	Health Education	Parents speak. The burn-out syndrome. *Journal of Autism and Developmental Disorders 9*(1) (1979): 111-126.	Frustration; ill health; feels helpless; depressed; emotional exhaustion; isolated
Valle, S.K.	Health	Burn-out: occupational hazard for counselors. *Alcohol Health and Research World 3*(3) (1979): 10-14.	Alienation from job, apathy; ill health; fatigue; lowered self-esteem; highly anxious; insomnia; withdrawn; isolated
Van Auken, S.	Health	Youth counselor burnout. *The Personnel and Guidance Journal Association 58*(2) (1979): 143-144.	Ill health; fatigue; highly anxious

Personality Factors	Characteristics of Organizations	Job Characteristics	Task Related
Being all things to all people	None	Isolation. Lack of feedback	High emotional involvement; caseload size
A belief of idealism— loving and respecting others is all that counts	High turnover rate; alienation; span of super- visory control; job design; accountability and support; formalization of rules; inflexible rules	Lack of power	High emotional involvement; caseload size; noncreative work
Feeling they must try harder	Accountability and support	Isolation. Exces- sive demands on energy, strength, resources	Repetitive work; high emotional involvement; caseload size
None	High turnover rate; job design	Inadequate train- ing. Lack of feedback	High emotional involvement; caseload size; repetitive work
None	Accountability and support; job design	Role conflict. Work overload	Repetitive work; high emotional involvement; caseload size

Author	Field(s)	Source	Symptoms and Indicators
Veninga, R.	Health	Administrative burnout—causes and cures. *Hospital Progress 60*(2) (1979): 45-52.	Excessive overtime; anger, ill health; fatigue; high resistance to going to work every day; drug or alcohol abuse; projects problems on others; unrealistic expectations of self; paranoid behavior toward self; emotional exhaustion; marital conflict; insomnia

Personality Factors	Characteristics of Organizations	Job Characteristics	Task Related
Individuals who burn out tend to be idealists	High turnover rate; formalization of rules; centralization of authority; span of supervisory control; job design; inflexible rules	Inadequate authority. Lack of feedback between line and staff	Noncreative work; repetitive work

Bibliography

CHAPTER 1

Bennett, J.G. *Gurdjieff: Making a new world.* New York: Harper & Row, 1973.

Browne, H. *You can profit from a monetary crisis.* New York: Macmillan, 1974.

Commoner, B. *The closing circle: Nature, man and technology.* New York: Alfred A. Knopf, 1971.

Dow Theory Letters, Inc. Debt will soar in 1980s, an investment banker predicted. *Dow Theory Letters,* December 5, 1979, 6.

Goodman, E. You can go home again. *Working Mother,* January 1980, 72-73.

Korda, M. *Power.* New York: Ballantine Books, 1975.

Laszlo, E., & Bierman, J. (Eds.). *Goals in a global community: A report to the Club of Rome* (Vols. I and II). New York: Pergamon, 1977.

Manning, D. Inflation, education and the after-school job. *Wall Street Journal,* March 11, 1980.

Matthiessen, P. *The snow leopard.* New York: Viking Press, Penguin Books, 1978.

O'Neil, N., & O'Neil, G. *Open marriage: A new lifestyle for couples.* New York: New American Library, 1972.

Prather, H. *Notes to myself.* Moab, UT: Real People Press, 1970.

Rubin, Z. Seeking a cure for loneliness. *Psychology Today,* October 1979, 82-90.

Ruff, H.J. *How to prosper during the coming bad years.* New York: New York Times Book Company, 1979.

Schumacher, E.F. *Small is beautiful: Economics as if people mattered.* New York: Harper & Row, 1973.

Slater, P. *The pursuit of loneliness.* Boston: Beacon Press, 1976.

Smith, A. *Powers of mind.* New York: Random House, 1975.

Terkel, S. *Working.* New York: Pantheon, 1974.

Toffler, A. *Future shock.* New York: Random House, 1970.

Wylie, P. *Generation of vipers.* New York: Farrar Rinehart, 1942.

Yankelovich, D. *Changing youth values in the 70s.* New York: McGraw Hill, 1974.

───────────── . New rules in American life: Searching for self-fulfillment in a world turned upside down. *Psychology Today,* April 1981, 35-91.

CHAPTER 2

Berkeley Planning Associates. *Evaluation of child abuse and neglect: Demonstration projects, 1974-1977* (Vol. XI). Springfield, IL: National Technical Information Service, 1977.

Brecher, E.M. et al. *Licit and illicit drugs.* Boston: Little, Brown and Company, 1972.

Brown, C., Holder, W., Giles, D., & Schmolke, L. The battered worker syndrome: Everything you wanted to know about staff morale but were too burned-out to ask. In M. Lauderdale, R. Anderson, & S. Kramer (Eds.), *Child abuse and neglect: Issues on innovation and implementation* (Vol. II). Proceedings of the Second Annual National Conference on Child Abuse and Neglect, Washington, DC: Department of Health, Education, and Welfare, 1977, 214-225.

Daley, M.R. Preventing worker burnout in child welfare. *Child Welfare,* 1979, *58*, 443-450.

Freudenberger, H.J. *The staff burnout syndrome.* Washington, DC: The Drug Abuse Council, Inc., 1975.

───────────── . The staff burnout syndrome in alternative institutions. *Psychotherapy: Theory, Research and Practice,* 1975, *12*, 73-82.

───────────── . Burnout: Occupational hazard of the child care worker. *Child Care Quarterly,* 1977, *6*, 90-99.

Garte, S.H., & Rosenblum, M.L. Lighting fires in burn-out counselors. *The Personnel and Guidance Journal,* 1978, *57*, 158-160.

Heider, F. *The psychology of interpersonal relations.* New York: Wiley, 1958.

Lamb, H.R. Staff burnout in work with long-term patients. *Hospital and Community Psychiatry,* 1979, *30*, 396-398.

Mailer, N. *Of a fire on the moon.* Boston: Little, Brown & Company, 1970.

───────────── . Job burnout: How people cope. *Public Welfare,* 1978, *36*, 56-58.

Maslach, C. Burned-out. *Human Behavior,* 1976, *16*, 16-22.

Maslach, C., & Pines, A. Burnout, the loss of human caring. In A. Pines & C. Maslach (Eds.), *Experiencing social psychology*. New York: Random House, 1979, 245-252.

——————— The burn-out syndrome in the day care setting. *Child Care Quarterly*, 1977, *6*, 100-113.

Mattingly, M. Sources of stress and burn-out in professional child care work. *Child Care Quarterly*, 1977, *6*, 127-137.

Pines, A., & Maslach, C. *Burn-out in mental health professionals*. In M. Lauderdale, R. Anderson, & S. Kramer (Eds.), *Child abuse and neglect: Issues on innovation and implementation* (Vol. II). Proceedings of the Second Annual National Conference on Child Abuse and Neglect, Washington, DC: Department of Health, Education, and Welfare, 1977, 239-245.

——————— Characteristics of staff burnout in mental health settings. *Hospital and Community Psychiatry*, 1978, *29*, 233-237.

Rosow, J. The worker of the '80s: Manage him like an asset. *Inc.*, February 1981, 72-74.

Rotter, J.B. Generalized expectancies for internal versus external control of reinforcement. *Psychological Monographs*, 1966, 80.

Warnath, C., & Shelton, J. The ultimate disappointment: The burn-out counselor. *The Personnel and Guidance Journal*, 1976, *55*, 172-175.

CHAPTER 3

Armstrong, K. How can we avoid burn-out? In M. Lauderdale, R. Anderson, & S. Kramer (Eds.), *Child abuse and neglect: Issues on innovation and implementation* (Vol. II). Proceedings of the Second Annual National Conference on Child Abuse and Neglect, Washington, DC: Department of Health, Education, and Welfare, 1977, 230-238.

Emener, W.G. Professional burnout: Rehabilitation's hidden handicap. *Journal of Rehabilitation*, 1979, *45*, 55-58.

Erikson, E.H. *Childhood and society*. New York: W.W. Norton, 1963.

Fabun, D. *Dynamics of change*. Englewood Cliffs, NJ: Prentice-Hall, 1970.

Freudenberger, H.J. Staff burnout. *Journal of Social Issues*, 1974, *30*(1), 159-165.

Friedman, M., & Rosenman, R.H. *Type A behavior and your heart*. New York: Alfred A. Knopf, 1974.

Gunning, P. Burnout—as apathy replaces empathy. *Connection*, 1977, *2*, 1-2.

Holmes, T.H., & Rahe, R.H. Social readjustment rating scale. *Journal of Psychosomatic Research*, 1967, *11*, 213.

Levinson, D.J. et al. *The seasons of a man's life*. New York: Ballantine, 1978.

Maslach, C. The client role in staff burn-out. *Journal of Social Issues*, 1978, *34*, 111-124.

——————— Burned-out cops and their families. *Psychology Today*, 1979, *12*, 59-62.

Maslach, C., & Jackson, S.E. Lawyer burnout. *Barrister*, 1978, 5, 52-54.

National Center on Child Abuse and Neglect. *Worker burnout among child protective services workers*. Washington, DC: U.S. Children's Bureau, Administration for Children, Youth, and Families, Department of Health, Education, and Welfare, 1979, 1-19.

Peterson, I. Hysteria on the assembly line. *Austin-American Statesman*, July 15, 1979.

CHAPTER 4

Selye, H. *Stress without distress*. New York: J.B. Lippincott, 1974.

Wolfe, T. The 'me' decade and the third great awakening. *New York Magazine*, 1976, *23*, 26-40.

Woolfolk, R.L., & Richardson, F.E. *Stress, sanity and survival*. New York: Sovereign, 1978.

CHAPTER 5

Leakey, R., & Lewin, R. *People of the lake: Mankind and its beginnings*. New York: Anchor Press, Doubleday, 1978.

Marx, K. *Das Capital*. New York: International Publishers, 1967.

Parsons, T. Differentiation and variation in social structures. In T. Parsons, E. Shils, K.D. Naegele, & J.R. Pitts (Eds.), *Theories of Society* (Vol. I). New York: The Free Press, 1961.

Shorter, E. *The making of the modern family*. New York: Basic Books, 1977.

Smith, A. In E. Cannan (Ed.), *The wealth of nations*. New York: Modern Library, Inc., 1937.

Taylor, F.W. *The principles of scientific management*. New York: Harper and Brothers, 1911.

CHAPTER 6

Katz, D., & Kahn, R. *Social psychology of organizations*. New York: John Wiley and Sons, 1966.

Massie, J.L. Management theory. In J.G. March (Ed.), *Handbook of organizations*. Chicago: Rand McNally, 1965.

Ollman, B. *Alienation*. (2nd ed.). London: Cambridge University Press, 1976.

Perrow, C. *Complex organizations: A critical essay*. Chicago: Scott Foresman and Company, 1972.

Pirsig, R. *Zen and the art of motorcycle maintenance*. New York: William Morrow and Company, 1974.

Roethlisberger, F.J., & Dickson, W.J. *Management and the worker*. Cambridge, MA: Harvard University Press, 1939.

Simon, H.A. *Administrative behavior*. (3rd ed.). New York: The Free Press; Macmillan, 1976.

Sutermeister, R.A. *People and productivity*. New York: McGraw-Hill, 1976.

Taylor, F.W. *Scientific management*. New York: Harper and Row Publishers, 1911.

CHAPTER 7

Bensman, J., & Lilienfeld, R. *Between public and private: The lost boundaries of the self*. New York: The Free Press; Macmillan, 1979.

Bruney, J. *On knowing essays for the left hand*. (Exp. ed.). Cambridge, MA: Harvard University Press, 1979.

Carroll, L. *Through the looking-glass and what Alice found there*. New York: The Heritage Reprints, 1941, 159.

Garfinkel, H. *Studies in ethnomethodology*. Englewood Cliffs, NJ: Prentice-Hall, 1967.

Genet, J. *The maids and the deathwatch*. (B. Frechtman, trans.). New York: Grove Press, 1954.

Goffman, E. *Frame analysis*. New York: Harper & Row, 1974.

———————— *The presentation of the self in everyday life*. Edinburgh, Scotland: University of Edinburgh, 1956.

Gouldner, A. *The coming crisis in western sociology*. New York: Basic Books, 1970.

Hartnell, P. (Ed.). *Oxford companion to the theatre*. (2nd. ed.). Oxford, England: Oxford University Press, 1957.

How Japan does it. *Time*, March 1981, 39.

Ionesco, E. *Three plays*. (D. Watson, trans.). New York: Grove Press, 1958.

Jaynes, J. *The origin of consciousness in the breakdown of the bicameral mind*. Boston: Houghton Mifflin, 1976.

Kanter, R.M. *Men and women of the corporation*. New York: Basic Books, 1977.

Loeb, M. Ideas from a matchmaker. *Time*, December 17, 1979, 72.

Maccoby, M. *The gamesman*. New York: Simon and Schuster, 1976.

Miller, D.C., & Form, W.H. *Industrial sociology: Work in organizational life*. (3rd ed.). New York: Harper & Row, 1980.

Pirandello, L. *Tonight we improvise*. Oxford, England: Samuel French, 1932.

Riesman, D. *The lonely crowd: A study of the changing American character.* New Haven, CT: Yale University Press, 1950.

Sellers strikes again. *Time*, March 1980, 64.

Whyte, W.H., Jr. *The organization man*. New York: Simon and Schuster, 1956.

CHAPTER 8

Bennett, J.G. *Gurdjieff: Making a new world*. New York: Harper & Row, 1973.

Castaneda, C. *Journey to Ixtlan: The lessons of Don Juan*. New York: Simon and Schuster, 1972.

_____. *The teachings of Don Juan: A Yaqui way of knowledge*. Los Angeles: University of California Press, 1968.

Farb, P. *Man's rise to civilization*. New York: E.P. Dutton, 1968.

Foster, G.M. *Traditional cultures and the impact of technological change*. New York: Harper & Row, 1962.

Keynes, G. (Ed.). *Blake—complete writings*. New York: Oxford University Press, 1969.

Kluckhohn, C. *Culture and behavior*. New York: The Free Press, 1965.

Kubler-Ross, E. *On death and dying*. New York: Macmillan, 1969.

La Barre, W. *The peyote cult*. New York: Schocken, 1969.

Levy-Bruhl, L. *The notebooks on primitive mentality*. (P. Riviere, trans.). New York: Harper & Row, 1975.

Lewin, K. *The practical theorists*. A.J. Morrow (Ed.). New York: Basic Books, 1969.

Macarov, D. *Incentives to work*. San Francisco: Jossey-Bass, 1970.

McClelland, D.C. *The achieving society*. New York: The Free Press, 1961.

Ornstein, R.E. *The nature of human consciousness*. San Francisco, W.H. Freeman, 1973.

O'Toole, J. *Work, learning and the American future*. San Francisco: Jossey-Bass, 1978.

Slotkin, J.S. *The peyote religion*. Glencoe, IL: The Free Press, 1956.

Zurcher, L.A., Jr. *The mutable self*. Beverly Hills, CA: Sage Publications, 1977.

CHAPTER 9

Adams, J.D. (Ed.). *Understanding and managing stress: A book of readings*. San Diego, CA: University Associates, 1980.

Asch, S.E. Studies of independence and conformity: I. A minority of one against a unanimous majority. *Psychological Monographs*, 1956, *9*, 70.

Edelwich, J.A., & Brodsky, A. *Burnout: Stages of disillusionment in the helping professions*. New York: Human Sciences Press, 1980.

Freudenberger, H.J. *Burnout: The high cost of high achievement*. New York: Doubleday, 1980.

Gazzaniga, M. *The bisected brain*. New York: Appleton-Century-Crofts, 1970.

Holmes, T.H., & Rahe, R.H. Social readjustment rating scale. *Journal of Psychosomatic Research*, 1967, *11*, 213.

Maier, N.F.R. *Frustration: A study of behavior with a goal*. New York: McGraw-Hill, 1949.

McLeon, A.A. *Work stress*. Boston: Addison-Wesley, 1979.

Pines, A., & Aronson, E. *Burnout: From tedium to personal growth*. New York: The Free Press, 1980.

Rose, S. *The conscious brain*. New York: Alfred A. Knopf, 1973.

Sherif, M. *The psychology of social norms*. New York: Harper & Row, 1936.

Sherif, M., & Sherif, C. *Social psychology*. New York: Harper & Row, 1956.

Thoreau, H. In F. Torrey & F.H. Allen (Eds.), *The journal*. New York: Dover Publications, Inc., 1906.

CHAPTER 10

Blake, R., & Mouton, J. *The managerial grid*. Houston, TX: Gulf Publishing Company, 1964.

Mitchell, M.D. Consultant burnout. In J.E. Jones & J.W. Pfeiffer (Eds.), *The 1977 annual handbook for group facilitators*. San Diego, CA: University Associates, 1977, 143-146.

Pines, A., & Kafry, D. Occupational tedium in the social services. *Social Work*, 1978, *23*, 499-507.

Pirsig, R.M. *Zen and the art of motorcycle maintenance*. New York: William Morrow and Company, 1974.

Yates, J. *Managing stress*. New York: AMACOM, 1979.

CHAPTER 11

Bath, B.H.S. van. *The agrarian history of Western Europe*. London: Edward Arnold, 1963.

Bishop, M. *Penguin book of the Middle Ages*. London: Penguin Books, 1971.

Blake, W. Auguries of innocence. In J. Sampson (Ed.), *Blake's poetical works*. Oxford, England: Oxford at the Clarendon Press, 1905.

Bloch, M. *Feudal society*. Chicago: University of Chicago Press, 1961.

Bronowski, J. *The ascent of man*. Boston: Little, Brown and Company, 1973.

The Cambridge ancient history (Vol. 1-3). Cambridge, MA: Cambridge University Press, 1968.

Cipolla, C.M. *The economic history of world population*. London: Penguin Books, 1964.

Clark, G.C. *The Stone Age masters*. New York: McGraw-Hill, 1962.

Clark, G.C. *World prehistory: A new outline*. London: University Press, 1965.

Clark, G.C., & Piggott, S. *Prehistoric societies*. London: Hutchinson, 1965.

Darlington, C.D. *The evolution of man and society*. London: George Allen & Unwin, 1969.

Dobzhansky, T. *Mankind evolving: The evolution of the human species*. New Haven, CT: Yale University Press, 1962.

Grunbaum, A. *Philosophical problems of space and time*. (2nd ed.). Boston: D. Reidel Publishing Company, 1973.

Huizinga, J. *The waning of the Middle Ages*. New York: Anchor Press, Doubleday, 1954.

Johnson, F.R. *Astronomical thought in Renaissance England*. New York: Octagon, 1968.

Krantzberg, M. *Technology in western civilization*. Oxford, England: Oxford University Press, 1967.

Leakey, R., & Lewin, R. *People of the lake: Mankind and its beginnings*. New York: Anchor Press; Doubleday, 1978.

Mallowan, M.E.L. *Early Mesopotamia and Iran*. New York: McGraw-Hill, 1965.

Mellaart, J. *Earliest civilizations of the Near East*. New York: McGraw-Hill, 1965.

Moret, A. *The Nile and Egyptian civilization*. London: Routledge & Kegan Paul, 1927.

Neugebauer, O. *The exact sciences in antiquity*. Princeton, NJ: Princeton University Press, 1952.

O'Leary, D. *How Greek science passed to the Arabs*. London: Routledge & Kegan Paul, 1949.

Pilbeam, D. *The ascent of man: An introduction to human evolution*. New York: Macmillan, 1972.

Pirenne, H. *Medieval cities*. New York: Doubleday, 1956.

Polanyi, K. *The great transformation*. Boston: Beacon Press, 1957.

Robinson, J.M. *An introduction to early Greek philosophy*. Boston: Houghton Mifflin, 1968.

Sagan, C. *The dragons of Eden: Speculations on the evolution of human intelligence.* New York: Random House, 1977.

Saggs, H.W.F. *The greatness that was Babylon.* New York: Mentor Books, 1962.

Sauer, C.O. *Seeds, spades, hearths to herds.* (3rd ed.). Boston: MIT Press, 1972.

Schrier, A.M., Harlow, H.F., & Stollnitz, F. (Eds.). *Behavior of nonhuman primates* (Vol. 2). New York: Academic Press, 1965.

Shirley, J. The contention of Ajax and Ulysses for the armor of Achilles. In R.L. Armstrong (Ed.), *The poems of James Shirley.* New York: King's Crown Press, 1941.

Tax, S. (Ed.). *Evolution after Darwin.* Chicago: University of Chicago Press, 1960.

Thomas, L. *The medusa and the snail.* New York: Viking Press, 1979.

Toynbee, A.J. *A study of history.* Oxford, England: Oxford University Press, 1962.

Ziegler, P. *The black death.* London: John Day Co. Inc., 1969.

CHAPTER 12

Anthony, R.N. *Planning and control systems: The framework for analysis.* Boston: Harvard University Press, 1965.

Argyris, C. *Interpersonal competence and organizational effectiveness.* Homewood, IL: The Dorsey Press, 1962.

Boring, E.G. *A history of experimental psychology.* (2nd ed.). New York: Appleton-Century-Crofts, 1957.

Brady, R.H. MBO goes to work in the public sector. *Harvard Business Review,* April 1973.

Carroll, S.J., & Tosi, H.L. *Management by objectives.* New York: Macmillan, 1973.

D'Espagnat, B. The quantum theory and reality. *Scientific American,* 1970, *241* (5), 158-181.

Drucker, P. *The practice of management.* New York: Harper & Row, 1954.

Fine, S.A. A systems approach to manpower development in human services. *Public Welfare,* January 1970, 91-97.

Gouldner, A.W. *The coming crisis in western sociology.* New York: Basic Books, 1970.

Hall, C.L. *Essentials of behavior.* New Haven, CT: Yale University Press, 1951.

Hersey, P., & Blanchard, K.H. *Management of organizational behavior: Utilizing human resources.* (3rd ed.). Englewood Cliffs, NJ: Prentice-Hall, 1969.

Herzberg, F. *Work and the nature of man.* New York: World Publishing Company, 1966.

Herzberg, F., Mausner, B., & Schneiderman, B. *The motivation to work.* (2nd ed.). New York: John Wiley and Sons, 1959.

Hinrich, H., & Taylor, G. *Program budgeting and benefit cost analysis.* Santa Monica, CA: Goodyear Publishing Company, 1969.

Kuhn, T.S. *The structure of scientific revolution.* (2nd ed.). Chicago: University of Chicago Press, 1970.

Levinson, H. Management by whose objectives? *Harvard Business Review,* July-August 1970, 125-134.

Lewin, K., Lippitt, R., & White, R.K. Patterns of aggressive behavior in experimentally created 'social climates.' *Journal of Social Psychology,* 1939, *10,* 271-299.

Likert, R. *The human organization.* New York: McGraw-Hill, 1961.

Maine, H.S. On states and contract. In T. Parsons et al. (Eds.), *Ancient law.* New York: The Free Press, 1961. (Originally published 1885.)

Mantoux, P. *The Industrial Revolution in the eighteenth century.* New York: Harper & Row, 1962.

Marx, M.H., & Hillix, W. *Systems and theories in psychology.* New York: McGraw-Hill, 1963.

Maslow, A. *Eupsychian management.* Homewood, IL: Richard D. Irwin and The Dorsey Press, 1965.

_____. *Motivation and personality.* New York: Harper & Row, 1954.

Massie, J.L. *Essentials of management.* Englewood Cliffs, NJ: Prentice-Hall, 1971.

McGregor, D. *The human side of enterprise.* New York: McGraw-Hill, 1960.

Meyer, H., Kay, E., & French, J. Split rules in performance appraisal. *Harvard Business Review,* 1965, *43,* 123-149.

Morley, J.E. Job enrichment and participation in work. In G.M. Stephenson & C.J. Brotherton (Eds.), *Industrial relations.* New York: John Wiley and Sons, 1979.

Odiorne, G. *Management by objectives.* New York: Pittman, 1965.

Oppenheimer, J.R. *Science and the common understanding.* New York: Simon and Schuster, 1953.

Popper, K.R. *Conjectures and refutations: The growth of scientific knowledge.* New York: Harper & Row, 1965.

Raia, A.P. Goal setting and self control. *Journal of Management Studies,* 1965, *2,* 34-53.

Roche, W.J., & MacKinnon, N.L. Motivating people with meaningful work. *Harvard Business Review,* 1970, *48,* 97-110.

Skinner, B.F. *Contingencies of reinforcement: A theoretical analysis.* New York: Appleton-Century-Crofts, 1969.

Spence, K.W. *Behavior theory and learning.* Englewood Cliffs, NJ: Prentice-Hall, 1960.

Steiner, G.A. *Top management planning.* Con Mills, Ontario, Canada: Collier-Macmillan, Ltd., 1969.

Stinchcombe, A.L. Social structure and organizations. In J.G. March (Ed.), *Handbook of organizations.* Chicago: Rand McNally, 1965.

Tolman, C. Principles of purposive behavior. *A study of science, Vol. 2, General systemic formulation of learning and special processes.* New York: McGraw-Hill, 1959.

Watson, J.B. Psychology as the behaviorist views it. *Psychological Review,* 1913, *20,* 158-177.

Weber, M. *Economy and society: An outline of interpretive sociology* (4th ed.). G. Roth & C. Wittich (Eds.) (E. Fischoff et al., trans.). Totowa, NJ: Bedminster, 1968.

Whyte, W.F. et al. *Money and motivation: An analysis of incentives in industry.* New York: Harper & Row, 1959.

CHAPTER 13

Ashvaghosha. *The awakening of faith.* (D.T. Suzuki, trans.). Chicago: Open Court, 1900.

Berger, P., Berger, B., & Kellner, H. *The homeless mind.* New York: Viking Books; Random House, 1974.

Etzioni, A. *A comparative analysis of complex organizations.* New York: The Free Press, 1975.

Faucheux, C., & Rojot, J. Social psychology and industrial relations: A cross-cultural perspective. In G.M. Stephenson & C.J. Brotherton (Eds.), *Industrial relations.* New York: John Wiley & Sons, 1979.

Goffman, E. *Asylums.* New York: Doubleday, 1961.

Krutch, J.W. *The modern temper.* New York: Harcourt, Brace, 1929.

Illich, I. *Medical nemesis: The expropriation of health.* New York: Bantam, 1976.

Likert, R. *The human organization.* New York: McGraw-Hill Book Company, 1961.

Marris, P., & Rein, M. *Dilemmas of social reform.* New York: Atherton Press, 1967.

Marx, K. Critique of Hegel's philosophy of right. In L.D. Easton & K. Guddat, (Eds. and trans.), *Writings of the young Marx on philosophy and society.* New York: Doubleday, 1967.

_____ *Economic and political manuscripts of 1844.* New York: International Publishing, 1964.

Perrow, C. Demystifying organizations. In R.C. Sarri & Y. Hasenfield (Eds.), *The management of human services.* New York: Columbia University Press, 1978.

Seeman, M. Alienation and engagement. In A. Campbell & P. Converse (Eds.), *The human meaning of social change.* New York: Russell Sage Foundation, 1972.

_____ On the meaning of alienation. *American Sociological Review*, 1959, *24*, 783-789.

Skinner, B.F. *Beyond freedom and dignity.* New York: Alfred A. Knopf, 1971.

Szasz, T. *The myth of mental illness.* New York: Hoeber Harper, 1963.

Weber, M. *The Protestant ethic and the spirit of capitalism.* (T. Parsons, trans.). New York: Scribner, 1958.

CHAPTER 14

Adair, J., & Vogt, E. Navaho and Zuni veterans: A study of contrasting modes of culture change. *American Anthropologist*, 1949, *51* (4), 547-561.

Bennis, W.G., & Slater, P. *The temporary society.* New York: Harper & Row, 1968.

de Schweiniz, D. *England's road to social security.* New York: A.S. Barnes and Company, 1961.

Rogers, E.M. *Diffusion of innovations.* New York: The Free Press of Glencoe, 1962.

Tennyson, A. By an evolutionist. *Demeter and other poems.* New York: Macmillan, 1889.

Wesson, R.G. *The Soviet state: An aging revolution.* New York: John Wiley, 1972.

CHAPTER 15

Albert, E., Denise, T.C., & Peterfreund, S.P. *Great traditions and ethics.* New York: American Book Company, 1953.

Beck, W. *Modern science and the nature of life.* New York: Harcourt, Brace, 1957.

Beston, H. *Outermost house.* New York: Holt, Rinehart and Winston, 1971.

Bledstein, B. *The culture of professionalism: The middle class and the development of higher education in America.* New York: Norton, 1976.

Dewey, J. *Intelligence in the modern world: John Dewey's philosophy.* New York: Modern Library, 1939.

Durand, J.D. The modern expansion of world population. In C.B. Nam (Ed.), *Population and society.* Boston: Houghton Mifflin, 1968.

Ehrlich, P.R. *The population bomb.* New York: Ballantine, 1968.

Hayes, J. Research, teaching and faculty fate. *Science*, 1971, *172*, 227-230.

Heilbroner, R.L. *The worldly philosophers.* New York: Simon and Schuster, 1961.

Kahn, H. *World economic development.* Boulder, CO: Westview Press, 1979.

Lasch, C. *Haven in a heartless world.* New York: Basic Books, 1977.

——————————— *The culture of narcissism.* New York: W.W. Norton and Company, 1978.

Machlup, F. *The production and distribution of knowledge in the United States.* Princeton, NJ: Princeton University Press, 1962.

McKeown, T. Determinants of health. *Human Nature,* April 1978, 60-67.

Milgram, S. Behavioral study of obedience. *Journal of Abnormal and Social Psychology,* 1963, *67,* 373-378.

Mill, J.S. *Utilitarianism.* London: Longmans, Green, and Company, 1897.

Moore, W.E. *Industrial relations and the social order.* New York: Macmillan, 1951.

Moynihan, D.P. *Maximum feasible misunderstanding.* New York: The Free Press, 1969.

Mumford, L. *The culture of cities.* New York: Harcourt Brace Jovanovich, 1939.

Reisman, D. The changing American campus: Beyond the 60s. *The Wilson Quarterly,* Autumn 1978, 59-71.

Sale, K. *Human scale.* New York: Coward, McCann and Geoghegan, 1980.

Stine, H.G. *The third Industrial Revolution.* New York: G.P. Putnam's Sons, 1975.

Tucker, W. The next American dust bowl. *The Atlantic Monthly,* July 1979, 38-49.

Veysey, L.R. *The emergence of the American university.* Chicago: University of Chicago Press, 1965.

Wallerstein, I. *The modern world system.* New York: Academic Press, 1976.

Woodberry, G.E. Man and the race. *The torch.* New York: Macmillan, 1912.

CHAPTER 16

Ashvaghosha. *The awakening of faith.* (D.T. Suzuki, trans.). Chicago: Open Court, 1900.

Back, K. *Beyond works: The story of sensitivity training and the encounter movement.* New York: Russell Sage Foundation, 1972.

Beagle, P. *The last unicorn.* New York: Viking Press, 1968.

Bell, D. *The coming of post-industrial society: A venture in social forecasting.* New York: Basic Books, 1923.

Benedict, R. *Patterns of culture.* Boston: Houghton Mifflin, 1935.

Bennis, W. Response to Shariff: Beyond bureaucracy baiting. *Social Science Quarterly*, 1979, *60*, 20-24.

Berlin, I. *Four essays on liberty.* New York: Oxford University Press, 1970.

Blundell, W.E. In Europe the sullen eighties. *Wall Street Journal*, July 15, 1979.

Boulding, K. *The image: Knowledge in life and society.* Ann Arbor, MI: University of Michigan, 1956.

Capra, F. *The Tao of physics.* Boulder, CO: Shambhala Publications, 1976.

Cartwright, D., & Zander, A. (Eds.). *Group dynamics: Research and theory.* (3rd ed.). New York: Harper & Row, 1968.

Cornish, E. (Ed.). *1999 the world of tomorrow: Selections for the futurist.* Washington, DC: World Future Society, 1978.

Eiseley, L. *The unexpected universe.* New York: Harcourt Brace Jovanovich, 1964.

Fiedl, E. Society and sex roles. *Human Nature*, April 1978, 68-75.

Gerth, H., & Mills, C.W. *Character and social structure.* New York: Harcourt Brace Jovanovich, 1953.

Gould, S.J. Evolution's erratic pace. *Natural History*, May 1977, 12-16.

Granet, M. The Tao. In T. Parsons, E. Shils, K.D. Naegele, & J.R. Pitts (Eds.), *Theories of society* (Vol. 2). New York: The Free Press, 1961.

Hayek, F. *The road to serfdom.* Chicago: University of Chicago Press, 1944.

Heisenberg, W. *Physics and philosophy: The revolution in modern science.* New York: Harper & Row, 1958.

Hoijer, H. (Ed.). *Language in culture.* Chicago: University of Chicago Press, 1954.

Husserl, E. *Phenomenology and the crisis of philosophy.* (Q. Lauer, trans.). New York: Harper & Row, 1965.

Meyer, M.W. "Debureaucratization?" *Social Science Quarterly*, 1979, *60*, 25-34.

Michels, R. *Political parties.* Glencoe, IL: The Free Press, 1949.

Nicolis, G., & Prigonine, I. *Self-organization in nonequilibrium systems: From dissipative structures to order through fluctuations.* New York: John Wiley, Wiley-Interscience, 1977.

Pickson, P. *The future of the workplace: The coming revolution in jobs.* New York: Waybright and Talley, 1975.

Rule, J.B. *Insight and social betterment.* New York: Oxford University Press, 1978.

Shariff, Z. The persistence of bureaucracy. *Social Science Quarterly*, 1979, *60*, 3-19.

Shipman, H.L. *Black holes, quasars and the universe.* Boston: Houghton Mifflin, 1976.

Wheeler, J.A. Beyond the black hole. *Science Year*, 1975, 76-89.

Work in America. Report of a special task force to the Secretary of Health, Education, and Welfare, prepared under the auspices of the W.E. Upjohn Institute for Employment Research. Boston: MIT Press, 1973.

Index